Witmer Stone

The Fascination of Nature

Scott McConnell

Book website: witmerstone.com

Author email: witmer.stone@gmail.com

Library of Congress Control Number: 2014913017

Printed in the United States of America

Witmer Stone

The Fascination of Nature

Scott McConnell

"It has always seemed to the writer a duty of present-day ornithologists to save from oblivion as many of the facts as possible concerning the lives of those who long ago laid the foundations of our science…concerning whom little or no record has appeared in our published literature."
  — Witmer Stone, *The Auk* 36(4):464-72

"Most of us have but a faint idea of the extent of all you have done."
  — J. Hooper Bowles to Witmer Stone, July 30, 1931; ANSP Collection 450

"Appreciated as he was for his long service to the Academy of Natural Sciences, and honored as he was by his fellow ornithologists, he was never appreciated as he should have been."
  — Cornelius Weygandt on Witmer Stone, *On the Edge of Evening*

"How many 'mute inglorious Miltons' would be rescued from the merciless sea of obscurity, if their worth was but recognized by the thoughtfulness of such men as you, who are actors on the passing stage of existence!"
  — Mahlen Kirk to Witmer Stone, July 19, 1904; ANSP Collection 450

"Now I don't want you to throw cold water, as Shakespeare says, on this notion, Quixotic as it appears. I have been so long accustomed to the building of airy castles and brain windmills, that it has become one of my earthly comforts, a sort of a rough bone, that amuses me when sated with the dull drudgery of life."
  — Alexander Wilson to Alexander Lawson, March 12, 1804, on his early plans to produce a book on American birds

"It is slow, tedious work to uncover the history of those who have passed on a few years ago."
  — T. George Middleton to Witmer Stone, February 15, 1938; ANSP Collection 2009-031

"It will be a work of years, however, solitary and alone as I labor."
  — John Cassin, *Cassinia* 5:3

"The verification of all references alone was a tedious and day-consuming responsibility."
  — James Rehn on Stone's work on the fourth AOU check-list, *Cassinia* 31:8

"It has been a great pleasure to personally plan and manage the production of such a work and to see it take form just as I had planned."
  — Witmer Stone to T.C. Stephens, in Stephens's review of BSOCM, *The Wilson Bulletin,* 50(2):147.

"A work of this kind is never complete, and if it paves the way for more thorough work along similar lines, its purpose will have been accomplished."
  — Witmer Stone, preface to *The Plants of Southern New Jersey*

Contents

Notes on the Text

Witmer Stone (1866–1939) lived his entire life in Philadelphia. He attended Germantown Academy, then received three degrees from the University of Pennsylvania: an A.B. in 1887, an A.M. in 1891, and an honorary doctorate in 1913. In 1904, he married Lillie May Lafferty; they remained married until Witmer's death did them part. He worked at the Academy of Natural Sciences of Philadelphia for 51 years, as an ornithologist and in a variety of administrative positions. He was very active in the American Ornithologists' Union, serving on a number of committees, as vice president and president, and as editor of its journal *The Auk* for 25 years. He was one of seven founders of the Delaware Valley Ornithological Club and edited its journal *Cassinia* for several years. He was also a founding member of the Philadelphia Botanical Club, and he published *The Plants of Southern New Jersey*, a flora of the New Jersey Pine Barrens, in 1911. Shortly before he died, Stone published *Bird Studies at Old Cape May*, a two-volume work detailing the ornithological research he and members of the DVOC had conducted in the area for the previous 50 years.

In quotations from correspondence, I have retained the original punctuation as much as possible, including ampersands. All emphases (including single, double, and triple underlining) have been retained, and in the single instance where I have added my own emphasis to a quote, I have noted it as such. Bracketed comments or insertions within quotes are my own, and any parenthetical ones are the original author's. I have sometimes replaced old bird names with ones more familiar to modern birders, and have put the newer names in brackets (e.g., "Merlin" for the older "Pigeon Hawk"). I have done some silent editing of obvious spelling and punctuation mistakes.

For brevity's sake, I have inserted a period instead of a more technically correct ellipsis when cropping the end of a sentence in instances where the meaning of the section quoted isn't changed by the edit. Also for brevity, I have sometimes used a dash for a range of dates, instead of using the "from…to…" construct. I have capitalized all proper plant, animal, and bird names. Beginning in 1901, AOU membership classifications, in order of decreasing class size and increasing prestige level, were Associate, Member, and Fellow. I have capitalized AOU and DVOC membership categories because of their ambiguous nature in uncapitalized form (e.g., "three AOU Fellows" describes three people of unspecified gender in a specific AOU membership class; "three AOU fellows" are simply three chaps from the AOU). Please note that there is a "cast of characters" appendix that provides a brief description of some of Stone's contemporaries who are frequently encountered in the book.

The following acronyms are used throughout the book:

AMNH	American Museum of Natural History
ANSP	Academy of Natural Sciences of Philadelphia; often referred to here as "the Academy" (In 2011, the institution's name was changed to The Academy of Natural Sciences of Drexel University.)
AOU	American Ornithologists' Union
ASM	American Society of Mammalogists
BEPNJ	*The Birds of Eastern Pennsylvania and New Jersey*
BOU	British Ornithologists' Union
BSOCM	*Bird Studies at Old Cape May*
CMP	Cape May Point
DVOC	Delaware Valley Ornithological Club; I often refer to members as "DVOCers" (i.e., "dee-vee-oh-SEE-ers")
MCZ	Museum of Comparative Zoology
NAAS	National Association of Audubon Societies (now the National Audubon Society)
NJAS	New Jersey Audubon Society
NWR	National Wildlife Refuge
OSNA	Ornithological Societies of North America
PANSP	*Proceedings of the Academy of Natural Sciences of Philadelphia*
PAS	Pennsylvania Audubon Society
PBC	Philadelphia Botanical Club
PGC	Pennsylvania Game Commission
PSNJ	*The Plants of Southern New Jersey*
TBNJ	*The Birds of New Jersey*
UP	University of Pennsylvania
USBS	United States Biological Survey (now the U.S. Fish and Wildlife Service)
U.S.	United States
USDA	United States Department of Agriculture
WNSA	Wilson Natural Science Association

Note that the museum called the U.S. National Museum in Stone's time has, for the sake of brevity and simplicity, been called "the Smithsonian" throughout, as it has always been part of the Smithsonian Institution.

In Witmer's Shadow

Sometime in the early 1980s, I was browsing in the Old Salt gift shop on the Ocean City, New Jersey boardwalk and came across the two-volume Dover reprint of *Bird Studies at Old Cape May* (*BSOCM*) by Witmer Stone. I'd never heard of the title or its author, but as I thumbed through the pages I decided to shell out the $4.50 for each volume. I think it was another year or two before I really got into the book, and like so many before and after I fell under the spell of Stone's idyllic prose in describing the landscapes of coastal New Jersey in the late 19th and early 20th centuries – the "old Cape May" that had long since vanished. The now densely packed borough of Wildwood Crest was, at that time, inhabited only by the men of the Coast Guard station, and on some days a herd of wild cattle could be seen standing in the surf. Whip-poor-wills called from the roofs of cabins in the pine woods at Cape May Point. East of Cape May City, the Cape Island Sound oyster beds were marked with stakes and worked by men using tongs. I was even fascinated by the crude, grainy photographs that illustrated the books: for just the instant the shutter was open, I was transported back in time to some long-vanished Jersey coastal location. Buried forests rose up out of sand dunes that today are crowded with houses and hotels; early incarnations of coastal towns loomed behind mudflats covered with blurry blobs that the captions assured me were flocks of shore-birds; I was walking along the beach on a DVOC outing with other members who were nattily dressed in jackets and ties, which was apparently the habit in those days. I immediately started wondering about the author, and a pipe dream began that had me writing his biography one day.

"The history of ornithologists is quite often as interesting as the history of ornithology, especially when it descends from the stilted formality, so charac-teristic of history, and gives us pictures of real life, full of humorous anecdotes and good-natured fun."[1] So wrote Stone in 1929, and I read this after I'd already decided that, even though biographies of dead ornithologists are unavoidably going to have their share of "stilted" historical material, readers bold enough to launch into a book of natural science history are entitled to a little spice and levity. Stone himself had a keen sense of humor which he didn't suppress when he didn't have to. It was Witmer Stone as a person, after all, I was trying to uncover; the agonizingly detailed minutiae of hundred-year-old scientific theo-ries, taxonomical quarrels, and scientific organization bylaws weren't things I was overly interested in, and I wouldn't expect readers to be, either. So while covering the (for some) drier aspects of Stone's work, I've made an effort to include some of the more interesting or humorous nuggets that turned up in the research. The stodgier ornithological historians may frown on me for this, but it's my book and I'll smile if I want to. Heaven forbid someone should try to make a book on ornithological history interesting, instead of dry as a mouthful of sawdust like most of 'em.

The author of a work such as this is like a paleontologist. It has often been said that the changes over time in ancient faunas – the rising and falling away of species, and their lineal relationships – are like a movie; the fossil record provides only occasional frames from that movie, and the task of the paleontologist is to try to reconstruct the movie based on the occasional frames. Similarly, Witmer Stone's life can be thought of as a movie, and the correspondence and articles that I've examined during the research for this book serve as occasional frames. Outside of one short magazine article about his youth, Stone – decidedly unlike some of his contemporaries – left nothing in the way of autobiography or memoir, and he had no children. His only sibling died before marrying or having children. That particular stirp screeched to a halt by 1940. It has been a cold trail to follow, and this book has been constructed, by necessity, "from scratch." It's been akin to building a house one brick at a time – nothing prefab here. There are undoubtedly instances when some missing frames, if found, would alter some of the storylines or theories and opinions presented here, and any work that contains as much historical data as this one is inevitably going to have its share of errors, but I have done my best to reconstruct the movie of his life as accurately as I could with the material at my disposal.

Because so little has been written about Stone, most of what follows is based on original research, mostly his correspondence. I have summarized a letter's contents in places, but often let the cast do the talking, telling this particular history in their own words. People in those days wrote with wit, politesse, intelligence, and eloquence the likes of which are rarely encountered today (they even knew how to construct sentences and spell!), and because we have precious little in the way of audio or video from the principals involved, reading their words is the closest we'll come to conversing with them, or meeting them personally. And I want anyone who reads the book to go away with more than just a head full of facts, dates, and other similarly dry information about Stone. I want them to have at least a vague impression, as I do now, that he's someone they've actually met, even if it feels as though it were fleeting, and a long time ago, like an old uncle you remember vaguely from childhood Christmas dinners. I want them to feel as if they've brushed up against "the innate goodness of the man."[2]

Many times while researching this book, particularly when reading a personal note from Stone's own pen, I've felt like I was stretching my hand back in time (I was born 23 years after he died), almost making actual, personal contact with the man, as in the Michelangelo fresco of God reaching out to touch Adam's finger. As Roger Tory Peterson wrote of Audubon in the introduction to the Dover reprint of *Bird Studies at Old Cape May*, he "now seems real, a man who actually lived – not merely a legend."[3] As I bird around the Cape May area today, it may be the historian in me – and most of the modern-day listers and rarity chasers with their pricey boutique optics and modern electronics gadgets would think I was nuts – but I can't help but feel the shadow of those who have gone before. And because Stone discovered the place and its migration phenomenon first, spent more time there, wrote it up at greater length, and described it better than the rest of them, it is, to borrow from Dickens, his spirit that is constantly at my elbow. He casts the longest shadow. (Stone was the same way: he imagined "the shade of Nuttall" arising before him when he found a species of plant at a location where the famous ANSP botanist had discovered it decades before.)[4]

Sometimes it's as casual as comparing a heavy Cape May flight of today with descriptions from Stone's time, or wondering how a particular Cape May or Pine Barrens vista appeared to him. Other times it hits closer to home, and I can feel a kinship with a long-departed kindred spirit. I have always been amused by Stone's description of a flock of Black Terns at Cape May Point on August 27, 1926: "[W]hile watching them, I was impressed by the similarity of their flight and general wing action to those of the Nighthawk, and to my astonishment I presently realized that one of the birds actually was a Nighthawk."[5] I've often thought of that while watching Black Terns at the Point, and then one evening while studying a flock of them kiting at the far end of a jetty, *I* was astonished to find a nighthawk in their midst.

Although most birders do their Cape May Point hawk watching from the lighthouse parking lot platform, in the 1990s I started watching the flights from the dune crossover walkways at the beach, oftentimes keeping notes on the weather conditions, and on which raptors were crossing and which ones were turning back. It is the characteristic water-crossing behavior of the different raptor and other species under varying weather conditions, after all, that produces the Cape May flights in the first place, and the beach is the best place to observe it – that's where the game is being played. I'd pick a raptor heading out and stay on it until it either turned back or disappeared from view heading south over the Bay, which could sometimes involve 5–10 minutes of continuous observation, binoculars glued to my eyes, shoulder muscles burning. Then reading the Eastern Kingbird account in *BSOCM* one day I realized a certain somebody had been similarly engaged 75 years before: "Flocks [of kingbirds]… would rise from trees on the Bay side and start out, widely scattered, across the water bound for the Delaware coast.…A few individuals which were kept in sight with the glass turned back and came to roost again but most of them kept on flapping their wings continually as they ascended at a very steep angle and attained a considerable height before advancing horizontally."[6]

While living in the Philadelphia area, I used to spend time watching, counting, and sometimes following by car crows that were heading to roost in wintertime, and I did the same thing with ravens in Wyoming – not something of interest to most birders. Then I came across an *Auk* article in which Stone recounted studying the same thing on the Delaware River with other DVOC members, "when the long straggling flights [of crows] may be seen winging their way homeward, sometimes in the bright glow of a winter sunset, at others in the teeth of a blinding storm, but always stubbornly heading for the particular roosting ground that generations of ancestors have used before them"[7] – the same phenomenon to be noted and wondered at in the same vicinity years later by a birdwatcher of a future generation, following in the footsteps of his ornithological ancestors.

I read through all of Stone's archived correspondence at ANSP while preparing this book, and shortly after reading Charles Richmond's letters I read Stone's fine *Auk* memorial for Richmond, which drew freely on the same correspondence. Having read it recently, I recognized most of the passages used by Stone, and some of the ones Stone particularly liked and quoted were ones that had struck my fancy as well. (Some are found in the pages to follow.) It occurred to me that he had sat down and gone through the same correspondence 80 years before, and that Stone and I were probably the only two who had *ever* read through all of it.

Maybe you've experienced the same consciousness of parallel experiences with Stone or other historical personalities, and hopefully after reading this book you'll find yourself with a heightened awareness of its occurrence. Many times I'll wander the Cape May Point area at dusk as the chill of a fall evening settles over the woodland, beach, meadow, and marsh, lost in the timeless enchantment of Cape May autumn magic, not wanting to be anywhere else in the world; I'll detect the whirring, whistling silhouettes of ducks winging by in the deepening twilight, espy a flock of herons heading out high over the Bay, destination Delaware, and thrill to an owl in the distance, hooting the day's benediction and ushering in the nightfall…and then "there flashes out, at regular intervals, the brilliant yellow star of the Cape May Light, and night settles down over the meadows."[8]

In Witmer's shadow, indeed.

1

An Enthusiasm Centered on Birds

As Union and Confederate armies collided head-on in the fields around Gettysburg in early July 1863, initiating three days of horrific casualties, a smaller but historically significant engagement briefly played out on a nearby stage. J.E.B. Stuart's Confederate cavalry attacked the town of Carlisle, Pennsylvania, on the evening of July 1, after Union Major General William "Baldy" Smith refused to surrender the town despite holding it with forces comprising only Pennsylvania and New York militia. The Confederates were short on artillery ammunition, but for the next several hours their artillery laced the town, "causing more noise than harm" according to one account.[1] The Union barracks outside the town were burned down before Stuart, hearing of the battle now raging at Gettysburg, withdrew his forces to head off in that direction. (The scars inflicted by Confederate cannons can still be seen on the Carlisle courthouse.)[2]

One of the Union militia members present at the shelling, serving with Pennsylvania's First Regiment Infantry – the famed "Gray Reserves" – was Frederick Stone from Philadelphia. He later described some of the particulars of the battle to a friend, including the mortal wounding of a soldier right behind him and the wounding of another nearby, and "how startling was the impression of the nearness of death and wounds produced by the sound of falling muskets and the sight of men staggering to the ground."[3] Had one of the Confederate shells taken a slightly different trajectory, Pennsylvania could have lost one of its most important budding young historians. Looking further into the crystal ball, 20th-century American ornithology may have missed one of its leading figures, and the future written record of an era of New Jersey natural history could have been sadly impoverished.

Frederick Dawson Stone was born in Philadelphia on April 8, 1841 to John Stone, born in Liverpool, England in 1786, and Mary Stone *née* Whittle, born in 1807 in Germantown, Pennsylvania. Frederick attended the Union Academy, located then at 11th and Market Streets. Upon the death of his father in 1859, he went to work with his older brothers as a salesman in the family millinery and silk-importing business, John Stone & Sons, at 45 South 2nd Street, and later at 805 Chestnut Street.[4-5] On November 9, 1865 he married Anne Witmer, born August 29, 1842 in Paradise, Lancaster County, Pennsylvania, to Adam Kendrick Witmer and Hannah Witmer *née* Steele. Frederick and Anne were distantly related: her grandfather on her mother's side (John Dutton Steele) and his grandmother on his father's side (Margaret Steele) were brother and sister.[6] Frederick never became a partner in the family firm, and in 1876 his brothers liquidated the business and retired.[7]

In a classic case of someone turning his avocation into his vocation, Frederick Stone then became the librarian of the Historical Society of Pennsylvania (HSP) in February 1877 and served in that capacity until his death. Selling "silks, bonnet ribbons, flowers, laces, crapes, etc." was drudgery for him; meanwhile, he had been an active amateur historian for several years, and had become increasingly involved with the HSP. He eventually became a member of several historical societies.[3-4]

Frederick and Anne had two sons. The first, born in Philadelphia at 6 a.m. on Saturday, September 22, 1866, they named Witmer (no middle name), following a common practice at the time of naming boys using their mother's or grandmother's maiden name as a first or middle name.[8] In later years Witmer told a friend, "[W]hile I try to spell my name the same, other people take all sorts of liberties with the first half of it, which gives me the benefit of a little variety."[9] That is true – in his correspondence one comes across all manner of misspellings: Whitmer, Wittmer, Whitmere, Whitmore, Whitmar, Whitman, even Wilbur and William, among others. Audubon Society president T. Gilbert Pearson in particular was all over the place in his renditions of it. A catalog of the vertebrate zoology literature housed at the McGill University library, compiled and published by a friend who knew Stone well, nevertheless renders Witmer's name three different ways.[10] One encyclopedia publisher kept writing to ask Stone to author some biographies for him, and it doesn't appear that Stone took him up on the offer – possibly due to his letters being addressed to "Wilmer" Stone. Similarly, a Philadelphia newspaper article covering the 1899 American Ornithologists' Union meeting, being held for the first time in Philadelphia, included a sketch of "Wilmer Stone." Stone's closest acquaintants – for example his lifelong friends the Brown brothers – addressed him in correspondence, and presumably in person, as "Wit." "Stones" and "Sax" were two more of Witmer's boyhood nicknames.

Witmer Stone was not born into wealth. Samuel Pennypacker, Pennsylvania governor 1903–1907, recalled in his 1918 autobiography that Frederick Stone had failed at business and had little money, but was capable nonetheless; another contemporary said Frederick had an impressive collection of historic prints despite "the limited means at his disposal."[3,11]

Witmer wrote an autobiographical piece about his youth in the Academy of Natural Sciences of Philadelphia's (ANSP) *Frontiers* magazine in 1936. It is so full of information on this period of his life, found nowhere else in this kind of detail, that I quote it at length:

> The first six years of my life were passed in the old residential section of Philadelphia, near Sixteenth and Pine Streets [317 S. 16th Street], in an environment of red brick houses and brick sidewalks,

white marble door steps and cobble-stone streets [similar to its current appearance].[5,8] There was nothing but the sky above to furnish any contact with Nature. Frequent walks with my nurse took me to nearby Rittenhouse Square, where there were at least trees and green grass, and to the more remote Logan Square (now Logan Circle). The Square was then surrounded by a high iron fence, behind which were a pair of deer. These deer still remain vividly impressed upon my memory, for there was in those days no exhibit at the Zoological Gardens, and these were the first wild animals ever seen by a little Philadelphia boy of 1870.

One day in mid-winter I was greatly excited by the discovery of a sick English Sparrow in our narrow brick-paved side yard. The sparrows had only been introduced a few years before and this was the first wild bird that I had ever seen in the city. In spite of our best efforts it died, but the incident was so impressed upon the mind of the small six-year-old that he set about recording it, printing his words in large block letters and fastening the several sheets together in a sort of pamphlet entitled on the cover "The History of the English Sparrow, By W.S." This, my first literary effort, is, I believe, still extant.

From my earliest recollection I spent the summer months at my grandparents' home in the village of Paradise, near Lancaster, Pennsylvania, and there, with extensive gardens, orchards and open farm country to roam over, my interest in Nature developed apace. I learned to know by sight the familiar birds, such as the Robin, Grackle, Catbird, Dove and Baltimore Oriole and was told the names of the common garden flowers. There were also occasional walks with my grandmother, who was an excellent botanist, to the meadows bordering the nearby Pequea Creek to gather bunches of wild flowers and to see the water flowing over the mill dam. Here I became acquainted with the Milk-weed, the Iron-weed, and the Touch-me-not, and with the Kingfisher and Fly-up-the-creek (Green Heron) and many butterflies. I was fascinated with the bull-frogs which leaped into the still pools, the mud turtles which I even succeeded in capturing and the water snakes coiled on rocks at the dam breast. This interest was not encouraged by my gentle guardian, whose chief care seemed to be that I should not fall into the water.

My uncle [John], who had a good cabinet of minerals and knew the common butterflies and other insects, was interested and amused at my early studies of Nature. He provided me with a butterfly net and showed me how to spread my specimens. He also furnished a sheet of cork upon which to pin my beetles, and gave me a small bottle of alcohol in which to kill them.

These seemingly endless summers were to me the most delightful periods of my life. Even more wonderful were the two or three weeks spent every year at my great-grandfather's [John Dutton Steele] farm [Stock Grange] in central Chester County [Pennsylvania] where lived, at that time, five maiden great-aunts [sisters of Witmer's maternal grandmother], whose principal interest seemed to consist in entertaining the young people of the family. My oldest aunt [Mary Steele] was an amateur ornithologist and botanist of no slight attainments. ["She possessed a knowledge of the natural history of Pennsylvania... equaled by but few persons of her generation," and was also a beekeeper.][6,12] She had formed a collection of birds' eggs....Once, at least, during each visit I was shown this collection carefully preserved in pasteboard boxes with partitions stitched in to divide them into little square sections. She also possessed a copy of the colored plates of [Alexander] Wilson's "Ornithology," and this, too, was shown to me on each visit, and as we turned the pages she read me the name of each bird until I almost knew them by heart long before I ever saw the birds in life. She also explained to me the differences between the leaves of the various forest trees and showed me how to make impressions of them....By the time I was seven years old, thanks to my aunt, I was possessed of a small box of eggs ranging from that of the Guinea fowl, whose harsh cackling to this day recalls that old farm, to the small brown egg of a Wren, and with a small series of minerals from my uncle my museum was begun. I can well remember, as I grew older, the pride with which I showed my aunt a specimen of a bird that she had only known from Wilson's painting or a wild flower that she had never found on the farm.[13]

When I was seven years of age my family moved out to Germantown [a former suburb which had recently been incorporated into Philadelphia]. Here opportunities for nature study were far greater than in the city, but the association with other boys and the varied interest that ensued diverted me to some extent except during the summers in the country. One memorable event when I was about eight or nine years old was a visit to the Academy of Natural Sciences, then located at Broad and Sansom Streets. I still remember the awe with which I examined the collections of birds, shells, minerals and other material....After that I never came into the city without going to the museum which had then been moved to its present location.[14]

Ironically, Witmer's great-grandfather, Charles Stones (the final "s" was dropped by his immediate descendants) emigrated to America in 1795, died of yellow fever in 1798, and was buried in Logan Square, which was a potter's field at the time.[3] A natural history museum was later built adjacent to the square, and Charles's great-grandson would begin a long career there almost a century after the emigrant's death.

Witmer also visited the Philadelphia Zoo as a youngster. Immediately after one visit in April 1878, he wrote an essay describing all the critters he encountered; shortly before his death he sent it in to *Fauna*, a magazine published by the Philadelphia Zoological Society, where it appeared posthumously.[15] He had his first close look at a Bald Eagle on a boyhood trip to the zoo, but was disappointed at the listless, waddling misfit he saw in its cage, which was at odds with its reputation and the typical artistic representations of it.[16] Later in life Witmer served on the zoo's board of directors.

Witmer's uncle, John S. Witmer, was an original member of the Tucquan Club, a group of outdoor enthusiasts in Lancaster which is still in existence, and he took his nephew on nature outings.[17] Six-year-old Witmer's enjoyment of outdoor activities with Uncle John is evident in an 1873 note: "Dear Uncle John; We are out of apples. I wish I was up with you to go sledding. I can't write more for I must put my pen behind my ear. Wit. Stone."[18] Stone had another uncle with the same name as that of a well-known oyster cracker company, and as a youngster he assumed that all the crackers he saw stamped "Exton" belonged to that uncle.[19] This was likely Adam Exton Witmer of Paradise, the "Uncle Eck" Stone referred to in letters written during his summer stays in Lancaster County.

According to University of Pennsylvania (UP) English professor and long-time friend Cornelius Weygandt, Witmer Stone was "of the Chester County Quaker–Pennsylvania Dutch cross that has given us so many of our botanists and ornithologists, paleontologists and chemists. The Quaker opposition to art drove, from our early days, many young men of questing minds and a love of the out-of-doors into field-work in the sciences. If such young men could not make something beautiful out of the work they saw beautiful and found good, they could at least put on record its truths."[20] In a memorial of George Spencer Morris in *Cassinia*, Stone attributed at least part of Morris's interest in natural history to "the wide spread love of nature so firmly established at all times in the Society of Friends and nurtured in their schools," and credited the same source for fanning the same interests in John Cassin and Thomas Jackson.[21-22]

After the move to Germantown, the Stones eventually settled in a house at 215 East Logan Street.[23] From 1877 to 1883, Witmer attended a Quaker school, Germantown Academy (GA), located then at the corner of School House Lane and Greene Street.[24] Maybe he was serenaded with "ribald rhymes" (like "'Quaker! Quaker! Mashed pertater' and all its unquotable addenda") by neighborhood boys on his daily walk to GA, as Weygandt was, because "Quakers were considered proper game by the juvenile humorists."[25]

Germantown had long been a bucolic suburb of Philadelphia, and although it was made part of the city by the 1854 Act of Consolidation, it still had lots

The Home Guard. Frederick (*left*) and Witmer c.1874. ANSP Archives.

of wide open spaces and a rural flavor. In an address to the Art and Science Club of Germantown in 1930, Weygandt described the Germantown of 1880 as "the age of horses; Germantown wagons; gas-light chandeliers; sherry and plum cake set out for neighbors when they called of an evening; family doctors;... an age of buckwheat cakes of mornings and real supper at night; of cows kept in the back yard; of greenhouses from which you cut flowers for your tables all winter long; of Quaker bonnets and broadbrims; and many country cousins in town during Yearly Meeting Week." Some still practiced the old trades, including blacksmithing; the town had a general store "where you could buy almost everything from a needle to an anchor"; and occasionally a covered wagon laden with wares set out for a distant country store.[26]

Witmer's boyhood gave clear indications of the path of his future life and career. He showed an early interest in all things natural and was an inveterate collector, like many boys at the time.[27,28] On the occasion of his 67th birthday, a Philadelphia newspaperman reported that Stone couldn't "recall a time in his life, even in his earliest childhood, when his enthusiasm hasn't centered on birds."[29] Stone was a boyhood friend and schoolmate of two (of the seven!) Brown brothers, Amos (b. 1864) and Stewardson (b. 1867). Their family rented the historic "Restalrig" home in Germantown, and the estate bordered miles of open farmland that the boys roamed, satisfying their collecting appetites ("our happy hunting grounds," as Witmer later wistfully described them after they were built over).[14] Wister Woods, still extant, was one of Witmer's local spots for bird study.[30] He had much in common with Amos and Stewardson, including "a love of nature, of music and of out-door athletic exercises," and he later recalled, "[W]e became inseparable companions. Indeed for a period of more than ten years we spent almost our entire spare time at Restalrig or in the immediate vicinity mainly in collecting and studying specimens of plants, animals, and minerals….Our aim was to become familiar with all of the animal and plant life of that part of Germantown as well as the minerals and rocks, and I think we nearly succeeded."[31] The Stone and Brown boys were so tight-knit from common interests that they didn't bother much with other GA classmates outside of school.[32]

Witmer described his early experiences in bird collecting:

> When I was about fourteen years of age I was allowed to have an old muzzle loading shot gun that had been my father's. Immediately I began to convert the Wilson pictures into realities. There were no binoculars in those days, and no thought of becoming acquainted with birds by any means except by shooting them. The only book by which I could identify my specimens was the bulky and rather formidable volume of the Pacific railroad Surveys containing Baird, Cassin, and Lawrence's "Birds of North America." I went laboriously over the descriptions and was usually successful in naming my birds, but a Pine Warbler and a Brewster's Warbler long remained unidentified.[33]

George Spencer Morris later described the gun Stone was using in the 1890s (and earlier?) for collecting as "a curious little contrivance which he calls a gun; in reality it's kind of a cross between a pea shooter and a slingshot, but when handled by an expert like the owner, it becomes a deadly weapon…. It has many good points (this is a tribute to Stone's marksmanship) and goes up the sleeve nicely; it is well-suited to suburban collecting; its gentle crack is doubtless not an unfamiliar sound in the wild back yards of Germantown, and for aught I know, it may have made the welkin ring in the trackless wastes of Logan Square."[34] Germantowners certainly heard it: in his journal entry for January 2, 1888, Stewardson Brown wrote, "Saw a large Red-tailed Hawk down by the Big willow and Stones got a shot but did not kill him."[35]

Witmer's early attempts at creating bird mounts were fraught with failures borne of ignorance. He was not allowed to use arsenic, so he used cayenne pepper instead. "The result was that upon my return home at the close of the summer [from Paradise and Stock Grange] my mounted birds consisted only of the hemp stuffing, the wires and a pile of feathers left by the moths."[14] Eventually, Elliott Coues's instructions for making skins in *Key to North American Birds* provided the necessary know-how.

One of the dangers of his boyhood collecting was recounted in an article Stone wrote about spiders in 1890: "While digging one of them [a wolf spider,

Hogna helluo] out of its burrow some years ago I was bitten on the end of the finger. The pain was rather more intense than that experienced from the sting of a
bee, and extended through the whole forearm. It did not last, however, more than
half an hour, though the finger remained swollen for some time."[36] Their mothers
must have gained experience in a variety of first aid situations with all the running, climbing, falling, knee skinning – and spider handling – the boys did.

A second son, Frederick D. Stone Jr., was born to Frederick and Anne in
1872. In their school days, the two Stone brothers and four of the Brown brothers (Amos, Stewardson, Herbert, and Francis) formed the Wilson Natural Science Association (WNSA – the boys pronounced it "Wansa"), named in honor
of Witmer's favorite ornithologist.[37] The Stone home held the club's natural
history collection, of which Witmer was the "curator" (along with his duties
as club treasurer). An opossum and a chicken skeleton were the "outstanding
exhibits" of the collection.[14] The club met weekly at the Stone house, where
papers were "read with all the formalities of a more serious organization."[31]
Their papers, preserved in the ANSP archives, covered an amazing variety of
topics in all the fields of natural history, from "Anatomy of lichens" to "Respira-
tion of insects" to "What is a diatom?"[38] Stone shared his findings (often with
drawings in his own hand) of, among other things, the microscopic inspection
of butterfly scales, the species of Curculionidae weevils he'd found in the past
year, a chart showing his 1884 locations (Germantown, Stock Grange, Paradise) for "diurnal Lepidoptera," and a botanical subject on which he was still
publishing 20 years later: violets, discovered in localities around Germantown
and at Stock Grange.

The young men drafted and lavishly produced a constitution, which defined
the purpose of the club: "[T]he study of natural science in all its branches,
including Zoology, Botany, Mineralogy, Geology, Physics and Astronomy." In
the "President's Address" one year, Amos said that physics, mineralogy, and
geology (his pet subjects, coincidentally) had not received sufficient attention;
he also advised that the club's collection was getting quite large and should
be burdened no further with "'curious growths' and other trashy specimens."[39]
Stone's "Treasurer's Reports" for various years included items that presaged a
couple of future situations with the American Ornithologists' Union (AOU): at
one point, he noted that he had 227 papers on hand submitted by club members, and both Amos and Witmer, in their respective reports, commented with
some condescension on the manuscript contributions and lack of progress of
"junior members [i.e., younger brothers]."[38] Years later, Stone had a perpetual
backlog of papers as *Auk* editor, and AOU members in the more prestigious
membership classes of the AOU caste system often assured each other of their
superiority to the lowly Associate members.[40]

The Stone parents deserve credit for their willingness to indulge the neighborhood boys' interest in nature, and for having the museum in their house.

As Witmer later recalled, "The Browns spent their summers at the seashore [Point Pleasant, New Jersey]. When we all assembled in the autumn there were always many additions to the Museum to be labeled and installed, and also many losses to be deplored, for the insect boxes which we made were by no means moth-proof. Many of our alcoholic specimens had spoiled because we had used Methylic alcohol [instead of a more expensive, but more effective, solution]….The highly odoriferous collection had to be surreptitiously carried down through the house and disposed of over the back fence."[14]

─────────── ∿ ───────────

"When we all assembled in the autumn" wasn't just about the Browns coming back from the shore: surviving correspondence with Stewardson indicates that Witmer, from at least his mid-teens through his college years, spent most or all of the summer moving back and forth between Paradise and Stock Grange, not returning to Germantown until late August or September. Between the two places, Witmer got in his share of botanical and zoological collecting, as well as experiencing rural lifestyle staples such as runaway farm animals, excursions in his handmade canoe (interestingly named "The Flirt"), and watching meteor showers.[12,41-43]

When visiting Paradise, Witmer also worked at his grandfather's warehouse, A.K. Witmer and Sons, where lumber, coal, and ice were sold; he spent even more time there once his grandfather took ill in the summer of 1886. (Adam Witmer died in 1887.)[44-45] Witmer's Uncle John, who may have worked at the warehouse, was in the berry business ("Uncle John has shipped 150 quarts of Raspberries to Lancaster"), and was the secretary for the Lancaster County Mutual Insurance Company.[46-47] Witmer must have been working for Uncle John in the summer of 1887, for he reported in mid-July, in a tone that implies he would rather have been out chasing birds and riding in his canoe, "Most of my time so far however has been taken up with picking raspberries & 'writing insurance.'"[48] His botanical knowledge was well-known enough that at least one Paradise farmer asked him to inspect his farm for the presence of the notorious invasive Canada Thistle.[45]

Frederick Stone's great-uncle, John D. Steele, bought the 600-acre Stock Grange estate in West Bradford Township, Chester County from the heirs of Revolutionary War general Richard Humpton in 1805. Steele built an addition on the east end of the original house, planted trees and shrubs brought over from his home in England, and ran a dairy farm on the property.[3] Frederick used to tell a friend of his love of the place and its exhilarating, out-of-doors, country living; "a jog-trot on a plough-horse with jingling chains, a moonlight ride in a hay wagon, a swim in the mill-dam, gigging for eels or fishing for bass in the Brandywine, the undulating motion of cradling wheat in the 30-acre lot" were some of his Stock Grange memories. In Witmer's youth, the aforementioned great-aunts lived there, and Stone and the Brown brothers were frequent visitors, exploring the surrounding fields and woods, fishing in the streams, collecting birds, frogs, and mammals, and climbing to hawk nests.[3,49-51] Stone found Turkey Vulture nests in the area, and in 1885 he described two that he found in 1882 – one along a tributary of the Brandywine Creek, the other on Stock Grange – in his first serious ornithological publication, "The Turkey Buzzard breeding in Pennsylvania" in *The American Naturalist*.[52] Interestingly, a January 1884 note in *Ornithologist and Oologist* recorded some recent finds of Turkey Vulture nests in Chester County. The author said vulture nests had rarely been found in the county away from Welsh Mountain, and he mentioned one nest found "this spring [1883], by boys, on the Brandywine Creek."[53] Assuming the author had his date mixed up by a year – not much of a stretch – this could very well refer to one of the nests found by Stone, and little would the author have suspected the future ornithological career of one of the "boys."

Twenty years after Stone's death, his longtime friend and colleague Henry Fowler, curator of fishes at ANSP, wrote a brief essay about a two-week stay at Stock Grange with Witmer in the early 1900s. At the time, only two of the maiden great-aunts (Dorothy and Esther) were still alive and living there, along with their sister, Stone's widowed (since 1887) maternal grandmother, Hannah. Fowler recounted that one day, when Witmer was trying to shinny up to a Broad-winged Hawk nest in a large oak tree "which did not have any branches until about thirty feet from the ground," a farmer in a nearby field was "chanting a most monotonous theme, simple, and very exasperating when repeated incessantly." The tune irritated Stone so much that Fowler whistled it to him on subsequent attempts to scale the tree, and "it so inconvenienced Witmer that every time he got up about twenty or twenty-five feet, he would slide down again" – so that particular hawk nest remained unrifled.[51] There are plants in the ANSP herbarium collected by Stone at Stock Grange as late as 1903. Dorothy and Esther both died in January 1910. (Hannah lived until 1911, dying at age 103, but was living in Philadelphia with Anne by then.) By September 1910, Witmer's cousin Hugh was sending him a letter asking him to set a date for moving the house's contents out.[54] This is apparently when the days of the Steele family living at Stock Grange came to an end. Just a few days before Stone's death, while chatting with a friend, he recalled an incident with a catbird from his Stock Grange days.[55]

Stock Grange was later owned by the actor Claude Rains, and Bette Davis often stayed there.[56] Local lore has it that Charles Lindbergh had to make an emergency landing in a nearby field once due to fog. Most of the grounds have now been developed, but the original house and 120 acres around it are still intact, and the current owners have done a wonderful job restoring it.[57] As I toured the grounds one fine winter day with the owner, crossing the wetland that teems with peepers in the spring, seeing the enormous old oak and Black Gums that remain from Stone's time, and spotting a Red Fox contentedly sitting by a hedge in the sunshine, I thought about what it would be like to have Witmer there now strolling along with us. I imagined he would be like Scrooge walking the old school road with the Ghost of Christmas Past, "recognizing every gate, and post, and tree," and exclaiming, "Good heaven! I was bred in this place! I was a boy here! Remember it?! I could walk it blindfolded!"

Some of the WNSA gang wanted to take a trip to the Susquehanna River in Pennsylvania in 1886, and a friend of Uncle John recommended the vicinity of York Furnace.[58] Their June trip was beset by rain, however, so three years later they tried again, with better luck. They produced an impressively formal book (handwritten accounts and drawings in a notebook) about the June 23–30, 1889 jaunt, complete with an overview of the trip written by Witmer and individual articles on the various natural history branches. Witmer reported on the reptiles, beetles, spiders, and other invertebrates, Frederick on butterflies, and the Brown brothers divvied up plants, shells, and birds (the latter illustrated by Witmer, who showed some fine artistic talent in his younger days). They investigated wind caves, watched a Bald Eagle soaring over the river, and one evening they sat on some riverside rocks and "made the night hideous" to the accompaniment of a banjo. Amazingly, many of the local features the club

Witmer (*center, facing right*) on front steps of Stock Grange c. 1895. Four of the maiden great-aunts are at left. ANSP Archives.

enjoyed that week can still be seen in an area that hasn't changed dramatically since then: Tucquan and Otter creeks, Bair's Island, Chickies Rock, and McCall's Ferry. The latter, after 80 years in the McCall family, had recently passed into ownership outside the family, and today the McCall Ferry Farm is on the National Register of Historic Places.[59] Some of the boys would have been young – Frederick was 16 – and it seems that by the end of the week they'd had enough of the hiking and exploring.[60]

All the club's procedural and "publishing" formality is initially amusing until you consider the future academic and scientific careers of the older members (the younger boys didn't pursue scientific careers). These were just the earliest indications of lives to be spent immersed in academia, research, and publishing. Amos Brown became a geology professor at UP and published on mineralogy, fossils, and snails. His studies with the microscope contributed to his co-authorship of the important 1909 report, "The crystallography of hemoglobins."[61] Stewardson worked for the Lehigh Valley Railroad for 15 years, but natural history was his first love. He became the assistant curator of the botany department at ANSP in 1900, published extensively on botany, was very active in the Philadelphia Botanical Club, and edited their journal *Bartonia*. In fact, Stone later wrote that although the WNSA studies were "very local in scope, I have since been impressed with the admirable basis that they afforded for our future work."[31] And it's easy to see the progression from WNSA→DVOC→AOU – for example, with *Proceedings of the WNSA*→*Cassinia*→*The Auk*. Similarly, WNSA drafted a formal and artistically impressive constitution; in 1895, Stone was on the DVOC committee to draft a new constitution; and later he chaired a committee charged with revising the AOU bylaws.[62]

The WNSA met regularly until the older boys went off to college, and remained active until they were young men.[14] Some of the WNSA collections ended up at ANSP. In 1894, Stone and the Brown brothers donated 96 trays of mollusks from New Jersey shore locations, and 33 jars of frogs, toads, and reptiles from Pennsylvania and New Jersey, although Stone was mortified when the reptiles faded and lost their color within a year after being stored in a room at ANSP with too much sunlight.[63] A club report penned by Witmer, undated but early in his ANSP days, is a striking testament to the zeal and industry the young men brought to their natural history studies, and reveals how at least some late-19th-century youths spent their time long before the advent of television, cell phones, the Internet, and computer games:

> The entire rearrangement of the society's Herbarium and the revision of the nomenclature has resulted in the detection of a number [of previously unidentified species]. In all cases of doubt the specimens were compared with the [ANSP] Herbarium....Among the lower plants considerable collections were made. The Lichens, Uredineae, Hymenomycetes & Gasteromycetes [the latter three are fungi] were

the only divisions which received systematic study [and] lists of most of these have…been made out….[T]he Vertebrata (Fishes excepted) have been so thoroughly studied in former years that new species are at once recognized. The same may I think be said of the diurnal Lepi-doptera and the Orthoptera. The other orders of Insects have never been carefully studied though most of the species are identified…. The Hymenoptera & Coleoptera I think are nearly complete as far as local forms are concerned. The Spiders have received considerable study and new forms are at once recognized in nearly all the groups. [In fact, Witmer would shortly publish on the local spiders in *PANSP*.] Diligent study has also brought the Mollusca up to the front in this respect and at least two of the members are now familiar with all the local forms thus far discovered & probably all that occur in the imme-diate vicinity. [Witmer] has identified all the Planarian worms found in the immediate vicinity. [Some insect orders], many of the worms, the polyzoa, sponges, mites & crustaceans are the only groups which are "unworked." While among the Plants the Mosses & Liverworts & lower fungi & algae remain to be studied.[64]

Clearly, the Wilson gang wasn't just some kids catching salamanders in the creek and putting bugs in jars. They were collecting the salamanders and bugs (and the fungi and the mollusks), preserving them, poring through the available literature to identify them and learn of their life habits (pre-Internet…pre-*field guides*), and writing up their findings in formal, semi-scientific papers which they read to each other at their formal, semi-scientific meetings. In "I Remem-ber," Stone summed up his boyhood and WNSA days:

While I always derived the greatest pleasure from the arrangement and study of the specimens that I collected, this did not compare with the actual contact with the outdoors and the study of living nature. I shall never forget the anticipation with which I looked forward each year to the opening of spring and the recording of the arrival of the first Robin, Bluebird and Grackle or the blooming of the Skunk Cabbage, the Hepatica and the Blood-root.

As I look back on those early years I am surprised at the amount that we accomplished, for we engaged in all of the usual pastimes of boys of our time – cricket, baseball and other sports. We also spent the usual amount of time on our school work, but back of it all was the fascination of Nature which left us never an idle moment.[14]

Witmer was particularly close to Stewardson, whom he often referred to in letters as "Old Buck" – a curious nickname for a fellow teenager. When he got back to Germantown at the end of summer in 1887 with a slew of great stories to relate, he found that Stew had gone off to the mountains for a vacation. He wrote to Stew, "I tell you what old buck I have so many things to [tell] you that if you don't get home soon I shall certainly bust."[37]

———————— ∾ ————————

At the Germantown Historical Society's March 23, 1934 meeting, Stone gave a talk about *The Gossip*, which was yet another endeavor he and Stew undertook as youths that foreshadowed their future professional activity.[65] Stone recalled that both he and Brown had printing presses on which they produced "preserve labels for our mothers, visiting cards for our friends, and various other typographical wonders." One summer day in 1881, Stew, then 14, printed off a one-page newsletter he titled *The Gossip*; when Witmer saw it, he suggested they team up to start printing issues on a weekly basis, using the printing press at the Stone house. When winter came, they moved the operations to Brown's house and started printing a larger issue on a monthly basis. *The Gossip's* printing room there was also used by Amos for chemistry experiments, and sometimes a particularly malodorous concoction sent the boys gasping and tumbling out of the room. Stone recalled, "On another occasion to our great joy a large shelf suspended from the wall which served [Amos] as a work table collapsed, precipitating hundreds of bottles in a mass on the floor."[32] It makes you wonder why the Browns had seven boys first before coming to their senses and having a couple of daughters.

The periodical was intended only for distribution among the boys' families, and covered family activities, the doings at Germantown Academy, snowstorms, cricket matches, and even some local and national news, such as famous deaths (Darwin, R.W. Emerson, President Garfield, H.W. Longfellow). Each issue had puzzles and riddles for readers to respond to with written answers. The Stone parents seem to have encouraged the boys' enterprise: they were often listed as having given correct answers to all the previous issue's riddles, and the only paid ads the boys ever garnered were when Mr. Stone placed ones for HSP publications. Three budding young future scientists also had their first "pubs" in *The Gossip*: future botanist Stew on "The Germantown Flora," future ornithologist Wit on the nesting of the Turkey Vulture (presumably the basis for his *American Naturalist* article), and future geologist Amos's very interesting contribution on Cuban mud. It seems mud loaded as ballast onto a ship sailing from Cuba was later used as fill for a railroad bed in Germantown, and Amos found it teeming with sea shells and microscopic diatoms, sponge spicules, and foraminiferans. How many of the "real" Germantown newspapers at the time caught that one? And has there ever been another time, before or since, when a teenager in Germantown thought to examine fill dirt with a microscope?

Perusing the *Gossip* issues turns up some amusing items, including a warning to a neighborhood boy who had been bad-mouthing the *The Gossip* that he "had better keep clear of the office or alarming events may take place." They bid good luck to a new major periodical, *Our Continent*, which nevertheless seems to have been short-lived. One issue announced that the Harty Cricket Club, formed by the boys, had recently held a meeting, "[b]ut no business of importance was transacted." You don't say…

After a little over a year of printing *The Gossip*, the boys tired of the activity and decided to concentrate on "job printing" – almost every issue had included an advertisement for their services printing cards, labels, letterheads, etc. – and they announced its demise in the October 1882 issue.[66] But it had been a great exercise in start-to-finish journalism and publishing: in addition to writing the articles, the boys printed the issues and even cut the letters for the blocks used for the headings. Stone (*Cassinia*, *The Auk*) and Brown (*Bartonia*) went on to edit scientific journals; in 1934 Stone reflected that the *Gossip* experience was a good training ground for future editorial work, "for we knew what the printer had to do as well as the writer, we knew what types were like as well as how handled, we knew how easy it was to make errors & how hard to detect them, & [knew] the importance & the tediousness of proof-reading."[32]

As a teenager, Stone contributed to a local monthly leaflet titled *Short Notes on the Birds of Germantown*. He also mailed spring and fall migration records of local birds (including Germantown and Stock Grange sightings) seen by him and Stewardson and Herbert Brown to the Division of Economic Ornithology and Mammalogy, the larval stage of today's U.S. Fish and Wildlife Service.[67] One of Stone's points of contact at the Division was its founder and head, C. Hart Merriam, and some of the brief notes Merriam sent the young Stone at the time are interesting. He thanked Stone in 1885 for contributing to the Division's bird stomach collection, then in its nascent stages. (The collection eventually included 230,000 stomachs and produced a mountain of data on bird diets; although most of the stomachs are long gone, the index cards recording their contents are still in existence and efforts have recently begun to preserve them.)[68] In 1887, Merriam queried Stone about an animal previously unknown to science – or, at least, one of its colloquial names was previously unknown to Merriam: "In your communication, received some time since, in regard to the economic relations of mammals, you speak of the injury done to beans by 'Ground Hackies.' Will you have the kindness to inform us to what animal you refer?"[69] A "Ground Hackie" is, of course, a chipmunk, as anyone living in Germantown in the 1880s could have told him.

Nature wasn't the only thing that occupied Witmer in his high school and college years. As mentioned earlier, he and the Brown brothers loved music and sports. During at least some of his summers in Paradise, he played flute and piccolo in the Paradise Orchestra (actually a nine-piece ensemble). In fact, his letters to Stewardson in the summers of 1883 and 1884 suggest that he was about as occupied with music as he was with nature. There appears to have been a big concert each summer, and the 1884 one sounds like quite a production: "[T]he Orchestra practices three nights a week, and the other nights the vocalists and soloists practice; besides six orchestra pieces I am in for a Flute duet with Steve and two quartets (2 flutes, violin & cornet)."[42,70] He also played piccolo in the Paradise Cornet Band, whose repertoire included "Shouting the Battle Cry of Freedom," "Old Hundred," and "Pleyel's Hymn."[71] It appears that the Paradise Orchestra was inactive in 1885, but was revived in 1886, sans flutes.[42] Years later, Francis Cope Jr., a Germantown Academy grad 12 years Witmer's junior, reminisced to Stone, "You made us all happy in the evenings with your flute."[72]

Young Witmer also played the ocarina, a woodwind instrument of ancient pedigree that sounds like a recorder. He formed the WNSA into a group named (not very imaginatively) the "Ocarinas."[37] This seems to have taken up much of his time during his summers after his involvement with the Paradise Orchestra ended. In 1886 he took to arranging songs such as "Woodland Pleasures Quickstep," "Bluebird Gallop," "City Cadets' March," and "Snow Flake Waltzes" for the Ocarinas while working at the family warehouse in Paradise. By the end of the summer he had arranged 15 pieces for six ocarinas, covering 104 sheets of paper – quite a bit of work.[42,45-46] The Wilson gang must have done some singing as well, for in trying to induce Stew to pay a visit to Stock Grange in August 1887, Witmer wrote, "Moreover I am dying to have some 'Restalrig Glee' selections and where would we be without our Basso?"[73] During their trip to York Furnace in 1889, the fellows entertained the locals with their singing in the evening on the hotel porch.[60] The scrawled lyrics and chord changes for "Little Annie Rooney" show up on the back of an 1890 letter, possibly for an Ocarinas or Restalrig Glee performance of the tune.[74] I haven't found any references to Stone playing the flute or ocarina in later years, although it was recorded that as the DVOCers on the 1897 Decoration [now called Memorial] Day outing, including Stone, sailed back home on the Delaware River, they were regaled by a club band consisting of voice, harmonica, and ocarina.[75]

There are a few references to sports. The WNSA gang also had a cricket/athletic club, the Harty Cricket Club, whose members used a cannonball reputedly from the Battle of Germantown for their shot-put. Witmer had some interesting background information on just how the historical article came into the possession of the club. He said it "had been purchased at the sale of old Freddy Flickenstein's effects on the death of that aged individual. He had become ill in his hermit-like home…& was taken care of by some well-meaning ladies' organization of Germantown who insisted upon his being washed & it was insinuated by some uncharitable individual that this belated & unaccustomed application of water was the cause of his demise."[32] So much for the pedigree of the boys' cannonball, but Flickenstein was known to have a trove of historical knickknacks in his old curiosity shop of a house.[76] On their 1889 York Furnace trip the gang played baseball in front of the hotel for the entertainment of the locals.[60] Track and field events were held in Paradise in the summer, and Witmer once wrote to Stew from Paradise, "I have exercised a little in the orchard in the way of high jumping & having 'got on to' the regulation modus for 'standing high' I have raised my record to 4 ft. (no leg swinging)."[43,48]

Frederick Stone Sr. was involved in many of the celebration events in the Philadelphia area from 1876 to 1889, including the centennials of the nation, the Constitution, and the inauguration of George Washington, and the bicentennial of the landing of William Penn. A Centennial Exhibition ticket survives that was made out for a Frederick Stone, and it may have been his; it seems impossible that young Witmer and his family didn't visit the grounds at least once.[77] Frederick was secretary of the Committee of Arrangements of a group of local men of prominence associated with UP and other city groups who successfully invited President Grover Cleveland to a banquet at the Academy of Music on September 17, 1887, during the Constitution centennial.[78] (Fifty years later, his son Witmer was on a committee involved with the 150th Constitution celebration.)[79] In 1893, Governor Robert Pattison appointed him a member of the Valley Forge Park Commission, which was charged with creating a state park at the historical site. In 1895, Frederick received an honorary Litt.D. from UP.

What was it like having your father involved with presidents and centennial celebrations? Just listen to Witmer reporting it all to Stew in September 1887: "I tell you, for the last week…the city of Phila. did not know what end it was standing on. The place was just packed with people, & the parades beat anything I ever saw, especially the military.…Dad was rushing things I tell you, he had charge of the Dinner at the Academy of Music, which was the grandest thing of the kind ever given in the city, so it is said, and it certainly was gorgeous.…The President, all the Diplomatic Corps from Washington, the Chinese etc. in full costume…"[80]

The Browns moved out of Restalrig, which they rented, in 1900; sadly, it burned down in 1912, and the site, by Wayne Junction, has been built over.[81] Stone stayed close to the Browns throughout his life, and he wrote memorials for Amos and Stewardson.[31,61] In fact, when Amos died in 1917, Herbert thanked Stone for attending the funeral and wrote, "[Y]ou were always a member of this family," and another brother, Hazen, wrote, "I do not think there is anyone who really knew Doc [i.e., Amos] as well as you did."[82] Stewardson suffered from stomach ailments beginning in 1913, and, after a stint in Germantown Hospital for a slow-to-heal broken leg suffered in a fall near his home, he died on March 14, 1921. Stone expressed his devastation to a friend: "I am grieved to tell you that Stewardson Brown died suddenly.…Heart failure as result of his long string of operations etc. He was almost like a brother to me as we had known each other intimately since 1878."[83] George Spencer Morris, who knew

Stewardson from the DVOC, wrote to Stone, "It's pitiful to think of all the pain and suffering that he has had to endure during the past few years – only to be snuffed out at last. And he was so plucky and cheerful with it all too. There was something very lovable about Stew. He was modest and unassuming & kindly, yet so intelligent and so full of a quiet humor that I always felt strongly drawn toward him. I don't wonder that anyone who was as close to him as you were should feel his loss deeply."[84] A few years after Brown's death, a mutual friend remarked to Stone, "A kinder man never lived."[85] Herbert Brown lived many more years, and contributed pen and ink drawings to *BSOCM*.

———————— ❧ ————————

Witmer's younger brother, Frederick Stone Jr., doesn't seem to have had any involvement with the DVOC, and was never a member.[86] But he had at least an early interest in nature: he was a member of WNSA, and is credited in *BSOCM* with collecting a Savannah Sparrow at Cape Island Sound on July 6, 1891 while accompanying Witmer on one of his early visits to the Cape.[87] A *Gossip* blurb mentioned a poem he wrote at about the age of 10 called "Dame Duck and Her Family," so he must have had the Stone penchant for witty poetry. The Stone brothers even wrote and illustrated a privately published book about the family cats in 1881.

Herbert Brown was Frederick's Germantown Academy classmate.[88] Another classmate and good friend of Frederick was future UP president Thomas S. Gates, and they worked together on the school newsletter.[89] It was called *The Academy Monthly*, and was published by the school's Philomathean Society, of which Frederick was the business manger.[90] When he graduated from GA, he was listed as 5'6" and 115 pounds, which sounds small now but was average then, and similar to Witmer at the same age.

Tragically, Frederick died of typhoid fever on February 14, 1896, aged 23, three years after receiving a B.S. degree from UP, and two years after receiving a civil engineering degree there.[6,91] Philadelphia was notorious for its polluted water supply and high incidence of the disease.[92] ANSP president Samuel Dixon wrote Witmer a poignant note at the time, mentioning other young men of his acquaintance who had recently died of typhoid and admonishing Witmer, "Now my dear fellow I do hope you will take care of yourself. Be very careful about the water you drink." Witmer must have stayed home with his brother during his final illness, for Dixon concluded with, "Every morning the men around the A.N.S. come to me to know if I have heard from you and have all been hopeful – they will be sad this morning."[93] AOU founder H.A. Purdie told Witmer he was "sorry indeed for your loss. I very nearly lost a brother (sick with typhoid pneumonia) a few years ago, but he was spared as I wish your brother could have been."[94] Another feeling note came from DVOCer Mark

Wilde, who wrote, "I was not acquainted with your brother, but what affects you touches me, since you have been such a kind friend to me."[86]

Later in 1896, Witmer privately published a 40-page book his brother had been working on at the time of his death, *The Descendants of George Steele*, which traces the family's genealogy and history.[6] The title suggests an interest in history on Frederick's part similar to his father's, and toward the end of his short life his interests were more historical than zoological. This is further borne out, along with the possibility of the father's demise a year later being linked to the son's death, in a memorial (at times melodramatic) of the senior Frederick: "The death of the younger, who bore his name, at a time when he had learned to sympathize with his father's tastes and to aid him in his work, was a blow from which he never recovered. The dart which the insatiate archer had aimed at the boy passed through his body and entered the father's breast, and though he struggled manfully to pluck it out…he [had] received, in the enfeebled condition of his heart, his deathwound."[3]

It is interesting that the younger boy was named after the father, and in their memorials of Witmer written years later, James Rehn, Wharton Huber, and Robert Cushman Murphy incorrectly recorded that Witmer was the second son.[28,50,95] This may be simply because they assumed that the son named after the father must have been the elder, and it may have remained uncorrected in their minds because Witmer spoke so infrequently, if ever, about his late brother, even with people he spent as much time with as Rehn and Huber – perhaps he was as pained by the unexpected early separation as his father reportedly was. Thirty years after his brother's death, in an interesting aside in a letter, Witmer said that young Frederick had amassed quite a collection of U.S. stamps, and Witmer had recently been adding to it "more as a matter of sentiment than anything else."[96] An item in the will of Witmer's wife Lillie – three pen sketches by Frederick of the famous "Rip Van Winkle" actor Joseph Jefferson – suggests an interest in theater.[97] Witmer wrote in a biographical sketch at the beginning of his brother's posthumously published book that Frederick "exhibited a great interest in all matters related to engineering, and continued his studies in spare hours after graduating. He was a devoted alumnus of the University, and it was one of his greatest pleasures to follow the history of the college, the doings of the students and the successes of the athletic teams." Note the lack of a mention of any strong interest in nature; Frederick was working as an engineer at the Pencoyd Bridge Works, so the brothers had headed down very different career paths.[6]

Shortly after their son's death, Frederick and Anne were offered a two-month trip to Europe, to be paid for by some wealthy friends. Frederick declined, however, saying there were "responsibilities of a private character resting on me at present that would make me so anxious, if far away from home, that I would find neither benefit nor pleasure in the trip."[98] What those responsibilities were is not known – it may be a reference to his son's death – but a few years later one of the friends, William Brooke Rawle, a noted Civil War veteran and author, rued Frederick's decline of the offer, saying he'd probably still be alive if he'd taken it.[99] At the time of his death from heart disease on August 12, 1897, Frederick's health had been troublesome for several years.[3,100] Witmer described his father's end: "He had a bad attack of his trouble [in the] Catskill[s]…and wished to come home. We came through yesterday & he seemed better & cheerful & stood the journey well.…He had only been in the house a little while when he suddenly died. It was over in an instant."[101] Curiously – and probably agonizingly, and solely for pecuniary reasons – two months after his death, Anne and Witmer auctioned off many of Frederick Stone's effects and moved away from Germantown; an article in the *New York Times* about the auction described "the large and valuable library, together with several hundred fine engravings" including much George Washington-related material.[102]

Witmer once wrote that "we are wont to trace back our characteristics to ancestral sources," and a familiarity with some of the traits of Frederick and his eldest son would indicate that the nut didn't fall far from the tree.[21] The father was described as "ruddy, stout, and sandy" – similar to descriptions of Witmer.[11] Both had heart troubles, which may have been at least partly genetic, but Witmer seems to have inherited, in some way, some of the personality traits and interests of his father as well. Frederick Stone was a historical writer of note, particularly on the subject of the early history of Pennsylvania, and his resumé included a long stint as editor of *The Pennsylvania Magazine of History and Biography*. A *Publishers' Weekly* memorial summarizing his works gives an idea of the breadth of his expertise:

> He was the author of the chapter on the early history of Pennsylvania in "Narrative and Critical History of America".…Dr. Stone [co-] edited a volume entitled "Pennsylvania and the Federal Constitution 1787–1788".…Of his later writings are a monograph on the Battle of Brandywine, being an address delivered on the battlefield before the Pennsylvania Society of Sons of the Revolution, in which he definitely fixed the location of the various brigades, which had not before been satisfactorily done; supplemental chapters to Wood's "History of the University of Pennsylvania," in which he cleared up the long-pending dispute as to the foundation of that institution; a supplemental chapter to a new edition of Etting's "Independence Hall," and "A Plea for the Study of Genealogy," which is now going to press.[103]

Like his historian father, Witmer Stone was one of the leading, if not *the* leading, ornithological historians of his day.

As a student at Union Academy Frederick Stone wrote poetry, and he later recalled, "We all did it; we could not help it. It was in the air, and we took it as we did the measles."[3] Several of Witmer's friends remarked on his gift for humorous poetry.[20,104] Like Witmer, Frederick "was a capital *raconteur*, and his wit and humor, both of which he possessed in abundance, added greatly to the interest of his conversation and his writings."[3] Frederick was known to have some artistic skill, and Witmer displayed serious drawing talent in his younger years.[3] His high school sketchbook, with depictions of people and buildings, survives in the ANSP archives, along with WNSA papers which feature his fine natural history drawings, many in color and principally entomological and botanical in scope. He also illustrated his diary of an 1890 trip to Mexico, but doesn't appear to have pursued the craft afterward. His correspondence in later years rarely included a sketch, and those that he made were hasty and crude. The senior Stone was a lover of fine books, and was very knowledgeable about the details of bookmaking; in his *Auk* literature reviews, Witmer often commented on a book's paper stock, artwork reproductions, and other production qualities, and when he wrote of one that "[i]n all respects it is the sort of book that lovers of handsome publications like to have," it was clear that he included himself among the bibliophiles.[3,105] He was an ardent admirer of the Academy's library, and he also had a large and eclectic home library.

Reportedly, Frederick Stone hoped Witmer would also become a historian, but his son's fascination with birds won out.[106] However, having borne the drudgery of an occupation he detested, Frederick was dead set against forcing a boy away from his natural calling and into a different field for merely pecuniary reasons, and it's likely that he only encouraged Witmer's interest in natural history. Frederick, after all, was a lifelong lover of nature as well.[3]

On the eve of his 21st birthday, Witmer wrote a letter to Stew Brown. He had graduated from UP in June, had just gotten back from a summer spent traveling back and forth between Stock Grange and Paradise, and was full of stories he wanted to tell Stew. He was flush with money, having made some over the summer and anticipating more on the way for his birthday. And he knew just what he was going to do with it, too. A night on the town with the boys? Splurge on a new suit of clothes? Not even close. The WNSA insect collection had been ravaged by beetles over the summer, and on the morrow he would buy the material to build some new glass-covered drawers to house any future collections.[37] His formative years had been spent in a wide range of zoological and botanical endeavors – collecting, identifying, curating, researching, and publishing – all of which had served as the perfect training ground for his career in the natural sciences that lay just ahead.

2

Class of '87

Stone graduated from Germantown Academy in 1883, then entered the University of Pennsylvania (UP) that fall. He later described the initiation of the young men into college life, when they took their entrance exams in late spring:

> About the middle of June 1883 the future Class of '87 approached the main entrance to College Hall and passing through the portals guarded by "Dan'l Webster" and "Pomp" were confronted by a series of examination papers....There were then only the three green stone buildings used by the College, Medical and Dental Departments and the Hospital and Vet. buildings (the latter since removed). The campus was surrounded by a dilapidated wooden fence and was overgrown with tall grass in which some sheep were being pastured. There was but one flower bed and no trees except a weeping willow by the path leading to the South Street bridge; the famous Rockery however adorned the northeast corner, while some ornamental members of '86 reclined on the front steps.[1]

Those few sentences are packed with a lot of UP history. "Pomp" was the nickname of Albert M. Wilson, a messenger, janitor, and lab assistant at Penn for 50 years who was very popular with the students.[2] "Dan'l Webster" could be a flippant reference to John B. Webster, the "Clerk to the College Faculty" who was involved in administering the test.[3] The long-gone Rockery was a display of different types of rocks from sites around Philadelphia, grouped on the ground in the shape of an oak leaf, and it served as a geology exhibit for instruction purposes.[4] It was built by Eli K. Price, a local lawyer and UP trustee who was also one of the prime movers behind the creation of the nearby Woodlands Cemetery. Only two of the green serpentine stone buildings mentioned by Stone (College Hall and the old Medical Hall) are still standing. Regrettably, the sheep are also long gone.

Stone earned an A.B. degree from UP in 1887 after attaining second or third honors in each semester of his attendance.[5] His final semester "report card" from UP listed Intellectual and Moral Philosophy, Physics, Mathematics, German, Latin, Political Economy, and English Composition as classes taken, along with a graduation thesis titled "Evolution."[6] His degree was in arts, not science or biology, but the science classes at the time emphasized mineralogy, mining, metallurgy, and chemistry, and the biology courses were intended for pre-med students.[7] Stone wasn't a member of the university's Scientific Society, although he attended at least one of its lectures.[8] He was strangely uninvolved in activities outside of class. He had always enjoyed athletics, including the high jump, and was fond of music, but there's no record of him participating in sports, fraternities, the glee club, drama, or any other extracurricular organizations at UP.[5]

The UP Class of 1887 produced several men of outstanding attainments, including George Wharton Pepper, later a U.S. senator, and business executive and Episcopal church leader Samuel F. Houston.[9] Another UP classmate was Clement Griscom, whose son Ludlow became a renowned ornithologist and a good friend of Witmer.

Stone completed an A.M. degree (again, in arts, not science) at UP in 1891, and the university later conferred an honorary Sc.D. on him (just as it had conferred an honorary Litt.D. on his father) during its 1913 commencement at the Philadelphia Metropolitan Opera House.[10] Samuel Dixon, UP Trustee and ANSP executive curator and president, had recommended Stone and ANSP malacologist Henry Pilsbry for consideration for an honorary degree, saying of Stone that he was "possibly the nearest second to [Joseph] Leidy of any Naturalist we have in this country."[11] With a recommendation like that, how could UP say no? Pilsbry had already received an honorary doctorate from the University of Iowa in 1899, and would receive one from UP in 1940.

Stone and others wasted no time in referring to him as "Dr. Stone," despite the honorary nature of the title.[12] In the 1913 *Cassinia*, the abstract of the proceedings referred to him as such (after "Mr. Stone" previously); he wrote in his annual migration report that information on migration should be sent to "Dr. Stone" at ANSP; and the members list had "Sc.D" after his name. A 1913 *Bird-Lore* article referred to him as "Dr. Stone," and *Bartonia* and *The Auk* began referring to him as "Dr. Stone" in their 1914 issues.[13] The *PANSP* listed him in indexes with "A.M." after his name in the early 1913 numbers, but by the end of the year had changed it to "Sc.D." Stone's gravestone reads "Witmer Stone, Sc.D." Seventy years after Stone's death, Dale Twining, the last living person to have a set of *BSOCM* inscribed to him by Stone, still referred to him as "Dr. Stone"– evidently that's what everyone called him when Dale, about 15, first joined the DVOC and met Stone in the mid-1930s.

Today, many universities, including UP, often draw media attention to their commencement ceremonies by spicing them up with the conferment of honorary doctorates on celebrities. The practice has devalued the perceived merit of honorary degrees. Stone's honorary doctorate was for his outstanding work in the natural sciences. His *Plants of Southern New Jersey* alone was probably at least the equivalent of a Ph.D. in terms of fieldwork, research, herbarium work, and writeup. He had also been editor of *The Auk* for a year, in addition to his other ornithological work and publications.

After graduation, Stone was active in the semiannual Class of '87 reunions. The class selected a new slate of officers each year; Stone was president 1910–1911, and served two terms as class secretary, 1908–1909 and 1912–1939. An extraordinary example of Stone's creativity, industry, and love of his class and Penn history survives in the form of six remarkable, large Class of '87 scrapbooks in the UP Archives. Stone saved every scrap he could find about his class including newspaper clippings; University class records and schedules; and attendance registers, minutes, and even the catering bills from reunions, supplemented with similar material from classmates. Stone pasted it all into scrapbooks, and added titles, introductions, and whimsical minutes, making the scrapbooks similar to the DVOC ones he also produced. Stone presented the class with the original volume in 1910, and members were so impressed with it they designated him permanent secretary beginning in 1912, at the completion of his term as president. He served in that capacity until his death.

At the 1932 reunion, he presented an additional three volumes; the class, clearly astonished at the completeness and size of the volumes, tendered him a resolution of heartfelt thanks. The men believed that no other college class possessed such a complete record of its doings.[14] Stone referred to the scrapbooks as "a regular '87 Thesaurus'" and said they would eventually reside in the UP library. Lillie was happy to see the hefty volumes finally taking up space somewhere besides the Stones' home.[15] Stone presented the class with the partially completed fifth volume at its 50-year reunion in 1937; in a snapshot in the scrapbook, Stone is seen standing next to Pepper in UP's Frank Furness library during the presentation, and another photo shows Pepper and Stone perusing the scrapbooks. A newspaper article at the time stated, "Probably no University class has been more cohesive throughout the half century after graduation," citing 82 reunions that had taken place.[9]

After Stone's death, his UP classmates remembered his "modest silence" and recalled a "shy, modest and exceptionally able man who endeared himself to us by his friendliness and his unselfish services to the Class."[1] Pepper, the class's first president, its valedictorian, and its de facto leader for the duration of its existence, was also probably its last surviving member; he presented the scrapbooks (with little material added after Stone's death) to UP before he passed away at age 94.

The fellows had fun at their reunions. They marched with flags, wore silly hats, sang to the accompaniment of bands, sat down to big meals, and played a ball game annually until they got too old for that. In 1908, they took a cruise on the Delaware and Schuylkill rivers, then marched from the South Street wharf to the UP campus, where they met up with classmate Sketch Elverson, straight from the hospital after having his appendix removed! He insisted on being driven to the campus to sign the reunion attendance roll. For his loyalty, the class presented him with a loving cup. The scrapbooks record,

Witmer (*rear*) and George Wharton Pepper (*front*),
detail of UP Class of 1887 senior class photo.
University of Pennsylvania Archives.

"He attempted to respond but was overcome and someone promptly stepped into the breach with the remark that the rest of the speech would be found in the Appendix!"[1] The class's Ivy Day plaque can be found on the north side of College Hall, just a short distance west of the front entrance. Interestingly, the scrapbooks record that at one reunion the class put a loving cup in the care of the university, to be presented to the Class of 1987 at its commencement. The cup's whereabouts, however, is unknown, and no one I contacted at Penn, including Class of 1987 officers, was aware of the planned gift.

As far as institutions are concerned, Stone's involvement with UP is second only to his involvement with ANSP. He became a member of the chapter of the Society of Sigma Xi in 1912, and served on the Alumni Society's "Committee of One Hundred" from 1920 to 1923.[16] (The latter was formed in response to some looming crises at UP c. 1920: the sudden departure of Dr. Edgar Fahs Smith as provost, and a proposal to [gasp!] put UP under the control of Pennsylvania and have it function as a state-run, not a private, university.)[17] He was president of the Alumni Society of the Graduate School in the early 1920s.[18] The university also presented Witmer with the Alumni Award of Merit on Founder's Day at the 50th reunion of his class on January 23, 1937.[19-21]

Stone remained active to some extent in academia. He was a lecturer on natural history at Germantown Academy for a few years in the 1890s, and gave the commencement address in 1935.[20,22] He lectured at Woods Hole Biological Laboratory from 1900 to 1904.[19-20,23] A 1913 letter from C.W. Stiles, secretary of the International Commission on Zoological Nomenclature, congratulated Stone on "the good work that you have done in lecturing at the University of Pennsylvania, in the line of Nomenclature," which indicates Stone was at least an occasional UP lecturer at that time.[24] The university made an arrangement with Stone in 1927 to send interested graduate students to him at ANSP, where they could receive credits for ornithological training; he was thereafter listed as a "Lecturer in Zoology" in the UP graduate school through at least the 1936–37 school year.[25] However, Stone did not actually lecture at UP (which offered no ornithology course at the time) on a regular basis, and he would probably be termed an adjunct faculty member today. A 1933 AOU publication noted that UP allowed graduate students to specialize in ornithology, but had none so engaged at that time, although it appears that one or a few students were involved in the program before then.[26]

In June 1934, Stone told a friend, "Last Wednesday I did my duty as a member of the Faculty of the Univ. of Pa. & went to the commencement & sat in my academic regalia while [Cornelius] Weygandt delivered the oration."[27] Stone may not have participated in commencement exercises annually, and his "duty" may have been more to his friend Weygandt and to Academy managing director Charles Cadwalader, who received an honorary M.S. degree that day, than to the university.[28]

In addition to lecturing in an academic setting, Stone delivered lectures to local clubs, schools, and ANSP audiences.[29] He gave talks at many AOU meetings and spoke frequently at DVOC meetings – sometimes as the featured speaker of the evening, at other times with shorter presentations or general remarks and observations. He gave his first ANSP lecture in about 1892, when he pinch-hit for a scheduled speaker who was unable to appear.[30] His Academy lectures were sometimes given to schoolchildren; for example, Stone and other ANSP staff spoke to 356 schoolchildren at the Academy in April 1935.[31] Samuel Dixon, ANSP president and famed as a tuberculosis researcher and physician, even arranged for Stone to give a talk at his Mont Alto sanatorium.[32]

Stone was very involved with the Ludwick Institute, which has had an interesting history. Christopher Ludwick was the Baker General for the U.S. Army during the Revolutionary War. In his will he left money to the city of Philadelphia for the education of poor children, which was granted to the Philadelphia Society for the Establishment and Support of Charity Schools. They built and ran some schools during the 1800s, but by 1894, the society, which had since changed its name to the Ludwick Institute, decided to get out of the school business and to instead sponsor natural history education. That led to an alliance with ANSP, where the institute began sponsoring an annual program of free lectures on science topics. Academy staff delivered most of the lectures, and Stone lectured for the Ludwick Institute from 1895 to 1938.[33-34] He had been active in the organization since 1890, and was secretary from 1920 until his death.[35-36] Stone's Ludwick lectures were mostly on local birds and plants, such as "Natural History of the New Jersey Pine Barrens," "Some Familiar Birds of the Philadelphia Area," "Wild Flowers of the Philadelphia Area," "Bird Life of the New Jersey Sea Coast, Past and Present," and "Philadelphia Bird-Life on Migration."[34,37] More than 100 people waded through a snowstorm to attend the latter lecture, and the talks regularly drew hundreds of people.[38] Marie Hochstrasser, daughter of Stone's good friend and Ludwick board member Art Emlen, remembers her father driving the family to Ludwick lectures and picking up Stone at his home on the way.[36,39] The Ludwick Institute became the Christopher Ludwick Foundation in 1995, and still sponsors education programs for the city's youth, including some ANSP programs.[40]

Stone's public lecture philosophy and style can be inferred from a note he penned in *The Auk* in 1917: "The writer has always maintained that a lecture or an article can be scientific without being tiresome or unintelligible to a popular audience. In other words, scientific facts can be presented in popular language without losing any of their force, but the man who does this must know, in the first place, what he is talking about."[41] A DVOC member recalled of Stone, "His communications were frequently interrupted with explanatory remarks, always interesting, when he would remove his glasses and carry us along into whatever field we were exploring."[42]

Stone lectured enough that he had a circular printed sometime prior to 1913 listing three lectures he could give, presumably for a fee.[43] (He charged $15, plus expenses, for a lecture given at an Audubon Society meeting that year in Washington, D.C.)[44] He must have been a popular lecturer, because he was often asked for a return engagement, and was sometimes even invited on outings by listeners (one of whom described him as "a very delightful lecturer").[45] A Lafayette College biology professor requesting a talk in 1902 tried to entice Stone by telling him, "We can give you an interesting audience of about 100 intelligent people."[46] What more could a lecturer ask for?

In the spring of 1923, he said that he had "received about two dozen requests to give free lectures on birds since the first of the year," but was turning down all except his ANSP lectures.[47] He was getting tired of requests for himself and others to give free lectures, anyway, telling one supplicant that someone "who is able to gather sufficient information for a lecture, and who purchases lantern slides, does so at considerable personal expense, and it always seemed to me that asking him to lecture for nothing is very much like asking business men to give us their wares, or doctors and lawyers to give their services without compensation."[48]

Stone may have been on Philadelphia radio stations as well. In 1927 he was invited to give a 10- to 12-minute talk about Cape May birds and flowers on WIP,[49] and in 1936 he was asked to give a short talk on conservation on WFIL.[50] There's no indication whether Stone accepted the offers, but either would be a priceless archival recording to hear.

3

My Establishment Will Not Go On

Stone visited the Academy of Natural Sciences of Philadelphia (ANSP) many times while growing up, beginning in 1874, and eventually worked there for 51 years.[1-2] He served the Academy well, in positions of increasing importance and responsibility. He began as a Jessup student in 1888, then from 1892 to 1908 Stone was an assistant curator, a curator 1908–1925, and executive curator 1918–1925; director 1925–1928; conservator of the ornithological section 1891–1925; and curator of vertebrate zoology, 1918–1934. Three titles (with year of appointment) held by Stone at the time of his death were vice president (1927; "and could have become president following the death of Doctor [Samuel] Dixon had he not declined"), emeritus director (1928), and emeritus curator of birds (1938).[3] He was also a member of the *Proceedings of the Academy of Natural Sciences of Philadelphia (PANSP)* publication committee 1901–1926, and served on numerous other minor and/or transient committees during his tenure.

Stone worked briefly at his father's workplace in the library at the Historical Society of Pennsylvania (HSP) after graduation from the University of Pennsylvania (UP) in 1887. Then in February 1888 he was appointed a Jessup Fund student at ANSP. At that time, Joseph Leidy was the Academy president. D.G. Brinton, the famous anthropologist and a professor at both UP and ANSP, provided Frederick Stone with letters of introduction for his son written to Leidy and to head curator Angelo Heilprin; the latter notified Frederick that his son had been awarded the Jessup position.[4] Note that both of these communications were made to Frederick Stone, and it's conceivable that he was the impetus behind Witmer's obtainment of an Academy position. Frederick had a long professional interaction with Academy personnel in his position as HSP librarian, and he may have been the one who steered his oldest son, the one smitten with natural history, in their direction for employment and training.[5]

Leidy was a giant among nineteenth-century American scientists, and excelled as an anatomist, paleontologist, physician, parasitologist, naturalist, and pioneering microscopist. He taught at several colleges and was president of ANSP from 1881 until his death in 1891.[6] Years later, Stone recalled his interview at Leidy's home on Filbert Street: "I can still clearly see his fine profile as he stood by the bowed window at the back of the parlor reading the letter. Then he asked me kindly about my studies in ornithology and botany, while he explained the opportunities offered at the Academy if one had the proper kind of interest in natural history."[7] Witmer, of course, had it in spades. At that point, Leidy only had a few years to live, and little did he know the impact the young man before him would have on his museum. It may have seemed like just another job interview to Leidy at the time, but it's fascinating to contemplate its historical significance – a passing of the torch, in a way, from Leidy to one of the young men (along with Henry Pilsbry, Henry Fowler, and James Rehn) who would do such extraordinary work at ANSP over the next half-century.

Witmer's first day of work at ANSP was on February 27, 1888, and he occupied Titian Peale's old room, which still had specimens lying around from Peale's round-the-world voyage with the U.S. Exploring Expedition 50 years earlier.[8,9] Just outside the door of his room was a case of books including Mark Catesby's *Natural History*, in which he quickly became immersed. Stone's familiarity and delight with the treasures in the Academy library had begun.[10]

The Jessup Fund was started in 1860 with funds supplied by the three children of the late Augustus E. Jessup, who had been an active member of the Academy. The fund provided $120 a year for the Academy's publication fund, and $480 a year "to be used for the support of one or more deserving poor young man or men who may desire to devote the whole of his or their time and energies to the study of the natural sciences."[11] (ANSP took the "men" part literally: one prospective student was told she couldn't apply for a Jessup position simply because she was a woman.[12] But the 1892 Jessup report recorded that Clara Moore, Jessup's daughter, had added $5,000 that year to be used to hire women for similar positions.[11] ANSP maintained gender-separated funds for another hundred years.)[13] The Academy's rules for awarding Jessup funds stipulated that beneficiaries would receive $20 a month for no longer than two years, unless a special extension was granted.

Stone later referred to the Jessup Fund as "a foundation which has made it possible for a number of naturalists to make a start in their chosen field, such as Charles H. Townsend, Samuel N. Rhoads, Samuel Wright and the writer, among ornithologists."[14] To this list he later added students who became full-time staff, including Pilsbry, Fowler, Rehn, and Francis Pennell, and others who found better opportunities elsewhere, including Spencer Trotter and Earl Poole.[15] Interestingly, both Rehn and Fowler began their long Academy careers with Stone in the ornithology department, but soon turned their attention to other fields where they became experts. Rehn became an entomologist specializing in Orthoptera, and, as Stone later recalled, Fowler "went along as an excellent ornithologist until I inadvertently suggested that he catalogue the fish collection which was in my care, and since then nothing else has given him serious concern!"[15] (Fowler's 600 principally piscine publications, including descriptions of 1,400 previously undescribed fish species, attests to that.)[16] Both Rehn and Fowler worked at the Academy until their deaths in 1965.

In 1911, Stone described the Jessup program at the time of his apprenticeship, and the changes since then:

The "Jessup Fund" was established...with the object of aiding young men who desired to devote their lives to scientific work. The idea was to give them benefit of the opportunities offered by the Academy's library & collections while they fitted themselves for such positions as were offered by museums, government institutions, etc....[I]t was understood that part of the time of the incumbent should be devoted to assisting in the Museum work of the Academy. The subsequent establishment of biological schools [i.e., biology departments in universities] all over the country & the possibility of getting good positions as teachers of biology, has drawn most applicants away from the Academy & the "Fund" & of late years it has been filled by young men who contemplate remaining here at the Academy....The intention was never to provide an advanced "Fellowship" such as we see today in college, but to aid the beginner.[17]

The work journal of James Ives, who served as a Jessup student at ANSP at about the same time as Stone, provides excellent insights into the tasks the young men performed. For every day when Ives seemed to be doing something interesting, like "Cleaned up Mastodon bones presented by Dr. Morris and fitted pieces together ready for gluing," or (especially) "Attended to young ladies with specimens to identify," there were several other entries that sounded like a much less exciting day at the office: cleaning out the labels cabinet, arranging and sorting the keys in the key cupboard, cleaning out Leidy's old office, running errands to purchase supplies and pay bills, even one red-letter day when he "bought a brush for cleaning water-closet [i.e., bathroom]." He also busied himself on several days with what must have been the least pleasant job for the Jessup students: changing the alcohol in the specimen jars. Stone did his share of that one in his Jessup days.[2] In what sounds like junior staff having to do senior staff's dirty work for them, Ives and Stone were once chosen to tell the janitor that Academy curator (and soon president) Samuel Dixon had decided to fire him.[18] In addition to training young men in the basics of museum operations and work, the Jessup program also served to weed out the ones who lacked the inspiration to make a career out of it. (Stone later referred to it as "a fund whereby [young men] could get [paid] while doing preliminary work which would show their capabilities.")[15] Stone worked 4½ years as a Jessup student before being offered an assistant curator's position, and undoubtedly his passion for natural history carried him through the more tedious days.[19-20] The Academy still awards Jessup funds, although now they are for postgraduate, Academy-based research, not for what were essentially internships in Stone's day.[21]

Academy work wasn't all indoor drudgery, however, and Stone must have been thrilled to participate in a couple of ANSP trips to exotic locations. He was part of a collecting expedition led by geologist Angelo Heilprin to Bermuda in 1888 (described by Heilprin as "a brief sojourn with a class of [geology] students from ANSP"), where Stone and Ives collected corals. On returning to Philadelphia, Stone studied and identified the crustacea collected on the trip.[9,22] Stone also served as ornithologist and botanist on the Academy expedition to Mexico February 15–April 22, 1890, comprising five individuals including leader Heilprin.[23] They left New York on February 15 and, after a brief stop in Cuba, where Stone got his first taste of tropical bird life, they arrived in Yucatan on February 22.[24] Stone collected birds with fellow expedition member Frank Baker. On April 6–7, the naturalists and their local guides attempted to ascend Mt. Orizaba, the highest mountain in Mexico. Stone and Baker were "compelled to desist from the final attack upon the mountain" when 300 feet below the summit.[25] (The thin air was too much for their East Coast, sea-level lungs.) Heilprin went another 100 feet and then the guides dragged him with ropes "up a steep incline of loose lava and dust to the rim of the crater which he reached at 5 P.M."[26] Stone doesn't describe exactly how Heilprin was "dragged," but it may have been similar to part of Stone and Baker's descent. When they reached the end of the snowline, an "immense incline of dust and fine particles of lava" lay before them. "The guide here unfolded the sheet of matting which he had carried and fastening a rope to the front end motioned to Baker and me to sit down which we did 'toboggan' fashion. The Indian then started to slide down the mountain pulling us after him; how he kept his feet was a miracle."[27]

Heilprin made accurate elevation measurements for the peaks of both Mt. Orizaba and Popocatepetl (an active volcano), although he offended the natives with his measurement of Popocatepetl: in a case of nationalistically-inclined calculating, they thought it 3,000 ft. higher.[28] Heilprin also published on the expedition's botanical collections.[29] Once the party returned to Philadelphia, Stone identified the birds he and Baker had collected, and he quickly published "On birds collected in Yucatan and southern Mexico" in *PANSP*. Stone had, for the first time, seen some familiar old friends on their non-breeding grounds, and he also enjoyed tropical species of hummingbirds, flycatchers, orioles, swallows, and even flocks of soaring frigatebirds.[30]

Stone's diary from the trip describes the local life, including the food. For some reason, he disliked all the bell-ringing in most towns, sometimes at sunup and sundown.[23] He grumbled about one town that the locals had "no regularity about ringing them, jingling first one and then another and when you think all is over they begin again all together and worse than ever. To make matters worse the military post has to fire off a cannon and play an 'overture' on a very bad bugle and a broken drum at the same time."[31] Stone and the party were also unimpressed with a bullfight they attended in Mexico City on the return trip, where the bull goring blindfolded horses was part of the entertainment.[32]

Stone had some photos taken at Philadelphia's Gilbert & Bacon photography studio at the time of his 1890 trip to Mexico. ANSP Archives.

In 1895, Baker, who had moved on to the Chicago Academy of Sciences, published a book about the expedition, A Naturalist in Mexico, which drew freely on the accounts Heilprin and Stone had published in PANSP without properly crediting them. Stone wrote a note in Science pointing out Baker's plagiarism on this and one previous occasion, along with other supposed inaccuracies in the book, including Baker's exaggerated description of their physical duress while ascending Orizaba.[33] Baker wrote personally to Stone, and replied publicly in Science, that he had prepared an insert for the book, naming his sources, and that all future books sold would have the insert. He defended himself well enough on everything but the plagiarism, on which count he pleaded unconvincingly that he hadn't intentionally plagiarized – that he'd read the others' accounts so many times their phrases became planted in his mind, and they came out when he wrote.[34,35] Six months later, Baker asked Stone why he might be getting the cold shoulder from the Philadelphia crowd, including Pilsbry, whom Baker had also (again, "unintentionally") plagiarized.[35-36] Stone's reply must have been pacifistic, and the matter soon blew over, although Baker had undoubtedly learned a tough lesson early in his career about plagiarism. Baker went on to become an eminent and widely-published malacologist and paleontologist, and held curator positions at three different museums in Illinois. Stone and Baker maintained a cordial, if infrequent, correspondence over the years. Baker was a scheduled speaker at ANSP's 1937 "International Symposium of Early Man"; if he indeed attended, that was likely the last time he and Stone saw each other.[37]

In the years immediately after the trip, Stone gave a few talks about the Mexico trip to the DVOC,[38] and in 1929, almost 40 years after the expedition, he presented another one, complete with a slide show and skins of the birds collected.[39] In 1938, a newspaper reporter interviewing Stone at home noticed a sombrero from the Mexican trip hanging on the wall.[40] Stone took several shorter trips later to U.S. localities, but the Yucatan trip would be his only long collecting expedition, and other than the Bermuda trip and a few AOU meeting-related trips to Canada, would be the only time he would leave the country. Museum and editorship duties were destined to take up much of his career. He never attended the foreign meetings of any international zoological organizations, and didn't travel to distant locations for fieldwork like his friend and AMNH ornithologist Frank Chapman did in Panama on a regular basis.

⌒

The first burst of ornithological activity at the Academy occurred in the mid-1800s. Academy trustee Thomas B. Wilson purchased and donated many collections of various taxa, including the Rivoli and Gould bird collections, and John Cassin's access to them made him feel he was in an "ornithological farieland."[41] Cassin gained international standing as an ornithologist, and his work with the DuChaillu collection gave him particular expertise with African birds.

Ornithology went onto the back burner at the Academy after Cassin's death in 1869, however, and when Stone arrived "there was no one there who had the slightest interest in birds."[9] In a response to Chapman's request for the loan of the Academy's grackle skins in May 1891, Stone apologized that "there has been such a lack of interest in Ornithology here during the past 20 years that we are woefully weak in our N. Amer. collections. I am now organizing an Ornithological Section [=Department] of the Academy & have hopes of obtaining an endowment for it."[42] Stone and 11 others, noting the recent dormancy of the study of ornithology in Philadelphia, formally applied for the section, and the Academy established it on September 14, 1891, with Stone as conservator.[43] He wrote in his first "Report of the Ornithological Section" in *PANSP* in 1891 that "the primary objects in organizing the Section were the encouragement of the ornithological study at the Academy and the improvement and enlargement of its ornithological collections."[44] He laid out his plans to renovate and modernize the Academy's bird collection, and described some recent additions, including the DVOC's collection of nests and eggs of local birds. The newly hatched (1890) DVOC would continue to play a major role in the early history of the department, with members serving as officers and doing much work with the cataloging, skin preparation, labeling, and maintenance of the collection, as well as contributing specimens, nests, and eggs to it.

Stone hoped to create a $10,000 endowment, the interest from which could be used to hire a curator and purchase more specimens. Isaac Martindale, a successful businessman with Academy ties, put up almost a quarter of the amount in his will before he died in early 1893.[45]

Stone inherited an ornithological specimens collection which, in recent times, had not been cared for properly ("in a state bordering on chaos," as Spencer Trotter described it, and he was familiar with it from his own earlier Jessup internship).[14,46] Stone said that the collection had received "no attention from an ornithologist since the death of John Cassin twenty years before and was practically in the condition in which he left it"[47]– and even that left a bit to be desired, for as he told AMNH's J.A. Allen in 1894, "Mr. Cassin left no notes or catalogues by which the history of the specimens could be fixed at first sight, but after several years study of such lists etc. as we have together with the labels & tags I have a pretty good knowledge of the several collections."[48] The collection's days of neglect were over, for Stone had no sooner been hired than he jumped with both feet into sorting and assessing its contents.[49]

He discovered that some rare eggs had been purloined from the North American egg collection at a time preceding his arrival at ANSP.[50] Another telling egg mishap which indicates the chaotic conditions that prevailed during the Cassin–Stone interim is detailed in several letters from Charles Bendire, the famous oologist, concerning the whereabouts of a California Condor egg Bendire had seen during an 1880 visit to ANSP, lying unmarked and uncared for in an open box of unidentified eggs. Bendire remarked to an Academy employee at the time that greater attention should be paid to such a rare specimen; however, ten years later Stone couldn't locate it and neither could Bendire when he stopped by ANSP in September 1890.[51] Bendire assumed it had been either broken or stolen, and a few years later when he heard of such an egg in the possession of a collector with a shady reputation he thought he recognized the fate of the one he'd seen at ANSP.[52]

Most of the specimens Stone inherited were mounted on T-perch stands, not prepared as study skins, because in Cassin's day all specimens were put out on display, where they were subjected to sunlight, insects, and city grime. The mounts were crammed into the exhibition cases, and over half of them bore no species label.[9] Some specimens had been inadvertently destroyed when they were put into an oven in ANSP's basement to rid them of insect pests and eggs. Instead of labels, data about the specimens were often written on the bottom of the stands, where Cassin had also sometimes included personal notes of no particular ornithological relevance, for example "Just heard of the downfall of the French Empire, Vive la Republique." Some had exhibition labels prepared in about 1850 which, Stone later recalled, had "colored borders representing the continent from which the specimen came and conforming so far as possible to the color of the natives. North American specimens had red-bordered labels, African, black, and Asiatic, yellow. Here, however, this resemblance ceased, as the Australian specimens bore green-bordered labels."[47]

Stone's affection for old study skins and their historical connections was apparent in his 1899 essay in *The Osprey* titled "An old case of skins and its associations," in which he described the contents of the Turnbull collection left to the Academy by Edward Drinker Cope. Stone wrote that examining the skins brought on a "feeling of close contact with the past," connecting with his love of ornithological history.[53] Notice was given that the long-neglected Academy collection was being cared for and utilized when Stone published three articles about the collection in *PANSP* in 1889, including "Catalogue of the Muscicapidae [Old World flycatchers] in the collection of the Philadelphia Academy of Natural Sciences."[54] Allen reviewed that paper in *The Auk*, noting that Stone, "a promising young ornithologist of Philadelphia," was "not only bringing [the specimens] into an orderly condition, but making known the contents of the collection."[55] Stone also published on the Academy's collections of owls, crows, and some recently acquired (through purchase or ANSP expeditions) collections.

Stone's efforts, beginning in 1891, to salvage the ornithological (and other) collections by converting the mounts into study skins, storing them properly, and cataloging everything, were nothing short of heroic, and the Academy, although hardly cognizant of it, owes him a debt of gratitude to the present day. Not only was little funding available for the endeavor, but space was at a premium as well: Stone later wrote that "no quarters for study collections were provided…in the plans for the present Academy building which were drawn in 1876."[47] Some specimens were historically valuable, including types from pioneering ornithologists and mammalogists, but it was a challenge to identify these because older naturalists had not always identified their type specimens as such. (A "type" is the specimen used in the first written description of a species that is new to science.) James Rehn later wrote, "In this laborious work, very largely done with his own hands, Stone located over 600 types of Gould, Cassin, Townsend, Audubon and a score of other authors; he developed the nucleus of a modern housing method in the Academy and saved for posterity many hundreds of exceedingly rare and in some cases extinct species of birds….For the greater part of twenty years the major official activity of Witmer Stone, aside from direct administration, was that of bettering, with limited help and even more restricted funds, the condition of priceless collections and their conservation for students in years to come."[56] The size of the Academy's bird collection increased fivefold during Stone's tenure, from 25,000 specimens to 143,000 (not that Stone was responsible for all accessions).[3,47,56] Many of his ornithological section reports in *PANSP* from that time documented the growth of the collection as well as efforts to maintain it, and by 1904 Stone was able to proudly report, "The ornithological collections of the Academy were never in better condition nor more accessible to the student than at present."[57]

After visiting some of the large bird collections in the United States in 1857, the eminent British ornithologist Philip Sclater wrote, "The collection of [ANSP] is certainly the best zoological collection in the New World, and in the particular department of Ornithology, and perhaps one or two other points, is probably superior to every Museum in Europe, and therefore the most perfect in existence."[58] Almost 40 years after Sclater's remarks, another British ornithologist, R. Bowdler Sharpe of the British Museum, recognized the critical work Stone was doing with the criminally-neglected ANSP collections. He wrote to Stone on November 12, 1894:

> I am delighted to hear that you are un-mounting the types of the Museum at Philadelphia, and if you are taking steps to preserve the treasures in the possession of the Academy, you will earn the gratitude of every zoologist in the world.
>
> The [ANSP] is possessed of priceless treasures, but is, at present…taking so little care of its types, that many are <u>missing</u>, and some of our ornithologists, who have journeyed to America, have found these types destroyed by moths and no longer in the collection. [Sharpe then related that he once told ANSP president Leidy that he and other European ornithologists were so alarmed at the lack of interest shown by ANSP in their ornithological collection that, if ANSP paid his travel expenses, he would personally visit and put all the types in protective storage. Apparently Leidy didn't take him up on the offer, and Stone later related that Leidy considered the Academy's bird collection a white elephant, anyway.][47] A great public body like the Academy of Philadelphia will be held responsible in future ages for the care of the specimens which the public spirit of Edward Wilson [Thomas's brother, who helped ANSP acquire the Gould and Rivoli collections] placed in its care. Gould told me himself that he regretted that in a moment of pique at the unexpected refusal of the British Museum to buy his collection, he allowed it to go out of the country. Were I in possession of the Gould types, I would treat them with the utmost care, and place them all in cabinets at once.[59]

This was not a case of Stone undertaking the work after being ordered to do so by his supervisors – quite the opposite. Leidy's purported disinterest in the collection has been noted above, and it actually took some cajoling by Stone, with backing by Sharpe and J.A. Allen (who had given Stone cataloging advice and been supportive of his restorative work on the Academy bird collection since 1889), to convince the Academy brass that the specimens would be better preserved as skins than mounted and that Stone should be allowed a free hand to do the necessary preservation work.[9,60-61] Stone told Allen in October 1894 that his efforts had been criticized by "certain members of the Academy (<u>not</u> <u>ornithologists</u>) who think every bird in the place – type or not – should be stuck on a stand & exhibited in the museum & consequently exposed to light & dust. I contend that my views are right & in accordance with the practice at other institutions & I should be greatly obliged if you would drop me a line or two confirming my position."[62] Allen responded that all AMNH bird types had been unmounted and put in insect-proof drawers five years previously, and that no more than 20% of AMNH's collection were kept as mounts.[63]

Stone's 1891 description of the salvage work getting under way reads like a defense of his plan – emphasizing that the remaining mounted specimens were seen to better advantage due to less clutter and more light, and that visitors had commented favorably on the change – which indicates he may have been meeting resistance from the outset.[44] Similarly, in 1893 he said the best specimens were preserved as display mounts, and only "unsightly specimens and duplicates unnecessary for display" were made into study skins.[64]

In those early days of Stone's efforts to salvage and systematically arrange the bird collection, he also asked for and received advice from other prominent ornithologists besides Allen and Sharpe, including the Smithsonian's Leonhard Stejneger and Robert Ridgway.[65] The latter recognized the importance of Stone's exertions, and offered encouragement in an autumn 1894 letter:

> I am exceedingly sorry that the work you have been doing to improve the Academy's collection of birds should be criticized by some of the authorities of that institution, for the condition of the collection before you took it in hand was nothing less than a disgrace to the Academy – a statement which may appear rather strong, but one which I am sure will be borne out by every ornithologist who is asked for an expression of opinion on the subject....It was a perfect chaos of birds on stands, most badly mounted, and neither a delight to the eye of the unprofessional visitor nor a satisfaction to the specialist....I sincerely hope your good work will not be impeded, much less stopped, for there was some hope that through your intelligent labors what was <u>once</u> the best bird collection in existence…might be restored in great measure to its original rank – a consummation to be reached only by the process of revision and renovations which you had carried so far to completion.[66]

Ridgway, like Allen, also advised Stone to turn most of the mounts, particularly the types, into study skins. Once Stone had all the types unmounted, he began studying their individual histories and preparing a list of them, which resulted in "A study of the type specimens of birds in the collection of ANSP, with a brief history of the collection," published in *PANSP* in 1899.[67] The production of that paper was an adventure, as Stone explained when Charles Richmond noticed some curious nomenclatural errors in it after its publication. The Academy decided to use Stone's paper as the guinea pig with a new printer who had not published scientific material before. Being unfamiliar with zoological syntax, he made a mess of the first proof, which Stone had to revise twice, then the printer lost the manuscript altogether! Stone had to hastily put another one together "with nothing to go by, as a check."[68]

Stone reflected years later on the whole collection restoration experience, and noted a side-benefit to all the work: "The opportunity of handling this vast mounted collection enabled me in a short time to become acquainted with birds from all parts of the world and to recognize them at sight, an experience that I could not have obtained in any other way."[9] It was certainly fortuitous for the Academy – which would indeed, as Sharpe averred, have invited well-deserved censure had it continued to neglect its priceless collection – that the curators happened to hire a young man at the time with enough knowledge of, and appreciation for, ornithological history to recognize the urgent need to salvage the collections and immediately house them with modern methods. He was willing to personally spearhead the necessary efforts in the face of managerial opposition – and this wasn't a seasoned curator with long museum experience, but a bargain-basement Jessup student. Contemplating Stone's efforts today, one can only wonder what would have been the fate of the bird collection if the Academy hadn't been providentially provided with the right man in a time of a crisis, the magnitude of which he alone recognized.

In addition to the usual specimen acquisitions via exchange, purchase, and collecting expeditions, a few specimens had a more interesting provenance. At a 1914 DVOC meeting, "Mr. Stone reported that he had obtained from a Market Street Restaurant a species of Siberian Grouse which was not in the Academy Collection."[69] This may have been the Nineteenth Street Market, where Stone used to eat.[70] One non-bird in the Academy collections, a Sonoran Desert Toad (*Bufo alvarius*), met its fate by making the unfortunate decision to hop into a restaurant in Maricopa, Arizona that was being patronized by ANSP malacologist Henry Pilsbry, who was as happy to collect a toad as he was to collect a shell.[71] A Red-throated Loon was found in the street in Philadelphia one morning and brought to the Academy, and Stone and others watched it after placing it on the floor. It couldn't walk or fly, of course, and struck out viciously at anyone who got near it.[72] The bird's fate isn't recorded, but it doesn't appear to have ended up in the collection.[73]

The herpetological collections also received much-needed attention from Stone, Fowler, and Rehn; their work was heroic and, at times, adventurous. After his WNSA collection faded inside its glass cases in the Academy's sun-

drenched storage room, Stone convinced the board of curators that the herpetological collection should be moved to the basement and stored there in
the dark. Shortly thereafter, a deluge of rain hit Philadelphia and flooded the
Academy basement, which suddenly had jars of dead reptiles floating everywhere. Fortunately, Fowler had just gone over the whole collection and inserted
a slip of paper into each jar indicating each specimen's place in the Academy
catalog.[2]

Then ANSP came into possession of the late Edward D. Cope's personal
collection of reptiles, batrachians, and fishes, much of which had, like most
everything else at Cope's home, received little curatorial care. In some of the
jars the alcohol had not been changed in so long that it had the consistency of
molasses and the specimens had disintegrated. Stone and Fowler worked on
salvaging that collection all through the summer of 1898, although the odor
they encountered upon opening some of the jars forced them to flee the room.
Stone recalled, "It was some weeks after the completion of the work before the
herpetological odor which had penetrated all the pores of my hands & arms
wore off. Meanwhile, I was a social outcast."[2]

By the mid-1890s Stone felt that his position as assistant to the board of
curators was too clerical and was keeping him away from his ornithological
work, so he applied for a position as professor of natural history at Girard College in Philadelphia in 1894.[61] Girard was not actually a college, but a boarding
school for fatherless boys. It was the brainchild of the wealthy Philadelphia
merchant Stephen Girard, who willed millions to the city for its establishment.
It opened in 1848 and still exists as a coed boarding school for students in
grades 1–12. Stone asked Allen for a referral in March 1895, saying he would
still be in charge of the Academy's bird collections (i.e., would retain his position as conservator of the ornithological section), and would be giving up only
his salaried position, which he described as "a sort of a 'business director' of the
museum."[74] Stone thought the Girard position would allow more free time for
research, but he notified Allen shortly thereafter that the opening had already
been filled by someone the city apparently had in mind from the outset.[75] How's
that for a "what-if"? Would Stone have had the same career – *Auk* editor, AOU
classification committee, author of two natural history classics, etc. – if he had
been working as a schoolteacher instead of at ANSP? It doesn't seem likely,
although he may have had more free time for his own studies.

Academy administrative work continued to keep Stone away from original
research, as it increasingly would during his lifelong tenure there.[76] He told
William Brewster that he wouldn't be able to attend the AOU annual meeting
in Cambridge in 1896 because a newly built Academy wing had just opened

"and as I am now practically in charge of all the museum work and our force of assistants is small, I find so much work on hand that I cannot see my way clear to get away."[77] He told Sharpe and Chapman in 1898, "[M]y duties as general custodian of the Museum here take so much of my time that original work among the birds is seriously interfered with," and made the same complaint to Sharpe in 1905.[78] In 1901, while he was still an assistant curator, his time was mostly spent helping out curators in other departments.[79] In 1911, a friend wrote Stone a prescient note with good advice which, ultimately, Stone didn't heed: "What a wonderful man you are – to shoulder so many loads, and to carry them so lightly and so steadily. But, if I were you, I would look out for my back! It won't stay limber forever under such treatments."[80] In 1912 Stone referred to a recent "wretched annual business meeting" he had been compelled to attend, indicating his distaste for administrative work.[81]

By then, however, he must have been settled into an Academy career, for in 1909 he turned down a job offer from the ornithologist Charles Cory to jump ship and work at the Field Museum in Chicago.[82] (Wilfred Osgood eventually took that position.) In 1913, Joseph Grinnell offered Stone the position of "executive of the California Academy of Sciences," with the job to begin as soon as possible.[83] Stone, however, quickly and firmly turned down that offer, vaguely citing "a number of personal reasons."[84]

The period when Witmer had the heaviest load of executive work must have been 1918–1928, when he served as executive curator (1918–1925) and director (1925–1928). As early as 1909, Stone noted the demands on his time "in looking after other departments."[85] In early 1918, he told Chapman that his workload had increased since the previous summer when both Academy president Samuel Dixon and secretary-librarian (since 1869!) Edward Nolan were incapacitated due to bad health: "As they together practically 'ran' the institution, the present situation leaves few who know much about the general conduct of affairs, except myself & I have had a series of responsibilities on my shoulders all the time."[86] At the time of his 1918 "promotion," he said, "I see that I am likely to be in full what I have been to a great extent for some time, the executive curator, and there are a lot of things to be attended to. I am not looking for this sort of responsibility but see no hope of escaping it & it does not mean any increase in compensation."[87] Stone expected the new position to further curtail his chances to do research, and it did.[88] In 1921, after forgetting to mail Alexander Wetmore a letter he'd written, Stone said, "I have been so terribly busy this winter my brain is working badly – & none of the work is research which is maddening! Executive work just goes on & on increasing at every turn."[89] By 1923 he was telling Chapman, "I certainly do envy you the opportunity for undisturbed work. In spite of all the efforts I make here to reach such a position, I do not seem to succeed."[90] He blamed administrative stress for a bout of ill health in early 1924, but told a colleague, "I cannot see my way clear however to do differently as I must keep on the job or my establishment will not go on."[91]

In 1922, in response to a letter requesting separates of all *PANSP* ornithological articles, Stone wrote, "I am sorry to say that as I am the ornithologist here, and my time is so entirely taken up with executive work, that no practical papers have appeared in our 'Proceedings' for some time past."[92] Far from being unique to Stone, museum curators saddled with executive responsibilities that interfered with original research were the norm at the time. Joseph Grinnell, director of the Museum of Vertebrate Zoology, wrote in a 1915 *Condor* editorial, "In the great majority of cases nowadays, when a young man reaches an advanced degree of proficiency in bird-study, the ability thus developed makes him desirable in some executive berth, and the matter of salary concludes the argument. At present, there appear to be practically no purely research positions in ornithology, offering anywhere near an adequate livelihood, available to the talented and ambitious young student anywhere in America. Very nearly all the published ornithology turned out is a by-product of busy men's activities, which are by necessity centered elsewhere."[93]

The Academy appears to have been a bit unsettled when Dixon died in 1918 after 23 years at the helm. In 1921, Stone told T.S.Palmer, "We are having the deuce of a time in Academy politics & it takes all my efforts to keep things going smoothly. It is hard to run a present day institution on Bylaws of a generation or two ago & equally hard to change them!"[94] An Academy administrative reorganization in 1924 created the new position of director, and Stone was chosen to fill it. That only increased the administrative workload, of course, and in December 1928, Stone resigned the position and was appointed emeritus director.[95] Charles M.B. Cadwalader, named managing director, succeeded him, and said, "The ANSP owes Dr. Stone possibly more than any other living man. I am fortunate in having been associated with him."[96] The move was made so that Stone could concentrate on research, but was also at least partly due to Stone's declining health brought on by the stress of administrative duties.[96-97] When the 1928 move was imminent, Florence Merriam Bailey wrote, "We are delighted that there is a proposal of you being relieved of administrative work. Tell them you <u>won't do</u> it!"[98] It's hard to imagine Stone putting his foot down like that, but a friend told him shortly after the change that he hoped Stone would "still persist in your determination to <u>give up</u> some of your too numerous responsibilities at the Academy."[99] It was certainly time to let someone besides one of the country's leading ornithologists deal with things like coal deliveries and broken typewriters.[100]

In his Stone memorial, ANSP corresponding secretary J. Percy Moore wrote, "In his later years and with failing health Stone felt the burden of administrative routine....To relieve him of these burdens and to free his time for writing, the new administration made him director emeritus in 1928. Among the products of this relative leisure were his finished *Bird Studies at Old Cape May*...and the Fourth AOU Checklist of North American Birds, prepared by a committee of which he was chairman and editor."[3] The year 1928 is also the first time in ten years that we find Stone describing an Academy collection, and he described several more in the ensuing years – his administrative duties had prevented him from doing that kind of research in the interval.[101] Stone said in 1935 that he had been able to concentrate solely on scientific work since being relieved of director responsibilities.[102]

───────────── ∼ ─────────────

Stone's main curatorial duties in the ornithological department involved maintaining the collection. In the early days the task was to get a large, historically valuable but long-neglected collection into proper shape, using modern storage cabinets and methods. Later, the work entailed cataloging and labeling new accessions and incorporating them into the collection, or sometimes reidentifying old ones; rearranging the collection as taxonomic revisions were made; publishing descriptions of new accessions, or taxonomy articles based on his study of the collection; corresponding with other museums concerning the sale or exchange of duplicate specimens between the institutions (museums had lists of desiderata for each of their departments); and arranging for loans of specimens with other institutions. And there was, of course, the never-ending job of simple maintenance, including rehousing the collection as better cabinets were purchased, and moving it during times of museum-wide rearrangement. As curator of the vertebrate zoology department (1918–1934), he performed similar work with the mammal collection.

Stone was virtually a one-man show in the Academy's ornithology department for much of his time there, but that began to change when James Bond and Rodolphe Meyer de Schauensee became affiliated with the museum beginning in the mid-1920s. Both were independently wealthy men without college-level zoological training who held various nonsalaried positions at the Academy (including de Schauensee's ornithology curatorship of several decades). Bond became an authority on birds of the West Indies, and de Schauensee sponsored and/or participated in many collecting expeditions around the world that added thousands of birds to the Academy's collection and gave it much greater international scope. Both men were active in the Academy until their deaths in the 1980s.[103]

Many other men passed through the department in Stone's time, including W. Wedgwood Bowen, who served for a time as an assistant curator until Depression finances led to his being let go, despite Stone's pitch to retain him.[104] Exasperated that Bowen, an expert in African birds, remained an AOU Associate while others less deserving were promoted to Member, Stone successfully pushed for Bowen's promotion to the higher class in 1931.[105] Stone did what he could for Bowen after he left ANSP. Bowen served a brief stint at the Smithsonian after Stone recommended him to Alexander Wetmore ("you will get a treasure in him"), then was a zoology professor for many years at Dartmouth College, after Stone had written a letter of recommendation for him when he applied for that position.[106]

Stone also made a pitch to keep Melbourne Carriker, who began an association as a collector with the Academy in about 1915. He joined the Academy staff in 1929 and made several collecting trips to South America. Stone went to bat for Carriker in 1933 when his job was on the cost-cutting chopping block, telling Cadwalader that Carriker's fieldwork in Peru was "one of the outstanding pieces of work that our institution has been able to carry out," and that the birds he collected for ANSP in Peru represented the finest Peruvian collection in the world. Given his vast experience with South American birds, Carriker knew the identity of a specimen as soon as he collected it, and its potential importance to the Academy collection; in other words, he was "an ornithologist in the field instead of a mere collector who [doesn't] know what he has secured until museum ornithologists have worked up the collection."[107] Stone's appeal may have helped get Carriker a reprieve, but unfortunately he was let go in 1937 for the same financial reasons that spelled Bowen's fate, although some today suspect it was due to political intrigues in the ornithology department. Carriker went on to collect extensively for the Smithsonian.[108] Wharton Huber was an associate curator in the vertebrate zoology department with Stone for a number of years, and was a skilled worker and good friend.

Some of the routine matters Stone dealt with in his Academy work included answering queries from people seeking positions, and endless letters from people who had mounted moose heads, bird skins, minerals, etc. – sometimes recently inherited from a deceased relative – that they wished to donate or sell to ANSP. As executive curator and director, Stone was also involved in the purchase and acceptance of animals for the diorama displays, and for the planning and arrangement of the displays, including the hiring of the background artists.[109]

The Academy's outstanding library was the envy of other scientists. D.G. Elliot of the Chicago Field Museum wrote to Stone, "What a great thing it is to have such a library as yours at one's elbow."[110] Academy entomologist Morgan Hebard believed the unmatched library was a perk that kept at least some scientists from taking better paying or higher positioned jobs elsewhere.[111] Stone received many requests to copy or verify some passage or tidbit from one of the library's rare works. Gerrit Miller of the AMNH was at least coy about it in a 1911 request, writing, "I do not like to trouble you again with a reference to verify, but I know how much you enjoy demonstrating the superiority of the Philadelphia Academy Library."[112] Copying something in those days meant just that – sitting down and writing it out longhand. It appears that Stone some-times did that himself, particularly in the early days, although he may have had subordinates do it at least some of the time.

Stone also served as a point of contact at the home base for collectors out in the field in distant corners of the globe, and was involved in logistical issues such as collecting permits and keeping track of specimens sent. Sometimes Stone had to hound customs brokers to free a shipment of specimens stuck in customs, or track down a shipment that had gone missing.[113] A real beauty in the latter department occurred when two collections of birds sent by Carriker from Colombia, where he lived at the time – one intended for ANSP, the other for the Carnegie Museum in Pittsburgh – got crossed in shipping and each institution ended up with the other's order.[114] Carriker was involved in another mix-up that points to the difficulties in communication with distant collectors at the time. He voiced his displeasure in a 1916 letter about not hearing from Stone for a year, during which time he had sent two shipments of birds to the Academy, writing, "[I]f you do not want my birds kindly let me know and I will not collect any more for you." For billing purposes, he understandably wanted Stone to at least acknowledge when his skins arrived. It turned out Stone had deposited money for a previous shipment into Carriker's bank account months before, but notification from Stone or the bank had never reached Carriker, who was living on a coffee plantation in Colombia.[115]

Work on Chinese collections could be a challenge, for a few reasons. One collector wrote to Stone in 1925 about the difficulties of collecting during Chi-nese civil war strife, where "the soldiers...object to anyone having a gun but themselves."[116] Working on a writeup of birds from China's Sichuan Province brought back by the Brooke Dolan expedition, Stone told a colleague, "It is no small job to decipher Chinese localities written by a German [ornithologist Dr. Hugo Weigold] & then find them on <u>any</u> map!"[117]

Stone was also active in fundraising, starting with his efforts to raise an endowment for the ornithological section in 1891, when he was still a young Jessup student, and his congenial, likable personality must have served him well.[44,118] Although he was not born into Philadelphia's upper-crust society, his connection with it through his father's Historical Society of Pennsylvania and civic endeavors (e.g., the Constitution centennial celebration at the Academy of Music) doubtless taught him the requisite politesse in interacting with the town's blue bloods. Clearly, Stone had a fluid roster of people with money who could be approached to fund the purchase of a collection, or contribute to any number of Academy causes, and he had at least some success with his efforts.[119] Stone's correspondence contains numerous references to him raising money for the purchase of new acquisitions such as the Josiah Hoopes col-lection, purchased in 1899, the Lindsey Jewel collection of Panamanian birds in 1916, and the Rufus Lefevre collection of Chinese birds in 1928.[120] But

Hebard once argued that scientists should be asked to do what they do best – research – and the fundraising should be done by those with expertise and experience in that area.[111]

Occasionally Witmer would have to clear up squabbles about whether people donated ("presented") material to ANSP or simply loaned it – sometimes ANSP thought it was donated and suddenly the donor wanted it back.[121] Relations between ANSP and other institutions, particularly in the Washington-to-Cambridge corridor, were generally peaceable because the men knew each other well, but in 1919 there was a major dustup with Thomas Barbour, the MCZ herpetologist and eventual director, over the type specimen of a lizard (*Celestus phoxinus*) that Barbour claimed was loaned to ANSP in the 1860s by Louis Agassiz, the MCZ founder, at Cope's request.[122-123] Cope never returned the specimen, and Barbour and the MCZ, who now had it on loan from ANSP, wanted to keep it as rightfully theirs, contending that Agassiz never gave away type specimens.[124]

At ANSP, Henry Fowler, the curator of reptiles and fishes, "nearly exploded" when he received Barbour's initial volley, and James Rehn had to intervene with some diplomacy to convince Fowler not to send the hotheaded reply he initially drafted. Stone, who was away in Arizona for the summer when the hostilities commenced, eventually consulted with Fowler, and they determined either that the specimen's provenance could not be definitely established, or the time interval was such that the specimen was now legitimately the Academy's ("outlawed in time," as Rehn put it).[125] Barbour was really irritated: in a September 15 letter he laid out the proof of his assertions, and told Stone that "in judging of these matters I claim to be a more competent judge than either you or Mr. Fowler....Cope's habits in handling borrowed material are so well known that we are all more than surprised that the Academy through you and Fowler should take this stand." (This wasn't the first time Stone had heard of Cope's laxity in returning specimens.)[126] Barbour insinuated that Cope had deliberately stolen the specimen, threatened to give publicity to the feud so that other museums would be aware of ANSP's (asserted) dishonesty, and asked to have his Academy membership immediately canceled.[127] At the same time, MCZ director Samuel Henshaw told Stone that he would no longer allow MCZ specimens to go out on loan to Academy researchers.[122] Barbour even mentioned the specimen, complete with an MCZ catalog number he had piquantly assigned to it, in a July 1919 article in the *Proceedings of the New England Zoological Club*.[128]

Stone wrote to Henshaw on September 17, saying that Barbour's letter of the 15th had for the first time laid out the proof that the specimen rightfully belonged to the MCZ, and that ANSP would allow the specimen to remain in Cambridge. Although he chalked it up to a simple misunderstanding, he also voiced his displeasure at Barbour publishing an article about the specimen with an MCZ-assigned catalog number.[129] After this shakeout, Barbour sent a chummy letter that all was forgiven (he was even canceling his ANSP membership resignation), Henshaw apologized for the inappropriately-published catalog number and told Stone that these things were bound to happen when you had "young and enthusiastic assistants [i.e., Barbour] who are apt to regard any restrictions as needless red tape," and all involved remained on good terms thereafter.[130] The specimen, an innocent bystander in all the commotion, still resides at MCZ.[131]

In 1926, Dr. Joseph Clubb of the Liverpool Free Public Museum seemed to be itching to kick up another such squabble over a type specimen at ANSP of the Black Honey Buzzard (*Henicopernis infuscatus*), which Clubb had proof should have been in the Henry Tristram collection housed in the Liverpool museum.[132] Stone quickly nipped that one in the bud, informing Clubb that there had been a second Tristram collection sold by his daughter to the Academy shortly after his death in 1906, and that the buzzard specimen had always been part of the latter collection.[133]

The Academy had a collection of Australian birds that Australian ornithologists, although doubtless recognizing it as rightfully the Academy's, at least *wished* was housed in their own country. In 1848, Thomas B. Wilson purchased the collection of 1,500 Australian birds from the British ornithologist John Gould. The collection had many type specimens, so Australian ornithologists in Stone's time were in the unfortunate position of having many of their country's type specimens housed at the Academy (others were in England), instead of in their own museums. In 1923, Stone worked with Australian ornithologist A.J. Campbell on matching the Gould types in the Academy collection with birds in Australian collections that most closely resembled them, so that the Australians could at least have pseudo-types to use for comparative purposes. In an *Auk* note, Stone expressed sympathy with the handicap under which the type-less Australian ornithologists labored, but you can bet that the scenario of selling the collection back to the Aussies never came up in any correspondence Stone had with them during their work with the Gould birds.[134] (Some of the Gould types made a brief visit to their homeland in 2004 as part of an Academy traveling exhibition.)[135]

———————————— ∽ ————————————

The Academy has never been the coziest place to work, and management hasn't always made things easier. The minutes of an 1890 board of curators' meeting noted, "Resolved that the janitor shall lock the water closets in the Museum on Saturday at 5 p.m. and open them again not until Monday 9 a.m., except on special application of members."[136] This edict may have called for some real forethought and discipline by members and staff – by the time someone made an "application" (supplication?), wouldn't it likely be too late? In 1891, the curators deemed it "inexpedient to introduce in the Academy the Electric Light."[137] The cost of lighting ANSP today might make that seem like not such a bad idea. Stone, of course, worked at the Academy before the advent of air conditioning, and the rooms on the upper floors must have been unbearable in the stifling Philadelphia heat. Fowler, who had worked at ANSP in the 1890s and knew what summers there were like, commented to Stone in an August 1902 letter from California, "Well, I suppose it is as hot as ever about the Academy!"[138] Wharton Huber, the ANSP ornithologist/mammalogist, told Stone, summering at Cape May in 1923, that he wasn't able to "get the heat out of this top floor [at ANSP]. Perhaps the roof is still radiating."[139] Stone summered annually at the Cape starting in 1916 to get away from the city heat; vacating a museum to escape summer's heat and stuffiness was a common practice at the time at ANSP and other museums.[140] Summer heat wasn't the only thing Academy workers had to deal with: one correspondent commented in 1933 on a recent Stone illness that "it is out of the question for you to work in an unheated building."[141] The Academy had a heating system long before 1933, but it must have been malfunctioning.

For much of Stone's time at ANSP, scientific staff worked 5½ days a week, including a half-day on Saturday, and in 1913 ANSP president Dixon even made a flippant remark to Stone about the Academy's "aristocrats" working *only* the half day on Saturday.[142] The practice must have been in place by at least the 1890s, because Fowler told Stone concerning his lab work at Stanford University in 1902, "I take Saturday when ever I want it. You see things are a little different in this to the Academy."[143] As might be expected, Saturday work could be a contentious issue. Huber once told Stone about the matter coming up in a staff meeting: "[Managing director] CMBC[adwalader] made inquiries amongst the staff [illegible] only certain members as to closing Saturdays in July & August. All seem in favor of closing except JAG R[ehn] who thought it was very important to have some one in every dept. (Boot licking for favor) so that balance of the staff will have to suffice so he can curry favor. I shall make it a point to see that he takes his turn or there will be an eruption."[144] In 1930, Cadwalader told Stone that effective immediately all staff, including Stone, would work Saturdays.[145] Three hours on Saturday was still the norm for the rest of the staff in 1938, but by 1933, at least, Stone didn't go in on Saturday "as a rule."[146]

The Academy was underfunded and frustratingly understaffed during Stone's time. In the 1920s, plans to hire help for mundane clerical work were being considered; incredibly, the scientific staff was doing it. Stone estimated he spent 80% of his time on administrative work at the time, and half of that could be handled by clerical staff.[147] Ten years later, however, Stone said the scientific staff was still burdened with the clerical work involved in maintaining the collections, which could be handled by assistants if they were available, and the staff accordingly had little time for research.[148]

In 1936, Cadwalader queried the scientific staff about time spent answering questions from the general public, and might have been surprised by some of the answers he received. Rehn reported that between May and October a very large part of the entomologists' time was wasted responding to "elementary entomological inquiries." Some people thought they had discovered some rare insect, when it was actually a large, showy, but common one, and wouldn't be put off from trying to sell it to the Academy. Rehn said it took valuable research time away from the entomologists, and "the technical knowledge of our men, which has for each required a life-time to acquire, is being lost to the Academy and to science."[149] Huber gave a couple of examples of some of the roughly 200 "foolish" questions he was peppered with each year: "Is crow good to eat and have you ever eaten it? What is the period of gestation of the elephant, horse, cow, sheep, hog?"[150] Stone also said that "the constantly increasing requests for information from newspapers, schools, and the general public" kept the staff from research.[148] (Mercifully, the Internet relieves some of the pressure from today's museum scientists.)

It appears that Stone got on well with Academy presidents Dixon (1895–1918), John Cadwalader (1918–1922), and Richard A.F. Penrose (1922–1926), all of whom were older than Stone (though Penrose by only three years). Dixon sent Witmer a sympathy note that was very paternal in tone when his brother Frederick died.[151] Penrose told Stone he enjoyed the cordial relations he had always had with the scientific staff, and he once remarked that not only were Stone and John Cadwalader "the closest of friends," but that Cadwalader had been friends with Witmer's father as well.[152]

It was a different story, however, with Charles M.B. Cadwalader (managing director 1928–1937; president 1937–1951; distant relative of John Cadwalader), who took the Academy reins in 1928 after Stone, 19 years his senior, stepped down as director to an emeritus position. Cadwalader had a business, not a scientific, background, and he worked hard to increase Academy membership and improve the displays – areas that had been lately neglected while the museum was run by scientific men like Stone, with their noses in the moth balls, whose backgrounds and temperaments were more suited to strictly technical and scientific work, not public outreach.[111,153] (An Academy memo stated that AMNH had 915,000 visitors in 1929, the Chicago Field Museum 1,168,000, and ANSP fewer than 20,000!)[154]

Stone and Cadwalader had such contrasting personalities that tensions were unavoidable. In early 1931, Stone complained to Palmer, "I thought an 'Emeritus Director' had no duties, but with a 'Director' who is full of questions & requests for assistance the job still takes most of my time!"[155]

Cadwalader had become an Academy life member in 1908 at the age of 23.[156] He became formally involved with the Academy in 1925, and his fine work chairing a committee charged with increasing Academy membership led to the managing director position.[157] It's possible that Stone felt Cadwalader was a bit of a Charlie-come-lately who was too assertive with his ideas of running the museum. Cadwalader had an overbearing, micromanagement style that the scientific staff was unaccustomed to – and didn't like. He didn't waste time making waves with his brusque management style.[158] In 1930, he ordered (there's no other word for it) Stone to begin submitting weekly reports detailing any time missed by the staff in his department of vertebrate zoology.[145] Memos and notes from Cadwalader to Academy staff often had a line at the bottom with "Received" followed by room for the recipient to sign, "proving" they had received it, as if it was all being saved as potential future legal evidence.

Dixon and Penrose seem to have been quick to agree to Stone's Cape May leave-of-absence (LOA) requests (although they may have been considered, or represented as, more collecting or research jaunts than vacations), but Cadwalader liked to be more evasive about it.[159] Stone made a lengthy and somewhat plaintive request for the Cape May LOA in 1934, spelling out how important it was to his health, and noting that arrangements for the cottage needed to be concluded within a week.[160] Cadwalader cagily replied that he would put it before the board of trustees at their next meeting a week hence, noting that Huber and Dave McCadden would be on duty in Stone's department (vertebrate zoology) during the summer – the clear implication being that otherwise Stone wouldn't be granted the Cape May leave.[161] (The LOA was granted.) After Stone pleaded his case for the Cape May getaway in 1936, complete with the need of a prompt answer in order to rent the cottage, Cadwalader used the trustees meeting put-off again and six weeks passed before Stone got an affirmative response.[162] In 1937, the day after he became ANSP president, Cadwalader told Stone, "Referring to your note of April 27th, I will arrange that you may have leave of absence from the Academy during the months of July and August, in order that you may follow out your physician's suggestion as to a sojourn at Cape May. Would appreciate having a talk with you before you actually leave in order that I may have a better understanding of just what work you propose to do during the summer."[163] Although it is all too easy to read a certain tone into a written communication, Cadwalader's note could be interpreted as "You can summer at Cape May on your doctor's recommendation, but I expect you to continue to do ANSP work while you're down there."

Cadwalader often did advise Stone to get some real rest while at Cape May, and Stone often (over-?) emphasized in his letters to Cadwalader from Cape May how closely he was heeding the admonitions to do so, as if it were all Cadwalader's idea, and also how much Academy-related work he was getting done. A few months before *BSOCM* was published, Cadwalader said he had a dim recollection of Stone having told him about the planned work, but immediately (and rightly) asserted that the book wouldn't have been possible without Stone's annual LOAs, and that Stone should mention the Academy's role (which he did).[164] When the book was published, Stone left a set on the president's desk, and Cadwalader, in a warm note of thanks, said he was "flabbergasted" to find them.[165] He was probably as stunned by the book itself as he was by the gesture.

In 1931, Huber, an Academy curator with much field experience, told Stone that Cadwalader was angry at him for sending in small mammal skulls from New Mexico (where Huber was on a collecting trip) that were not fully worked up and ready to put in cases on arrival at ANSP. Huber said, "Nothing ever seems to please." He planned to stop at a few places on his way back to Philadelphia after his fieldwork was done, but told Stone he wasn't telling that to Cadwalader, whom he expected would instead order him home straightaway.[166] The next summer, Huber was collecting in the Southwest again while Stone was at Cape May, and in early August he told Stone, "It won't be long now until we both return to the turmoil" – an obvious reference to conditions at the Cadwalader-run Academy.[167]

Stone indeed must have dreaded going back to ANSP at the end of his Cape May summers, especially during the Cadwalader years. A letter the managing director sent him in late August 1937 ended with a little pep talk about all the work Stone could look forward to pitching into when he got back to the Academy in a week:

> There is a huge amount of work to be done this winter, and I find it very difficult to accomplish all that we should. We must bear in mind that we have a great opportunity here, but I am frank to say that in my opinion it has been shamefully neglected over a long period of years, and now we must work doubly hard to make up for lost time [Stone was Academy director for the four years before Cadwalader assumed the job, so must have felt this criticism was at least partly aimed at him]....I sincerely trust you will be in fine shape when you return and all set to assist in studying out [*sic*] and trying to solve some of the Academy's problems.[168]

That sounds like a fired-up young V.P. at a Fortune 500 firm rolling out the latest sales plan, and Stone must have been looking forward to his Academy return as if it were a dentist appointment.

Stone also got in the habit of sending "if there are no objection" notes to Cadwalader when he wanted to attend the annual AOU meetings, saying that the Academy should be represented, and that he would pay his own expenses; in 1937 he even used the fact that he was still on the AOU Council as a reason he should attend.[169] (Contrast this to 1915,when the Academy appropriated $100 to cover Stone's railroad expenses to the AOU meeting in San Francisco.)[170] It is more than a little ridiculous when one of the country's leading ornithologists should feel compelled to defend, to the head of the natural history museum where he is employed, his desire to attend the annual meeting of the country's leading ornithological society, in which he has been one of the principal leaders for decades. Cadwalader was no scientist and likely didn't realize how well Stone's *Auk* editorship and other AOU involvement reflected on the Academy. As one example, Stone was a "homer" as an editor – he had no reservations about using his literature reviews and the "Notes and News" section to pitch not only DVOC doings, but also recent papers by Academy staff (usually in the Academy's *Proceedings*), and, in particular, the Academy bird collection, frequently mentioning its type specimens and historic importance.

I have also found several instances in Stone's correspondence with Cadwalader in which the older man seems to be overly complimentary about an idea or action of the younger administrator, or a little too zealous in his professed enthusiasm for ANSP, to the point of being ingratiating. It is easy to imagine that Stone felt vulnerable, particularly given his age and precarious health, and was worried that if he didn't show the proper enthusiasm and team spirit, Cadwalader might entertain the notion of letting him go. A. Brazier Howell told Rosalie Edge in 1935 that he had heard though the grapevine that Stone was "scared to death of C[adwalader] and will do anything the latter says."[171]

In about 1937, Cadwalader developed a sudden infatuation with the German ornithologist and systematist Erwin Stresemann – or at least was suddenly infatuated with the idea of luring him to work at ANSP. Stresemann, who has been called "the most influential ornithologist of the twentieth century" and whom Stone deemed "the leading systematist of the ornithological world," visited the Academy in 1936, and Cadwalader told Stone he wanted to talk about trying to get Stresemann to join the Academy staff. Stone advised him that Stresemann was editor of two German ornithological journals (including the renowned *Journal für Ornithologie*) and was very attached to his work at the Zoological Museum in Berlin, where he ran the ornithology department, and that it was highly unlikely that Stresemann would jump ship. (He was offered a research professorship at Yale University in 1934, but turned it down.)[15,172]

A couple of months later, Stresemann had Cadwalader all worked up about having the 1940 International Ornithological Congress (IOC) held in Philadelphia. Stresemann had told him "confidentially" that Philadelphia would be much more suitable for the meeting than New York or Washington, and Cadwalader wanted Stone to dig up all the information he could in the Academy library about previous meetings (not realizing that Stone probably had most of the information in his head) and get back to him with it as soon as possible. The Academy president had never heard of the IOC, and wasn't entirely sure of its name ("the International Ornithologists Congress, or whatever their exact title is") – he just knew that Stresemann had suggested it, and that it was an opportunity to try to further impress the German and induce him to consider a workplace change.[173] Stresemann was 23 years younger than Stone, who may have felt he was being moved closer to the door as his managing director raved to him about the younger, hotshot ornithologist, and you have to wonder about Cadwalader's motives in the matter. At any rate, the rising Nazi menace in Germany would lead to events ensuring that the 1938 IOC meeting was the last one held until 1950, and the loyal Stresemann would remain at the Zoological Museum in Berlin for the rest of his career, right through World War II and the hardships of its aftermath.[174] But it was one more episode with Cadwalader that may have made Stone's last years at the Academy a lot less pleasant than they could have been.

Stone was not getting rich working at ANSP. As a Jessup student he made the standard $20 a month, although his Jessup salary was increased to $35 shortly before his $50 assistant curator position began in the fall of 1892.[20,175] By 1896 he was making $1,000 per year, and his salary was up to $1,960 by 1917.[176] In 1919, rumors were afoot of possible salary adjustments for ANSP staff to bring them in line with what other similar institutions were paying, and Rehn told Stone he was "in favor of an upward revision, which is now a necessity to off-set starvation, ejectment or arrest for indecent exposure" – in other words, ANSP salaries at the time made the acquisition of food, shelter and raiment a challenge. Salaries did indeed jump, across the board, in 1920 (and Rehn got his "upward revision" to the tune of a 30% raise), and Stone's annual salary went up to $3,000, and to $4,000 in 1926.[177] In 1932, however, as fallout from the Depression, his salary was cut 10%, along with all other Academy salaries, but that cut was restored in 1936.[178]

Beginning in 1920, Stone received $200 annually as secretary of the Ludwick Institute, which had Academy affiliations.[179] Additionally, Stone received an honorarium for editing *The Auk*. It was initially $300 a year, then $500 (1920), and $600 from 1929 until Stone's *Auk* retirement in 1936. Although Stone's salary increased quite a bit in 1920, and may have been a decent amount of money during the Depression, he appears to have been supporting his wife and, at least some of the time, his mother as well. Anne lived with Witmer and Lillie for the last 10 years of her life, and I haven't found any indication that Lillie worked.[180] But the Stones' finances were touch-and-go during the Depression, like almost everyone else's, and the *Auk* honorarium was a real lifesaver, especially after the 10% ANSP cuts – the honorarium just about made up the difference.[181] Stone almost missed a couple of AOU annual meetings in the early 1930s because he couldn't afford the cost (telling one friend, "The cut in Academy salaries hits us hard"), and attended the 60th anniversary celebration of the Nuttall Ornithological Club in 1933 despite being "about 'broke.'"[182] J.H.

Fleming wrote to Stone in 1933, "Lessening incomes are a condition common to us all, but it is doubly unfortunate in your case, you had reason to look forward to a comfortable retirement if not an affluent one."[183]

Stone was wistfully contemplating retirement as early as 1927, when he returned from his Cape May summer and told a friend, "The change from the quiet of Cape May with woods & ocean & birds so close to me, to the wrangle of the City & the 'wrangle' of the Museum is very disheartening. If I could afford it I should like to retire & move to some quiet spot like that for my remaining years."[184] The *Auk* editorship was enough of a hassle that Stone got to the point where he wouldn't have minded letting go of it, but he needed the money.[185] He even envisioned a doomsday scenario of the Academy going under and he and Lillie having to live on the *Auk* honorarium alone.[186]

By the mid-1930s, Stone wanted to retire and concentrate on bringing to press his Cape May and American ornithology manuscripts, but ANSP didn't have a pension plan of any kind and he simply couldn't afford to stop working.[187,188] In an undated but clearly mid-1930s letter, Stone said he felt like "a veritable antique at the Academy when everything is in the hands of a new outfit quite unfamiliar with the traditions of the place, but they are very generous in keeping me on, as we have no retirement system."[189] Wealthy bird enthusiast E.A. McIlhenny told Stone in 1937, "I think it is a shame that the Academy of Natural Sciences does not retire you on full pay, so that you could have a free rein to continue your writings, which would be a lasting benefit to naturalists."[190] Huber told Joseph Grinnell in early March 1939 that Stone was about to return home from the hospital after a serious operation and had "retired from active service in the Academy" to pursue his writing, but a week later, the day after his hospital discharge, Stone was assuring Cadwalader that he would be working from home shortly. In a March 31 letter to ANSP assistant secretary John Bowers, he thanked the Academy trustees for continuing his paychecks, saying it was practically the only income he had, and that he was "back at work every day now," doing Academy-related work at home.[191] So much for being retired from the Academy and working on his own projects. He could barely walk, couldn't leave the house, and was in pain from the illnesses and the aftereffects of a major surgery – in short, he was dying – and still felt he needed to do work so that the Academy would continue to pay him, because he couldn't afford to retire.[188,192] He continued clinging to his position, until his death in May put him beyond the aggravation at last.

——————— ∽ ———————

William Maclure, Thomas B. Wilson, and Joseph Leidy are some of the giants in the Academy's history, and their contributions, be they scientific or philanthropic, should never be forgotten. Nor should Stone's. He revived the dormant ornithology department and salvaged its world-class bird collection (and other ones) from ruination. His eminence as an internationally known ornithologist put a spotlight on the Academy's collections and ornithological vitality. He produced a classic Pine Barrens flora that highlighted the Academy's botanical collections and lent further luster to the recognized expertise among Academy staff. His long, faithful, and varied service to the museum, as both a renowned scientist and capable, industrious administrator, certainly earns him a place as one of the outstanding figures in its history. Even today, the Academy receives some incidental limelight from Stone's enduring popular legacy. In a memorial minute published in *PANSP* after Stone's death, J. Percy Moore wrote, "While it would be difficult and perhaps impertinent to attempt to appraise the relative values of individuals who have benefited the Academy in different ways and at different times, I think that it can be stated fairly that Stone's aggregate services to the Academy have never been exceeded."[3]

JACKRABBIT DRIVES AND HIS HOLINESS SLIDES

Stone's archived correspondence and other reference materials contain, in addition to matters related to his normal duties as curator and director, some less mundane ANSP matters:

• While preparing a 1903 *Cassinia* biography of the late Philadelphia-born ornithologist John K. Townsend, Stone had asked Townsend's brother-in-law Mahlen Kirk for some information. Kirk liked the article so much that he offered to Stone and ANSP some of the curios brought back by Townsend from various parts of the globe, which Kirk thought could be better cared for at a museum. They included "a small collection of <u>poisonous</u> arrows John obtained from some tribe of Indians in the far North West, and a water-proof cloak or garment from [Hawaii], made from the intestines of some fishes that inhabit those waters."[1] It doesn't appear that Stone took him up on the offer, missing an opportunity for ANSP to acquire some interesting display items that would probably get high yuck-out scores with school kids today.

• From the "one person's trash is another's treasure" department: In 1901, four years after her husband's death, Annie Cope, widow of the famous Philadelphia paleontologist (and pack rat) Edward D. Cope, was cleaning out their Pine Street houses and arranged for ANSP to come by and pick up some of her late husband's effects.[2] She got off a note to Stone that included, "When the wagon comes on Monday for the two boxes I am going to take the liberty of sending three [additional] small boxes which contain specimens (fragments) of Jurassic Dinosaurs. If upon examination you find you would care to keep them and would like more we would gladly send you ten boxes which contain like material from Wyoming. It will go to the dump heap if you do not wish to have it [!]…[T]here is good material in the lot, and if you can use it we shall be glad."[3] Evidently, when you've had dinosaur bones lying around your house for 35 years they start to seem about as valuable as a box of scratched-up LPs or a dusty old set of golf clubs. The recorded Academy accessions for the year 1901 note many fossils from the Copes, and hopefully they include the ones threatened with a date with the dump.[4]

• Stone had a great recollection of Cope's visits to ANSP to compare specimens: "I have often seen him busily engaged in such comparisons, all the while whistling whole passages from grand opera, or else counting the scales on the back of a lizard, while he conversed in a most amusing manner with some small street urchin who had drifted into the museum and was watching in awe with eyes and mouth wide open."[5]

• How to never get loaned a specimen by anyone again – ever: Hubert Clark of Olivet College had requested the loan of some Academy hummingbird specimens. Immediately upon receiving them he wrote to Stone that, by the way, he intended to pluck every one of them clean, adding, "If you do not wish me to do so, will you please let me know at once. If I do not hear from you by Monday next [i.e., one week from the date of Clark's letter], I shall conclude it is all right for me to go ahead, so you will not need to write unless you want to stop me."[6] Clark's subsequent *Auk* article on the feather tracts of hummingbirds thanked Stone for specimens, so either Stone was fine with the plucking, or he didn't receive, discover, or respond to the letter in the brief time period that Clark had not so graciously given him.[7]

• The old museum's wear and tear was noted in 1917 by Philip Calvert, who found a chunk of plaster on the floor when he came to work one day in the entomological department. He decided to chance another fall, but when the next chunk fell the sound reminded him of the 1910 earthquake in Cartago, Costa Rica that he'd lived through, so he removed to a lower floor. He asked Stone to have the problem addressed, wryly noting that "blinding or other physical injury to the worker is a slight matter as compared to the loss of precious <u>types belonging to</u>

the Academy which can never be replaced, whereas another student is likely to appear in 50 or 60 years if the plaster kills."[8] Falling plaster was a common problem around the Academy at the time.[9]

• Just when you thought you couldn't have any higher admiration for Leidy than you already did: Shortly before his death in 1920, the noted physician, botanist, and UP professor Horatio Wood related a great Joseph Leidy story, telling Stone, "When I was about 14 years old I had the use of the Library of the Academy, but no allowance was given to open the cases. The famous Professor Leidy came past me one day when I was crying because I could not have a case open. He asked me what was the matter. I told him that I was wild to handle the specimens, and that was the cause of my sorrow. He reflected that he would soon remedy that, and gave me a [written] order to have any case in the Academy opened as I wished."[10]

• Harry Swarth of the California Academy of Sciences in San Francisco sent Stone a recent article from the *Berkeley Daily Gazette* about the Colorado delegation traveling to the upcoming American Legion convention in Philadelphia. The group planned to capture thousands of jackrabbits in Colorado, then release them in towns through which they passed while traveling to Philadelphia. The newspaper described the "trench drive" that would be used to capture the rabbits: "The rabbits will be driven into trenches, where the largest can be captured alive and caged to be taken with the delegation." The delegates planned to release 2,000 jackrabbits onto the streets of Philadelphia once they arrived there.[11] With a wisecrack that only a fellow museum curator would cook up, Swarth instructed Stone, "Read the enclosed clipping, and then prepare to dig some trenches for yourself to gather in a series of the mammals thus being provided for you."[12] (In museum curator parlance, a "series" is a collection of specimens of the same species that includes a range of sizes, sexes, ages, etc.)

• The Academy had photographic slide collections that were used by staff in their public talks, and they were sometimes loaned or rented to other institutions. Witmer was very helpful in response to an unusual request from Reverend Mother Jane Saul of the Convent of the Sacred Heart in Philadelphia, telling her, "I regret that our lantern slides deal almost entirely with natural history subjects, and we have no lecture or slides relating to Rome" before suggesting some other possible local sources for such photos.[13]

• Some museum operations must have been a little more relaxed in Stone's time than now. Glover Allen of the MCZ wrote to Stone in 1934 about a recent shipment of Chinese mammals from ANSP's Brooke Dolan collection. Allen couldn't find all the skins and skulls listed on the ANSP packing list, and asked Stone, "Is there not some mistake about these specimens? I am certain that the skins mentioned did not pass through my hands, and our janitor who unpacked the lot is very careful to examine all wrappers, so I don't think it possible they could have been missed."[14] The janitor is unpacking the loans??

• Because of his Academy position, Stone was featured with some regularity in local newspapers, which noted his birthdays and Academy anniversaries, and also called on him for expert opinions on a range of natural history topics, including conservation. One 1908 article noted that a recent bird talk by Stone included an anecdote about a Chuck-will's-widow swallowing a Yellow Warbler, which it mistakenly took for a butterfly (or so it may have been thought at the time – their predatory habits are well known now). Stone joked with his audience that the dubious narrative might get him labeled one of Teddy Roosevelt's despised "nature fakers," and the article's title was a humorous "Not a Nature Faker: No! No! No! No!"[15] In another 1908 article, he was decidedly (and hypercritically) uncharitable in his opinion of the new Saint-Gaudens-designed U.S. double eagle ($20) coin, saying, "That picture on the reverse side of the coin is a bird, but I am at sea to decide what kind. If I might be real lenient I might concede that it's a bird of prey, which might show it to be a distant relative of the eagle; but an eagle, never!"[16] He expressed healthy skepticism at the report of a live Brontosaurus discovered in central Africa in 1919, but he only called it "extremely improbable," as if he was hesitant to discredit the report outright.[17] Asked about a massive Gray Squirrel migration taking place in Massachusetts, Connecticut, and eastern New York in 1933, Stone said he had heard of such migrations by Gray Squirrels in search of food, but had never seen one and was unaware of any such migration under way in the Philadelphia region. That was a lucid, factual counterbalance to some hooey from C. Emerson Brown, director of the Philadelphia Zoo, who said that Gray Squirrels sometimes moved to find new food sources, but also because "they always run away from Red Squirrels," which were "noisy and too active." Gray Squirrels were "dignified and quiet by nature," and the "chattering of their red cousins makes them so nervous they will migrate for miles to get away from it."[18]

4

Characters I Have Known

S tone was one of the founding members of the Delaware Valley Ornithological Club (DVOC) in 1890, and although it seems to be widely believed that he started the club, that was decidedly not the case.[1] An earlier bird club had been formed in 1884 at Haverford College, and its six members included William L. Baily. That club quickly foundered, but in December 1889, Baily and J. Harris Reed, a fellow employee at an architectural firm, discovered they had a mutual interest in ornithology. They soon asked some other local amateur ornithologists – Spencer Trotter, Samuel Rhoads, and George Spencer Morris – to "join with them for the purpose of keeping combined lists" of local birds.[2-4] Blank check-lists were sent out, to be completed and mailed back to Reed, who (so the plan went) "was to compile the [daily lists] and furnish a copy to each [member]." Trotter came up with an idea: why not form a club and hold meetings at which papers could be read and discussed?[5]

Stone was not even at the original meeting of five (Baily, Trotter, Rhoads, Morris, and Reed) of the eventual seven (including Stone and Charles Voelker) founders, held January 22, 1890 at a vacant house owned by Baily's father at 1624 Arch Street in Philadelphia. Right next door was the spectacular (if structurally shaky) Willis Hale-designed clubhouse of the Athletic Club of the Schuylkill Navy.[6] (Both buildings have since been demolished.) At the invitation of Trotter, the only member he knew, Stone attended the third meeting of the club two weeks later, on February 3, and became the last of the seven founding members to join.[3,5,7] The club offered membership to Philip Laurent in March, presumably as a founder, but he declined on the grounds that he "couldn't perform satisfactory work for the club as a member."[8-9] The men used Stone's quill pen fashioned from a Golden Eagle feather to sign the club's constitution and bylaws.[10]

William Collins had influenced the early ornithological interests of Trotter, Morris, and Rhoads, and would have been a founding member, but he died just before the formation of the club.[11-12] He and Trotter had collected birds around the Collins farm in the Frankford section of Philadelphia. One day in October 1876 the two boys started off for the Centennial Exhibition, collecting gun in hand ("just in case," presumably). They never arrived, however, for on the way they stopped at a local woodlot, found and shot a Saw-whet Owl, then returned home to stuff it.[13] Twenty years after the club formed, Collins was still fondly remembered. In 1909, Rhoads gave a talk to the DVOC on "Memories of a Departed Bird-lover – William L. Collins," with additional reminiscences by Morris and Trotter. Morris's *Cassinia* paper on club history the same year mentioned Collins, "whose early death we still mourn."[12,14] That Collins was an industrious collector is evident in Rhoads's *Cassinia* Dickcissel paper, which contained many Collins records.[15]

Trotter's "What the DVOC Means to Me" essay (doubtless the "letter" read at the January 1910 annual meeting)[16] recalled the pre-DVOC days of his youth and medical school, when many of the members' paths crossed for the first time:

> Then I met dear old Will Collins and we were as David and Jona-than in our love for ornithology. Through Collins I first learned of Sam Rhoads and heard rumors of George Morris – a youngster who dwelt at Olney – not far from the hunting ground of Collins....When I die I would ask nothing better than to go bird-hunting again with Collins in Elysian Fields....I knew William L. Baily in those days too – but he caught the fever later when at Haverford [College]....[Trot-ter recounted meeting "Billy" Hughes, an early DVOC member, and Philadelphia taxidermist Chris Wood]....The fire of ornithology had smoldered in my being through the medical years. Strangely enough it was not Wood that rekindled the flame – but Stone – The Stone – the only Stone – Witmer Stone. The old spark flashed into light when my steel struck Stone.[17]

Although Baily may be rightly credited as "not only one of the founders, but...par excellence *the* founder," Trotter was considered the ornithological big gun at the beginning ("stood higher than any of us on the ornithological ladder").[11,18] Stone later recalled that Trotter "was the first ornithologist I had ever met [in March 1888] – the first man who knew more about birds than I did," and "Trotter has the honor of proposing the name of the Society but to W.L. Baily belongs the inspiration that resulted in its founding."[19] After first meeting in homes, the DVOC began meeting in the Council Room at ANSP on March 3, 1891, and moved to the ornithological room on November 19, 1896.[11,20] In return for the use of ANSP rooms for meetings, the DVOC presented the Academy with a collection of local bird skins, nests, and eggs, and club members made frequent additions to it in the following years.[21] The collection reportedly fell into disuse after Stone's death, but the skins, at least, were incorporated into the Academy collection in the 1970s.[22]

At the time of the founding of the DVOC, Trotter was a biology professor at Swarthmore, Voelker a taxidermist, Rhoads a New Jersey farmer, and Baily, Morris, and Reed were architects.[11,19] Stone, a Jessup Fund student at ANSP, was closer to being a professional ornithologist than were any of the others. All the founding members were between 23 and 32 years of age, and, with the exception of Stone and Voelker, were members of the Society of Friends (as Collins evidently had been also – he published in the Quaker weekly *The Friend*).[23] Voelker had been born in Germany, so he could hardly be expected to be a Quaker, unlike Witmer, who had attended a Friends school.

Stone had no sooner joined the DVOC than he headed off on the ANSP expedition to Mexico. He was back in time to give a talk about the trip on May 19, complete with newly collected specimens.[11,24] At that same meeting he made the first move toward his inevitable leadership role when he volunteered to write a notice of the new club for publication in *The Auk*.[9] Reed showed some early interest, and seems to have considered himself one of the leaders. By the end of the DVOC's first year, however, it was clear that Stone was the de facto leader, and he was elected president after Baily cited business pressures in bailing on a second term.[25] Baily wrote to Stone at that time, "If it was not for you I would be very anxious about the welfare of the club."[26]

In January 1891 the club adopted Stone's system for recording migration waves, using a sample set of common migrants.[24] Two weeks later the cream really rose to the top, as recorded in the DVOC minutes for the meeting: "Mr. Stone surprised the Club by presenting two blue-print copies to each member of a complete list of the birds observed in 1890 with their time of occurrence and relative abundance. Also a map of the 'D[elaware] V[alley]' district and a separate list showing the arrival of 40 commoner species during the spring migration and giving hints for '91. Mr. Stone was unanimously tendered a vote of thanks for this excellent piece of work and requested to hand in his bill and present a copy to the Department of Agriculture. Mr. Reed announced, amid great [obviously derisive] applause, the completion of his long-delayed 1890 list."[27] It had been Reed's job originally, before Stone even joined the nascent club, to compile a list of everyone's observations. By the time he produced it, Stone had taken that ball and run a lot farther with it than the rest of them could have imagined. If there was any one incident that established Stone as the DVOC's leader early on, that was it. The other fellows were, to varying degrees, active amateur bird students, but Stone was immersed in it every day at the Academy, and that, combined with his greater innate interest in the subject, led to his inevitable assumption of the role as the club's leader, a position he retained until his death. Only Voelker, working daily as a taxidermist, was exposed to bird work on as regular a basis as Stone at that time, but it was not of a particularly scientific nature, and he was certainly nowhere near the all-around (fieldwork, research, publication, museum position, AOU involvement, etc.) ornithological package that Stone was.

Early club meetings were held the first and third Tuesdays of each month, but owing to potential conflicts with Academy meetings (many DVOCers were also ANSP members), it was decided in 1893 to make Thursday the meeting night. Stone ran the planned change past the Academy curators, and his assurance that he and Rhoads would "be responsible for locking up the building &

the proper behavior of the members of the Club" makes you wonder whether the DVOC didn't already have a reputation for shenanigans by that early date.

It didn't take long for Stone to start working on what would prove to be the DVOC's first big splash in the ornithological world. In the fall of 1890 he asked Rhoads, Baily, Reed, and Morris to add the dates of occurrence from their own records to a list of birds known to occur in Pennsylvania and New Jersey, with the idea of publishing a complete list for the area. Stone had circulars printed for distribution to gunners and sportsmen along the coast to solicit information about water birds, with whom the gunners would be familiar.[20,28-29] Stone wasn't a hunter, but he readily gathered data from those who were, and he would use gunners' records in *BSOCM* 40 years later.

By the end of 1892 the plans for a list had become plans for a book, and Stone gave a progress report to the DVOC in December; the following June, he read extracts from the manuscript to Active members at a pre-meeting council.[30] When *The Birds of Eastern Pennsylvania and New Jersey (BEPNJ)* was published in late 1894, the DVOC attained its place on the national ornithological map.[31] B.H. Warren, the state ornithologist for Pennsylvania, had produced two editions of his fine *Birds of Pennsylvania*, but previous efforts at cataloging New Jersey's birds had left much to be desired.[32] In an *Auk* review, Frank Chapman wrote that the new DVOC book "may well stand as a model for works of this nature," and concluded, "[W]e congratulate Mr. Stone and his associates on having performed their task in a manner which demands the highest commendation."[33] By 1897, AOU founder Charles Batchelder was beginning a letter to Stone with, "As you are generally understood to have charge ornithologically of Pennsylvania and New Jersey..."[34]

During the first 11 years of its existence, the club occasionally published an *Abstract of the Proceedings of the Delaware Valley Ornithological Club of Philadelphia*, produced by Stone.[35] This was simply a brief description of recent meetings held, but with the third issue, for the years 1898–1899, the club started including some papers read at the meetings. In 1901 the club morphed its *Abstract* into a periodical named *Cassinia*, after John Cassin. Stone served as editor from 1901 through 1910, when he began preparing to assume editorship of *The Auk*.

Even when he wasn't technically the editor, however, Stone was still very involved in *Cassinia* production, because his vast editorial and publishing experience was relied on by later editors. Stone anonymously edited the 1922–24 *Cassinia*; as he worked on it he vowed, "I hope someone will be found to keep it going, for after [it appears] I shall retire absolutely. I did this [i.e., retired] some years ago but have had to help out ever since."[36] One hindrance to Stone getting relief was finding someone to take the *Cassinia* editor position and stay with it. Robert Moore, who replaced Stone and edited *Cassinia* for a time before eventually moving to California, told Stone in 1927, "It is certainly too bad that the younger men do not take the interest in keeping up Cassinia. Certainly no one could expect you to continue with the responsibilities of Cassinia after you took over the Auk."[37] After retiring as *Auk* editor, Stone co-edited one last *Cassinia* issue before he died.

Moore confronted a problem early in his editorship that must have bedeviled Stone at times: how to tell one of your bird club pals that their article isn't up to snuff. It's one thing to reject, via letter, an article for *The Auk* from someone in another state whom you may never or rarely see; but to tell someone you see at club meetings on a regular basis, probably accompany on field trips, and who might even be your friend, that his article doesn't cut it is a little tougher. That was Moore's problem with a manuscript he received from DVOC vet Charles Pennock. Moore told Stone, "Pennock's paper has arrived and has nonplused me! Frankly I do not know what to do with it, it is so entirely without point! I would like to ask him to confine it to Lapland Longspurs and [Horned Larks] but hardly dare. I wonder how you steered *Cassinia* so long and remained popular and acceptable."[38] Moore must have been a little short of material a year later when he asked Stone, "In case I should need another paper [for the upcoming *Cassinia*], will you have any crumbs dropping from the overflowing table of the Auk?" – but things probably didn't quite work that way.[39]

Cassinia and the DVOC fell on hard times occasionally. In 1908, Stone had to solicit funds to keep the publication's head above water, and people responded.[40] One member sent money and told Stone to ask for more "if the life of Cassinia continues to be despaired of."[41] Samuel Wright, the DVOC treasurer at the time, lent the club money to produce one issue.[42] It appears that Morris also helped out with *Cassinia* finances, both in raising funds and supplying them, and Stone recalled Morris's generosity in the *Cassinia* memorial he wrote after Morris's death.[43,44] The DVOC was still in the red in 1915, and the high cost of printing and the club's dire financial situation ("The Club was about bankrupt last year [i.e., 1921]") led to combining the 1920 and 1921 *Cassinia*s into one issue.[45] Stone said in 1920 that he was trying to find a printer "who will print it for something less than the German indemnity."[46] Club finances in Stone's time seemed to be on a better footing after that, even through the Depression. *Cassinia* continued to be published on an erratic schedule, but that may have been due to the editorship bouncing from one busy senior member to another, and a lack of interest on the part of the younger men to get involved with it.[37] Today the DVOC is on much better, if not worry-free, financial footing, and *Cassinia* is still its major expense.[47]

Fellow club members were unstinting in their open appreciation for Stone's leadership. In 1904, Rhoads noted the "untiring and skilful labors of our business manager, Mr. Witmer Stone" as the main reason for the success of the club.[3] Mark Wilde told Stone in 1910, "I consider that your untiring efforts and devotion have kept things going along at 'full speed' and the goodly feeling among the boys has been largely inspired by your zeal and friendship which is greatly appreciated."[48] Morris said of Stone at the 20th anniversary meeting of the club, "And there is Stone, ever at the tiller, quiet in manner, but potent in influence. No matter who may be President, we all recognize him as the person behind the throne. With infinite tact, he gives a push here and a pull there as occasion requires, keeping us all in line. In our hearts we know that the guiding hand of Stone has made the DVOC what it is."[12] In 1910 Trotter said of the club's early days, "Baily, Rhoads, Morris, [Reed]…Voelker and I were in attendance, but we called in Witmer Stone who pulled the baby into the world and has been its guiding light ever since."[17] In 1912 he added, "I believe that I voice the sentiment of all who know him that he is the bright and particular star in our ornithological firmament, and that the life and vigor of our Club has been in largest measure due to his broad knowledge and untiring zeal."[49]

------------ ∾ ------------

Until late 1982, DVOC membership, meetings, and field trips were restricted to men.[4] In 1910, "any respectable male bird student" was a potential candidate for membership.[11] Rhoads wrote in the early days of the club that "visitors of the male sex may attend any of our meetings on invitation of a member. It was at one time debated that a form of honorary lady membership should be instituted, but the establishment of Audubon and other societies about that time seemed to cover the ground so well that no action in this matter is ever likely to be taken."[3] (And he was right for a very long time!)

The debate Rhoads referred to occurred in 1891, when he wrote to Stone in March concerning the creation of an honorary membership for women. Stone had already told Rhoads that it didn't make sense because women wouldn't be allowed to attend the club meetings, so of what benefit would it be for them? Rhoads said there could be one or two special meetings each year open to the general public, which women could attend, but that attendance at meetings shouldn't be the main point of consideration – he didn't think the women would want to regularly attend meetings with men, anyway. Rather, the idea was to allow women to have an association with the club whereby they would more readily benefit from the DVOC's expertise, encouragement, and instruction.[50] At the next DVOC meeting, Rhoads proposed "that an Honorary Membership be established to which ladies might belong. The plea did not however meet with much enthusiasm from the Society as it was generally considered that it would not be best for such members to attend our regular meetings. They could not therefore reap much benefit from the club, but would nevertheless add considerably to the work of our already busy officers."[51] Harrumph!

At least some in the club were able to poke fun at themselves about it, as they did in 1939 when Ed Weyl, writing the minutes for a joint meeting with another local (and more progressive) natural history club, wisecracked, "A notable feature of the evening for the monastically inclined members of the DVOC was the presence of the ladies of the Philadelphia Botanical Club."[52] Members of the latter group got started on their slippery slope of women's membership early on when they accepted Dr. Ida Keller as a member in 1892, after unanimous agreement that, despite their unwritten rule of excluding women from membership, Dr. Keller, who was to publish in *PANSP* on botany and co-compile *Handbook of the Flora of Philadelphia and Vicinity* in 1905, was enough of a scientist and botany enthusiast to be admitted to their ranks.[53] One little moment of weakness…

Actually, it's easy to beat up the old-timers for being misogynistic grumps, but society was different then. Stone doesn't seem to have had any reservations about women's abilities as bird students or museum workers. Women were among the field observers whose records he compiled for the migration reports in *Cassinia*, and he of course accepted their manuscripts for *The Auk*. In the "Birds" section of the annual curators' report in *PANSP* in 1917, Stone wrote that "the services of Miss Emma P. Merrick were secured as an aid in the ornithological department, and with her help, Dr. Stone was enabled to make a great advance in the arrangement of the study series of birds."[54]

An earlier woman worker under Stone, however, Ada Apgar, found the Academy experience unpleasant enough that her father, Austin, wrote to Stone asking if she could continue her (unspecified) work at home. He said that her eyes were strained from the poor light in the work area, but also that her presence "is not always pleasant either to her or to the other [male] workers." This may have been the statement of an overprotective father (Ada was about 23 at the time), but she must have felt tension from at least some of her male colleagues. Austin Apgar thanked Stone for "all your kindness to her in her work," so Stone was not the source of the tension.[55] Austin was a natural history author, and Ada carried his last book, *Ornamental Shrubs of the United States*, to press after his death.

In 1900, the women formed their own bird club, the Spencer F. Baird Ornithological Club, reportedly inspired by the Pennsylvania Audubon Society, with which there was some personnel overlap.[56] The club constitution decreed two meetings per month, November through April; membership limited to 25; and each member to present at least two papers per year. No mention was made of a journal or newsletter.[57] Stone was in favor of the new organization; in fact, AOU secretary John Sage told the club's president, Julia Robins, "I'm glad to know about the new Club and shall watch its progress with interest. The Stone Chats would not be a bad name."[4,58] Stone and other DVOC members gave talks at Baird Club meetings.[4,59]

When Robins passed away suddenly in 1906, a tribute to her was read at the October DVOC meeting and recorded in *Cassinia*.[60] Stone also penned a short notice in *The Auk*, because Robins had been an Associate member of the AOU.[61] One Baird member told Stone, "I rather think the S.F. Baird Club has perished with her," but it soldiered on for several years.[62] Stone led the club on a tour of ANSP in 1909, and the 1910 *PANSP* noted that club meetings were being held in the Academy.[63] Mention of the club in a 1913 *Bird-Lore* article indicates that it was still in existence then but, as Phil Street aptly summarized its history years later, "[A]fter an enthusiastic beginning, interest waned, and the club eventually folded."[4,64] About 70 years after the Baird Club's demise, the DVOC – not without a fight – voted to allow women members, and they have played an important and welcome part in its subsequent history.

———————— ❧ ————————

The DVOC in Stone's time comprised a colorful, if all-male, cast of characters – that is obvious from its 20-year history souvenir booklet published in 1910, for which no author is listed, but appears to have been written by Stone.[4,11,16] AOU Fellow Ruthven Deane told Stone, "The genial wit and humor shows to me very plainly that you were the chief cook and bottle washer of this publication."[65] In addition to providing invaluable information on the early days and members of the club, it's highly entertaining with its witty, irreverent prose and captions. One gem: "Then there were questions of nomenclature, some used one name, some another. 'What do you mean by an "Irishman"?' said Baily. 'Why, a Shoveler, of course!' replied Reed, and the Club shouted its acquiescence." (A Shoveler is a duck with a broad, shovel-like bill; 19th-century Irish laborers were frequently engaged in digging canals and railroad beds.) Batchelder received a copy, and he summed up the state of the DVOC at the time when he wrote to Stone, "I am impressed not only with the substantial scientific results of the members' activities – and they are large – but much more with the indications I see of their attitude toward each other…. A club that serves well as a scientific clearing-house, or even as a school of friendly mutual criticism, is always a reasonable possibility, almost anywhere, but in Philadelphia you evidently have aimed at something better than that, and your ideal has been realized very fully."[66]

The fellows did have fun together. Some bird clubs could be stuffy and proper, but not this one. Stone assured one visiting ornithologist, while inviting him to the upcoming DVOC 25th anniversary dinner, that "this is positively not a dress affair. Just an ordinary free & easy DVOC gathering."[67] A member razzed Stone about missing a recent DVOC outing to Cape May: "Have you ever heard the song: 'Oh! 'tis fine to get up in the mornin'/But it's better to lie in your bed.' We had a fine trip to the Cape. Sorry you couldn't go," to which Stone shot back, "As to your scurrilous remarks about the song, I have no reply except to say that I was up at 2 A.M. and again at 6 A.M., and hardly thought that there were enough fools prepared to go out in such a snow storm to make it worth my while to go down to the ferry."[68] One member referred to another DVOC winter outing – apparently an icy one – as "the slipperiest day that ever dawned since Adam fell!"[69] Julian Potter once sent Stone the limerick, "A wonderful bird is the seagull/He can fly most as high as the eagle/As he eats on the strands/If he sits or he stands/You can not tell a he from a she gull." (It ended up on an Abbott and Costello program in 1945, so it must have been making the rounds.)[70] On one club outing, Sam Scoville asked Baily whether some distant ducks might be Wood Ducks; Baily said that if they saw something in the water they wanted to eat they wood (would) duck. Cue up the laugh track.[71]

Someone put together video footage of a few of the club's 1920s outings; this was transferred to DVD by the club in 2004. Members are seen canoeing in the Pine Barrens, birding at the shore, playing some sort of "field hockey in a box" game (that would be my description) – but mostly hamming it up for the camera. There are some witty intertitles, such as "Birds seem to be scarce in this section, but here is proof that the woods are being carefully searched," followed by footage of a dozen guys sitting on a bridge railing, doing ostensibly little.

Richard Miller and Turner McMullen were eggers who frequently collected together and whose nest records were used extensively by Stone in *BSOCM*. Longstanding DVOC member Alan Brady remembered that Miller and McMullen were like Mutt and Jeff: Miller was about six feet tall and gangly, whereas McMullen was about five feet tall, with a high, squeaky voice. (His *Cassinia* death notice recorded that he weighed 100 pounds, and was a horse jockey and tightrope walker at various times.)[72] Alan said that they used to sit at the back during DVOC meetings, and nobody wanted to talk to them because they were "just eggers," but they were a fountain of bird lore.[73] Alan recalled McMullen bragging about the size of his Black Rail egg collection and said McMullen once led a DVOC outing in the New Jersey marshes looking for their nests. Everyone was walking around poking into what they thought were likely spots, except for McMullen, who was down on his hands and knees sticking his whole arm into rail trails through the grass. He advised that if you just followed the runways, eventually you'd come to the nest. He then found a Black Rail nest with trampled, broken eggs and assumed that one of the DVOCers had stepped on it, whereupon he proceeded to throw the men out of the marsh – he told them all to leave.[73-74] (McMullen was a self-described "hot-headed little Irishman.")[72] McMullen rubbed some members the wrong way by collecting nests and eggs on other DVOC outings. John Gillespie, for one, thought it set a bad example for young birders, and he was against eggs being collected for pecuniary, not scientific, reasons.[75]

The enigmatic Richard Miller remains a true DVOC legend. Alan said, "Miller never worked a day in his life" (he was, essentially, a professional egg collector), and he corroborated Charlie Wonderly's assertion that Miller rarely used binoculars – he could see as well with the naked eye as others could with their binoculars.[74,76] That may be a bit of hyperbole, but the binoculars in those days weren't up to today's standard. Charlie told me that Miller lived on a dump at Tinicum in south Philadelphia ("in a shack made out of waste tin that was carried to the dump," as Cornelius Weygandt remembered it), and that he (like Stone) never owned a car and took trolleys and trains everywhere.[77]

Charlie, who joined the DVOC in 1947 and used to say kiddingly that he was going to write a book about the club some day titled *Characters I Have Known*, told me a story once about Miller. In the wee hours of a morning in the early 1940s, Miller was out birding, using binoculars on this occasion. He used to keep a list of birds on his outings, but instead of writing species names he just wrote down the corresponding numbers from the AOU check-list – he had the numbers memorized.[76] The police came along and asked him what he was doing. Miller had a speech impediment, and couldn't get it out that he was birding, which – particularly in those days – probably wouldn't have done much to allay suspicion anyway. Then they saw the list of numbers. During World War II, people walking around with binoculars at offbeat hours, carrying a list of numbers, and unable to explain their doings were considered suspicious, so poor Miller was hauled off to the police station. (Egg collectors marked their eggs with the corresponding species number from the AOU check-list, which is why Miller was so familiar with them; Brady said of Miller and McMullen, "When they talked to each other, they conversed in numbers.")[73,78]

The artist Al Nicholson, remarking on the dedication of the Stone-era birders ("they were *close to it*"), had another Miller story that he told to author Jack Connor: "I remember one time meeting old Richard Miller at Tinicum when I was a kid. It was the middle of the winter and he was looking for owl droppings. 'Have you seen any excrement?' he asked me. I didn't know what he said. 'Have you seen any *excrement*?' I could hardly understand him because he had no teeth; he talked like he had marbles in his mouth. But his eyes were lit up and excited. He was *close to it*."[79] And for all his eccentricities, one only has to read Miller's *Cassinia* and other journal articles, or his nest records in *BSOCM*, to recognize that he was indeed "close to it." Miller's collection of 4,959 egg sets was eventually housed at the Western Foundation of Vertebrate Zoology, after a residence at Louisiana State University.[80]

Another DVOC character, John D. Carter of Lansdowne, corresponded frequently with Stone, sending letters full of typical – and endearing – Quakerisms, such as "Thine hastily" and "Thine cordially" as signoffs, and writing "third month" or "ninth month" instead of the names of the months. In a note accompanying a Barred Owl manuscript submission for *The Auk*, Carter wrote that he thought the article might be suitable for inclusion, but assured Stone, "If you think quite differently, I shall be well content," which isn't a sentiment encountered very often by journal editors.[81] Stone did not think quite differently: he published the note. Carter was also president of the Lansdowne Natural History Club, and he invited Stone to present a lecture to the club in 1909. After some exchanges concerning the date and topic, Carter shot off the following on February 24:

> Dear Stone: –
> I think the subject proposed – "Birds nests and nestlings" – would be very satisfactory.
> We have a man to operate the lantern [i.e., projector].
> A little daughter arrived here this evening at 7:10 and seems to be doing nicely.
>
> Thine sincerely,
> Jno. D. Carter[82]

His wife had just given birth at home, and he was worrying about a nature club talk? And he didn't even sign off "Thine hastily" – it must have been just another day on the home front for Mr. Carter, with domestic distractions like childbirths serving only as background noise to the more important business of organizing nature club meetings.

Things will never be dull in your bird club as long as you have a J. Dryden Kuser on the rolls. Kuser was born into wealth and was quite a precocious ornithologist. He was approved for membership in the DVOC in 1911 when he was 13 and posted a short article in the *Cassinia* issue announcing his membership.[83] He published a short note in *The Auk* at 14, privately published *The Birds of Somerset Hills* at 15, then *The Way to Study Birds* (published by Putnam, drawings by famed artist Louis Agassiz Fuertes) at 20.[84] He was also, as a teenager, president of the Somerset Hills Bird Club and editor of its short-lived periodical, *The Oriole*. His father, Anthony, served a stint as president of the New Jersey Audubon Society (as Dryden later did), sponsored William Beebe's Asian expedition and the sumptuous series of pheasant monographs that followed, and in 1923 donated his home and surrounding 10,000+ acres to New Jersey, which became High Point State Park.[85]

In 1919, Dryden married 17-year-old Brooke Russell, but the marriage was rocky from the start. They had a son, Anthony, but Brooke said that Kuser was a drunken womanizer who occasionally beat her, and she divorced him in 1930.[86] When she remarried, her new husband adopted Anthony, whereupon Kuser sued his own son in an (unsuccessful) attempt to get back child support payments.[87] (Years later, Brooke married Vincent Astor and became the Brooke Astor of New York philanthropy fame.) Kuser reportedly married four times, was the victim of a kidnapping plot, and lived a life troubled with booze, gambling, and debt.[88-89] All this made him perfect material to be a New Jersey politician, of course, and he was – he held a state Senate seat for six years, which ended when one of his many affairs came to light, but during his tenure he managed to get the goldfinch named the New Jersey state bird.[89] Kuser maintained a DVOC membership through 1934 (or, because of his blue blood, perhaps the DVOC maintained one for him), and after his death a part of High Point State Park was named the Dryden Kuser Natural Area.

BSOCM featured ten photographs by Norm McDonald, and numerous drawings by the artist Conrad Roland. In the late 1980s, Charlie Wonderly told me another old DVOC yarn concerning the two of them, and I present it as it was told to me, with no claims to its veracity (although Charlie was friendly with McDonald, from whom he'd probably heard it). Roland was a typical artist: he found aesthetic flaws with everything. One evening at McDonald's home, Roland told "Mac" that the he was annoyed by the white cement between the bricks in the fireplace because it was too bright, and he was leaving. McDonald told him to wait, then showed him the Earl Poole Osprey painting used as the frontispiece of Volume 1 of *BSOCM* and asked him what kind of fish the Osprey was holding. (It was of no particular species.) An argument ensued over whether or not it mattered if the fish was an exact species or an artist's generic fish – McDonald said it mattered, and Roland said it didn't. When two artistic naturalists get together, they clearly find better things to bicker about than sports, religion, or politics.

Some characters Stone knew included DVOC stalwarts (*left to right*) J. Fletcher Street, George Stuart, William Baily, John D. Carter, and Stone's longtime physician William Hughes. DVOC Collection, ANSP Archives.

Alan Brady told me another story with the same two characters. One evening McDonald was visiting Roland at his home near Hawk Mountain. A policeman knocked, and Roland answered the door with one of his pet pigeons perched on his shoulder. The cop wanted to ask a few questions of Roland, who turned to the pigeon and asked, "Well, Pidgee, what do you think? Should we let the officer in?"[90]

On a side note, the DVOCers were techie trailblazers in at least one way: they may have a claim to being the first digiscopers. Young John Emlen Jr. illustrated a couple of his DVOC talks with photographs that he had taken using his binoculars as a telephoto lens.[91]

———————— ᙣ ————————

One of the strangest stories in the DVOC's history is the disappearing act by Charles Pennock of Kennett Square, Pennsylvania, who joined the club in 1895, was an avid egg collector, and served as the first secretary of the American Bird Banding Association. He was also a good friend of Stone, who helped him get appointed as the Delaware State Ornithologist in 1903.[92] After the May 15, 1913 DVOC meeting, Stone and Pennock headed over to the Broad Street Station together, with Pennock complaining of a headache. They parted, and Pennock...vanished. Maybe not immediately, however, as Stone related to a concerned colleague: "We heard Monday night that he had stopped at a farm house about 50 mi. N.W. of Phila. for a drink of water...& his son went there immediately, he followed the road from Pottstown & found several people who identified Pennock beyond a doubt, but in spite of a search by parties in autos all yesterday they have lost their trail completely. I fear he has been taken very seriously ill & is lost in the woods. He was evidently deranged when he spoke to some of them who saw him."[93]

Coming from one of his sons, however, the events described are open to question, because things quickly got a little fishy with the Pennock family. Stone was hearing from many concerned people who feared the worst – Charles Richmond had been reading in the Washington, D.C. newspapers of men disappearing mysteriously in Philadelphia recently, and thought Pennock might have been the victim of some foul play; *Cassinia* editor Robert Moore asked Stone whom he should get to write Pennock's obituary – but there were indications that the Pennocks might know something others didn't.[94] His son Richard hinted at an expected future return when he wrote to Stone in November about his father's AOU dues, asking, "Would the fact that they are not paid now make any serious difference to him if at any future time he should wish to continue as a member?...We continue to have no news from, or of Father but have not given up the idea that he will yet be located."[95] Samuel Palmer, DVOC treasurer and a Swarthmore botany professor, told Stone in January

1914, "A day or two ago Jean Pennock paid us a visit here, and she seemed to me especially happy for one who is supposed to have a father wandering in some unknown region."[96] Another DVOC member related a rumor to Stone in February 1914 that there was "pretty good evidence that Charlie Pennock's family knows where he is, though they will not admit it. It is generally believed that he is with his brother in Porto Rico, and we most certainly hope that it is so."[97] So early on there were indications that Pennock was not deranged or dead, but had merely run off.

And run off he had. Pennock had earlier spent time collecting in St. Marks, Florida; he moved there after fleeing Philadelphia, shaving his beard and changing his name to John Williams. He had dabbled in all sorts of occupations in Kennett Square, including a nursery business, a general store, and real estate. This varied occupational background served him well in Florida, where he was the business manager for the W.F. Linton Fish Company ("Salt[ed] and Pickled Mullet a Specialty"), a notary public, a lighthouse keeper, and a county commissioner.[98-102] He even drilled a local company of troops for service in World War I.[103]

"John Williams" first contacted Stone in September 1915, asking if Stone was interested in bird skins from the St. Marks area. He said he'd been collecting there "for a good while but lost the most I had a few years ago." Then he added an interesting postscript, saying that he got Stone's name "long ago from a Mr. Pennick [note the deliberate misspelling], who was here about 1890. He showed me about making skins."[98] Thus began his alter ego's habit of mentioning Pennock. Stone must have replied quickly to the first missive, for by October 26 Williams was back at it, talking about skins but adding, "What you tell me about Mr. Pennock is very sorrowful….We would be interested to know more about him if there was any notice about him at the time he went away that we could get."[104]

Stone later recalled that when the U.S. Biological Survey forwarded a John Williams note for publication in *The Auk* ("Williams" published 15 papers, mostly in *The Wilson Bulletin*), he recognized the handwriting as being Pennock's, confirming earlier suspicions. Stone didn't say when he received the note, but the first *Auk* publication for Williams came out in the last issue of 1919, so it was likely sometime early in 1919. "Williams," of course, had been writing to Stone since 1915, and the handwriting is different enough from Pennock letters pre-1913 and post-1919 that it would have been difficult to make the connection, but similar enough to suggest that Pennock wrote them and was deliberately altering his handwriting in notes intended for Stone.

Handwriting aside, if the earlier communications, with their curious and consistent references to Pennock, didn't get Stone wondering about a Williams–Pennock connection, a couple of letters in autumn 1919 pushed Stone's skepticism past the tipping point. In late October, Williams placed an order for the latest *Cassinia*, noting his interest in a Pennock article mentioned in Stone's *Auk* review of that issue.[101] Stone strongly suspected by now that Williams was, in fact, Pennock, and he asked Ludlow Griscom, who had done fieldwork in the Tallahassee area, what he knew about Williams. Griscom replied that he had never met Williams, but that he could make inquiries of people he knew in the area in a way so as not to arouse suspicions. He suggested that Stone contact the U.S. Lighthouse Board for background on Williams, because he was the lighthouse keeper at St. Marks.[99]

Stone also wrote to Robert Williams of the USDA, who, along with T.S. Palmer, had visited Williams in Florida earlier in the year. Robert Williams's reply makes you wonder how he didn't realize who John Williams really was: "He went to St. Marks about eight years ago from New Jersey. He was well acquainted with Mr. Pennock. About his previous private life I learned very little – not more than that he has a son from whom he has not heard for many years." Both he and Palmer were very taken with the man. He said he was going to Tallahassee in mid-November and expected to see John Williams then.[102] It is particularly surprising that Palmer didn't recognize Pennock, for he must have met him at AOU meetings held in Philadelphia.[105]

John Williams again wrote to Stone in early November after receiving the *Cassinia*, saying, "It has been believed here that Mr. Pennock was dead. You may be assured that I will be most willing to deliver your message and if Mr. Pennock comes here and makes himself known will do what I can to have him communicate with you direct or through myself. It would seem unlikely he is alive if unheard of for so long a time or else he must strongly desire to remain unknown & your assurance of holding in strict confidence any word of or from him should be a satisfaction and an inducement for him to let you know of himself." It's easy to hear Pennock almost pleading with Stone to recognize him, and Stone's scrawled "= C. J. Pennock" across the top margin may well have been added at the time of his first reading the letter.[106]

Things got a little cloak-and-dagger after that. Robert Williams wrote to Stone on November 28 saying that he would see John Williams shortly, and would try to determine whether John Williams was Pennock.[107] Five days later he told Stone he would be back in Washington, D.C. soon, and "it is worth-while, I think, for someone who is interested to come to Washington to see me. Whoever comes, however, must come of ~~their~~ his own free will, without any feeling that I compel ~~them~~ him to do so."[108] The vague, rambling letter continued with fuzzy instructions about the planned clandestine meeting. Stone wrote at the bottom of the letter that Robert Williams, who now realized who "John Williams" was but hadn't yet told Pennock, was worried about upsetting Pennock by exposing his identity. Stone went to Washington on December 11 and talked the matter over with Robert Williams, then contacted Pennock's brother-in-law, Dr. Richard Phillips, about the situation. Phillips went down to Florida to bring Pennock back.

Pennock's wife, Mary, thanked Stone in mid-December for "the great thing you have been doing for us," and said she would do whatever Stone thought best.[109] Charles Pennock was heading home by Christmas. He wrote to "Dear Old Stone" on Christmas Eve, saying, "Well you did the job in good shape! [– confirming that Pennock wanted to be recognized] I am really feeling in fine shape and most anxious to see my people and you must know I leave explanations until I see you and I believe you will still have <u>some</u> respect for me.... Remember me to Rehn and Fowler and Dr. Trotter etc. and believe me <u>always</u> your friend 'John Williams' (← for the last time), CJP."[110]

Just as he had done in letters to Stone, in the last article he wrote as John Williams – about the birds of Wakulla County, Florida, which appeared in three parts in *The Wilson Bulletin* beginning in autumn 1919 – he mentioned Pennock by referencing a Pennock nest record from 1890.[111] Wilson printed the article over three issues; by the time of publication of the third part, Williams was back to being Pennock, but *Bulletin* editor Lynds Jones appended no comment to the articles about the situation.

Pennock said that overwork and business worries had put him in some sort of deranged state, and that after finding himself in Baltimore on the night of his disappearance, he proceeded by stages to St. Marks. The amnesia story cooked up by Pennock and his family is hard to believe, however, considering their curious behavior during his absence, and Pennock's own comments to newspapers after his return: "There is not much to say. I had been working too hard and my health gave way. All of my affairs were in good shape and I simply wanted to go away."[112] Concerning the name change, he said, "I felt that I wanted to start anew and I did not want to be bothered," and he refused to discuss family matters.[113] That sounds like a planned respite by someone unhappy with their home life, with the amnesia excuse concocted as a way to cover that up.

Pennock had 'em fooled – and worried. Just before he heard of Pennock's reappearance, Chreswell Hunt, a DVOCer who had moved to Illinois, sent Stone a clipping from the *Chicago Tribune* about a man found on the streets of Lambertville, New Jersey, "wandering in rags and babbling childishly," who reportedly could remember events from 10 to 20 years earlier, but knew of no recent ones. Hunt said it reminded him of "the sad case of Mr. Pennock," whom he obviously pictured in a similar state, unaware that Pennock had essentially gone on an extended birding jaunt for six years and was now back at home as if he'd never left.[114] In fact, he returned to St. Marks with his wife for a visit in March 1920 – the first of what became annual winter stays in Florida – and he stayed put with his family for the duration of his life.[105,115]

Pennock's relationship with Stone after his return seems to have been cordial enough, but there was a little kickup about Pennock's bird skins and books, and the surviving correspondence is ambiguous about some of the points in the matter. Mary Pennock wrote to Stone in 1916, in response to either a letter from, or conversation with, Stone about what to do with Pennock's books and skins collection. She wrote, "I do not at present see the way to disposing of either," so she had decided to keep the books (appraised by ANSP librarian William Fox) and follow Stone's suggestion to let the skins go to ANSP as a loan, where they would be stored properly. The fact that she did not want to permanently part with either indicates that she may have expected Pennock's return at some point. Her letter doesn't indicate whether the topic was initially raised by her or by Stone.[116] By 1917 Pennock's skins and possibly some eggs were at ANSP, and, like distant relatives coming out of the woodwork at an estate settlement, the egg collectors were already asking Stone for duplicates.[117]

In August 1921, Pennock asked Stone for the return of the books and tendered a long list of skins he wanted as well.[118] Stone responded that although he had no problem with Pennock taking some skins of common local birds for lecture purposes, Pennock was asking for "practically everything of value" from the collection. Stone reminded Pennock that there would be no collection had ANSP not spent time salvaging it while Pennock was away, and that when he returned from Florida Pennock had approved of the collection being given to the Academy.[119] Pennock quickly replied, "About those skins. There will be no trouble over them – will send for the books in a few days," so the issue appeared to be solved.[120]

But the problem reared up again 12 years later, when Pennock, recalling the 1921 incident with some petulance, asked ANSP managing director Charles Cadwalader for one skin each of an Ivory-billed Woodpecker, Carolina Parakeet, and Passenger Pigeon (all rare or extinct birds).[121] Stone got involved and gave Pennock the same rebuttal he did earlier, saying that even if the specimens had been loaned to Pennock for lectures it was not desirable to have rare specimens leave the Academy for such purposes.[122] Pennock wasn't happy, but said he would let the matter drop for the present (he didn't live much longer anyway) because Cadwalader "prefer[red] to hold the word of the ANSP for less than the value of three bird skins."[123]

After Pennock's death in 1935, Stone asked his daughter Jean – the same one who had raised eyebrows at Swarthmore by showing no signs of concern over her father's disappearance – to help fill in some details of the Pennock memorial he was writing for *Cassinia*. She said her father was born and died "in Kennett Square, Pa. which was his home during his life except for a few years when his parents moved to Ithaca N.Y. that their three sons might attend Cornell" – no mention of a six-year working vacation in Florida![124] At the DVOC annual meeting in 1936, the men, like children pleading to hear their favorite bedtime story again, asked Stone to regale them with the tale of the Pennock affair – what Arthur Conan Doyle might have titled "The Curious Case of the Missing Ornithologist."[125]

———————— ❧ ————————

Then there's the equally curious case of the missing book. Plans to produce a book on the birds of the Delaware Valley, as an update and expansion of the DVOC's *BEPNJ* effort, had been announced at the annual meeting in January 1905.[126] Stone, of course, chaired the committee for collecting data.[127] In 1910, "A Prospectus" in *Cassinia* reported that the original plans for the book to include technical data on "distribution, abundance, migration, nidification, etc." had recently been broadened to include articles in a more popular vein for each species. Ten DVOC members had each been assigned five or ten species to work up, and drafts of them were read at some of the meetings around that time, but with some authors things didn't look very promising.[128] Chreswell Hunt wrote to Stone in 1909, "You remember the five birds that were given me to write up? Well at first opportunity I'm going to write up what little I know about them and turn same in to you. There might be something in it worth gleaning out." Shortly thereafter, he told Stone that he was too busy to work on the accounts, and ten years later, long after he had moved to Illinois, Hunt sent Stone a couple of the biographies.[129]

In a January 1914 talk to the club Stone referred to the book as *Birds of the Delaware Valley*, and, in a bit of hyperbole, said that the biographies submitted ranked among the best of their genre (studies of the living bird) in ornithological literature.[130] Things seemed to have been moving along by 1918, when Stone told Julian Potter "The 'Club Book' is now in the midst of the Warblers and the call is going out for any additional data on the species as far as the genus Dendroica....Very shortly I am going to pass along the finished sections for you [and others] to read and criticize. I have about thirty-six species practically done including all the thrushes, tits, wrens etc."[131]

Spencer Trotter announced at a March 1919 meeting that the book was nearing completion, but there was a tip-off as to one possible reason that never happened: reference was made to the "historical, descriptive and distributional data" accompanying each biography, and Stone spoke about his methods for compiling this "greatly scattered data."[132] Sure enough, Stone was compiling the information on distribution, song, habitat, migration, nest/eggs, plumage, and "history" to each biography – in other words, adding greatly to the complexity and workload of the project, and doing the lion's share of it himself.[133] Then, at a 1920 meeting, Stone said that more information was needed on the

Some more DVOC members on a June 1900 outing. *Left to right*: Charles Pennock, James Rehn, Stewardson Brown (*foreground*), Herbert Coggins, William Hughes, David McCadden, Witmer Stone. DVOC Collection, ANSP Archives.

nest structure and Pennsylvania distribution of warblers in areas of the state where they had received little study, presumably the western counties and the mountainous areas.[134]

Stone referred to the book in his Morris memorial in the 1922–24 *Cassinia*, still calling it *Birds of the Delaware Valley*,[44] but in 1926 Scoville asked Stone, "Do you still want my biography of the Carolina Chickadee or have you in desperation given it to someone else?," which indicates that the biographies had not been completed by that late date.[135] In the same year, Robert Moore, the former *Cassinia* editor now living in California, told Stone, "I am very sorry to hear that the birds of the Delaware Valley is still held up. It would seem as though there are enough interested to raise initial funds to start the publishing. Personally, I should be glad to contribute with the rest and would place myself for an amount somewhere between fifty and a hundred dollars towards this fund to be paid when a sufficient number of others have made pledges to warrant publishing of the first volume."[136] Thus, it appears that some combination of Stone biting off too much work on the project; authors taking too long to complete the bird biographies, which probably ran the gamut of quality, given such a large group of contributors; and funding issues all resulted in the book never coming to fruition. Stone was also at work on *BSOCM* by this time.

It might have needed a last push to the finish line from Stone, who was too involved in other things to give it the needed attention.

Cornelius Weygandt, for one, became tired of waiting. He'd been assigned 10 species for biographies in 1910, and seems to have had the last one finished by 1913.[137] In 1929, when the book still didn't seem close to making an appearance, Weygandt told Stone, "The time has come when I can use those bird sketches of the DVOC book which was projected but now seems likely never to come into being."[138] Witmer wasn't ready to give up, though, and replied, "The case is perhaps not so bad as you think, as everything from the beginning of the Warblers to the end of the Thrushes has been completed for some years and all typed ready for the printer. It simply awaits the energy necessary to secure the funds and put it through the press. Now that I am relieved of executive work here [at ANSP], there is hope that this may be done in the not far distant future."[139] But a year later Weygandt's new book, *The Wissahickon Hills*, appeared, complete with bits and pieces of several of the bird biographies originally written for the "long dreamed of" DVOC book.[140]

It's possible that Weygandt's using his material elsewhere may have been the last straw – Stone may have figured "Why bother?" when so much of the material was now already in press. Another tack would have been to get other authors to handle Weygandt's species, but that would have meant starting from scratch on about 10 biographies. At any rate, the book effort fizzled and never saw the light of day as a DVOC publication.

———————— ∾ ————————

World War I reached into all spheres of life for the nations involved, and the Academy and the DVOC were affected as well. In January 1918, Stone told Frank Chapman, "We have a service flag up in my [ANSP] room where the DVOC meets with 17 stars on it – so much for the old Club which celebrated its 28th anniversary last Thursday."[141] Twenty-seven DVOC men served, with one, Archibald Benners, killed in action at Belleau Wood after being wounded in two earlier battles.[142-143] Trotter and Baily had sons who went off to the war, and *The Auk* listed AOU members serving, and dying, overseas.[144] Stone gave bird lectures during and after the war at the Camp Wissahickon barracks and naval hospital at Cape May.[145] Keeping journals afloat was challenging, and coal was in short supply at the Academy and in Stone's home.[143,146] At work, the ANSP staff was huddled together in a few rooms; Stone said the rest of the building was "as cold as Greenland."[69] The Belgian Ornithological Society lost two officers to the war, including a treasurer murdered by the Germans in Louvain during their pillage of that city.[147] Jonathan Dwight commented about the German U-boat atrocities that it was "so stupid of the German beasts to make sure of everybody hating them for their evil deeds – for all time!"[148] Stone told a friend, "I get very much depressed sometimes & begin to think that even when the war is over it will take so long to get back to the good old times that I shall hardly live to see it."[149]

But it wasn't as bad as all that, and there were some good old times, and some bad old times, ahead for Stone and for his beloved DVOC. By the mid-1920s he was one of the club's senior members, and there had been a lot of turnover in membership from the early days. In early 1926, he hoped Baily would quickly recover from an illness and return to DVOC meetings, telling him, "I found that I was the only original member at the annual meeting!"[150] The old stalwarts were breaking down, moving away, or dying, and Stone worried about the club's capacity to attract and handle another AOU Philadelphia meeting.[151] He still loved his club – after a good turnout at a January 1926 meeting, despite a downpour, he told a friend, "It seems to take more than a deluge to dampen those fellows' enthusiasm!" – which he described at that time as being "composed largely of young men and boys beginning the study of birds."[152] As early as 1915, Stone had said that the DVOC tried to recruit young men of high school and college age and get them active in the club.[153]

There are indications that toward the end of his life Stone sometimes felt that there was a widening gap between him and the younger men in the club. In late 1935, he complained to T.S. Palmer that at the latest DVOC meeting the secretary [Gillespie] told him not to give his usual report about the recent AOU meeting because he didn't think the club would care: "They had [Warren] Eaton over from New York [NAAS] talking Hawks! Instead of encouraging the young members to speak and so develop ornithologists the present trend of the Club seems to be to invite outsiders who can make an interesting address. I guess I am behind the times there also!"[154] However, at that meeting a committee was appointed to find a way to publish *BSOCM*, and Stone wasn't even in attendance (due to pique?), and the next meeting was devoted entirely to the AOU meeting, with Stone and others talking.[155] In1936, he was miffed when his request to the DVOC membership for photos for *BSOCM* yielded few responses, and he groused that the young men coming along were more interested in running up lists than in detailed studies or photography.[156] In 1937, he told Potter he was going to try to cajole Norm McDonald into accepting his election as club secretary, saying it was the first time in the its history that someone had "refused an election to an office in the club – everybody [before] thought it an honor – what are we coming to anyhow!"[157]

He was still affectionately regarded. In 1936, Stone was "almost prostrated" at the turnout for a dinner at the Art Club of Philadelphia that the DVOC held to celebrate his 70th birthday.[158-159] The attendance sheet for the event listed 87 people, including Charles Batchelder and A.K. Fisher, two of the four remaining AOU founders.[160] Stone said it included 57 "DVOC boys too, many of whom I started on their ornithological careers, [which] made me feel very happy."[158] As the most distinguished ornithologist in the club, he was unquestionably the leader. In fact, demonstrating its dependence on his leadership to the end, a month before his death the club appointed him to make revisions to the bylaws.[161]

What became of the seven DVOC founders over time? Interestingly, they were rarely all at a meeting together – in the DVOC minutes I have found only three such occasions.[162] Reed, who had shown so much early interest, was the first casualty. By early 1892 his attendance had fallen off enough that he must have been asked for an explanation, for in mid-March he wrote to Stone, "In regard to my attendance at the club meetings, it was not photography but masonry that has captured my time, which I feel very sorry for on account of the Club."[163] The DVOC minutes for the June 6, 1893 meeting, at which Reed gave a talk about a recent trip he and Mark Wilde had taken to Cape May and Cumberland counties, note, "Among other noteworthy species Mr. Reed recorded seeing a Swallow-tailed Kite and that he had found nests supposed to be of the Wild [=Passenger] Pigeon and Pileated Woodpecker," then add, with understandable cynicism, "Mr. Reed did not however produce specimens of the birds or their eggs."[164]

By 1896 he hadn't been to a meeting in two years, was slow to pay his dues, and was transferred from the Active to the Associate list in April because of "continued unnecessary absences from the meetings of the Club."[165] Reed requested to be moved back to the Active list in early 1897, but at a business session the Active members declined to do so, with Morris acerbically recommending that Reed be told that there was an opening in the Active list and he could "prove himself eligible in the manner usual with Associate Members."[166] Morris had never liked Reed, anyway, for whatever reason.[167] Reed was more of a participant for the next few years, even giving talks at a few meetings, but in May 1905 he resigned.[126]

Another hint about Reed's falling out may have come in some remarks from Wilde, who told Stone in 1898 that he and Reed were not so friendly anymore.[168] In 1909, he provided more information about the break: "I note you have given friend 'Reed' credit [in the recently-published *The Birds of New Jersey*] for the Swallow-tailed Kite I noticed and called to his attention while collecting in South Jersey. This is all right as I know he reported it in his own name and since he gave me much good instruction in my early days I am perfectly satisfied that he take all the credit as I had the pleasure, the joy, of study with him. My only regret is that he did not adhere to the teachings of the Society of Friends from which stock he came and appreciate the value of the truth and a life of virtue which failing was the final cause of our separation."[169] Reed was presumably still alive in 1937, because in a list in the *BSOCM* preface of DVOC members who contributed in some way to the book, Stone placed Reed among the living (i.e., he was not asterisked as "Deceased"), but Stone may have long fallen out of touch with him by then and perhaps the exact state of his existence was unknown.[170]

Charles Voelker never distinguished himself in the DVOC (possibly due to no particular desire to do so). He was also transferred from the Active to the Associate list in 1896, doubtless because of truancy – he attended only three meetings between January 1895 and April 1896.[171] By 1911 he was telling Stone that he hadn't attended many DVOC meetings lately because of the pressures of business – he was still a taxidermist, and one of the "pressures" may have been all the mounts people wanted of the recently introduced Ring-necked Pheasant.[172] He doesn't seem to have been active in the club for most of his life, but was still on the rolls at Stone's death. He died in June 1947, and had by then taken up clay modeling of birds, perhaps as a progression from his taxidermy work.[173]

George Spencer Morris remained an architect with a strong interest in birds. He lived his whole life on the Olney property where he grew up, and was active in the Society of Friends, the Boy Scouts, and the Pennsylvania Audubon Society. He was the first of the founders to pass away, too young, in 1922.[174]

Spencer Trotter, the Swarthmore biology professor, had a very active involvement with ANSP and the Wagner Free Institute. He almost died of typhoid fever in 1892, and resolved to "take life easy" in the future because he felt he had run himself down too much and was consequently more vulnerable to disease.[175] He became an enthusiastic world traveler, and served a stint as ANSP librarian late in life.[176] His health broke in 1926 when he had a nervous breakdown and a bout with uremic poisoning, and worsened until his death in 1931.[177]

Samuel Rhoads did prodigious amounts of ornithological and mamma-logical fieldwork in his younger days, in many U.S. locations as well as Latin American countries.[178] On an 1892 collecting trip to the state of Washington he worried Morris, also along, who said, "Sam is an indefatigable worker, and to my way of thinking does more than there is any sense in, for a fellow must have some regards to his health, though S[am] seems to forget that the human body is a machine to be broken or spoiled by the acts of the owner."[179] Rhoads was always interested in birds, but eventually became more well-known as a mam-malogist (or, as Stone put it in the DVOC 20-year scrapbook, "The main trouble with him was that he ran to rats and there was some fear that he would never again look a bird in the face").[11] He spent 11 years preparing and writing his monumental *The Mammals of Pennsylvania and New Jersey*, published in 1903. By then he had opened the Franklin Book Shop in downtown Philadelphia. He suffered a nervous breakdown of some sort in 1926 and lived out his days (all 90 years' worth – he was the last founder to die, in 1952) in a sanatorium.[178]

By the mid-1930s, Stone and Baily were the only founders still active in the club. Baily had remained an architect, and several buildings he designed are extant on the campus of his old alma mater, Haverford College.[180] In 1900 he was appointed Inspector of Birds and Mammals at the Port of Philadelphia – work that he must have done in addition to his architectural work. He was a pioneering bird photographer and was active with Stone in the Pennsylvania Audubon Society, serving as treasurer. His interest in birds never flagged, and late in his life he presented Haverford College with a list of 207 species he had identified on the campus over the years.[181] An uncle of the same name, who died in the same year that Baily was born, was an author and artist of no small skill, and produced a staggeringly beautiful four-part work on humming-birds, employing a technique he had perfected using gold and silver leaf to produce a lifelike sparkle in the plumages and gorgets.[182] Shortly before he died, DVOC founder Baily and his relatives presented this stunning unpublished, unique manuscript with original watercolors to ANSP, where it is preserved in the archives.[183] Rhoads outlived him, but Baily was the last founder to remain active in the club before passing away in 1947.

───────────── ❧ ─────────────

The DVOC continues to be an active bird club today (and still maintains its conviviality and sense of humor), with meetings still held at ANSP. It has regularly scheduled outings (originally Stone's idea), is involved in local conservation issues, and continues to publish *Cassinia*.[184] It was also responsible for the field trips scheduled for the 2009 AOU annual meeting held in Philadelphia, and two members were involved in presentations at the meeting.

However, the DVOC never became the organization that Stone may have envisioned in 1913, when he commented in *The Auk* on a recent editorial in *The Wilson Bulletin* by Lynds Jones that outlined plans for the Wilson Ornithological Club to start holding annual meetings in the central U.S. "The Cooper Club on the Pacific side, the AOU on the Atlantic, and the Wilson Club in the Interior" was Jones's vision for the near future of the major American ornithological societies.[185] Stone preferred "The Cooper Club on the Pacific side, the Wilson Club in the Interior and the Nuttall and Delaware Valley Clubs in the east," with the AOU as an umbrella organization over the whole.[186] Stone obviously saw the DVOC on a par with the other three regional clubs mentioned.

Today, the Cooper Ornithological Society's *Condor* and the Wilson Ornithological Society's *Wilson Journal of Ornithology* (for years *The Wilson Bulletin*) are in an elite group of peer-reviewed ornithological journals, published on a quarterly basis in an increasingly technical, quantitative style. The Cooper and Wilson societies (notice that they're not "clubs" anymore) have become leading research organizations, with officers immersed in academia, and their journals have moved away from a regional emphasis (as defined by Jones and Stone) to a worldwide one.[187] The Nuttall Ornithological Club, from which sprang the

AOU, may be the most elitist bird club in America today, but it continues to produce important ornithological research and historical publications.

Meanwhile, the DVOC today is heavy on "birding." The most recent volumes of the irregularly published *Cassinia* have some nice historical articles, but contain much in the way of local lists, rarities/vagrants, and county/state records, and you won't find a *p*-value anywhere between the covers. There is, of course, nothing inherently wrong with the DVOC having remained simply a local birding club – with an infatuation for things like the World Series of Birding, rarity alerts, and even an annual award for the member who has ticked the most Delaware Valley species in the past year – but you have to wonder if it hasn't traced a retrograde motion compared to where Stone thought it was headed in 1913. Cooper and Wilson have, ornithologically speaking, grown to adulthood, while the DVOC, by comparison, dawdles in adolescence.

Stone might have steered the DVOC onto a more narrowly scientific course had he not become so involved in other efforts, including his 25-year *Auk* editorship, ANSP administrative duties, and the fourth AOU check-list, but then again he may not have: as discussed elsewhere, there was some criticism during his *Auk* editorship that the periodical was not rigidly scientific enough under his direction, and that he was not pushing the science forward. A note in the 1933–37 *Cassinia*, however, unsigned but likely written by editors Stone (in his last involvement with a *Cassinia* issue) and C. Brooke Worth, indicates that an effort was begun at that time to move the club into a more scientific direction. The note stated that "as time goes on, the mere recording of migration dates or unusual occurrences of birds becomes a narrower and narrower field for the acquisition of new information. Modern field ornithology is concerning itself more and more with the problems of birds' daily lives. Our Club membership is slowly turning its attention to this new kind of investigation." A call to fieldwork along those lines was given, with project plans and results to be presented in *Cassinia*. It was reasoned that this would lead to *Cassinia* "becoming a forum of advanced ornithological thought."[188] Seventy-five years on, however, lists and rarities continue to dominate *Cassinia*, which has hardly become anybody's idea of "a forum of advanced ornithological thought."

But maybe the DVOC was just where Stone wanted it in 1913, and although he may have eventually called on the club to take the next step beyond lists and vagrants, he may not have had any grand vision of it becoming the sort of organization that Wilson and Cooper are today. At the DVOC's 20th anniversary, Morris felt certain that "at no time in the history of bird study in this country has a body of men been able to keep up so full and persistent a line of investigation of the ornithological conditions of a given region for almost a quarter of a century."[12] Maybe simply describing the geographic and temporal distribution of the local avifauna was all Stone and the early DVOC aspired to.

The club certainly achieved that, and its current members continue to involve themselves in such study.

They also remain deeply interested in their rich history. Among many other nods to their past are two annual awards for which members are eligible: a Julian Potter Award, for field ornithology, and a Witmer Stone Award, for published research. Club members also recently spearheaded efforts to have two signs mounted at Cape May Point – one about Stone's life, and the other about the 1935 creation at the Point of the Witmer Stone Wildlife Sanctuary. Stone and his fellow club founders and pioneers are long gone from, but far from forgotten by, the DVOC today.

5

Conservation Battles

Witmer Stone was a conservationist at heart, and early in his ornithological career he was actively involved in conservation work with both the AOU bird protection committee and the Pennsylvania Audubon Society (PAS). The original PAS was formed in April 1886, and incorporated on August 21, 1886.[1-2] It produced a periodical, *The Bird Call*, which Stone described years later as having been "published in Philadelphia by the original PAS in 1887. So far as I know, only six numbers were issued, from January to June of that year. They had no title, the cover being printed across the top of the first page, and they covered eight pages each, the last page being devoted to advertisements. The subject matter was almost entirely quotations from other journals, largely those of the Society for Prevention of Cruelty to Animals [SPCA]. I am not sure who was the Editor, as no name is given, but I think the late Mrs. Brinton Coxe was the responsible one. I know during the summer of 1887 she requested me to assume the editorship, but it did not meet with my approval at the time, and I had nothing whatever to do with the journal. I have copies of [numbers] 3, 5 and 6, and these are the only ones that I have ever seen."[3] An 1887 *Auk* announcement of the magazine noted that Miss A.C. Knight was president of the PAS, and that *The Bird Call* would "plead for mercy to God's messengers of beauty, use, and song" and fight their use in women's fashions.[1] Like the rest of the original national Audubon movement, however, the first PAS quickly petered out.

This was at a time when the use of birds in women's hats was all the fashion rage. Sometimes it was only a few feathers; other times it was the whole bird (unappealing as that may seem now). Terns were particularly in demand for this purpose, and accounts from the period mention East Coast gunners knee-deep in piles of dead terns for the millinery market. Egret and heron breeding plumes were also in demand and their colonies were being decimated everywhere for the sake of fashion. In 1903, DVOCer John Carter wrote to Stone about an article he'd just read in *Scientific American* about Laysan, and wondered whether it couldn't be protected while it was still unspoiled. He quipped, "Fashion is so thoroughly irrational that we can not tell at what moment it may require the wearing of half a dozen Laysan Albatrosses by every one of its devotees."[4]

The rebirth of the Audubon Society (actually, local Audubon societies) in 1896 was a reaction to the crisis brought on by the current whim of women's fashion. The second Audubon movement began with the formation of the Massachusetts Audubon Society in February 1896,[5] and in October the second incarnation of the Pennsylvania Audubon Society rose from the ashes.[6-7] The original meeting was at the home of Julia Stockton Robins, who became secretary; Stone was elected president and remained in that position for the duration of the organization's existence.[8] Fellow DVOC members Francis Cope Jr., George Spencer Morris, and Stewardson Brown were added to the board of directors in 1899.[9] Another DVOCer, William Baily, was the longtime secretary of the PAS.[10-11]

The history of the second PAS is difficult to trace, but can be pieced together with its archives and some of Stone's correspondence at ANSP, along with some material in *Bird-Lore*. In short, it seems to have been fairly, if irregularly, active for the first half of its 40-year life span, then almost dormant for the second half. For the first 10 years or so, members held annual meetings at the Academy, made efforts (like the "Hat Show") to discourage women from wearing birds and feathers in their hats, worked with schools on activities such as "Bird-Day," and offered public lectures by Stone and others.[10,12,13] They also printed circulars, including 10,000 copies of Stone's *Hints to Young Bird Students*, and his pamphlet on the practices of the millinery trade.[14] (The latter may have been culled from a manuscript I found in a private collection titled "The Aigrette Plume and What Its Use Involves," in which Stone quoted ornithologist W.E.D. Scott extensively about the heron slaughter in Florida.)[15]

The PAS was the only state society at the time to not charge membership fees; Stone felt it led to a larger, more effective membership and that funds could be raised in other ways.[16] After some wrangling, the society created a "sustaining" membership class which involved a onetime $1 fee, but people could still join for free.[17] Membership steadily increased to more than 7,000 by 1902.[18]

There is an interesting line in the minutes of a 1900 meeting at which new bylaws were being drafted: "The meetings of the Society shall be held ~~annually in January~~ at such time and place as may be fixed by the Board of Directors."[19] This could have simply been indecision at the moment, due to trying to work a meeting into everyone's schedule, but maybe some of the initial enthusiasm had dimmed after a few years. Hilda Justice, in charge of the PAS's "traveling libraries," asked Robins in 1904, "How is the Audubon Society – or isn't there any? Since we gave up annual meetings and annual reports, there doesn't seem to be much news."[20] The PAS also didn't become officially affiliated as a member in the National Association of Audubon Societies (NAAS) until 1916, after some prodding from NAAS secretary T. Gilbert Pearson.[21]

As PAS president, Stone's dual involvement during his years on the AOU bird protection committee ensured that the PAS would be in the thick of things, but Robins was the real central character. When she died rather suddenly in July 1906 (she had been ill for several months but had told few of her illness), Stone, who said that the PAS had been founded "entirely through her energy" and that she was de facto in charge of its work, thought it spelled the end of the organization.[22] In fact, Robins's death stopped the PAS temporarily in its tracks until an April 1907 meeting when a major reorganization took place.[23] Some of the curiosities of the 1907 reorganization were described by Stone almost 30 years later. The original PAS in 1886 was incorporated, but the second one was not. He said that the second one was formed with no knowledge of the first one, but Stone clearly knew of it; he may have meant they didn't realize that the first one was an incorporated entity with a legal right to the name. He recalled, "Now in 1907 it was thought advisable to [re]organize as a continuance of the original [PAS] established and incorporated in 1886 and 1890[?]. We had legal advice as to how this was to be accomplished and it was done, the sole survivor of the directors of the original Society, Mr. N.E. Janney being present. We thus <u>became</u> the original Society and Mrs. Robins' unincorporated society of 1896 went out of existence. We automatically came under the provisions of the Charter and By-laws of the original society which were essentially the same as those of Mrs. Robins' society."[24]

The new (or more exactly, return to the old) setup doesn't seem to have breathed new life into the organization. A landmark bill outlawing the sale of aigrettes and other feathers was passed in Pennsylvania in 1913, and Stone appeared at a hearing in Harrisburg in support of it; however, the effort was spearheaded and mostly carried out (financially and otherwise) by the NAAS, and PAS's involvement appears to have been limited.[25] By 1914, the PAS had hired Henry Oldys to canvass the state to drum up memberships and funds in an effort to revitalize the PAS.[26-27] He did occasional work along that line for a few years, but despite his continual predictions that a blockbuster donation was just around the next corner, even as he operated at a loss to the Society (Oldys was once characterized as "a decided optimist"), he didn't bring in funds to warrant his PAS paycheck, and the society ended the arrangement at the end of 1916.[27-28,29] So much for revitalizing the PAS. Oldys renewed his offer a few times over the next several years, usually with a caustic comment about the "moribund" or coma-like state of the PAS.[29-30] It seems that local Audubon societies around the state, like the Western Pennsylvania Audubon Society, were doing fine and there was no real need for an overarching statewide organization; in fact, NAAS's Pearson told Stone as much.[31-33]

In 1917 another founder of the second PAS, Elizabeth Wilson Fisher, who took over as secretary after Robins's death, experienced some sort of breakdown. By 1921 the Society was so dysfunctional that Stone told Seth Gordon, secretary of the Pennsylvania Game Commission (PGC), who had inquired about the PAS membership mailing list, that the society didn't have much of a membership list anymore.[29,32] In 1922 Stone said that the NAAS had "taken over the work of bird protection to such an extent, that but little is left for the State Societies to do. We keep up a form of organization, however, in order to step in whenever it is necessary to enforce important legislative action, or to fight any undesirable bills. I do not know of anything at the present moment that seems worthwhile for us to undertake."[34] He told Pearson the same thing in 1926, and added that PAS did no educational work.[35] He told Oldys in 1924 that the PAS was "concentrating [its] efforts" [?] on the Philadelphia area, having recognized the impracticability of a statewide organization.[31] In 1925, Stone reported that the PAS had "practically gone out of existence" and had no dues coming in.[36] In 1928, Stone once again told Pearson that the PAS existed only for emergencies such as a harmful bill pending in the state legislature; it was apparently dormant otherwise. Stone said he was a only a figurehead, and was "ready to drop out" if someone else could be found for the job.[37]

The second incarnation of the PAS eventually wound down its affairs, although the final dispensation of its funds is difficult to trace with certainty. At the AOU meeting in Philadelphia in 1929, Stone, probably at the Council meeting, said that he thought some of the PAS funds could be transferred to the AOU.[38] By then, Baily and Fisher, the PAS treasurer and secretary, were the only board members Stone knew to be living or for whom he had contact information. (No wonder – Fisher told him that the last meeting for which she had minutes had been in 1919!) Stone wanted the money to go to the AOU bird protection committee, but delays were caused by uncertainty as to how much money PAS still had to its name, and Fisher's dalliance in replying to letters.[11,39] In early 1936, she found there was more on hand than originally realized – about $5,000 all told, mostly in the form of public utility securities.[11,40] Stone was still trying to close things out; of the remaining funds he wanted $2,000 to go to publication of *BSOCM*, $1,000 to the AOU bird protection committee, and the remainder, roughly $1,500, could he held for a possible newly revised PAS. The latter was an idea that some of the DVOCers, particularly Richard Pough, were drumming up, but which ultimately died a-borning.[11,41] Baily, wisely, was more cautious about disbursing the funds, trying to make sure that he, Stone, and Fisher were proceeding correctly in a legal sense.[13]

The trail goes cold at that point in trying to find out where the money in the PAS accounts went, other than $100 being paid to Old Swedes' Church in Philadelphia for the maintenance of Alexander Wilson's grave in early 1936.[40,42] Stone really pitched using some of the funds for *BSOCM* to Baily in January 1936,[24] and in May he told Baily, "As you know the [DVO] Club with the assistance of the [Pennsylvania?] Audubon Society and others is going to publish my Cape May bird studies," which may or may not indicate where some of the funds went.[43] No mention is made in *BSOCM*, however, about any publication moneys coming from any Audubon societies. At any rate, the second PAS lasted about 40 years and wound down in the mid-1930s.

———————— ∼ ————————

Stone joined the AOU Committee on Protection of North American Birds in 1895 and served as chairman 1898–1901.[44] There was much overlap between the committee and the state Audubon societies, in both efforts and personnel, and the war on the milliners' use of birds in women's hats was engaged on all fronts. Bachelor Stone was perfectly frank in placing the blame for the practice where it belonged in an 1899 talk at the AOU meeting: "As to the women, why, common sense has no chance when fashion is in the way. It's an outrage."[45]

An interesting bit of conservation sleuthing was recorded in a 1900 *Auk* article that detailed the efforts of Stone and others to derail (literally) an illegal shipment of bird skins to a millinery commission house:

> Early in March a notice appeared in a Philadelphia paper giving details of a contract between certain parties in Delaware and a commission house in New York [Al. Richardson & Co.],[46] by which the former were to procure and ship to the latter 20,000 bird skins for millinery pur-poses. The Chairman, Mr. Stone, in company with Mr. [A.D.] Poole, President of the Delaware Game Protective Association, visited Gov-ernor [Ebe W.] Tunnell of Delaware, and found him to be enthusiastic on the subject of bird protection. He proposed to have the Secretary of State issue a warning about shooting insectivorous birds. As the Pennsylvania Railroad system controls all the railroads in Delaware, a letter was written to the President, Mr. A. J. Cassatt, calling his atten-tion to the contract and also to the Delaware statute regarding com-mon carriers transporting birds out of the State. [The illegal shipment was then thwarted by railroad agents.] This agitation has aroused the whole State, and farmers are posting their land. The public press gave valuable aid, and it is probable that every person in Delaware now knows the reasons for bird protection.[47]

Stone was helped in this conservation effort by the owners of the ironically-named George W. Bush & Sons freight company in Wilmington, who sug-gested he contact Poole.[48] Stone reported that a state Audubon chapter had sprung up in Delaware in reaction to the incident, and a year later he was congratulated on a bird protection bill just passed by the Delaware Senate due in part to his earlier testimony before a House committee.[49-50] The incident also kicked off private correspondence, as well as salvos in the press, between Stone and Charles Farmer of the Millinery Merchants' Protective Association (every exploitative industry has to have its lobbyists), who protested that the reported shipment was a plant to rile up opposition to the milliners, that the newspa-pers printed it without fact-checking, and that he had never heard of an "Al. Richardson."[51] Stone told Farmer that if the milliners would agree to stop using any American birds in their trade it would ease criticisms in the newspapers. Farmer and the milliners then made a proposal, which was printed in *Bird-*

Lore, to do just that, with the caveat that the Audubon societies and the AOU would not oppose their use of barnyard fowl, legally harvested game birds, and birds from other countries.[49,52]

That suited Stone, Frank Chapman, William Dutcher, and others who had "been active in dealing with the practical side of bird protection, especially legislation," but others, including some members of the protection committee, would not stand for a compromise that allowed the milliners to kill foreign birds with impunity.[49] Stone received an earful from them. Louise Stephenson told him that "our" birds migrate to foreign countries, so if milliners were allowed to use foreign birds they could conceivably be killing "ours" on their wintering grounds in South America. She also predicted that the Audubon societies would not agree to the deal, because they were interested in protection of *all* birds, foreign or otherwise.[53] (Stone told Dutcher in May, "[M]y experience with these [Audubon] societies is that it is practically impossible to make them pull together. You may remember that NY & Mass. refused my gift of 1,000 Hints to young Bird Students [pamphlets] because there was a line in the circular saying that a boy might under certain circumstances kill a bird!")[54] Stone thought Stephenson's position was extreme, and he told her, "We sometimes in our enthusiasm sacrifice the very things we are trying to benefit for the sake of principle. I fear many others hold the same views that you do and that it will be impossible to explain the state of affairs except to those who have had personal contact with the milliners." He said that the deal was the best that could be hoped for at the time, and that the gulls and terns along the East Coast would soon be wiped out without it.[55] He groused to T.S. Palmer of the U.S. Biological Survey (USBS) about "persons who would apparently rather see all our birds destroyed than back down one inch from their 'principles'!"[56]

Otto Widmann wasn't about to compromise, telling Stone, "War is my cry. War until all the trade in bird feathers is prohibited....No, no compromise by which the birds in general gain next to nothing and the milliners all....To stop the importation of foreign, as well as the sale of home grown birds, that should be our aim as it is that of the Audubon Soc."[57] Olive Thorne Miller was frustrated about the proposed compromise, and she asked Stone, "Am I the only member of the Committee to protest against this agreement?"[58] No, she wasn't. There were enough other dissenters on the committee and in some of the Audubon societies to scuttle the deal, and the two sides dug in their heels again. It was to be long after Stone's tenure as protection committee chair that the fashion for using dead birds in ladies' hats would finally die out.

Stone's experience with museum ornithological collections served him well with some additional sleuthing. He related in a 1901 AOU bird protection committee report that he had recently examined feathers at a Philadelphia millinery house – feathers that, according to recent legislation, were supposed to be taken exclusively from domestic fowl, not from wild birds of any country of origin. Stone, however, found feathers of "the Indian vulture, Nicobar pigeon, great bustard, Baikal teal, Indian pheasant, Impeyan pheasant, and gull [species]."[59]

One upshot of Stone's work with the AOU protection committee was a tiff with his good friend and fellow DVOC founder Samuel Rhoads, with whom Stone had done some rodent trapping in New Jersey in the early 1890s. In addition to his ornithological collecting, Rhoads went on to make his mark as a mammalogist, and Stone suspected that Rhoads took umbrage with Stone's defense of hawks and owls in his AOU committee work "as being entirely unfair to the mice" on which they preyed. Rhoads aired his pique in a couple of curious articles in 1898 in which he questioned the merits of the USBS's methods for determining which raptorial birds were of benefit or harm to agricultural interests, based on studies of their diets.[60] Rhoads singled out A.K. Fisher, the Survey's economic zoologist and author of a seminal pamphlet on the subject, but Stone felt that at least some of the argument was directed at him.[61] Even if the incident was at all serious, it didn't cause any long-term strain on their friendship; however, it was another example of how prickly and emotionally charged the conservation arena could be.

Stone's years of involvement with the AOU bird protection committee were easily his most active in conservation work. His correspondence with Dutcher, who both preceded and succeeded him as chair of the committee, and who became president of the NAAS when it was formed in 1905, contains several references to planned sting operations. They appear to have been cooked up by Dutcher, and often featured Stone posing as a dealer interested in skins. In one, Dutcher had his Dutch up over a shady dealer named Murgatroyd, and he hatched a plan for Stone and some DVOC associates to catch him. William Baily was to write Murgatroyd "a foxy letter…so as to get him in the trap"; the vulpine missive would state that Rhoads had recommended Murgatroyd as a skins dealer, and would include a request for a protected bird. If the requested specimen was sent, it could be given a tag marked by a notary and used as evidence.[62] Dutcher was snorting like a racehorse, telling Stone, "[I]f I do not make [Murgatroyd's] hair stand up like the quills of a fretful porcupine before I get through with him it is because my name is not Dutcher, and if I find that Mr. [John] Rowley [AMNH's head taxidermist] is in the slightest degree involved in this he will get such a calling down from the authorities of the American Museum that he will wish that he had never been born."[63] Murgatroyd took the bait and sent the bird, but T.S. Palmer (Dutcher was known to say, "I do nothing without first consulting Palmer"), who as an employee of the USBS would have brought it to trial, decided the case was too small to risk losing, which could have jeopardized future efforts. Dutcher believed that the incident had at least rattled Murgatroyd.[64]

Dutcher was often imperious and brusque in his letters to Stone, for example in this one from 1909: "I have just received a letter from Western Pennsylvania calling my attention to a very vicious bill introduced by Dr. Kalbfus [head of the PGC, and whom Dutcher distrusted] to codify the Pennsylvania game law. Are you doing anything about it, if so, what? Kindly let me hear from you as soon as possible."[65]

In 1900, Stone was made an as-needed USDA inspector of birds and animals entering the Philadelphia ports, checking that no prohibited species or ones requiring a permit were passing through.[66] A few months later, Stone and Palmer visited some of the milliners' Philadelphia warehouses to ensure that protected birds weren't being used.[67] A newspaper article in 1902 stated that Palmer, Dutcher, Stone, and Chapman would be helping authorities in seven states "in the identification of plumage birds," and in prosecuting persons found shooting them.[68]

There was a subtle humorous undercurrent to a court case in which Stone was involved in 1907. A hapless dealer named Henry Crumley was nabbed selling two mockingbirds and three cardinals. The mockingbird was protected, but no penalty had been written into the law, so Crumley was off the hook for that one. There was a $10 fine, however, for a long list of birds, including the "grosbeak" (which means "large [gros=French for 'big'] beak"). The debate, then, was whether or not the bird indicated by the law was the cardinal or another bird or birds. "Learned Ornithologists" (this is where Stone came in) testified that "grosbeak" covered a number of birds, including the cardinal; bird dealers, of course, countered that the "grosbeak" and cardinal were two different birds.[69] The judge turned to Warren's *Birds of Pennsylvania* for the final word. The text of the cardinal account referred to it as the "Cardinal," "Winter Red-bird," "Red-bird," and "Red Corncracker," but, alas for Mr. Crumley, the color plate had the caption "Cardinal Grosbeak," and he suddenly found himself out of $30 and costs.[70]

Sometimes man does more damage by introducing an exotic species than by removing the odd cardinal or mockingbird. In 1897, William T. Hornaday got wind of a plan by an ecologically illiterate fellow named Fulton to import and release exotic, pugnacious European Starlings in Pittsburgh, hoping they would drive out the exotic, pugnacious House Sparrows that had already been unwisely introduced. Hornaday passed the information on to Dutcher, who forwarded it to Stone.[71] Others had asked Fulton not to act on his bad idea, but Stone must have been more persuasive, and at his behest Fulton scrapped the plan.[72]

Of course, the flock introduced to Central Park in New York in the early 1890s had multiplied and spread and the species would conquer the continent in short order, causing untold harm to native species. But at least Stone, Dutcher and Hornaday made the effort – ultimately futile – to check the spread of a species they rightly recognized as a potential catastrophe. (Almost 30 years later, after the species had spread about a third of the way across the U.S.,

Stone presciently told Alexander Wetmore that, despite the USBS's assertions to the contrary, it would soon be "an infernal nuisance & a serious menace all around.")[73-74] Hornaday, in fact, sounded a theme that would be well to heed over 100 years later: "I am opposed to reckless & ignorant interference with the balance of nature....After our experience with the [House] Sparrow, I have no patience with the people who propose to make fool experiments in the same line."[72,75] The rampant proliferation of exotic and invasive species of every taxonomic class, introduced to North America intentionally and otherwise, presents one of the greatest challenges in modern conservation efforts.

Stone, with his noncombative nature, was probably not really cut out for the rancor of pitched conservation battles. As Dutcher, a giant in the field and a participant in many clashes, once told Stone about trying to get bird legislation passed in New York, "I tell you that it is hard work to get protection for birds."[76] Stone quickly tired of the protection committee chairmanship.[77] He told Dutcher in mid-March 1900, "Like you this thing seriously affects my work & the authorities here [at ANSP] while in sympathy with the work think it interferes with what I am paid for so next fall I will absolutely resign the chairmanship."[78] AOU vice president C. Hart Merriam wrote to him in October 1900, "I regret to learn from your letter respecting the chairmanship of the AOU Committee on Protection that you find the duties of this position so onerous that you will be unable to continue as chairman."[79] By year's end, Stone had changed his mind and agreed to serve another year, but that may have been simply because he was stuck with the hot potato after Dutcher told him in early December that he had no intention of taking the chair back, and that T.S. Palmer, the other possibility, wouldn't take it either.[80] In April, however, Stone told Dutcher that he would give up the chair at the next AOU meeting "without fail." He said that Dutcher and Palmer were doing all the work anyway, and that it was "absurd for [him] to pose as chairman."[81] Dutcher didn't want the job back (he thought they might be able to rope Palmer into taking it), but finally acquiesced.[82]

After giving up the chair, Stone immediately asked Dutcher to remove him from the committee altogether, begging off with the excuse that he had just been appointed to the AOU classification committee, and "a man should not be on too many committees." He said he would do as much or more conservation work as head of the PAS, and that he was sure there were many others who would want to be on the protection committee.[83] He was surely glad to be off of it, and seems to have felt about conservation work as Thoreau felt about charity: that it was one of the professions that was full, and that he had tried it fairly, and, strange as it may seem, was satisfied that it did not agree with his constitution. In some of his bird protection correspondence with Palmer, Stone is clearly trying to persuade Palmer to perform the onerous task of attending meetings with politicians and legislative committees because Stone doesn't want to do it; he uses flattery ("I think you are the only man who can talk the committee over & have <u>no doubt</u> but that you can do it") and assurances that, in essence, he and the PAS will be cheering Palmer on mightily from the side-lines.[84] In 1910, Stone said that defective bird protection laws in several states were the result of politicians at every session tampering with (i.e., weakening) previously enacted legislation.[85] Years later, Stone recalled having to deal with "hard-headed legislators," which he must have considered one of the more distasteful aspects of conservation work.[86]

Stone may have also quit the AOU committee in part because of complaints from eggers who thought he was too critical of their activities.[87] Like Stone, Dutcher also tangled with the militant collecting arm of the AOU, which eventually gained control of the committee and rendered it ineffective for a couple of decades.[88] When the NAAS formed in 1905 as an umbrella organization for the state societies, many of the people who had been on the AOU bird protection committee during its active phase became leaders in the NAAS. (It was headed by Dutcher.) Stone served on the advisory council of the NAAS for years, but wasn't particularly involved with it – in fact, he wasn't even a member.

Working on the classification committee, which he eventually chaired and remained a member of for 30 years, was more suited to Stone's temperament and interests. After his service on the AOU protection committee, he was busy with his botanical research; then *The Auk* and ANSP duties took his time. His response to a 1923 request to chair a committee on conservation of Pennsylvania songbirds serves as an excellent summary of his career in conservation work: "Many years ago, I acted as Chairman of the [AOU] Committee which ultimately developed into the [NAAS] and most of my work in bird conservation was done during those years. Of late years, since I have been the President of the [AOU] and Editor of…'The Auk' my whole time has been taken up with this more scientific side of Ornithology, although my sympathies with the conservation work have remained unimpaired. It seems to me, however, that a younger and more active man who is not tied up with technical and executive duties should be in charge of this Committee's work."[89]

Stone was indeed sympathetic to conservation work, and he remained involved in the cause, if somewhat peripherally. He used his work and personal contacts to forward conservation matters. He corresponded with the PGC's Kalbfus about pending Pennsylvania wildlife legislation, suggesting changes that he felt were necessary. Legislation targeting Great Egrets and Great Blue Herons because of their reported depredations at fish hatcheries seemed to particularly irritate Stone. Kalbfus and his successor, Seth Gordon, often sent animal skins, some of which had been turned in for bounty, to ANSP personnel for them to verify identification, and Stone tipped them off when he heard of wildlife protection law violations.[90]

Gordon contacted Stone in 1921 about a Pennsylvania House bill to add the bobwhite to the songbird list (i.e., remove it from the list of hunted birds). Gordon asserted that hunters were to be credited with the species' continued existence in the state, and that without hunting pressure, "the birds run together, inbreed, lay in the same nest, etc."[91] Saying nothing about the curious inbreeding theory, Stone replied that as far as he was concerned, almost all the bobwhites in Pennsylvania were released birds and could be hunted as much as any other introduced birds.[32] Assuming Stone was on the PGC/hunters' side on the issue, Gordon responded with enthusiasm about Stone's "splendid" letter, and asked him to testify at an upcoming House hearing on the matter.[92] Showing his pacifist streak, Stone replied that he was in the embarrassing position of having been pressured by both sides in the debate to testify for them, "therefore, I felt the best thing I can do is to remain out if it entirely." But then he let Gordon have it about the inbreeding: "I gave you my personal attitude in my letter of recent date, but my experience would compel me to take exactly the opposite ground from that taken by the sportsmen as to the necessity of killing quail in order to prevent inbreeding, therefore, I think that you would prefer not to have me present."[93]

Stone used his USBS contacts as well – for instance, alerting E.W. Nelson, chief of the Survey, about alleged illegal snipe shooting in Delaware in the spring of 1923.[94] In 1926, Stone wrote to his friend and UP classmate, U.S. Senator George W. Pepper, urging opposition to a bill that would allow grazing on national forest land in opposition to the wishes of the U.S. Forest Service.[95]

Although Stone was not slugging it out on the front lines of the conservation wars after his involvement with the AOU bird protection committee ended, as editor he used *The Auk*, particularly the "Notes and News" section, as a bully pulpit for his conservation views and to get the word out about needed action on pending conservation issues. He wasn't going to take many lumps preaching to the AOU membership choir, yet even then there were times when he was mired in the middle ground. He agreed with the assertions of the USBS's W.L. McAtee that sapsuckers should be killed when caught damaging lumber trees.[96] A common theme with Stone concerning crows and birds of prey was that it was appropriate to kill ones caught damaging crops, taking livestock, etc., but extermination of the species should not be a goal. For example, after noting the bounty system in Australia that led to the killing of thousands of Wedge-tailed Eagles, Stone wrote, "There is some justification in this slaughter as the birds are very injurious to lambs, but let us hope that this fine bird may be saved from absolute extermination!"[97] (Subsequent studies have found that this species rarely kills lambs.)[98] In a 1920 review of some USBS reports about bird damages to agriculture and fisheries, Stone wrote that "several species regarded as beneficial when the effort toward bird protection was initiated must now be regarded as injurious at certain times and places and necessary steps taken for their control."[99] One could fairly argue that Stone was simply being pragmatic instead of dogmatic, but he was hardly a conservation tiger roaring.

In 1930 he penned "The hawk question" as one of the leading articles in the April *Auk* issue, saying that although it was true that some hawks committed depredations on poultry and livestock, they were mostly beneficial and part of nature's balance. He called for involvement in legislative and educational efforts on behalf of the persecuted raptors, and singled out arms manufacturers, sportsmen, and state game agencies as waging the campaign against the birds. Citing correspondence from conservationists William Adams and Beecher Bowdish, he called for a change in the composition and mission of state game agencies, which Bowdish said needed to become state wildlife agencies and not just focused on game species. Stone called on *Auk* readers to get the results of empirical studies into the discussion, in order to negate the biased opinions and misinformation that the sporting magazines were "only too glad to publish," by sending letters that contained the results of scientific investigations to those magazines.[100] Before and after he published the article, however, Stone was openly pessimistic in *The Auk* about the chances of saving the birds of prey from extermination, writing bluntly in 1929, "It would seem therefore that the case of the Hawks and Owls is hopeless."[101]

Stone was no "sportsman," and although he sometimes collected birds for study, he never shot them for food or sport.[102] Stone of course had no time for the law-flaunting hunters of the day, and he often acerbically criticized sportsmen in his *Auk* literature reviews and the "Notes and News" section, saying they were being duped by ammunition and arms manufacturers into wiping out hawks and overharvesting ducks. As one example, in a review of some Emergency Conservation Committee educational material on hawks and ducks, he wrote that it was imperative to teach schoolchildren the facts about conservation, for not only were today's children tomorrow's lawmakers and voters, they were also "open minded while the sportsmen often are not."[103]

In the early 1900s, the USBS became involved in predator and rodent control via trapping and poisoning in the western U.S., and by the mid-1920s it had become a heated issue between biologists inside and outside the Survey. Survey chief Paul Redington was adamant about the effectiveness and necessity of the program, but the American Society of Mammalogists (ASM) took a strong stand against it.[104] Stone mentioned the program and its results a few times in his *Auk* reviews of Survey annual reports, giving it tacit approval by never voicing any objection to the slaughter, aside from one comment that he hoped the indirect results of the extermination of so many mammal species had been considered (and of course they hadn't).[99,105] He started to change his tune when he served as ASM president from 1929 to 1931, however, and found himself in the middle of the fray.[106] He shot off a letter on the subject to the *Philadelphia Ledger* in June 1930 that was half mammal conservation, half ANSP sales pitch (the Academy was installing new mammal exhibits). Stone blasted the "outrageous poison campaign being waged in the interest of stock raisers," saying that it also killed nontarget animals and birds.[107]

Stone was hearing plenty from A. Brazier Howell, the ASM secretary, who wanted him to come out strongly against the poison campaign and didn't think he was being sufficiently militant. Redington, meanwhile, felt that Howell had slighted him in print and was trying to get Stone and the ASM Council to demand an apology from Howell.[108] Stone, characteristically, was straddling the fence with all his might, telling Redington he didn't feel his grudge was justifiable but that he appreciated the impossible situation he was in. Stone was getting so many letters on the issue, because of both his ASM and *Auk* positions, that he felt he should publish at least some of them, but eventually decided to write an editorial in *The Auk*.[109] Joseph Grinnell, who had written a *Condor* editorial condemning the poisoning (as had Jean Linsdale), urged him not to pussyfoot: "Now, in the strong editorial which I hope you will run in July Auk, I counsel no attempt at maintaining an 'impartial' attitude, as you intimate. The facts before us are many and convincing. The Auk and the AOU are powerful; and courageous, out-and-out condemnation of Redington and Co's animal-destruction policy cannot help but have effect sooner or later."[110]

Stone began his editorial by citing the Linsdale and Grinnell pieces, and their bleak numbers about the vast destruction of nontarget wildlife. He didn't adopt a combative tone in his editorial, and in fact made excuses for the Survey – it was unaware that thallium was being used, Redington didn't realize how many birds were being killed – but he was unequivocal about where he stood:

> It seems to us that it is impossible for an agency actively interested in the conservation of wild life to be at the same time actively engaged in its destruction and it is deplorable that the Biological Survey which has done and is still doing such admirable work on various scientific and economic problems should be involved in this wretched business of destroying life….By its present activity in adopting and encouraging the poison method the Survey is being brought into disrepute to an extent that its officers apparently do not realize and we sincerely hope that it may abandon at once any further participation in this nefarious work….It looks as if this "Ten Year Program" would be as disastrous to wild life in America as the Russian "Five Year Plan" bids fair to be to human life in Russia.

Stone recommended that state legislatures decide whether or not to poison, because he felt that those who were in favor of poisoning were in the minority, and he urged AOU members to send their views, either in letters or editorials, to local newspapers.[111] Clearly, he didn't want to receive a flood of responses demanding *Auk* space.

Howell was delighted with the editorial, telling Stone, "Copy of the Auk received within the hour and your editorial aroused my unbounded admiration and elation. If that doesn't lift them out of their seats I will begin to think the whole thing hopeless and impossible. You must be experiencing that self-satisfied glow."[112]

However, the editorial drew some heat from Redington and from Stone's longtime friend, and AOU founder, A.K. Fisher, who was in charge of the Survey's predator control efforts. Fisher, ten years older than Stone and a Survey biologist since its nascent USDA Branch of Economic Ornithology days in 1885, lectured Stone, "You know nothing personally of, in regard to our placing poison, the situation of the bait stations or in fact anything more tangible than you do regarding the actions in Hell!…An eminent zoologist who read your Auk tirade said: 'Someone near Stone should warn him not to copy Grinnell in being an ass.'" (The editorial was anything but a tirade.) Fisher defended the poison campaign as necessary for the livelihood of ranchers and for ensuring the nation's meat supply, and was scathing in his opinions of those publicly opposed to it, especially Grinnell.[113]

Stone sent a conciliatory letter, saying that many prominent AOU members had sent in letters to *The Auk* that were inflammatory in tone, and that he thought it better to write his own even-tempered editorial than to publish some of the letters. He felt that he and Fisher were not really that far apart on their views of the matter.[114] Fisher, however, was having none of it, telling Stone, "[I]n considering generalities you have become involved in false premises. I am sure you do not know of the contemptible methods used in expending propaganda and the false inferences used to gain points." In other words, he was telling Stone he'd been duped.[115] It was difficult for Fisher to lay it on his old friend; they remained on cordial terms, although it seems their correspondence cooled a bit until near the end of Stone's life. Fisher was the only fellow ornithologist to send greetings on what proved to be Stone's last birthday, and was one of the last people to whom Stone wrote shortly before he died.[116] The poison debate was another example of how high feelings could run on conservation issues.

AOU treasurer W.L. McAtee, also a Survey biologist but not connected with the poisoning campaign, seemed embarrassed at the boondoggle. He responded privately to Stone's *Auk* editorial, saying that he was a conservationist, and that he and other Survey biologists did care about protecting wildlife, but the organization was not being run by biologists, but by men who put business interests foremost. McAtee did some grumbling but had to be careful – then as now, personnel who bucked the company line in a government agency could face consequences.[117] The battles over federal agencies' involvement in poisoning predators in the western U.S. were just getting heated up, and would continue after Stone and his contemporaries were long gone.

Fisher, of course, had a rather dismal record in the conservation arena. He authored an 1898 publication that generally defended the food habits of raptors.[118] In the early 1900s, though, he grumbled that the AOU bird protection committee was too preservationist and too closely allied with the Audubon movement, and he became the committee's head after Dutcher and Stone had thrown in the towel, taking it in the opposite direction.[119] During Fisher's all-too-lengthy tenure the committee was largely inactive, and if it exhibited a concern for anything it was in continuing the collecting privileges of ornithologists.[120] Stone once complained that much wasted time at AOU Council meetings could be saved if they could get Fisher to stop droning on about the "Protection of Ornithologists" (i.e., protecting their collecting rights).[121] As AOU president from 1920 to 1923, Stone heard from some of the more conservation-minded in the AOU about the ineffectiveness of the committee, but he didn't seem particularly bothered by it. He told Beecher Bowdish in 1920 that the committee was under the thumb of the USBS, which was on a "vermin" crusade, but to break up the committee would cause "considerable ill feeling which would be very unfavorable from the standpoint of the AOU."[122] Stone must have thought that keeping the AOU in good stead with the Survey was more important than whether or not the committee was effective in its mission.

A year later, Waldron DeWitt Miller suggested a change in the committee, or "at least cease the hypocrisy and pretense of the present committee."[123] Miller must have been discouraged by Stone's noncommittal answer: "I shall give the matter of the Bird Protection Committee serious consideration. It seems to me that the unions should take a definite stand as to whether or not they wish to take an active part in matters relating to bird protection, if so, of course the Committee should be an efficient one. As far as I can, I shall canvass the council for their opinion before the session convenes [at the upcoming AOU meeting]."[124] It would be a few more years, however, with Joseph Grinnell serving as AOU president, before the committee would get some new blood and renew the Union's commitment to conservation.[125]

Stone had some involvement in the Pennsylvania State Conservation Council, which was formed by Pennsylvania State University (PSU) faculty members and administrators in 1922 to serve as an umbrella organization for the many state conservation organizations.[126] In 1923, he was on the Song Bird and Executive committees and helped with the Publicity Bureau.[127] He attended the 1924 meeting at PSU and stayed at a fraternity house, which makes you wonder how much sleep he was able to get. The frat brother who hosted him, Alfred Folweiler, later became the director of the Texas Forest Service after a stint on the faculty at Louisiana State University, so Stone got stuck with a studier, at least.[128] Then the organization was renamed the Conservation Council of Pennsylvania, with headquarters in Harrisburg, and things started getting a little comical at Stone's end. He responded to a letter from the new secretary, a very naïve chap named Vorse, by saying, "I was a little amused at your offer to explain to me just what the Council is, as I was invited some years ago to serve on the Executive Committee which I did; but at the reorganization a year ago things were so arranged that I was forced out, though I am at present, I believe, one of the members of the Song Bird Committee. I am, therefore, fully aware of the activities of the organization."[36] He served on a bird committee in 1926,[129] and Vorse's invitation to that year's annual meeting, emphasizing the important work to be discussed and the need for a good attendance, concluded with an admonishing "You are respectfully reminded that you are a member of the Birds committee."[130] Not surprisingly, Stone's involvement with the council seems to have petered out about that time.

———————— ∼ ————————

Stone had plenty to say about conservation issues in *BSOCM*, including the loss of coastal habitat to resorts; the draining, ditching, and oiling of wetlands by the local mosquito commission; and the shooting of hawks, shorebirds, and crows. Along with other DVOC members, Stone had quite an affection for crows and often protested local extermination efforts. He asked the DVOC to investigate local crow roosts as early as 1891, and he presented the talk "Crow Flights and Crow Roosts" to the DVOC in October 1898, based on investigations with Joseph Tatum.[131] Stone used a map that showed not only the locations of southeastern Pennsylvania/ New Jersey roosts, but also lines of flight taken by the crows to and from the roosts.[132] Stone was aware of former roosts on Pea Patch and Reedy Islands in the Delaware River at the mouth of the Bay that had formerly held an estimated half-million birds, but which were now abandoned due to building on the islands. In an 1899 *Bird-Lore* article, Stone recounted searching for, and finding, the location to which the crows now repaired on winter evenings, somewhere near Salem, New Jersey. Three times, Stone and his companion (probably Benjamin Carpenter) deliberately startled the crows into flight, then "were glad to leave them in peace."[133] He had heard that this roost was "little molested," and hoped it continued that way – evidently shooting them would be molesting them, but putting them to flight three times was not.[134] Herbert Coggins later facetiously wrote that for the 1899 *Bird-Lore* article, "government postmasters, respectable private citizens and lighthouse keepers, who were suspected of possessing any information upon the subject of Crows, were promptly and effectually besieged" by Stone.[135] In a rambling 1903 *Auk* article, Stone described Philadelphia-area winter crow roosts and the local practice of trapping crows for use in trap shooting contests in lieu of pigeons. (He also shared that bird skeletons placed on the roof of ANSP to bleach in the sun were pilfered by Fish Crows living in Logan Square.)[136]

In 1924, in a transparent effort to increase gunpowder sales, DuPont (originally manufacturers of gunpowder, before "better living through chemistry" beckoned) offered a $2,500 prize to the person or club that killed the most crows and other "vermin" in a three-month period.[137] DuPont sent a group to coastal Virginia; they reported back about crow depredations on the eggs of gulls and rails. Stone took issue with the report in an *Auk* note, pointing out that high tides could have been responsible for washing the eggs off the nests, to be feasted on by the opportunistic crows; that the crows in question were Fish Crows, not the widely maligned American Crows; and that the reporter's trip was sponsored by a gunpowder manufacturer (without naming DuPont directly). Stone concluded, "By all means let the farmer kill Crows when damaging crops but do not let us exterminate an extremely interesting species of bird on the advice of ammunition manufacturers."[138] He protested to USBS chief E.W. Nelson about the DuPont contest, and the company's habit of twisting Survey publications to its purposes in its sales pitches; further, he wrote to NAAS president T. Gilbert Pearson requesting that Audubon come out against the campaign.[139] In another *Auk* note later in the year, Stone singled out DuPont by name for the crow defamation crusade, and told a friend in 1926, "If DuPont would train their heavy artillery on the Starling instead of the Crow I would be with them."[74,140] He pitched the latter idea again in a 1932 *Auk* note, adding that starlings were good eating![141]

Killing crows at their roost sites was a favorite pastime with some of the "sportsmen" in those days, and at a February 1927 meeting, the DVOC decided that Stone should contact the New Jersey Game Commission to protest crow shoots.[142] A brief article, "Dr. Stone Denounces Crow Slaughter in New Jersey," appeared in the Philadelphia *Evening Bulletin* shortly thereafter.[143] In *BSOCM* he called the habit of slaughtering crows at their roosts "despicable" and "an outrage."[144] He thought that the crow should be forgiven his occasionally destructive food habits, saying that studies had shown that the crows did at least as much good as harm: "[H]e is as beneficial as he is injurious and he is economically, as we so often see him in actual life, on the fence!"[145]

———————— ∽ ————————

Collecting was another area with conservation overtones. Stone, as an ornithologist, editor, and museum administrator, was right in the middle of the debates and changing attitudes that swirled around the subject in his lifetime. People collected to add to personal or museum collections, and to establish a verifiable record of an unusual find. Stone collected throughout his life. The WNSA had a small "museum" of its specimens in the Stones' house. In 1897, Witmer deposited his personal collection of over 2,000 skins of local birds with the Academy, and in 1901 he and Henry Fowler donated "several hundred" skeletal birds – but he collected more than birds.[146] In *Pennsylvania and New Jersey Spiders in the Family Lycosidae,* Stone discussed his extensive spider collection at length.[147] His *PSNJ* fieldwork included the collection of thousands of specimens. The *PANSP* frequently listed recent accessions that came via Stone's fieldwork. As one example, on a two-week trip in May 1914 to South Carolina, Stone brought back reptiles and amphibians, fishes (identified by Fowler, list published by Stone), an insect collection, crustaceans, 13 trays of mollusks, and 500 plants (some specimens of the latter two groups were from Pennsylvania).[148] The variety was typical: *PANSP* noted all manner of things added to the museum's collections by Stone. Besides the expected birds, plants, and mammals, there were also rocks, marine invertebrates, shells, leeches, crayfishes, and even "parasitic worms from the intestines of Cooper's Hawk."[149] Stone continued to collect for the Academy while traveling; as late as 1935, a trip to Ed McIlhenny's Louisiana estate netted 196 fish, 40 crustaceans, 1,350 insects, 22 amphibians, 50 plants, and 7 nestling herons.[150] Toward the end of his life, Stone turned his attention during summers in Cape May to insects, and Lillie presented the Academy with his collection of more than 10,000 insects after his death.[151]

George Spencer Morris wrote about Stone making the welkin ring with his little collecting gun as a youth, and early DVOC literature is replete with examples of a cavalier, almost sneering attitude about collecting birds. The following are some examples from the DVOC 20-year history booklet (mostly or entirely written by Stone):[152]

"McCadden has always been in demand when anything had to be killed and he responds nobly."

"[B]ut far from being terrified by McCadden, [Fowler] stuck to the job and even acquired some of his peculiarities, notably the thirst for gore. He nearly exterminated the Purple Grackles and Yellow-billed Cuckoos at Holmesburg in his zeal to secure a good series of skins, and was visited by a committee of ministers and other outraged citizens to protest against the further activity of his ten-bore."

"Oh! what a slaughter of Sharp-tailed Sparrows there was in pursuit of Nelsons and Acadians [by Norris DeHaven and Stone]."[6,153] The word "slaughter" is used frequently by collectors in Stone's correspondence, for example when Bill Shryock told Stone he was contemplating a trip to Cape Charles, Virginia "to slaughter Ducks, Geese, and Ipswich Sparrows,"[154] or when, collecting for the Academy in Colorado, Robert Young asked Stone's help in getting a permit for "scientific slaughter."[155]

At a DVOC meeting in 1893, Morris read "A Day in the Salt Marshes," wherein he, de Haven, and Stone ("Stone was always bloodthirsty") blasted their way through the Atlantic City-area avifauna.[156] The tone of the talk is what you might expect from a teenaged redneck chortling about some illegal hunting with his buddies, not from a supposed "ornithologist" collecting in the name of science. (Even the DVOC minutes for the meeting noted that Morris "depicted in graphic style the capture [i.e., killing] of several treasures now on exhibition in the Club collection at the Academy.")[157] In another tale of powder-burned feathers, Morris recounted a trip to Tinicum in south Philadelphia, where several birds were collected, including a female Golden-winged Warbler. He wrote, "I watched it with intense delight, but all the while I knew that it was the fate of that little bird to lie for years to come in a dark drawer by the side of [another] one shot twelve years ago." Morris offered that the opinions of naturalists who didn't kill anything were, scientifically speaking, "hardly worth considering."[158]

Morris sent Stone a couple of letters while on a collecting trip in the Pacific Northwest in the spring of 1892.[6,159] In one, he wrote, "Tomorrow the slaughter begins in earnest," and a few days later he told Stone about some of the amenities of the house in which they were staying: "'Tis a pleasure to be able to shoot ducks & geese out of the windows of your house, or to stand on the front porch & plunk with your revolver at the seals as they go down the channel."[160] There was a noticeable absence of this primitive mentality after Morris got married (and had four daughters!); he implied as much in his 1894 talk to the club about sentiment in nature.[6,161] Maybe the worst thing that can happen to a collector is the same worst thing that can happen to a fighter, as Mickey told Rocky in the famous film: they get civilized.

Another DVOC founder, J. Harris Reed, wrote to Stone in 1891 about a recent trip to Beaver Swamp, New Jersey, where "like true ornithologists we [Reed and Voelker]…amused ourselves in shooting swallows. I shot 4 in 6 shots, among them was a bank, cliff, and [tree]."[162] Amusing, indeed. At a 1900 DVOC meeting, Stone read a letter from Otto Behr, of Lopez, Pennsylvania about some birds he had just collected. Behr said that "it was difficult to procure the White-winged Crossbills [because] they roosted high, and when wounded they grasp the cones and branches of the Coniferous trees on which they feed, and to which they would cling, [and] it was difficult to recover them."[163] Notwithstanding, Behr had sent seven crossbill skins. Did anyone at the DVOC that night feel a pang of sympathy for the birds clutching the branches while their lives flickered out, or did they all, like Behr, just consider the birds' death throes an irritating collecting inconvenience? A.K. Fisher spoke at the 20th anniversary DVOC dinner about a subject dear to his heart:

the necessity of allowing and encouraging boys to collect. The minutes then record that William Hughes, a DVOC member since 1891, who once shot nine Ipswich Sparrows in a day, "arose to state his preference for study through an opera glass, but not until the specimen had been shot, unless, perchance, he could procure it in the egg" – which, presumably, set off a few rounds of "Hear, hear!" and "Well said!"[164]

In 1913, a collector asked Stone for a Philadelphia location to find Kentucky Warblers, and Stone recommended Darby Creek.[165] A short time later, there were three fewer Kentucky Warblers brightening the edges of Darby Creek than there were before Stone's kindly tip.[166]

Not everyone looked on the collecting favorably, of course. One bird-watcher was regularly seeing a flock of Evening Grosbeaks near Browns Mills, New Jersey in 1917, but refused to tell anyone the location for fear the birds would be shot by collectors.[167] Princeton University ornithologist Charles Rogers was hesitant about revealing the exact whereabouts of a Piping Plover nest he'd found at Barnegat City, New Jersey, asking Stone, "If I publish this record with the exact locality, do you think there would be any danger of [Richard] Harlow or [Richard] Miller or some other egg shark going down next season and snitching a 'clutch'?"[168] Stone must have thought there was such a chance, for the subsequent *Auk* note didn't get any more specific with the locale than "the central part of the New Jersey coast."[169]

Stone made the welkin ring not only in Germantown as a youth, but also on the hallowed ground of Cape May Point in later years. The Stone archives at ANSP contain Pennsylvania and New Jersey collecting permits for Stone as late as 1936, and Stone made sure he had his permit with him when visiting Cape May for the summer.[170] He collected extensively on his earliest trips to Cape May, and he did some collecting there in later years as well. In the Northern Shrike account in *BSOCM* Stone noted that he "saw one daily on the Fill January 8–10, 1922, which was eventually collected" – in fact, Stone collected it on the 10th.[171] He collected a Yellow-throated Warbler in July 1920, a Savannah Sparrow in July 1921, an Olive-sided Flycatcher in September 1924, and doubtless others.[172] A Gray Kingbird was observed during a DVOC outing on May 30, 1923, and Stone wrote in *BSOCM* that he went down two days later and searched for it, but he disclosed his full intent only in a letter to AMNH ornithologist James Chapin: "There was no gun in the crowd [on 5/30], and although I went down two days after (<u>with one</u>) I failed to see any trace of the bird."[173]

However, attitudes were changing. In 1900, *The Osprey* stated, "The blood and thunder days together with those of the embryo hook [used by egg collectors], have given way or are giving way to the more esthetic side of bird study. We seem to be emerging above the mere collecting or amassing craze, and are beginning to view the birds from a more philosophic standpoint."[174] As early as 1891, Stone wrote in *The Auk* that DVOC members were "using the glass [i.e., binoculars] much more than the gun" in their daily spring migration counts.[175] In his *Hints to Young Bird Students* pamphlet in 1899, he advised students to shoot as little as possible for purposes of identification, and to instead learn to identify birds visually and by their call notes and songs. He wrote that "those who undertake any special line of study will soon learn what specimens are required and collect accordingly, instead of amassing a large number of specimens with no particular object in view."[176]

By 1914, Spencer Trotter was bemoaning the passing of professional bird collectors and what he facetiously referred to as "the absolutely illogical desire to get out and shoot specimens," which had given way to the study of the live bird.[177] In a DVOC talk that year, Stone said that studies of plumages, taxonomy, and ranges – which validated collecting for a previous generation – were now "almost a completed book."[178] In another talk before the DVOC in December 1922, Stone emphasized "the importance of studying and recording the habits, behavior, and characteristics of the living bird, not merely the record of its presence or the getting of a mere skin or set of eggs."[179]

In a 1923 talk, Stone said, "[L]et anyone, even an old collector – and I speak from experience – set out upon an intensive study of the birds of his immediate vicinity or of any limited area, with a good pair of binoculars, and he will be amazed at the amount of data on migration, behavior, habits, etc., that he can collect and the things he can learn, that skins would never have taught him. And yet he should have a handy collecting-gun in his sack." He didn't rule out any place for collecting in modern ornithology, but said that an increased knowledge of field characters of living birds would make future identifications more certain and further decrease the need to collect for identification purposes.[180] In another DVOC talk in January 1933 titled "Two Kinds of Ornithology," he contrasted "old collecting methods with modern field studies of birds."[181]

In the *BSOCM* preface, Stone wrote, "During the period of my field work at the Cape the greater perfection and more general use of the binocular glass has entirely changed the method of the field ornithologist and there are today no collectors of birds skins in southern New Jersey [including, one would assume, Stone]. The modern glass brings the bird so close to the observer that the experienced student can identify practically all of the birds that he sees at a reasonable distance but the less experienced and less conscientious observer certainly cannot."[182] He also mentioned Roger Tory Peterson's "admirable" recent field guide as a good reference for identifying birds.[183] (If you think "admirable" sounds like shallow praise for a book regarded as revolutionary today, Chapman's tepid *Bird-Lore* review went so far as to say that Peterson had "done a fine job.")[184] Stone rolled with the changes, from being an avid collector himself to using, and recommending, the field glass for identification instead of the gun, although some state laws that were enacted based on the AOU's

Model Law, and federal ones such as the Migratory Bird Treaty Act of 1918, had removed shooting as an option for all but permit holders anyway.

Stone was of course as interested in obtaining rare bird skins for his museum as the next curator; his correspondence includes inquiries about Heath Hens, Bachman's Warblers, Ivory-billed Woodpeckers, and Kirtland's Warblers – all of which were extremely rare.[185] In fact, although the Kirtland's Warbler hangs on, the other species are certainly (Heath Hen, although now considered a subspecies of the Greater Prairie Chicken) or probably gone. And a few years after the last Heath Hen had disappeared, there was Stone in the local paper, pitching the Academy's stuffed-specimen display of the now extinct birds.[186]

───────────── ❧ ─────────────

Excessive collecting, especially egg collecting, negatively impacted local bird populations. Collectors of both skins and eggs in the late 1800s were ruthless, and sometimes their attitudes could be comical if their actions hadn't been so devastating. An 1883 note in a collecting magazine reviewed the previous raptor breeding season around Norwich, Connecticut, when the author took 104 eggs: "And from other nests in my circle of observation were taken or destroyed by farmers, hawk-hunters and others, sixty more eggs and young birds. So until a more favored breeding range is made known I shall claim this [area] to be the home of the Buteos."[187] "Home" for how long, with that kind of theft and pillaging going on? Far from being a "home," the area had probably become a population sink, to use today's ecological terminology. Charles Shick's 1890 *Auk* article about collecting on Seven Mile Beach referred several times to unrestrained egg collecting and decreasing numbers of breeding birds with no indication that the author thought there might be a correlation. For example, Roseate Terns (they reportedly formerly bred in New Jersey, although Shick may have misidentified the terns as to species) were not as plentiful as five years earlier, "when it was an easy to task to go out and gather several bushels of eggs in a few hours"; Black Skimmers were now scarce, when previously Shick could "go out during the breeding season and take all the [egg] sets [he] desired."[188] Declining numbers notwithstanding, Schick told Stone in December 1890 that he had collected more than 4,000 eggs in South Jersey that year.[189]

Stone always took a dim view of such excessive egg collecting. It appears that he had no axe to grind with "eggers" early in his career. He posted a note in *Ornithologist and Oölogist* in 1892 at the request of J. Parker Norris, a prominent oologist, about the birds and eggs collected on the recent ANSP-sponsored Peary Expedition.[190] Later, Stone had no problems with occasional egg or specimen collecting for truly scientific purposes by legitimate investigators, but rightly despised collecting just for collecting's sake under the guise of scientific inquiry.

In his first report as chairman of the AOU bird protection committee, Stone's criticism of the slaughter of small birds for market and the use of egrets and terns for millinery purposes would not have offended any ornithologists, but he also criticized excessive specimen and egg collecting. About the former, Stone wrote that it was no longer necessary for every ornithologist to have a collection, as large museum collections were now accessible to interested researchers, and worthwhile studies could be conducted without a gun. He also decried the use of a collecting permit merely to sell birds to a taxidermist. But he saved his harshest criticism for the "fad" of egg collecting, writing that the excessive egg collecting by boys and "egg-hogs" (a term that had been in use for some time by oologists) contributed little to ornithological knowledge.[191]

At about the same time as his bird protection committee report, Stone published "Hints to young bird students" in *Bird-Lore*, which expressed similar sentiments, including, "[Y]ou will see what an insignificant matter the formation of an egg collection is in comparison with real ornithology."[176] The essay was signed by 10 leading ornithologists besides Stone. They included William Brewster, who signed off on it but told Stone he didn't believe that egg collectors did as much damage as was attributed to them, and that the vast majority of eggs and nestlings succumbed to natural predators – but that he still found egg-hogs "despicable." He also estimated that domestic cats killed hundreds of thousands of birds a year in Massachusetts.[192]

The Pennsylvania Audubon Society printed the "Hints" essay as a pamphlet and distributed 10,000 copies.[193] It received wide circulation, and was mentioned in periodicals as remotely located as *The Wyoming Tribune*.[194] One Pennsylvania oologist, J. Warren Jacobs, needled Stone about it while asking for a copy: "I have heard so much about this paper I am sure it will interest me, for, while I am not a beginner, the thought occurred to me that, possibly, I was one of the old [egg] hogs and naturally wished to see the sort of sty I belonged to."[195]

The "Hints" pamphlet was commended in a *Condor* note as being practical and without "unnecessary sentiment."[196] However, the AOU report and the pamphlet incurred the wrath of J. Parker Norris Jr., who shared a huge egg collection with his father. Stone referred to the senior Norris (although not by name) in his pamphlet as an egg-hog for having 210 sets (917 eggs) of the Kentucky Warbler in his collection. (*The Condor* opined that the Norris warbler egg collection was "probably…the finest [= largest?] in America.")[197] The senior Norris had published his warbler egg numbers in *The Oölogist*, and Stone either got his numbers there or from William T. Hornaday's essay "The destruction of our birds and mammals," which took Norris to task by name.[198] Norris Jr. felt that in Stone's case it was a stab in the back from a friend.[199] He privately published a lengthy rebuttal in a pamphlet, in which he wrote, "I do not consider Mr. Witmer Stone the proper man to be at the head of any committee for bird protection, as he is neither sincere nor consistent." He defended his sizeable Kentucky Warbler egg collection on the grounds that (1) he was preparing to publish "an elaborate monograph on the breeding habits" of warblers, which would include "numerous colored plates of the eggs" (the monograph was never published) and (2) there was much more variation in bird eggs than in bird skins, so the former needed to be collected in greater numbers (e.g., he planned to show about 175 figures of eggs for each of several warbler species in his monograph, but thought that the Worm-eating Warbler's plumage variations could be covered with 12 to 15 skins).[200]

Norris argued that the Kentucky Warbler had actually increased in the area where he collected all his eggs, and that Thomas Jackson, another Chester County oologist, would vouch for that. However, Jackson told Stone that he hadn't discussed Kentucky Warbler numbers with Norris.[201] ANSP had just purchased Josiah Hoopes's bird collection, which Norris said contained "a drawerful" of Worm-eating Warbler skins collected over two seasons in Chester County, and that their numbers in the area had plummeted because of it. So who was Stone to criticize his egging when Stone was buying skins from someone who had decimated a local population to get them? The "drawerful," however, actually amounted to nine skins.[201] And if Worm-eating Warbler numbers were, in fact, declining in the area, Norris might have first pointed a finger at a couple of his fellow Chester County egg thieves. During the 1887 breeding season, Samuel Ladd literally walked until his feet were blistered in his pursuit of Worm-eating eggs, racking up 24 sets (!) totaling 113 eggs.[202] That blow to the local warbler population was in addition to Jackson's pilfering of at least 10 sets.[203] The West Chester area was a tough place to pull off a brood if you were a Worm-eating Warbler.

This was not the only time Mr. Norris took someone to task for criticizing the large numbers of eggs collected by him and others. The pages of ornithological journals often saw the feathers fly with accusations and rebuttals between him and others (e.g., his testy "A reply to the Rev. W.F. Henninger" in *The Osprey* – not even the clergy was safe), and Norris's pamphlet attacking Stone set the ornithological world atwitter.[204] AOU Member Ruthven Deane told Julia Robins that Norris's "tirade against Mr. Stone was quite as amusing as it was weak."[205] Charles Richmond was more sarcastic in a note to Stone: "I see J.P. Norris Jr. is out with a blue book denouncing the chairman of the AOU committee on bird protection! You have probably prevented his amassing a series of 917 eggs of the worm-eater & he is sore at not being able to show more than ½ the variation in that species."[206] Chester Barlow, the *Condor* editor, told Stone that Norris had published little of worth, considering the size of his collection, and Barlow correctly predicted that Norris would never finish the warbler monograph.[207] Stone read Norris's pamphlet to the DVOC at an October 1899 meeting, "calling particular attention to a number of misstatements made by Mr. Norris in his article."[208] Stone doubtless read it as much for the members' amusement as their instruction, and the guffaws must have been flying.[209]

In any case, Mr. Norris's defense was more earnest than convincing, and he softened his pique about Stone in later years: he became a DVOC member in 1916, the same year that Stone authored a commendatory *Auk* notice of his father's death, and in 1929, just before his own death, he supplied Stone with information the latter needed for a short writeup about Connecticut Warbler nests. The fabled, coveted, celebrated, condemned, notorious, and excessive (more than 100,000 eggs!) Norris collection was eventually divvied up and scattered after the death of the younger Norris.[210]

In his 1909 book *The Birds of New Jersey*, Stone again addressed the issue of excessive egg collecting by "so-called 'oologists'" and the impact it was having on local bird populations, noting that it had wiped out the breeding Osprey population of Seven Mile Beach, where they had formerly been numerous. He wrote, "Science does not countenance this sort of collecting and no good comes of it."[211] In the Least Bittern account, he criticized the harassment of the few remaining rookeries of the species in New Jersey by, among others, egg collectors, asking, "Of what possible good to science is the gathering of dozens of egg shells of a bird whose breeding habits have been known and described for a hundred years, and whose eggs have been measured over and over again!"[212] In a January 1914 talk to the DVOC, he asked, "[H]ow many ornithologists have watched a young bird emerge from an egg? Hundreds of thousands of young birds have been blown out of egg shells by so-called 'Oölogists' but a recent author has been able to find but two instances in American Ornithological literature where the natural hatching of a young bird has been described."[213]

In his *Auk* literature reviews he often made caustic comments about the lack of any worthwhile scientific insights being published by egg collectors. In one review of a study of egg incubation periods, he wisecracked that there had been few studies on the subject, "most oologists being more anxious to secure the egg shells intact than to ascertain how many days will elapse before the young break out of them."[214] Stone never softened his stance: at a 1936 DVOC meeting, after Fletcher Street had given a talk on "The Case of the Oologist," Stone offered that there was little of scientific value in the oological magazines "in spite of the fact that egg collecting permits were granted for scientific purposes."[215] In *BSOCM* he blamed eggers in part for the declines in Bald Eagles and Ospreys breeding in New Jersey.[216] However, Stone freely used the nest records of Turner McMullen and Richard Miller in *BSOCM*, and they made their living as eggers.[217]

───────── ❧ ─────────

Another bone of contention involving collecting in Stone's time was the reliability of sight records compared with collecting a bird for identification confirmation. Stone lived through the transition from collecting to sight records; the differences of opinion tended to split along generational lines, with the older ornithologists feeling that a specimen was the only indisputable proof of a record. In 1902, William Brewster, an avid collector, coauthored a complaint in *The Auk* that too many questionable sight records from unknown observers were being published.[218] Chapman wrote an interesting *Bird-Lore* editorial on the subject in 1902, arguing for the validity of sight records by wondering what the range of the mockingbird would be if every individual or nest found outside the "normal" range hadn't been collected, or how much more we might know about the mysterious Brewster's Warbler (a rare hybrid) if they weren't always shot on sight by ornithologists more interested in the bird dead than alive. Chapman stressed the need for reliable field identification, but ended with a thought that would be at odds with the current emphasis by modern birders on vagrants: "After all, the discovery of one new fact in the life history of the most common species is of greater importance than the capture, with glass or gun [or camera], of a bird which, like thousands of birds before it, has lost its way and wandered to parts uninhabited by its species."[219]

When Stone became *Auk* editor, one longtime AOU Fellow pointed out several instances of questionable sight records published recently in its pages and expressed the hope that the new editor would be more discriminating with them than the previous one.[220] Stone noted the unreliability of "sight records" in a July 1917 *Auk* "Correspondence" editorial, specifying two categories of concern: identifications of subspecies when the forms were difficult to differentiate in the field, and records of individuals from locations where they were rare or unknown. He said that dubious records had slipped into not only the minor journals (who "consider that all is grist that comes to their mill and publish any records" submitted), but the majors as well, and he urged editors to use criteria such as observer ability and viewing conditions in decisions about unlikely sight records.[221]

In November, Stone reiterated his comments on the topic in a talk at the AOU annual meeting, saying he'd only found one person who seemed to have read his July *Auk* comments. He stated that the rise in the number of bird students had the unavoidable consequence of increasing the number of questionable sight records; even common birds were misidentified by "persons with limited experience who feel that they have a mission to publish their observations to the world."[222] Stone's only interest in the unusual records was as material for local avifaunal lists, which he felt were of increasingly less importance anyway.[223]

The problem didn't disappear in Stone's lifetime, however. In one of the last *Auk*s he edited, he reviewed Ludlow Griscom's recent *Bird-Lore* article about the problems of sight identification, and Stone criticized the dilettantes and their ornithologically valueless daily lists and "big day" competitions.[224] He wrote in *BSOCM* that even though it was now possible, using binoculars, for an experienced observer to identify most birds, not everyone was so experienced or careful, and that the Christmas Bird Count (CBC) and similar efforts, "into which the spirit of rivalry enters," further made incorrect identifications likely.[182] (He expressed similar sentiments in *The Auk*.)[224] Stone had fueled that fire himself, however, with annual *Auk* notices of CBC results, invariably singling out the Cape May count as having one of the highest totals. He noted that for the 1929 count the Bronx Club had a higher total than the DVOCers at Cape May, "but did not confine its observations to the prescribed 15 mile diameter" – the lousy cheats![225] So much for concerns about the spirit of rivalry driving up the numbers.

Digital photography has made verification of sight records much easier, although records of vagrants have long since passed out of the serious ornithological literature and are now confined to listserves, birding magazines, state birding journals, and the like.

—————————— ∾ ——————————

Stone was in the middle of the drama and intrigue that surrounded the creation of Hawk Mountain Sanctuary in the 1930s. Hawks had been killed wantonly for decades – opportunistically at any season both by farmers who hung the carcasses in rows on barn walls, and "sportsmen" who saw them as competing for scarce game; and methodically, if mindlessly, by gunners at migration concentration points. At a 1904 DVOC meeting, Norris DeHaven reported a spring hawk migration site near Paterson, New Jersey where local gunners had recently shot 126 in one day.[226] Ruthven Deane told Stone of a fall flight in New England in 1908 with "everybody popping at them – my brother writes that one man in walking a ¼ mile counted 380 which had been shot. Don't know the species."[227] Long before hawk migration counters and photographers began using owl decoys to bring hawks in for a closer look, Justus von Lengerke, a wealthy proprietor of hunting and fishing equipment, used one (complete with moving head and wings) to shoot hawks by the bushel on the Kittatinny Ridge in Sussex County, New Jersey.[228-229] He told Stone that in the winter of 1916–17 he killed 16 Northern Goshawks; as of December 1926, he had killed 30 that winter, and had handled 75 killed by others.[230] Von Lengerke donated many of the hawks he shot to museums, including ANSP, and Stone was not only appreciative, but put in requests for desired species.[228,231] The PGC recorded 812 goshawks turned in for bounty between 1922 and 1933 (~68 per year).[232] At a December 1935 DVOC meeting, Richard Pough reported that more than 400 goshawks had been turned in to the

PGC for bounty in November, their peak fall migration month.[233] (That total sounds high, and may have included all birds turned in for the goshawk bounty, including other species misidentified by gunners.) At another DVOC meeting in early 1937 some hawk specimens were on display that had been sent by the PGC to the Academy the previous fall, including 20 goshawks and a few Red-shouldered Hawks. Someone (probably Stone) penciled into the margins of the minutes, "These represented about ⅒ of the number the Academy has received this Fall."[234] Cape May, of course, was another place where raptors were killed in great numbers each year.

These examples, some of which involve only one person, one day, or one location, are indicative of the barrage raptors faced at the time, particularly on migration, when a slaughter of hundreds of hawks on one day could represent the birds from thousands of acres of the breeding range of these low-density nesters. Maurice Broun wrote that before he became curator at Hawk Mountain he used to see only 40 to 50 hawks "in an entire year of active birding."[235] That sounds like an extraordinarily low number today, but it's easier to believe when you realize so many were being shot at the time that they were probably greatly reduced in at least some parts of their ranges.

Locals had been shooting hawks for years from a spot on the Kittatinny Ridge near Drehersville, Pennsylvania. The gunning locale had even been mentioned in the ornithological journals, beginning with references to it in a couple of articles by the PGC's George M. Sutton.[236] When Pough and Henry Collins reported the shooting, which they had just witnessed and photographed, to a joint meeting of the Linnaean Society and the NAAS in October 1933, along with the terms and contacts for buying the property where the shooting was done, the reaction of NAAS brass present led some at the meeting to assume that the NAAS planned to buy the property and end the slaughter.[237-238] Nothing had been done by the following spring, however, and Pough and Rosalie Edge, chair of the very small, but very active and effective, Emergency Conservation Committee (ECC), met with the real estate agent for the property, and Edge and the ECC soon had a lease with an option to buy. Pough later recalled, "What then followed was rather amusing. Mrs. Edge said that as the land was in Pennsylvania, she did not see why she, a New Yorker, had to raise the money. She said she thought the members of the DVOC ought to raise it. This I reported at the next meeting of the DVOC [October 4] and asked, 'How about it?'…[T]heir reaction was okay – if the Audubon Society would take over the project, as they had heard unfavorable reports about what they called that 'crazy' Mrs. Edge."[239-240]

The caveat about Audubon Society ownership doesn't seem to have been there from the beginning, however. The first two times the matter was brought up at DVOC meetings, the plan was to raise money for the purchase and give it to Edge and the ECC; Edge later asserted that Stone had told her just that in an October 1934 letter.[241,242] Club sentiment quickly shifted to a preference for NAAS ownership, however. John Baker, NAAS executive director, visited Philadelphia and the Drehersville location in early November; around dinner that evening DVOC members pledged the necessary funds, with Stone eventually holding the subscriptions after the DVOC formed a committee to raise the money.[239,243-244]

Baker contacted Edge after his Philadelphia visit and told her that the NAAS had the money necessary for the purchase if she would turn over to them her lease and option to buy. He said that the Philadelphia group had specified that its pledges were good only if the NAAS, which was an incorporated body with an endowment, made the purchase.[245] Edge, however, who was famously described by a colleague as an "indomitable hellcat," had other ideas. She had been wrangling with NAAS leaders for years, and didn't like the way they were running some of the sanctuaries they already had, so she had no intention of handing her lease over to them. That's when the fun started, and Witmer was caught in the crossfire.

He had known Edge for several years, and their relations were cordial. Edge had asked him in 1932 to consider being on the ECC's consulting board, but Stone politely refused, citing health issues.[246] He contributed $5 to the ECC in early 1934 – not a piddling sum during the Depression – so he must have admired the ECC's work.[247] He gave favorable reviews of ECC publications in The Auk.[248] Stone was one of the signers (along with many other DVOC members) of a petition in 1934 to have Edge admitted as an Associate member of the AOU.[249] Edge had tried to join for years, but animosity toward her among some of the AOU brass, probably because of her battles with the NAAS, was such that she was not admitted until 1938.[250] Longtime – and domineering – AOU secretary T.S. Palmer had issued a standing threat that the minute she was admitted he would resign, which probably had some in the AOU hoping they'd make her a Fellow.[251]

Baker asked Stone in mid-November 1934 to inform Edge that the money raised for Hawk Mountain's purchase had already been turned over to the NAAS, in an effort to get Edge to see the futility of the ECC attempting to purchase it, thus hastening her "capitulation." Stone replied that no money had been raised, only pledges, and they weren't earmarked for the NAAS but were being held for any organization meeting club approval that might eventually buy the property. He told Baker, however, that he hoped it would be the NAAS, and in an editorial blip in the next Auk he cajoled Edge to give the lease to "some permanent incorporated body" – an obvious reference to Audubon.[252] Clearly, by mid-November Stone and most of the DVOC had decided that Audubon was better placed to purchase and maintain Hawk Mountain.

Edge told Stone in December 1934 that the ECC had voted to form a trusteeship to run Hawk Mountain, and she invited Stone to be a trustee.

Anticipating what would prove to be a sticking point for Stone and others, she advised, "The financial responsibility would be negligible as the ECC would stand behind the project though the trust would be an independent entity."[253] The trust agreement, however, stated, "The trustees shall at all times pay within three months after same becomes due, taxes of whatever nature or description that may be assessed against the said premises," which could have been open to an interpretation that the trustees would ultimately be on the hook for the finances. It also stipulated that should the trusteeship fail, the property would revert to the Pennsylvania SPCA, and, should that arrangement fail, to the state of Pennsylvania.[254] The SPCA seems like a curious choice, although in 1932 it had provided, at Pough's request, technicians to euthanize hawks at Hawk Mountain that had been mortally wounded by the gunners.[255]

In early 1935, Stone told Edge that health issues forced him to decline a trustee position; he also said he was no businessman and recommended Pough instead.[256] He was concerned about the provision that the property could ultimately revert to the state, because the PGC had always been in favor of shooting, not protecting, raptors.[257] He also told her that the DVOC Hawk Mountain Committee, which he chaired, would meet soon to discuss the trust arrangement and "just how much funds are available under this arrangement."[256]

Edge referred to the Baker–DVOC meeting in November 1934 as the "Affair of the Supper Party." On February 8, 1935 there was another interesting supper party, which might be called "Affair of the Supper Party II." "Mrs. [Eliza M.?] Cope" of Germantown held a dinner to give Edge an opportunity to pitch her vision for Hawk Mountain to a gathering of Philadelphia gentlefolk."[238,258] Witmer and Lillie attended, along with Pough and soon-to-be Hawk Mountain trustee A. Brazier Howell. Witmer reported the particulars to John Baker a few days later:

> Howell outlined the plan of forming a Board of Trustees to take over the title. Then quite naturally someone asked why some existing incor-porated body should not take it over and someone else suggested the Audubon Society! Then the fat was in the fire. She said Hawk Mt. was her child and she was not going to give it up....She was then asked by several lawyers present as to the details of her trust arrangement and it developed that it was a very flimsy plan at present but after the Trustees had signed up to take over all responsibility the details could be altered or elaborated! The upshot of the whole matter was that an audience predisposed to be friendly to anything she suggested was pretty well convinced that her plan was impracticable and as our Com-mittee [i.e., the DVOC Hawk Mountain Committee] had raised the money once it did not seem worthwhile to raise it again.[259]

Stone told Baker that he would ask the subscribers whether they wanted their money to go to Edge and her trusteeship; he thought they wouldn't, but he would maintain their subscriptions in case Edge decided to let NAAS acquire the lease/option.

On the morning after the dinner, Edge met with two wealthy Philadelphia men, Frank Foster and ANSP's Charles Cadwalader, about the $1,000 they controlled for the Hawk Mountain purchase. They told her that they would have nothing to do with the trustee proposition, which led to her remarking to Stone, "They would give more money to the Audubon Society because it already has $1.7 million and so commands their respect. They would give nothing to the ECC which has only a record of work accomplished to its credit."[259-261]

Edge realized by then that the Philadelphia money was slipping away, and she asked Stone for a list of the people who had pledged money for Hawk Mountain – pledges that, in at least some cases, were intended only for the NAAS or some similarly large, incorporated body.[261] Stone, of course, was not about to provide her with such a list, and the request initiated some comical cat-and-mouse moves between Stone and Edge: she kept asking for the list, and Stone kept offering to send the DVOC membership list, cagily telling her that most of the people who made pledges could be found there.[242,262] At one point, Edge suddenly asked for not only the list of donors, but also their pledge amounts – that request, of course, went nowhere.[242] By mid-March, Edge knew that the pledges raised by the Philadelphia group were not coming to her, and she wrote to Stone, "Do I understand that after writing me so kindly in October that you would collect money among the DVOC members to help the ECC buy Hawk Mountain that nothing further is to be done in this matter?"[242]

Edge soldiered on, though, and by the end of 1935 she had raised the necessary amount on her own to buy the Hawk Mountain property. The land was acquired, kinks such as property boundaries were worked out, the gunners went elsewhere (unfortunately, hawks were still shot at other places along the ridge for many years), crowds started showing up on fall weekends armed with binoculars and cameras instead of shotguns, and Hawk Mountain Sanctuary was on its way. Edge's maligned trusteeship went into place and served well enough for the first few years until the Hawk Mountain Sanctuary Association was incorporated.

In August 1936, Stone learned that hell hath no fury like a hellcat feeling scorned. In May, Edge had asked him for an *Auk* review of the latest version of the ECC pamphlet *Framing the Birds of Prey*. Stone obliged by writing a favorable review in the July issue (giving it publicity in the process), but concluded by wondering why the annual hawk slaughter at Cape May had not been mentioned in the publication. This brought on a mid-August missive (missile?) from Edge, who started things off by saying that a mutual friend had recently told her that Stone's "feelings were hurt" by the lack of a mention of the Cape

May Witmer Stone sanctuary in *Framing the Birds of Prey* – the first of two affected references to Stone's supposedly wounded feelings. She said that the ECC had wanted to include something about the sanctuary, but the idea had been opposed by Warren Eaton of the NAAS organ The Hawk and Owl Society. He was concerned that efforts to get a law passed banning hawk shooting from New Jersey highways (drafted with Cape May Point's Sunset Boulevard in mind) might be hampered if the Cape May sanctuary was portrayed in *Framing* as a hawk haven. Edge then pretended to try to assuage Stone's "hurt feelings," but her sarcastic, vindictive tone is unmistakable in the masterpiece of fact bending, disingenuous flattery, and subtle digs that followed:

> No one appreciates more keenly than I do that you deserve recognition from the Audubon Society for diverting to them the money you collected for us; but I had not guessed how much naming the Sanctuary after you meant to you. Your name represents so much that is fine that its inscription in one or another place can add very little to its glory. You appreciate, of course, that I have never shown to anyone your letters to me, telling me that you were collecting the money for us. It is always sad to us conservationists that men in scientific institutions are forced to yield to political pressure. Believe me, we have a most sympathetic understanding of their ["your"] difficulties.
>
> You told me that your health would not permit you to climb Hawk Mountain. I do wish, however, that you could drive up there…and sit by the trail and greet your friends. I am sure that you would be delighted and encouraged at the interest and enthusiasm displayed in hawk protection. Mr. [Henry W.] Shoemaker has told me how he appealed to you to preserve Hawk Mountain…but that you were not able to do anything to preserve the hawks at that time. This was the period when Dr. Sutton was so gaily shooting hawks at Hawk Mountain…Time marches on – and at Hawk Mountain it marches in the right direction.[263]

Edge's claim that a mutual friend told her that Stone's feelings were hurt, and her jab at his supposed vanity about the sanctuary name, are unconvincing. The friend must have made reference to Stone's *Auk* review, and there's no petulancy anywhere in that, only Stone rightly pointing out the inexplicability of a pamphlet about current raptor protection efforts not mentioning the work at Cape May. The whole Cape May situation was probably a sore spot for Edge to begin with: it was her nemesis the NAAS, after all, that was doing all the work there (Hawk Mountain curator Maurice Broun once told Edge that her hatred of the NAAS amounted to a mania), and the New Jersey Audubon Society had provided funds for the Cape May work, but had reportedly refused to do so for Edge's Hawk Mountain purchase.[243] Either she hadn't read the *Auk* review of *Framing*, or she had and was deliberately distorting it, because Stone, with every opportunity to do so, didn't even mention the Cape May sanctuary. In fact, Edge was probably irritated that the review, although favorable and published at her behest, ended with a reference to "the good work of the NAAS" at Cape May.[264]

I have never located Stone's October 1934 letter to Edge, but certainly by mid-November, at least, he was up front about the fact that money was being pledged for the purchase of Hawk Mountain, not for the ECC specifically, and that the Philadelphia pledgers, who assumed that the NAAS would buy the property, were uneasy with the thought of it being managed by the ECC. That, and not "political pressure," was why the pledges were never collected, and the accusation (made twice) that Stone personally diverted money collected for the ECC was untrue. And although Sutton, in his 1928 *Wilson Bulletin* article, reported examining hawks that were shot while migrating along the ridge that would be the future home of Hawk Mountain, there is no indisputable evidence that he personally shot any – happily or otherwise – although he certainly didn't register any objection to the activity.

Seventeen months after expressing to Stone her feeling of betrayal over the failure of the Philadelphia pledges to be redeemed for her, Edge was obviously still smarting, and now that the ECC owned the property and appeared to be free of the need for Philadelphia/DVOC funds, Edge was letting Stone know that hellcats, like elephants, never forget. But at the end of the day, bully for Edge. She stirred decisive action at Hawk Mountain while the NAAS executives twiddled their thumbs, and she made heroic fundraising efforts to get the area purchased and protected. She stuck to her guns in maintaining complete ECC control of Hawk Mountain, and one cannot contemplate the sanctuary and its history and not recognize that her instincts were dead-on. The naysayers, John Baker, all the potential donors who didn't have faith or trust in her or her blueprint for the sanctuary's future, the Blue Mountain locals who were angry at outsiders for coming in and meddling with their hawk shoots – Rosalie Edge gets the last laugh over all of them. Even though we'll never know how the subsequent Hawk Mountain story would have played out if the NAAS had bought the property, the sanctuary's long, inspiring history began with a plan and a setup based on Edge's ideas and convictions. Her picture of just what she wanted "her child" to be when it grew up was presciently painted in a 1935 letter to Stone that not only reads as a forceful crystallization of Edge's vision for Hawk Mountain, but also shows her at her persuasive, fund-raising best. Note also her defense of her trusteeship idea, and the references to the NAAS and its policies:

> We want Hawk Mountain not to be merely so-many acres from which trespassers are excluded but a centre from which shall radiate the spirit of bird and animal protection.
>
> We want it to be a mecca for bird-students. Also, a place where those who are opposed to us in principle will be kindly received (only

they must leave their guns in their cars!) and persuaded to think over the benefits to be derived from the protection of hawks and other predators.

We want our Trustees to be the nucleus of a group that shall lead in the movement of a new kind of sanctuary – the sanctuary that shall maintain ecological conditions and not be for the protection of one species at the expense of others [a reference to the NAAS policy of fur trapping at its Rainey Sanctuary in Louisiana].

We want a group alert to extend the movement for hawk protection and for better sanctuaries for all species, to advance, to lead.

A small group of earnest and enthusiastic people can do these things. It is seldom that a big established organization is alert and keen to seize every opportunity for service.

We feel that Hawk Mountain, the world's first sanctuary for the birds of prey, deserves its own organization – that as a separate entity it will better make its demonstration and lead other groups [i.e., NAAS] to greater and more intelligent activity.[265]

Rosalie Edge richly deserves the accolades for her Hawk Mountain efforts, even if the NAAS wasn't actually as nefarious and ineffective as she charged and Witmer Stone didn't really renege on promised funds. Collins and Pough were the early sleuths who got the word out, and Pough (who went on to be one of the 20th century's most important conservationists) helped Edge get the lease; Stone and the DVOC thought it was a worthwhile cause that they were willing to assist financially, and many members contributed funds for its maintenance after it was established; the NAAS eventually, belatedly acted; Willard van Name was an important adviser for Edge and put up early money – but the catalyst was Rosalie Edge. She had the vision, the passion, the urgency, and the industry to end the slaughter at that location and bring Hawk Mountain Sanctuary into existence.[266]

Witmer Stone never visited Hawk Mountain, and his heart condition at the time certainly would have precluded him hiking up to the North Lookout. Despite the ruffled feathers with Edge, Stone was undoubtedly pleased at the protection offered to migrating raptors by the sanctuary, and would be delighted with the crowds that throng the spot each fall, aiming cameras and sometimes even applause at the passing hawks. Stone was an interested, if not always an overly active, conservationist. With his PAS and AOU bird protection committee work at the turn of the 20th century, he was unquestionably among the leaders in the movement that led to the formation of the NAAS. But battlefront conservation work doesn't seem to have suited his personality, and after resigning from the AOU protection committee he focused his efforts on work that was more narrowly scientific.

6

The Beautiful Science

Witmer Stone was interested in birds from childhood, and is rightly remembered today primarily as an ornithologist. He had a long association with the American Ornithologists' Union (AOU). He was elected an Associate in 1885, and, with Spencer Trotter, attended his first annual meeting in 1889 in New York.[1] There he met many distinguished contemporary ornithologists for the first time, including C. Hart Merriam, Edgar Mearns, Robert Ridgway, J. A. Allen, Frank Chapman, D.G. Elliot, and William Brewster.

In a 1923 talk to the Nuttall Ornithological Club, Stone related how much of an effect Brewster had on him in subsequent years. He said, "[T]he inspiration that I received from William Brewster I cannot adequately express," and of their correspondence, "I treasure [it] as one of my most valuable possessions."[2] He even had a photo of Brewster over the desk at home at which he sat to do *Auk* work.[3] Stone sent the dying Brewster a letter while on a trip to Arizona in 1919, but it arrived at Brewster's Cambridge home too late. Stone's feelings were not unique. Frederic Kennard, an amateur ornithologist in Cambridge, wrote to Stone on the day of Brewster's funeral that he wished he had been able to know the reserved Brewster better, adding, "But I believe I thought more of him and his opinions than any man I ever knew except my own Father."[4] Those sentiments were echoed by Merriam, who told Stone, "Brewster was one of the men who leave a hole that can never be filled."[5] Charles Batchelder recalled Brewster running Nuttall Club meetings, when his "Jove-like presence, his deliberate manner and his judicial attitude of mind, gave him an impressiveness that was not to be trifled with."[6]

Stone seems to have also had a great rapport with the other older ornithologists, which isn't surprising given his disposition and his respect and affection for ornithological history. His fortuitous meeting at the Academy in 1898 with septuagenarian Dr. Samuel Woodhouse brought that eminent explorer and naturalist out of seclusion and into not only the DVOC, where he became a much-admired elder statesman, but the AOU as well; he was able to spend the last years of his life enjoying the company of fellow naturalists who looked up to him as a near-legendary link to the ornithologists of old.[7] Stone also struck up a ten-year correspondence with British ornithologist Alfred Newton, sending his author separates to Newton until the elder ornithologist's death in 1907. Newton was a founding member of the British Ornithologists' Union and edited its journal *The Ibis* 1865–1870, but Stone probably also regarded

Newton, who had met with Cassin on an 1857 visit to Philadelphia, as a living link to the Academy's storied ornithological past.[8]

Another individual on whom Stone made an impression was longtime AOU secretary John Sage, almost 20 years Stone's senior. On one of his first trips to Philadelphia, Sage perused Stone's incipient library and noticed that Stone was missing the first two volumes of *The Auk*, which were out of print and hard to come by. Stone received a package the following Christmas from Sage containing the needed volumes, and a note that read, "I have fed these birds for many years and think they are in proper condition for your Christmas dinner. Please accept them with my compliments."[9] The kindly Sage recognized how much the junior ornithologist would appreciate and use the prized journals. Years later, Stone spearheaded the production of a bound book of appreciative letters from all living AOU Fellows, with a frontispiece by Louis Agassiz Fuertes, to mark the occasion of Sage's 25th year as AOU secretary.[9-10] Stone also authored Sage's *Auk* memorial.

In 1890, Stone attended the AOU annual meeting in Washington, D.C. and announced the formation of the DVOC. He also read a paper for the first time at an AOU meeting, presenting "A study of bird waves in the Delaware Valley during the spring migration of 1890," and was encouraged when Merriam had high praise for his system of recording the migration.[11-12] (Ernest Thompson Seton had read a Stone paper on charting migration at the 1888 meeting in Stone's absence.)[13]

Stone, only 26, was elected an AOU Fellow in 1892.[14] In 1896, he told Brewster that he wouldn't be able to attend the upcoming annual meeting in Cambridge, adding, "I trust you will not consider it any lack of interest in the work of the AOU, as I should like nothing better than to be able to take a more active part in its work."[15] Little did he know then how many chances he would get, and he grabbed most of them. He was a member of the Council 1898–1913, a vice president 1914–1920, and president 1920–1923. He served on several committees of various sizes and importance over the years, including the Committee on Protection of North American Birds 1895–1901 (chairman 1898–1901), and the Committee on Classification and Nomenclature of North American Birds 1901–1931 (chairman 1915–1931).[16] His interest in bibliography led him to participate in AOU efforts to index *The Auk* and its precursor, the *Bulletin of the Nuttall Ornithological Club*.[17] Last but not least, Stone edited the AOU's journal *The Auk* for 25 years, beginning in 1912. Wishing to support the AOU, which he felt had given him "about all the honors at its disposal," Stone became a life member in 1922, and Lillie, who joined as an Associate in 1920, became a life member in 1936.[18]

The AOU held seven of its annual meetings in Philadelphia during Stone's lifetime.[19] The DVOC had been hankering to host a Philadelphia AOU annual

meeting since at least 1894; the vibrant activity of the Academy's ornithological section, especially the restorative work being done with the historic collection, undoubtedly encouraged the AOU to accept the invitation to hold its
annual meeting in Philadelphia for the first time in 1899.[20] An editorial in *The
Osprey* before the meeting described the decline of the Academy's bird collection and the recent resurgence led by Stone, who, it was hoped, would "take
the place in Philadelphia so long ago vacated by Cassin."[21] Witmer's *Auk* pitch
for attendance at the 1916 Philadelphia meeting, with a description of the
social and historical amenities to be taken advantage of, revealed a salesman's
streak, and he always sent personal notes to leading (and lesser) ornithologists
inviting them to attend Philadelphia meetings.[22] Stone and the DVOC made
sure to introduce the visiting ornithologists to their favorite haunts. The 1916
and 1921 meetings featured trips to the New Jersey Pine Barrens (in both
years, AOU Fellows were invited to the New Lisbon cabin owned by DVOC
members), and 165 attendees took a special train trip to Cape May during the
October 1929 meeting, where they rang up 102 species.[23] Alexander Wetmore
was amazed at the total, and told Stone, "I remarked to [James] Peters that it
was a day on which the birds at Cape May could expect little privacy."[24] Imagine how violated they must feel today on a busy Cape May autumn weekend.

Echoing the sentiments of others, AOU founder Batchelder told Stone
on more than one occasion that the Philadelphia meetings were the best. In
fact, in 1916 he told Stone in advance of the meeting that he was so ill he
feared if he attended he would leave Philadelphia midweek in an ambulance;
he nearly did, for he attended anyway and was bedridden with bronchitis as
soon as he returned home – but he told Stone it was worth it.[25] Conversely, the
prospect of the first Philadelphia meeting in 1899 had a restorative effect on
Brewster, who wrote to Stone three days before the meeting that he was too
sick to attend. Stone scrawled a note at the bottom of the letter: "But at the
last minute he changed his mind & arrived in Phila. before the letter!"[26] Joseph
Grinnell said in 1915 that Stone's "joviality and social qualifications have made
Philadelphia famous as headquarters for successful AOU meetings."[27] Robert
Cushman Murphy of the AMNH, trying to cook up something amusing for
the upcoming 1933 AOU meeting being held in New York, told Stone, "Our
principal problem seems to be to devise anything half as amusing as the stunts
arranged by our Philadelphia hosts. Your meetings seem to stick in everybody's
memory as high spots."[28]

By contrast, the first time the meeting was held on the other side of the
state, in what Stone referred to as "the Smoky City," Kennard told him, "I
think we all had a mighty good time in Pittsburgh, but what a God-forsaken
hole! Please don't railroad us down there again."[29] Stone protested that he had
nothing to do with the selection, and it was close enough to the Washington–
Philadelphia–New York–Cambridge corridor that the meeting was held there

again in 1936.[30] Kennard was ill and a few months from his death at that point, so missed out on one last visit to the God-forsaken hole.

It's easy to assume that AOU meetings circa 1920 were decorous, staid gatherings. The group photos that survive don't suggest otherwise, with rows of serious-looking aristocratic gents in formal attire, but in sending his regrets to Stone for his inability to attend the 1916 meeting in Philadelphia, Kennard, who was present at these things and we weren't, makes you wonder what else might have been going on: "I wanted to listen to some of the classics perpetuated by Fisher, Nelson and Chapman, et al. Possibly you will 'can' some of those stories for me, and if not too outrageous, please try and perpetuate some of the yarns from those rough-necks Fuertes and Job. Buy them all a little Scotch on my account and send me the bill, but for heaven's sakes keep Fuertes off the table top until the ladies have gone to bed."[31]

The AOU celebrated its 50th anniversary in 1933, toward the end of Stone's active involvement in the organization. Chapman, probably to his everlasting regret, proposed at the 1930 AOU Council meeting that the union produce a volume to mark the occasion. The Council appointed a committee of Chapman, Stone, and T.S. Palmer to draw up a plan for such a work.[32] Authors were solicited to write chapters on various topics of importance in American ornithology since the AOU's founding; Chapman, for example, would write about museum collections, and Stone on ornithological literature. But by early 1933, funds were short, and for some of the authors, at least, it felt like a homework assignment. Stone griped to Chapman in January that the whole project should be scrapped due to finances, and that Palmer, who was then seen as the driving force behind it, should just publish a pamphlet for the occasion: "The proposed volume would not sell & there are a stack of Check Lists unsold!" Stone and Wetmore hadn't even begun work on their chapters yet.[33] Stone vented at poor Palmer in March, saying he was "all at sea" about it, asking Palmer who was in charge, who should write what, and whether the volume would even follow the earlier plans or just be a short memorial to the founders. Stone said he wasn't sure he could produce a manuscript "at this eleventh hour," but a month later he was telling Peters, "I have not had any enthusiasm about that memorial volume but suppose I must do my bit soon."[34]

He continued to waffle, however, as he headed to Cape May for the summer, saying that he couldn't write anything there without his library at hand. He eventually produced a thorough, if uninspired and tedious, review of American ornithological literature since the AOU's inception.[35] He got more involved as the effort came down to the wire, serving as point of contact for the printer and reading proofs. Somehow in the lapse of time it had been forgotten that Stone had been on the original committee, and Chapman and Palmer, neither of whom wanted to own up to being in charge of the project, welcomed his help.[36] In the end, however, Stone, for whatever reason, told Palmer not to list him as being on the committee, and Palmer complied.[37] Chapman sent some articles to Stone for the printer in October, grumbling, "[T]he Jubilee Volume – was there ever any publication more misnamed?...I confess that I never wrote anything with less pleasure, or felt that it was more inadequate, than the one I am sending you."[38]

Whatever birthing pangs were involved in the volume's production, it serves today as an interesting historical reflection, from some of the principals involved, on the occasion of an important anniversary in American ornithological history. The authors are a mix of older ornithologists and some of the younger ones (Herbert Friedmann, Arthur A. Allen, George Miksch Sutton) who would soon be among the leaders in the field.[39]

Stone did quite a bit of original research early in his ornithological career, and his publications on migration, taxonomy, molt, and the Academy bird collection were important contributions to what he referred to as "the beautiful science."[40] His lifelong wonder with migration is discernable in a remark to a newspaper reporter in 1936 that "young birds leave their birthplace in the north and journey thousands of miles to winter homes they never have seen, traveling on their own initiative and without guidance, and in the following spring return to the spot from which they started."[41] From 1883 to 1889, Stone and Herbert and Stewardson Brown submitted their local bird migration records to the U.S. Dept. of Agriculture's Division of Economic Ornithology; after 1890, Stone sent the DVOC migration reports instead.[42] His first contribution to *The Auk* was a note about flocks of migrating hawks he witnessed over Germantown on two separate days in late September 1886.[43] Stone thought that several species of hawks were involved, but they were too high for him to identify positively. He might not have had binoculars at hand at the time he spotted the birds, but 50 years later he still referred to those flights as being at "a great height."[44] The birds were certainly mostly or all Broad-winged Hawks, which migrate through Pennsylvania in flocks in the second half of September.

Some of Stone's early contributions to *The Auk* were articles about making graphs to record migration.[45] His *Auk* announcement of the formation of the DVOC mostly covered its efforts at monitoring the spring migration; the first publication of the DVOC stated that "the primary objective of the Club during the first year of its existence was the recording and comparison of data relating to [local] bird migration" and that "many of the meetings of 1890 were devoted entirely to the discussion of the local migration."[46-47] At the October 20, 1890 DVOC meeting, Stone gave a talk on the local spring migration of 1890, using data collected by club members, and speculated on the likely flight paths of migrants through the region.[47] He gave the same talk a month later at the annual AOU meeting.[11]

Stone felt that the published migration records in *Cassinia* were a great lasting contribution of the club.[48] Early issues, starting with Volume 6 in 1902, contained reports compiled by Stone on the Delaware Valley spring migration, based on data submitted by dozens of local observers. Each observer kept data for the area in which they lived (their "station"), and Stone was always on the lookout for potential observers. Rachel Allinson was recruited after sending Stone detailed notes about a Long-eared Owl roost by her house in Yardville, New Jersey, and was a regular until her death in 1915.[49] The famous architect Frank Miles Day, of Art Club of Philadelphia fame, was also a participant.[50] William Fair sent Stone a note expressing an interest in birds and was immediately roped in for spring migration duty. It doesn't seem that Stone was concerned about level of expertise – maybe he just took whatever came along and hoped for the best, and Fair couldn't tell a dead goshawk from a Peregrine Falcon.[51] Stone must have figured that if anything too unusual turned up in someone's observations he could just reject it. In taking Edward Forbush to task in an *Auk* review for not weeding out questionable sightings from a migration report, Stone wrote that he knew "from personal experience what a large proportion of the records submitted by a miscellaneous lot of observers has to be ignored in preparing a record of scientific value."[52]

The willingness of potential recruits for this endeavor undoubtedly varied, but at one end of the spectrum would be Charles C. Abbott, who wrote to Stone in early 1909 that his blank spring migration chart, which Stone mailed to all participants, had not yet arrived: "This is well as I'm damned tired of having any task set before me such as it suggests. If it was an oversight or the chart went astray in the mail, <u>do not</u> try it again. It won't hurt the birds' feelings."[53] Alas, 1909 was the last year C.C. Abbott was listed as a contributing observer. (In his *Auk* notice of Abbott's death in 1920, Stone wrote that he "was of very peculiar temperament and caustic in his comments so that he made enemies or rather drove away many who would have been fast friends.")[54]

Similar efforts weren't made with the fall migration, the unconvincing excuse being too few observers afield in the fall.[55] The real reason can be discerned in Stone's 1889 *Auk* article concerning his pre-DVOC studies of the spring migration in Germantown: "Similar observations were carried on in the fall, but owing to the difficulty in recognizing many species at that season on account of the thick foliage of the trees, the results were much less accurate and therefore less interesting."[56] The trees leaf out earlier in some springs than in others, but the invariably thick late summer/early autumn foliage does hamper efforts to get good looks at the southbound passerines. However, the difficulty of identifying some species in their nonbreeding plumage, particularly "confusing fall warblers," at a time when distinguishing field marks had yet to be worked out, might have had as much to do with the spring emphasis as obscuring foliage.[57] Spring migrants can also be detected and identified by their songs; fall birds rarely sing. In 1927, Stone wrote that spring migration still fascinated him, with no mention of any interest in the fall version.[58] There is a curious dearth of warbler records in *BSOCM*; Cape May was and is one of the best places in North America to see them during fall migration, which suggests that Stone wasn't putting in much time looking for them there.

Stone thought that having the *Cassinia* migration observers count (or estimate) the number of individuals of each species on each date would be beyond the abilities or time constraints of most, and that numbers of individuals for a given species across all stations would increase dramatically on weekends and holidays because of more observers afield, making it appear that there was a migratory push on those dates when there may not have actually been. Instead, he had observers simply record the arrival dates (the first date seen at their location) for each species. Of course, arrival dates might be clustered around weekends and holidays as well, or on days with the best weather. For example, in the 1907 report he wrote about four dates in March when there was a spike in temperature, and two-thirds of the March arrivals were recorded on those days or the one that followed.[59] Although a warm southerly flow may certainly have caused an influx of new arrivals, it could have also induced more birders to be out in the field on those days. In the 1913 report he noted that April was rainy until the 17th, with a "marked migratory movement" on April 18–19, and another on April 25–26 and again on the April 30. May 3–4 saw an "enormous migratory movement."[60] However, the end of the rain in mid-April probably brought the birders out en masse, and April 18–19 and 25–26 and May 3–4 were weekends. But these are the problems that bedevil any "citizen science" study of the sort, when it's difficult to control for variables such as consistency of effort.

In the early years of the project, Stone looked for (and thought he saw) differences in arrival dates between southern and northern locations around Philadelphia. He discontinued this comparison after a few years, and later said the differences at such a small spatial scale were negligible and due to happenstance as much as anything else.[61] Thereafter, he simply compared the current year's bulk arrival dates (i.e., the first date on which a species was found at half or more of the stations, not just the first date an individual was detected at any station) with previous years. The effort peaked in 1914, when 80 observers turned in reports, but interest – including Stone's – waned after that. The published reports grew increasingly shorter and were discontinued after the 1929–30 *Cassinia*. Stone and his observer teams put a great deal of work into the DVOC spring migration reports, and they shouldn't be overlooked as the best data set we have for spring migration in the Philadelphia area during the early 20th century.

In a fascinating 1906 *Auk* article, Stone reported a March 27 flight of nocturnal migrants he detected by the light of a conflagration at the McIlvain lumber yard near his home in West Philadelphia.[62] An electrical short circuit started a fire that burned 12 million board feet of lumber and caused $350,000 in damages.[63] Reportedly, "the glare in the sky, which was almost prismatic, ranging from blood orange to pale yellow, was visible at points twenty miles from the scene," and "anxious inquiries were received from points as far distant as the New Jersey shore."[63-64] Stone wrote that "the nature of the fuel produced a tremendous illumination with very little smoke – practically none of the dense black clouds that usually accompany fires in a large city," making conditions ideal to spot anything flying over the fire.

He first noted bats and House Sparrows, which had likely been roosting in the lumber yard structures, flying around the fire. Soon he detected migrating birds, heading southwest to northeast, and at the flight's peak at 10 p.m., he estimated there were 200 birds in view at any given moment. He thought most of them were passerines (and later identified some remains of juncos and Song Sparrows found at the scene); he presumed some heavier-bodied birds were woodcocks or rails. He was able to positively identify a Sharp-shinned Hawk circling over the fire and a flock of Common Mergansers flying east, probably heading from the Schuylkill River to a reservoir in Fairmount Park. Some of the birds passed low enough over the fire that they caught fire themselves, and "a slender thread of silvery smoke came trailing out from the unfortunate bird, like the unfurling of a skein of yarn; it would fly wildly and then, bursting into flame, fall into the roaring furnace below. I saw twenty or thirty birds perish thus during the evening." Stone watched until only 11 p.m., but heard later that the flight continued until at least midnight.

I was transfixed the first time I read the article, and I wasn't the only one. Stone must have been thrilled by the letter he received from fellow migration aficionado William Brewster:

> May I offer you my hearty congratulations on what I consider to be one of the most interesting and best written articles on birds that I have ever read. I refer, of course, to your "Some Light on Bird Migration" in the July Auk. Your observations are intrinsically of thrilling interest and profound information and you have done them full justice in your manner of reporting them. Indeed you have told the story so picturesquely and effectively and with such exquisite literary taste and finish that the reading of it must be to anyone who is appreciative of such perfect composition, a great delight. Even now then let me congratulate you on the production of an article which will be regarded, if I am not mistaken, as one of the most notable and admirable papers that have appeared for very many years.[65]

Stone remained interested in migration, and studied it during his summers at Cape May later in life. *BSOCM*, of course, contained data and theories about fall migration at that location, both in the species accounts (e.g., flicker and Eastern Kingbird) and in some of the essays (e.g., "Bird Migration at the Cape" and "The Autumn Hawk Flights").

Stone was interested in the molt of birds throughout his career as an ornithologist. His first paper on the subject was "The study of molting in birds" in *Science* in 1893.[66] Stone laid out the basic types of molt patterns, and lamented the lack of skins available from the molting period for most birds. That article later became the basis for his monumental "The molting of birds with special reference to the plumages of the smaller land birds of eastern North America" in 1896, in which he gave an overview of molt, then discussed families and species for which he had examined sufficient numbers of skins to draw conclusions.[67] The state of knowledge of the molts of birds was primitive enough at the time that Stone actually spent several pages refuting the notion, still being espoused by some contemporary ornithologists, that the seasonal changes in the plumages of some birds were due to the feathers actually changing color, not to their being replaced. (He was still refuting it in an *Ibis* article in 1901 – European ornithologists were apparently slow to give up pet theories.)[68] An *Auk* reviewer of the paper referred to it as an "important paper on a hitherto almost neglected branch of American ornithology," and added, "Mr. Stone deserves great credit for the present paper, which is a good basis on which to build a better knowledge of plumage changes."[69]

In 1897, Stone published "On the annual molt of the Sanderling."[70] He noted "the great variation in the time of the molt" of the skins examined, but the specimens came from a variety of locations in the U.S. and Britain, and it hadn't yet been discovered that the timing of the postbreeding molt varies for different populations of Sanderlings depending on their wintering grounds.[71]

In 1844, English naturalist Charles Waterton referred to the mysterious postbreeding molt of drake Mallards, when their plumage is quite similar to the females', as a period when the "drake goes, as it were, into an eclipse."[72] In 1899, Stone addressed this "eclipse" plumage (although never referring to it by that term) in "The summer molting plumage of certain ducks." In examining birds collected by Edward McIlhenny at Point Barrow, Alaska, Stone realized that Red-breasted Mergansers and four species of eiders (Pacific [Common], Spectacled, King, and Steller's) could be added to the list of waterfowl in which the eclipse plumage occurred. He reasoned that, because the dull plumage is acquired while drakes of many species are flightless due to the simultaneous molting of all the flight feathers, "a dull blended plumage would naturally be important in rendering the bird inconspicuous and thereby protecting it, and such I think is the explanation for this curious summer molt."[73]

J.A. Allen, in his *Auk* review of the paper, thought Stone had "clearly described" and explained the reason for the peculiar plumage for the first time (and the explanation is still accepted today). However, a few years earlier Alfred Newton had offered a similar, if less succinct, explanation in *A Dictionary of Birds*, writing, "Most of the…Ducks, Geese and Swans, shed their quill-feathers all at once, and become absolutely incapable of flight for a season, during which time they generally seek the shelter of thick aquatic herbage, and….the males…at the same period lose the brilliantly-colored plumage…to resume their gay attire only when, their new quills being grown, it can be safely flaunted in the open air."[75] Stone gave two talks on molt at the AOU meeting in Philadelphia in 1899: "The Summer Molting Plumages of Eider Ducks" and "The Molt of the Flight Feathers in Various Orders of Birds"– further evidence of the attention he was devoting to the subject at the time.[76]

Another contemporary ornithologist studying molts was Jonathan Dwight; Stone wrote a favorable and thorough review in *The Auk* of Dwight's 1900 paper, "The sequence of plumages and molts of the passerine birds of New York," which expanded on Stone's "The molting of birds" paper.[77] Stone's molt publications petered out around the turn of the century, but Dwight continued his studies and publications and was probably considered the leading authority on the subject of molts and plumages among American ornithologists at the time.[78]

By the time he started editing *The Auk*, Stone had earned a reputation as one of the country's leading ornithologists. An informal Cooper Ornithological Club poll in 1916 placed Stone among the top five American ornithologists "in terms of scientific output." (Another poll ranked popularizers of ornithology.)[79] He also eventually had an international reputation enhanced by his Academy work and his long *Auk* editorship. He was one of a few American ornithologists consulted for R. Bowdler Sharpe's *Hand List of the Genera and Species of Birds*, starting with Volume 2 in 1900, indicating that he already had international standing at that time.[80] He was elected to honorary membership in the British, French, Dutch, and Hungarian ornithological societies, and was awarded the Hungarian organization's Otto Hermann Medal in 1931 for "outstanding work in the science of ornithology, particularly as applied to bird migration."[17,81-82] When DVOC member Henry Collins visited Russia, he reported that all the ornithologists he met there "spoke of Dr. Witmer Stone in glowing terms!"[83]

Stone was an honorary member of the Linnaean Society of New York, Nuttall Ornithological Club, and the Zoological Society of Philadelphia, for which he served on the board of directors' executive committee for the Philadelphia Zoo.[81,84] Stone was a Fellow of the American Association for the Advancement of Science, and was elected a member of the American Philosophical Society in 1913.[85] Some other organizations to which Stone belonged, listed (by no means exhaustively) here for insight into the extent of his interests, are the Philadelphia Mineralogical Society, the American Entomological Society, the American Society of Ichthyologists and Herpetologists, the Historical Society of Pennsylvania, the Philobiblon Club, the Boone and Crockett Club, the Science and Art Club of Germantown, and the Franklin Inn Club.[86] All these organizations are still extant.

Stone was also active in less scientifically oriented bird organizations. In addition to his involvement in the DVOC and the Audubon movement, Stone was an honorary member of the West Chester (Pennsylvania) Bird Club and president of the Wissahickon Bird Club.[87,88] The Wissahickon Creek flows through a wooded area of Fairmount Park in northwest Philadelphia and has long been a popular location for birdwatchers. The club began as the Fairmount Park Bird Club in 1922, and in its early days club secretary Caroline Moffett, a schoolteacher unfamiliar with the demands on the time of world-renowned zoologists, breezily ordered Stone to whip out a newsletter, with suggested topics, to be given to her in a month.[89] Stone quickly straightened her out: "As I told you when you elected me President of the Bird Club…I would merely be a <u>figurehead</u> and could not possibly find time to [engage in] any active work.…I have all that I can do both day and night.…If the Club is to be a success, we shall have to find some real, hard workers to undertake this part of our duties."[90] It must have been a vibrant organization: 486 schoolchildren attended the club's spring meeting at ANSP in 1936, and upkeep of a bird sanctuary in Carpenter's Woods (an area of Fairmount Park) was credited to students of the Henry School in Philadelphia, about 200 of whom belonged to the club.[88,91] The club also had regularly scheduled bird walks in the Wissahickon. In 1945, the Wissahickon Bird Club merged with the conservation organization Friends of the Wissahickon, which is still very active today.[92]

An interesting aspect of Stone's ornithological career was his relative isolation in Philadelphia for much of the time. The Smithsonian and the Biological Survey in Washington, D.C. always had several prominent ornithologists connected with them, as did the AMNH in New York and the MCZ in Cambridge. Until Rodolphe de Schauensee and James Bond began at ANSP in the mid-1920s, however, Stone was the only prominent ornithologist in Philadelphia, and he felt it early on. In 1898, he asked Charles Richmond, who worked with Robert Ridgway at the Smithsonian, "What is Mr. Ridgway's new book? I am so isolated here that I do not hear what you are doing down at the Capitol except so far as <u>war</u> is concerned!"[93] In 1918, in an interesting aside to W.L. McAtee, who had, along with Palmer, pointed out some flaws in the latest *Auk* index, Stone said he had forgotten a few details during the publication rush, then complained, "My trouble is that I have too much to do and have no one here to make timely suggestions on Auk matters – so as to keep me straight!"[94] Think of that: if he'd been editing *The Auk* at the Smithsonian, AMNH, or MCZ, he would have had several ornithologists to kick ideas around with in a casual, conversational way on a regular basis, including their reminders and opinions about *Auk* affairs. Instead, in the days before email or even regular telephone usage, he had only the occasional letters. If he wasn't quite editing *The Auk* in a vacuum, he was at least missing out on the daily, "watercooler" interactions with other professional ornithologists that the Washington, New York, and Cambridge crowds enjoyed as a matter of course.

Stone tried to get the DVOC men involved in the AOU, and to move beyond the Associate level. (The membership classes, low to high, were Associate, Member, and Fellow.) Many of them joined, and some moved up to higher classes. In 1928, Stone nominated Bond, Fletcher Street, and George Stuart for AOU Member class in an effort to ensure that Philadelphia would be better represented.[95] (Street and Stuart were elected that year, and Bond in 1929.)[96] Stone successfully pushed for de Schauensee's election to Member in 1933, after one or two prior attempts to do so, and tried unsuccessfully to get Melbourne Carriker made a Fellow in 1934.[97] Richmond ribbed him in 1929 about the fact that Stone was the only Fellow in AOU history from Philadelphia: "You should have more….It does not look right to me that the Phila. Academy, the former premier bird collection of the world, should be represented by only one man. The American Museum [of Natural History] was represented by [eight men]. Build up your local organization! Doesn't Philadelphia politics teach you anything?"[98] At a 1935 DVOC meeting, Stone encouraged the men to join the AOU, and to attend AOU meetings, not only for the ornithological and social benefits, but also to improve their chances of being promoted.[99] Possibly the DVOC men didn't attend enough "away" meetings to place themselves in the better graces of the AOU higher-ups.

---- ∾ ----

Probably owing to his Aunt Mary, who introduced young Witmer to Alexander Wilson's *American Ornithology*, Stone had a lifelong affection for the pioneering American ornithologist. The DVOC's 20-year history whimsically noted that Stone "was brought up on a copy of Wilson and consequently worshipped a different ornithological god from [George] Morris [who favored Audubon], and long years of amicable discussion has failed to shake their allegiance."[100] AOU Fellow Walter Faxon, also a Wilson enthusiast and expert, began one missive to Stone with the salutation, "Fellow Philo-Wilsonian!"[101] Stone wrote short biographies of Wilson for several periodicals, encyclopedias, and the like; his allegiance to Wilson was evident to a humorous extent in one article, which concluded with, "[T]here have been few if any influences as great as that of Wilson in developing our widespread interest in bird study."[102] That Audubon guy doesn't even deserve mention as a close second? Stone thought that the author of one Audubon article embellished details about the (in)famous Wilson–Audubon meeting in Louisville, Kentucky in 1810, including the assertion that Wilson was "grouchy" and "selfish," and in his *Auk* review of the article Stone looked to set the record – and the author – straight.[103]

In a 1913 *Auk* note on the centenary of Wilson's death, Stone, echoing an earlier biography he'd written in *Bird-Lore*, lamented Wilson's premature demise and wondered what influence Wilson would have had on the careers and writings of Thomas Nuttall and (particularly) Audubon, had he lived.[104] Stone gave a talk about Wilson at the 1913 AOU annual meeting in New York, and gave another one on Palm Sunday in 1936 to the Sunday congregation at Gloria Dei Church (Old Swedes' Church) in Philadelphia, where Wilson is buried.[105] The latter talk came about after Stone had made some of the funds of the defunct Pennsylvania Audubon Society available for the maintenance of Wilson's grave; Stone told the congregation, "I feel a particular sympathy with [Wilson] and his work because he labored in the same field of science to which I have devoted most of my life, and also perhaps because of the coincidence that his birth was just 100 years before mine and that he came to America in the same year that my ancestors left England for Philadelphia."[106] (Wilson had actually arrived the previous year.)

DVOC member Norris DeHaven thought that the male Savannah Sparrow depicted in Wilson's *American Ornithology* was actually an Ispwich Sparrow. (The Ipswich, larger and paler, is considered a subspecies of the Savannah now; in the 1890s they were considered separate species.) The Savannah Sparrow was first described by Wilson in 1811; the Ipswich was "discovered" in 1868 and described in 1872, so if one of the "Savannahs" that Wilson figured was really an Ipswich, that would have moved its discovery up by about 60 years. Stone agreed with DeHaven, and they presented their find to the DVOC at the January 17, 1893 meeting.[107] Stone contemplated writing the matter up in *The Auk*, and wrote to editor J.A. Allen on January 18 to get his thoughts on it.[108] Allen looked at the Wilson plates with Chapman; they thought that the "male" was a spring-plumaged Savannah, and the "female" was an autumn one, which accounted for the apparent plumage difference. (The sexes are not actually separable by plumage.) Allen noted that Wilson gave the same measurements for each sex (an Ipswich would have been larger), and considered the "male," although paler than the "female," not pale enough to be an Ipswich.[109]

Allen's response ended Stone's plans for an *Auk* announcement of his "scoop," but he wasn't done yet. In early 1898, Elliot Coues, associate editor of *The Osprey*, invited Stone to "'rake up some old personalities' for a pleasant gossipy article" (specifically, something on the Wilson/Annie Bartram love interest).[110] Stone had a better idea, and trotted out a paper on the theorized Ipswich/Savannah mixup. He said there was little difference in Savannahs between spring and fall, and that ornithologists in Wilson's time were careless in their measurements, thus pooh-poohing Allen's earlier, privately expressed objections.[111] Wilson's "male" *is* paler than the "female" – it looks more "Ipswichy," if you will – but Wilson's artistic skills were not quite up to the difficult task of depicting sparrows, and it's hard to hang your hat on either figure being one (sub)species or the other. But that was Stone's story and he was sticking to it, and in DeHaven's *Cassinia* memorial 25 years later, and in *BSOCM* even later, Stone was still pitching it as though it were an open-and-shut case.[112] It was too good a story to let the dissenting opinions of other ornithologists get in the way.

In 1913, Alexander Milne Calder, the famous sculptor whose William Penn statue graces the top of Philadelphia's City Hall, notified ANSP that he had a 4-foot statue of Wilson which had been displayed at the Pennsylvania Academy of Fine Arts when that building was completed about 1880, and which he was now looking to give away.[113] Stone wrote in *Cassinia* in 1913 that the work was placed in the ANSP library.[114] The statue had a very interesting subsequent history after going on permanent loan to Cornell University, and was ultimately lost. A smaller plaster duplicate donated to ANSP by Alan Brady and the DVOC in 1995 now greets visitors outside the library.[115]

The statuette isn't the only Wilson memento at the Academy. In late 1922, the St. Andrew's Society of Philadelphia, a Scottish heritage organization, offered to commission and donate to the Academy a tablet commemorating Wilson. The will of a recently deceased Philadelphia physician and Society member, J. Cameron Lawson, had included the idea and the funds for the tablet.[116] Stone and ANSP agreed to it, and on May 17, 1923 the tablet was dedicated in a ceremony at the Academy.[117] Everything was ice cream and balloons – until the next day, when Stone wrote to John Croskey of the Society that there was still patching up to be done in the wall where the tablet was installed, and it was clear that he expected the Society to take care of it.[118] It did, but its troubles weren't over. A couple of weeks later, Stone notified Croskey that the year of Wilson's death on the tablet was incorrect. The Society had put the dates in Roman numerals, probably for artistic effect, and lucky Wilson belatedly had an extra 20 years tacked on to his life – if only he'd been able to cash them in.[119] Plans were immediately formed to fix the date, but a note placed in the Academy archives years later by researcher Venia Phillips indicates that in 1959 the date still had not been fixed and the tablet was collecting dust under a staircase, out of public view.[120] The tablet is faring a little better these days, uncorrected date and all: in 2013, it was leaning against a wall in the ornithology department, which is arguably an improvement over sitting under a staircase.

Witmer was interested broadly in ornithological history, not just in Wilson. The interest might be traceable to his historian father, and he came to it early. In the late 1890s he was, for a time, engaged in compiling an index of ornithological writings, similar to a larger Coues effort, but this was left uncompleted while other matters took his time.[121] In 1904, *Bird-Lore* announced that some ornithological biographies would soon appear courtesy of Stone, who was possessed of an "unusually keen and sympathetic insight into the lives of early American ornithologists," and brief sketches of Wilson, Mark Catesby, William Bartram, and Benjamin Smith Barton followed.[122] Stone produced numerous biographies of historic ornithologists and obituaries of recent ones for *The Auk* and *Cassinia*. His correspondence includes many letters from family members and descendants of deceased ornithologists whose lives Stone was in the process of researching.

Stone expressed his interest in ornithological history at the beginning of his *Auk* biography of Jacob Giraud Jr.: "It has always seemed to the writer a duty of present-day ornithologists to save from oblivion as many of the facts as possible concerning the lives of those who long ago laid the foundations of our science, and he has accordingly from time to time prepared biographical sketches of some of the older American ornithologists, concerning whom little or no record has appeared in our published literature."[123] He described his affinity with his ornithological antecedents in his William Gambel biography in *Cassinia*: "The history of American ornithology or of the men to whom it owes its development is always fraught with interest to those of us who continue to cultivate the same study and to follow in the footsteps of predecessors whose minds ran in the same channels, whose thoughts are now our thoughts, and whose enthusiasms arouse our sympathy."[124]

Since at least 1904, if not earlier, Stone had been planning to write a book on ornithological history in America.[125] In 1924 he told Casey Wood, "I have a lot of material gathered together for a sort of history of American ornithology (or ornithologists), some of which has come out in Cassinia but I feel that a volume, with a readable account of the development of our knowledge, the careers of the men who did it etc. would be well worth while, but The Auk & the Academy take my every moment & I don't know how or when I can get it in shape."[126] As *BSOCM* neared completion, Stone turned his attention to his ornithological history book again, particularly during his summers at Cape May, telling Palmer in 1934, "I am actually rounding up sections of that proposed history of American ornithology & ornithologists which I have threatened to get at these many moons. Did something on it this summer. Plan to describe the discovery of N.A. birds with personalia of the discoverers worked in. Shall want your criticism when it gets in a little better shape."[127] His comment in a 1935 letter from Cape May that he was "getting a lot of typing done in [regard to] 'historical research'" was likely a reference to this work.[128]

Stone was still working on the book a few months before he died, and reportedly had a manuscript ready for the publisher at the time of his death.[129] However, he told Charles Cadwalader in January 1939, "I have made great progress getting all my notes on the history of American ornithology in sequence and am writing up special parts of it – maybe not in exactly 'Green Laurels' style but readable, anyway."[130] If that's as far along as he was in January, it seems impossible that he would have had a manuscript ready for a publisher by May, particularly given the state of his health in the interim.

It's a pity that the book never saw the light of day, because many sections and fragments of it – some handwritten, some typed – are in the ANSP archives, and they make interesting reading. Of particular interest is an undated document that includes the planned introductory page for the work: "For some years past I have been collecting data for what might be called a chronological history of the Ornithology of North America, the idea being to trace the first discovery of each species on this continent with any correlative data and biographical sketches of the men responsible for the discovery – a discussion as it were of both ornithology and ornithologists."[131] When Cadwalader bought Stone's correspondence and papers from Lillie's estate after Witmer's death, the word "manuscripts" was crossed out on the sale receipt.[132] That may be a hint as to the eventual whereabouts of the American ornithology manuscript (assuming that a version existed that was more complete than the fragments extant in the Academy archives), or at least an indication as to why it didn't end up at ANSP.

———————— ∾ ————————

In 1900, *Bird-Lore* editor Frank Chapman proposed a humane alternative to the "side hunt," a barbaric practice that featured bands of hunters going out into the field on Christmas Day and competing to see which group could shoot the most wildlife. Chapman invited *Bird-Lore* readers to go out on Christmas Day and count birds and send their lists to the magazine, thus initiating the Christmas Bird Count (CBC), which has been going strong ever since and now has tens of thousands of participants each year.[133] Stone spent some time on Christmas morning of the inaugural count tramping around the Delaware River marshes below Philadelphia ("Alex. Wilson's old haunts," as he told Chapman), and did two more counts with DVOC companions over the next four days.[134] For some reason Stone wasn't much of a participant thereafter until later in his life, when he became involved in the DVOC's Cape May CBC. He and Lillie stayed with Otway and Edith Brown in Cold Spring at Christmas starting in the late 1920s, if not earlier, and Brown and Stone were a team for the Cape May CBCs.[135] Unlike Stone, Brown drove a car, and chauffeured Stone on the CBC and other Cape May outings.[136]

Alan Brady used to tell the story of seeing a Merlin on the 1936 Cape May CBC, but being told by Stone at the roundup dinner that evening, "Alan, we don't see them on the Christmas Count" – and that was the end of that. Alan was 16 at the time and may have been too young and unfamiliar to Stone for the latter to believe the sighting. There is a Merlin recorded on that count for that year – someone might have put it into the final tally despite Stone's censure, but maybe another party had one, possibly the same one Alan saw.[137] (A few years earlier, Stone had done the opposite. Phil Livingston's favorite story was said to be the time he reported a Wood Thrush on the 1933 Cape May CBC at a DVOC meeting. Wood Thrushes are usually wintering in the tropics at that time, and the old-timers hooted in derision until Stone stood up and defended the sighting, whereupon it was immediately accepted.)[138]

Some 1924 correspondence with Franklin and Marshall College professor Herbert H. Beck, a frequent contributor to *The Auk* at the time, indicated that Stone was skeptical of Beck's winter Merlin sightings as well, so Alan shouldn't feel singled out.[139] In fact, in *BSOCM* Stone wrote, "I am inclined to think that [Merlins] are always rare in November and I have so frequently been deceived by the dark appearance of young female [American Kestrels], under poor light conditions, that I am skeptical of the alleged sight records of [Merlins] in December which appear on several of the Christmas censuses. There is no positive record of [Merlins] in winter, I believe, north of southern Florida."[140]

That is decidedly not the case today, but the field guides and other bird books in Stone's time (including the Stone-edited fourth AOU check-list) recorded the Merlin's winter range as the Gulf states and southward, although A.C. Bent cited numerous winter records of birds found in the U.S. and southern Canada which "extend[ed] the range much farther north."[141] Either Stone was unaware of the wealth of winter records north of Florida, or he didn't consider them "positive records," but such records, including collected birds, had been noted in *The Auk* for years.

Stone has rightly been called "an extraordinarily diligent observer of birds," and he was a patient, careful watcher and recorder of wildlife.[142] His attention to the minute details of bird behavior is apparent in his *BSOCM* discussion of whether the cowbird/cattle association was due to the (still) widely-held belief that the cattle stirred up insects on which the cowbirds fed: "As a matter of fact, however, after many careful studies of such flocks with the binoculars at close quarters, I have been unable to detect the birds in the act of catching any insects nor have I seen the cattle stir up any form of insect life from the short grass of the pastures. On one occasion…when I was but a few yards away, I could see that the feet of the cows were covered with flies but the Cowbirds continued to peck at the ground and paid not the slightest attention to them nor were the flies disturbed by the progress of the cows."[143] Be honest, now – when was the last time you carefully inspected the flies on bovine hooves in your quest to better understand *Molothrus* commensal relationships? He studied a migrant Lincoln's Sparrow (an unusual find) in his West Philadelphia yard for an hour, and he once stood so quietly near a swirling flock of Tree Swallows that their wings almost brushed against his face.[144] He spent 20 minutes re-locating a Yellow-billed Cuckoo he had seen fly into a tree in Cape May, and he found a cock pheasant after carefully following its tracks through a field.[145] He watched a weasel go back and forth from a swamp to its burrow with captured mice for about 40 minutes, and watched a Saltmarsh Sparrow at Cape May for a half hour, hoping to hear it sing ("but he never opened his mouth!").[146] He suspected a thick tangle at Cold Spring would harbor woodcocks, and came face to face with one while crawling through the thicket on his hands and knees.[147] He not only discovered that the local Chimney Swifts favored a particular row of cherry trees along the railroad in Cape May to gather twigs for their nests, he also noted that he had seen them so engaged from May 28 to July 3, covering a number of years.[148] Anyone keeping track of the dates on which they've seen Chimney Swifts gathering nest material at a particular location over a period of years certainly qualifies as meticulous in note-taking and record-keeping.

In *BSOCM*, Stone made several references to the appearance of birds under varying light conditions, something to which he paid close attention. In 1926, ANSP's J. Percy Moore thought he might have seen an almost-extinct Whooping Crane during a visit to Massachusetts, and was told by an incredulous Stone, "I have had a great deal of experience in the last few years in watching birds flying over head in various kinds of light and am astonished by the deceptive appearance presented by many of them."[149] (The light in Moore's case wasn't as deceptive as Stone may have thought, however, for the bird was a free-flying Red-crowned Crane from Japan – similar in appearance to a Whooper – which lived at a nearby estate with its wing-clipped mate.)[150]

In what could be a reflection of both the wariness of birds so recently subjected to intense hunting and the inadequacy of birding optics at the time, *BSOCM* is full of accounts of Stone crawling or creeping along, often behind shielding vegetation, to get a closer look at birds. He once used a tool shed as cover to sneak up for a better view of a Turkey Vulture feeding on a dead cat on the Cape May golf course, although why he'd want a closer view of that is hard to understand.[151] In another instance, he was creeping up on herons and egrets at a pond with when he spotted a Great Blue Heron eyeing him over the tops of the grass; Stone quickly "sank down behind a convenient bush," and the heron eventually went back to feeding, its suspicions quieted by the seeming disappearance of its stalker.[152] In fact, concealment seems to have been a knee-jerk reaction: he sometimes immediately dropped to the ground when he saw birds fly toward him, in the hope they wouldn't spot him.[153] One evening he hid in a woodlot being used by roosting herons and watched as they came in and landed in the branches over his head, stretching their legs and preening – it's a wonder he didn't walk out covered in whitewash.[154] Another way to get a closer look at a bird was by producing strange sounds to entice a bird to pop out of cover for a peek, as today's pishers do – in Stone's case, possibly a "sucking sound" similar to the one he described as resembling a Brown Thrasher's alarm note, or else a squeak produced by loudly kissing the back of the hand.[155]

Stone kept a list of birds he found in his yard, and while living on Hazel Avenue in West Philadelphia he used to watch birds at nearby Black Oak Park (now Malcolm X Park).[156] In a find that is sadly unthinkable today, he discovered Red-headed Woodpeckers nesting there in 1908.[157] Nesting starlings would be a better bet now, although there are still many huge, majestic old trees which were doubtless there in Stone's time. Due to a heavy workload, he was doing less birdwatching around Philadelphia by 1921, and by 1924 was telling Sam Scoville, "I have seen so little of the [spring] migration myself that I cannot give an opinion upon it."[158] Partly because of failing health, Stone spent less time birdwatching and more time on Auk, check-list, ornithological history book, and BSOCM work during his last several Cape May summers. Although he was a knowledgeable, experienced, attentive, and diligent birdwatcher, he appears to have pursued his field studies in a comparatively relaxed fashion, closely studying the birds and the conditions. The DVOC's birder par excellence, Julian Potter, seems closer to an early prototype of the gung ho, rarity-chasing modern birder.

Although Stone participated casually in the first DVOC May Run (a precursor to today's birding competitions), he was not much into listing.[159] At a 1929 DVOC meeting, he made a plea for the study of individual birds, rather than simply running up lists.[160] In 1936 he complained about the lack of DVOC responses to his call for photographs to be used in BSOCM, saying, "I fear that the rising generation is too much in a hurry to make a big list and do not take the time for either detailed study of activities or photography."[161]

Automobiles were making it easier to run up a list, and serious bird students didn't like it a bit. Robert P. Allen, on his way to becoming one of the most important American field ornithologists and conservationists of the 20th century, told a colleague about a fieldwork committee organized by the Linnaean Society that "it has been our feeling that this business of getting better and bigger lists was just about run into the ground and it seemed a shame that an active group of field ornithologists…should play around with birds as if they were ping-pong balls for amusement only, when so many vital ornithological problems remain unsolved."[162] Conrad Roland's take on a May Run engaged in by him and a friend also has great resonance decades later. He told Stone, "Our list of 101 [species] you see was the leisurely finding of only two gentlemen ornithologists & did not involve 15 persons rising in a body at 1:30 a.m. & moving about stealthily in a posse of motor cars till dawn & then 'hiking' furiously till dusk."[163] That sounds like today's 24-hour birding contests, except for the hiking part – they are done more by car now. Stone had his yard lists, and he kept lists at Cape May every summer, but was less than impressed with the craze of scurrying around in cars trying to run up a count.[164] In *BSOCM* he wrote about all the walking around the Point he used to do when he was younger and healthier, and compared it to the new trend of birding by car: "It is questionable however, whether the ornithological results of a day's outing under present conditions are as important or as thorough as in the pedestrian days, although of course a far greater area can be covered."[165]

7

The Custodian of the Bowl

Witmer Stone, almost 38, married Lillie May Lafferty, 32, on August 1, 1904. Wharton Huber described their marriage as "an ideally happy union."[1] Witmer gave her a large silver vase on their silver anniversary, and despite getting married somewhat late in life they'd almost made it to 35 years when Witmer passed away.[2] They had no children; a possible hint about the reason for that may be contained in a remark Witmer once made about some classical music concerts he was enjoying in Cape May one summer from which "bawling brats [were] excluded."[3]

Lillie was born April 30, 1872 at Harrisburg, Pennsylvania, one of 11 children of Isaac H. Lafferty and Ellen Penn Lafferty *née* Coart.[4] Her father (b. 1843), who served on the *U.S.S. Black Hawk* during the Civil War, had lived for a time in Altoona, Pennsylvania, and moved his family back there shortly after Lillie's birth. He opened the Lafferty Market, a produce store, on 17th Street, and tended it until his sudden death in 1893. Ellen's interesting start in life, in 1848, took place on the Atlantic Ocean aboard the ship *William Penn*, and presumably explains her curious middle name.[5] Her English parents, James and Anna Coart, were on their way to America at the time.

Witmer and Lillie had known each other for some time before their marriage, but I've not been able to find any information about how they met or how long they knew each other before commencing a romance.[6] Lillie was living in Philadelphia by 1893.[7] At any rate, their marriage was clearly a sudden shock to his acquaintances. His DVOC buddies had never even met Lillie.[6,8] Congratulatory letters, like the one from cousin Hugh Stone, indicate that the family had given Stone up for a hopeless bachelor, and that the courtship was a brief one: "I don't have to feign surprise at your news of last week, in fact am just recovering from the shock, but we are as pleased as we were surprised. I think it is splendid and should like to congratulate the lady also, even though that is not quite 'according to style.'"[9] George S. Morris was vacationing at Eagles Mere, Pennsylvania, when the news reached him: "The shock of your announcement is beginning to wear off & the doctors now think they will be able to pull me through. The bomb struck me at this quiet mountain resort, where everything is favorable to my recovery – but my dear boy this is so sudden….You say you have known Miss Lafferty for a long time. That's the right way to begin….[My wife and I] are sure that the best sort of love is that which is founded on long strong friendship. Someone is liable to get hurt when the matrimonial gun goes off at half cock. Mrs. Morris is almost as much tickled over your announcement as I am....[I]t's a lucky girl that marries Witmer Stone."[6] A.K. Fisher said, "You are a sly boy – but nonetheless I am hastening to send my congratulations....We were surprised but pleased that one more of the crowd had crossed over to the respectable majority."[10] Spencer Trotter welcomed Stone to "the happy brotherhood of Benedicts – It was quite a surprise – but then surprises are in order along that line – Both Mrs. Trotter and I extend our hearty congratulations."[8]

Shortly after Stone's marriage, Morris sent the following notice to fellow DVOC members:

DVOC SECRET SERVICE COMMITTEE

As you are probably aware, one of our most esteemed members, Mr. Witmer Stone, under the auspicious guidance of the Leap Year, has taken advantage of the dull molting season and committed Matrimony. [Many birds molt in late summer.]

Nevertheless, to show our appreciation of his past services to the Club, individually and collectively, and to render the new environment as harmonious as possible with the old, the Committee proposes to give an informal supper in his honor, to be held in the Academy on the night of the first Club meeting, October 6.

To insure its success we would be very glad to have you contribute to the cause to any extent which you may feel moved, the same in no case to exceed one dollar....Needless to say, it is our earnest wish that no mention of the matter be made to Mr. Stone.[11]

The club responded with a nice turnout, and the minutes for the meeting record, "The large attendance of members at this meeting, surpassing in this respect any heretofore held, is not to be credited entirely to a revival in the love of our chosen study, nor to 'loaves and fishes' of which there was some showing at the end of the meeting, but was prompted by the desire to give expression to our feelings of regard for one of our Active members. The interested reader is referred to corresponding date in the biography of Witmer Stone."[12]

Lillie appears to have done at least some birdwatching with her husband.[13] In a *Cassinia* note, Witmer listed the birds seen in his West Philadelphia backyard in 1913 "by Mrs. Stone and myself."[14] Witmer and Lillie arose early on October 17, 1920 and took an excursion train to Cape May. There they hiked seven miles, had lunch in the woods, and got up a nice list of birds for the day. It included a pair of Sanderlings that dropped into a small pond near the lighthouse, looking distinctly out of place away from their usual location at the ocean's very edge, and, in another unusual sighting, three adult Ring-necked Pheasants in low flight over Lake Lily.[15] The only mention of Lillie in *BSOCM*, other than "To My Wife" on the dedication page, is in the "Bird Migration at the Cape" chapter, in which Witmer recorded that he and Lillie witnessed a heavy flight of birds coming in off the ocean one fall morning when "Red-breasted

Nuthatches and Brown Creepers alighted on our shoulders and backs as we stood on the sand, apparently taking us for tree stumps."[16] (Both Lillie and Witmer were stocky, so the birds' confusion is understandable.)

Lillie became an AOU Associate in 1920 and a life Associate in 1936.[17] She had previously attended annual meetings with her husband (including the 1915 one in San Francisco) and continued to do so for years. She is not only listed as an attendee in many *Auk* meeting summaries, but can also often be spotted in annual meeting photos (even those of the American Society of Mammalogists).[18] Her interest in birds had a reasonable limit, however, unlike that of her husband. Stone once told a friend about a flicker "which comes to play jazz on the corner of our tin roof every morning about 5 a.m. & [Lillie] is real bloodthirsty in her denunciation of the poor bird!"[19]

Stone's correspondence rarely mentions Lillie by her first name; instead, as was customary with other men with whom he corresponded in reference to their wives, he usually called her "Mrs. Stone," even with people who knew the Stones well. Curiously, Witmer and Fisher hit upon the nickname "Custodian of the Bowl" for Lillie, and for years, until Stone's death, they both unfailingly referred to her as such, eventually shortening it to "the Custodian." One of the few hints to the name's origin is a reference to her by Witmer as "custodian of the 'Jardinaire [sic].'"[20] Stone occasionally included crude little drawings of "the bowl" in letters to Fisher, and they do look more like some sort of jardinière than, say, a punch bowl.[21] Lillie's will mentioned a white and gold jardinière given to her and Witmer as a wedding gift, and that was presumably "the bowl" that endlessly amused the boys.[2]

Some Lillie miscellany is provided here to help round out the picture of her. She made several kinds of jelly at Cape May, and was known for her lemon meringue pies. In 1917, Stone named a newly discovered Columbian bird species from an ANSP collection, the Sapphire-bellied Hummingbird (*Lepidopyga lilliae*), after his wife.[22] Unfortunately, the species is now listed as "critically endangered" by the IUCN.[23] In 1920, Lillie voted in an election for the first time, as did many other women; also like many of them, and making her husband proud, she voted for Warren Harding.[24]

Lillie helped out to a small extent with Witmer's home office, where he did his *Auk* work, sorting the index slips and keeping Witmer's correspondence and pamphlets in order.[25] However, she doesn't appear to have worked outside the home: the 1920 and 1930 censuses list her trade/profession as "none," and I haven't found any reference in Witmer's correspondence to her working. In both census years there is a servant listed for the residence (and Witmer mentioned a servant occasionally in his correspondence), as well as a relative or two living with them.[26-27]

After his father's death in 1897, Stone and his mother Anne had to vacate the Logan Street house in Germantown, presumably because they could no longer afford the rent on one salary.[28] Witmer was 31 at the time, and there's no indication that he had ever lived anywhere else but his parents' home. By the 1900 census, Anne, Witmer, and a servant were living at 4520 Regent Street in West Philadelphia, not far from Bartram's Garden and just a stone's throw from Clark Park, where Stone must have done some birding.[29] Anne was noted as the head of the household, but had no occupation listed.[30]

When Witmer and Lillie married in 1904, they moved into 5044 Hazel Avenue in West Philadelphia, right around the corner from Black Oak Park, where Witmer watched birds.[31] He bought the house in 1908 after renting it for a few years.[32] One of the improvements he made to the property was the addition of chicken wire to the fence lines to keep marauding neighborhood cats away from his avian visitors.[33] Anne continued to live in the Regent Street house and was joined by her aging mother, Hannah, sometime after 1900, possibly when Stock Grange was sold.[34] In 1911 Stone told a friend, "I…have been much upset lately by the illness and death of my venerable grandmother of whom you may have heard me speak – she was in her 104th year. The death breaks up my mother's household & she is coming to live with me."[35] The 1920 census recorded Anne living with Witmer, Lillie, Lillie's niece Margaret, and a servant at 5044 Hazel.[26] The Hazel and Regent houses, still the same structures today, are about a mile apart.

Unhappy with troublesome neighbors, the Stones suddenly sold 5044 Hazel in September 1921 and embarked on a yearlong sojourn of moving from place to place, including a stay in at least one boarding house. November was one of the most severely trying times of Witmer's life: Anne passed away, aged 79, and Lillie reacted with a fit of hysteria ("was severely prostrated & I had fears for her condition for a time") – all while they were living in temporary quarters.[36-37] Publication of *The Auk* was delayed due to a printers' strike. To make matters worse, the AOU meeting was held in Philadelphia in early November, and a threatened railroad strike that would have crippled the travel plans of many attendees was added to the usual stresses of organizing the meeting.[38] Stone said of the ordeal, "The strain of the meeting and the shock [of his mother's death] nearly finished me & with the printers strike and everyone clamoring for their Auks I was about ready to give up….For 55 years I have seen my mother almost daily & it has left a terrible gap."[37]

Witmer and Lillie rented George S. Morris's home, "Birdfield," in the Crescentville section of Philadelphia in the winter of 1921–22 while the Morrises were in Florida, but that ended abruptly in early April when Morris was stricken with his final illness and returned home on very short notice. By early June, the Stones were living in Germantown and were contemplating buying a house there.[39] They went to Cape May for July and August, and on September

14, 1922, a year after their hobo odyssey began, they moved into a newly built house at 452 Church Lane in Germantown, where both would live out their days.[40] Witmer told a friend all about their new digs, and it's clear that the Stones were thrilled with their new home:

> You know I lived in Germantown for 22 years not a mile from where I am now & the woods where I learned my ornithology reaches from one spot to the other. It is now a city park [Wister Woods] which is being kept as a forest & bird sanctuary, but a drive runs through the middle [Belfield Ave., recently built][41] & countless houses cover the former open country to the east. There ought however to be good [bird] lists to be had in migration. We are surrounded by large estates where we now are & can see Robins, Grackles, Flickers, Nighthawks, Jays, Starlings & Gray Squirrels from the porch at any time!...I hung 73 pictures Saturday so we are beginning to look like home. As I wander about Germantown I feel like Rip van Winkle. It is 25 years since I lived here & while the old place is still here so much has changed as to details & persons! Mrs. S is tickled to death with a brand new house, hardwood floors, hot water heat & electricity & wallpaper & fixtures of her own selection![42]

There were large trees around the place, including a Kentucky Coffeetree with pods and two enormous Ginkgo trees by the door.[43] In a 1923 letter, Stone playfully scribbled "Germantown Under the Jinkgo Tree" in the upper corner, as if it were the name of an estate from which he was writing.[44] The Ginkgos, a male and a female, are still there, towering over the house. There is also a long, low mica schist stone wall supporting flower beds, which may be the very structure Stone referred to in 1926 when said he was having "a wall of rough stone substituted for a terrace...which will give me an additional flower bed."[19]

Stone had many guests, especially visiting ornithologists, at his Church Lane home over the years. He once had to tell one of them some sad news about a notable Germantown feature: "With the change in line of railroad & elevation to avoid grade crossing, our station 'Wingohocking,' the name of which you so admired, has disappeared entirely!...I did like that little station & the birds around it, however"[45] – like the Blue Jays that nested right by the tracks.[46] It was the station Stone used for his travels to and from ANSP. More than just a train station with a charming Indian name, however, it was one of the many Frank Furness-designed buildings around Philadelphia that have, sadly, been demolished.[47] Today, the main walkway entrance to the old station can still (barely) be detected on the north side of the intersection of Baynton and East Coulter streets.[41]

Witmer took advantage of the American Society of Mammalogists' annual meeting in Philadelphia in May 1923 to show off his new house, telling friends that he "had the visiting 'quadrupeds' to the number of thirty out here at my new home in Germantown…and there was still room to move around & eat some ice cream."[48] Although he had to downsize his library at the time of his move back to Germantown, he still had an impressive and eclectic one.[42,49] Shortly after moving in he wore himself out building bookshelves in his study, declaring, "I don't get enough exercise to take carpentry easy!"[50] Joseph Grinnell complimented Stone on his library after a 1929 visit, saying, "And your own 'den' there, was a most interesting and restful place. I could have spent hours browsing among the many historic and literary and ornithological items in it."[51]

ANSP was initially interested in buying Stone's personal library after his death. After examining it, however, the Academy realized that it already had most of the material the library contained. One inventory of it by an Academy librarian broke it down into three parts: separates (i.e., article offprints) and books (12,000–13,000 titles); complete and incomplete sets of periodicals/journals (150 titles); and sets of old rare and obscure natural history journals (115 titles).[52]

Lillie instead sold the complete library to the Reading Public Museum (RPM) shortly before she died. A newspaper article at the time noted 2,500 books and a complete set of the *Proceedings of the Academy of Natural Sciences*, among other gems. Lillie reportedly wanted to keep the library intact and didn't want to sell it off piecemeal.[53] Unfortunately, that seems to have been its eventual fate. The RPM held an annual book sale for many years until about 2010, and it appears that much of the Stone library, including some of the separates, was deaccessioned and sold off in that period. That would be unpleasant news to Stone's friend Earl Poole, the Berks County artist and RPM director who arranged the purchase, and Henry Janssen, the philanthropic Reading industrialist who funded it.[54] I examined some unprocessed material one day at the RPM storage site, and it included dozens of small boxes of separates – the sad, small remnant of Stone's library. Each box bore two labels on the spine, one describing its topical contents (e.g., "Birds of Utah," "Bird Migration"), and the other marked with a number that was part of the library classification system Stone used. A newspaper article from 1938 on the occasion of Stone's 50th anniversary at ANSP includes a photo of him at home sitting in front of his bookshelves, and some of the separates boxes now at the RPM are visible behind him.[55]

The Stones' beloved old 452 Church Lane house, the north half of a duplex, still stands. After years of such neglect of the southern half that I expected the structure to be demolished, both halves have recently been fixed up and look like new again. On a visit in the summer of 2012 I walked up to the main entrance at 452 and was astonished to find the same door that can be seen in the Stones' 1926 Christmas card – still in place since the house was built 90 years earlier![56]

8

Such a Natural Flower Garden

Although he is rightly remembered primarily as an ornithologist, Stone had a deep interest in other branches of natural history, and certainly made his mark as a botanist. He was a founding member of the Philadelphia Botanical Club (PBC) and was on the original publication committee of its journal *Bartonia*.[1,2] His knowledge of systematics of the local flora was "surpassed only by that of Simon-pure botanists," and his concentration on ornithology was pronounced a "definite loss" for botany by a later eminent botanist.[3-4] For approximately 10 years, beginning in 1900, Stone concentrated on botanical fieldwork more than at any other time in his life. His efforts resulted in *The Plants of Southern New Jersey, with Especial Reference to the Flora of the Pine Barrens [PSNJ]*, published in 1911 by the New Jersey State Museum. The book, Stone's botanical pièce de résistance, remains an important baseline reference for New Jersey Pine Barrens botanists today, and marks his greatest contribution to the natural sciences outside of his ornithological work. ANSP botanist Francis Pennell counted 20 botanical publications from Stone, and said that his Yucatan, South Carolina, and Louisiana collections were the "most extensive and notable" of the many he assembled during his travels.[5] Certainly Stone's Philadelphia-area violets and Jersey Pine Barrens collections were also impressive.

Stone cut his teeth as a botanist at Stock Grange with Dr. William Darlington's *Flora Cestrica: An Herborizing Companion for the Young Botanists of Chester County*, and the ANSP botanical collections contain many Stone specimens from the Stock Grange area.[6] His boyhood interest in plants was encouraged by the Stone family physician, Dr. James Darrach, who, along with Joseph Leidy and a few others, informally organized the Botanical Club, which met at ANSP and preceded the PBC by a few decades.[7] Stone's Wilson Natural Science Association (WNSA) talks, essays, and even artwork were often botanical in nature.[8]

Stone collected plants on the ANSP trips to Bermuda and Mexico, and later took part in the weekly field trips led by ANSP botanist Dr. J. Bernard Brinton.[5,9] On one such outing, on July 21, 1889, Stone visited the Pine Barrens of New Jersey for the first time.[10] He was immediately smitten by the flora, as his Orange Milkwort (*Polygala lutea*) entry in *PSNJ* makes clear: "I well remember my first visit to the Pines, when the low moist spots were all dotted with the brilliant heads of the *Polygala*, with here and there stalks of white fringed orchis, and the small orange fringed orchis, so like the *Polygala* in color, with *Xyris* [yellow-eyed grasses] and *Eriocaulon* [pipeworts], and a host of other things hitherto unknown. The mosquitoes and heat were nothing, when such a natural flower garden lay before one's eyes, and the poor flora of my upland pastures seemed to sink into insignificance beside such riches."[11] Thus began Witmer's love affair with the Pine Barrens, where he could go birding, botanizing, and even mousing; dig to exhaustion in futile quests to find the far ends of *Euphorbia* roots; and fall asleep counting Whip-poor-will calls – the Pine Barrens version of counting sheep.[12]

The PBC was formed in December 1891 by men, including Stone, who had been involved in informal botanical research in the Philadelphia area for some time, and who thought it was time to take things a step further. Their stated goals were to advance the interests of botany and to establish a herbarium and check-list containing all the plants occurring within 50 miles of Philadelphia.[2] Another impetus for the club's formation was that the men who ran the Academy botanical section were older (the conservator, John Redfield, was 75 in 1890), and some were not overly disposed to helping the younger men in their studies. The latter formed their own group in which they could have a say in things.[13]

Stone lasted only two years in the club, however. On November 23, 1893, he wrote to club secretary Stewardson Brown that he would not be at the meeting that night due to a bad cold, and continued, "My connection with the Club is, I'm afraid, developing into a farce. The fact is I have no time anymore for Botany & may as well acknowledge the fact. I have blamed little for Birds or anything else this year with the orders, accounts, labeling, etc [i.e., his ANSP duties]....I never was ornamental to the Club and am becoming useless as well, so I wish you would accept my resignation from the Active List tonight as I don't think it is right to lumber it up with inactive members."[14] Stone remained off the rolls until 1907, when he rejoined the club, and was thereafter listed as a "founder" in the *Bartonia* membership lists, despite the lengthy membership gap.[15]

He began his 1894 "Summer birds of the Pine Barrens of New Jersey" article in *The Auk* by briefly noting that the area was long renowned among botanists.[16] This casual aside to the botany of the Pine Barrens is fascinating in hindsight, because although Stone was not botanically active for most of the 1890s, after a joint outing of the Philadelphia and Torrey Botanical clubs to Toms River on July 4, 1900, he resolved to write a flora of the Pine Barrens.[10] Over the next decade, Stone turned more intensively to botany than at any other time before or after, making "several hundred" collecting trips to southern New Jersey and amassing 5,000 specimens for his personal herbarium.[17-19] In 1908, he took on the monumental task of critically examining all 14,000 of the South Jersey specimens in the ANSP herbarium; all told, he consulted 33,000 specimens from various collections for the book.[19-20] Presumably, this work was done on his own time outside his usual duties at the Academy.

The commencement of Stone's intensive study of the Pine Barrens flora coincided with his involvement in the construction of a cabin near Medford, New Jersey. Stone, along with George Spencer Morris (also the building's designer), Stewardson Brown, Francis Goodhue Jr., and one other person built "Catoxen" cabin on the Rancocas Creek, near the western edge of the Pine Barrens, in 1899.[21] Stone sometimes used Catoxen as a springboard for botanical excursions into the surrounding area, and some distinguished American ornithologists were his guests at the cabin over the years.[18,22] Stone told a 1905 DVOC meeting about a recent (May 14) trip to Medford, and reported that the dawn bird chorus reached its peak at 4:10 a.m. (pre-daylight saving time) – picture Witmer standing outside, or maybe even lying inside on a cot, referring to his watch in the dim light of dawn as the birds sing lustily in the woods surrounding the little cabin.[23]

He recalled the Catoxen life years later in his *Cassinia* Morris memorial: "Here it was possible to live the life of the back woods whenever a day or two could be spared from the activities of business; when trees could be felled, meals cooked over the camp fire, a little game obtained, bird lists made up or the wild creatures of the woods tracked in the winter's snow."[24] And it was "back woods," all right – right down to the deer mice that broke in and ruined the blankets.[25] Mice weren't the only uninvited house guests. On December

Witmer the woodchopper, Lillie (*center*), and unidentified woman at Catoxen cabin door. ANSP Archives.

29, 1900, Stone and three others conducted a Christmas Bird Count around Catoxen, and he told count compiler Frank Chapman, "You should especially appreciate that trip to Medford. Some miscreant broke into our cabin & stole all our bedding so that we nearly froze [that] night."[26] (A later thief filched the cutlery.)[27]

It's easy to imagine that a cabin full of DVOCers would be something like *Animal House*, and a later reminiscence to Stone by Herbert "Curly" Coggins doesn't suggest otherwise:

> The picture of the cabin in the [Rancocas] stirs many recollections, but none were more tender than of the day when with a carefully made composite of mash potato and table scraps I lay in wait for you beside the door, with the view of donating the whole to you without the formality of a presentation speech. And I have never gotten over the ingratitude with which you surreptitiously stole out the other door and around the corner of the cabin and from that point of vantage & distance delivered the two half boiled potatoes which you had secretly been cherishing for your cold blooded purpose.[28]

Almost 20 years later, Coggins recalled the incident again – this time Stone was an "unprincipled, pussyfooting prowler" sneaking around with a baked potato that "not only had been improperly cooked but still retained all of its original ruggedness." He continued with some more cabin recollections: "I have visions of strawberries and milk in wholesale quantities, of a chicken cooked by amateurs that chewed up into 'cuds' and defied all ordinary digestive maneuvers, of nature lovers who discarded unnatural clothing but just as naturally turned to it again with the advent of a small portion of a feminine picnic, of after-dinner noises that my untrained ear at that time classed as music, and of acrobatic efforts that threatened the security and safety of the above mentioned viands."[29] Sounds like the boys were having a regular old hoot out in the wilds of Medford.

The original owners spent a day at Catoxen in 1914 repairing the roof – the first time they'd been there together at the same time since the cabin was built. They suffered sore muscles later as a consequence, but had a great time, with Morris cooking up fried chicken and hot cakes "in his best style."[30] By 1921 the structure was in need of serious repairs, but the owners were older and probably had less time and enthusiasm for camp life than they had previously.[31] In 1927, Catoxen and the surrounding area were bought by the Arch Street Friends Meeting (Philadelphia) for use as a camp.[32] Amazingly, the cabin still stands near its original location, as a part of Camp Dark Waters, a Quaker youth camp; despite its continuous use by rambunctious boys since the late 1920s, it is in remarkably good condition. A 1908 *Cassinia* article included a photograph of the original fireplace, which is brick-by-brick recognizable today as the same one from more than 100 years ago.[33] Catoxen was obviously built to last.

One of the notable trips Stone took through the Pine Barrens at the time, leaving from Catoxen, was a weeklong jaunt with Coggins and James Rehn in June 1901. Coggins wrote about the trip in *Cassinia*, including their visit to "the Plains," where the trees came up only to their knees; the endless persecution from mosquitoes and heat; and the hot, thirsty trudge back to Catoxen on the last day.[34] Stone's description of the trip in a letter to the ANSP curators, although written with an eye to reimbursement of expenses, gives an excellent summary of their adventure:

> About 75 miles of country was covered and abundant notes on the distribution of animal & plant life were taken. A series of reptiles & batrachians were taken including the [Carpenter Frog], hitherto only known from types. Specimens of the Southern Red-backed Mouse…were also obtained.…A series of all the most characteristic insects was secured. In the way of plants about 400–500 sheets were collected, the specimens being selected to show variation in the species in the various regions traversed. A new locality for the rare [Curly-grass Fern] was discovered & many other interesting species obtained. In addition a number of photographs were secured which will be used later in illustrating a communication before the Academy.[35]

The DVOC 20-year souvenir booklet had a great photo of the three travel-worn naturalists during their trek, with the caption "Unwashed and Uncombed, 1901."[36]

Some of the collecting trips, like this one, were made at least partly in mule- or horse-drawn wagons.[18,34] A further glimpse into the transportation agenda in those days is provided in Stone's description of an August 1909 train trip aboard the "botanists' special" to Palermo, New Jersey, at the edge of the Pine Barrens near the coast: "The early morning rush to the ferry [to cross the Delaware River to Camden], the mouthful of breakfast swallowed hastily at a 'hash house'.…We leave the train at this solitary station [Palermo] to the astonishment of the excursionists, who in another moment are speeding away for the beach."[37] Another traveler recalled that the ride across the river took 10–15 minutes; when the boat docked the people were in a rush, fearful of missing their train, but the pilot showed only amusement at their impatience: "Then a dash across the Camden station, along the platform to rows of iron gates marked Cape May, Wildwood, Ocean City, and Atlantic City." Once on the train, "cigar smoke and cigarette smoke filled he air. A boy hurried down the aisle calling, 'Ice cream, sandwiches, soft drinks – next stop a long while ahead.'"[38] Stone recorded conspicuous plant species spotted from the train while traversing southern New Jersey (as well as Tree Swallows, kestrels, and Ospreys).[20,39]

He once listed some of the unpleasantries of summertime collecting in the humid, coastal Barrens, including "the hordes of blood-thirsty mosquitoes, swarms of persistent deer flies, the apparently endless roads of deep white sand, and the broiling sun of midsummer" – all too familiar to those who do fieldwork there today.[40] But he loved it all the same, as this entry from the *PSNJ* introduction makes clear: "At the same time thoughts of the pungent odor of the pines, the cool shade of the cedar swamp, where the road runs through, with its white bridge spanning the dark tea-like water of the stream; the refreshing draught of the water itself, always palatable in spite of its dark color; the fragrance of the magnolia, azalea and clethra, and the beauties of the ever attractive pine barren flowers, all tend to obliterate the memory of clouds of mosquitoes and dripping perspiration and draw the naturalist back again and again to this wonderful wilderness."[41]

Stone's fellow botanists on many collecting trips were Bayard Long and the enigmatic Samuel Van Pelt, who was a capable but reluctant collector due to his belief in the sanctity of all life. Stone said Van Pelt "protested volubly against my collecting one hundred or more specimens in a day" for the

Unwashed and uncombed: Rehn, Stone, and Coggins (*left to right*) on a week-long New Jersey Pine Barrens trip, June 1901. ANSP Archives.

PSNJ material. Van Pelt had a rare talent for mounting botanical specimens, and his were considered by Pennell "the most beautiful that I have ever seen. He developed a special technique for rapid drying, so that color has in many cases persisted remarkably well. He had also an artistic sense for the effective display of plants on the herbarium sheets." Van Pelt was an accomplished organist and violinist, and used to attend classical music concerts with score in hand, following along.[42] Long not only checked many of Stone's identifications, he almost single-handedly prepared the *PSNJ* sections on the flowering and fruiting phenology of each species by exhaustively (and probably exhaustedly) checking dates on thousands of herbarium specimens.[20,43]

Stone's intensive New Jersey fieldwork resulted in several short notes and articles that appeared between 1902 and 1911, initially in the Torrey Botanical Club's *Torreya*, then in *Bartonia* once that journal was hatched in 1908. Many of them described the discovery or rediscovery of a rare plant species in Pennsylvania or New Jersey, and the findings were due to the zealous fieldwork being done in the area by Stone and other members of the PBC. Stone had been studying the local violets since at least his WNSA days; his first botanical publication was a 1902 *Torreya* article on the first Pennsylvania record for a species of violet (*Viola renifolia*) he had found growing in Sullivan County, Pennsylvania during one of his visits with the Behr family in Lopez.[44]

In 1903, Stone really put himself on the botanical map with his 53-page *PANSP* article "Racial variation in plants and animals, with special reference to the violets of Philadelphia and vicinity," in which he referred to his personal collection of "several thousand" violet specimens. Stone presented the characteristics of 30 Philadelphia-area species from the genus *Viola*, which he had studied intensively during the previous three years. He identified a couple of specimens from Chester County as LeConte's *V. septemloba*, but in 1905 botanist Homer House disagreed and described Stone's specimens as a new species, *V. stoneana*.[45] Far from being flattered by having a species named for him, Stone thought the new description was arrived at too hastily; indeed, *V. stoneana* is today synonymous with *V. palmata*, which is a hybrid.[46]

In "Racial variation," Stone noted the proliferation of newly described species in the past 10 years, particularly in botany, where the distaste for trinomialism led to the naming of new "species" for what were often only varieties. In a humorous aside, he asserted the *Crataegus* genus (hawthorns) had undergone too much splitting into supposedly valid species (over 200), adding, "While there are admittedly a large number of species in eastern North America...I have seen sets of specimens collected from six bushes and submitted to three leading specialists on the genus returned as belonging to twice that number of species, due to the difference in their identifications."[47]

When Stone's 1903 violets article appeared, Nathaniel Britton, founder of the New York Botanical Garden, wrote, "I congratulate you cordially upon your invasion of the vegetable kingdom, and only wish that you would come into it altogether."[48] John Small, also of the Garden, wrote, "Many thanks for your Violet paper. It is certainly refreshing to see some real work begun in connection with our violets. Your paper represents the first definite results thus far reached."[49]

The paper also initiated much correspondence with Ezra Brainerd, the president of Middlebury College and a violet expert, who wrote, "It is to me a very great pleasure to come into contact with one who has studied this genus as critically and thoroughly as you have."[50] Stone collected violets at numerous localities around Pennsylvania, including in the Sherwood area near his home in West Philadelphia, and also at Ivy Hill Cemetery near Germantown. Violets are still a tough nut for botanists to crack, and their variation and propensity to freely hybridize increase the complexity level exponentially. Brainerd visited Stone and his violet haunts in early September 1905, and was particularly struck by the violets growing at Ivy Hill, saying it was "full of mysteries," a "hopeless confusion," and "by all odds the worse [*sic*] mess that I have encountered."[51] Within a few years of his "Racial variation" article, Stone apparently lost interest in splitting violet hairs, despite additional prodding from Brainerd to continue his studies with that group, and their correspondence petered out at about the time of the release of *PSNJ*.[52]

Stone's primary interest in botany was the distribution of plants. In 1907, he published "The Life-areas of southern New Jersey," which proposed a division of the Carolinian Zone in the region into finer zones based almost entirely on their characteristic flora (which he described for three of them), although some vertebrates and invertebrates were also mentioned.[53] The "Life-areas" discussion was fleshed out further in the *PSNJ* preface. In a 1908 article about plants in the coastal strip of New Jersey, Stone noted that some plant species that grew in eastern Pennsylvania and northern and western New Jersey, but were absent from the Pine Barrens, also grew in the narrow coastal strip between the Barrens and the coastal marshes. He wrote, "The problem of discovering how they got there is not one to be solved by a season's work, nor a hastily conceived theory, but is rather dependent upon a thorough knowledge of the components of this coastal flora and the distribution of each species. This is the side of botany which has always appealed most strongly to me, and the accumulation of facts for the elucidation of such problems is more gratifying than the discovery of new species."[37] He reiterated in the *PSNJ* preface that studying distribution was more interesting to him than simply making annual visits to rarities at known locations, although the former involved intensive fieldwork over a wider area.[54]

The 1908 coastal strip article was published in the PBC's inaugural issue of its journal *Bartonia*, for which Stone served on the publication committee. (Stewardson Brown was the editor.) Stone told a colleague, "I was placed on the publ[ication] committee & did what I could to make the first number what I thought it ought to be, but I am not taking an active part in the future issues unless it may be to contribute something now & then."[55] He served on the committee through at least 1914, however. In the coastal strip article, Stone described a 1908 trip with Van Pelt to the Palermo area, where they found Eastern Grasswort (*Lilaeopsis lineatea* [=*L. chinensis*]) growing at or near the location where Thomas Nuttall had found the state's first – and only previous – record of the species almost 100 years earlier. The botanist Walter Deane commented on Stone's coastal strip article, "Your pleasant way of telling it makes the reader a companion on the trip."[56]

In mid-1909, Britton, for one, was unaware of the botanical tome Stone was preparing. He told Stone in June, "I have known of your great interest in the South Jersey flora and realize that you must have brought out a great amount of additional information. Whatever you can send me to illustrate distribution of species made known by your collections I shall be very glad to have at your convenience either from South Jersey, or from eastern Pennsylvania."[57] Stone gave a talk to the PBC in November 1909, displaying some rough maps of the distribution of several plant species in southern New Jersey based on collecting locations.[58]

The minutes for the May 26, 1910 PBC meeting record that "Mr. Stone announced his intention to publish a book on the distribution of Southern New Jersey plants."[59] In August 1910, Stone told a friend, "The N.J. State Museum wants me to prepare a flora of the southern counties covering the Pine Barrens & I am preparing to look up some odd corners that I have not visited before – providing the mosquitoes permit."[60] A month later, he was "grinding out [a] final manuscript now with blanks for revised list of localities."[61] Stone gave another plant distribution talk to the PBC in January 1911, and in April he spoke to the club again, this time about the forthcoming book. Ever the historian, he said that biographies of botanists for whom plants were named would appear after the plant descriptions.[62] (Ultimately, they weren't used.) Stone credited the club members whose fieldwork contributed so largely to the book (just as he would call *BSOCM* "the DVOC book" years later). He had kudos for the club herbarium as well, saying that "no local flora has ever been issued based on such exhaustive material, so much of which is in the Club's herbarium."[63]

He also showed some of the watercolors by Hugh E. Stone (Witmer's first cousin once removed) that would illustrate the book. Hugh was working as a bank teller in Coatesville, Pennsylvania at the time.[64] He later worked as a research associate at ANSP, and published *A Flora of Chester County* in 1945.[65] Cousin Witmer had asked him in early June 1910 if he would prepare drawings for the book. Hugh responded that he didn't have much of the New Jersey flora in his sketches, "but would be very glad to try my hand on your material."[66]

———————— ❧ ————————

Stone's extensive research resulted in *The Plants of Southern New Jersey*, published in 1911 as part of the New Jersey State Museum's Annual Report for 1910 (and not actually off the press until February 1912), which "is the only comprehensive floristic treatment for southern New Jersey and it continues to be used today [2002]."[67-68] At the time of Stone's death, Pennell wrote of *PSNJ* that "it stands forth increasingly with time as the most careful geographic study of any comparable part of the flora of eastern North America."[5] In a review of the 1973 Quarterman Publishers reprint, Dutch botanist Frans Stafleu referred to Stone's botanical tome as a "surprisingly detailed and thorough work" whose main value was "the precision of the keys, the amount of phenological, geographical and ecological information, the precise documentation, and the careful integration of fieldwork and herbarium studies."[4] Sydney Greenfield, founder of Rutgers University's botany department, also in a review of the Quarterman edition, wrote, "This is a very valuable reference because of its comprehensive coverage of mosses, ferns, grasses, sedges, rushes, trees, shrubs and native wildflowers...still unequalled as a guide to the plants of the New Jersey Pine Barrens and adjacent regions....[T]he book remains the most valuable reference for the area covered."[69] Another Quarterman review was given in *Castanea* by its longtime editor, Earl Core, who wrote that Stone "knew the area and its plant life better, perhaps, than anyone before him or since.... [A]fter more than sixty years this book stands alone as the single great work on the subject."[70]

Contemporary and modern botanists are uniformly critical of the finer points of Stone's nomenclature, which was based in part on a zoological instead of a strictly botanical system.[4-5,71] (Gerry Moore gives a thorough treatment of Stone's *PSNJ* nomenclature in a 2002 *Bartonia* article.)[68] Stone said that American botanists were "on the horns of a dilemma" as to which botanical code they should employ. He predicted that the botanists would eventually change some of their nomenclatural rules to come more into line with the zoologists, but 100 years later that still hasn't happened. (And Stone's statement that zoologists had been studying nomenclature longer and more seriously than botanists probably rubbed some of the latter the wrong way.)[71] H.H. Bartlett reviewed *PSNJ* for *Rhodora* in 1912 and was critical of some of the work, especially the nomenclature, which he found "thoroughly objectionable." Overall, he offered a favorable review, writing that, nomenclature aside, it was "a remarkably pleasing work" that would be "indispensable" to "students of the coastal plain vegetation."[72] Bartlett was especially impressed with the illustrations in the book by Hugh Stone, whose willingness to "try his hand" had resulted in some beautiful work, although his watercolors were unfortunately reproduced as halftones. Stone took his lumps at the time concerning the nomenclature, but he remained interested in the subject and later served on the Botanical Society of America's Committee on Nomenclature.[73]

Perhaps Stone's favorite "review" came from a woman named Mary Brown, who wrote to him that she had been so "charmed" and "enthused" on reading his *PSNJ* that she made two trips to Bennett's Bog, New Jersey, where she collected the Low Pinebarren Milkwort (*Polygala ramosa*). The plant was identified by Stewardson Brown, who declared it the first record for Cape May County (and Stone didn't have it in *PSNJ*). Miss Brown wrote, "Of course I was delighted with my find, but if it had not been for your book perhaps never should I have visited the Bennett bog or found the Polygala."[74]

Other naturalists also complimented Stone on his work, which brought him international as well as national standing as a botanist.[75] The naturalist and mammalogist Vernon Bailey wrote, "I doubt if any, even the botanists, appreciate a work like this more than we in the Biological Survey who are working along the line of distribution problems. We rarely have a chance to do such careful detailed work as you have done in this region, and for that reason we appreciate it all the more."[76] Paul Bartsch, curator of mollusks at the Smithsonian, wrote to Stone, "Why, reading it fairly made me your companion in your rambles."[77] Ornithologist A.K. Fisher wondered, "I do not see how you have found time to prepare such an elaborate treatise on the plants of New Jersey."[78]

Silas Morse, curator of the New Jersey State Museum, told Stone shortly after its release, "Everyone is praising [*PSNJ*]. I would like to show you some of the excellent letters I have received, from Ex-governor Griggs, and what Ex-Governor Voorhees and others say about it. I am receiving applications for it from all over the country, and have to say no to most of them, except in cases where they are interested in the work."[79] Morse sent Stone 50 unbound copies of the book in 1913, presumably for Stone to distribute as he saw fit, and the book was reportedly reissued in bound form in 1917.[80] It may have been out of print by 1919, and Stone answered a 1921 request for a copy by saying that it might be possible to get one by writing the State Museum, but that there had been a great demand for the book.[81]

Other members of the PBC made strong contributions to *PSNJ*, particularly Long and Van Pelt, and club members were not slackers when it came to fieldwork: Stone mentioned in the Snowy Orchis account that "the systematic efforts of the members of the…Club to explore all the bogs of this region that were marked on the maps were responsible for discovering the locality" of the orchid.[82] That sounds like a lot of bog-trotting. Stone was also not the only club member to contribute to the local botanical literature. John Harshberger wrote *The Botanists of Philadelphia and Their Work* in 1899, and published *The Vegetation of the New Jersey Pine-Barrens* a few years after Stone's *PSNJ*.[83] Ida Keller and Stewardson Brown compiled the club publication *Handbook of the Flora of Philadelphia and Vicinity* in 1905.[84]

PSNJ is a fairly straightforward flora, as dry and technical as any good flora should be, but Stone marked it with his individual stamp. He brought a conservation element into it, lamenting the decimation of mistletoe and cedar swamps, and the escalating intrusion of roads and settlements into the Barrens' inner sanctums. As historian, he gave an excellent summary of the history of botanical exploration in the Pine Barrens, and of the discovery and subsequent increase in knowledge of the haunts of the famed *Schizaea* (Curly-grass Fern). There's even a little dry humor in the Sweet Pepperbush description: "At Manahawkin it is called Soap Bush, from the idea that the flowers when rubbed together in water make a sort of soapy lather. Our results have not been very startling, however."[85] His 1911 *Bartonia* "Abama americana" article contained some wonderful word paintings; in *PSNJ* we get glimpses of some of the descriptive writing style that Stone later displayed in *BSOCM*, for example in the Pitch Pine account. His description of a bog location along the Wading River revealed Stone's love of the Barrens (some of the scientific and common names used by Stone have been changed to modern common names):[86]

> A low, scattered growth of Pitch Pines slopes down on either side to the moist savanna, through which flows the rapid, tea-colored stream. On the edge of the moist ground is a dense, low, shrubby growth of White Azalea, three or four species of huckleberries and the Inkberry....White Cedars mark the course of the stream, now forming dense clusters, now scattering, with young ones standing out here and there in the grassy, open stretches, and with the cedars along the bank are Red Maples, Wax Myrtles and beds of Royal Fern, Livid Sedge and Tuberculed Spikerush.
>
> The "Savannas" are covered with the tall stalks of Smooth Wild Oatgrass, while the denser growth below contains Britton's Panicgrass, Beaked-rushes of several species, Slender Nutrush [named for science by Stone], etc., all rising from a bed of sphagnum or from patches of wet, white sand and scattered all about in definite clumps are the Pitcher Plants, with pitchers of all shades and combinations of green and crimson, and the button-topped stalks of the Flattened Pipeworts and Ten-angled Pipeworts – the former at this date, July 4, scattering its chaff at the slightest touch, the latter only in bud. With them, but not so definitely tufted, are the yellow spikes of the Bog Asphodel, the white, gummy-stemmed Viscid Asphodel and beds of the downy, wooly heads of the Goldencrest. There are crimson Grasspinks and

Rose Pogonias starring the grass here and there, and where shallow, rusty, iron-stained pools are formed on either side of the rapid-flowing stream there are solid masses of *Utricularias*, shining like beds of gold in the sunlight. And in the deep water are white pond lilies and velvety leaves of the Golden Club, now gone to seed, erect emerged spikes of Bayonet Rush and Congdon's Yellow-eyed Grass and great beds of Seven-angled Pipewort and Water Club-rush, their leaves and stems ever swaying in the steady current. Truly one of nature's flower gardens, and it stretches for miles, following the course of the streams through the wilderness of pine, cedar and white sand, now narrowing, now widening out into broad stretches.[87]

Stone's friend Cornelius Weygandt was so taken with this passage, and the descriptions of the Plains elsewhere in the book, that in March 1914 he asked Stone to take him on an excursion to the area, and Stone obliged.[88]

───────────── ᪱ ─────────────

At the time of the publication of his botanical masterpiece in early 1912, one could argue that Stone was almost as much a botanist as an ornithologist. He had just spent the last 12 years doing intensive botanical fieldwork in the Pine Barrens and writing an 800-page book about it. The botanist and aquarist William A. Poyser told Stone upon receiving his copy of *PSNJ*, "I surely congratulate you, but I don't like that 'Never again' sign! Can't believe you mean it."[89] However, Stone told fellow ornithologists that, after all the work the book required, he'd had his fill of botany.[90] Although these declarations may have been due to a feeling of having a millstone off his neck, Stone clearly turned his professional attention almost entirely to ornithology at that point. Amazingly, with the exception of death notices of club members he occasionally wrote for *Bartonia*, *PSNJ* proved to be his last botanical publication. He simply became too swamped with Academy and AOU responsibilities. Pennell wrote that it was the call to become editor of *The Auk* in 1912 that turned Stone's attention from botany after the Herculean botanical efforts over the preceding 12 years that led to *PSNJ*: "He only gradually relinquished active interest in botanical collecting and attendance at the meetings of the PBC, but for nearly twenty years pressure of administrative duties [at ANSP] and then increasing physical incapacity have made him a rare visitor with us....Sometimes, although more and more rarely, he would stop in the botanical department of the Academy to tell of some plant he observed."[5]

Stone gave nine talks to the club during the period 1915–1923, which would indicate he was still active in it; however, the club secretary noted in 1917 that Stone no longer attended meetings.[91-92] He continued to do at least some botanical fieldwork: the *PANSP* often recorded some later collecting, such as a note in 1918 that "Dr. Stone spent several weeks in making an exhaustive collection of the flora of southern Cape May County, N.J." (and he presented those findings in a talk to the club in early 1919).[91,93] Stone asked for his plant press to be sent to him from ANSP while he was summering at Cape May in 1932.[94] He also collected plants for the Academy's herbarium in the Chiricahua Mountains of Arizona on a summer 1919 trip that was funded by the Academy's Redfield Memorial Herbarium Fund.[95] He brought back over 1,000 sheets of plants, in addition to several nonbotanical collections.[96] Stone said in October that the plants were being mounted, "after which I hope to tackle <u>portions</u> of it anyway," which indicates he worked on identification of at least some of them.[97] He had left some of his other Arizona plant specimens (*Senecios*, *Cactaceae*, etc.) at the Smithsonian for their botanists to identify, presumably because the staff there had more expertise with those taxa than did Academy botanists.[98]

However, in response to an invitation to lead a field trip for the Torrey Botanical Club in 1922, Stone declared that "my duties here at the Museum are such that I have had no time for Botany for some years past, and it is very seldom that I can get out in the field at all."[99] In 1924 he told the famous Harvard botanist M.L. Fernald that his botanical work was "a thing of the past," and in 1927, in response to a request for a plant identification, he said, "I have been out of botanical work so long that my opinion would be worthless."[100] By the time he published *BSOCM* in 1937, Stone seems to have even forgotten the name of his botanical tome: he referred to it as *Flora of Southern New Jersey*, which is a nice encapsulated description of it, but not the correct title.[101]

That Stone never lost his love for the Pine Barrens, however, is clear in Weygandt's description of a trip taken there some time after the book was published: "It was good to see him on 'The Plains' and to hear his say-so on pixie and sand myrtle, arbutus and sand heath, golden club and Schizaea....How his eyes danced as he followed the darts and dashes of the lizards across the sand between the scrub oaks and up their trunks! What satisfaction he had, too, in the scent of cedar chips that filled holes in the road, and in the sight of white drifts of plum blossoms tumbled by golden bees."[102]

Stone and Cape May botanist extraordinaire Otway Brown entered a display in the Cape May Flower Show for at least a few years, and they always won in the wildflower category. There are indications they were involved in some sort of Cape May flower show as early as 1923, and Witmer greatly enjoyed the event.[103] In 1929, he told Wharton Huber, "They had a flower show here last week & Otway Brown & I put up a Wild Flower exhibit, by going in car to where we <u>knew</u> good things were to be had we got bunches of 60 species which were displayed in milk bottles & suitably labeled. It caused <u>some</u> stir (we gave no localities!!) We got a 1st prize & a special award etc. $5 + $2 + 1 gal. Marsh

Mallow Whip!!!"[104] The display reportedly was such a hit that they were asked to prepare the same exhibit for the New York Flower Show.[105] At the 1930 Cape May show, held at Convention Hall, they exhibited 78 species of native New Jersey wildflowers, including "orange milkwort; many varieties of orchids; scarlet gilia, a western flower also found [as an escaped exotic] in the pine barrens of Ocean county; sea pink and butterfly weed; some insectivorous plants, such as the oblong-leaved sundew, found in the cranberry bogs." Stone said the plants had been gathered July 22 "in red hot temperatures."[106]

Poor health caused Stone to miss the 1931 show, but he and Brown were back in winning form in 1932, and Stone told a friend he won "a silver loving cup for a collection of wild flowers (85 varieties in vases) at the Flower Show here! I may not be able to compete in the Olympics but can still pull in a prize!"[107] (The Olympics were held in Los Angeles that summer.) And in 1933, Brown and Stone won again – "as usual," according to one observer.[108] When you think about it, with the two preeminent Cape May botanists teaming up for a display, did anybody else really stand a chance?

Members of the PBC were treated to a tag team of South Jersey botanical giants at their April 25, 1929 meeting, when Brown presented "Flora of Cape May County, New Jersey." He spoke of his early days of botanizing with little in the way of books, knowledge, or instruction; eventually, through contact with PBC botanists and countless hours of fieldwork, he was able to amass a list of 1,700 plants for Cape May County. The walls of the meeting room were hung with many of his specimens, especially the rarer ones. Stone followed with "Botanizing in Cape May County," which included a brief talk on distribution of South Jersey plants, complete with anecdotes and reminiscences of his work on *PSNJ*.[109] Modern Pine Barrens botanists would dearly love to have an audio or video recording of *that* meeting.

Stone also had an interest in lichens, at least in his younger days, and the following excerpt from his *Bartonia* memorial of John Eckfeldt recounts his initial meeting with the amateur botanist and lichen expert:

> When I first came to the Academy in 1888 I frequently noticed a short, quiet man visiting the herbarium across the hall from my room and examining the case containing the lichens. In my botanical studies I had attempted to gain some knowledge of all the groups and had collected a number of lichens although I had been unable to name them. The next time the visitor came I had my specimens there and took them to him for assistance. He gladly named them all and expressed both surprise and pleasure that I had shown any interest in such plants, for students of lichens, he told me, were very few.[110]

Eckfeldt even gave Stone a key to his lichen collection cabinets.[111]

Stone's 10-year obsession with the distribution of plants in the New Jersey Pine Barrens led to the publication of a book which was remarkable for the amount of detailed field and herbarium work that went into it, and it also cemented his legacy as a botanist. Silas Morse was the curator of the New Jersey State Museum during the time that Stone was writing his mammals, birds and plants books for the museum's annual reports. In 1917, when he was no longer curator, he wrote Stone a poignant letter about a recent visit to the museum, where he felt he saw his life's work ruined. The museum's emphasis had originally been natural history, but in 1912 archaeology was added to the mission, and Morse was apparently uncomfortable with the resultant changes.[112] But, he told Stone, "I have the satisfaction of knowing that they cannot wholly undo the good work done for the State and the Course of Education, for the reports you and Mr. [Henry] Fowler and others so kindly prepared for me will live after we have passed on to the other land where I trust politics will have no hold."[113]

Morse was presciently correct, for although *The Mammals of New Jersey* may have always been of limited importance, and *The Birds of New Jersey* was superseded by *Bird Studies at Old Cape May*, Stone's monumental *The Plants of Southern New Jersey* is a local flora of unquestioned botanical and historical importance. It continues to serve as a critical baseline reference in a state that finds itself on the horns of its own dilemma as it nears build-out while constantly wrestling with the issue of the value of its irreplaceable natural heritage versus economic and development agendas.

9

An All-round Naturalist

J ames Rehn and Wharton Huber called Stone one of the last of the "general naturalists," in an era that saw increasing specialization in the biological sciences.[1-2] Rehn wrote, "Equally at home with birds or mammals, he also possessed a good knowledge of reptiles, of mollusks, particularly our local land and marine forms, of many of our insects and crustaceans, as well as critical ability in the systematics of our local flora." Botanist Francis Pennell noted Stone's expertise in ornithology, mammalogy, and botany, but added that one of his earliest memories of working at ANSP was being sent to Stone for identification of a myriopod (millipedes and centipedes).[3] Stone even knew shells: a search on the Academy's malacology department collection database turns up numerous shells donated by Stone, from locales that cover many of the places he visited in his lifetime.[4]

Witmer and the Wilson Natural Science Association (WNSA) boys, of course, studied pretty much everything they came across out of doors. Stone told Stewardson Brown in 1887 that he had over 50 phials and bottles of spiders that he'd collected around Germantown, Paradise, Stock Grange, York County, and the Browns' summertime stomping grounds, Point Pleasant. Three years later he published his only arachnological manuscript, "Pennsylvania and New Jersey spiders of the family Lycosidae."[5] Stone, as a "fellow arachnologist," received a letter of congratulations and encouragement to further studies (not forthcoming, however) from the Smithsonian's Nathan Banks, later a noted entomologist.[6]

Two passages from the article reveal the kind of down-in-the-dirt natural history study the WNSA crowd was into, and some of the minute details they uncovered that wouldn't be apparent to a casual observer. In the Sand Spider (*Trochosa cinerea*) account, Stone wrote, "On the night of Aug. 12th, 1889 while catching Amphipods and other small crustacea which abound on the [N.J.] beach after dark, I caught a number of these spiders which appeared to run down after the retreating waves in search of food. Some of these were females that had already deposited their eggs while others were not more than half grown." It's a safe bet that of the millions of people who visit the Jersey Shore these days in summer, absolutely none of them is crawling around the beach in the dark studying crustacea and the habits of spiders. And you have to spend a lot of time hanging around spider holes to learn all this about one of the burrowing spiders (*Lycosa aernicola*):

This species I have met with only in the sandy districts of New Jersey, especially near the coast. Here they make tube-like burrows in the sand, usually lining them with silk. Numerous specimens were collected at Pt. Pleasant August 13th, 1888. Both males and females were found in the holes, but only one spider in each. The females were not fully grown, and had not yet deposited their eggs. The tubes were made in the loose sand, and were eight to ten inches deep, with a slight silky lining inside, but no collection of sticks or rubbish around the opening. My friend, [Amos] Brown, made a careful study of these spiders at the same locality some years before, and states that most of the burrows examined by him had silky linings which extended out from the mouth of the hole, and the sand adhering to them formed flaps. These flaps, he noticed, were always drawn over the hole during rain or high wind, nearly covering the mouth of it, and serving as a protection to the spider within. Burrows situated in grassy localities some distance from the beach often had a few pieces of grass or small sticks collected around the mouth, but nothing like the turrets found by [previous researchers].

In 1892, Stone presented ANSP with his collection of 160 species of spiders in 400 vials.[7]

Stone made some contributions to mammalogy, though they were not nearly as numerous or as important as his ornithological and botanical studies. In the 1890s he frequently collected rodents with Samuel Rhoads, particularly in New Jersey. In the fall of 1892, they took turns naming new rodents found in the Mays Landing area after each other, with Stone proposing the subspecies *Evotomys* [=*Myodes*] *gapperi rhoadsii* for a series of Southern Red-backed Voles, and Rhoads naming his find *Synaptomys stonei* (now considered a subspecies of the Southern Bog Lemming, *S. cooperi*).[8] Stone also described a new species of woodrat (*Neotoma pennsylvanica*) from specimens obtained by J.G. Dillin near Carlisle, Pennsylvania; the species was later determined to be conspecific with *Neotoma magister* (Allegheny Woodrat).[9] In 1900, Horace Jayne, director of the Wistar Institute of Anatomy and Biology at UP, asked Stone to look over some mammals collected in the East Indies, and Stone named two as new species: a rabbit, *Caprolagus furnessi* (now *Pentalagus furnessi* and still a valid species), and a flying squirrel, *Sciuropterus harrisoni*, which is no longer valid.[10] Similarly, in 1917, at the behest of a museum in Honolulu, Stone examined some recently collected material and described a new species of rat from the

Hawaiian Islands, the Hawaiian Rat (*Rattus hawaiiensis*), which he surmised was native to the islands but had been much reduced after the introduction of Norway and Black rats.[11] He considered it a distinct species from the Polynesian Rat (*Mus* [=*Rattus*] *exulans*) because of Hawaii's oceanic isolation, but it's now recognized that wide-ranging fishermen introduced *R. exulans* to the Hawaiian islands, and Stone's "Hawaiian Rat" is considered conspecific with the Polynesian Rat.[12]

Stone had plans as early as the late 1890s to write a popular mammal book.[13] He approached the publisher Doubleday, Page, and Company, in 1901, suggesting that it publish a handbook of American mammals along the lines of Frank Chapman's *Handbook of Birds of Eastern North America*.[14] Doubleday was hesitant to do so, and editor Henry Lanier told Stone that it was almost impossible to find scientific men who wrote well in a popular vein. At Lanier's invitation, Stone submitted an outline and some sample chapters to indicate what he had in mind.[15] After perusing the material, however, Lanier told Stone that it was just as they'd feared: the writing was spot-on as far as scientific accuracy was concerned, but "it smacks too much of the museum, and not enough of the woods. One does not get an intimate feeling of the life of the wild creatures in their home....[I]n a word, the personality and the surroundings of the wild animals are rather neglected at the expense of the definite statements regarding their relations and habitat."[16]

Shortly thereafter, William Everett Cram offered a collection of mammal essays for book publication, and Doubleday contacted Stone again to work with Cram on preparing a book. Cram was a nature and historical writer who lived his entire life (1871–1947) in Hampton Falls, New Hampshire.[17] He had already written another popular animal book, *Little Beasts of Field and Wood*, which was principally a compilation of articles he had previously published in magazines, and he followed that with *More Little Beasts of Field and Wood*.[18] For the Doubleday book, Cram authored the accounts of the more common and well-known species (e.g., Little Brown Bat, Red Fox, Virginia [=White-tailed] Deer, Muskrat, etc.), and they are full of long-winded, homey accounts of his personal experiences with the animals. Stone tweaked some of Cram's accounts, and he also handled the less common species, as well as animals such as rodents and bats that Cram, in the preface to *Little Beasts of Field and Wood*, said he hadn't yet written about. Stone's accounts are more concise, and drier, leaving out the personal nature adventures. He also prepared the accounts for species outside of the range of experience of either writer (e.g., Bison, Musk Ox, Mountain Goat, Pronghorn Antelope); many of those accounts contained long passages from Audubon, C. Hart Merriam, and others. The mix of authors and styles made for an uneven presentation of the material. Stone also handled the more technical sections like subspecies descriptions, taxonomic group overviews, distribution, and keys.[14,19]

Their collaboration produced *American Animals*, published in 1902.[20] This was one of Stone's more ambitious forays into popular nature writing, and although the book could be considered a blight on his resume, he was still pitching it 12 years later in *The Auk*.[21] The book didn't make either author rich: Cram wrote to Stone in 1913 that Doubleday was bringing out the whole Nature Library set, of which *American Animals* was a part, in smaller volumes that would be sold cheaply compared to the original books. Under the new arrangement, Stone and Cram would receive five cents per volume to be divided between them![22]

Stone authored *The Mammals of New Jersey* in 1907 as part of the annual report of the State Museum at Trenton.[23] The book was an exercise in compilation of other authors' work, with Stone leaning particularly heavily on Rhoads's *Mammals of Pennsylvania and New Jersey* from 1903. One could have guessed as much from Stone's preface, however, in which he wrote that Rhoads's work "completely covers the subject and leaves practically nothing to be said on the New Jersey species" – which leaves one wondering why Stone and Silas Morse, the New Jersey State Museum curator and de facto editor of the annual reports, bothered to cook up another one just a few years later. Stone seems to have had personal experience with only the more common species. In one of the interesting nuggets in the book, he described a plan hatched in New Jersey in 1894 to harvest dolphins for their oil; happily, that quickly came to naught and today they are still, as in Stone's time, abundant off of Cape May, "plunging and rising again just beyond the breakers."[24]

Stone was a founding member (along with many other ornithologists), councilor, vice president (1927–1929), and president (1929–1931) of the American Society of Mammalogists.[25] He told Joseph Grinnell after the society's 1930 meeting that he hadn't intended to take the presidency for another year "as I am not now a mammalogist except in sympathy," but consented to another term for the sake of organizational stability.[26] Huber listed 19 mammal-related publications in his Stone memorial in the *Journal of Mammalogy*, many of them collection descriptions published in *PANSP*.[2]

--------------------------- ❧ ---------------------------

Stone was interested in herpetology as well. In a 1901 talk to ANSP staff, Stone reported a specimen of the Pine Barrens Treefrog that had recently been donated to the Academy. Earlier in the year he had heard some unidentified frogs calling near Medford, New Jersey (doubtless at or near Catoxen) and suspected they were this species; he thought more intense searches would turn up additional locations (it had only been found at five to date – four in New Jersey).[27] In 1906, he published "Notes on Reptiles and Batrachians [i.e., frogs/toads] of Pennsylvania, New Jersey, and Delaware" in *The American Natural-*

ist.[28] This was a list of species from Stone's personal observations and from the ANSP collections, to which Stone had donated specimens. Occasionally, he would tackle an unprocessed Academy herpetological collection, identifying the specimens and publishing a description of it in *PANSP*.

Stone was a member of the American Society of Ichthyologists and Herpetologists, and in 1932 he published an interesting account in its journal *Copeia* about the discovery of the burrowing habits of Eastern Spadefoot Toads. It is reproduced here in its entirety because it presents such an interesting glimpse of Stone and other prominent contemporary naturalists making a fortuitous natural history find:

TERRESTRIAL ACTIVITY OF SPADE-FOOT TOADS

Following the Philadelphia meeting of the American Society of Ichthyologists and Herpetologists, several members, associated with members of the Society of Mammalogists, spent the weekend of May 15–17, 1931, as the guests of Mr. Arthur N. Leeds [PBC founder and fern expert], at Four-ways Cabin [still extant] on the Egg Harbor River in the heart of the New Jersey pine barrens. About ten o'clock at night Mr. Arthur C. Emlen told us that a week previous he had discovered, with the aid of a flash light, a number of small toads out under the pines, by following up the pink eyeshine of the batrachians. This statement caused considerable interest and in a few minutes it was abundantly verified. Dr. Remington Kellogg [a cetacean specialist and assistant, later head, curator of the Smithsonian], judging from an experience in the west some years previously, predicted that these Jersey toads would prove to be spadefoots (*Scaphiopus holbrooki*), and sure enough our specimens were at once recognized as this species. On this and the following night we found the open pine woods fairly well populated with the toads and a number of specimens were obtained all of which seemed to be about half grown (body length 1.50 inches). They evidently burrowed in the dry sand during the day and came forth only late at night. Some were caught in the act of emerging from their burrows and were photographed successfully by Mr. Francis Harper [a widely-published naturalist and photographer] with the aid of a flash light apparatus. Others subjected to the glare of the light rapidly dug themselves in, sinking "tail first" into the sand, and were a couple of inches down in as many minutes. Some individuals which I brought home and placed under a bell glass on a box of soil at once disappeared in the earth but came forth again late the following night. Previous to this experience my knowledge of the spadefoot was as a loud-voiced species usually frequenting temporary pools in early spring which, after pairing, disappeared no one knew where but probably to remain buried until the following spring. Their appearance in these dry pine woods was, therefore, to say the least, surprising although others have perhaps been aware of their nocturnal terrestrial habits.[29]

∾

Stone came to entomology early. He gave talks to WNSA on the subject, covering butterfly wing scales, beetles, dragonflies, and even barklice. Stone also showed some early talent for drawing insects (see book cover). He eventually became a member of the American Entomological Society and collected insects on trips around the country, including several thousand insects on his 1919 trip to Arizona.[30] In an arrangement still common today among research institutions of sending specimens to friends and colleagues who are experts in a particular field, he sent his Arizona Hymenopterans (wasps, bees, and ants) and Hemipterans (true bugs) to W.L. McAtee and Henry L. Viereck at the

Some all-round naturalists gathered at Four-ways Cabin, May 16, 1931. *Back row, left to right*: Art Emlen Sr., W.E. Saunders, Arthur H. Howell, E.A. Preble, Remington Kellogg, Witmer Stone, Francis Harper, Arthur N. Leeds; *front row, left to right*: Art Emlen Jr. (standing, with butterfly net), W.E. Sanderson, E.M.S. Dale, Howard [last name illegible]. Photo courtesy of Ruth Fisher/Pat and Clay Sutton.

USDA in Washington, D.C., for identification.[31] In late May 1920, Stone told McAtee, "The Coleoptera [beetles] are all done & the Orthoptera [grasshoppers/crickets/locusts] & Lepidoptera [butterflies/moths] nearly finished [presumably worked up by ANSP entomologist James Rehn]….I think it might be worth while to publish the several lists with such field notes as I have, all in one article with all due credit & thanks to those who did the [mounting and identification] work."[32] It doesn't appear, however, that the planned publication was ever produced.

Stone also did some entomological fieldwork closer to home. A species of grasshopper, Stone's Locust (*Melanoplus stonei*; still a valid species), was named for Stone by Rehn in 1904, after they collected the type series in the New Jersey Pine Barrens.[33] The University of California, Berkeley coleopterist Edwin Van Dyke once paid a visit to the Academy to study its collection; he and Stone took a field trip with their wives to Pink Hill, now part of the Tyler Arboretum, west of Philadelphia. The boys "turned over innumerable rocks and logs and investigated a dead dog in the pursuit of rarities." The ladies were more interested in the blooming Moss Phlox that gives the location its name than in dead dogs and dirt, and they spent the time picking flowers.[34]

During his 1935 visit to Edward McIlhenny's Louisiana estate, Stone and his host set up an insect trap. McIlhenny enthusiastically sent ANSP the Coleoptera collected in the trap all through the summer, which is why so many beetles in ANSP's collection today have "Avery Island, Louisiana" on their tags.[35] McIlhenny's September 24 note to Stone would break the heart of a museum lepidopterist: on that morning there were "thousands upon thousands of moths of various kinds. It was hard to get the coleopteran separated from them."[36] (The beetles were the only things being collected; the moths were discarded.)

In his last years, when declining health curtailed strenuous fieldwork, Stone turned his attention more to entomology and he "collected insects assiduously even through his final summer at Cape May."[37] Rehn sent Stone a cyanide bottle and a lens in July 1933, advising him, "I can fully realize that you must do some hunting, and the 'small game' which you can get nearby can be just as interesting as larger stuff. I know there is quite a little in the Orthoptera of Cape May which is of interest and I shall be glad to see anything you gather in. However, do not try to track down the fast flyers [for health reasons]."[38] Stone sent his Cape May Hymenopterans and Dipterans (true flies) to Harold Morrison at the USDA Bureau of Entomology for identification; H.G. Barber at the Smithsonian worked up the Hemipterans when McAtee was too busy to help.[39] After Witmer's death, Lillie presented the Academy with his collection of over 10,000 insects from the Cape May area, which Huber described as "the most complete collection of this region, beautifully prepared, in existence."[40]

That Stone's contemporaries recognized his broad knowledge of natural history is apparent in a few letters from the bound collection presented to Stone in honor of his 20th anniversary as *Auk* editor and the completion of the fourth AOU check-list. Paul Bartsch, the Smithsonian malacologist and pioneering bird bander, wrote:

> When I look over the group of active naturalists in this wonderful land of ours, I am impressed by the fact that most of them are engaged on needlepoint efforts, trained excellently in the study of transverse and longitudinal sections – let us say the hair of an elephant – but so well specialized and pointed that they would fail to recognize one of these animals were they to meet it in their daily route! I have therefore found it most refreshing whenever I have had the pleasure of a little while with you, whether in the laboratory, the parlor, or field, to meet a man whose outlook is of that old, antiquated type…which still enables one to enjoy the handing out of a peanut and to watch the pachyderm enjoy the titbit…without thinking of the scant hirsute covering of the beast and its histological structure….[W]hat a joy it is to spend a bit of time afield with a man who knows the things that surround him on his daily route as you do.[41]

C. Hart Merriam, one of the last of the general naturalists himself, wrote about Witmer and Lillie's 1915 visit with the Merriams at their Lagunitas, California home ("our little shack in the Redwoods," as he called it): "That visit was a revelation to me. Previously I had known you as an ornithologist with a side interest in mammals. But the day you came I discovered my mistake, for from early morning till dark you were perpetually hunting – not for Birds, for you seemed to discover them without searching, but for small mammals, lizards, snakes, scorpions, insects, and unfamiliar plants. In other words, you were that rare thing – an All-round Naturalist! Your enthusiasm, your persistence and your knowledge were a surprise and a delight. I was deeply impressed."[42]

10

I Am Asking for More!

S tone had an early interest in taxonomy. At the beginning of his ornithological career, "the height of his ambition" was membership on the AOU
Committee on Classification and Nomenclature of North American Birds.[1] He
later realized just that: he served on the classification committee beginning in
1901, was appointed acting chairman of it in 1915, and served as chairman
1919–1931.[2-3] The committee was chaired by the indefatigable J.A. Allen in
Stone's early years, and produced the third AOU Check-list of North American
Birds in 1910. The fourth edition of the AOU check-list, published in 1931,
was 526 pages long and took many years of fits and starts to complete; the
work was overseen, and largely written, by Stone.[4] He was also a member/
commissioner of the International Commission on Zoological Nomenclature
(ICZN)1927–1939.[5]

Stone published many articles on taxonomy and nomenclature, beginning
shortly after his arrival at ANSP and tapering off after he started editing *The
Auk*. As he delved into the long-neglected bird collection early in his Academy
career, he compared selected specimens there with closely related specimens
from ANSP and other museum and private collections, which led to several
publications on proposed taxonomic revisions.[6]

Discovering the North American avifauna was the order of the day for
American ornithologists in the mid-19th century; by the end of the century,
naming and classifying the discoveries was the task at hand. Witmer took an
active, even feisty, part in some of the bickering about priority and species
splitting that prevailed at the time, before a measure of stability was reached.
By nomenclatural rules, the scientific name associated with the first formal
description of a species is the name to be used ever afterward; the name is
said to have "priority." It was almost a game among some ornithological taxonomists in Stone's time to dig into obscure, old publications, including foreign
ones (e.g., a rare, little known Polish work from 1821, or a similar German
one from 1804), to try to find an earlier description of a species than the one
formally recognized as the first one; the earlier description would inevitably
have a different scientific name, which would then trump the later, recognized
one.[7] Sometimes there was disagreement over exactly which species was being
referred to in a typically inadequate description from an old journal. Sometimes a newly discovered, older name was deemed to have priority, but had no
sooner been accepted than someone found another, even older one, usually in
an even more obscure publication.

Stone happily joined the fray in his younger days and published several articles on the subject over the years. For example, in an 1899 *Auk* paper, Stone asserted that John Kirk Townsend's scientific name for what we now call MacGillivray's Warbler, *Geothlypis tolmei*, appeared in Townsend's published journal a couple of months before Audubon published the accepted name of *Sylvia macgillivrayi* in the fifth volume of his *Ornithological Biography*, and should therefore have priority. (Remarkably, after some nomenclatural wandering and wobbling over many years, the species' latest name is actually – for the moment – *Geothlypis tolmei*.)[8]

Such articles, and his taxonomic revision ones, garnered Stone a reputation with some at the time that was at odds with his later one. In 1905, Jonathan Dwight complained to Stone about the lack of name stability that hampered check-list efforts, saying, "[F]or us to suffer endlessly at the hands of such nomenclatural highwaymen as [Charles] Richmond & [Harry] Oberholser & yourself & some others is asking too much."[9] Years later, Stone would be seen as a conservative antidote to the likes of Oberholser, although more in the area of species and genus splitting. In a talk at the 1928 AOU annual meeting, Stone gently ribbed "those who claim [nomenclature] as their chief indoor sport."[10]

The biological sciences move through periods when the trend is either for previously separate species to be combined into single species ("lumping"), or divided into ever greater numbers of species or subspecies ("splitting"). Late 19th/early 20th century ornithology was definitely a time of splitters ("feather-splitting," as some called it), not only of species but also of genera, and scientific names were in great flux.[11] As early as 1899, Stone made a gibing reference to the constantly changing names, saying that collectors wrote the name last on a species label, "perhaps because we fear it will be changed by the AOU Committee before we get it written!"[12] In an *Auk* paper in the same year about the various plumages of the Rose-breasted Grosbeak, Stone argued that at a time when describing new subspecies was all the rage, the seasonal plumages of common birds were only imperfectly known.[13] Stone expressed similar sentiments in his address to the Nuttall Ornithological Club in 1923, saying, "It is conceivable that a species may be divided into an innumerable number of local groups, but the human senses are limited in the degree to which they can discriminate between them."[14] Stone voiced no protest at his friend Frank Chapman naming a grackle subspecies after him, however.[15] *Quiscalis quiscala stonei* has survived as a valid form, if on shaky legs.[16]

Stone wasn't the only one who was vexed with the subspecies mania, and American ornithological journals at the time carried frequent complaints about their proliferation. Frederic Kennard told Stone, "I shall never forget talking with William Brewster a few weeks before he died about this hair-splitting business, and the constant changes of nomenclature. Brewster sat up in his chair with all the old fire in his eye, and said, 'Kennard, it makes me ashamed to be an ornithologist.'"[17] Some of it could get pretty silly, as in a 1919 Joseph Grinnell article about subspecies recently added to the California list, which Grinnell wrapped up with, "We are still decidedly behind Texas, with its 605 species and subspecies, but we are steadily catching up!"[18] The state with the biggest list wins?

One of the upshots of the flood of new subspecies descriptions was that it was suddenly more difficult for ornithologists – both amateurs and museum professionals – to assign their specimens to a particular form. Because the purported plumage differences between some of the described forms were so negligible, ornithologists often simply went by range, but the ranges given for the forms did not, of course, blanket North America. There were gaps between, which made assigning difficult. Stone asked Robert Young, collecting for ANSP in Colorado in 1904, for location data for some of the specimens he'd sent to the Academy, so Stone could identify the form. (The genera listed indicate that Stone was trying to figure out the species for some of the specimens, and subspecies for others.) Young shot back, "[P]ermit me to ask what an ornithologist is good for if he can't identify species without data, and what a species is good for it if can't be identified by a good ornithologist, without the data?"[19] Young comes across as a smart aleck in other correspondence, and it's difficult to know just how serious is his sarcasm here, but he makes a good point. He's essentially asking, "If you can't tell which form it is by just looking at it, but instead need to know the exact location in order to look up which form is supposed to occur there, then a) how specialized or superior is your ornithological knowledge and b) how valid is the form?" And Stone probably largely agreed with him.

However, Stone also defended the feather-splitters at times. In a 1914 talk to the DVOC, he said the depth of knowledge of the taxonomic specialist would "astonish" the amateur who thinks they are merely out to rack up more names.[20] Twelve years later he used an *Auk* review of three weak papers by J.D. Figgins, which were critical of the subspecies craze, to defend the specialist again:

> The reviewer [i.e., Stone] has no more personal use for subspecies separated on minute characters than has Mr. Figgins, because they do not happen to concern the work in which he is most interested, but that is no reason why he should object to others describing them or using them in their work, nor does it give him any warrant to doubt the accuracy of their work. Neither is he interested in the minute and detailed nomenclature of the muscles nor is he able to distinguish them but he realizes that others can do this and reach important results from their anatomical study. Why this rather general clamor against subspecies on the part of field ornithologists, collectors, oologists, etc., it is hard to understand. If subspecies do not pertain to their work why bother with

them? Let them be satisfied with the species but do not try to hamper the work of those who can and do make use of them for the advancement of scientific knowledge.[21]

As work on the fourth check-list neared completion, Stone, perhaps trying to head off inevitable criticisms of the number of subspecies, called for a truce: he asked *Auk* readers in the January 1929 issue to begin the new year by resolving not to attack the "manufacturer[s] of subspecies" in print, and not to quibble over the species splits in the forthcoming check-list.[22] In one of his last remarks on the subject, however, he told AMNH ornithologist James Chapin in 1936, "[L]ike you, I have less & less use for subspecies, the more I see of them. I suppose they are a 'necessary nuisance,' but the job of the future will be to cancel a lot of them instead of making more!"[23]

If Stone was somewhat ambivalent about the proliferation of subspecies, he came down squarely against genus-splitting. In a 1915 *Auk* note, he wrote that taxonomy should be used as much to show similarities as to show differences. (He had made similar arguments in *The Plants of Southern New Jersey* and elsewhere.)[24] He pointed out that in some groups of birds there were already numerous genera that contained a single species, so the genus was superfluous and gave no indication of the species' relationship to other birds. He advised the use of broader genera, and taxonomists who wished further generic splits could make use of a sub-genus (a term used by John Cassin), which would not appear in the scientific name.[25-26] Stone reiterated the same points in a 1920 *Science* article, "The use and abuse of the genus." He again called for the use of a sub-genus, suggesting that taxonomists "use the broader generic terms of a few years ago for *nomenclatural* purposes and use another term, call it sub-genus or what you will, for further systematic refinements, without incorporating it in the [scientific] name....The main point would be to check the excessive generic subdivision which is today rampant in certain quarters. If some such reform be not inaugurated technical nomenclature will soon be – if it is not already – useless to anyone but a narrow specialist."[27] In modern taxonomy, there are actually two categories in use between genus and species, namely subgenus (as suggested by Stone) and superspecies, both of which are used in taxonomic discussions but do not affect the scientific name.

He gave a similar opinion in response to an *Auk* letter from systematist Robert Ridgway in defense of genus-splitting. Editor Stone inserted a comment after Ridgway's letter that included, "[I]t is just as important from the viewpoint of evolution to indicate a common resemblance as a well-defined difference, and every time we divide a group of species [i.e., a genus] into two…we lose, in our name, all trace of several common characters which bind these two groups together as distinguished from other groups….The only other method would seem to be to abandon the use of scientific names entirely except for technical systematic work, a course which is already being forced upon us more and more as our Latin names become meaningless to all but a comparatively few experts."[26]

On another related issue, in the January 1913 *Auk* Stone rightly took Oberholser to task for naming 104 "new" subspecies from Sumatra in a Smithsonian periodical without giving adequate descriptions of them. With gentlemanly politesse, Stone had dropped Oberholser a note beforehand telling him about the criticism in the upcoming *Auk*, and his reason for doing it. In both the letter and the article, Stone said he was criticizing the practice, not Oberholser, but that wasn't really true: in the article, he said that publishing new forms (species or subspecies) without sufficient written diagnoses, as Oberholser had done, was "absolutely worthless," and that the only reason for doing so would be "the desire to secure [via priority] the species to an author or the types to an institution."[28] Both Oberholser and Richmond protested to Stone about his remarks.[29]

Chapman blew off some steam about the practice in a December 1915 letter to Stone, saying, "We both know also that in the majority of cases these 'preliminary' descriptions are never followed by detailed ones and that in reality they are slipshod, unscientific and unpardonable means of securing priority." He mentioned a recent case in which the author didn't even indicate the nearest allied species to the "new" one he was describing.[30] He asked Stone to take up the cudgels about it in *The Auk*, and Stone did just that in the January issue, blasting the "inexcusable, slovenly work" of ornithologists and museums more interested in ringing up new names and types than in genuinely advancing science. He called for at least a minimal comparative description relative to closely related taxa, including measurements and colors, instead of the practice of some who simply cited the type specimen and collection locality.[31]

He often bluntly criticized the practice in his *Auk* literature reviews when he detected it in publications. In 1916 he said that ornithology would become the laughingstock of zoologists if the practice didn't cease.[32] It was particularly irksome when authors didn't even indicate where the type specimen was located, because that inhibited the ability of future researchers to make comparisons.[33] He wrote in 1932 that it was easier to publish hastily described subspecies than to get rid of them later, but "institutions and individuals sponsoring faunal work desire collections to be worked up quickly and novelties described before someone else gets ahead of them!"[34] He asserted that if the subsequent rejections of dubious and ultimately untenable subspecies were given as much notice as their initial announcement as "new forms," science would be better served.[35] With his interest and expertise in taxonomy, Stone knew what headaches those preliminary descriptions would give future researchers, and he was firm in taking the guilty parties to task for it.

As part of his interest in systematics, Stone also spearheaded efforts to keep the *Zoological Record* afloat after the Zoological Society of London announced in *Science* in 1923 that its continued publication was in jeopardy. The *Record* had been around since 1865, and provided an exhaustive register of the names of all recently described species in the various fields of zoology, and a bibliography of articles describing new species. Systematists relied heavily on it, but it fell on difficult financial times when World War I disrupted its funding network.[36] Stone sent out a form letter to numerous institutions asking for contributions, and raised funds locally for at least a few years that were sent to London in ANSP's name to help with continued publication of the *Record*.[37] He also continued to pitch the *Record* and the necessity of funding it in *The Auk*, as he had been doing for years.[38] The efforts of Stone and others helped tide the publication over the rough patch, and it still exists today in an online form.

───────────── ∾ ─────────────

Stone joined the AOU classification committee in 1901 and was involved in its work on the third AOU check-list. Such undertakings are always a tremendous chore, and J.A. Allen was hampered by committee members who didn't complete their assigned tasks (something that Stone would experience later when he was chairman).[39] William Brewster was supposed to work on bird ranges for the check-list, but he never got started, so Allen asked Stone to take on the heavy assignment.[40] In April 1907, Stone told Brewster, "I have been almost overwhelmed by the job I undertook last fall of making out the geographic distributions for the new Check List. Every spare evening and most of my Sundays have been spent at it ever since December last!"[41] Stone used Ridgway's *Birds of North and Middle America* and state lists as his sources; the Biological Survey's W.W. Cooke later tweaked the ranges using additional records, including (to Stone's irritation) some questionable sight records that Stone had ignored.[42-43]

Some very interesting internal squabbling took place during the preparation of the third check-list, with Stone asserting himself as a leading ornithological taxonomist. He had been doing a great deal of work on the synonymy of bird genera and the fixing of their types; by mid-1906 he had reviewed all the genera of the world up to 1840.[44] Allen, the oldest member of the committee, was opposed by Stone, one of the youngest, on the preferred method to be adopted for fixing generic type species (i.e., designating one species as the type for the genus to which it has been assigned, akin to designating a particular specimen as the type for a species).

Stone was usually kindly and pacifistic, but he was exasperated over the issue with Allen, who – in addition to being an admirable gentleman – was one of the three prime movers (along with Brewster and Elliott Coues) behind the formation of the AOU, and an intelligent and insightful ecologist and conservationist before the terms were even coined. Allen's grandfatherly disposition was nicely captured in a story by Frank Chapman about his early days of working for Allen at AMNH: Chapman was tasked with sorting a bird collection one day, and he recalled, "Every few minutes I found some specimen of such exquisite beauty that I could not resist the temptation of showing it to Dr. Allen as though I had made an actual discovery, and he, in his quiet way, shared my pleasure though he had doubtless seen it before."[45] Allen had also been one of the senior ornithologists to whom Stone had reached out for advice as he tackled ANSP's neglected bird collection early in his Academy career.

But Stone could be uncharacteristically testy with Allen at times. In 1900, Allen reviewed an article by Stone's ANSP colleague James Rehn about the priority of the generic name for the American Opossum. Allen disagreed with some of Rehn's reasoning, and correctly pointed out an error in the name and date of one of Rehn's citations.[46] Stone unwisely published a short note in *Science* that took Allen to task over the title of the citation (Stone was unsure about the date), even stating bluntly that Allen had tried to mislead readers of the review.[47] Allen sent Stone a gracious note gently confirming that Rehn and Stone had, in fact, gotten the title wrong.[48] Stone apologized in a letter to Allen, saying that in his "zeal" he hadn't noticed Rehn's incorrect title.[49] He said he hadn't intended to criticize Allen, but it certainly read that way, and the upshot was that Stone came across as hasty and inattentive to detail, even a tad hot-headed, compared to his serene, meticulous senior. Score one for Allen.

On the classification committee, Stone and Allen started locking horns over the proper method for fixing generic type species in early 1906, and before the year was out they had taken it public by initiating a series of back-and-forth papers in *Science*, each arguing his position.[50] The committee's laundry was being aired in public. Allen told Stone in November 1907, "Your letter of yesterday is received. You say you are 'very sorry that we cannot seem to see anything relating to type fixing in the same light.' You cannot regret this more than I do, and I am sick and tired of the whole business. Your letter, however, only confirms me in my belief that the position I have taken is the correct one."[51]

Allen favored the "elimination method," which was the choice of the ICZN, and which the AOU committee had historically used; Stone favored the "first species rule."[52] Elimination involved subjective decisions and gave uneven results; first species was objective and gave uniform results, and was favored by the AOU Council and the U.S. Biological Survey.[53] Stone pushed for having the ICZN revisit generic fixing and decide on the best method. The upshot was that the AOU adopted the first species rule, but when the ICZN got around to taking another look at elimination, it settled on a third method, "subsequent designation." In the interest of international uniformity, and because subsequent designation was also objective and gave definite results, the AOU adopted it in place of the first species rule.[54]

Charles Batchelder, AOU president during the tussle, told Stone, "I am thankful you fought your fight out on the checklist, though of course disciplining an old dog isn't wholly pleasure."[55] The haggling wasn't over, however, as there was soon another dustup in early 1910 about the centering of the names in the check-list. Stone told Brewster that Allen was getting things so mixed up that he thought Allen's memory must be failing, and, "The continual series of protests that Dwight & I have been forced to make is very distasteful to me."[56] Dwight told Stone, "The wonder is you have always been so temperate with [Allen] with all the 'elimination' & other Check-List matters. The real trouble with him is he resents that anybody knows more than he does about matters that he has considered as his own preserve, so to speak. I have talked to him pretty plainly at times & I find that he pays heed to what I say, now, for I have proved him wrong after he insisted he was right, just as you have repeatedly."[57] Well, that's one insider's take on it, although Dwight was firmly on Stone's side throughout. Certainly, however, Stone had shown not only great aptitude for the committee's work, but leadership qualities as well in taking on Allen and pushing his agenda home, which no doubt led to him being appointed chairman of the committee a few years later.

The check-list was finally published in 1910. Allen must have been as relieved as he was after the first AOU check-list had wrapped up in 1886, when he told Ridgway that he felt like jumping over the moon.[58] In his early years as *Auk* editor Stone sometimes defended the new check-list from criticism.[59] South Carolina ornithologist Arthur T. Wayne, who was wont to whine about such things, complained to longtime classification committee member Brewster that some of his local records had been ignored in the check-list, but Brewster replied that "it was much easier to criticize such a piece of work than to produce it!"[60]

———————— ∾ ————————

In 1914, Allen retired from the classification committee and was replaced as chairman by Chapman, who called it quits before the year was out.[61] Stone was asked to serve as acting chairman in 1915, then became chairman in 1919 when a new, streamlined committee was formed (reduced from 12 members to five – Stone, Dwight, Oberholser, T.S. Palmer, and Richmond).[3] At that time, there was no new check-list effort under way, and the committee's work consisted of issuing occasional supplements to the 1910 check-list, listing changes it had agreed upon in nomenclature or classification. The committee was largely inactive after Allen retired; in fact, in late 1918 Stone wasn't even sure just who was on the committee. He wrote in a 1919 *Auk* note that it hadn't met for several years – when it had, participants grew bored with the work and were more interested in lunch break – and after a supplement in 1912, none was published until 1920.[62] The committee (usually Oberholser) also published occasional *Auk* articles listing the latest *proposed* changes to the 1910 list by various researchers, but produced little else.

Dwight expressed at least part of the problem to Stone around the time of the new committee appointment in 1919: "I know how tired you must be & how little you get out of the members of the Committee. ...The trouble with our old committee was that none of us went to class <u>prepared with our lesson</u> – hence loss of time and much irrelevant discussion."[63] In other words, committee members who were assigned to research certain topics or cases were showing up at meetings without having done their homework. Stone referred to the committee as a "joke"; with "semi-fossils" in its membership, it was "dying of dry rot."[64] He had tried to get work out of people, on or off the committee, "with no result. Present day ornithologists have been far less willing to sacrifice time & energy on this work than the older men did some years ago....I invited everyone to publish views on <u>any</u> of the cases but the response is almost nil."[43] Another reason for the committee's inactivity during this time was that a raging world war, of course, interfered with daily lives and work agendas, including those of scientific classification committees.[65]

By early 1923 there were murmurings about a new check-list, but the new committee was still bogged down enough that Stone was contemplating shutting things down and letting a new group have a go at it.[66] In July 1924, he told a colleague that the committee hadn't met recently and didn't seem likely to accomplish anything, and that he should retire as chairman because "I have been a failure so far as accomplishment goes." Members of the committee were overworked with museum and other duties, *The Auk* occupied all his free time, and being director at ANSP left him almost no time for bird work.[67] In an August 1924 letter about the committee's failure to produce a new check-list, and growing discontent with its performance, he told AOU president Dwight that the Council should decide whether to keep on the present course or make changes: "In order to relieve the Council and yourself of any possible embarrassment in taking up this matter I beg to present my resignation as a member of the Committee with the assurance however that I stand ready to render any service in my power to the Union in preparing the Check-List if my services are desired."[68] A month later, however, Palmer was prodding Stone to continue as committee chair.[69]

Shortly before the AOU annual meeting that fall, Stone told Dwight that he didn't think the committee process was working, and that having one man making the decisions would be better, but he was concerned that if he made statements to that effect, it would be perceived that he was gunning to be that one man. He described some of the weaknesses of the committee idea during his 22 years of experience with it, and the problems caused by time constraints, travel, and basic human nature foibles: "You know as well as I do that we never got satisfactory results in the past and never would have held any meetings had we not fixed upon the date that brought Dr. Allen to the National Academy meeting and Brewster to his Washington dentist....The Washington men would never go to New York or anywhere else....Our attitude was different before and after lunch and results were different [depending on] whether [C. Hart] Merriam was there or not and in recent years whether <u>you</u> were present or not."[70]

At the AOU meeting, however, the committee concept stayed in vogue. Stone was chosen to lead a new one comprising members of his choosing; he added Alexander Wetmore, Waldron DeWitt Miller, and Joseph Grinnell to the existing committee, giving it eight members.

———————— ∾ ————————

What seems to have finally gotten the check-list ball rolling was the work of the Wetmore–Miller subcommittee, which laid out the classification scheme, down to subgenera, that the committee would use for the new check-list. Stone asked for the scheme as soon as Wetmore started producing sections of it in early 1926, and he and the rest of the committee followed with the species/subspecies work for each genus. The committee suddenly had a good work plan to follow, in contrast to the ad hoc manner in which it had been operating.[71] Stone was almost ecstatic when Wetmore sent a draft manuscript of the new classification, which appeared in *The Auk* a few months later: "<u>Ms</u> received! Well! 'The world do move.' Many, many thanks. I can now see my way clear to rush the check List just as soon as I get a list of genera to show sequence & limits."[72] Stone later told Grinnell, "I have always thought the appointing of Wetmore & Miller to draw up a classification down to genera was my master stroke!"[73]

Stone may have felt that he was now in a position to "rush the check List," but further delays were inevitable. The Wetmore–Miller relationship seems to have been cordial, but Miller habitually dragged his feet.[74] Both Miller and Grinnell eventually wanted some of "their" proposed subspecies, which the committee had already rejected, to be reconsidered, but Stone said no on both counts, as well as to Grinnell's "sesquipedalian" vernacular names, such as "Slender-billed White-breasted Nuthatch" and "Boat-tailed Great-tailed Grackle."[75] (Today's birders and banders can be grateful to Stone that they don't have to cook up any four-letter codes for those two, at least. As he once put it, by the time you got done trying to point out a bird with a name that long to a field companion, the bird would have already flown away.)[76] Stone told Wetmore in 1928 that Miller – alone – no longer responded to the questionnaires sent to committee members for their votes and opinions on check-list issues; one wonders if this wasn't some pique associated with not having his pet subspecies reconsidered, but Miller seems to have been slow to respond to things anyway, and it may have simply been a case of having too much on his plate.[77]

The committee as a whole had a lot on its plate. Stone's method for dealing with changes proposed since the 1910 check-list was to solicit the views of one or two members of the committee whom he felt were the experts on the particular case, then put their recommendation(s) to vote by the rest of the committee. Stone said in a 1930 *Auk* note that almost "500 proposed new forms, proposed cancellations and changes in rank or status" were voted on.[78] Stone was frustrated by having to pull teeth to get responses from some committee members, telling Chapman in late 1927 that although some parts of the check-list were about ready to send to the printer, and he didn't foresee major changes to the rest of the material, "It is an awful job to get replies from the Committee & some of them when received are just expressions of personal preference without rhyme or reason. I am convinced that the <u>next</u> checklist should be done by a 'one man' committee. He could <u>ask</u> advice right & left but would not be tied to a committee."[79] A month later Dwight told Stone, "I am sorry you have such a neglectful committee on N. Am. birds but it is always so with committees."[80]

Some of the delays were due to the same type of caviling that had bedeviled work on the third check-list. Dwight had fought to retain the use of apostrophes with the third check-list committee (e.g., Swainson's Thrush vs. Swainson Thrush), and took to the pages of *The Condor* in 1909 to make his case; in 1926 he told Stone, "Sorry you raised the question of apostrophes. I thought we had killed that viper," so the apostrophe debate must have been on again for the fourth check-list.[81] For the third one, in addition to the "nomenclatural stupidities," Dwight had also gotten worked up over things like Allen's insistence on centering the species names in the check-list.[82] Stone's committee haggled over the use of a single vs. double "i" in species names, just as the earlier committee had found any number of technicalities to quibble about, because that's what such committees are supposed to do.[83] Allen told Stone in 1910, "Oh, the joy of being editor of the Check-List! Each member of the Committee had his own notions about punctuation, use of capitals, and the number of the's [*sic*] it was necessary to employ."[84] Stone sounded similarly beset in a letter to Robert Cushman Murphy in 1930, in the midst of the printing of the fourth check-list: "With twenty sets of galleys returned by twenty men of nearly twenty minds I am having a glorious time marking up a final set for the printer. However, like Oliver Twist, I am asking for more!" – and he proceeded to ask about the ranges of some pelagic species, which was Murphy's area of expertise.[85]

The check-list effort didn't need any more drama, but got it anyway in the person of poor Harry Oberholser, an over-the-top taxonomist who reputedly never saw a bird he couldn't describe as a new subspecies. Dwight in particular had no time for Oberholser's nomenclatural gymnastics. One of the many gems

Dwight shared with Stone was this one from 1915: "Hail! genus Oberholseria! – rhymes with hysteria I suppose – I doubt if the Latins would have let any of their language survive them, if they had known what crimes of nomenclature were to be committed!"[86] (Scientific names employ Latin rules of grammar, and often Latin words.) Fellow ornithologists complained of his habit of announcing his proposed taxonomic splits in many different journals, including small regional and nontechnical ones; Stone said *The Auk* was too backed up to handle Oberholser's flood of submissions.[87] Oberholser also used the lesser-known journals to sneak in spurious claims of Smithsonian type specimens. In 1921, Stone rightly criticized him in an *Auk* review for claiming, in the obscure *Ohio Journal of Science*, that the type of the Audubon's Warbler (now a subspecies of the Yellow-rumped Warbler) was in the Smithsonian, when in fact the Smithsonian specimen was a duplicate of the type long known to be housed at ANSP.[88] Grinnell applauded Stone's efforts to put the spotlight on what he said was a frequent Smithsonian practice, for the Museum of Vertebrate Zoology had also sent duplicates there that were later declared by the Smithsonian to be the types.[89]

Many, even those Oberholser rubbed the wrong way with his work, conceded that he was an astute and diligent laborer in the field of North American avian taxonomy.[90,91] Even Dwight, who was critical of Oberholser's nomenclatural "flights of fancy," acknowledged his industry.[92-93] Oberholser prepared a check-list supplement for *The Auk* in 1922 that had Grinnell, at least, concerned that the committee was being taken over by one man; Stone assured him that the manuscript would have to be approved by the entire committee first, and he told Oberholser, in unusually pointed terms, that it was too long and that some of its material hadn't been agreed upon by the other members.[94] It eventually came out in the July 1923 *Auk*, signed by the committee as authors; how different it was from Oberholser's original manuscript isn't known, but one would assume it was much less adventurous.[95] Certain it is that by 1925, Oberholser was in a bit of a sulk and wouldn't participate in check-list work, although he was still on the committee; maybe he felt ostracized because the rest of the committee wasn't nearly in accordance with his comparatively radical views.[93,96] It took a couple of years for him to come back into the fold, possibly under pressure from his employers at the Biological Survey, and he seems to have been welcomed like the prodigal son.[91,97]

Stone, typically, always had cordial relations with Oberholser; in fact, at the height of Oberholser's discontent with the committee, Stone accompanied him on a Biological Survey boat trip of several days' duration in New Jersey, surveying water birds from Barnegat Bay to Cape May.[98] And Oberholser was gentlemanly in his correspondence with Stone, telling him in 1922 that he didn't want Stone to resign the committee chairmanship, and that he would help with the workload as much as he could.[99]

The new check-list couldn't please everyone, of course, and other feathers were ruffled. The crotchety California ornithologist Louis Bishop, to whom Stone was sending some galley proofs for comment, declined to do any further reviews when he felt his suggestions weren't being heeded.[100] Peters told Stone, "I hardly know what to make of [Bishop]. He seems to have worked himself up to the point where he is entirely unreasonable; some of his remarks are almost incoherent! I'm glad you told him what you did, but as you say, I fear he has got to the stage where nothing will suit him except some of his pet ideas. He is out for trouble and will not be diverted."[101] J.H. Fleming, the AOU vice president, told Stone, "Bishop is bound to protest or he would not be Bishop."[102] Grinnell, responding to news of Bishop trying to stir up a "protest" in California about the forthcoming check-list (Stone heard reports of Bishop "flaying us all alive in a blistering harangue at the Cooper Club meeting"), passed it all off as a lark: "I really think that his onslaughts are to the good, in that they constitute good advertising for the new Check-list. Everyone will want a copy!"[103] Harry Swarth, who lived in California and was familiar with Bishop, was also flippant in a letter to Stone at the time, saying, "I can quite understand your feeling of fed-upedness on this job; it must have been awful. It has occurred to me that I might write to Dr. Bishop and get him to send you a brief summary of his ideas of the whole list. Do you think it would prove helpful?!!"[104] Let's take it easy on Dr. Bishop, though – there's a sizeable stack of his typed comments on the check-list proofs in Stone's correspondence, thoroughly done and with no acerbity. He did a lot of good, careful work – and, of course, none of these guys were getting a dime for their efforts.

Other glitches were more serious. In 1929, both Dwight and Miller died. Dwight was 70 and had been ill; Miller, only 50 and a talented ornithologist and passionate conservationist, was tragically killed in a motorcycle accident.[105] They were replaced by AMNH's John Zimmer and MCZ's self-effacing James Peters, who sent some galley proofs back to Stone in 1930 with the wry comment, "If there is any danger of my being 'last man' to get all his proof back drop me a postal and I'll try to get the old bread wagon running in high gear."[106] Zimmer, a future *Auk* editor, had an eye for things like punctuation consistency, making him invaluable for reading proofs; Peters was working simultaneously on his own *Check-list of the Birds of the World*, and clearly brought much-appreciated expertise to the AOU project.

As part of his work with the fourth check-list, Stone performed a massive 1920s version of a cut-and-paste operation: once the material to be revised had been decided upon, Stone "drew up the text of the new Check-list using cut-up copies of the third edition as a basis with all new material typed and properly inserted."[107] He described it further to Wetmore: "I have all of the old list cut up & pasted in accordance with the 'new order' with necessary rearrangements of subspecies, authorized changes & additions, etc. and with all 'proposed changes' indicated in margins."[108] (Imagine Stone's amazement if he could see the hocus-pocus immediacy of a cut-and-paste with a modern word processor.)

He was about as busy as he ever was as the check-list work neared completion, particularly before being relieved of his ANSP director responsibilities, and the loose ends to be tied multiplied apace like so many hydras' heads. In 1927 he said, "I get discouraged because it seems physically impossible to make much progress [on the check-list] with the Auk bobbing up every 3 mos. & so much else for me to do at the Museum."[109] In 1928, in addition to his other responsibilities, he said his health was weak, "and this Check List, which I <u>must</u> carry through, has nearly floored me as I cannot work at night as I used to."[110] In 1930 he groused, "I have the January Auk about off my hands & can then plunge into the Check List until about Feb. 20 when April Auk will call for attention. One damn thing after another!"[111]

Chapman told Stone in April 1930, "It is certainly a great pity that you have been saddled with the final responsibility for the production of the Check-List. At the best it is a thankless task."[112] At the same time Stone complained that the committee was "slow even at answering questions (some don't reply at all) & there is no one to do the real work but yours truly."[113] That may have referred to Stone's preparation of the index, which Grinnell opined "must be just about the last word in <u>drudgery</u>!"[114] While spending most of his 1930 Cape May summer vacation on check-list work, he told Wetmore, "[W]hile I am anxious to make it as perfect as possible, I am thoroughly fed up on it! I have moreover given up everything else this summer in order to push it through."[115]

A letter from Swarth in late 1930 indicates that at least some major revising went down to the wire. Swarth had just seen a "second revise" proof of the check-list, and wrote to object to the treatment of the *Branta canadensis* (Canada Goose) group, the taxonomy of which is still fluid and challenging today. Swarth made a convincing and lucid argument that the arrangement was contrary not only to what he had seen in the first check-list proof, but also to research published in the ornithological literature (a reference to his own *Auk* article on the subject).[116] He argued that the check-list should be based on published material, not private whims and impressions, so that future researchers could at least read the publications on which the work was based. He elaborated on a few of what he considered taxonomical blunders, plus a sloppily worded distribution one: *Branta c. occidentalis* (today's Dusky Canada Goose) was said to "'probably' occur on the Pacific Coast of southeastern Alaska. Is there an Atlantic Coast to that region? And if *occidentalis* does <u>not</u> occur in southeastern Alaska in Heaven's name where does it occur? The few of us who have done field work in that region have come to believe that it occurs hardly anywhere else."[117] Stone agreed with the points raised, for the final version was changed in agreement with all but one of them. That was probably one instance among many of the endless loose strings and last-minute revisions.

Stone queried A.L. Pickens with check-list questions about some bird ranges in South Carolina. Pickens was a pastor who had frequently published articles about the state's avifauna, but he told Stone, "Unfortunately my ornithological labors there met an untimely end following an attack on my theological views as to the literalness of the Adamine rib."[118] Yes, even in today's Deep South you have to be very careful what you say about the Adamine rib. Pickens was briefly in exile in California before returning to South Carolina and resuming his ornithological labors.

As he worked on page proofs in April 1931, Stone said that once that was done, "I shall heave a sigh of relief & retire to receive the bitter criticisms of the public at large!!"[119] His relief was great when the endless task was finally over. As he crossed the finish line, he told Chapman, "I am through with Checklists, for ever & ever, Amen!"[120] (And he really was – he resigned from the classification committee once the check-list was published.) Wetmore sent Stone a congratulatory note when he received his check-list, and Stone responded with a printed "Hallelujah, Brother – Hallelujah!" that he'd cut out from some publication and pasted to a sheet of paper.[121] Grinnell also congratulated him, and said, "I marvel at the huge amount of last-minute work upon it you must have done during the past summer – and this despite [health] handicaps!"[122] (Stone had been increasingly troubled by heart disease.)

Stone provided a nice summary in *The Auk* of the work behind the check-list at the time of its appearance, enumerating the changes from the third check-list. Most of the scientific name changes were due to genus or species/subspecies changes; few were due to the law of priority, as the old literature had been pretty well combed over by that time. There were 1,420 species and subspecies, as against 1,200 from the previous check-list; that

Thanking heaven that the check-list is done, or blessing the loaves? Stone looking pensive on a DVOC outing c. 1930. DVOC Collection, ANSP Archives.

was mostly due to increased exploration in California (which was the theater of the subspecies-prone Grinnell). The number of genera had not increased much since the previous check-list (395 vs. 382), and the new genera were due entirely to new vagrants discovered in North America; in fact, the number of generic splits (12) exactly equaled the number of generic combinations.[1] That was due at least in part to the influence of Stone, who often railed against generic splitting, and who had asked Miller and Wetmore to use subgenera in their classification scheme. It probably led to more clutter in the check-list, but at least it avoided having a slew of "new" genera.[123]

The check-list's publication coincided with Stone's twentieth anniversary as *Auk* editor, and in October 1931, the AOU presented him with a bound collection of letters expressing congratulations and appreciation from fellow members. The book featured a George M. Sutton painting of a European Stonechat on the cover and a stunning Ruddy Turnstone painting by Allan Brooks as the frontispiece. (Note the "stone" theme.) The letters were full of the affection and praise to be expected on the occasion.

The AOU had hoped to present the book to Stone at the annual meeting, but Stone's health prevented his attendance. Curiously, he found the book awaiting him in his office one evening when he went in to the Academy for a DVOC meeting. He took it to the meeting to show to the club. He suspected that Chapman was the hand behind the gift, and wrote to him immediately: "I am overwhelmed!...[W]ords fail me when I try to express my deep appreciation. Nothing could please me more than these letters and paintings and the affection and good will that they express." A check was included, which Stone said would help pay for the illustrations in his forthcoming Cape May bird book.[124]

Possibly Stone's favorite missive in the book was "Owed to a Stone," supplied by Arthur A. Allen of Cornell, which, though not to be found in *The Norton Anthology of Poetry*, is clever and whimsical and – for what it matters – historically and ornithologically sound:

> The rocks of the Atlantic were the stronghold of the Auk,
> For meat t'would eat the finny fleet, its song a raucous squawk.
> But sailormen devoured it – It was a bird ill-fated;
> Its claim to fame, Oh what a shame! A bird now extirpated.

> For forty years it lay extinct with nothing but a blessing,
> Then rose anew for A.O.U. in quite a different dressing.
> A Journal now where scribes may print their observations curious,
> Or try to tell their reasons well for being quite so furious.

One Stone of Quaker City is the stronghold of this Auk;
Its food are observations good; its song like pleasant talk.
And A.O.Usters guzzle it and love the Master clever,
Its name, his fame, one and the same; may they go on forever.

Another bird that Stone has stirred – the Check-list now completed,
Another gift from Witmer's thrift that well ought to be feted.
So let me raise my word of praise for deeds so nobly done,
Let Auk and Check-list cheer for Stone when I am dead and gone.[125]

James Rehn later gave an excellent summary of Stone's labors on the fourth check-list:

His years between 1924 and 1931 were crowded with check-list labors....Few but those associated with him in this project, or close enough to him officially to know its virtually day-to-day demands, appreciate what a great amount of his time and energy this task consumed. The verification of all references alone was a tedious and day-consuming responsibility, while the refurbishing of the distributional statements to include the enormous increase of recorded information since the previous check-list was, in itself, enough to deter any but the most serious student. To those of us who knew him well, Stone's work on the Fourth Edition of the AOU Check-list seemed to afford him a deeper and more lasting personal satisfaction than any other purely technical undertaking with which he had been associated.[126]

The latter sentiment was apparent in Stone's own summary of the effort, in which he indicated that the check-list effort brought together some of his greatest passions in ornithology, including taxonomy, history, and the AOU:

As one turns the pages of the Check-list he seems to read between the lines the whole history of American ornithology. In the names of the birds and the authors appear almost all who have contributed to our science, while the type localities recall the itineraries of the early and later explorers. One sees in the "Check-list," too, a sort of epitome of the hard work of the AOU and cannot but realize its tremendous influence in welding the Union into the cooperative organization that it is today, while it emphasizes that accuracy of detail which has always characterized the development of American ornithology.[1]

11

The Brave Old Bird Goes On

S tone replaced the long-serving J.A. Allen as editor of *The Auk* in 1912 and held the position for 25 years. His tenure was marked by severe financial woes exacerbated by World War I and the Great Depression, and by disagreements over the journal's content, with some AOU members favoring more scientific rigidity and others wanting to balance that with popular appeal. Other nettlesome matters included the institution of authors paying publication costs, the annual printing of the lengthy and expensive members list, a bird banding organization whose insistence on having a banding section in *The Auk* nearly compelled Stone to quit his post, and Stone's unfortunate decision to add to his workload by taking on the business management of the journal. In addition to his editorial duties, which were time consuming enough in the pre-computer/email/Internet age, he also had to deal with such mundane matters as authors' separates, and mailing and membership problems. His workload was further weighted by his accommodating editorial style. The result was that much of his spare time was taken up with *Auk* work.

Stone's first foray into editing was with *The Gossip*, the small newsletter he and Stewardson Brown produced as teenagers. In 1887, he was offered the editorship of *The Bird Call*, the short-lived organ of the original Pennsylvania Audubon Society, but he declined it.[1] He edited the DVOC's first four proceedings abstracts, and edited *Cassinia* for its first 10 years. He became an associate editor of *The Osprey* in 1899 and served in that capacity for the remainder of the periodical's short existence.[2] He authored many articles in scientific publications, especially *The Auk*, and also contributed material to Frank Chapman's popular *Bird-Lore*, including biographies, bird articles, and literature reviews.

In late 1911, he was one of a handful of people considered qualified to take over *The Auk* from Allen. AOU Council member Ruthven Deane told him, "In my correspondence with several members of the Council your name has been [the] choice in 4 out of 5."[3] AOU treasurer Jonathan Dwight hoped Stone would take the position, telling him, "Chapman don't want it & nobody is as well qualified to fill the position as you are."[4]

The Smithsonian's Charles Richmond later recounted for Stone the behind-the-scenes machinations (no doubt embellished) of his November 13, 1911 election to succeed Allen during the AOU annual meeting, held in Philadelphia that year. "In a weak-minded moment" Richmond was put up as a candidate for the position by a Washington contingent scheming to have *The Auk* headquartered in their backyard:

I do not recall that we had heard of any other candidate at the time, so I feared the worst. When the [AOU] Council met at the Academy on that fatal [sic] morning there was a stack of printed matter on the table labeled "Preliminary Program," with an explanation (presumably by you) that the Postal authorities had trailed its origin to my lair…and you diagnosed the trouble and prescribed its cure. I did not attribute any Philadelphia politics to this "Preliminary Report" at the time, but it now looks as if that "cure" was a P.P.S. (peanuts, pretzels, steins) set out as bait for the voters present. In any event, they all voted for you on the one and only ballot, and so did I.[5] [The ballot vote was actually nine votes for Stone, three for Richmond, and one for Dwight.][6]

Stone later said that he was elected with the help of the New York and Cambridge coteries, with the Washington crowd trying to get control of the journal.[7] And surely his years as *Cassinia* editor and his growing reputation as an ornithologist had more to do with his election than did P.P.S.

Stone's editorship hit a bump in its first year in the form of a donnybrook that involved, among others, Teddy Roosevelt himself. Roosevelt published an article on concealing coloration in the *Bulletin of the American Museum of Natural History* that took Abbott and Gerald Thayer to task over their book on the same subject.[8] Francis Allen published a rebuttal of sorts to Roosevelt via the pages of the October 1912 *Auk*.[9] Roosevelt and Deane wrote letters to Stone objecting to the tone and some of the arguments of Allen's paper – Roosevelt with all the indignation and fire you'd expect from the ebullient former president – and Stone published what was essentially an apology in the next *Auk* for allowing some of Allen's more questionable and opinionated phrases to stand.[10] Roosevelt, who had been justifiably sore, was mollified by Stone's apology, but the editor did allow Allen to get in one last shot before deciding that enough was enough and pulling the plug on the whole tussle.[11]

It was just one more dustup in an ornithological periodical – they were commonplace in those days – but, perhaps because of the eminence of one of the parties, Stone got to fretting about how his fitness for the editorial chair might be perceived by the AOU brass, querying AOU Fellow Chapman, "While I do not think anything like this will be possible again, I wish you would advise me if the Fellows of the Union feel that my negligence in this matter unfits me for the position of Editor."[12] Chapman responded, "I do not think you need give yourself a moment's uneasiness for I have heard no criticism whatever."[13] Stone had nothing to worry about, but the incident indicates that he may have understandably felt a little unsure of himself in his early days in the big chair at *The Auk*.

Stone often asked for Chapman's opinion – from one editor to another – about *Auk* affairs. He also ran ideas past J.A. Allen, or asked for the senior ornithologist's advice.[14] They had locked horns in the past, but Allen, in the evening of his life, and ever the gracious gentleman, was very complimentary of Stone's editorship.[15] In 1919, two years before he died, Allen told Stone how thankless editing *The Auk* could be: "For long years I felt the need of words of approval when I was your predecessor in this arduous work, but rarely was I favored with such expressions from anyone, either spoken or written, and at times I felt their absence keenly."[16] Stone soon savored the infrequent pats on the back he received during his editorship.[17-18]

After consulting with Allen, Stone expanded the material reviewed in the "Recent Literature" section in the April 1912 issue from a few selected articles to include a number of ornithological journals, both domestic and foreign, because Stone felt that the average *Auk* reader had limited access to such material.[19] Allen had considered doing the same in the past but space, funding, and time constraints prevented him.[15,20] During his years as *Auk* editor, Stone had less time for original research and publication; by 1921, ANSP duties limited his ornithological work solely to *Auk* editorship.[21] However, as James Rehn related in his *Auk* Stone memorial, "[D]uring the years of his editorship we find the number of critical reviews of current literature from his pen running into several thousand, between 1911 and 1920 alone totaling nearly eight hundred, while in addition *The Auk*'s pages include from his pen a very considerable number of obituaries of American and foreign ornithologists who passed away during those years."[22] His current literature reviews were much appreciated, and a fellow ornithologist remarked that they were "in most cases…really distinct articles in themselves."[23,24]

Until the late 1920s, Stone often reviewed faunal works, and most of his critical comments were in the areas of nomenclature and taxonomy. For the last several years of his editorship, his reviews were rarely critical and more often were simply summaries. The section was lengthy, and it's hard to imagine that today so much space would be wasted on simple notices and summaries of material in *other journals*. Additionally, his reviews of popular nature books by friends such as Sam Scoville and others, sometimes written for children, had no place in a serious ornithological journal; his reviews of Cornelius Weygandt's books, particularly his two-page notice of *The Wissahickon Hills*, were little more than plugs.[25]

Stone was said to be too lenient in his reviews, but he didn't mince words when he didn't like something.[26] He considered one *Ibis* article the most remarkable one he'd ever seen in an ornithological journal: it extensively quoted a field journal verbatim – abbreviations, symbols, and all – and Stone said "life [was] too short" to waste time trying to decode it all.[27] He asserted that a short biography of Audubon was so bad that the author should have remained anonymous and should immediately withdraw the publication from circulation; the author soon told him he planned to do just that.[28] Stone found much wrong with a book about Louisiana birds, commenting drily on a "so-called 'key' to the families of perching birds [that] constitutes a puzzle worthy of the serious attention of a cryptogram expert, to which the printer in spacing and punctuation has added not a little. We fear the 'key' will not unlock the treasury which lies beyond!"[29]

———————— ∾ ————————

It is a stated expectation of scientific journals today that when a manuscript is submitted for consideration, it hasn't been submitted at the same time to another journal (or already been accepted or published by one). In Stone's day, publishing etiquette was in a much more primitive state, and Stone was perturbed when papers submitted to *The Auk* were submitted or published elsewhere. He was confronted with it early and often in his editorship, and the offenders were sometimes prominent ornithologists who could have been expected to know better.

Stone was "mortified" when he discovered that part of a R.W. Shufeldt article appeared elsewhere at almost the same time. Shufeldt haughtily told Stone that he had no right to gripe, because the article was published in the other journal *after* it appeared in *The Auk*; Stone, of course, didn't want it coming out anywhere else before *or* after its *Auk* appearance.[30] A.C. Bent published an identical note about Yellow-billed Loons in both *The Condor* and *The Auk* in 1915; after Stone put him on the right path he sent apologies to both Stone and *Condor* editor Joseph Grinnell.[31] However, when Grinnell later had to straighten out John B. May on the subject, May responded with some heat, prompting Grinnell to tell Stone that May would not get anything published in *The Condor* again – and he didn't.[32] In 1929, Stone once again had to chide contributors about manuscripts submitted simultaneously to *The Auk* and other journals.[33]

Stone, Grinnell, and Chapman alerted one another when it appeared that the same article had been submitted to more than one of their respective journals.[34] In fact, at the outset of Stone's *Auk* editorship, Grinnell suggested they keep each other informed of articles they'd rejected to prevent authors from turning around and publishing it in the other editor's journal (and clearly Grinnell was thinking of *Condor* rejections that would end up in *The Auk*, as, according to him, they did under Allen).[35] That was Grinnell's way of keeping up the quality of manuscripts, and he was still informing Stone of articles rejected by *The Condor* as late as 1931.[36]

Frederic Kennard carried on a witty, self-effacing ("I know I am a nuisance, but I was born that way") correspondence with Stone.[37] In 1914, Kennard sent Stone a revised *Auk* manuscript submission – his first one during Stone's editorship – saying that Stone's no-nonsense editing of it made him laugh until he was sore:

As a matter of fact, I never expected to "get by" with all that "lingo," but when you wrote me last spring to send you a readable article, the temptation to break away from the morgue-like solemnity of Dr. Allen's standard was more than I could resist....I submit, however, that the phrase "cruising" about the swamp was a little bit more apt than your commonplace "searching," and I am quite certain that those Florida Crows and Fish Crows were "hanging around," as well as "present," they were simply waiting for the cook to throw out some swill....I am now engaged in rubbing out all the bright spots in the next chapter and reducing that also to the dead, dry monotony of Dr. Allen's standard.[38]

Kennard published several articles and notes in *The Auk* during Stone's editorship, and this was the first of many gibing Kennard references to "shades of Dr. Allen," or similar expressions, in their correspondence over the years.

One of the striking differences between Stone's style as *Auk* editor compared to his modern counterparts was his willingness, even preference, to edit manuscripts himself. A manuscript submitted to a scientific journal today is initially assessed by the editor; if it passes muster at that stage, it is sent on to people with expertise on the paper's topic. They review it and advise the editor about its suitability for publication, and whether it needs rewrites, reanalysis, clarifications, and the like. Editors lean on the reviewers' opinions to varying extents, running the gamut from some who use them in a supplementary fashion while reviewing a paper themselves, to others who take the reviewers' opinions as gospel while simply serving as a conduit between reviewers and authors. Authors can make a case against suggested edits that they don't agree with, but it is up to them to make all the necessary edits and then resubmit their work.

Stone started babysitting manuscripts early in his tenure, and it became so much the norm that authors seemed to take it for granted that he would tidy up their messes for them. Alfred Bailey, the director of the Chicago Academy of Sciences and a frequent contributor to ornithological journals, accompanied a 1928 proof return with "I am returning the proof of my heron notes. I was a little in doubt as to what was intended on the third sheet, and I fear I smeared the proof up without making myself clear, and I'll have to leave it to you to straighten out," comically followed by a contemplatively contrite, "I suppose I am one of the many readers of the Auk who have not realized the thankless job, and the enormous amount of work that the Editor has" – to which Bailey had just added more![39] Bailey is just one instance among many in Stone's correspondence in which someone said, "I hate to add to your workload, but..." – and then added to it anyway.

Stone was known to be accommodating, however. One author, after condensing a manuscript at Stone's suggestion, told him, "You may yet be forced to take it in hand and condense it still further; if you think it necessary, I shall be glad to have you do so."[40] Another actually gave permission, with stipulations, to *allow* Stone to condense a manuscript for him, saying, "I…will approve any cutting you wish to make which will not weaken the argument or leave important points unanswered," then making a suggestion as to what could be left out.[41] Those authors weren't being demanding or petulant – that was just the way Stone did things. In fact, in 1933 he spelled out in *The Auk* that authors of short articles could expect him to edit the articles for length if necessary, without changing important details or facts.[42]

Authors came to expect it, and is it any wonder? Listen to Stone politely, almost meekly, asking permission to condense a 1921 article: "Would you consider it an intrusion if I suggested some alteration in the order and manner in which the facts are presented?…If it would meet with your approval, I can make the suggestions and return the paper to you for your approval or disapproval."[43] The editor asking the author for permission to edit his article for him, with the final disposition of the paper up to the author, would be unthinkable today. Stone told one author whose paper needed condensing, "This is the meanest part of an Editor's job – cutting the cloth to fit."[44] In another place he said that "many a weary hour of editorial time is devoted to saving certain papers and notes containing really important matter which is buried in a mass of superfluous verbiage."[45] If a modern editor thought such papers had merit, they would send the submissions back to the authors with instructions to condense and resubmit. Incredibly, some articles came to Stone as part of a letter, and he would then rewrite them in a suitable format for the printer.[46] No wonder his *Auk* duties used up so much of Stone's time (and probably some of his psychological and physical health).

Stone's *pro bono* edits could bring him more grief than it was worth. Although the majority of authors probably either appreciated them or didn't care, some were not pleased. Josselyn Van Tyne got hissy with Stone about a 1933 article, telling him, "I wish to protest most emphatically against your unauthorized alteration of my note on the [Western] Kingbird in Michigan. If my manuscript is not satisfactory you should refuse it or ask me to change it, but I cannot agree that any editor has the right to publish altered manuscript without the author's permission. I have no criticism to make of your choice of material for the Auk but when you accept a contribution of mine I certainly expect you to use it as I sent it or ask me to change it."[47] The 30-year-old van Tyne was a recently minted Ph.D. with the hubris of youth, and he may have served as an indication to Stone that the younger, graduate-schooled ornithologists had different views and expectations concerning the publication process. Ironically, van Tyne would later serve as editor of *The Wilson Bulletin*, and a 1957 *Bulletin* memorial shortly after his death noted that "diplomatic handling of authors who consider their manuscripts sacrosanct" had been one of the trials of his position.[48]

Leonard Wing used a Harry Oberholser-invented Common Raven subspecies name in a 1935 *Auk* submission, and gave Stone permission (!) to add a footnote if he disagreed with the subspecies designation.[49] Stone instead added a sentence in mid-article that stated the form was not recognized by the latest AOU check-list, with no indication it was an editorial insert.[50] Wing was not happy, and probably rightly so. He told Stone, "I realize that the Editor of a Journal has the right to require that articles conform to the editorial policy, but to change anything over an author's signature is exceeding the authority he possesses."[51] Wing demanded a correction in the next *Auk* and got one from an apologetic editor, but Stone defended his policy of changing names not recognized by the AOU check-list unless authors explicitly asked for an exception and gave a good argument for it.[52]

Stone offered to condense a paper for J.A. Farley, the assistant ornithologist in the Massachusetts Department of Agriculture, in order to keep it at General Notes length and thus get it published sooner.[53] But Farley responded petulantly that there had been other long papers in the General Notes section, and why not this one? While he was at it, Farley complained about "countless errors" in *The Auk*, backed with two piddling examples, and told Stone that when *The Auk* was printed in Cambridge (Cosmos Press) there were few typographical errors.[54] Stone's take-the-blame reply was a model of turning away wrath with a soft answer, but there was an undercurrent of sarcasm as well:

> While you were quite right in referring to typographical errors in the 'Auk,' you are mistaken in charging them against the printer, as they are the fault of the Editor. From the time that I took hold of the 'Auk,' the New England members were in a constant clamor to change the printer, and take the 'Auk' away from Cambridge. Apparently, you were not one in agreement with them. However, I do not think you understand the situation. The editorship of the 'Auk' is an entirely different matter from a state position, or any other office where the editing is the man's principle job. The 'Auk' has always had to be edited in <u>spare</u> moments and is mainly a <u>Labor of Love</u>. Inasmuch as the size has been almost doubled since the old days, the opportunity for error is very much greater and from what I have learned the previous Editor had more time to attend to the 'Auk' work during the day than has the present incumbent.
>
> It would be very nice, of course, if someone could provide funds sufficient to employ an Editor who could give all of his time to the work – then we could get one who would be thoroughly competent and satisfactory, but under the present circumstance, I fear we shall have to get along the best we can.[55]

Stone was not saying "labor of love" lightly. After pointedly asking the Council not to cut honoraria at the annual meeting a few months before, in early 1934 he proposed to cut all AOU salaries and honoraria starting in May, to resume when the new fiscal year started in October, in order to have funds available for the July *Auk* – a drastic step that ultimately wasn't taken.[56] Stone also paid for *Auk* office expenses out his own pocket in 1935 and 1936 to the tune of about 20% of his honoraria.[57]

It is also striking how often authors submitting a manuscript assumed it would be accepted. A Lawrence Hicks cover letter that accompanied a submission was typical: "Attached is a note for the Auk – would like to have it appear as early as the Jan[uary] issue if possible. Please order me 100 reprints of same."[58] Note that he not only assumes it will be published and puts in his order for reprints along with the submission, he even tells Stone he wants it published as soon as possible. The university professors, professional ornithologists, etc. (Hicks was a wildlife biologist) who submitted articles probably did have most of them published, so their acceptance assumptions weren't arrogance but simply based on past experience; the laity probably felt less self-assured. Some authors could be unreasonably testy about how long it took Stone to acknowledge a submission; although Stone was sometimes guilty as charged with failing to respond in a timely fashion (if at all), one author was indignant at not having heard from Stone about a submission he'd mailed only 10 days before.[59]

Stone was already spending enough time on *The Auk* in those pre-computer days. He counted – not with a word processor's toolkit, of course, but by hand – not only the words in each General Note, condensing them in an effort to keep that section under 30 pages, but in early 1936, at least, and possibly at other times, he "gathered together all the papers on hand and counted their word-content (almost as bad a feather count!) and arranged them in order of receipt and then divided them up according to our estimated income. They just fill four numbers."[60-61] In other words, he counted the words for an entire year's worth of *Auk* articles and arranged the issues accordingly! That *would* be on a par with a feather count, in which an investigator plucks and counts the feathers from a specimen, and the totals run into the thousands.[62]

Stone's gentlemanly nature caused him other editorial headaches as well. He and secretary T.S. Palmer corresponded endlessly on the subject of delinquent AOU members and what to do about them, particularly in the early 1920s. Dwight, the AOU treasurer, knew what to do, and early on he advised Stone, "I stopped sending Jan[uary] [*Auk*] number to those who had not paid before Jan 1st, or rather held up their Jan. number until they did. It has saved us from those who drop out."[63] Dwight was still harping on it in 1921 as he was retiring as treasurer, telling Stone, "Send to nobody (nor Library) until they pay for 1921. We can only judge safeness by dollars."[64] His advice fell on deaf ears:

a year later, Palmer and Stone were agonizing about dropping members from the *Auk* mailing list when they hadn't paid up.[65]

The modern peer-review practice was probably not quite as formally institutionalized in Stone's day. He may have been the sole referee for most of the shorter notes, but he at least sometimes sent the longer, more technical articles ("leading articles," which appeared at the beginning of the issue) out for review. He used Richmond, A. Brazier Howell, Ludlow Griscom, and R.M. Strong, among others.[66] While reviewing one article, Strong told Stone, "Am saying nothing about it to any one else, and I quite approve of your policy of silence concerning my examination of it," which indicates an editorial policy similar to the modern practice of anonymous reviews.[67]

Stone also had a network of ornithologists in each state whom he could consult when he received an unusual sighting from their region by an observer Stone was unfamiliar with, but he eventually gave up on it when his queries were answered after long delays, or not at all.[68] If he trusted the person doing the vouching, however, he could be convinced of something highly unusual, such as the nearly extinct Whooping Crane that AOU Associate Edward Court thought he saw. Before publishing the record in *The Auk*, Stone checked with Alexander Wetmore, who knew Court and seems to have thought it was a valid sighting. Stone responded, "I am afraid you have a more lenient mind than I have in re[gard to] Whooping Cranes – they might I suppose have been Fla. or SandHill [Cranes], but ye Gods! However if you say so in it goes."[69] Wetmore replied that Court was reliable, but he would check with him again; ultimately, the sighting wasn't published.[70]

——————— ∾ ———————

Stone unwisely took on more responsibilities and aggravation in 1920 when he took it into his head to assume some of the AOU treasurer's duties from Dwight, who threw in the towel after threatening to do so for years. Dwight told Stone, "I have broken in six assistants [over the years] and am tired of it." They kept getting higher-paying jobs elsewhere.[71] Stone thought that having a more centralized arrangement, with both AOU financial matters and *Auk* operations headquartered in Philadelphia, would make things easier all around.[72] W.L. McAtee, the U.S. Biological Survey (USBS) economic ornithologist, took over the treasurer position from Dwight, but the new plan was to have the treasurer's chores handled jointly by McAtee, Stone, and Edith Clark, Stone's secretarial assistant hired in 1920 to help with *Auk* clerical work. Some idea of the particulars came in a note from Dwight to Stone in late 1920: "During the past few days I have sent you everything essential in the AOU machinery & tried to explain so that your assistant [Clark] might go ahead. I am about to write McAtee & explain to him – but he has so little to look after. He puts the money you send him into the bank, [and] draws checks against it."[73] McAtee wrote to Stone at the same time, "As I see it I will handle bank account, checkbook and securities, and that otherwise the Treasurer's duties of the past will be handled in Philadelphia. For this relief much thanks."[74] Stone was optimistic as the new arrangement with him as business manager got under way, even if Dwight – who said, "I used to have trouble enough when everything was in one town" – was not.[75-76]

A sentence from a December 1920 letter to McAtee was a portent of things to come. Stone wrote, "With regard to several items on your receipt, the 50 cents, the donation, has not to be returned; it was presented by DeLury [a Canadian member] to cover exchange charges and was not to be sent back."[75] The AOU president, *Auk* editor, and ANSP executive curator was wasting his time over the history of a 50-cent donation? The extra work soon began to overwhelm Stone, and the split-office arrangement only exacerbated things.[77] Dwight was having none of it, telling Stone that they were not running things as he had advised at the beginning, and "I do not see where the cog slipped.... The matter is no joke....I am sorry you should be so burdened & I don't wonder you think you might crack. Cut out something!"[78]

McAtee could be opinionated and stubborn, and that may have added to the pacifistic Stone's difficulties.[79] He told Dwight that his treasurership had been ideal, but "whether the [current] divided office will be able to duplicate it, I somewhat doubt....[McAtee] is decidedly fixed in his ideas of how to do things, and how not to do them."[80] He sarcastically referred to McAtee's treasurership to date as "the reign of St. Mac the First."[81] After two years of the extra duties, Stone got out of the whole mess, saying it was "a physical impossibility for me to continue with this burden," and McAtee took over as business manager.[46,82] Stone must have reflected that his dedication to the AOU and propensity for taking on too much had given him much unnecessary tribulation during the preceding two years. McAtee had an interesting take on it years later: he believed that the split-responsibilities arrangement with Stone was made because some thought McAtee was too young (he was in his midthirties) to handle the full treasurership load. He noted that after taking on full responsibility he served longer than any previous AOU treasurer.[83] (Recall, however, that McAtee had originally thanked Stone for relieving him of some of the treasurer duties.)

———————— ∽ ————————

Stone was in for some additional editorial aggravation in 1922 when the New England Bird Banding Association (NEBBA) began clamoring for the AOU to have a supplement in each *Auk* covering NEBBA's activities. Stone went back and forth with Edward Forbush and Charles Whittle (NEBBA president and councilor, respectively) about the matter; Stone was adamant that he couldn't take on any more work as *Auk* editor.[84] The ANSP archives contain a letter dated February 28, 1922 in which Stone tells Forbush that he plans to query the AOU Council about the matter; if the Council decides to begin regular publication of the supplement that NEBBA desires, Stone will quit his editor post. He continues, "In order not to influence the Council I have therefore placed my resignation in their hands as I cannot let my personal convenience or limitations affect the AOU in an important matter of policy such as this."[85] The letter, however, is a rough draft that was never sent, and a letter dated March 1, which was the one Stone sent to Forbush, had some of the same material as the draft, but did not include Stone's threat to resign.[86]

A letter from Dwight to Stone in July 1922 indicates that Stone did resign as *Auk* editor, at least for a time, probably upon publication of the July issue. Dwight thought that Palmer might take over the position ("although I rather fear the outlook"), but a month later Stone had changed his mind.[87] AOU Fellow J.H. Fleming told Stone in October, "I am relieved that you are not to drop out of the editorship of the 'Auk.'"[88] The matter was still simmering in December, however, and Stone once again threatened to resign. He told the other members of the AOU publication committee that NEBBA was trying to strong-arm articles into the January *Auk*, but most of its material didn't merit publication: "There are a great many notes that simply record the number of birds banded by this man or that, and other little, personal incidents of no ornithological value; just such things as appear in 'Forest and Stream' in connection with hunting trips, and these are the sort of items I should insist on omitting."[89]

The matter managed to blow over in early 1923. Frederick Lincoln, the USBS's bird banding director, told Stone that he convinced NEBBA to publish its material in his *Bird Banding Notes* periodical, and that there would be no more demands for a section of *The Auk* to be devoted to it.[90]

Stone wasn't against bird banding *per se*, but he didn't see it as an end unto itself, and probably had mixed feelings about the banders who were drawn to bird study only by the pleasure they got from handling live birds. One AOU Fellow referred to bird banding as a "fad."[91] (And it's still an enduringly popular one 100 years later.) In rejecting one weak *Auk* submission from a bander who wondered whether the journal had a banding department, Stone said he welcomed manuscripts that shed light on bird biology via banding returns, but that there was no more need for a banding department "than maintaining a department for shot-guns and opera glasses, or any other method of study that may be in vogue."[92]

However, he urged the DVOC to get involved in bird banding in 1923, and was on the council of the Eastern Bird Banding Association when it formed later that year.[93] In a December 1923 talk to the Nuttall Ornithological Club, he offered that bird banding was the most important of the new methods of ornithological field study, and even went so far as to say that many of the people drawn to banding had not been interested in ornithology before, and "[t]hey look upon the older ornithologists, I fear, as a precious lot of conservatives, and many of our methods as antiquated; and in many cases they are right, and the remedies and innovations which they propose should be welcomed."[94] Most of this, admittedly, occurred after the controversy died down, but at the height of the NEBBA/*Auk* brouhaha he told Whittle, "We all feel very much interested in the success of the Bird Banding movement, and I am sure 'The Auk' and the AOU will wish to cooperate to the fullest extent."[95]

Stone was on friendly terms with the banding crowd afterward. Late in 1923, Fleming correctly predicted that the bird banders would start their own journal; after NEBBA changed its name to the Northeastern Bird Banding Association, it started publishing its own *Bulletin of the Northeastern Bird-banding Association*, which eventually morphed into today's *Journal of Field Ornithology*.[96] Ironically, the first issue of the *Bulletin*, in 1925, kicked off with the passage from Stone's Nuttall Club address extolling bird banding.[97] Stone had needed to put his foot down about not having more work added to his *Auk* load, but he wished the association all success with its new journal.[98]

The *Auk*'s perennially shaky fiscal footing during Stone's editorship was a constant headache for him.[99] The general havoc — financial and otherwise — produced by World War I didn't help, but the magazine, though reduced in size, remained afloat.[100] Some wished that a wealthy benefactor could be found who would shore up the journal's finances.[101] One AOU Fellow told Stone in 1914, "It's a great pity that your finances are so low now-a-days; we should scare up some rich patron, and let him bail into our coffers a few ladlefuls of double eagles [i.e., gold coins worth $20]."[102] It wasn't quite that easy, of course, and no angelic "rich patron" was forthcoming. In 1920, Stone facetiously predicted, "Unless money is forthcoming we will have to clip the wings of the old bird further & make an Apteryx [i.e., Kiwi] out of it!"[103] He told *Auk* readers that a $25,000 endowment would double the size of The *Auk* and put it on sound financial ground.[104] Funds were still so low in 1924 that Stone was told by treasurer McAtee to drastically cut the size of the July and October issues.[105] In 1925, Stone was grousing about the continued lack of an endowment, saying that one was needed "but someone has to get it and have authority to go after it and that never seems to be granted [by the AOU Council]."[44] The endowment was a pipe dream that never came to fruition in Stone's time, and he was still asking for an endowment fund at the end of his editorship in 1936.[106]

He was also irritated that the Council wouldn't dip into permanent funds for The *Auk*'s benefit.[44] At the 1925 AOU annual meeting, McAtee had suggested using some funds held by the trustees to shore up *Auk* finances, but Stone said the outcome was that no voice "was raised in behalf of the Magazine & so we have been forced to get along on a greatly reduced amount of funds."[107] Stone told one author, "Now owing to the shortness in funds and the disinclination of the AOU Council to do anything to relieve the situation it will be necessary to cut the 1926 Auk about one quarter to one third its size....It is an awful job to publish a journal of insufficient funds and you get 'cusses' from all sides no matter what you do."[108]

The Great Depression, of course, further strained the AOU's publication resources, and Stone was looking for fat to trim. He thought deaths of Associate members could be treated with "a mere statement of death, unless they did some real ornithological work, instead of [AOU secretary] Palmer's long… obituaries, dealing with business & religious activities etc. etc." (which Stone was also guilty of writing).[109-110] Stone's buddies in the Fellows class, however, warranted special treatment, and when one of them died, a long memorial appeared in a subsequent *Auk*. Stone wrote a 22-page memorial of Charles Richmond at a time when the "Notes and News" section contained editorial grumblings about the shortage of *Auk* funds and the backlog of articles.[111]

In June 1933, Stone announced that 500 AOU members had been unable to pay their annual dues, leaving the publication of the July issue in doubt. The AOU trustees said they could supply an emergency fund of $500 for the July *Auk* if the Council voted to release the funds.[112] Some of the Council members, however, were skeptical about the inability of members (read "Associates") to pay their $3 annual dues. Thomas Roberts, an original (but not technically "founding") member of the AOU, told Stone, "I am greatly surprised at the very large number failing to pay dues. I warrant they go to movies, fights, guzzle beer, etc." – which is a good indication of what some of the AOU Fellows thought of the lower membership classes.[113] Grinnell told Stone, "I am astonished that so large a proportion of the AOU membership is delinquent. I seriously wonder if the policy of scrambling for members of only passing interest is a good one.... Better, perhaps, to have a smaller membership, of steadier interest."[114] Stone raised some funds on his own by soliciting donations from concerned, wealthy AOU members, contributed $50 himself, and the July issue came off.[112,115] Funds were still tight a year later, however, and Stone told one *Auk* contributor, "The editor's job under present conditions is not an enviable one and I can assure you I wonder why I hold onto it!"[116] But he did – money shortages and all – for another two years.

───────────── ❧ ─────────────

Problems with the printers were another nuisance. The Cosmos Press in Cambridge, Massachusetts, was printing *The Auk* when Stone became editor, but he immediately shopped around for better prices.[117] The AOU's patience with Cosmos was eventually exhausted when the owner, Edward Wheeler, grew old and his business started falling apart. Stone had to rush the October 1919 *Auk* to press because of printer delays; he predicted that the issue might feature some "rhinoceroses and okapis" mistakenly inserted by Cosmos and missed by Stone in his haste to read the proofs.[118] The last straw was a price increase Wheeler put into effect just as the January 1920 *Auk* was heading to press.[119] In 1920, Intelligencer Printing of Lancaster, Pennsylvania began printing *The Auk* and did so through Stone's tenure and well beyond. Intelligencer and other eastern publishers were hit by a printers' strike in 1921 that also affected *Science*, among other scientific journals.[120] As if Stone's *Auk* labors weren't hectic enough, the strike, which lasted from May 1 into August, caused the publication of the July issue to be delayed until October, and the October issue until December.[121]

After the strike ended, the AOU–Intelligencer road was still rocky, and Stone threatened more than once to take the printing elsewhere.[122-123] Intelligencer was doing shoddy work, and Stone's irritation rose proportionally. He could be uncharacteristically blunt and critical, almost acid, at times in his letters to his long-suffering contact at Intelligencer, A.E. Urban, telling him in April 1922, "I need hardly tell you that the last batches of proof are exceedingly unsatisfactory. It is perfectly evident that they came to me without any proof-reading whatever....[T]o have whole lines omitted, and all kinds of absurd errors, shows that no attention could possibly have been paid to the proof in your office....You cannot expect us to pay for the corrections in the galley proofs...as there were not over a half-dozen that were in any way our fault."[122] Stone received his July 1922 *Auk* at Cape May, where he was summering, and assumed everyone else had gotten theirs too, but when he made a visit to Philadelphia on July 19 he found that was not the case. He railed at Urban, "I came up to Philadelphia today, and was thoroughly disgusted to find that no 'Auks' had been received by anyone here....You do not realize, perhaps, the annoyance that this is to me, and everyone blames me for not receiving their magazines."[124]

By November, however, Stone was telling Urban that he was keeping Intelligencer as the *Auk* printer, and that its work "when properly supervised is entirely satisfactory, and I hope that you will be able to get competent supervision in the future."[125] All was quiet on the printer front, and despite the usual price increases, and quotes from rival publishers, Intelligencer printed *The Auk* until 1961, and was also engaged by Stone to print the AOU semicentennial retrospective volume in 1933 and his own *Bird Studies at Old Cape May* in 1937. [126-127] It is still in business in Lancaster today.

Some grumbling about publication delays must have reached Stone's ears in 1923, leading to an interesting *Auk* note detailing some of the trials of editorship, which Stone delivered in almost a lecturing tone, like an exasperated teacher or parent would use. He said that AOU members needed to understand that the editors and managers were busy men who performed their *Auk* labors in such time as they could find apart from already busy schedules, and he cited a bout of personal illness during the past year. Stone then laid down the law for future submissions, lecturing on timeliness of submissions, uniformity of style and format, paper length limit (20 pages), and conciseness in writing.[46] Today, of course, journals define an exact format in their instructions to authors, and a manuscript submission that wanders too far from it may be peremptorily returned.

In 1924, Stone asked that all future *Auk* submissions be typed, if possible, rather than written out longhand.[128] The typewriter had been around since before the AOU formed, and calling for its general use for *Auk* manuscripts was a long-overdue step. But typewriters were apparently not as ubiquitous as one might expect. James Peters at MCZ summed up the situation perfectly, telling Stone, "Your ultimatum concerning typewritten manuscripts for the Auk is going to make it hard for some of us poor cusses up here who don't own either a typewriter or a secretary, only not nearly so hard as it was on the Editor before the edict went into effect."[129]

∾

The annual printing of the AOU members list in the April *Auk* was a sore spot with Stone; he constantly butted heads over it with the AOU Council, and particularly with secretary Palmer. Stone's correspondence indicates that most of his fellow ornithologists agreed with him that publishing it annually was a waste of space and money. But the rite was sacrosanct with Palmer, who wielded great influence and was a wily political infighter. Stone and Palmer started locking horns over the list's annual publication in 1921.[130] Stone didn't print the list in 1926, after framing the argument as "Do you want 45 pages of names, or 45 pages of ornithology?"[131] Stone had gotten permission from AOU president Dwight and treasurer McAtee first, but it still drew a slap on the wrist from the Council at the annual meeting in October, which directed that "in future the Editor publish the annual list of members until otherwise ordered" and "to omit the list only on authorization of the Council."[132] Stone was still smarting from that one four years later, telling Palmer during another set-to about the list in 1930, "While the Council went to some trouble to order the Editor to publish the list they entirely ignored his suggestion of appropriating funds to carry it through."[133]

With *The Auk* in dire straits in 1932, Stone was on the warpath again to omit the members list, which he said would take up 63 pages and cost $340, or about all the funds he had on hand to publish the April *Auk*.[134] He may not have been exaggerating much when he told Wetmore, "The omission of the list this year is absolutely necessary, otherwise there will only be the list, one paper & the Cover in April Auk! A fine thing for the Editor, surely!! But − !!"[135]

Stone had informed the Council of the critical situation at the AOU annual meeting in 1931, and the only reply he received was from Palmer telling him there was no crisis.[134] In his correspondence with the Council, Stone put the blame for much of the mess on Palmer; Peters, for one, told Stone, "You can count on my support to make the Auk a journal of ornithology, not of necrology and statistics" − an obvious reference to "Tomb Stone" Palmer's endless obituaries and his minutely detailed, numbers- and names-laden reports on annual meetings and general state of the AOU.[135-136] Stone won that particular battle, and announced in *The Auk* that the list would not be published for 1932 ("much to our regret," in a sarcastic aside), but by March 1933 he was telling Peters, "[T]hat infernal List of Members ate up about a quarter of our available funds for April. But my hands are tied, the Council (=TSP) ordered it!"[137] He told Chapman that Palmer once again claimed that funds would be found for publishing the list, as he had argued on previous occasions, "but by following his advice in 1931, we were short $900 at the close of the year and I had to get out and raise $600 to square matters."[109,135]

Stone, as *Auk* editor, at least had the advantage of getting in the last word, and he did so − literally − in 1935, when, just before the 61-page members list, he wrote, "The present issue contains a smaller number of leading articles in order to make room for the long list of members which has to be published unless omitted by order of Council. Its compilation is responsible for a delay in the appearance of the issue."[138] The Council members could make him publish the list, but they didn't think to tell him not to carp about it in print. His 1935 *Auk* comment that 80% of a recent British journal publication was taken up with a members and donors list, "but this perhaps is a necessity required by the management as in some publications in America," was a thinly veiled dig at the AOU Council.[139] Stone was granted permission to leave the list out again for the 1936 volume − like a going-away gift in his last year as editor.[140]

Well, bless Palmer's heart anyway − his lists and other minutiae are an invaluable source of information for ornithological historians. These days, the Ornithological Societies of North America (OSNA) publishes *The Flock*, a membership list for several ornithological societies, including the AOU, which frees modern editors from one more headache that their predecessors such as Stone had to deal with.

——————————— ∾ ———————————

Stone's *Auk* editorship also saw the rise of authors paying publication costs for their manuscripts. By the early 1920s, Stone found himself between a rock and a hard place as *Auk* editor: he had a backlog of papers to publish, and no funds with which to increase the size of the journal to publish them.[141] A very long manuscript by Wetmore was ready for publication in early 1920, but its length would necessitate bumping other manuscripts from the April issue. Stone told Wetmore that he wanted to print it "but it will make 51 pages! & unless I [want to] face assassination at the hands of some 20 others who are expecting to see their papers in April I shall have to divide it in two" (which he did, spreading it over two issues).[142]

Some authors began covering page costs in order to get their manuscripts to the front of the long queue. Paying some or all of the page costs is expected of authors today, but it smacked of "pay to play" (or "pay to publish") at that time, even though Stone was up front about the practice – both in *The Auk* and in correspondence – when it got under way.[143-144] For example, he told one author in early 1922 concerning *Auk* submissions that "if you have funds to help pay for them, they can be pushed ahead of any paper that may be waiting."[145] That raises the question of whether papers that would not otherwise have been accepted were published simply because the author agreed to pay for them up front, but Stone was notoriously uncritical of *Auk* submissions and likely would have wanted to publish most articles anyway. Still, some worried that paying for publishing costs might be misperceived. In 1932, one author who didn't want it known that he was paying for part of his article told Stone, "I wouldn't for the world have anything printed merely because it was paid for, and I want most carefully to avoid grounds for such a criticism."[146]

Stone's correspondence is full of references to authors paying for articles submitted to *The Auk* (and for accompanying illustrations, which were costlier to print than text).[126] Stone heard grumblings about it, and argued that authors paying page costs actually benefited all the other authors with manuscripts in the pipeline, because papers with the page costs covered by the author were added to the latest issue in addition to those already slated for inclusion, and thus it actually helped decrease the backlog.[147] *Auk* funds were so short that sometimes articles paid for by authors actually fleshed out issues that otherwise would have been quite a bit smaller.[44,148]

AOU Fellow John Phillips told Stone in 1926, "It is rather too bad that small articles have to be excluded from the 'Auk' unless they are subsidized. I am afraid if this got to be generally known it might make for a rather bad feeling. However, I do not see that there is anything we can do about it."[149] Phillips, though, was one of the men of means – such as Robert Moore and John Rockefeller – who could more easily afford to have their articles published, at the length and with the illustrations they wanted, than the average *Auk* contributor could.[150]

Pay to publish took a shady turn in June 1921, when NAAS president T. Gilbert Pearson arranged to place an advertisement for the NAAS youth programs, disguised as an *Auk* editorial, in exchange for a $250 NAAS contribution to the journal.[151] That amount wouldn't go far today, but in 1921 it was enough to cover a lot of red ink. Pearson said he'd give Stone the general facts he wanted to have included. Stone mentioned a recent contribution by the NAAS in the July *Auk*, and the "editorial" appeared in the October issue's "Notes and News" section, but the *quid pro quo* arrangement wasn't mentioned.[143,152]

None of this was really nefarious. Stone had often used the "Notes and News" section as a bully pulpit for conservation, and the majority of the *Auk* readership would have been sympathetic to the efforts of the NAAS youth programs – unlike the similar shenanigans Pearson dragged the NAAS into with arms manufacturers. Stone insisted that the money was "a "gift," and certainly Pearson could have gotten the blurb placed with the promise of a lot less than $250, but the Pearson rent-an-editor incident wasn't entirely aboveboard, either.[153]

Stone's unusual relationship with Edward "Ned" McIlhenny, the wealthy Tabasco tycoon, made for some interesting *Auk* decisions that reverberate today. McIlhenny got together an expedition to the Arctic in 1897, and the mammals and birds he collected there came back to the Academy. McIlhenny wanted to sell it all off for $6,000 initially, promising Stone a 10% commission if he could find a buyer.[154] McIlhenny later agreed to offer it piecemeal, but Stone received so many queries from a variety of interested (and semi-interested) parties that he must have considered it a bother.[155] All of it eventually sold (ANSP bought some of it), with some buyers satisfied with the specimens' quality, and others not so much. A Short-eared Owl in the collection looked like a new form to Stone, and McIlhenny asked outright to have it named after himself.[156] Collectors can always *hope* that a new form based on one of their specimens gets named for them, but to blatantly ask for the honor is cheeky, if not unprofessional. Stone acquiesced, although the subspecies is no longer given consideration.[157]

In 1912, McIlhenny submitted an article to new *Auk* editor Stone on Little Blue Herons – or, as it appears, he was testing the waters with the new editor to see if he could ram a shaky article through. He pompously announced to Stone in August, "I would like to give your publication the benefit of my study of the dichromatic phase of the Little Blue Heron," and apparently expected the article to be accepted before he even sent it in.[158] Stone told him that wasn't the way things worked; McIlhenny responded that he would send in the manuscript, and because it was sure to be accepted, he instructed the editor to reserve a place for it in the October *Auk*.[159] McIlhenny's article was titled "A new species in the making," which indicates the slippery slope he was on with his misunderstanding of the Little Blue's plumage sequences.[160-161] It appears that Stone accepted the paper at first (at least, that was McIlhenny's impression), but he sent the manuscript to Chapman to get his opinion of it.[162] He told Chapman about his predicament: "The photos are all right, and I must confess that I have not seen any faking in McIlhenny's recent conversations [so clearly he had in previous ones], so I felt safe in regard to them. I am in rather an embarrassing position regarding the man as his friends & relatives in Phila. are prominent in affairs here & also in the Academy and have great confidence in McIlhenny!"[163]

Chapman read it over and would have none of it, finding it too full of material that ranged from dubious to absurd.[164] Stone rejected it, using the excuse that there were too many photos (19, five of which were full-page – yes, that's a lot of photos), but heaven only knows how bad the text was.[165] Years later, McIlhenny was still completely mixed up about the molt sequence of the species, even though it was understood by then, and that misunderstanding was the starting point for the problems with his 1912 manuscript.[161,166] The paper never saw light of day in any serious ornithological journal, if it was published anywhere.

Things were quiet on the McIlhenny front for about 20 years, until he probably saw an opportunity to use *The Auk*'s Depression-era financial woes to his advantage. He paid for publication of a Blue Goose article in 1932, telling Stone, who was pulling rabbits out of hats to pay for the journal at the time, "If at any time I can assist you with the AUK financially or otherwise, please command me."[167] He sent a check for $200 and told the *Auk* editor to keep the change, if there was any.[168] (Tabasco sauce must be a Depression-proof business.) He continued to contribute articles and money, sometimes simultaneously, over the next few years.[169] Additionally, McIlhenny first invited Stone to visit his Louisiana estate in 1931, and, after a few more invitations, Witmer and Lillie made a trek there in the spring of 1935, with expenses paid by McIlhenny.[170] If Stone had his doubts about some of the material with which McIlhenny was suddenly peppering *The Auk*, his reservations may have been soothed by the openness of the author's purse.

McIlhenny certainly seems to have been an interested observer of birds, and he did a splendid job with "Bird City," the sanctuary for waterfowl and wading birds that he created on his Louisiana estate. He was one of the first to publish on the skewed sex ratios of North American waterfowl, which was supported by later researchers.[171] He was a generous Southern gentleman to boot. However, he had a reputation for playing loose with the truth.[172] Frederic Kennard told Stone in 1935, "Ned McIlhenny and his wife are certainly delightful hosts. I like the fellow. The only trouble is truth seems to be foreign to his makeup. I was compelled, years ago, to make up my mind never to quote him. It's just too bad."[173] McIlhenny's publications were a mixture of fact and fiction, and some of his *Auk* material should never have been accepted. He added to the confusion about the ranges of Boat-tailed Grackles with brown vs. golden eyes with the erroneous assertion in one article that their eye color changed from gold to brown when they were being handled in banding operations.[174] He published an article in 1937 (after Stone retired) about a supposed

Turkey Vulture–Black Vulture hybrid that he caught in a trap in Louisiana; the bird, which would have represented the only known instance of hybridization between the two species, reportedly later proved to be a Black Vulture with red paint applied to its head.[175]

Given the questions about his reliability by folks who knew him, it's unfortunate that the recent *Birds of North America (BNA)* series authors and editors included his Purple Gallinule and Boat-tailed Grackle predatory behavior reports in their species accounts.[176] One of the gallinule *BNA* sources was a McIlhenny *Auk* article, which could be expected to be reliable – at least it was reviewed by an ornithologist, although his cozy relationship with the editor may have greased the publication wheels for him – but another source cited was McIlhenny's *Bird City*, which was a children's book saturated with anthropomorphisms.[177] In the book, McIlhenny depicts the gallinule as "Public Enemy No. 1 of Bird City," a "thief and murderer" that makes all the other birds "bristle with rage" when it walks past, and he has the gallinules stealing eggs and ripping apart half-grown nestling Snowy Egrets.[178] That's pretty vicious stuff compared to their usual diet of plant matter and invertebrates, although *BNA* cited a recent study in Costa Rica that reported them eating frogs. The *BNA* gallinule authors did not quote McIlhenny's 1937 Boat-tailed Grackle article, and were likely unaware that there he reported gallinules routinely depredating grackle nests.[179] He also reported male Boat-taileds depredating nests of conspecifics and preying on other birds, as well as eating carrion, and the *BNA* grackle account quoted him, although other researchers haven't reported those behaviors for the species. Some of McIlhenny's questionable published material from the 1930s is being given credence decades later by ornithologists who may not know about the skepticism with which he was viewed by his contemporaries, or the particulars of his relationship with *Auk* editor Stone.

Paying the costs of a manuscript's publication in Stone's day was a new concept; some authors found it uncomfortable, some found it prohibitive, some thought it had a bit of an odor about it, and some used it to their advantage. Today it has become more of a norm, and authors are often expected to help defray page costs when a manuscript is published.

———————— ∿ ————————

Any editor who serves 25 years will face criticism, and Stone heard enough of it – everything from missing *Auks* and publication delays to journal content and editorial style. In *A Passion for Birds: American Ornithology After Audubon*, Mark Barrow Jr. summarized the last years of Stone's editorship, based in part on an interview with Ernst Mayr. The latter was portrayed, along with Herbert Friedmann, as one of the younger ornithologists pushing for reform in the AOU at the time, trying to move it away from the collecting and systematics emphasis and toward more modern studies of the living bird, and Stone was portrayed as one of the old-guard ornithologists who were too set in their ways to move with the scientific times, particularly in his duties as *Auk* editor:

> Witmer Stone had been a popular choice to take over management of the journal when founding editor J.A. Allen finally decided to step down in 1911. At the time Stone was a respected avian taxonomist with a decade of experience editing *Cassinia*. However, by the early 1930s he was in his mid-sixties, suffering from chronic heart disease, and (according to his critics) increasingly out of touch with modern ornithological trends….The reservations about how Stone was editing *The Auk* were varied. Several AOU members regretted his failure to exercise more editorial discretion. Stone had a reputation for writing lenient book reviews and accepting for publication nearly all the manuscripts that came across his desk. The result was a large backlog of submissions, long delays in publication, a decline in quality, and the imposition of a twenty-page limit for most articles. In the face of these problems, many graduate-trained ornithologists – especially those pursuing more innovative life-history, behavioral, physiological, and ecological studies – sought other channels for their work….Beyond these complaints was the concern that in an effort to maintain a healthy subscription list, Stone catered far too much to the large contingent of associate members who paid the bulk of the AOU's dues. According to the critics, the end of the "Stone Age" [Mayr's term] of the *Auk* was long overdue.[180] ["Stone Age" was not original to Mayr, nor was it always used derisively.][181]

As in any other branch of science, all the major American ornithological journals have become more technical and quantitative over time, as younger researchers continually build on the work of the previous generations and move the field into a more narrowly scientific and quantitative direction. By 1936, Stone had received his college and graduate education almost 50 years previously, and his doctorate was honorary. He would not have been up to speed on the latest methods and advancements in science (e.g., genetics) and statistics being taught at the universities. In 1915, he called for the academic experimental biologists (the younger guns) and the museum systematists (Stone's generation) to work together on understanding the mechanisms of evolution, making a case for what today might be termed cross-disciplinary research.[182] But in 1924, Stone and Smithsonian botanist William Maxon grumbled to each other about the lack of systematics training at universities, where the graduates, said Stone, couldn't identify even common species of plants and animals, and "the present-day overwhelming majority of geneticists, physiologists and the like [in academic positions] is evidence of the way things are going."[183]

His ANSP duties and *Auk* and other AOU labors took up so much of his time that he had little time for any original research of his own. He was conservative by nature, and was unlikely to take the journal in any new directions, as indicated in his 1935 *Auk* musings lamenting the way other journals were changing their appearances. He liked the conservatism of *National Geographic* and the stability of *The Ibis*, with the same cover illustration since the 1800s; he hoped *The Auk*'s Louis Agassiz Fuertes drawing would remain on the cover in perpetuity – an idea first suggested by Chapman.[184] By the time he retired as *Auk* editor, it was probably time for Stone and his generation to step aside and let the younger folks carry the torch forward. Twenty-five years is enough time for anyone to get bypassed by the advances in the science of the journal he is editing.[60]

The nature of *Auk* content was an ongoing issue throughout Stone's editorship. He tried to maintain a balance between technical and popular material, because he felt it was necessary to engage a broad readership in order to get enough *Auk* subscriptions (i.e., AOU memberships) to keep it afloat, which he did, Great Depression and all. (J.A. Allen had been through the same popular vs. technical issue as far back as the *Bulletin of the Nuttall Ornithological Club*, and *The Ibis* – and doubtless other bird journals – was having similar content tussles contemporaneously with Stone's *Auk* editorship.)[185] The younger men such as Mayr and Friedmann could push for their idealized vision of what the journal should be like, but reading Stone's correspondence about the *Auk*'s finances, particularly with AOU president Fleming during the 1930s – when they were dealing with economic catastrophe and delinquent members – it's clear that it was a constant burden to keep the journal's head above water during a time of grueling financial hardship. Stone, for one, was raising money and putting up his own, all the while hearing the gamut of opinions about the nature of the content. (Friedmann, ironically, considered starting a rival journal that would be more technical, but realized it would be impossible to finance given the limited potential readership for it.)[186]

Stone moved articles of what he felt were important new findings or descriptions of new species to the front of the queue, but he also felt that the AOU needed to maintain a healthy membership base; the vast majority of AOU members, of course, were at the Associate level, and they were thought to be more interested in material in a popular vein, such as the shorter communications and faunal lists.[187] He summarized his views in a 1920 *Auk* note: "'The Auk' is a journal and not merely a work of reference, and as it appeals to a very wide range of readers, it is necessary to keep the matter in each issue as varied as possible. What might be called 'readable' articles are therefore arranged in one series and technical papers and geographic lists in another and the aim of the Editor is to mingle the two judiciously in every issue….[P]apers are accepted for their historic, literary, biographic and economic value as well as for their intrinsic scientific worth."[104]

That prompted one AOU Member to write to Stone that, given some of the recent articles in *The Auk*, Stone might be "giving the literary quality undue consideration."[188] But McAtee at the USBS responded to the same note with, "Don't worry! most of us here, at least, highly approve of the present status of The Auk. The last volume was the best ever. Variety is necessary to cater to all brands of ornithologists, but also has the drawback of offering points of attack for several different classes of kickers."[189] (In the parlance of the day, to "kick" was to complain, as when one reader told Stone his *Auk* workload was excessive, and asked, "Why don't you kick?")[54]

Auk content did change over the course of Stone's editorship. A comparison of the 1913 volume, in Stone's first full year as editor, with his last one, the 1936 volume, reveals a notable decrease in faunal articles (e.g., simple regional lists of birds, with some notes added), and a large increase in the proportion of articles concerned with facets of species' natural history. That was a reflection of a concurrent movement away from museum-based systematic studies toward the study of the living bird, but *Auk* content still wasn't moving in the direction of hard-boiled science quickly enough for some.

Joseph Grinnell gave Stone his two cents about *Auk* content in 1922, saying it should be more rigidly scientific, even if that meant losing members who were more interested in the lighter fare, and that Stone wouldn't have such a backlog of articles if he were more selective.[190] Stone, typically accommodating, responded that he entirely agreed with Grinnell, asserting unconvincingly that Palmer was the one who wanted a large membership, even if it consisted mostly of people with nontechnical interests, which meant Stone had to cater to them to some extent ("places me in a rather ambiguous position" of trying to appeal to both audiences). He also maintained that when good material was scant he put in the popular fare, then would get hit with a deluge of better manuscripts and a backlog.[191]

Grinnell again expressed his concerns about *The Auk* and the state of the AOU to Stone in 1930; Stone again defended *Auk* content, as well as the scientific mettle of the AOU membership and meetings, and the performance of the bird protection committee. He said that he hadn't heard any of the complaints Grinnell was hearing, which is difficult to believe.[192]

In a 1927 *Auk* note discussing the current state of the periodical, Stone wrote that because of the increased volume of manuscript submissions, articles would have to be shorter (8,000-word limit), and all would have to await their turn in the queue, but he made no indication he would be more selective about manuscript acceptance.[193] Some of the material in *The Auk* at the time, particularly the shorter communications, would be listserve fodder today, and one wonders why, when pressed for space, Stone would continue to publish the likes of "Blue Jays gathering twigs for nests" and "A comparatively tame Eastern Green Heron."[194] (In earlier years, his literature reviews could be excessive – for example, a 6½-page whopper of the first volume of William Beebe's pheasant monographs, or a 7½-page one of Gregory Mathews's *Birds of Australia*, but he reined things in considerably when *Auk* funds dried up during the Depression.)[195]

He did reject submissions, of course; his minimum standards for acceptance must have been somewhere above one paper he rejected in 1921 with a gentle "I regret to say that owing to the number of contributions already waiting publication, I am unable to accept your manuscript on 'Bird Pets.' I am therefore returning it, in the hope that you will be able to find a channel of publication elsewhere."[196] Stone maintained that oftentimes when he rejected a paper, the authors would pitch their case to an AOU officer or councilor, who would then appeal to Stone with "a long argument why this paper must go in!!"[197]

However, Stone largely believed that if someone took the time to write something up and submit it, it should be published, and he was too lenient when separating the wheat from the chaff. In 1936, he received a manuscript that described a new subspecies of screech owl from Colombia, based on some specimens in the Academy's Rivoli Collection. Stone told a colleague, "I am perfectly willing to publish it, although I am very skeptical about its being a new form, as it is from one of the best-collected localities in Colombia & the alleged differences are very slight!" He published it anyway (and the form is no longer valid).[198] After McAtee expressed skepticism at some recent *Auk* material from a particular author, Stone told him, "I don't believe in his ideas any more than you do but like H.C.O[berholser] & others when he presents them in scholarly form it is up to the editor to publish them & someone else can knock them!"[17] Stone was probably being placative with McAtee to some extent, but certainly his willingness to publish an article if he didn't agree with its content would astonish present-day editors (and authors). If an editor doesn't agree with an author's arguments or conclusions today, the author either comes up with a major rewrite or one heck of a sales pitch; otherwise, the manuscript doesn't get published in that journal.

Friedmann sent Stone a manuscript in 1935 by T. Hume Bissonnette and Alphonse Zujko about ovary changes in starlings during the onset of the breeding season.[199] Stone must have told Friedmann that the paper was too long or technical, or both, and an irritated Friedmann convincingly made his case for publication: "I have a feeling that the complaints made by many of our Associate members to any technical article will have to be discounted. After all, the primary object of the journal is the publication of serious contributions to ornithological science, not light reading for amateur bird students....I think in the past there has been entirely too much attention given to their criticisms, not by yourself but by others....I doubt very much if the majority of them read the [leading] articles anyway. They probably read the reviews and short notes."[200] Stone must have been swayed by the perfectly valid argument, for the manuscript was published within a year.[201]

After it appeared, McAtee told Stone that he liked the article, and Stone responded that he didn't receive many technical papers like the Bissonnette and Zuijko one:

> I asked Bissonnette for something at the last New York meeting and this is what I got. I infer from your note that the "younger Folkes" want more of this sort of thing but no definite demand has come to me. The fact is that I have published all the technical matter that has come to hand. The trouble is that it does not come. On the other hand if we put in too much of it we shall lose Associates by the dozen and they are the ones who provide the means for keeping "The Auk" going! Up to date you are the only person who has written his enjoyment of the above paper [but the issue had been out less than two weeks] while I have had several protests against publishing papers of the sort – to which I of course pay no attention.[202]

The "protests" don't seem to refer to letters about this particular article, but to ones he'd received over the years decrying other similar ones. Stone's remark about routinely publishing all technical papers is suspect, however, given that Friedmann had to cajole him into publishing this one.

But whatever any of the "younger Folkes" may have thought of Stone's editorship, many contemporary ornithologists expressed admiration for his work. On the occasion of Stone's 20-year anniversary as editor, Ludlow Griscom wrote of the difficulties of trying to please all members of a readership that ran the gamut from inexperienced amateurs to world-renowned ornithologists. He asserted that Stone had "produced one of the great ornithological magazines of the world, satisfying as nearly as humanly possible all the varied interests represented in the Union, and I think any reasonable-minded member would agree with me on this."[203]

    Ironically, one of the papers that came across his desk that Stone seemed unimpressed with was C.W.G. Eifrig's "Is photoperiodism a factor in the migration of birds?"[204] Rev. Eifrig was a Lutheran minister who taught at Concordia Teachers College (now Concordia University Chicago, where the building that houses the Natural Sciences and Geography Department is named Eifrig Hall). He was a frequent contributor of mostly short notes to *The Auk* and *The Wilson Bulletin*, and served for a time as president of the Illinois Audubon Society.[205] In a paper he read at the AOU annual meeting in Chicago in 1922, he proposed that changing day length may be the stimulating factor for the onset of bird migration, just as some recent articles had shown it to be in the reproductive schedules of plants.[206] Eifrig submitted it for publication in *The*

Auk twice, hoping to be the first one to publish the idea, but Stone, not recognizing the paper's insights, told him both times that it would be put into the queue with everything else.[207] The second time he recommended that Eifrig publish it elsewhere if he was in a hurry, and referred him to a paper in *The Ibis* "on somewhat the same topic," suggesting to Eifrig that Stone was telling him someone had already beaten him to it.[208] After some more prodding from Eifrig, Stone published the paper in the July 1924 *Auk*.

But not only was the *Ibis* paper not on the same topic, Eifrig had also hit the nail on the head with his theory and was cited by a later author on the subject as being the first to put it into print.[209] (He wasn't – E.A. Schafer proposed it, almost as an aside, in a 1907 migration article in *Nature*, but his remark seems to be have been overlooked for many years.)[210] Granted, his paper was entirely conjectural – Eifrig simply had a hunch that the same controlling factor shown in plants might be at work in birds. He didn't advance any physiological mechanisms nor present any experimental evidence for the phenomenon in birds (others would soon do that), and his assertion in a 1924 letter to Stone that he had observed Passenger Pigeons on five recent occasions, including a pair, wouldn't have encouraged Stone or anyone else about his scientific temperament.[211] Maybe it was a case of a blind squirrel finding a nut, but Eifrig's photoperiodism/migration idea has long been accepted as correct, and a curiously disinterested Stone almost lost the chance to have the idea first fully proposed in *The Auk*.[212]

A cautious Stone similarly rejected another paper with original insights, and the story is notable for the admirably stubborn conservation ethic of its unsung central character. Fred M. Jones submitted a note on the nesting of the Swainson's Warbler in rhododendron thickets in the mountains around Bristol, Virginia to *The Raven*, the state ornithological journal, in 1932. The species was known to nest only in coastal plain canebrakes, so *Raven* editor J.J. Murray rejected the note.[213] Jones submitted it to *The Auk*, where it was met with more editorial eyebrow raising.[214-215] Stone thought it might be a Worm-eating Warbler nest, so Jones mailed him a nest and eggs with permission to send them out for expert opinion. Stone had them examined by Wetmore and J.H. Riley at the Smithsonian, and their verdict was that although it certainly looked like a dead-ringer Swainson's nest and eggs, an inland nest in rhododendron "would be decidedly out of the ordinary." Wetmore advised Jones to collect one of the adult birds for identification in the next breeding season.[216]

Jones thought otherwise. In an even-tempered but firm letter, he told Stone to throw away the manuscript about the Swainson's nest, as he had no more information to furnish concerning it. He had previously told Stone that it would be "a useless waste of bird life" to kill one of the adults for identification purposes, and that he'd seen them sitting on the nest at a distance of a few feet.[214] He had enough field experience that he could accurately identify birds without collecting them. Now he told Stone, "Science demands the killing of the bird when they depart from the customs of their forefathers, or what is known of their customs; with me in their chosen haunts they are safe." He emphasized that he respected Stone's knowledge and experience, and he realized that in requesting a specimen Stone was following standard procedures. But Jones wasn't about to kill a bird to get the publication.[217]

In 1935, Murray published an *Auk* article about his discovery of Swainson's Warblers breeding in the mountains of North Carolina. They had previously been known to breed only in the coastal areas of the state, but Murray didn't collect the birds or the eggs to back his identification.[218] Jones resubmitted his southwest Virginia Swainson's Warbler notes to Stone at that point, saying he assumed Stone's "policy in the matter of publications may have been moderated."[219] Stone, however, had already told Wetmore, "I have a couple of Swainson's Warbler nest records from inland spots but not yet in Rhododendron thickets so I do not feel that I shall have to swallow my rejection of that record (?) of Mr. Jones – not yet anyway!"[69]

Justice came, belatedly, to Jones in 1939, when Murray published a short notice in *The Raven* that recounted his original rejection of Jones's Swainson's Warbler notes in 1932, and the recent finding of the species during the breeding season in a swamp with hemlocks and rhododendrons in the Tennessee mountains not far from Jones's location. The Tennessee birds were discovered by a Smithsonian team whose finds were published, ironically, by Wetmore.[220] Murray graciously admitted his mistake and congratulated Jones on being the first to discover the inland, rhododendron breeding habitat of the species, which is well known today.[221]

Jones wasn't averse to killing hawks, and in fact was on a mission one breeding season to kill as many of the detested, bird-killing Cooper's Hawks as he could. (He got "only" six.)[222] But he'd stuck to his guns about not wanting to collect the Swainson's Warblers. He told Stone in 1932 that he was submitting the Swainson's notes because the part of the state where he was doing his work was little known to ornithologists, and his records would help to fill in distribution gaps in the 1931 AOU check-list – perfectly good reasons to publish one's findings.[214] These days, of course, Jones would find the nest with the bird on it and whip out his digital camera and be done with it, without having to kill anything. But bully for him for standing firm on his conservation principles, at the risk of losing publication priority of his distribution findings, and they were put on a back burner for seven years by ornithologists who weren't familiar with the rugged and remote areas of the southern Appalachians that Jones had clambered and sweated all over. And Stone, the skeptical *Auk* editor, spent way more time at a desk in a museum than he spent outside doing fieldwork.

———————— ❧ ————————

The grind of editorship took its toll on Stone. As early as 1917, in closing a letter to an *Auk* author, he wrote, "I trust you will appreciate the difficulties under which an editor labors when funds are short, and make allowances for his apparent shortcomings," and told another correspondent, "I tell you for the five weeks previous to the appearance of an Auk I have not any time to spare either Sundays or evenings."[223] Evenings in particular were a tough time to do *Auk* work, because he was tired after a day at ANSP and his mind wasn't fresh.[17] A few years later, the other seven weeks were being impinged upon as well: "Now the editorial job is getting clear beyond me. I have tried & I think succeeded in making the journal the leading one in the world…with the result that I am in receipt of letters, papers for review, comments, requests for copies & exchanges, etc. from every quarter that requires all my spare time between 'issues' to attend to."[224] In 1922 he asserted, "[I]t is a physical impossibility for me to edit a magazine of more than six hundred pages per year. The job is getting so big, that it seems to me before long an editor must be provided who will be able to spend at least half of his time on this work."[225] In 1925 he gently chided a new AOU member, "You, perhaps, do not know that the entire work of 'The Auk' is done on Sundays, evenings and holidays, as most of my time is occupied as Director of the Museum here. This has prevented my doing practically any scientific work for the past ten years."[226] It never let up, of course: as he neared retirement, Stone told Wetmore:

> When I took over the job 25 years ago I realized that I must do it entirely at home in spare time and I have held to that religiously. As time has gone on the work has grown apace until I have to take all my spare time, and even then for the past couple of years I cannot keep up with it. The correspondence required has become tremendous and while for a time I could sit up to all hours of the night to 'balance the budget' so to speak I cannot do it now [for health reasons]. I do not believe anyone has a clear idea of what the job really is at present.[227]

Stone's insistence on bearing most of the editorial workload made things unnecessarily difficult for him and everyone else.[24] In 1919, he requested clerical help from the AOU, and in 1920 Mrs. Edith Elliott Clark was hired to work at ANSP as Stone's secretary for AOU matters.[228] She handled member address corrections and dues payments, AWOL *Auks*, some of the Intelligencer Printing correspondence, and similar matters.[229] Clark must have helped to some extent in the short time she was employed, but Stone still had the rest of the editorial workload to deal with.

His bout of severe heart troubles in 1931 gave everyone a scare when they suddenly realized that their trusty old editor was mortal and would not be around forever. AOU president J.H. Fleming asked Stone in October if he wanted an assistant to help in editing *The Auk*, and told him in early 1932, "Get all the help you need I mean stenographers it would ease things for you." (Fleming wasn't much on punctuation.)[230] But an interesting 1934 letter from Fleming to Stone's ANSP colleague Wharton Huber indicates Stone had other ideas:

> I have had a letter from Stone re-iterating his belief that he can carry on for years to come and repudiating any idea of a successor or in need of a co-laborator, I only wish it were so and I feel there is a stone wall between facts and the inevitable. If Stone would only accept suggestions we might get somewhere. Stone means so much to us that any difference of opinion as to articles in 'Auk' had best be left unsaid.... [I]n the mean time I have to depend on you for the real facts as to Stone's ability to carry on. Many of my confidants are alarmed that there is no one able to succeed Stone if the inevitable happens.[231]

Fleming felt it necessary to treat Stone with kid gloves and not rattle him with talk about *Auk* content and a potential replacement, but he had Huber reporting from inside the compound, so to speak. Stone, meanwhile, was getting a little paranoid that Fleming and the AOU were planning to oust him before he reached 25 years, despite assurances to the contrary.[60,232]

One account of Stone's last years as editor said that "Stone had earlier pleaded to be allowed to serve for 25 years" as *Auk* editor; however, in the 1935 letter cited for the assertion, Friedmann wrote only that he'd had a recent conversation with Stone, and "[t]he outcome is just this – he wants to continue until his span of editorship has reached 25 years," which hardly sounds like pleading.[233-234] Friedmann, curator of birds at the Smithsonian, was one of the many young men whom Stone had helped when he was a budding ornithologist, and he was soon to become the AOU president.[235] He had really gotten under Stone's skin and added some unnecessary irritation to his last year as editor by suggesting, during the Council session at the 1935 AOU annual meeting in Toronto, that all honoraria for AOU offices should be discontinued, including that of the *Auk* editor. The matter was referred to the Finance Committee for consideration (and came to naught), but Stone told Chapman:

> No matter how this Committee may report I should not care to carry on after an objection of that sort had been made. It never occurred to me that there was any feeling that I was taking funds that might better be applied to actual publication....Having expressed my willingness to retire at any time after the end of 1936 I was surprised that this method of getting rid of me should have been employed....I do not think many people realize the tremendous amount of time that it involves and as I had to do it all at home it came out of the time I should have liked to devote to something else.[236]

Chapman responded, "It is too bad that you cannot be permitted to finish your editorial term in peace."[237]

Stone saw it, perhaps rightly, as part of an attempt to get rid of him and the rest of the old guard, for he told longtime AOU secretary Palmer, "The action of the Toronto meeting makes it look as if the AOU was anxious to get rid of <u>us</u> and I think that in <u>my</u> case it will be wiser to get out than be kicked out....[I]f the Council thinks that no honorarium should be paid and Friedmann is willing to do the job for nothing he had better go to it. However we shall see what we shall see."[238] There was a movement afoot to boot Palmer, and Stone – who, like almost everyone else, found Palmer difficult to deal with at times – reportedly agreed, in private, that it was time for Palmer to go, which he grudgingly did in 1937.[234,239]

Finally, at the end of 1936, after 25 years as editor, Stone turned over the reins of *The Auk* to Glover M. Allen of the MCZ. Among their "passing of the baton" correspondence Allen wrote, "I think you must feel like throwing up your hat and giving a loud shout at the end of 25 years!"[240] Indeed, among other feelings, Stone must have felt relief. One frequent *Auk* contributor wrote to Stone at the time about his pending retirement, "I shall be sorry to lose you as editor of The Auk. You have become an institution."[241] A British ornithologist congratulated Stone with "Well, you have had a wonderful 'innings' as we say in cricket parlance."[242]

J.A. Allen had served as editor of the *Bulletin of the Nuttall Ornithological Club* for eight years, and after it morphed into *The Auk* he continued to edit it for another 28 years – an amazing 36 years of editing essentially the same journal. At Stone's retirement, *The Auk* had seen only two editors in its first 53 years. (*The Condor* had two during one 60-year stretch.)[243] Stone felt at the time that it wasn't good for the journal to change editors too frequently, but there were 14 editors in the next 45 years, with the longest tenure being nine years by Oliver Austin Jr.[244] Either the AOU wants the gene pool refreshed a little more often than twice every 53 years, or editors are no longer able or willing to put in the time Allen and Stone did. Austin was the last museum man to hold the position; the editors since then have all been principally university professors, and the demands on their time are such that they have generally served in five-year slots.[245] That may get them to right about their breaking point.

Stone announced his retirement as *Auk* editor at the 70th birthday dinner given by the DVOC at the Art Club of Philadelphia.[246] A month later he made some remarks at the AOU annual meeting banquet when he was honored for his *Auk* service.[247] He told those gathered that not all the *Auks* during his tenure were Great Auks – some were only Dovekies. He said he had inherited the "sacred trust" of editing *The Auk* from Dr. Allen of Cambridge, and that he was pleased to hand it back to Dr. Allen of Cambridge "although there is a slight change in initials." This was one of several times Stone, ever the ornithological historian, referred to J.A. Allen, and he admonished, "There seems sometimes in these days too little remembrance for the work of our predecessors whose pursuit of the beautiful science we follow."

He also said he had published all "technical" articles submitted (territory, bird banding, migration, and anatomy and physiology), but that limited funds forced him to make the "embarrassing choice" of which nontechnical papers to reject. This was one of a few mentions of the dire financials straits *The Auk* was in: Stone asserted that finances were the chief burden on the editor and other officers, and cited the need for an endowment to better ensure continued publication. He characterized the past 25 years as the "golden age of North American ornithology," adding, "We have the men to make each next age an improvement over the last." He finished by saying that the personal contacts and friendships he'd made in the course of his *Auk* editorship had made for the happiest years of his life, and were something he'd always treasure.[248]

———————— ✍ ————————

Stone concluded his talk, "Present Day Tendencies and Opportunities in Ornithology," given to the AOU at its annual meeting in 1922, with this nugget about the current state of *The Auk* in challenging times: "Meanwhile, brethren, the brave old bird goes on as if nothing had happened, and we continue to entertain while we instruct our constituency in the pleasing Science of Birds by editing the best illustrated magazine of ornithology the world has ever seen."[45] There were more troubled times ahead for the brave old bird, with the Great Depression still several years away. The reference to *The Auk* being the world's best ornithological journal was a bit hyperbolic, although it may have been the most prestigious American one, and one of the top two or three in the world – the same position it occupies today. Today's journal editors have their own set of headaches to deal with, but at least the OSNA office takes care of membership and journal distribution (which is increasingly electronic) for the AOU and several other organizations. *The Auk* enjoys a healthy endowment today that would have seemed like manna from heaven in 1935.

But being cognizant of what editors like Stone had to go through in their day – the flak he took for making *The Auk* readable enough to appeal to a wide audience and keep it afloat during lean financial times, all the "spare" time he spent editing it and dealing with all the mundane details that today's editors need not worry themselves about, putting his own money into it when necessary – let's give a tip of the hat and three cheers for the Allens, Stones, and others for their heroic efforts to keep alive and pass on to future ornithologists that brave old bird that has a continuous record of publication for 130 years… and counting.[249]

LIME-LIGHTS, SQUARE ROOTS, AND PREMEDITATED ASSAULTS

Stone's *Auk* correspondence is full of the usual manuscript submissions, queries about *Auks* gone missing in the mail, and *endless* requests for separates (i.e., article offprints) – the latter usually from the authors, but some from nonauthors as well, including all manner of instructions as to where and to whom to send them. Stone's penciled calculations for cost charges for the separates appear in the margins of some letters. Some of Stone's other *Auk*-related correspondence, however, was a little more interesting or humorous:

• William Bergtold, a Denver medical doctor and an AOU Associate, congratulated Stone on his election as *Auk* editor in a February 1912 letter, and rightly predicted about Stone's new position, "I feel sure [it] will not be without some 'grief.'"[1] Bergtold personally saw to that in short order. Six months later, he asked for Stone's advice on whether a manuscript he was submitting would be more likely to get him promoted to Member if it appeared in *The Auk* or was presented at the next annual meeting instead, thus officially kicking off his campaign for promotion to that class.[2] He later pointed out one of his stellar qualifications for Member status: "There is but one [M]ember in Colorado."[3] He was elected a Member in 1913, but as Stone probably fully expected, in a 1917 letter he started in on Fellow, sounding a familiar argument: "In thinking this over, don't fail to recall that there is no Fellow in all the region between St. Louis and San Francisco."[4] Well, bully for Bergtold anyway – his fine book *A Study of the Incubation Periods of Birds*, published in 1917, may have been what led to his election as AOU Fellow in 1921. He was also a serious student of Colorado bird life and published a book on the subject.[5]

Arthur T. Wayne, the South Carolina ornithologist of Wayne's Warbler fame, was another one who pestered Stone for years with his obsession, tinged with paranoia about who was plotting against him, for getting elected a Fellow; that finally happened in 1928, doubtless to Stone's great relief.[6] In one 1921 letter pitching his ornithological accomplishments for AOU president Stone's consideration, Wayne included, "Have seen and taken [i.e., killed] more Ivory-billed Woodpeckers than any man who ever lived" – which, if it got him any points with the AOU at the time, certainly earns him the censure of history now.[7]

• Seems lots of folks were getting all het up over their class of membership. J. Warren Jacobs, who was an AOU Member and the proprietor of a company that sold birdhouses, received a past due bill for AOU annual membership, priced at the Associate level. He told Stone, "I am conscious of having accomplished my share of history of [*sic*] American Ornithology, and will not stand among the lists made up chiefly of the 'lime-lights' and fad bird students, after I had attained a more elevated standing of membership. Therefore I repeat…if it is intended that my name is to be enrolled with associates, then return the check and my name need stand nowhere on the membership rolls."[8] Whoever they were, those contemptible "fad bird students" were a frequent object of ridicule in Jacobs's written diatribes to Stone – the patient, pacifistic, paternal *Auk* editor and magnet for all AOU malcontents.

• Authors 100 years ago experienced at least some of the same joys of publishing enjoyed by modern ones. One contributor told Stone that a manuscript he was submitting was "begun with no idea of rushing into print (a thing I somewhat dread, as there is generally somebody ready to pick you to pieces)."[9] The more things change the more they stay the same, although today there's usually a phalanx of editors and reviewers ready to pick it to pieces before the general readership gets in on the feeding frenzy.

• In 1919, UC Berkeley ornithologist Tracy I. Storer suggested putting authors' addresses at the end of articles to facilitate correspondence from interested readers.[10] Stone agreed it was a good idea, and said he'd take it up with the members of the Publication Committee to see if they'd go for it. They did, and in January 1920, *The Auk* became the first ornithological journal – in America, at least – to include authors' addresses, which is *de rigueur* today.

• In 1921, the always-testy Louis Bishop was moving all around California on a collecting trip and peppering Stone with continually changing demands concerning the next address to which his *Auks* should be sent. He had also submitted a manuscript, and when it appeared in *The Auk* he notified Stone that he was "surprised and disgusted" that the article contained two paragraphs that were intended for a separate manuscript. "If you had sent me the proof I should have cut this out; but I cannot understand how you let it stay in yourself."[11] He later owned up that the proofs had arrived at one of the many previously specified addresses, but if he felt any sheepishness about the confession it doesn't come through in the letter.

• The following gobbledygook from Stone to one *Auk* author sheds light on the kind of headaches Stone and other editors went through in the days before email and with limited telephone access (ANSP had them installed in 1919): "I am sorry to say that there has been a series of mix-ups regarding your paper, due entirely to the late arrival of the original manuscript, and the instructions that were received from several sources regarding it; also, the failure to get all the pictures sent at one time. I surely understood from your letter that Oberholser advised cutting out the House Wren material and I edited accordingly. At the time I received your letter requesting that such of this matter as you had sent might be restored to the article, the whole thing had been made into pages and it was impossible to do anything. Regarding the pictures, I waited until the last moment, and failing to get the third one to which you refer, I imagined that you had changed your mind in regard to it. Now, however, I have gotten it..."[12] It goes on from there, but it sounds like it was another trying day for the long-suffering *Auk* editor.

• In addition to dealing it out, Stone had to deal with incoming gobbledygook as well, as in this tangled mess about past-due membership fees and *Auks* gone AWOL, courtesy of J. Warren Jacobs (still having dues issues): "I had a mix-up of dues in 1917, not remitting until 1918, at which time I received a receipt for 1918 dues, and duly received the Auks. Then later I discovered that my 1917 dues had not been paid, therefore I remitted another $4.00, and requested the Auks, but they never came, although I wrote the two gentlemen named. Last May, when I wrote, I received an extra for 1918 April, but to this date no 1917 issues ever came. I am also without the present Jan. issue, possibly because of my delinquency in sending in my present dues. If you can do anything in this matter, I will appreciate the favor."[13] At this point in time, Stone – almost alone – *was* the journal's office staff, and he had to deal with all this.

• In a portent of the current birding-world craze for Big Days, Big Sits, and the like, George Simmons submitted a manuscript in 1917 that detailed the results of his effort to break the "all-day census record. The attempt was a failure in so far as breaking a record went, but we did succeed in establishing a Southern record of 117, of which I observed or shot [!] 108."[14] (On today's counts, at least, the birds aren't shot with anything but a camera.) Stone frankly told Simmons that other papers in the queue were more important than someone's daily list.[15] Stone once said that the pursuit of big daily or life lists were "matters of personal amusement rather than contributions to science."[16] It's a pity the American Birding Association wasn't around yet to provide a proper publication venue for Mr. Simmons's exertions.

• Charles Cory, for whom the shearwater is named, submitted a manuscript to *The Auk* in 1919 that Stone couldn't get into print as quickly as Cory wanted. He decided to publish it elsewhere, telling Stone, "Thank you for your frank letter. I shall inflict it on the Proceedings of the Biological Society."[17] The same phrase appears several other times in Stone's correspondence. A little stronger expression was used by Robert Young, who did some collecting for ANSP in Colorado: "I am premeditating an assault on some publication with a few notes on my Colorado mammal work."[18]

• Frank Burns published a *Wilson Bulletin* article about egg incubation periods, and he wasn't altogether happy with Stone's *Auk* review of it. Stone commented that Burns should have cited his sources for the data given for each species.[19] Burns told Stone that it would have taken up too much space to cite all, and besides, "Guide posts are only placed at crossroads, not upon every panel of fence."[20]

• It's rare that a budding young ornithologist ends up being remembered as one of the country's most heinous murderers, but such was the fate of Nathan Leopold Jr. of "Leopold and Loeb murder" notoriety. Leopold lived in Chicago and was known as an expert amateur ornithologist: he had been an AOU member since he was 12, delivered ornithology lectures at the Chicago Harvard School, and had published eight papers or notes in *The Auk*. He and Richard Loeb abducted and murdered a young boy of their acquaintance in cold blood. Their trial, at which they were defended by Clarence Darrow, was a national sensation and is one of a number of cases frequently hyped as the "Crime/Trial of the Century."

While being questioned by law officers after his arrest for the 1924 murder, Leopold dropped Stone's name as an ornithologist with whom he'd had correspondence. Stone, in an interesting denial, told a Philadelphia newspaper, "I never met the boy and know nothing about him. Some few years ago I read a paper written by Leopold [he reviewed one in *The Auk*], but beyond that I know nothing. He is said to be quite proficient in ornithology, but I never have heard him lecture. Neither was he in any class conducted by myself."[21] Actually, as *Auk* editor, Stone would have read all of Leopold's manuscript submissions, and his archived ANSP correspondence includes 11 items from Leopold. Stone arranged (at Leopold's request) and attended Leopold's presentation of motion pictures of Kirtland's Warblers during a 30-minute talk at the 1923 AOU annual meeting in Cambridge.[22] It could be that Stone just didn't remember every instance of contact with Leopold, but the nature and earnestness of his denials almost makes you think you can hear a cock crowing twice in the background.[23]

The AOU also dropped Leopold like a hot potato. At the annual meeting in 1924, AOU Council members kicked him off the rolls with the logic that because he was jailed with a life sentence, he was "legally if not physically dead" (but they stopped short of moving him to the "Deceased" list). Leopold's father sent Stone an updated address to which his son's *Auks* could be sent – namely, the Joliet, Illinois hoosegow where Nathan was initially incarcerated – but the Council wouldn't have any of that, either.[24] They were willing to mail it to someone who could send it on to Leopold (how could they prevent that, anyway?), but they didn't want his infamous name and scurrilous address on any *Auk* mailing labels.[25] Elliot Coues had once wisecracked that the only requirements for being an AOU Associate were to be out of jail and have $3 for the annual membership fee, and Leopold was only meeting half of those requirements now.[26] (His rich daddy could surely spring for the $3.) Anyway, Leopold was a model prisoner, was paroled in 1958, and studied the Puerto Rican avifauna while living out his days there. He even had a note published in *The Auk* in 1961, and he published a check-list of birds of the island in 1963.[27]

• Stone found production of the April 1925 *Auk* particularly difficult. He told Frederic Kennard, "I never had a number that has caused me more trouble than this April issue. It seem [sic] bewitched."[28] He couldn't even write about the issue without the goblins getting into his spelling.

• Sometimes it seemed as though the AOU brass couldn't win for trying. In 1925, A.K. Fisher reported to secretary T.S. Palmer the death of Associate member Franklin Brandreth, whom Fisher had recruited to become a life member. Fisher was soon mortified to find out that Brandreth had been ill but was still alive. However, Palmer's latest AOU members list, with a "deceased" Brandreth, had already gone to the printer for the next *Auk*, and the race was on to hold the presses to make the correction. Palmer told Stone, "Fisher is swearing vengeance on the printer if he falls down on this matter and threatens to cease his search for Lifers if they are reported dead prematurely."[29] Of course, Fisher was responsible for the mess to begin with. The printer didn't fall down on the matter: Brandreth was still among the living, both in reality and on the AOU rolls, when the issue came out.[30]

Palmer had someone else in mind that *he* was apparently anxious to kill off early: DVOC artist Conrad Roland! Twice – in 1930, and again in 1931 – Palmer told Stone he'd heard of Roland's death. Stone responded the second time with, "Try again!?" Roland wasn't even ill, and would be very much alive for some time to come. Stone quickly assured Palmer both times that it was just another report of an AOU member's death that had been greatly exaggerated.[31]

• James Peters wrote to Stone in 1931 about a recent article in the German *Journal für Ornithologie* in which the author used a formula with square roots as part of his argument for conferring subspecific status on a shorebird population. Peters told Stone, "My own personal opinion is that when you have to use a formula [with] square roots to show that a subspecies is worth describing, it is no good."[32] Peters should see the mindlessly quantitative ornithological journals now, with articles that are such masterpieces of cabalistic and obfuscatory statistical claptrap and undecipherable equations that readers have to glance at the cover once in a while to remind themselves that they are, in fact, reading something that purports to be about birds.

• In (not surprisingly) his last effort at it, and employing a persuasive tack not likely to be endorsed by Dale Carnegie, Frank Hall of the Pacific Northwest Bird and Mammal Society, who had already asked Stone to join his organization on several previous occasions, cajoled him in 1934 with, "You are among the very few of the old ornithologists who have not become a member of our Society."[33] Come on, old-timer, get with the program.

• Stone queried AMNH's Frank Chapman in 1921 about one remarkable correspondent. Roy Curtiss of New York had sent Stone several long-winded, meandering letters expounding on nomenclatural issues, which were not very well-informed. Stone, who told Chapman, "He proposes to overturn the names of nearly all our birds," suspected that Curtiss was a child, and Chapman's response confirmed it:[34]

> The Roy Curtiss of whom you inquire is the most remarkable human phenomenon who has ever entered our gates. He is an eleven year old boy in knee trousers who devotes apparently

every available moment to the study of Linnaeus and kindred nomenclatural works in the study of which he evidently has the most intense and absorbing interest and on which he propounds questions which somewhat dismay his seniors. He adds to our amazement by informing us that his researches are made in the interests of an eight year old brother who is writing a book on birds![35]

The enigmatic Curtiss was precocious, if he was anything: he was reportedly reading and writing at age three, attended his first AOU meeting when he was nine, and taught himself Latin in order to read Linnaeus's original writings in that language.[36] Stone responded to one of Curtiss's curious missives in 1924, when the remarkable human phenomenon was almost 14, lecturing, "You do not know what binary authors are....You had better study the International Code of Nomenclature and the opinions pertaining thereto, which I am sure you can consult at the American Museum of Natural History." Curtiss came from money, and he sent Stone a copy of his privately published book about New England wildlife, hoping Stone would review it in *The Auk*, but Stone thought otherwise: "I cannot quite understand what your object is in publishing it. As a serious review of the New England [fauna] it is so far from complete that I would not wish to review it and I could in any case refer only to the birds so I think it best to return it as you desire."[37]

Alas, Curtiss's Christ-among-the-doctors early days careened off onto a path of middling natural history research and world travel while fathering seven children by a Tahitian woman whom he married when she was 14. He lived in a variety of mostly exotic locations including, ironically, Germantown for a brief stint in 1950.[36] But in his youth he certainly had the bemused attention of Stone, Chapman, and others.

12

Writing for Fun and Profit

In addition to his scientific publications, Stone published material in a popular vein, and there are indications he never got as involved in this type of writing as he wished. Frank Chapman started his popular periodical *Bird-Lore* in 1899, and Stone was casually involved in its early days. He told Chapman as the magazine got under way that he would author "a couple of papers a year," and would try to get DVOCers to contribute as well.[1] Over the first several years of the magazine, he contributed articles on the Carolina Wren, Gray Catbird, and Orchard Oriole, and several biographies of ornithologists, including Alexander Wilson.[2] Chapman frequently asked Stone for more articles, up until Stone's *Auk* work clearly limited his time. As Stone prepared to take the *Auk* reins, he appealed to Chapman, editor-to-editor, for an *Auk* contribution, saying that if *quid pro quo* were necessary, he would write something for *Bird-Lore*.[3] Chapman kiddingly responded, "If I had any idea that you were going to occupy the editorial chair in 'The Auk' so unpleasantly I should certainly have voted for some other candidate," and said he was too swamped at the moment to do an *Auk* article.[4] When *Bird-Lore* launched a new bird sightings feature called "The Season," Stone was offered the compiler position for the Philadelphia area, but he recommended Julian Potter instead.[5]

Shortly after Stone and Cram's *American Animals* appeared in 1902, Gebbie and Company, publishers of some of Theodore Roosevelt's voluminous output, contacted Stone about writing a popular text to accompany wildlife art by the American painter Alexander Pope.[6] Plans for the book were moving right along until the remuneration negotiations between Pope and Gebbie hit a snag and the whole project very suddenly came a cropper.[7]

In addition to numerous short ornithological biographies he prepared for *Bird-Lore*, *The Auk*, and *Cassinia*, Stone also wrote a "Roosevelt the Naturalist" essay for use in William Lewis's 1919 biography of the former president. Lewis included his own recollection of Roosevelt's visit to Philadelphia in 1913 to give a speech at the Academy of Music on behalf of the Progressive Party. Roosevelt added a visit with Stone to the agenda, and engaged him in an animated discussion (could T.R. have any other kind?) about animal coloration right up until it was time to give the speech.[8] Stone recalled their lively chat in an *Auk* notice of Roosevelt's death.[9]

In 1940, a grandnephew of Spencer F. Baird asserted that the Baird family had turned over a large collection of Baird's papers, letters, and manuscripts to Stone sometime before 1913, to be used by Stone for a biography of the great

Smithsonian naturalist. Stone never produced one – that task eventually fell to Baird's colleague William Dall, who published it in 1915 – and in 1940 Baird's heirs were trying to learn from ANSP what became of the material given to Stone.[10] However, in Dall's preface he gave an overview of Lucy Baird's efforts to produce a biography of her father before her death in 1913, and he didn't mention any Stone involvement. Stone's review of Dall's book in *The Auk* makes no mention of Stone ever having been asked to write the biography, nor is there any mention of it in the Stone–Lucy Baird correspondence in the ANSP archives.[11] In late 1899, Stone was viewing Spencer's original correspondence at Lucy's Philadelphia home, and making copies of letters that interested him; she was also sending to Stone at the Academy copies she'd produced of some letters but was averse to letting the originals leave the house.[12] Stone used that material for one short article and a talk at an AOU meeting.[13] His comment in a 1915 letter that he had given Dall his "storehouse of Bairdiana" indicates that Stone had returned any personal Baird material he may have still had at the time Dall was writing the book.[14] The 1940 complaints about unreturned material were apparently owing to a misunderstanding on the part of Baird's family.

Stone was occasionally involved in educational writing as well. He contributed articles on bird flight, plumage, ornithology, etc. to *The Encyclopedia Americana*.[15] He wrote about rodents (for $26.17 in payment, which was close to his weekly paycheck from ANSP at the time), lancelets, sea-squirts, and acorn-tongue worms for the American Educational Material Company's "The Specialist Plan" series.[16] He contributed a list of Philadelphia-area birds to Chapman's *Bird-Life: A Guide to the Study of Our Common Birds, Teachers' Edition*, and an article on bird migration to a *New York Teachers' Monographs* number devoted to nature study.[17] For Allen Johnson's *Dictionary of American Biography*, Stone wrote several ornithological biographies and edited others.[18] Johnson paid well, and it was easy money for Stone, who had either already published biographical articles about the ornithologists requested or had unpublished biographical material on them. In fact, in one letter Johnson expressed his astonishment that Stone had responded so quickly with an article, telling him, "You have beaten all records!" (Little did he know…)[19]

Stone also penned short biographies of Audubon and Wilson for David Starr Jordan's *Leading American Men of Science*.[20] The publisher, Henry Holt, tried to cajole Stone into writing an Edward D. Cope biography as well, but Stone said he was too busy. One of Holt's pressure tactics, amusingly, was based on the assumption that Stone took Philadelphian Cope's side in the infamous O.C. Marsh–Cope feud: "You, as a friend of Cope's, have more interest in the matter than I have, but I have enough not to wish to see his friends grieved by the book coming out without a biography of him….But isn't there enough of the disinterested interest among his friends somewhere to have a biography of him gotten up – or are Marsh's friends right about the controversy? I'm afraid that will be the inference if the book appears without the biography."[21] Stone was unmoved by Holt's sophistry, and someone else eventually authored the Cope biography.

Stone also sometimes reviewed books for authors before they headed to press. Charles Shoffner wrote a book for teachers that Stone reviewed, asking Shoffner that his name not be used. Stone probably didn't want to be associated with it – in one letter, Shoffner told Stone that he saw a Baltimore Oriole teaching its young one to sing.[22] But Shoffner sent a $25 check as "part payment on account of your work on my book," which was another nice paycheck for the amount of time Stone probably put into it.[23] He did a similar thing for Charles Shriner, a New Jersey Fish and Game protector who wrote a popular book on birds. Stone charged him $30 for reviewing it, which Shriner thought was low.[24]

Stone turned more to writing toward the end of his life. He finished *BSOCM* and was at work on his history of American ornithology. In the 1930s, *National Geographic Magazine* ran some articles about birds, and Stone asked Alexander Wetmore, who was one of the authors, to put a word in for him if the magazine was looking for additional writers.[25] He later wrote to editor Gilbert Grosvenor offering his services, but the magazine didn't take him up on it.[26] He did, however, publish a very brief biography of Wilson in *Nature Magazine* in 1936.[27]

Additionally, the ANSP archives contain some interesting rough notes written by him at that time – embryonic articles in a barely legible hand – on the subject of berry-picking around Cape May. They contain some fully fleshed-out paragraphs, but in other places there are only hastily jotted phrases and fragments of thought. (That Stone picked berries while in Cape May is known to close readers of *BSOCM*, because he mentioned it in the Whip-poor-will account.)[28] Only Stone knows where he may have planned to publish them, but the ANSP popular-style publication *Frontiers*, to which Stone contributed two articles and was preparing a third when he died, seems as likely an outlet as any.[29] The writing is descriptive and quite similar to the style of *BSOCM*. The following is a short example of part of one essay (edited slightly for readability):

> Fox grapes! How the very name seems to bring up visions of wild places. I have never personally seen Reynard or his gray cousin of these coast lands feasting on grapes but the fable of the fox and the grapes is too sacred to be gainsaid at this later day and the association too pleasing to be [rudely?] upset. At any rate he has left us plenty of grapes in Old Cape May to satisfy all who can go "fox graping" though there are of course certain seasons when the crop of grapes like that of all other wild fruit is a failure. Fox grapes are in season during the last days of August and the first of September, and of all the pursuits of wild fruit

"fox graping" is the most strenuous. This time of year seems to bring some days of excessive humidity and high temperatures following the usually cooler weather of mid-August. Days when there is not a breath of air stirring or just a light lazy breeze from the south – when mosquitoes and neck-and-ear flies swarm along the wood edges. Such at least are the conditions prevailing on all the fox graping expeditions that I recall. One starts early and the sky is overcast with mists and fog which the sun is trying to break through, and the rank early vegetation is wet with dew or with recent showers. We are soon wet to the skin though it is hard to say whether the greater moisture is from without or within as the slightest exertion produces a copious flow of perspiration, further irritated by the maddening persistence of the flies...[30]

As he retired from *Auk* editorship, Stone told a friend he "could have made a good deal more [money] had I been able to devote the time given to 'The Auk' to other writing! But I liked the Auk work and was glad to do it."[31] Given that he sold *BSOCM* at slightly above cost to make it affordable to the younger men studying birds, after spending countless hours writing it, one has to wonder just how much money he would have made.[32] Maybe *National Geographic* and *Frontiers* was the direction Stone intended to take with his writing, but by staying so long at the *Auk* helm and working at the Academy until he died, Stone seems to have lost a gamble that he could spend his golden years as a retired distinguished scientist, earning his living at his leisure while writing to his heart's content.

13

It Is Some Book!

For all his work as one of the leading ornithologists of his day, Stone's most enduring popular legacy is undoubtedly his monumental and charming *Bird Studies at Old Cape May: An Ornithology of Coastal New Jersey* (*BSOCM*). He had been working on the book for many years, and between the enormity of the task, other time-consuming responsibilities, and a lack of money to publish it, the book almost never saw the light of day. It was finally published by the DVOC in 1937, less than two years before Stone's death. The book is not only an indispensable reference and a must-read for anyone interested in the ornithology of the region, but also a classic of American time-and-place natural history literature.

BSOCM was preceded by two other regional ornithological books authored by Stone: the DVOC's *The Birds of Eastern Pennsylvania and New Jersey* (*BEPNJ*; 1894), and the New Jersey State Museum's *The Birds of New Jersey* (*TBNJ*; 1909). The latter was very much in demand when published, and it could be considered an earlier, shorter version of *BSOCM*, with more of a statewide focus.[1] A few years after *TBNJ* was published, DVOC member Richard Harlow offered to write a *Cassinia* article on birds he'd found nesting in Pennsylvania and New Jersey.[2] Stone encouraged the effort, and Harlow's "Notes on the breeding birds of Pennsylvania and New Jersey," which appeared in *The Auk* in 1918, served to some extent as an updated add-on to Stone's 1909 book.[3]

It's interesting to compare the three books as Stone's knowledge of the area they cover (principally New Jersey) broadened, through increased awareness of older written sources plus his field experiences, and those of others. As an example, compare the Marbled Godwit accounts. In *BEPNJ*, Stone briefly summarized seasonality and distribution information from older sources, citing only B.H. Warren (Pennsylvania) by name. In *TBNJ*, he fleshed things out a bit more by presenting the species' seasonal occurrence from New Jersey sources individually instead of summarizing them. The first part of the *BSOCM* account reads much like the *TBNJ* one, and then Stone presents a whole page of subsequent sightings, including his own.

The title for *BSOCM* may have been suggested to Stone by the "New Bird Studies in Old Delaware" talk given by a couple of fellow DVOCers at the AOU annual meeting in 1903, but that was long before the book even got under way, and maybe the use of "old" for place names was standard DVOC lingo.[4] In Stone's 1932 *Auk* death notice of his Cape May friend and fellow naturalist Walker Hand, he noted that Hand "was reared in the seafaring atmosphere of old Cape May."[5] Another possibility for the inspiration for the eventual title comes in a note from an AOU member who heard of the work-in-progress in 1934 and told Stone, "I think your book will help me back to the Cape May of old."[6] In the early 1930s, Stone's working title for the book was *Birds of Cape May* (with variations), although he referred to it as *Bird Studies at Cape May* in 1931.[7] The first reference I've found using *Bird Studies at Old Cape May* as the title is in a Cornelius Weygandt letter to Stone on April 1, 1936.[8,9-10] As far back as 1875 it had been said, "The curious feature of the little city of Cape May is that it combines the fashionable watering-place with the rude provincial settlement"; 60 years later, Stone wrote that it was the juxtaposition of the modern seaside resort with the ubiquitous implements and residences of generations who had made a hard living from the sea that gave Old Cape May its charm.[11]

BSOCM is an ornithological treatise covering southern New Jersey, with an emphasis on Cape May County, particularly the coastal areas. The bulk of the work consists of species accounts of all the birds that had been recorded in New Jersey at the time of the book's publication, with notes on their historical occurrence in the state, seasonality, habits, behavior, etc., gleaned from Stone's own notes and the records of fellow DVOC members. Stone took notes while in the field: in the *BSOCM* Black Duck account he wrote that a group of seven ducks he was watching "flushed suddenly while I was recording my notes and were out of sight when I again raised my head," and after listing some calls in the Herring Gull account he added, "I have copied the calls as I wrote them at the time."[12] During a talk to the DVOC in 1932 he "strongly advocated the jotting down of items in a small note-book when afield."[13] He responded to a query about some birds he had seen on a trip to South Carolina in 1922 with "I have just returned from a vacation [Cape May], and have not my note books with me, but as soon as I can, I will look up the exact dates and will be glad to send them to you."[14] I don't know whether he reworked field notes later – his field notes were reportedly sold at auction in 2004 – but he must have grouped them by species at some point in order to facilitate the writing of the *BSOCM* species accounts. It's also clear from *BSOCM* that he recorded numbers (sometimes estimates) of individuals seen for all or most species for each date.

Two events that figured largely in Stone's life and legacy took place in 1890: he was a founding member of the DVOC, and he made his first sojourn to Cape May. Stone was at the Cape from August 23 to September 1, and spent most of July and August of 1891 there.[15] His father accompanied him in 1890, and his brother Frederick was along for at least part of the 1891 trip.[16] (President Benjamin Harrison also summered at Cape May Point in 1890 and 1891, although it's unlikely he crossed paths with the marsh-tramping, gun-toting bird collectors.)[17] Witmer wasted no time in calling the DVOC's attention to the area. He gave a talk on "Birds of Beaver Swamp, Cape May County, N.J." in May 1891, and he gave two talks in fall 1891 on birds he'd collected in Cape May the past summer.[18] In the same year, references from Stone and others to Cape May trips began to appear in the minutes of DVOC meetings. In 1940, the DVOC's Fletcher Street said, "It was Stone's early realization of the importance of this area that led many other observers to it and to adjoining territories."[19]

———————— ∾ ————————

Stone's 1891 fall migration observations, which he recounted in his "Summer Birds of Cape May, N.J." talk to the DVOC on November 3, 1891, are the zero point on a timeline culminating with the thousands who now throng Cape May Point every fall to witness the migration spectacle.[15] Stone's talk that night is the first record we have of someone describing and attempting to explain the extraordinary fall flights there. He surmised that southbound birds following either the east side of the Bay or the Atlantic shoreline would have to head out over open water from the Point in order to continue, and he cited William Brewster's observations from Canada that birds reaching the termination of a landmark along which they'd been migrating stopped for a day or two before moving on, causing a congestion of birds at the location.[20] Stone continued:

> Now I have always imagined that the same occurrence might be noticed at the southern extremity of New Jersey…and the immense concourse of birds which I observed on Aug. 26th cannot, I think, be explained in any other way. The locality certainly did not seem to offer a superabundant food supply and I could see nothing whatever to attract the birds to it. Moreover the action of the birds was more that of a resting from a journey than of mere search for food. Again the great bulk of the birds seen were Kingbirds which are one of the earliest of our fall migrants and such a mass of Kingbirds as was here accumulated – more I think than I have seen all previous years together – could not be accounted for in any way but by considering them as migrants on their southern journey….Other species such as [Eastern Towhees], Wood Pewees, Robins, Cedar [Waxwings], Thrashers and a few early Warblers and [Veeries] accompanied the Kingbirds.[15]

He finished his discussion on a remarkably prescient note, which, with hindsight, is striking for its understatement: "These occurrences were of great interest in connection with our understanding of migration, and I think an observer stationed at Cape May Point could not fail to have some most valuable experiences during the migratory seasons especially as I have heard persons mention the occurrence of great hosts of birds coming into the town (Cape May) during [the] night, doubtless driven to shelter by sudden storms which are very prevalent about the mouth of the Bay."[15] Stone is grasping at the reason for the congestion of migrants he'd witnessed, and doesn't yet recognize the effect of regional weather patterns on the phenomenon – it would be Walker Hand who would eventually piece together the basic mechanics of it involving cold fronts and northwest winds – but he's close.

Stone's 1891 observations put Cape May Point on the map as an extraordinary place to study fall migration. He suspected it, confirmed it, studied it, theorized about the causes, and started getting the word out before anyone else did. The swirl of birding activity centered on Cape May Point every fall, with birders from all over the country and the world descending on the area like Tree Swallows swarming over a clump of bayberry bushes, pumping millions of dollars into the local economy; with the hawkwatch platform filled to capacity and the parked cars overflowing from the asphalt lot onto the lawn by the lighthouse; and with the shoulder-to-shoulder rows of birders lining the paths at Higbee's on a chilly morning, everyone clutching their binoculars and intently watching for any movement along the low treeline and thickets in front of them – it all started in 1891 with a rather short, unassuming, shy young man standing in front of a dozen colleagues in the Council Room of ANSP, reading his "Summer Birds of Cape May" essay, occasionally referring to his prepared map or to one of the bird skins lying on a table in front of him.[18,21]

Stone published "Winter birds of Cape May, New Jersey" in *The Auk* in 1892 after suffering through a late-January Arctic blast there with Samuel Rhoads.[22] He made some trips there over the years and was an annual summer resident, with leaves of absence from ANSP, from 1916 to 1938 (with the exception of the summer of 1919, when Stone was on a collecting trip to Arizona).

The obvious question, of course, is why, after discovering the fall migration phenomenon at Cape May Point and suggesting further research, he waited another 25 years to start studying it on a regular basis.[23] It may be simply that he wasn't inspired enough by his 1891 trip to undertake a study of it until years later when he started summering there. Even then, the emphasis on water birds in *BSOCM*, and the perplexingly sparse records of some expected passerine species, indicate that Stone and the DVOC may not have been giving the fall passerine flights a great deal of attention. He doesn't mention Cape May as a migratory hot spot in *TBNJ*, and there's no mention of the 1891 flight in the *TBNJ* or *BSOCM* Eastern Kingbird accounts – in fact, in the latter he says he "encountered [his] first notable migration of Kingbirds" on August 27, 1920.[24] He doesn't mention the 1891 flight in the *BSOCM* "Bird Migration at the Cape" chapter. He does mention some of his summer 1891 records in *BSOCM*, but it was almost as if the migratory flight he witnessed had slipped his mind.

Some of Hand's correspondence must have reminded him of it, like in 1903 when Hand mentioned the fall flicker flights twice, including a heavy flight he witnessed that year.[25] Hand wrote to Stone about another heavy flight on September 25, 1909.[26] But when Stone tells A.K. Fisher in late September 1917 that he's heading back to Cape May for the weekend to get some "pointers" on the migration, probably from Hand, and adds with deadpan understatement, "It is very interesting down there – a sort of point of congestion," does he regard that as a recent revelation, or something he's known for years?[27]

His apparent absence from Cape May in autumn in the 1890s is baffling. Day trips there were not particularly feasible in the 1890s, but he would have been able to take trips of a few day's duration if he'd been so inclined.[28] His fieldwork for the years 1900–1911 may have been devoted mostly to botany. He took what appear to have been short trips to Cape May in September 1910, and in the summers of 1913 and 1914, but he spent most of August 1912 in Minnesota and Wisconsin, and in 1915 his vacation time was used on a two-month, May-to-July jaunt to the West Coast and back.[29]

By January 1916, however, Hand was looking around for a house for the Stones to rent for the summer, and this was the beginning of their regular summer-long stays.[30] They loved it right out of the gate: Stone said of their first summer there, "We had a bully good time down there & kept out of the worst of the [Philadelphia] heat. I was up and down – mostly down – in fact I slept 47 nights at the shore against 13 in Phila[delphia]!!"[31] The first several summers he frequently traveled back and forth to the city (leaving Lillie at the shore), but over the years, Witmer increasingly stayed put at the Cape. The Stones usually headed down in late June or early July, after Witmer had wrapped up the July *Auk*, and stayed until early September. Through the mid-1920s, at least, Witmer would stay at Cape May for a week, then return to Phila-

Stone in 1916, the year he started summering annually at Cape May. University of Pennsylvania Archives.

delphia and the Academy for a week. By about the early 1930s, however, he was staying in Cape May for the duration, with occasional short trips to ANSP as needed. Also, Stone started making spring trips to the Cape in 1921, which is why in *BSOCM* he often gives Hand's spring arrival records (from Hand's annual participation in Stone's *Cassinia* spring migration study) up until 1920, and his own thereafter.

———————— ꙮ ————————

The Stones rented 211 Perry Street in 1920, 917 Queen in 1921, and 909 Queen in 1922. They stayed at 909 Queen every subsequent year except 1925, when it wasn't available and they stayed at 1009 Washington Street.[32,33] The 909 Queen Street house was owned by Sydney and Elizabeth Goff, who are mentioned in the *BSOCM* preface.[34] Sydney was a railroad employee, and the 1930 census reported him living at 909 Queen with his wife and a sister-in-law, so it seems likely they rented rooms or maybe a floor to the Stones, even though Witmer referred to it as "our house" and "our cottage."[35] The three-story duplex still stands, little modified, as do the sycamore trees in which Stone watched nesting robins, and saw the fall's first migrant Black-and-white Warbler in 1937.[36] He also noted a catbird feeding on caterpillars that had fallen from the sycamores onto the porch roof.[37]

Long gone, however, are the cornfield in which blackbirds on their way to their Physick estate roost used to stop and feed, with Stone peeking out his window at them, and the apple orchard behind the cottage where Stone saw 25 Baltimore Orioles feeding on August 29, 1932.[38] The nine-hole golf course on Lafayette Street, just a stone's throw from 909 Queen and often mentioned in *BSOCM*, is now the grounds of the Cape May City Elementary School.[39] Just behind the school, however, the Cape Island Creek meadows still stretch away southward into the town and north to the present-day canal. That must be where the meadowlarks that Stone could hear from his front porch used to breed, along with Marsh Wrens, Seaside Sparrows, Clapper Rails, Killdeers, Ospreys, and Tree Swallows, and Stone surely birded the area on many occasions.[9,40-41]

You'd be hard-pressed to find some birds breeding in the town today that did so in Stone's time: both Yellow-billed and Black-billed Cuckoos, Red-eyed Vireos, Eastern Wood Pewees, Brown Thrashers, Great Crested Flycatchers, and Yellow Warblers. Another indication of change is his mention of a Great Crested Flycatcher nest in Hand's yard that was constructed partly of cow hair and chicken feathers – building materials not likely to be found there now.[42] Cape May was more rural and less paved over and congested then, and it's clear from reading *BSOCM* that, although Stone birded Cape May Point, he also did quite a bit of birding in town. On September 17, 1932, Stone noted that he "[h]ad a great rush of birds…[and] personally saw 78 species about the town – including several Cape May Warblers at Cape May!"[43] His remark in a 1924 letter that he and David Baird "scour C.M. Pt. every Saturday" suggests he was only birding the Point once a week and was actually doing most of his birding in Cape May.[44]

The Stones loved the 909 Queen cottage ("Hotel Queen Street," as Witmer called it), and they housed and entertained many visitors there, including DVOC members and ornithologists such as Alexander Wetmore (and his wife Fay) and T.S. Palmer.[45] In a 1937 invitation to Julian Potter, Witmer boasted of the cottage's amenities compared to Cape May hotels: "We can rival the Windsor as to both beds and food I think! and can beat the Homestead all hollow!"[46] Their maid, "Anna" (probably the Anastasia McCaughy listed in their household in the 1930 census) stayed with them in Cape May at least some of the time.[45,47] Lillie made beach plum, huckleberry, wild cherry, elderberry, blackberry, and fox grape jellies; they sometimes had over 100 jars by the end of the summer. Witmer the berry picker kept her well supplied with the staple ingredients. He probably harvested the plums for her in the Higbee's dunes, where they still grow.[48,49-50] The Stones took the train back and forth to Cape May, and used an express company to get their baggage to and from the town for their summer stays. That meant they sometimes arrived in Cape May a day or two before the baggage arrived, and their 1925 vacation ended on a sour note when, as Witmer told a friend, "Lillie made 50 glasses of beach plum jelly & lost it all in transit home – some express man is living high!"[51]

Of course, renting to an ornithologist can result in some strange activity on the premises, and sometimes something other than jelly was brewing in the kitchen. In August 1928, a storm wiped out a tern and skimmer colony on Ephraim Island behind Wildwood, and on a visit two days later Stone picked up 14 dead Common Tern chicks and took them back to 909 for skinning. (They reside in the ANSP collection today.)[52] A friend told Stone, "I can well imagine the highly scented condition of at least a part of your house, after the 'tern episode.'"[53] What did the Goffs expect?

Lillie spent much time at the beach, and jellyfish stings and a bad knee didn't diminish her ardor for "bathing" in the ocean. Witmer seems to have spent less time there, and by the 1930s health issues were keeping him out of the water.[10,54] He took ribbing from fellow ornithologists about his summers spent at a famous resort town with its beach bunnies. Charles Richmond told him, "Yes, you have been very remiss, watching these Cape May bathing beauties all summer and not telling us about them; almost as silent as Geo. Ord and Alex. Wilson, and other former Cape May visitors."[55] The gist of a poem in *The Auklet* one year titled "The Beachcomber" was that Stone was really looking at the girls through his binoculars when at the beach, while pretending to look at birds. (This was one of several references in *Auklet*s to Stone's supposed girl watching.)[56] Whether or not he was guilty as charged (or guilty as razzed), his correspondence does contain the occasional wisecrack about girls on the beach, and one year he told Palmer he hadn't yet been to the beach but could tell by the newspapers that women's bathing suits were tiny, and that Quakers in Cape May that summer for a convention were "liable to get an eyeful!"[57] Lawdy, lawdy, he should see what they (don't) wear now…

Stone's correspondence includes a couple of items about his Cape May summers that are too interesting to leave out. In 1926, the mosquitoes were so bad that Witmer took to wearing a heavy canvas coat and wrapping his legs in newspapers in order to get in some birding.[58] He told Wetmore about a predawn hail storm on August 16, 1930, that "crossed the peninsula about 3 miles above the tip in a belt only about 200 yds. wide, stripped every leaf off the fields of beans & corn & piled up banks of hail stones along the roadside which froze into masses 6 to 8 ins. thick still in that condition at 9:30 a.m. Talk about 'cool Cape May' snow banks in August are going some!"[59] And DVOCer Bill Shryock responded to Stone's invitation to visit at Cape May with, "We are both looking forward to the inspection of your menagerie, including the skunk." A menagerie? The skunk?[60]

The 909 Queen Street house was right around the corner from the 1002 Washington Street home of Walker Hand (now the Inn at the Park bed-and-breakfast), Stone's good friend and an outstanding local naturalist and historian. Henry Walker Hand Jr. was born at Green Creek, Cape May County, on August 14, 1870, and was descended from Shamgar Hand, one of the original settlers of Cape May County. His grandfather was Christopher Smith Hand, and his father was Captain Henry Walker Hand, an abolitionist who served in the Union Navy during the Civil War and was later editor of the *Cape May Wave* newspaper.[61] His father and uncles were sea captains, and as a young man Walker worked in the fishing and oyster industry on Delaware Bay. His mother, Mary, who preceded him in death by a year, at age 95, once told Stone of a childhood visit to an egret rookery on a New Jersey coastal island, where she climbed to the top of some cedars and took in the view of the nesting white birds all around her.[62]

Walker Hand studied pharmacy in Philadelphia, ran drug stores in Cape May and Cape May Point, and eventually worked at the Cape May post office for 30 years.[63-65] The *Cape May Wave* reported Hand's marriage to Caroline Hughes, of Lafayette Street in Cape May, in April 1906; Hand was identified as "the very popular mail clerk at the local office."[66] Caroline, a Mayflower descendant, died less than a year later, and in 1913 he married Laura Wemple.[67] Stone became friends with Hand sometime in the 1890s, and Hand joined the DVOC as a Corresponding Member in 1900.[68] Stone later recalled, "Many were the delightful trips that we took together over the marshes and through the woods of Cape May, always enlivened by his reminiscences and anecdotes."[65]

Sam Scoville supplied some insights into Hand's life and personality in the "Desert Island" chapter of *Wild Honey*.[69] Hand was described as "[s]traight, slim, with lank black hair and coal-black eyes" indicative of his Indian heritage: his great-great-grandmother was a Leni-Lenape "princess." Hand told of a place "back on the dunes called 'Cow Pen,' where his great-grandfather drove his cows to hide them from the British" during the War of 1812.[70] Hand also told Scoville some humorous stories. He used to take his Irish setter on the local train to hunting excursions, and the conductor would always charge him a fare for the dog as well. Hand learned that charges weren't imposed for lap dogs, so the next time he took the train he hauled the setter up onto his lap and told the conductor, "He's a dog and he's in my lap, therefore he's a lap dog and I don't pay." Another time Hand, out quail hunting with a friend, espied two other hunters in the same field. He went up and ordered them off "his" property at once, and they complied; in fact, Hand had no idea who owned the land – *he* certainly didn't.

Hand once told Stone that several skunks had been hit by cars around Cape May recently, after which the drivers didn't need a horn.[71] (It might take a second or two to get that one.) He also included a short poem in a letter to Stone: "The north winds do blow and we shall have snow and what will the Dr. do then? Poor thing/ He'll to go the Point, search out every joint, and see many birds on the wing, wing, wing."[72] Not exactly up there with Shelley or Coleridge, or even Ogden Nash, but give him points for trying.

Hand was an avid outdoor sportsman ("one of the best shots at Cape May"), and hunting and fishing were probably his main reasons for going afield.[69] On several occasions he complained to Stone that the yellowlegs season should be longer to cover the time when the birds were in Cape May in peak numbers, and he once even asked Stone's help in getting a state law passed to place a bounty on hawks, which Hand was sure were responsible for a purported local decrease in small game.[73] He wasn't what we'd call a "birder" – in fact, he told Stone in 1902, "I don't know anything about the warbler family and mighty little about the fraternity of sparrows."[74] He learned at least some passerines as time went on, however, doubtless influenced by Stone, and he was familiar with enough bird species that both *TBNJ* and *BSOCM* are replete with Hand sightings and arrival/departure dates.

Hand certainly knew the game birds (including the shorebirds and ducks) well. The *BSOCM* woodcock account quotes a number of Hand records, and in a 1914 letter to Stone he bemoaned the recent loss or misplacement of a notebook in which he had kept voluminous notes on woodcock habits and feeding-ground habitats in the Cape May area.[75] He knew his fish, too, and

Henry Fowler's 1907 report on New Jersey fishes included records of many species obtained in the Cape May area by, or in company with, Hand.[76] He even led Stone to what the latter considered one of the only naturally occurring Bald Cypress trees in the state, after botanists had failed to find the species in their searches of South Jersey swamps, and Hand knew of two others nearby (one cut, one killed by saltwater intrusion). Stone wrote in *PSNJ* that some doubted the trees occurred there naturally, and believed they had been planted; Bayard Long, for one, had his doubts, but Hand told Stone that Long just didn't like it that someone else had made the discovery.[77]

Fred Ulmer, who worked at ANSP as a young man before a long stint as curator of mammals at the Philadelphia Zoo, recalled Stone telling him that one of Hand's cats used to bring in small mammals not previously recognized to occur in the region, thereby expanding their known range. Hand's cats weren't limited to mammals: *BSOCM* recorded that one of them brought home a female White-winged Crossbill, the only Cape May record of the species of which Stone was aware.[78]

Hand had a knowledge of local natural history minutiae only obtainable through years of close observation, and it's no wonder he and Stone hit it off so famously. In a report submitted to the DVOC for its 1907 spring migration study, he noted that on May 23rd he found "a 'curlew [i.e., Whimbrel] roost,' a place where they sit during the night. It was conspicuous from the tracks and droppings, the ground being quite white. Went out in the evening to see them come in. They came from 7:50 to 8 p.m. [pre-daylight savings] in big bunches with little or no whistling, but their wings roared like ducks. The flocks were so big I could not imagine where so many birds spend the day without being seen. Had it not been for the moon I could not have been able to see them."[79] He once told Stone he often noticed eelgrass that had been pulled up by the roots floating on the water when Black Ducks were feeding, but since he never found any eelgrass in the stomachs of the Black Ducks he had shot, he surmised they must be feeding on something found within the grass.[80] (It may have been various kinds of small animal food, or even the seeds of the eelgrass.)[81] Hand's description for Stone of a frog he had found buried in the ground included the observation that it smelled like freshly dug mulberry roots.[82] We all know that smell, right?

Another fascinating incident involving Hand appeared in *BSOCM*'s Tree Swallow account. In mid-September 1903, a huge flock of the swallows roosted in the trees of the Physick estate in Cape May during a windy rainstorm that struck in the middle of the night and knocked down trees and damaged buildings.[83] The next morning, an estimated 6,000–7,000 swallows were on the ground, drenched and unable to fly. Hand told Stone that "[l]arge numbers were gathered up in baskets and dried out and eventually all but about seventy-five recovered and flew off."[84] Just how many people were involved in the remarkable operation, and the manner in which the birds were dried off, is left to the imagination of the reader. (Picture Cape May clotheslines full of pinned, disheveled, and irritated Tree Swallows.)

Captain Horace O. Hillman, head of a New England shipping fleet that put up at Cape May every spring, collected 11 Red Phalaropes at sea for ANSP at Hand's request. Fleet members were very familiar with the species.[85] It's easy to imagine the sociable postmaster Hand, with his seafaring background, who probably knew every person in town – residents, visitors and transients alike – stumbling across the subject of the birds as he chewed the fat with the captain and crew.

Some of Stone's favorite Cape May outings were the ones when he lived in a gunning shack on the salt marshes studying the northbound shorebirds. He spent May 23, 1918 "in a blind on the marshes with decoys all about but no guns! We saw a goodly lot of shore birds including quite a bunch of Knot which I was very glad to note."[86] The first mention I found of an overnight trip is one planned for Frank Dickinson's shack on Taylor Sound (just north of Jarvis Sound) on May 22, 1920.[87] There were at least four later ones, all in the Jarvis Sound area: May 20–22, 1921, which Stone exquisitely described in the *BSOCM* "Birds of the Salt Meadows" essay; May 20–24, 1922 with Hand, who had earlier sent Stone the local May tide tables so he could pick the most suitable dates, and where Stone happily "saw more shorebirds than I ever expected to again"; May 16–19, 1924, when a full-moon tide flooded the meadows and waves lapped at the bottom of their shack, sending the Clapper Rails scrambling for higher ground; and a May 21–24, 1925 trip with Hand where, as on previous occasions, they let the tide run out, stranding their skiff, which they then used as a blind to watch the shorebirds feeding in the surrounding mudflats.[88]

Stone mentioned in the *BSOCM* preface that he used to stay in a stilted cabin with Dickinson, who had a farm in Erma, so at least some of the trips, if not all, were made to Dickinson's shack.[89] For the 1924 trip, at least, Lillie and Laura stayed in the "shooting shack" with their husbands.[90] During preparations for that trip, Hand told Stone, "It's about time we began to talk over our trip to the shack….Tell Mrs. Stone to bring her galoshes or rubbers. There are, as you know, no toilet arrangements but I guess we can make out all right."[91] Lillie and Laura probably had a pretty good idea what weekend getaways were going to be like when they married their nature-loving hubbies.

Hand was the first to correctly postulate about the subsequent movements of birds seen migrating north along the Bayshore on fall mornings with northwest winds. Some thought the birds continued north in search of a narrower place to cross the Bay. However, as a postscript to Allen and Peterson's 1936 *Auk* article on the Cape May Point hawk flight, editor Stone wrote, "[O]ur attention was first called to the *northward* flights of birds along the Bay shore by the late Henry Walker Hand…who had given them a life long study, and the information regarding them that the writer has presented at several meetings of the AOU was largely furnished by him. Mr. Hand was of opinion that the birds were not searching for a narrow crossing of the River or Bay, but simply spread out over the wooded areas to feed, and passed on southward from the Point after the northwest wind had abated."[92] That reference was to raptors and non-raptors alike; Stone reiterated Hand's insights in *BSOCM* in a discussion principally concerned with the passerine flights: "Walker Hand, who was familiar with the autumnal bird flights all his life, always maintained that at their conclusion at about 8:00 a.m. the birds scattered over the Bay side woods and thickets to feed and remained there overnight or until the wind shifted when they resumed their southward flight in the usual scattered formation and crossed the Bay from Cape May Point to Cape Henlopen."[93] That's still considered the most plausible explanation of the birds' behavior, although some raptors do continue north along the Bayshore to cross further north.[94]

John Nichols's "Angles and speculations on migration" article in *The Auk* in 1926 prompted Stone to write to him about the Cape May Point flicker movements. Nichols responded with his thoughts on it, and most interesting was his hand-drawn map showing the lines of flight curving around the Point and heading up the Bayshore. The map may very well be the oldest extant such diagram of the phenomenon, antedating the Allen and Peterson *Auk* article by 10 years.[95]

Hand died of a heart attack on September 14, 1932, aged 62, while waiting in the ferry house of the Reading terminal in Camden on his way to visit his doctor in Philadelphia. Hand "had been in poor health for some years past"; in fact, he was sounding pretty played out when he told Stone in early 1930 that arthritis was the latest of his aches and pains, but "a few additional handicaps won't make much difference, as the race is not much longer."[63,96] But he continued as an active naturalist right up until the end: his record of an American Redstart feeding a juvenile at Eldora less than two months before his death was noted by Stone in *BSOCM*.[97] He was survived by Laura and a daughter named Mary, and was interred at the Methodist-Episcopal cemetery at Cape May Court House.[63-64] The Hands also had a son, H. Walker Hand III (1917–1921), who died as a toddler after suffering from diabetes and kidney disease.[98]

Stone told a friend about Hand's death: "We had a sad ending to our summer….[Hand] was on his usual monthly trip to see his physician in Phila. who had done wonders in relieving his diabetic condition. Lately he has had severe pains in the chest – angina – I suspect & this was the final trouble. I had known him intimately for 40 years & spent Tuesday evening with him. He was in good spirits & I little thought I should be writing an obituary for the local paper the next day. It was a great shock to me." On the day of Hand's funeral, Stone had "the greatest bird flight ever" in Cape May, recording 78 species; he said his attendance at the funeral prevented him from possibly reaching 100.[99] It was as if the birds had also gathered to pay their respects to their old friend, referred to by Stone as "the 'resident ornithologist' of Cape May."[43]

In an obituary published in a Cape May newspaper, Stone wrote, "In his capacity as naturalist he was perhaps even better known outside of Cape May than in the city itself," where few "realized the extent and soundness of his natural history knowledge and the esteem in which he was held by naturalists elsewhere."[63] Stone wrote feelingly in the *BSOCM* preface of Hand that his "knowledge of the history and natural history of the region was unequalled. Through an intimate companionship of over a quarter of a century I feel that I owe to him much of my knowledge of the water birds, and of the lore of the Cape, and it is a matter of the deepest regret that he could not have lived to see the completion of this work in the planning of which he took such a keen interest."[100]

When visiting Cape May outside of the summer season, Stone stayed with the Hands, the Goffs, or the Browns.[101] It was Hand who originally put Otway Brown in touch with Stone in 1907, and Brown sent several batches of plants to Stone at ANSP to identify.[102] They met in person for the first time at the May 28, 1908 Philadelphia Botanical Club meeting, and Brown became a corresponding member of the club that year.[103] Brown was Cape May County's leading botanist, and his name appeared frequently in *Bartonia* and *PSNJ*. He was employed for a time by Erma florist Howard Nece, and was the grounds-keeper at the Physick estate in Cape May for several years. In June 1903, he married Edith Young, a Bartram descendant, at First Baptist Church of Cape May.[104-105] Later in life, he was district clerk for the Lower Township school district.[106] The Browns eventually lived in Cold Spring on New England Road just east of Bayshore Road. The house succumbed to neglect years ago after Brown's death, and the two 70-foot Sweet Gums that used to grow in the front yard are also sadly no longer there.[107]

The Stones were frequent Cape May guests of the Browns, and as early as 1929, if not earlier, the Stones stayed with the Browns each Christmas.[108] (They reportedly celebrated 14 Christmases together.)[104] Witmer and Otway were a team on the DVOC Cape May Christmas Bird Counts. Brown also knew his birds, and his observations were cited often in *BSOCM*, including one bizarre incident when his Cold Spring property was deluged with warblers one fall morning; many that struck a chicken-wire fence were promptly gobbled up by a flock of domestic ducks attracted by the sudden and unexpected manna-like repast.[109] Shortly before his death, Brown prepared a list of plants he'd collected in Cape May County; it was updated with supplemental records and taxonomically revised by Edgar T. Wherry, then published in *Bartonia* in 1970.[110] It's an invaluable baseline reference for the Cape May County flora, and is frequently consulted and cited by modern botanists.

Brown died on October 31, 1946, and was survived only by his wife; they had no children. Both are buried in the Union Cemetery by Trinity South Dennis United Methodist Church on Route 47. The Cape May Geographic Society, formed in 1946 shortly before his death and in which he was active, planted an avenue of Eastern Red Cedars along Madison Avenue between Michigan and Stockton Avenues in Cape May as a memorial.[111] Many of them are still growing there, weathered and noble looking, over 60 years later.

Witmer described the Stones' travel to Cape May in 1931: "We take a taxi from the house to North Philadelphia Station & get the Cape May train there & then a taxi to the cottage." That may have changed a bit through the years as rail lines came and went. According to longtime club member Phil Street, DVOCers traveled to Cape May in the 1920s via a ferry to Camden, then an excursion train to the shore (round-trip fare: $1).[19] Dale Twining and Alan Brady told me that the train they took in the 1930s was called the "Fisherman's Special," and you had to get on the right car in Camden, because the final destination was one of the other shore towns, not Cape May.[112] At different points along the way, the rear car would be disconnected and left on the tracks for a donkey engine to come and tow it the rest of the way to, for example, Cape May (or as Alan said, you *hoped* a donkey engine was coming along). Dale recalled that the Cape May car was detached in the Tuckerton marsh, and the DVOC men used to get out and bird while waiting for the donkey engine.

The Fisherman's Special came in to Schellenger's Landing. Two other stations were in the center of Cape May: one was at the location of the present-day Washington Street Mall, and the Grant Street Station was near the beach. When the latter closed down, one of Stone's Cape May friends asked him, "What will Cape May be without that [train] station on the beach? Nothing can ever take its place. The psychological effect of stepping on a train in a sweltering city and stepping off almost on the beach was a thrill I never experienced anywhere else."[113]

Those old-time DVOC outings around Cape May and other places were, physically speaking, quite a bit beyond the regimen of today's motorized birders. Until declining health forced him to bird from a car in later years, Stone's outings around Cape May were on foot and could cover 10–15 miles in a day, and his daily tramps ranged through what today would be all the area south of the canal.[28,114] One DVOCer told Stone, "I used to think the walk back to Cape May [from the Point] in the hot sun was a pretty stiff drill and never envied you that part of the experience."[115] An outing to Seven Mile Beach (now Avalon/Stone Harbor) featured an eight-mile round-trip tramp over the meadows from Cape May Court House to get to and from the beach.[28] A 1921 trip by Stone,

Hand, Scoville, Fletcher Street, Harry Parker, and Franklin Cook to Brigantine and Little Beach islands included wading an inlet up to their armpits and dealing with swarms of green flies that Scoville pulled out of his hair by the handful.[69,101,116] Julian Potter wrote about an August 1923 trip to Little Beach Island (still today one of the very few undeveloped barrier islands on the East Coast) with William Yoder and Henry Gaede. They left Atlantic City in a rowboat (!) at 7 a.m. and didn't arrive on the island until 1:30 p.m., after temporarily getting lost.[117] They found the Black Skimmer colony they had come to see. On the trip back they couldn't row against the outgoing tide or the wind, so they towed the boat from a sod bank at one point, gaining two miles in two hours. They eventually started rowing again and made it back after dark. Potter's dispassionate take on the outing was, "We covered 18 miles by boat, gained a lot of blisters and three severe backaches but we reached our Island and saw the birds, so what did the other trivial matters amount to?"[118] Trying to reach Browns Mills, New Jersey for an outing with a fellow DVOCer, but without the money to buy a train ticket, Richard Miller had himself rowed across the Delaware River from Philadelphia late at night, then walked the 30 miles to get to Browns Mills the next morning.[119] Samuel Rhoads's 1901 New Jersey birding-by-bicycle trip from Audubon to Salem, which must have been every bit of 35–40 miles one way, in the days before gears and gel seats, is further evidence of the kind of stuff those guys were made of, and the strenuousness of some of their excursions.[120]

Stone dealt with ANSP and AOU/*Auk* matters while summering in Cape May, although usually in a more relaxed fashion. He was handicapped without the near proximity of his library, particularly for *Auk* work, and the Cape May public library left a lot to be desired. Stone told a friend, "The library here contains only fiction. [T.S.] Palmer went in & asked for my 'Birds of N.J.' & was informed that it & other similar state reports were thrown out as nobody asked for them."[121] When James Tanner met Stone at 909 Queen in 1936, he noted that the room was "part living room, with easy chair, pictures, divan, and partly work room, a typewriter, few books, [papers?], and boxes."[122] However, in between his occupational duties, picking berries, putting out bread and water for the backyard birds, sitting on the porch and drinking ice tea, going to circuses, entertaining friends and relatives, listening to ballgames on the radio, attending classical music concerts at the old Convention Hall Pier, helping the local kids identify their seashells, writing up to 30 letters a day, swimming at the beach, listening to Walker Hand's stories of the sea, and collecting insects, Stone made time for his meticulous ornithological studies around Cape May.[40,50,123,124]

He had been planning and writing *BSOCM* for some time before its 1937 publication. He told the DVOC at the time of its release that it "was not for many years [after his initial 1890 visit] that he began to assemble his notes

Now *that's* how you dress for a Cape May bird outing. Stone and Fay Wetmore on the beach at Cape May Point, August 10, 1926. Smithsonian Institution Archives.

with the idea of putting them together in book form," and serious studies didn't begin until 1920.[125] In the *BSOCM* preface he wrote, "The 'studies' were written originally in 1920 and 1921, as the result of an intensive investigation of the bird life immediately about Cape May, and have been amplified in later years."[126] In 1922, Stone was compiling his Cape May bird notes, and by 1924 he had typed up many of his Jersey Coast species accounts and was thinking that "[m]aybe some day I can publish a 'Birds of Cape May' like Brewster's 'Umbagog' [*The Birds of the Lake Umbagog Region of Maine*]."[127-128] He clearly had a dawning conception of the book by those early dates.

He gave talks about Cape May, including early drafts of his *BSOCM* species accounts, at AOU and (particularly) DVOC meetings; he also put some of his Cape May sightings in *The Auk*. In 1925, he was "still amassing notes on Cape May birds & combining them into readable accounts – a combination of field & study work that is very agreeable."[33] In July 1928, he told Wetmore that he intended to incorporate sightings through the end of the year, then "call it a job" and finish the book.[129] So much for the best-laid schemes of mice and men: four years later, he was telling Wetmore that 1932 would be the year he would wrap everything up and try to get it published, and ditto in 1933 to James Peters.[130] Cornelius Weygandt recalled, "Those of us who had been following the writing of [*BSOCM*] were afraid it would never be completed. It had been written slowly during long years....It was almost a miracle that he was able to finish it in his ailing age."[131-132] James Rehn wrote that failing health in later years actually enabled Stone to devote more time to his work on the book.[133] (The evolution of the book is presented in Appendix 2.)

Once the manuscript was nearing completion, funding its printing became an issue, and Conrad Roland told Potter in 1934, "It seems a pity that Stone may never see his book published before he dies & all for lack of $2,500."[134] Stone was contemplating using $2,000 from the defunct Pennsylvania Audubon Society's kitty, reasoning that the NAAS wanted the book published to promote its Witmer Stone Wildlife Sanctuary in Cape May, so the money would essentially be used for conservation purposes.[135] He felt it was akin to the NAAS sponsoring *Bird-Lore* articles or John B. May's recently-published *The Hawks of North America*.[136] The DVOC, meanwhile, was looking into ways to finance the publication, and by late February 1936 had apparently agreed to do so, although it reportedly wasn't announced until September.[100,137,138]

Getting to the finish line with the book, however, was a daunting task; as with any such project, there were countless loose ends and small details to be taken care of. Stone told Palmer in early 1937, "All the rest of my home time has been taken up with the Cape May book which like everything else of the sort manages to grow as it advances. I had no idea that I had such a job bringing the thing up to date."[139] He told Wetmore the same thing: "I have had more than I bargained for however in getting that 'Birds of Cape May' ready for the press. There seem to have been about a million things to add & check in order to bring it up to [the end of 1936]....Mrs. Stone says it is worse than ten Auks!"[140] The decision to include records of birds along the entire New Jersey coast, not just Cape May County, as mentioned near the beginning of the *BSOCM* preface, was arrived at early in 1937, and that added to the enormity of the effort.[126,139] In an August letter to Potter, Stone, summering at 909 Queen, wrote "Publishing House of the <u>Magnum Opus</u>" at the top of the first page. He was clearly excited about the way the book was shaping up as it neared completion, telling Potter, "Actual printing will not start till all is in pages, so we can add a line here & there if you see a Roseate Cockatoo or a Green Bul-bul! It is some book!"[45]

The finished work has rightly been called "Stone's Tome," and it ran to over 900 pages.[141] Lillie compared its length to that of the recently published, and notoriously excessive, *Gone With the Wind*.[142] Stone used the type and format of Murphy's 1936 *Oceanic Birds of South America* as the model for his own book, which explains the distinct similarity in the appearance of the two works.[143] An August 1937 letter from his old friend Herbert Brown, one of *BSOCM*'s illustrators, indicated that Stone was pausing to smell the roses as the book neared completion. Brown wrote, "I rejoice to know of the 'Book's' progress and of the let up of the grind, with time known for bugs and bird excursions, and 'relaxing,' a word one gave little thought to in days of yore."[144]

Stone showed an advance copy of the book to some of the AOU members at the annual meeting in mid-November 1937.[145] He gave a talk at the December 2 DVOC meeting about the writing of *BSOCM*, and copies of the book hot off the presses were first distributed to purchasers at the next DVOC meeting two weeks later.[146] (An August 22, 1937 sighting of a Scarlet Tanager is included in the book – Stone was clearly making final edits right up until the book went to press.)[147] At a gathering at his home on December 15, Stone distributed complimentary copies to artists, photographers, and others who had contributed to the book.[148]

DVOC members contributed extensively to the work, with photographs and drawings in addition to the countless records of nests and sightings. In particular, Richard Miller, Turner McMullen, Hand, and Potter had provided reams of the latter. Potter, a career banker, was the hotshot birder in the DVOC – the Philadelphia version of Ludlow Griscom, if you will.[149] Stone and Potter were good friends, and Stone graciously informed him, "You figure quite a bit in this and 'Julian Potter' figures so often in the manuscript that I wonder who is writing the work!"[150] Potter proofed so much of the book that as it entered the printing phase, Stone told him, "There is a little bit more [to proofread] but I shall not trouble you with that, also the introduction which I think is the best part of the book and which I shall let you see when the book appears so that it will not <u>all</u> be 'stale'!"[46]

The species drawings by Conrad Roland (who had studied under the great Louis Agassiz Fuertes) and Earl Poole, and the landscape vignettes by Fletcher Street and Herbert Brown, still lend immeasurable charm to the work. Poole and Roland had distinct styles: Poole's drawings are delicate and lightly drawn using fine lines, with the subjects gracefully posed, almost retiring; Roland's drawings are bolder, with heavy black fill, the subjects looking more alert and animated. Stone had given Roland a list of species to illustrate, including suggestions about the characteristics of some species that he hoped Roland could bring out in his depictions. For the woodcock, for example, Stone said their flight resembled that of a giant mosquito, and he wanted Roland to try to capture that.[49]

Stone's initial call for DVOC members to contribute photographs was met with a tepid response, but they eventually came through, and the book included 240 photos from club members and others.[151-153] The quality of the photos is quite dated now, but at the time several reviewers were impressed with both them and the drawings, and the book was considered an artistic as well as a literary triumph. In fact, Stone, in a bit of overdone modesty, said the book's photos and illustrations "bid fair to be well worthwhile even if the text is not!"[152] Although Stone had pocket cameras, and was good at using them for general shots, he didn't move on to more serious equipment for bird photography, and no Stone photos of birds appear in *BSOCM*.[154]

———————— ❧ ————————

Contemporaries recognized the caliber of Stone's book. In a *Bird-Lore* review, Joseph Hickey said, "[*BSOCM*] is written in a style that is ever graceful, never pedantic, better than Brewster and approaching Thoreau. The book is a beautiful one which can be picked up by any reader, opened at practically any place, and read with considerable interest."[155] Robert Cushman Murphy wrote in a *New York Herald* review, "Here is a rare and beautiful book," and, "The science of the book is of the present...yet the flavor of the text is almost Elizabethan."[156] A review in *Bird-Banding* was more restrained, but still referred to "these fine volumes that constitute a mine of information," and opined that "Dr. Stone writes in simple, dignified English which at times in its beauty and vividness rises to literary distinction."[157] J. Percy Moore later wrote that *BSOCM* "reflects Stone at his best, both as a naturalist and a writer."[158]

Stone included a note in the set sent to T.C. Stephens, who reviewed *BSOCM* for *The Wilson Bulletin,* and an excerpt from it gives an idea of Stone's take on the book: "It has been a great pleasure to personally plan and manage the production of such a work and to see it take form just as I had planned.... I have tried to picture the environment of the various species and to get the atmosphere and the spirit of the Cape as I know it. (But have not been led into *verse*!!)"[159] One reader told Stone that what "crops out all through the book is 'the spirit of Cape May – the shore'"; Stone said he was very pleased to hear it because that was just what he was trying to evoke.[160] Some examples of Stone's succeeding wonderfully in describing environment and atmosphere are his captivating landscape essays at the beginning of the work and his depiction of the Hereford Inlet skimmer and tern colony at the end of the Black Skimmer account.

Weygandt, the UP English professor and a prolific author himself, was always unstinting in his praise of *BSOCM*. Several years after Stone's death, Weygandt wrote:

> There is no book about birds in America to put alongside of it....The book has not been accorded the praise it should have....Always heard in this writing is the voice of the sea, always haunting it is the mystery of the sea, always there is breaking out in it some bright beauty of light on white egret or glittering stretch of thoroughfare. Wafts of salt air and of air sweet of the pines wander through its pages. Kindly

faces of old seamen appear and disappear. The inexplicable in bird ways is candidly admitted. Scientific fact lies down with romantic wonder as quietly as lion and lamb on the old plates of "The Peaceable Kingdom."[161]

Weygandt wrote elsewhere, "Witmer Stone was not only of the brotherhood of Wilson and Audubon and Nuttall, but a fellow of Thoreau and Burroughs, Richard Jefferies and W. H. Hudson."[131] In an address before the Nuttall Ornithological Club in 1923 on the subject of the current state of ornithology, Stone said, "It seems to me that the cultivation of literary ability in describing bird activities and behavior, or in picturing ornithological backgrounds and habitats, is just as important as the cultivation of artistic skill in portraying them with brush or camera."[162] Stone practiced what he preached in *BSOCM*, with detailed, vivid descriptions of bird behavior, plumages, voices and habitats. Common Terns' tenacity in colony defense is described thus: "The innocent trespass of an occasional Turkey Vulture had amusing results as the entire [tern] colony arose and attacked him, from six to twenty continuing the pursuit far over the meadows. The great bird flapped his wings laboriously and twisted and turned to avoid the annoying assaults of the agile terns and in nearly every instance he disgorged part of his food although the terns paid no attention to this tribute."[163] His Thoreauvian depiction of the solitary habits of wintering and migrant Hermit Thrushes puts the reader right into the woods and onto a branch next to one of the birds, deep in the hermit's private little world.[164] Of the Piping Plovers on Brigantine Beach, Stone wrote, "As they took wing they uttered their plaintive *peenk!*; *peenk!*; like the stroke of some silver bell, clear cut and delicate as the little bird itself, and suited to the solitude of the spot with its broad stretches of white sand flanked by green-topped dunes, and with the distant pounding of the surf on the outer bar."[165]

The book is an ornithological tome, often dry and factual, but Stone included many "delightful word pictures," as Wetmore called them.[124] Weygandt singled out the close of the Herring Gull account for particular praise:[131]

I always associate them with winter and picture them in my mind's eye as accompanied by the angry roar of the surf and the rush of waters on some wild beach by the harbor's mouth, as they gather together for the night. Many times I have seen them on a narrow bar at sunset where they stand out silvery white and gray against the deep blue black of the darkening ocean, while every moment a long line of snowy surf boils up behind them as if to wash them from their narrow strand. Farther out other lines of surf appear successively and are lost again in the flood of waters. Every moment the pale yellow moon is growing brighter as the last rays of the sun die out in the west, and the night shadows creep closer and closer, while the great gulls stand there like a row of sentinels silhouetted against the sky until they are slowly and gradually swallowed up in the night.[166]

Potter particularly liked Stone's description of the constantly changing shape of scoter flocks on the wing, which birders today can witness at places such as Avalon and Cape May:[167]

> At the times of greatest abundance…we see Scoters from the beach passing constantly far out over the ocean, in long jet black lines, conspicuous against either sky or water. They literally "stream" along over the surface like slender wisps of cloud or mist, drifting with the wind. Now one of these wisps seems to swell out in the middle as the birds gather more closely together, and then it thins out and lengthens, then once again the congestion develops at the head or rear of the column. Now there are little knots formed at several points along the stream or perhaps it breaks up into small "clouds" which later drift together and form again the long slender line. The formation is ever changing but the streams of birds are always pushing steadily ahead as if driven by some unseen power behind them. Now and then a flock will rise twenty feet or more above the surface of the water and then drift down again low over the waves.[168]

Reading Stone's idyllic description of a May evening on his beloved Jarvis Sound, behind present-day Wildwood Crest, a reader can almost smell the salt air. I consider it the zenith of his descriptive writing in *BSOCM*:

> May 21, 1921. It was just sunset as we pulled our boat out from Weeks' Landing under the two silver poplar trees and floated slowly down the little creek and on out into the wider thoroughfare. It was nearly high tide and the water reached almost to the top of the banks, so that we had an uninterrupted view over the wide stretches of salt meadows. Far away to the east across the open sound was the low-lying shrubbery of Two Mile Beach with a glint of sand dunes here and there amidst the green, and the roar of the surf beyond. To the west lay the long border of the mainland woods growing black in the shadows. Great masses of kelp with its countless floating bladders lie in the water just below the surface as we slip quietly along between the slender stakes that mark the location of the oyster beds.
>
> There are many clouds on the western horizon but the fiery red orb of the sun comes into view for a moment between their dark masses, and lights up all the water and land to the eastward while across its disk, as if traversing a field of fire, a couple of Crows pass by. Almost immediately it disappears again and sinks below the horizon, but for fully ten minutes the fleecy clouds overhead and to the eastward are

all edged with crimson and pink, the color constantly spreading and changing, and all its varied tints are clearly reflected in the smooth glassy waters of the channel. The two poplars at the landing and a little oyster shack supported on poles become black silhouettes against the fading light and the far off woods are now merged with the shoreline in a uniform dusky band. The full moon already risen a little above the horizon is growing brighter with every moment as the sunlight fades, and makes a long path of yellow light on the water, broken by the ripples of a passing breeze. In the gathering dusk the last wild flights of little sandpipers wheel over the meadows; we hear the cackle of the Mudhens among the taller grass; and solitary Night Herons come winging their way across from the woods on the shore to drop into some shallow pool for their night's feeding. Then to the south there flashes out, at regular intervals, the brilliant yellow star of the Cape May Light, and night settles down over the meadows.[169]

Some other delightful word pictures include Stone's descriptions of the secret lives of Clapper Rails; the feeding behavior of Least Sandpipers; the magical cohesion of twisting, turning flocks of Semipalmated Sandpipers; the antics of a singing mockingbird; and the swarming fall flocks of Tree Swallows and Myrtle (= Yellow-rumped) Warblers.[170] He also provided an outstanding description of a classic Cape May Point autumn fallout flight from 1926, the details of which would be perfectly familiar to modern birders.[171]

Stone's dry humor isn't on display much in *BSOCM*, but it surfaces occasionally, as here in his description of an interesting encounter with a Clapper Rail ("Mud Hen"): "Once in early autumn, when standing on the meadows, a Mud Hen, alarmed at something, came running rapidly through the grass and crouched suddenly directly between my feet, doubtless thinking that he had found safety between two convenient lumps of mud, and I did not abuse his confidence."[172]

Another charming feature of the book is the use of the old gunners' local names for the water birds (e.g., "Mud Hen"). Stone clearly had an affection for the old names; he once wrote in *The Auk* that times were changing and the professional market gunners would soon be gone forever, and the bird names they used would go with them unless they were compiled and written down.[173] When Stone was gathering material for *BEPNJ* in 1893, he received a letter from Captain John Taylor, one of the old Jersey Shore gunners, who described the seasonal distribution of waterfowl on the Delaware Bay. He told Stone little if anything that was new, but Stone must have loved the vernacular names Taylor used: among others, Dusky (Black) Duck, Whistlers and Cub Heads (male and female goldeneyes), Mommy/O'Molly (Oldsquaw), Hairy Head (Hooded Merganser), Butter Ball/Dipper Duck

(Bufflehead), and Water Witch (Horned Grebe, but others used it for the Pied-billed).[174] Stone was put in touch with Taylor by Philip Laurent, whose recommendation included, "Capt. Taylor is a gunner among a hundred as he does not smoke, chew or drink, the only thing I know against him, is that the big letter D. will sometimes escape between his lips, this is particularly the case when he happens to miss an easy shot."[175]

John Mecray and Raymond Otter were two local Cape May gunners whose waterfowl records were quoted extensively by Stone in *BSOCM*. Mecray was a banker, and Otter had an upholstery business.[176] On October 7, 1932, at Pond Creek Meadows, Otter "shot about all the Rallidae possible in one day: Clapper, King, Virginia, Sora, Yellow & [Common] Gallinule."[177] That would be a tough list to match in Cape May today, for either a hunter or a birder, given the rarity of the King and Yellow Rails, and Otter got three Yellows that day and told Stone he'd seen others over the years (as many as eight in a day!).[178] Throw in Walker Hand's Corn Crake that he shot in Dennisville in 1905 and you'd *really* have "all the Rallidae possible."[179]

———————— ✑ ————————

Stone wrote in the *BSOCM* preface that he had been disappointed that ornithologists after Wilson had failed to leave an adequate record of the avifauna of coastal New Jersey, and his main object in publishing the book was to leave an account for future generations of the situation in his time. The Cape May Point area is one of the most important and well-known bird migration locations in the world, and *BSOCM* is the best baseline we have for the conditions there in the early 1900s. There is a wealth of dates for nests and number of eggs, Christmas Bird Count numbers, estimates of roosting Purple Martin numbers, and dates of arrival and departure – even dates when numbers increased due to an influx of migrants. Stone wasn't conducting scientifically rigid point counts or transects, of course, although he sometimes performed something repeatable, such as the number per minute of migrating Barn Swallows or flickers passing a defined point; the number of Tree Swallows lining the telegraph wires in Cape May, calculated by multiplying the number of birds per wire by the number of wires per span by the number of spans occupied; even a calculation of robin density on the Cape May golf course.[180]

The shorebird and waterfowl surveys by Charles Urner, Julian Potter, and others provide some of the best baseline data in the book. Urner was vice president of Urner-Barry, a commodity market reporting company still in business in New Jersey, and an outstanding field ornithologist. He died suddenly of heart failure in 1938, at age 56, after publishing articles about his ten-year study of New Jersey shorebird migrations in *The Auk* and in the

Linnaean Society of New York's *Proceedings*, as well as putting his count data at Stone's disposal for *BSOCM*. Robert Storer published the final data sets and an overview of Urner's shorebird study in *The Auk* in 1949.[181]

For all his interest in bird migration, Stone doesn't write much about its nocturnal component. Many birds, particularly the passerines, migrate at night; on nights with a heavy flight their chirps and twitters can be heard continuously as they pass overhead in the dark. A 1916 *Auk* article described the nocturnal calls of several species, so the phenomenon had been known for some time and was well studied by some.[182] But the *BSOCM* Swainson's ("Olive-backed") and Hermit Thrush accounts make no mention of the nocturnal flight calls of those species, which are such a prominent feature of autumn migration along the East Coast, although Stone mentioned that Hand and Audubon warden William Rusling heard Veeries calling on still autumn nights.[183] Stone heard migrating loons calling in the dark; Hand and Roland told Stone about hearing Black-crowned Night Herons, Upland Sandpipers, and other birds at night; and Allen and Peterson mentioned it in their *Auk* article.[92,184,185] So although Stone may have been too deaf to hear most of the calls himself very well, if at all, he was certainly aware of them, but there are few references to them in *BSOCM* (e.g., a brief mention in the "Bird Migration at the Cape" chapter). Dorothy Balme, a regular at Margaret Shaffer's Cape May Point house, where many visiting birders stayed in the mid-1900s, recalled listening to the nocturnal call notes raining down on cool autumn nights, and today Point birders study the phenomenon each fall.

The Auk and *Bird-Lore* featured several articles going back to the 1880s about studying night migration by watching the moon through a telescope, and Stone made brief mention of this practice (and of nocturnal call notes) in *TBNJ*, but in *BSOCM* he doesn't record that he engaged in it himself at Cape May.[186] James Tanner watched the moon with binoculars to detect migrants when he was the Cape May Audubon warden in 1936.[122]

Another notable feature of the fall migration that received curiously little notice in the book is the passerine flights. Stone devoted much more space to the water birds (shorebirds, ducks, herons, gulls/terns, etc.) than to the passerine and other "land bird" species. Particularly puzzling are the terse accounts of some of the songbird species. In early 1936 he noted that *BSOCM* was "nearly done now, up to the song birds, & they, with a few exceptions, can be dismissed quickly. They figure mainly as migrants."[138] Stone may have been more interested in studying the water birds when he visited Cape May because he felt that they were the prominent ornithological feature of the area, but it's also possible that Stone gave the passerines a somewhat short shrift, almost as an afterthought for complete coverage, in his haste to finish the book.[187]

It's also curious that Stone and the DVOC seem to have missed some warblers that he represented as rare (either with that designation or by listing few records) but which are common fall migrants today. These include Tennessee, Nashville, Black-throated Blue, Black-throated Green, Blackburnian, Chestnut-sided, Bay-breasted, Blackpoll, and Cape May Warblers. Rose-breasted Grosbeak and Philadelphia Vireo are two other species similarly, and inexplicably, thought to be rare fall migrants by Stone.

Certainly most neotropical migrant species had larger populations then than now, and must have passed through Cape May in greater numbers than today. Stone often returned home in early September, right about when the passerine flight was building, and the last few days may have been spent packing, not birding.[128,188] He admitted that the warbler migration was lightly covered.[189] His remark in the previously cited early September 1924 letter that he and David Baird "scour C.M. Pt. every Saturday" suggests that even early in his Cape May studies, when his health was still good, with the fall passerine migration in full swing (and Stone stayed until September 15 that year), Stone was only birding the Point – where the best passerine flights are concentrated – once a week.[44,128] As noted in an earlier chapter, Stone was more interested in the spring migration of passerines than the autumn flights. The NAAS wardens' reports from the 1930s indicate that they weren't paying particular attention to the warbler flights, either.

The spectacular monarch and dragonfly migrations through Cape May Point receive increasing amounts of attention today, as they well should. Their migration was recognized in Stone's time, and they each get a single, passing mention in *BSOCM*.[190] Hand made reference to the monarch flight in an undated letter to Stone, and Potter reported a September 17, 1922 flight in *Bird-Lore*, when monarchs by the million passed down the coast (they were also seen in great numbers in Atlantic City that day), covering the pines at the Point like leaves, just as they do today.[185,191] Allen and Peterson also mentioned the monarch and dragonfly movements.[92]

∽

In the Cerulean Warbler account, Stone mentioned a May 1926 sighting of five Ceruleans at Cape May Point reported in *Bird-Lore*. Stone dismissed the sighting outright, writing that it "need hardly be taken seriously," although he didn't single out the observer by name.[192] There were only two known records of the Cerulean Warbler in New Jersey when Stone published *BSOCM*; their breeding range was mostly west and south of the state (as it is today, although they became rare breeders in New Jersey after Stone's time). Stone considered the species an accidental straggler whose occurrence in the state was "unlikely."[189,193]

The poor chap who reported "a flock of five Cerulean Warblers" in *Bird-Lore* was one Walter Albion Squires (his teenaged son Leslie was listed as co-author of the note), who lived in Philadelphia but didn't belong to the DVOC. (He had belonged to the Cooper Ornithological Club and other wildlife/conservation organizations while attending seminary in San Francisco, and he published in *The Condor*.) Squires didn't give the sex composition of the flock, but wrote that the birds "were unmistakably identified, being viewed with binoculars at a very close range."[194]An anonymous *Cassinia* reviewer also questioned the sighting, noting that the species had never been seen in Cape May and didn't occur in flocks, and that the habitat was unsuitable. He wondered if the birds weren't Blue-gray Gnatcatchers. (The same reviewer questioned another Squires *Bird-Lore* report of three Yellow-throated Warblers at Kirkwood, New Jersey.)[195] *Birds of New Jersey* (published in 1999) noted a spring maximum of six banded Ceruleans on May 9, 1987 at Island Beach.[196]

Squires was a widely traveled Presbyterian minister who spent most of his career in the area of Christian education for the Presbyterian Church, and he wrote dozens of books and articles on the subject. He was located in Philadelphia for 13 years.[197] During that time, he authored some articles in *Bird-Lore* including "Birds which are coming back to New Jersey shores" in 1925, wherein he gave every indication of being a competent and knowledgeable field birder who had experience at several places along the eastern seaboard with the birds discussed in the article, who kept careful notes of his sightings, and who was aware of the historical literature on the subject.[198] In *BSOCM*, Stone mentioned a Black Duck nest that Squires had found and pointed out to him on May 9, 1931; Squires also wrote that up in *Bird-Lore*.[80,199] Five Cerulean Warblers together would be an extraordinary sighting, but considering the solidness of Squires's *Bird-Lore* notes, Stone may have been a bit blunt, if justified, in his *BSOCM* dismissal. However, he obviously had personal experience with Squires and saw fit to reject the record.[200] He wrote in the *BSOCM* preface that when confronted with a questionable sight record he "considered the personal equation and the experience of others in the same region and acted accordingly."[153]

Another sighting in *BSOCM* that has its doubters is Muriel Fisher's Man-o'-war-bird (= Magnificent Frigatebird). Stone had no doubt as to the bird's identity, based on her description – she had no idea what it was – but a later author of a book on Cape May birds did, saying the description in *BSOCM* was "unconvincing."[201] Fisher's written description in a 1928 letter to Stone, if not exactly field guide material, is at least strongly suggestive. (The day before her sighting, Stone had found an Audubon's Shearwater, another southern waif probably also driven north by the Nassau Hurricane of 1926.) The clincher, however, is what Stone couldn't practically include in his *Auk* and *BSOCM* accounts of the record: three small but perfectly convincing sketches in the letter of the beak, tail, and rear-view flight profile that leave little doubt that Fisher – sans binoculars, shortsighted and all, who couldn't tell a mockingbird from a magpie – is due credit for New Jersey's first documented record of a frigatebird.[202] (For an encore, she later found a Purple Gallinule in a Cape May privet hedge.)[203]

———————— ❧ ————————

There have been many changes in Cape May bird species composition and abundance since *BSOCM*. To name just a few, Brown Pelicans, Black Skimmers, Royal Terns, gulls (with man's help), and mockingbirds have increased, as breeders or visitors. Conversely, Henslow's Sparrows, Green Herons, Least and American Bitterns, kestrels, King Rails, meadowlarks, Barn Owls, chats, Hooded Warblers, and Ovenbirds have declined or disappeared as breeders around Cape May, and Loggerhead Shrikes, once regular fall migrants, are extremely rare now.[204]

The decline of the bobwhite is another sad change since *BSOCM*. Walker Hand noted an amazing bobwhite flight on October 21, 1902, like nothing we're likely to ever witness again, when he "saw a flock at Cape May Point, flying over the water a mile from any feeding ground; another flock was observed to run to the water's edge and take flight apparently for Delaware. There is always a large migration about the first week in October."[205] In *BSOCM*, Hand said of this same flight that the birds took off heading due south at an elevation that was quite high for bobwhites.[206] Any bobwhites in Cape May now are sedentary (and usually clueless and short-lived) stock birds, and even Stone wondered how many New Jersey birds were the original race, compared to more recently introduced stock birds.[207]

Another possible change concerns gull behavior, and one almost wonders if they weren't less belligerent and predatory in Stone's time. He reported Herring Gulls eating broken eggs and dead chicks after a tern colony was flooded, then curiously stated, "From the way in which the terns pursue them, when they fly near a breeding colony, they may also appropriate fresh eggs and living young if opportunity offers, but I have never actually seen them do so."[208] He recorded a Laughing Gull chasing a Common Tern and forcing it to drop a fish, but Stone wrote that he didn't "regard this as a common habit."[209] Garbage dumps and shopping centers have enabled the omnivorous gulls to flourish in the face of environmental degradation, and today their pirating and predation are a further bane to nesting terns and shorebirds already reeling from habitat loss and human disturbance at their breeding locales. Stone also said that Laughing Gulls fed on the beach "under exceptional circumstances," which anyone trying to eat a sandwich on a New Jersey beach today still wishes was true – or maybe beaches now thronged with sunbathers eating sandwiches represent an ongoing "exceptional circumstance" for the ravenous Laughers.[210]

———————— ❧ ————————

The DVOC published 1,400 sets of *BSOCM*, and Stone handled the sales out of his home. The books had been sent by the printer, Intelligencer Printing Company in Lancaster, to be bound and stored at Arnold's Book Bindery in Reading, Pennsylvania, and when an order came in and Stone had no sets on hand, he may have had Arnold's ship it from Reading.[211-212] He had also given the Academy a few dozen sets, and they filled orders that came addressed to them. Stone and the DVOC only charged $6 for a set, which Stone said was "at about cost." That made the book affordable to everyone, especially the younger men in the DVOC, and not "a rich man's plaything." By April 1938, almost 300 sets had been sold, and Stone thought another 300 or so sales would be the break-even point.[213]

Six months after Stone's death, the Academy received the 722 sets of *BSOCM* that were in storage at Arnold's, and the Academy and Art Emlen, Stone's estate executor, suddenly had to unravel the whole tangled web of legal issues surrounding future sales of the book.[214] After Lillie's death in 1940, it was suggested by one staffer that ANSP should buy the remaining sets from Germantown Trust Company, the executor of Lillie's estate, and use them – we're talking an ornithological classic, a Brewster Medal winner – as "magazine premiums, membership inducements, and on straight sale."[211,215] This was apparently not done, however; the Academy then proposed to continue to sell the book for Germantown Trust for a 33% commission.[216] That was probably the arrangement until 1947, when, with the inventory down to 180 sets, Germantown Trust agreed to sell the remaining sets to ANSP, which handled sales after that.[217]

Each original set of *BSOCM* has a number (1–1,400) stamped on the last page of volume two, permitting the identification of specific sets. Sandy Sherman published a *Cassinia* article in 2001 on the whereabouts of many of the original sets, and over a quarter of the sets have been relocated.[218] When Lillie died, the copyright to *BSOCM* was left to the DVOC.[219] The club eventually sold the rights to Dover Publications, and used the money as the nucleus of its endowment fund.[19] As the original volumes became harder to obtain, Dover (1965) and Stackpole Books (2000) published reprints.

――――――― ∾ ―――――――

In early 1938, Stone told Frank Chapman that "even Cape May in winter has lost its lure now that [*BSOCM*] is out and I am less able to face exposure."[141] He returned to vacation at Cape May for one last summer in 1938, but his health was frail and the weather wasn't cooperative ("July was a flood & August was hot"). Stone and his companions nevertheless managed to find some "additions to the Book," including Little Blue Herons nesting in Cape May County for the first time in decades, an Osprey nest on the ground, and a Cooper's Hawk nest at Cape May Point.[220] He even added the White M

Hairstreak butterfly to his Cape May list.[221] His last Cape May bird outing that I can find record of was on July 29, 1938, when he sat in a friend's car and watched a flock of shorebirds, including Killdeers, Greater and Lesser Yellow-legs, dowitchers, and Pectoral, Stilt and Semipalmated Sandpipers feeding at a rain puddle just a few yards from the car.[222] By the end of the summer, he was afflicted with a "urinary complication" that proved to be the beginning of the end, and when he returned to Germantown September 6, he had seen the last of his beloved Cape May.[220]

Stone had come a long way as a writer from the days when his writing "smack[ed] too much of the museum, and not enough of the woods."[223] *BSOCM* showed that he could mix detailed and accurate ornithological observations and data with riveting sketches that so wonderfully captured the charm of old Cape May and her feathered denizens. One has to wonder how much of his writing was inspiration and how much was perspiration. In any case, time ran out for Stone in bringing to publication some of the manuscripts of varying sizes he was working on in his final years. Thus, *BSOCM* will have to suffice as the only finished material that we have from the evening of his life to glimpse what Stone could have been as a writer. Weygandt wrote, "It is not many men [who] write better and better as they grow older. Witmer Stone always wrote well, but he surpassed himself in [*BSOCM*]....When it was finally published those of us who had awaited it so eagerly found it was even a better book than we had expected it to be. It is not only a complete and scientifically exact record of the goings and comings and stayings of all the birds of Cape May, but literature to which the only companion piece is Gilbert White's 'Natural History of Selborne.'"[131]

In a letter to Brewster in 1906, after receiving the famed ornithologist's *The Birds of the Cambridge Region of Massachusetts*, Stone wrote, "The work is I think about as near as we shall ever come to an <u>exhaustive</u> account of the birds of a limited area and as such it has a value peculiarly its own. I think we should all congratulate ourselves that one who has spent so many years in the painstaking labor of collecting such a mass of data, has been able to put it in final shape where it will be a constant source of pleasure and instruction to many generations of bird students."[224] It is remarkable how perfectly that description could serve for Stone's own account of Cape May's birds, the publication of which was 30 years into the future. At the June 1939 annual AOU meeting, Stone's *BSOCM* was posthumously awarded the Brewster Medal, given by the AOU for "the most important [recent] work" on "birds of the Western Hemisphere."[225]

I have often been struck that people *like* Stone so much even though they know next to nothing about him outside of having read *BSOCM* and maybe *PSNJ*, and I think it's simply because his personality – that twinkle in his eyes – comes through in the writing. Weygandt put it best, in as good a summary of the book as you'll find anywhere, when he wrote of *BSOCM* that it is "a scientific treatise of first importance, leavened by a pleasantness of personality and a revelation of the innate goodness of the man."[226] Elsewhere, in a similar vein, he wrote, "The winning personality that was to the fore in all his foregathering with his fellows informs [*BSOCM*]....[I]t is the man's kindliness and charm and poet's eye that give quality to the book."[227]

The descriptive writing style of *BSOCM* was not peculiar to, or original with, Stone – just read A.C. Bent's *Life Histories* series, for example the first paragraph of the "Marsh Hawk" account.[228] But *BSOCM*, although an ornithological – not a popular – treatise, does indeed sometimes rise to literary distinction, approaching Thoreau, and a reader can't help but wonder what other pearls of prose Stone may have produced had he retired from ANSP and *Auk* duties earlier, or been given another five or ten years of life to concentrate on writing. But at least we can feel fortunate that, with all the editorial and administrative responsibilities that consumed his life and his health, we were able to receive from Stone, in the nick of time, a timeless ornithological and literary classic that enables us to further recognize the astonishing breadth of the man's capabilities.

Witmer provides his own vignette: playful sketch of the Cape May lighthouse from a letter to Alexander Wetmore. Smithsonian Institution Archives.

14

A Sanctuary in Which to House It

Migrating hawks were shot on their passage through Cape May Point (CMP) for at least several decades before publication of *BSOCM*. A 1982 review of old newspaper accounts found an 1888 reference to the shooting, so it had been going on at least that long and probably longer. It also included an assertion by a local resident that the shooting used to extend up the Bay as far as modern-day Villas.[1] That whole area of Cape May County was quite rural in Stone's day, with farmers and fishermen who were avid hunters as well.

AOU president Stone was curiously tepid about the idea of protecting hawks migrating through CMP in a 1920 response to a query on the subject from New Jersey Audubon Society (NJAS) head Beecher Bowdish. He agreed with Bowdish that the hawks were not taking a higher percentage of songbirds while both were concentrated at the Point during the fall than they were at other times of the year when they were more dispersed. However, he didn't have a definite view as to the best course of action, didn't think the ineffective AOU bird protection committee could help, and wasn't opposed to leaving some "injurious birds" (probably accipiters) unprotected, but was only against plans to exterminate them. (Stone's 1920 letter to Bowdish also noted that passerines and raptors both got bottled up at the Point by unfavorable winds, so the flights' causes were recognized at least that early.)[2]

Hawk counts weren't conducted at the Point until the 1930s, but scattered records exist from before then, including mentions by Julian Potter in a *Bird-Lore* regional-sightings feature titled "The Season." In 1921, raptors were reportedly "abundant" at Cape May on October 9.[3] In his "Cape May Bird Life" talk to the DVOC in October, Stone spoke of one gunner having killed 64 Sharp-shinned Hawks (or "Sharpies," their usual moniker at Cape May and elsewhere) on a September day, and said that Walker Hand estimated 1,000 hawks were killed in the same week.[4] In 1922, Stone brought national attention to the raptor flights at CMP with a short *Auk* note that provided an early and accurate description of the flight conditions: hawks were wind-drifted to the southern tip of New Jersey on northwest winds; fearful of being blown out to sea, they milled around the Point before continuing north along the Bayshore. He stated that the same northwest winds were responsible for the songbird, flicker, and woodcock flights also seen at the Point, and that since the flicker shooting had been outlawed, local gunners had turned their attention to the Sharpies, which they also gathered up and ate. "Unfortunately," Stone noted drily, "while they may be epicures they are usually not ornithologists," and in addition to the Sharpies many other raptor and non-raptor species were killed.[5]

In 1923, Potter reported a "very heavy flight" on September 10, when about 900 hawks were shot, mostly Sharpies, with another good flight on September 16.[6] However, Hand reported a small flight of Sharpies on September 10, a large one on the 14th with 900–1,000 killed, and another flight of Sharpies on October 18.[7] In 1925, flights were reported by Potter on September 22 (237 raptors counted, mostly Sharpies) and the 25th. Two to three hundred hawks were estimated to have been shot on the former date, "not up to the high record of last year."[8] In a 1926 *Auk* letter about the widespread decline of hawks due to shooting, Henry Carey of Philadelphia mentioned the Potter records and wrote, "Only a few years ago, as many as a thousand Hawks could be seen at Cape May, N.J., in a single day." He called for the passage of state laws forbidding the killing of all hawks, at any time, other than those caught in the act of depredating at game farms or in the barnyard.[9] In 1927, flights were said to be "somewhat below normal," but shooters managed to kill about 200 hawks, mostly Sharpies, between September 19 and 24.[10] In 1928, heavy flights were reported for late September, with about 1,000 hawks killed, mostly Sharpies.[11] In 1929, Potter wrote that the hawk flights at Cape May were "about normal," and in late September "perhaps 500" were shot by the gunners – mostly Sharpies, but also Merlins.[12] Another witness to a few days of the flight in 1929 reported that he saw thousands of kestrels and Merlins shot by the gunners, although it seems unlikely there weren't a lot of Sharpies in the mix.[13] In 1930, Stone published "The hawk question" in *The Auk*, arguing the case for protection of hawks, which studies had shown were mostly beneficial, and condemning their slaughter on their migrations through Cape May and other locales.[14]

It is interesting that at these early dates, between Potter's *Bird-Lore* material and the Stone and Carey mentions in *The Auk*, CMP was getting *national recognition* for its hawk flights – albeit mostly as a place where they were being shot, not ogled by observers running season-long counts – yet some birders today still think the flights were "discovered" in the 1970s. Stone described the slaughter from his time in some detail in *BSOCM*; it featured "a small army of men," toting various models and vintages of guns, scattered around the Point but concentrated at the west end of Sunset Boulevard, with "everyone bent on the slaughter."[15] In later years, the automobile brought gunners from as far away as Pennsylvania, and their cars lined the boulevard on days when northwest winds brought a good flight. Stone wrote that "so frequent are the discharges that it actually sounds as if some sort of engagement or mock battle were in progress." The hawks were eaten ("much to the amusement of those not familiar with the gastronomic ability of the hardy residents of the shore"), and small boys combed the nearby woods for wounded ones they could snag for the table.[16] Locals carried home peach baskets full of dead hawks (and flickers).[17]

Along with some other DVOC members, Norm McDonald witnessed just such a slaughter on October 5, 1930, and a letter and photograph he sent to *Bird-Lore* were published in a January 1931 article on the situation. The graphic photo showed several dead birds – including hawks, a flicker, and a night heron – and numerous empty cartridge boxes. "For the last [i.e., west-ernmost] mile or mile and a half" of Sunset Boulevard, McDonald wrote, "the sides [of the road] were strewn with empty shells and cartridge-boxes....In the concentration of the Hawk-flight, the birds fly low and slowly at this point, and the slaughter is accomplished with ridiculous ease." McDonald and (in a separate letter) Walker Hand pointed out that many protected species of birds were shot illegally in addition to the unprotected species.[18] (Only the three accipiters and the Peregrine Falcon were unprotected by law.) Potter described the same event in another *Bird-Lore* article: "The remains of Sharp-shinned [hawks], [Merlins], and [kestrels] were numerous. One Cooper's Hawk, sev-eral [harriers], 2 Broad-winged Hawks, three Ospreys (1 flapping about with a broken wing), 1 Night Heron, and 1 Flicker were noted among the victims."[19]

Maybe McDonald's disturbing photograph was worth a thousand words, because after years of the hawk killing at CMP being generally known, the let-ter and photo brought immediate action. NAAS president T. Gilbert Pearson contacted the New Jersey Board of Game Commissioners, alerting it to the shooting and asking, "I wonder whether you have detailed any wardens who specially guard the region and warn shooters against killing protected birds?"[18] McDonald had asked Stone to pass on to Pearson any information he had on Cape May hawk flights, saying "[i]t may help Cape May birds which is what we are all after," but Stone wasn't mentioned in the *Bird-Lore* article, which suggests he didn't do so.[20] (McDonald had also asked Hand for his input, which appeared in the article.) In his *Auk* review of the *Bird-Lore* article, Stone sounded decidedly pessimistic that the state would do anything about the situ-ation.[21]

However, Pearson informed McDonald in April that the NAAS would fund a warden to work with the local game warden at CMP to prevent the killing of protected birds. Pearson asked the DVOC to recommend a warden, and it was probably Stone who suggested George Saunders, one of Arthur Allen's Ph.D. students at Cornell University.[16,22] Saunders was known to Stone and the club because of his participation as assistant ornithologist on an ANSP expedition to Africa in 1930, and had been recommended by Allen to Stone in 1929 for an ANSP Colombia expedition that was postponed.[23] He would be assisted at Cape May by the "sensible, efficient, and fearless" George Groves, a game warden from the New Jersey Game and Fish Department, and Dr. Thomas Winecoff from the Pennsylvania Board of Game Commissioners.[16]

The same conditions that led to a traffic jam of raptors at CMP produced a similar congestion of woodcocks in October and November, and those birds were also subjected to a merciless barrage. Stone squandered a chance to help protect them in 1927, when his old friend A.K. Fisher of the U.S. Biological Survey (USBS) told him that the Survey was concerned about the plight of the woodcock, and asked for information and recommendations concerning the CMP slaughter in fall – certainly the kind of golden opportunity a conservationist dreams about. Stone's reply, however, was mostly milquetoast. He confirmed the slaughter was taking place, but told Fisher he didn't know what to do about it – in fact, "it does not seem fair to take advantage of this great concentration of birds in one spot during the migration" was the extent of his indignation. He said that the Cape May hunters had already been "deprived" of flicker and spring duck shooting, and now had only the hawk flights and woodcocks "on which to expend their energy"; stopping the woodcock shooting "would meet with great objection." He made no recommendations to protect the birds, and ended by saying he didn't want his name used in any publications relating to the matter.[24]

Hand estimated that 3,000–4,500 woodcocks were killed in 1928, the year after Stone was asked what should be done about it.[25] In late 1929, Stone wrote to USBS chief Paul Redington about possible bag-limit violations during the woodcock shoots.[26] Then in an April 1931 *Auk* note, Stone called the autumn Cape May woodcock hunting an "outrageous slaughter" that needed to be checked by state or federal authorities, and he wrote that if CMP were made a sanctuary the illegal shooting of woodcocks and hawks could be halted.[27] The sanctuary suggestion was better late than never, but in 1927, when the Feds had asked for his input, he had fumbled the ball.

Stone wasn't the only one with the sanctuary idea. Wharton Huber proposed it during a talk he gave in early 1931 about the uncontrolled woodcock shooting at CMP, and it drew a query from the president of the Pennsylvania Parks Association, who asked for more particulars to pass along to an interested friend on the Pennsylvania Game Commission.[28] Huber responded that he thought it would be an easy thing for the New Jersey Game Commission to put an end to shooting in the Cape May area, and he welcomed any assistance with persuading the commission to help preserve the species.[29]

Protected hawks, at least, got a hand when the 1931 fall flights got under way with the wardens in place. An excellent *Bird-Lore* article provided a summary of the period (September 15–October 15) during which they were on patrol. Most of the shooting occurred along a 300-yard stretch at the west end of Sunset Boulevard. Saunders (whose presence Stone said was "heralded and bitterly resented in the local press") estimated that 95% of the gunners ate the hawks.[30] Early on, the wardens used shot specimens of protected species to educate the shooters about which hawks could be legally killed; thereafter only three hunters ("new arrivals" who had not been given the lecture with dead birds) were caught shooting birds illegally, and two of them stopped shooting altogether when threatened with arrest for future infractions. Italians and boys were particularly troublesome: they shot from the woods instead of the highway in order to escape detection, and were "much more indiscriminate in their shooting." Many shooters who couldn't differentiate between Sharpies and the two small falcon species (American Kestrel and Merlin) stopped shooting during the month of warden presence in order to avoid jail or fines.[16]

Saunders estimated that 10,000 hawks passed through the area between September 29 and October 15.[31] He reported 14,060 hawks for the entire season (not including Ospreys and Turkey Vultures, which were "common"), but it's obvious from the rounded numbers in his published counts that his figures were just seasonal estimates and weren't derived from daily count totals.[16,32-33] Saunders estimated that 1,000 hawks were shot, including about 925 Sharpies (of which only two were adults) and lesser numbers of other species. He examined stomach contents and found, among other things, that Merlins occasionally captured Eastern Red Bats![34] In its first year, the NAAS warden program was already quantifying the magnitude of the flights and the food habits of the raptors.

———————— ❧ ————————

In 1932, the NAAS hired Robert P. Allen as warden. He was assisted again by Groves, "without whom [Allen] would [have been] powerless to accomplish anything save a census of the flight." It was reported in *Bird-Lore* that, because of light flights and warden presence, the number of gunners was much lower, and the ones who did turn up cooperated with enforcement efforts.[35] Allen counted 10,611 migrating hawks from September 15 through October 29, of which 428, mostly Sharpies, were estimated to have been shot. Allen noted a heavy flight of 4,562 on October 21 on "very strong" northwest winds.[32,36] His season total was apparently summed from daily counts, although some of his buteo numbers were seasonal estimates: 400 Broad-winged Hawks and, somewhat suspiciously, 600 Red-shouldered Hawks. (Identification of immature buteos was problematic at the time.[37] Maurice Broun had trouble differentiating Red-shouldereds from Broad-wingeds during his first year or two at Hawk Mountain. As late as 1908, Stone thought the Broad-winged was resident in New Jersey – clearly some wintering hawks were misidentified.)[38] Allen estimated that most of the gunners (40% being natives and 55% Italians) were shooting for food and 5% were natives shooting for sport.[39]

The October 6 DVOC meeting was a historically notable one, whether or not the members realized it at the time: Allen and Groves spoke about that year's Cape May hawk flights, and the Hawk and Owl Society's Warren Eaton, who would soon figure largely in the Cape May story, spoke about raptor protection in general.[40] Allen, a twentieth-century conservation giant, went on to be appointed director of sanctuaries for the NAAS, and to do pioneering field and conservation work with Roseate Spoonbills, Whooping Cranes, and American Flamingos.[41]

In 1933 and 1934, no NAAS warden was present and there were no organized counts. Groves was present at least some of the time to enforce shooting regulations in 1933; when a protected hawk flew into range, gunners up and down the line would call out, "Wrong kind!" in order to induce the trigger-happy to hold their fire (and avoid a fine).[13] Point resident Charles Page told Stone in September 1933 about a recent hawk shoot: "Biggest flight of hawks last Monday [Sept. 18]. Rube & two others got 200. A taxi driver 80. Many other hunters. It would be illuminating to count the cartridge shells along [Sunset] Boulevard. It would be over 1,000 I think."[42] Jack Gerew, another Point resident, estimated 5,000 migrating hawks on September 10; 10,000 hawks on both September 18 (same date as Page's big flight) and 21; and 3,000 hawks on October 20.[43] (How Gerew made his estimates isn't known; his numbers are presented simply for comparison of relative magnitudes of the flights.) Potter reported heavy flights on northwest winds in September; Merlins were particularly common, with many seen during the September 10 flight.[44]

In 1934, Potter wrote that in early October there were heavy flights on northwest winds. On October 12, gunners told him they shot about 500 hawks, and Potter saw 50 Merlins in one hour on that date.[45] Gerew estimated 5,000 hawks on October 7, and a combined 18,000 for October 12–14.[43]

The artist Conrad Roland remained at Cape May in 1934 after Stone returned to Philadelphia on September 4. He later filled Stone in on the hawk flights and other things, and his comments on the gunners are enlightening. On September 12 he found "[h]awks in movement. Adult Bald Eagle, [Merlin] & Cooper's, etc." He told Potter he counted about 200 dead hawks that day, the most he'd ever seen. He put one wounded hawk out of its misery while the gunner who shot it "cautioned me tenderly – 'Watch out – they have sharp claws – it will get you.' Evidently he was not strictly pitiless, but simply not brave enough to kill it!...My mere presence & peculiar (as it seems to them) careful examination of the birds [he often kept them to use as models for his artwork] put the whole camp in uneasiness and acts, I do believe, to deter them from shooting everything that flies – for they think I must be a spy of some kind."[46] On the 17th, with northwest winds, he noted, "The hawks are increasing in numbers ([kestrels] abundant). The contemptible sportsmen are already having their fun, – among them today a shooting parson with a clerical collar

& a full <u>hunting</u> costume like opera bouffe." Roland said he was tempted to say something but didn't. (The comment he had in mind was, "It's a lot easier to bring down the birds than to get suckers to come into your church, isn't it?")[46] Roland saw another flight of several raptor species on the 19th, including "a large flock of Sharpshin and Coopers & other hawks," and two flocks of approximately 100 Broad-winged Hawks.[47]

New Jersey passed a law in 1934 extending protection to the Peregrine Falcon – a raptor that today might be *the* star of the show in autumn. With its regal bearing, electrifying presence, and spectacular and crowd-pleasing aerial athleticism, it has done exponentially more to pump money into the Cape May economy than catering to the shotgun crowd ever would have.[48]

It doesn't appear that Groves or any other law enforcement personnel were present at the Point in 1934. By early November, concerns about the hawk shooting prompted the Hawk and Owl Society (affiliated with the NAAS), the Emergency Conservation Committee (ECC), and NJAS to look into the possibility of leasing land for a sanctuary. New England conservationist Alexander Lincoln Jr. was dispatched to Cape May to examine the situation. He found that the Cape May Sand and Gravel Company (CMSG) owned much of the land at the west end of Sunset Boulevard. Lincoln met with company owner Ralph Stevens, but figuring he'd be rebuffed if the real purpose of his inquiries was known, he was so evasive with Stevens and other locals as to whom he represented or what their interest was that Stevens suspected Lincoln intended to start a nudist colony there. (That was prescient, given the area's later history.)[49-50]

———————— ∾ ————————

It appears that the NAAS alone then moved forward with the sanctuary initiative. Warren Eaton, founder of the Hawk and Owl Society before heading up raptor protection for the NAAS, was the point man who did most of the grunt work in making it a reality. He first contacted Stone about the recently announced sanctuary in November 1934, and quickly zeroed in on the CMSG property, which bordered Sunset Boulevard and where most of the shooting occurred.[51] By the following June, Eaton had negotiated a lease with Stevens to prohibit shooting on the property, but there was a catch: Eaton would have to pitch Audubon's sanctuary plans at a meeting of the Cape May County sportsmen's organization before Stevens would sign the lease. Eaton invited Stone to attend the meeting, or at least write something about the area's rare birds and plants that would benefit from protection, which Eaton could read at the meeting.[52] He made the same request in another letter a week later, just a few days before the meeting.[53] Eaton was working with Robert Allen on the sanctuary details; they both spoke on behalf of the NAAS at the June 21 meeting, at which Richard Pough seems to have been the only Philadelphia/DVOC attendee. When Eaton wrote to Stone a few days later to fill him in on the meeting, he didn't mention having received the twice-requested report from Stone, who presumably hadn't written it. He told Stone they had gotten some support at the meeting, but that "the thing did not go through at all smoothly."[54] Stevens signed the lease shortly thereafter, however, and the Cape May sanctuary was a go.[55]

In late July 1935, new NAAS president John Baker told Stone, "In view of your particular interest in this sanctuary development, and your long and intimate association with Cape May, as well as our appreciation of your great contribution through many years to the cause of bird preservation, we feel that it would be highly appropriate to name this the Witmer Stone Wild Life Sanctuary."[56] Stone immediately concurred, and he was clearly excited about it.[57] He told Alexander Wetmore, "That is one more name sake – there are already two boys [Shope and Hunt], a mouse [*Synaptomys stonei*], violet [*Viola stoneana*], snail [*Neptunea stonei*], grasshopper [*Melanoplus stonei*], fish [*Notropis stonei*], several birds [*Quiscalus quiscala stonei, Lurocalis stonei*, et al.] and some more live stock that I do not recall."[58] Wetmore replied, "My congratulations on the Wild Life Sanctuary. Not every man can have as extensive a personal zoo as you and also a sanctuary in which to house it!"[59] The sanctuary sign, next to which Stone famously posed for a Conrad Roland photograph, used the curious – and easily misinterpreted – "Wild Life" spelling in the sanctuary name (as had Baker and Wetmore), instead of "Wildlife." Stone told Frank Chapman that he was elated about the sanctuary, adding, "The large sign is quite impressive and motorists from all the states in the Union stop to read it. I fancy most of them are disappointed when they discover the nature of the 'Wild Life' & pass on to the Hotel Admiral where their brand is to be found in all its activity!"[60] (The Hotel Admiral was an enormous, lavish building in Cape May that was torn down in 1996 after years of decay.) AOU president J.H. Fleming told Stone, "Nothing I know of could be a greater tribute to you unless a genus of flowers was named for you."[61]

Stone's role in bringing about the sanctuary, and in Cape May conservation matters in general, is probably overrated today. As noted previously, he sometimes pushed a Cape May bird conservation issue in *The Auk*, but was lukewarm at other times when his opinion was solicited by someone in a position to make a difference. McDonald's letter and photo, published in *Bird-Lore*, provided the impetus for Pearson and the NAAS to hire wardens. Clearly, Eaton, Allen, Baker and the NAAS did the legwork to bring the sanctuary about, and Stevens was willing to lease his land to them. Stone brought some attention to the shooting at CMP and was involved to some extent in conservation issues in the area, and the Audubon folks freely drew upon his knowledge and long experience in the area when planning strategy, but to give him a large role in the establishment of the sanctuary or major credit for the end of the hawk and woodcock slaughter unfairly overlooks the efforts of many others who were more involved in the work than he was.[62]

Tragically, Eaton died suddenly in February 1936, at the age of 35, of complications from appendicitis, leaving behind a wife and daughter. Graduated *cum laude* with a history degree from Harvard, he became a businessman, but his love of nature and conservation pulled him inexorably into that field. He made intensive studies of the local avifauna wherever he lived, and had recently founded the New Jersey Ornithological Society, which appears to have died with him.[63]

———————— ∾ ————————

In 1935, a warden was once again present at CMP to keep watch over the hawk flights and the new sanctuary. William Rusling, secretary of the Montclair Bird Club and a member of the Linnaean Society, was a diligent recorder of birds that fall, and Stone used his records extensively in *BSOCM*.[64] Interestingly, of three alleged sightings of rare birds mentioned by Rusling in a December 1935 letter (Kirtland's Warbler, Common Eider, and two Sandhill Crane observations), Stone only included the eider sighting in *BSOCM*, clearly skeptical of the other two.[65] Rusling and Roger Tory Peterson counted 11,774 migrating hawks (1,080 shot), and analyzed the stomach contents of "a few" shot hawks.[31-32] The report of the AOU Committee on Bird Protection for 1935 mentioned the new Stone Sanctuary, and said that an estimated 60,000 hawks passed through on migration, with about 5,000 (mostly Sharpies) killed.[66] One has to wonder how those figures were derived, particularly as both are much higher than official counts at the time.

As the 1936 fall migration season approached, Rusling was again being considered for the warden position. However, Pough, now working for the NAAS, told Stone that, although Rusling's ornithological acumen had been excellent, he "was possibly a little weak on diplomacy," whatever that implies – maybe he didn't use enough finesse in dealing with the shooters.[67] Pough eventually sent Rusling off to study the hawk flights near Cape Charles, Virginia that fall, a more isolated locality where shooters and diplomacy were less of an issue.

Pough hired James Tanner (later of Ivory-billed Woodpecker fame) as the CMP warden for 1936. Tanner boarded with Francis Gerew's family, including son Jack, at their general store, which today is the CMP post office.[43,68] He counted 5,023 migrating hawks, of which he estimated at least 325 were shot. He believed both estimates were low because the gunners were more spread out than in previous years, meaning he had to move around more to keep track of their doings and couldn't make his counts from a favorable location.[69]

Tanner's journal also gives some interesting insights into hawk protection efforts around CMP at the time. In his first letter to Stone in 1934 about the proposed sanctuary, Eaton had broached the idea of getting a state or local law passed outlawing shooting from a highway, with the gunning along Sunset Boulevard in mind. (In 1935, Robert Allen wrote that "the air rights in a perpendicular line around the borders of the Sanctuary" would be protected against gunners legally shooting from Sunset, i.e., they could only shoot hawks in the air space over the highway.)[70] After continued efforts by the NAAS, just such a law was passed before the 1936 fall migration, outlawing firing a gun from or across a public highway.[57,71] Tanner wrote that the law was enforced easily enough, and it had two benefits: it weeded out the "sport" gunner, who preferred to shoot from the road with his buddies, and it probably cut down on the number of accipiters killed because the gunners were more spread out. Because the gunners were no longer massed in a group, however, it also made it more difficult for Tanner to check for protected species. Shooting was taking place east and south of the Stone Sanctuary, as well as along the railroad tracks north of Sunset Boulevard and in the vicinities of both Sea Grove and Alexander avenues. Tanner wrote that there were two main facets to his law enforcement efforts: keeping gunners out of the Stone Sanctuary and off the boulevard, and enforcing regulations concerning protected species. His highest gunner count for a day was on September 25, when 20 of them shot an estimated 84 hawks.[43]

To anyone who walks around the Point today and bemoans all the houses, and longs for the good old days of Stone's time, they should try to imagine the sounds of gunfire coming from Alexander Avenue north through the Higbee's dunes, sometimes north of where the canal is now, east to the Beanery and south to Lighthouse Pond. During heavy flights the firing was so continuous that local stores (including Swain's Hardware, still a fixture in town) ran out of ammunition.[1,50] Stone used to come upon gunners plucking the (nominally) protected Broad-winged Hawks so that the wardens wouldn't be able to identify them.[72] The barbarity of the fusillade that greeted Sharpies flying over the dunes north of Sunset Boulevard was well described by Allen: "A loud report is followed by the thin, high, rapid shrieks that the local gunners ignorantly attribute to a head-wound, and the little bird tumbles to earth, turning swiftly round and round, like a pinwheel. The brush is thick and generous with catbriar, so that many of the hawks brought down are lost. Small boys armed with sticks and a few dogs act as retrievers."[73] The wounded hawks fed upon each other, according to another observer.[13] Mercifully, the hawks aren't being shot these days, although now there are thieving falconers and meddling banders to contend with.

The railroad tracks were posted against gunning in 1937, further curtailing the toll on the hawks.[74] The 1937 warden, Richard Kuerzi, counted 8,377 hawks, including 4,281 Sharpies (475 killed). Tanner was there again for a few weeks early in the fall, banding hawks; Kuerzi took over that duty after Tanner left.

Allen wrote in *Nature Magazine* in 1936 that the sanctuary was 25 acres in extent, but that figure only included the land leased from the sand company.[75-76] Some CMP residents with land adjoining the sand company's tract gave permission to have their property posted against shooting as well, and the total size of the sanctuary changed over the years, sometimes even within a season, depending on how many local landowners were signed up at a particular time. An Audubon press release in 1935 stated that 62 acres had been leased; Allen was expecting it to get to 100–125 acres once he and Rusling got some more landowners signed up.[77] He sent a lease to at least one of them in August 1935, but Baker told Stone in early September that some properties had been posted after verbal agreements, which the landowners then broke, probably due to cold feet.[78-80] Tanner said one landowner, dairy farmer Bob Rutherford, changed his mind in 1936 because he was concerned that posting his land might irritate some of the gunners who were customers on his milk route.[43] Rutherford's son David, however, believes Tanner's story is incorrect. He told me his father posted all 18 acres that he owned, and that both of his parents "felt keenly for animals." In fact, his father once, at his mother's behest, confronted a boy who was shooting at hawks on their posted property, and although the kid huffed that his parents would stop buying Bob's milk, they didn't.[81] But clearly some landowners, in the first few years at least, waffled on the issue of just how they felt about the NAAS and the sanctuary, and the woodcock hunters were angry at losing some of their old shooting grounds.[82]

In an August 1935 letter to Potter, Stone expressed doubts that the lease would be renewed in 1936 (he later learned that the lease renewed automatically and annually for ten years), because sportsmen's groups had been vocal in their opposition to the sanctuary.[79] He wrote, "The woodcock shooting is the thing that caused the trouble." He referred to the townspeople as "a hardboiled lot" for their disinterest in the sanctuary, and described the gunners as "desperate and <u>mean</u>."[80]

The locals quickly grew accustomed to – and even liked – the new sanctuary, and the dust had settled enough by 1939 that a *Philadelphia Evening Bulletin* article about the sanctuary described it as "a 300-acre Federal [*sic*] bird sanctuary."[83] In 1942, Pough reported that it had increased to approximately 700 acres (and roughly 1,000 acres if adjacent federal and borough properties, also with trespassing and/or hunting restrictions, were included). He also noted the about-face Point residents had performed in their attitude toward the sanctuary, noting "the increasing interest in wildlife conservation on the part of local people who live on and near the Point. Within seven years of the establishment of the Sanctuary, the [Audubon] Society has won not only the full sympathy and approval of neighbors, but their active cooperation as well."

The NAAS footed the bill for most of the sanctuary expenses, with help from NJAS's Miller Memorial Bird Sanctuary Fund and income from a $2,000 fund established with the NAAS in 1937 by Gertrude Abbott in memory of her late brother William L. Abbott.[57,84] Stone was friendly with the Abbotts and was instrumental in bringing about that arrangement.[85]

The sanctuary was a beautiful place. Rusling listed several species of frogs, toads, turtles, and snakes, and noted the abundance of fence lizards. He also reported that Bobcats were occasionally shot by Raccoon hunters.[86] Allen wrote, "Typical plants include the prevailing Spanish Oak [i.e., Southern Red Oak], the pond pine, holly, purple lady-slipper and slender lycopodium [i.e., ground pine]."[75] A brief writeup by a sanctuary visitor in 1935 described a "wild beauty, which is still preserved as the Indians must have known it," with "[o]ld gnarled cedars, masses of shining holly and flaming ilex bushes."[87] The Torrey Botanical Club went on an outing to the Sanctuary in August 1936; according to Otway Brown, who led the trip, the sanctuary had "received some notoriety as a good place to find lichens, and which proved to be the home of a southern species of great interest to Mr. [Raymond] Torrey and his friends, *Cladonia leporine.*"[88] Older men of my acquaintance could recall the huge old Spanish Oaks and other trees that used to grow there.

Unfortunately, in 1942 a magnesite plant was built on the north side of Sunset Boulevard, and the plant's toxic emissions killed many of the sanctuary's large trees.[89] Magnesite was an essential ingredient in the manufacture of refractory bricks used to line open-hearth steel furnaces. Naval blockades during World War II made the previously imported magnesite unavailable, and with increased steel production for the war effort, the need for it was critical. The site along Sunset Boulevard was an ideal location for a magnesite plant.[90]

NJAS began administering the sanctuary in 1945, and did so until state legislation in 1959 led to protection for all hawk species; NJAS then let the leases expire.[91] It was touch-and-go with the old sanctuary area for a while, with everything from campgrounds to condos to golf courses proposed. Happily, most of the original core sanctuary ground is now part of the state's Higbee Beach Wildlife Management Area, created in 1978 largely to protect the historically outstanding woodcock hunting grounds there.[92] With all the other state land in the Cape May area, in addition to the Cape May National Wildlife Refuge farther north on the Bayshore, migrating birds can still find food and shelter when northwest winds force them down north of the Delaware Bay.

——————————— ∾ ———————————

The hawks and other birds have been piling up at CMP on northwest winds in autumn for probably thousands of years, way longer than there have been transplanted Europeans around to notice them, shoot them, eat them, photograph them, and count them. Today, of course, the Point is one of the most popular places in the world to watch migrating raptors in autumn, and is particularly famous for its accipiter and falcon flights. On a good flight day, if you want to see a hawk, just look up. The readers of a birding magazine recently voted Cape May their favorite place to watch hawks in North America.[93] Counters are employed by NJAS to monitor the daily flight from September through November, from a large, state-built cedar platform near the lighthouse that can accommodate a crowd of birders.

It's a long way from a mock battle raging and a mere handful of observers watching, not shooting, the hawks. Today's birders, along with the Cape May hospitality industry, should be mindful of Stone and (especially) McDonald, Pearson, Eaton, Stevens, Allen, Baker, Groves, and all the others who helped usher in a new, more progressive, humane, sensible, and exponentially more interesting era, in which migrating hawks at CMP are studied and admired by throngs of well-behaved and free-spending bird lovers, instead of blasted out of the sky and carried home in peach baskets by desperate and mean gunners bent on the slaughter.

Stone saw the ecotourism future with great clarity, and he expressed it in a remarkably prescient note in *BSOCM* at the conclusion of his discussion of the Cape May hawk flights. He wrote that it would be a mistake to allow the destruction of the hawks that passed through the peninsular bottleneck each fall, not only for those interested in wildlife, but also for "the hotel and business interests of the town, which could be vastly enhanced if these hawk flights and other natural attractions of the Cape were advertised as they deserve – to nature-lovers, not to gunners."[94] The work done in the 1930s to post wardens, protect the birds, and end the shooting marks that decade as a critical time in CMP's transformation from a killing ground to the world-renowned birding destination it is today.

☞ CONTEMPLATING COUNTS ☜

Comparisons are sometimes made between modern hawk counts and counts from the 1930s, but comparing modern numbers – gathered by a hawk counter with modern optics, attention fully focused on the sky many hours a day, often with the help of several other similarly focused birders – with 1930s "counts" is an apples-to-oranges situation. Some of the 1930s Cape May Point (CMP) wardens may have been more diligent in counting birds than others – William Rusling, the 1935 counter, seems to have been particularly focused, on hawks and everything else, and Robert P. Allen and Roger T. Peterson wrote about the "neck-breaking and eye-blinding job to obtain an accurate count" when the hawks were crossing at a great height – but the first duty of the wardens was to keep an eye on the gunners, not the hawks.[1]

The 1936 journal and field report of James Tanner are particularly enlightening.[2] He wrote that his count of 5,023 hawks, which was "the poorest since accurate counts of the flights have been kept and the poorest in the memory of many [CMP] residents," was due in part to the dearth of days with northwest winds that fall. He further related that because of the recent passage of the law forbidding shooting from a state or county highway, the gunners, who had formerly shot from the west end of Sunset Boulevard, now took to spreading out through the nearby woods. That resulted in Tanner spending a lot of time walking in the woods trying to locate and monitor dispersed groups of hunters, instead of being able to camp out at one spot with a clear view of the sky to keep an eye on both gunners and migrating hawks, as previous wardens had been able to do. But Tanner's journal entries make it clear that he spent quite a bit of time visiting local residents, politicians, newspaper editors, and game and law enforcement officials; maintaining the Stone Sanctuary and taking visitors on guided walks; taking off for birding trips to Wildwood and other places; and building and testing hawk traps for banding. In fact, Tanner's instructions from the NAAS were to band "as many hawks as possible," not *count* as many hawks as possible. (Fortunately for the hawks, he had difficulty with his traps and didn't catch many.)[3] Although he sometimes turned his attention to the hawk flights, it's clear that a lot of his daily "counts" (and estimates) were hawks he happened to notice while engaged in a host of other activities – a far different scenario from today's fully engaged hawk counter.

Rusling's notes from his 1936 season in the Delmarva Peninsula also reveal different objectives than a modern count. Rusling studied raptor movements there at widely different locations under varying wind conditions, and he conducted at least some of his observations from a tree platform he built for better visibility.[4] What a contrast to today's coastal counts, which for repeatability and comparison purposes are conducted from the same location each year; for which birds are watched just long enough for an identification to be made, then it's on to the next one; and in which the emphasis is on numbers, record high counts, and vagrants...And there was Rusling back in the 1930s, by himself, moving all around the peninsula and focusing on individual birds to determine how flight paths varied with wind direction, climbing trees for a better view, striving to uncover and *understand* the whys and wherefores of the flights, not just run up a count.

The 1930s Audubon wardens weren't present at CMP for the same range of dates each year. Keep in mind, also, that today's counter follows (to varying degrees) an established protocol, so that there is at least an effort being made to conduct the count using the same methods each year, for example counting only hawks moving south across a defined line; how the 1930s wardens counted isn't determinable and doubtless varied from one warden to another. This is why it's also not appropriate to compare counts from the 1930s with contemporary counts at other locations (e.g., Kiptopeke or Hawk Mountain vs. CMP), or between years at the same location.

Another factor complicating comparisons of historic versus modern counts is that the optics available in the 1930s were not of today's quality, and they were using only binoculars; probably few birdwatchers, if any, were employing the comparatively crude spotting scopes of the time. The more limited range of their optics must have limited the number of birds they could detect and identify. Some of the numbers from Stone-era accounts of what were considered big flights indicate that observers at the time canvassed a much smaller sphere of space around them compared to their modern counterparts; the size of that sphere is always going to be proportional to the quality of the optics being used. Additionally, knowledge of diagnostic field marks and behaviors has increased since then, and is available from a greater variety of sources.

15
A Genius for Friendship

Agood summary of Witmer Stone's physical and personality traits were provided by his friend and AMNH ornithologist Robert Cushman Murphy, who remembered Stone as being "of average build, sandy and freckled, and of aquiline countenance. His genial expression fitted a mellow and buoyant temperament. He was reticent, yet fundamentally merry and whimsical, fond of companionship....He understood 'good living' throughout all ranges, from the dinner table to the fine arts, and his knowledge and appreciation of music were highly developed."[1]

Stone wasn't provided with much of a head of hair. Even in photos of him as a young man, it appears thin and doesn't occupy much space atop his head. It looks dark in the old black-and-white photos, but it may have been strawberry blonde: George Spencer Morris called it both "blonde" and "red."[2] Whatever color it was originally, it thinned further and whitened with age. He was somewhat slight of build as well, at least in his youth. The results of a couple of physical education examinations in his college days described the 5'5¾" 130-pound Witmer, with his 34" chest and 27½" waist, as a little underdeveloped; sparring and weight-lifting were recommended to beef him up.[3] Stone appears stockier in photos taken in his later years.

He was spry and active until late in life, as some gleanings from *BSOCM* attest. In the Mourning Dove account he mentioned climbing a tree to a dove nest 12 feet off the ground on a date that was two weeks shy of his 58th birthday. One day at the beach, Stone noticed a bird he didn't immediately recognize "just beyond the surf" flying short distances and landing on the water again, as if unable to sustain itself in flight. (It was an emaciated and dying Audubon's Shearwater.) Stone casually recorded that he "[swam] out to it as near as possible" on a day when the surf was choppy – this was a month before his 60th birthday.[4] In a photo taken at the beach a few weeks after the shearwater incident, Stone shows a bit of a paunch, but the arms and legs still look brawny.[5] By the early 1930s, however, Stone's health was declining due to heart disease, and his studies around Cape May were conducted from a car.[6] Prior to that he had often done his birding by shank's mare, and he recalled that "one thought nothing of covering ten or fifteen miles on a day's tramp."[7] Tell *that* to today's birders motoring around the Point to their favorite hot spots and lounging on the hawkwatch platform! Stone didn't drive, and Ernie Choate, Charles Page, Otway Brown, Bill Shryock, Conrad Roland and others used to chauffer him around Cape May in his later years.[8-9] (Richard Erskine frequently took Stone

If you've ever tried to picture Witmer (*right*) swimming out "as near as possible" to the Audubon's Shearwater, make sure you have him in the swimming attire shown here. Lillie (*center*) and unidentified couple on beach at Cape May, August 29, 1926. ANSP Archives.

on auto trips, and Art Emlen used to drive Stone to the train station for work in Philadelphia.)[10]

Stone was well known for his keen sense of humor. James Rehn, his long-time Academy colleague, said that behind the serious scientist there lay "[t]he merry twinkle of the eye, the clever quips or even the touch of whimsy."[11] Sam Scoville echoed that in a comment to Stone after an AOU dinner in Philadelphia: "I never realized what an amount of delightful humor is concealed under your stratas of science."[12] Cornelius Weygandt wrote, "There is always in [his letters] some flash of humor or an interesting human anecdote. He accompanies a list made for you of the principal men in natural science of our state of Pennsylvania with a story of a drunk in Washington who stole an ocelot from the Zoo there."[13] (Alexander Wetmore told Stone the Ocelot story just as Prohibition was ending; Stone replied with a quip that D.C. must be serving beer stronger than 3.2, and that the drunk was probably looking for a "blind tiger" – i.e., a speakeasy.)[14]

In her foreword to the 1973 Quarterman edition of *PSNJ*, Elizabeth Wood-ford wrote, "I have repeatedly heard stories that Dr. Stone's sense of humor was a sharp one which made dreary parts of long trips easier to endure." She related Choate's story of Stone playing a trick on a fellow botanist by planting a nonnative tree at a location where he knew the botanist would discover it and think he'd found something growing well outside its normal range.[8] Stone played a similar prank during a trip to Little Beach Island, New Jersey with Scoville and some other DVOCers. As told by Scoville, who refers to one of the party simply as "the Collector" (i.e., a collector of birds and eggs), "[Stone] discovered two door knobs, one white and one brown, which he carefully placed in a hollow in the sand and then shouted to the Collector that he had found an unknown nest with two eggs. That enthusiast ploughed his way to him through the deep sand at a tremendous rate, and a few moments later [Stone] was fleeing for his life with said door knobs whizzing after him as he ran."[15] Stone was still at it less than a year before his death. He had been collecting insects for the Academy during his last few summers at Cape May, and he put three grasshopper specimens someone had sent him from Florida in with his Cape May specimens to "get a rise" out of Rehn and fellow Academy entomologist Morgan Hebard.[16]

Rehn recalled working with Stone on Edward D. Cope's long-neglected reptile collection. The alcohol preservatives had deteriorated, and it took painstaking work to remove them; Stone placed five-gallon jars for the disposal of the residue marked "gorum," "gee," and "goo" according to their consistency. When DVOC member Herbert "Curly" Coggins moved to the West Coast, Stone sent him a humorous four-page newssheet updating the doings of members, complete with "want ads, personals and cartoons."[17-18] One might expect a Quaker propriety to Stone's humor (or Spencer Trotter's, for that matter); however, Fletcher Street related, "Many times, when I would call upon Stone, I would detect a twinkle in his eye, and I sensed that I was about to be treated to one of Trotter's tales, and they were not always of the parlor variety."[19] Frederic Kennard, who carried on a jocular correspondence with Stone, once wrote, "As for your ribald joke, my stenographer is a lady, hence I scorn to reply," although Kennard was likely playing up the "ribald" nature of the joke, whatever it was.[20]

Witmer could be a wag when giving public talks as well. One of his greatest hits with the DVOC was his "Progging for Eagles" essay, first read – and rapturously received – at the March 20, 1919 DVOC meeting.[21] (According to the *Dictionary of American Regional English*, the verb "prog" means "to poke or prowl about in search of something," and a "progger" is "one who forages about marshes and beaches.")[22] The essay recounted, in a humorous vein, a March 1919 outing undertaken by Stone, Scoville, and Street, under the direction of George Stuart, to look for eagle nests in the vicinity of Clayton, Delaware (at or near today's Bombay Hook National Wildlife Refuge). Stone must have liked it, for he sent it to John Sage to read.[23] Stone read it again at the annual meeting in January 1931, and the club secretary recorded that "[i]nteresting and amusing anecdotes of those early days were related in typical Stone Style."[24] Witmer included some of the particulars of the trip, sans humor, in his *BSOCM* Bald Eagle account.[25] The "Progging" talk was mentioned in a tribute to Stone at the October 19, 1939 DVOC meeting.[26] A manuscript of the talk in a private collection was quoted in Woodford's *PSNJ* foreword, because she mistakenly thought it referred to a New Jersey Pine Barrens outing.[8]

Stone's sense of humor was not only appreciated but in demand at meetings. A. Brazier Howell cajoled Stone into participating in a humorous slide show at an upcoming American Society of Mammalogists (ASM) meeting featuring photos of members in "unstudied, and preferably unkempt, pose." He asked Stone to "act as master of ceremonies during the showing of this galaxy of beauty, holding forth in the amusing way which you know how to manage better than any member of the Society, apparently. The committee positively will not consider no for an answer."[27] Stone replied, "I felt that I had retired from such activity as you suggest, but as I feel unable to help the Society in any other way, I shall be glad to accept your kind invitation."[28] For the 1935 AOU annual meeting in Toronto, organizers asked Stone to speak at the banquet, after a couple of "serious" talks by T.S. Palmer and Joseph Grinnell. They wanted Stone to reminisce about previous AOU meetings, as a segue into lighter fare: "Your witticisms should, we think, taper off these more or less serious addresses to the less serious or nonsensical part of the program to follow."[29] Sounding witty after Palmer and Grinnell was probably not the tallest order in Stone's public speaking career.

Stone's correspondence is full of references by others to humorous flyers and menus he wrote for upcoming AOU meetings. Such drollery must have been included in Stone's circular for the 1907 Philadelphia AOU meeting, for after receiving it, Cambridge's Charles Batchelder wrote to Stone, "You fellows put the other AOU towns to the blush by your enterprise and cleverness."[30] Stone once jotted down some ornithologically punny menu ideas for the upcoming DVOC annual dinner, including "Venison Steak a la Killdeer," "Bucco and Dodo served in Faunal Zones," and "Whiskey Jack a la Brewer's Blackbird and Thrush (or any bird with Booted Tarsi)."[31]

Weygandt wrote of Stone's poetic side, "He developed a gift of ready-patter verse and delighted the gatherings of his college classmates by rhymed accounts of them and their doings."[13] When Stone distributed copies of his new *PSNJ* to a small gathering at his house, the botanist Francis Pennell, who was present, said there were "apt verses accompanying each, for Stone was a master of such improvisations."[32] I'd love to find a copy of the Stone poem mentioned in a short 1932 note from Charles Burr that began, "Your remarkable poem concerning Prohibition, or at least the drinking habits of men and animals, created such a sensation at the club that most of the members wanted copies."[33] (This may have been the Medical Club of Philadelphia, a UP organization in which Burr was active.) Commenting on the same poem, Edward Mumford, secretary of the UP Graduate School, told Stone, "Your verses, 'Wages of Sin,' have been much admired….You ought to print it, and if it were mine I would send it to the 'New Yorker.'"[34]

Stone was well loved for his kindly and gentlemanly ways. Pennell recalled that Stone's "wealth of experience was at the command of all, and his information always generously and genially given."[32] Weygandt wrote of Stone, "There is no man [who] will take more trouble in your behalf. He has a genius for friendship, and he regards it as part of a duty done cheerfully to help others working in any field that approaches his own."[13] Years later, Weygandt said of Stone, "He was to the end, after years of ill health, the same considerate helper of all and sundry who came to him for information."[35]

Weygandt also noted Stone's "genial and gentle and unselfish nature," and the way Stone never lost his cheerfulness, even through his deafness and health troubles.[36] He said Stone's characteristic facial expression was quizzical, masking his innate kindness.[13] Wharton Huber wrote that Stone's "dominant traits [were] kindliness and helpfulness," and that "[w]ith all the seriousness of his work there was always a lighter side, where a merry twinkle of the eye or a hearty laugh showed the buoyancy of spirit beneath the surface."[18] When DVOC favorite Coggins, long removed to the West Coast for health reasons, became president of the Cooper Ornithological Club, Stone sent Grinnell a dried flower bouquet and a congratulatory document from the DVOC, to be presented to Coggins as a surprise during the meeting at which he assumed office.[37]

Kindly as he was, Stone was not blind to people's faults. One summer while Witmer was at Cape May, Huber had to deal with a notoriously truculent ornithologist visiting the Academy, and he wrote to Stone, "You are very capable in sizing up humans – I agree with you – he is a damned conceited narrow minded egotistical ass….He sure is a colossal ass."[38] Sadly, we'll never know just which of those adjectives were Huber's and which were originally Stone's.

In his *PANSP* Stone memorial, Academy corresponding secretary J. Percy Moore quoted an unnamed "prominent ornithologist" commenting on Stone's demeanor, "I have never heard him open his mouth, either in private conversation or public speech, without saying something significant and worthy of attention."[39] Weygandt quoted an unnamed "Cornell [University] man" as saying of Stone, "I do not understand why everything is not made of him everywhere. He is…one of the few wholly just and true men humanity has produced."[40] Moore also wrote, "Doctor Stone was a pacifist and avoided controversy."[39] Although, admittedly, someone who didn't like Stone would be less inclined to correspond with him, the extent to which Stone's archived incoming correspondence is replete with expressions of geniality, respect, and affection is striking. When AOU treasurer Rudyerd Boulton notified Lillie of Witmer's posthumously-awarded Brewster Medal for *BSOCM*, he told her that Stone "well deserved the title 'the best loved member of the AOU.'"[26]

───────────── ∾ ─────────────

Stone seems to have been particularly close to fellow DVOCers Spencer Trotter, George Spencer Morris, Samuel Rhoads, Art Emlen, Fletcher Street, and Julian Potter; some of his closest AOU friends were William Brewster, Charles Batchelder, A.K. Fisher, Charles Richmond (about whom Stone wrote a warm *Auk* memorial), T.S. Palmer, Frank Chapman, Alexander Wetmore, and Frederic Kennard.[41]

Chapman, Wetmore, and their wives were good friends of the Stones.[42] Chapman and Stone each considered the other their "ornithological twin," because Chapman started at AMNH almost the same day that Stone began at ANSP.[43] Chapman sent Stone a warm note on the 50th anniversary of work at their respective institutions, writing, "Greetings to you on this our professional birthday. There is so much one might say that I will merely wish that we could have been together on this our day. Affectionately, FMC."[44] Chapman also invited the Stones to spend a winter at his Barro Colorado, Panama field station, writing, "[W]e could have a wonderful time together"; Stone declined with health excuses but said, "I appreciate your thoughts of me & nothing could be more enjoyable than to be with you at your 'Casa Mia.'"[45]

The Stones and Wetmores often stayed at each other's homes when in town, and the Wetmores spent time with the Stones at Cape May in the summer. However, Wetmore couldn't find the time to visit Stone during a January 1939 visit to Philadelphia during Stone's final illness – something he must have regretted afterward.[46] He was supposed to visit with Stone in Philadelphia again a short time later, but Stone's hospitalization for an emergency surgery nixed that, and Stone's death occurred shortly thereafter.[47] Wetmore then traveled to Philadelphia on short notice to attend the funeral.[48] He wrote a Stone memorial for the American Philosophical Society's *Proceedings*, and shortly before her own death, Lillie attended the wedding of the Wetmores' daughter, Margaret.[49-50]

Stone was also friendly with Joseph Grinnell, and the extent of the parallels of their lives on opposite coasts is remarkable. Both experienced Quaker-influenced upbringings, and both had long service with a museum and as editor of a major journal (Grinnell directed the Museum of Vertebrate Zoology in Berkeley for 31 years, and edited *The Condor* for 33 years).[51] Both were faculty members at a university, although Grinnell was full-time at the University of California and much more immersed in academia. They are the only two people to have served as president of both the AOU and the ASM, and each was known for their interest in encouraging younger men in their studies.[52]

As a grad student at Stanford, Grinnell heard much about Stone from Henry Fowler, who interrupted the early part of his long ANSP career to take some classes there. Grinnell told Stone in 1900, "It _is_ certainly a long ways between the Pacific & Atlantic coasts, yet I don't see why we cannot become better known to one another through correspondence at least. Our interests are somewhat in common, anyway....If I can be of service to you in any way, don't hesitate to let me know."[53] In 1903 he wrote, "I have come to express opinions to you rather bluntly. But I feel as though I know you almost intimately, and trust you to take my rantings with plenty of salt. Fowler told me so much of you, that I feel as though we had been personally acquainted. I hope we will meet some day."[54] Stone saw Grinnell on his two California trips, and Grinnell visited at the Stones' house at least once on a trip east.[55] They would have seen each other at many AOU meetings. When Witmer was unable to attend the 1931 meeting for health reasons, Grinnell, the current president, told him, "I most deeply regret your inability to be present at the...meetings, especially that of the Council. We (I) will miss your expressions of judgment as well as your most pleasant personal influence – which latter has a lot to do with making a business meeting go along smoothly."[56]

They were always cordial enough, but Grinnell eventually grew frustrated with Stone's lenient policy with _Auk_ content. He was among the ornithologists who participated in a dual celebration of Stone's 20th anniversary as _Auk_ editor and the long-awaited release of the fourth edition of the AOU check-list by writing congratulatory letters that were bound in a book and presented to Stone as a gift. Grinnell listed three things he liked about Stone's editorship: his reviews, the "Current Literature" department, and Stone's well-balanced conservation views. He expanded on each, then ended with "So – _on the above specific scores_, let me express to you my own personal high regard of your editorial services [my emphasis]."[57] It was scant praise, and by making it clear that he was only pleased with the few things noted, Grinnell seems to have been clearly implying that there was much about Stone's handling of _The Auk_ he didn't like. If others harbored any displeasure with Stone's editorship, they kept it under wraps for the occasion, and their letters are in the unreserved congratulatory tone you'd expect, which makes Grinnell's almost grudging regard more noticeable.

They remained friends, even if they didn't see eye-to-eye on everything. In 1931, Grinnell was prostrate from a double-hernia surgery at the same time Stone was flat on his back with severe heart troubles.[58] In 1938, Grinnell was stricken with his final bout of ill health at the same time Stone was with his, and their uncannily parallel lives came to a close when Grinnell suffered a fatal heart attack less than a week after Stone suffered one.[59]

Stone's "genius for friendship" is apparent in some of his written comments. In Norris DeHaven's *Cassinia* memorial, Stone recounted that DeHaven and the other DVOC members had been unknown to each other until DeHaven responded to a notice about the club in a local newspaper. He wrote, "In constituting that bond of union – the means of communication between kindred spirits – lies perhaps the most notable service that the Club has rendered."[60] He once said of the Philadelphia Botanical Club, "The ties which bind together the members of this Club are of a kind that are not easily severed. We know one another not only as participants in the meetings but also as companions in the field – on daily tramps, camping trips or summer vacations – in that intimate association which brings out a man's character better perhaps than it can be brought out in any other way. He who successfully passes this test is a friend indeed."[61] In the *BSOCM* preface Stone wrote again about the bond between kindred spirits:

> As I look back upon the many years that are identified in mind with Cape May I realize that my greatest pleasure has been in the delightful association with men of kindred interests. Whether while watching the shore birds from a skiff on Jarvis Sound with Walker Hand or living in one of those little stilted cabins on the meadows with Frank Dickinson, photographing Wood Ibises under a broiling sun with Fletcher Street or counting Skimmers and Terns on wind-swept Gull Bar with Julian Potter, the personal contact has always meant as much or more than the ornithological association. And there have been those gatherings for dinner at the Court House at the close of the Christmas Census with one party after another coming in half frozen from boats on the sounds and the Bay or from stations out on the end of the jetty or on remote ponds and in dense woodlands, to prepare their combined report.[62]

Another example of Stone's soft spot for his fellow DVOCers is a 1920 letter he received from Bessie Gardner, wife of Aston Gardner, who was certainly one of the lesser lights in the DVOC firmament. Mr. Gardner had been ill for eight months and landed in the hospital. He was unable to get outdoors or go to bird meetings during his illness, and Bessie asked Stone if he or other members could send her husband a "cheery letter."[63] Four days later she wrote to Stone again at her husband's dictation, thanking Stone for his "very interesting letter, it certainly had the effect of cheering me up quite a lot."[64]

"Witmer" is a bit of an unusual name to saddle a boy with, but it happened to two newborns whose parents were clearly taken with the original and hoped their sons would grow up to be like their namesake. Chreswell Hunt, a DVOCer who moved to Chicago, named one of his sons after his old Philly friend, and one of Lillie's nephews in South Carolina went through life as Witmer Stone Shope. It's a further testament to the kind of effect Stone's personality had on people.

Rehn said that Stone had a somewhat retiring disposition due to "deficient hearing, an aftermath of juvenile whooping-cough."[65] The minutes for a UP Class of '87 reunion in 1911 mention that Stone "referred to a prenatal defect in his hearing."[3] Both remarks indicate that Stone's hearing was subpar all his life, and by the time he was 50 it was getting worse. A friend told Stone in 1917, "I did not for a moment realize how deafness has been creeping on you. In fact, if anyone had asked me if you were troubled in this way I should have said no."[66] He was having more trouble with his ears ten years later, and Robert Cushman Murphy's wife Grace had some advice: "Though I know you hate hearing devices, & with good reason, still I must tell you of a new marvel which is simply making life over for me. I am going to see if I can't borrow one to bring to Washington [for the upcoming AOU meeting]....I know that you could hear all the AOU papers when [you get] used to it."[67] By 1930, however, Stone still had not found a satisfactory hearing aid, and because of his increasing deafness he was reluctant to preside over the annual meeting of the ASM, which as the standing president he was expected to do.[68] Stone said of the 1932 AOU annual meeting that "as I hear but little of the proceedings I only attended a few of the sessions."[69] James Tanner, the 1936 NAAS Cape May warden, met Stone in early September and described him as "a trifle short, thin gray hair above a ruddy keen face, large nose, sharp eyes, an interested, searching, but comfortable face. He was quite deaf, so that it was easier for him to do the talking, which he did well."[70] In a *Bird-Lore* photo from the 1935 AOU meeting in Toronto, Stone is seen listening to the sessions with headphones.[71] Deafness in his later years was also noted by Weygandt, who wrote, "He could no longer hear the [towhee's] twittering song, or the pine warbler's drawl, or the gurglings of the martins. Deafness had deprived him of that so great joy of the listening to bird song."[13]

Longtime DVOC member Alan Brady participated in a few 1930s Cape May Christmas Bird Counts as a teenager and recalled that Stone had "twinkling eyes" and looked like the grandfather of Alan's wife Elizabeth.[72] Dale Twining also remembered Stone from Dale's early days in the DVOC in the mid-1930s, and he said that, unlike some of the more aloof old-time members at the time, Stone made efforts to encourage the interest of the younger members of the club.[73] Stone had been doing that since at least the early 1920s. In 1922, 15-year-old Charles Mayer wrote to the "Del. Co. Ornith. Society" that he had an interest in birds and was contacting the club about membership at the suggestion of DVOC member Bill Shryock.[74] The letter ended up on Stone's desk, and he wrote back immediately that, based on Shryock's endorsement, he would nominate Mayer for membership at the March business meeting, and that if Mayer wanted to attend a meeting in the meantime, he could do so as Stone's guest.[75] Mayer joined the DVOC that year and was a member for a few years, by which time he'd probably realized that the kindly gent with no airs and graces who once offered to have him as his guest was one of America's most esteemed, and equally unpretentious, ornithologists.

At a DVOC meeting in 1923, Stone announced that some of the Active members had recently been discussing ways "of gaining the interest of the younger members and of attracting young men to become associates with the club. The younger men…should be encouraged to make reports and present papers even if such communications were brief or if these should appear of an ordinary character."[76] He similarly felt that the "General Notes" section of *The Auk*, in which shorter, nontechnical articles were published (oftentimes just sightings, such as you would see on a listserve today), was a good place for the younger AOU members to get something into print – to "get a start."[77]

Similar characterizations were made by others who knew Stone. Wetmore said, "Dr. Stone was always cheerfully helpful to others, willing always to assist not only his colleagues but also the younger students who might diffidently approach him."[49] Rehn wrote that Stone's "knowledge, wit, and kindliness made him beloved to the beginners and the seasoned 'wheel horses' alike."[11] Art Emlen Jr., the son of one of Stone's best friends, took an interest in entomology when he was just a lad. He still has a handwritten, two-page 1935 letter from Stone who – ever the systematist – outlined the basic orders of insects, which

Stone and his twinkling eyes contrast markedly with the dour expressions of the other DVOC old-timers on a c. 1930 outing. Sam Scoville at far left. DVOC Collection, ANSP Archives.

hardly seems like the appropriate tack for encouraging an eight-year-old's interest in entomology.[78] Roger Tory Peterson remembered Stone's demeanor toward Peterson and two other youths visiting Stone in Cape May: "Smiling benignly beneath his white moustache he seemed to enjoy thoroughly the three boys who plied him with so many questions."[79] Robert Moore, *Cassinia* editor for a time, wrote to Stone in 1931, "You did not realize what an effect you produced on me, when at the age of fourteen I attended the meeting of the DVOC. Your kindly way of speaking to the new members registered a pleasant surprise and put me at ease."[80] James Peters remembered his first AOU meeting in 1908, when Stone – alone among the senior ornithologists – went out of his way to make the young men feel welcome with "a friendly look and a kind word."[81]

A few of the young men who received help (to varying extents) from Stone early in their ornithological/scientific careers included Ludlow Griscom, whose father was Stone's college classmate; Richard Harlow, the college football coach whose heart seemed to be more into birds than pigskins; Smithsonian ornithologist and cowbird expert Herbert Friedmann; Wallace Grange, who worked for the Wisconsin Conservation Department and the U.S. Biological Survey; C. Brooke Worth, the medical man/naturalist extraordinaire; artist Conrad Roland, who used Stone as a reference when applying for teaching positions; John K. Terres, later editor of *Audubon Magazine*; H.A. Surface, a Penn State professor and state economic zoologist; and John T. Emlen Jr., an ornithologist and pioneering ethologist at the College of Agriculture in California (later UC Davis) and the University of Wisconsin at Madison.[82] As a 12-year-old at Germantown Friends School, Emlen cajoled his father into asking the principal to get Witmer Stone to visit and lecture the boys about birds.[83]

Eliot Underdown was a young man who knew Stone particularly well. The son of longtime DVOC treasurer Henry Underdown, he joined the club in 1923 at age 16, and later worked for two years under Stone in the ornithology department at ANSP before moving on to the same department at the Field Museum in Chicago.[84-85] Underdown seems to have been somewhat immature, a bit of a busybody, and someone who had trouble fitting in with the older men in the department, and he pushed Stone's patience on more than one occasion. During negotiations for the purchase of a James Bond bird collection, Stone told Huber to make sure young Underdown kept his nose out of it, citing his lack of discretion and inability to "stay out of things that do not concern him."[86] On a visit to Philadelphia after he'd started his new position in Chicago, Underdown told Academy managing director Charles Cadwalader that his new boss, Field Museum zoology curator Carl Hellmayr, wanted Underdown to look up some birds in the Academy collection. Cadwalader asked Stone, summering in Cape May, how to proceed; Stone firmly nixed it, saying he doubted Hellmayr had made such a request of Underdown and that the latter probably just wanted to see what new bird specimens the Academy had acquired since he left. "Moreover I feel sure when he finds that Haverford [College] boy there [John Emlen Jr.] he will immediately start to tell him all he knows or surmises about the Academy & the staff etc. which may seriously affect the boy's work....[Underdown] is only engaged as an <u>aid</u> to catalogue material, just like the boy we have only he is paid. In other words he has just the same job he had with us & I never thought of asking him to look up material elsewhere for <u>me</u>."[87]

The younger man may have lacked discretion at times, but he and the elder ornithologist had a warm relationship. Underdown used to visit the Stones in the summer at Cape May, and in a letter from him in September 1931, after he'd moved to Chicago, one gets a sense of the gratitude that some of the young men felt toward Stone, and some insights into Stone's personality traits. The 24-year-old Underdown's sudden death from pneumonia five months after he wrote the letter lends it a greater poignancy:

> I have never forgotten <u>most</u> of what you said to me in the two years I was at the Academy, both what was pleasant, and not so pleasant; particularly the latter have I remembered, for you taught me much in the way of what proved to be a rather bitter lesson. I am still in agreeance with you that I am not of a scientific temperament, but I am <u>very</u> sure that I will be able by hard work (and a love of what I'm doing) to attain a measure of usefulness in ornithology....I want you to know all this for you did much (and most) to further my ambitions, and when you had to bawl me out (I use slang for it expresses what I really mean) it was the best thing for me that was ever done, at any time in my life. I hate to think that it made you feel badly, as it obviously did. You had no call to exercise more than employer to employed, but I have always considered that you did show a very friendly, and more, spirit towards me. I have never forgotten, and never will. Your photograph...hangs at the side of my desk, and I often wish as I look at it that I might be [able to] repay you for what you did....Please do not think I have become swell-headed or anything like that. I'm not! And one reason is because of the example I saw in you, of your modesty, and temperance of criticism of the work of others....Anyhow, I want to say it again – I will never forget <u>all</u> you did for me, and have done.[88]

Underdown published some notes in *The Auk* and even had a posthumous publication in *The Ibis*. In his *Auk* death notice Stone made no mention of any lack of a "scientific temperament"; instead, he described Eliot as "a bird student who gave promise of excellent work in the field of technical ornithology."[85] Underdown's last publication was a short note that Stone kindly published as a leading article in *The Auk* in 1933. Today, the same springtime dawn bird chorus serenades the graves of the paternal mentor and his understudy in Laurel Hill Cemetery, where both Stone and Underdown lie buried.[89]

―――――――――― ∽ ――――――――――

Witmer Stone's kindly personality, twinkling eyes, and wit can be glimpsed in a 1937 article from the Philadelphia *Evening Bulletin*, reproduced here in its entirety because it's the best thing I've found for getting an idea of Stone in conversation. He was cajoled into participation in the piece by ANSP's John Fulweiler, who as membership secretary must have handled public relations. The newspaper wanted a story about what could be encountered by the average vacationer during a stroll along a Cape May beach.[90] Its title was "Scientist Takes a Busman's Holiday – With Variations: Bird Specialist, Caught Digging for Sea Life on Sands, Admits He Likes the 'Change'":

Have you ever seen a clam with his foot out or a mole-crab trying to burrow into Dr. Witmer Stone's index finger?

Dr. Stone is vice president of the Academy of Natural Sciences, 19th St. and the Parkway, in charge of vertebrates, and a director at the Zoo.

Caught in an informal moment at Cape May, squatted over a tiny tidal mole-crab which is as big as a coughdrop, Dr. Stone admits he ought to be spanked.

"Feel like I was playing hooky," he says. "Kind of an ornery ornithologist, for here am I, a bird specialist, digging for invertebrates – and liking it."

Suddenly Dr. Stone lunges into the sea and comes up sighing. The water has receded from his tidal lagoon, with no mole-crab in sight.

"Burrows into the sand," he explains, "when the tide goes out."

But his eyes light with sudden joy.

"Look! – a clam with his foot out!"

On the firm sand nearby, a clam has cautiously lifted his upper shell and covertly stuck forth something that looks like a cross between a fin and a teaspoonful of French vanilla ice cream.

"That's his foot, sure enough," says the truant scientist. "He navigates with that when the tide leaves him high and dry on the beach. He's trying to get back to the water."

But Dr. Stone has trapped his mole-crab and shows it happily. The crab immediately tries to dig its way into his captor's first finger. Failing in this, it shoots from the impenetrable digit to the sand and burrows in deep, before Dr. Stone can recover it.

A trip along the beach with Dr. Stone is a revelation. He knows more about crabs, shells, washed-up fish and flotsam and jetsam than Sally Rand knows about fans.

Swooping quickly as a wave withdraws, leaving enough sand to get a foothold on, Dr. Stone scoops up a boat-shell, a whole string of conches, several hunks of cork, a starfish studded with Cape May "diamonds" and a fistful of bladderweed.

"Each of these conch-shells should have a conch in but they've escaped. I remember when they used to line the beach by the thousands and you couldn't go in bathing without having them festooned around your collar bone and big toe. This cork is from fishermen's nets and the bladderweed is a species of sea cabbage which looks like bladders."

The tide recedes again and the scientist, making a quick swoop, comes up with a hermit crab.

"This fellow," he says, "is the original hobo of the shell-fish world. Always on the go. At an early age he takes up residence in the shell of a small dead snail. As he grows larger he moves to a larger shell and so on. He is always outgrowing his breeches."

At Cape May Point, Dr. Stone emerges again as an ornithologist and points proudly to a blue and white sign heralding the "Witmer Stone Wild Life Sanctuary," where birds in the fall halt on their way south to gain wind for the hop across Delaware Bay.

"In September and October," he said, "these thickets are jammed with woodpeckers, kingbirds, hawks, robins and woodcocks till it looks like the subway rush hour. You must come back then."[91]

In an accompanying photo, Stone sits on a log on the beach, holding up a small shark for the amusement and edification of two local boys. It was staged, but Stone was well known to, and well liked by, the Cape May locals, especially the kids.[92] Ida Schroeder, whose family summered at the Cape, asked Stone to autograph a copy of *PSNJ* for their daughter, Beatrice, saying she would "value it all her life. It will be something for her to remember years from now having met the author, who 'knew everything,' for we discovered in our public library your 'American Animals' [Stone probably rathered she hadn't]….Beatrice wrote on cards the names of the shells in Latin and English, which you gave her, and placed each shell beneath the name…and her brother who has a rock collection, after learning of your 'knowing everything' asked if you wrote a book on rocks, too."[93] A 1921 newspaper article reported that some fossilized animal teeth scooped up in a fisherman's net off of New Jersey were brought by the Coast Guard to Stone, summering in Cape May, for identification, so by then he must have already become known as the local natural history expert and the go-to for such matters.[94] In 1927, the Cape May city manager asked Stone to do a radio spot about the area's birds and flowers.[95] A Cape May teacher wrote to Lillie in 1935 that her students were excited about the new Witmer Stone Wildlife Sanctuary and had written letters of thanks to its namesake, which she hoped Lillie would pass along. The students were anxious for a reply, because then they would have "Dr. Stone's 'autograph.'"[96] They all got their chance, for Stone spoke to the combined schools at Cape May about the sanctuary in January 1936.[97] Caroline Moffett, the Wissahickon Bird Club secretary, once sent Stone a scrap of paper for his autograph at the request of a Germantown Friends School student who had been disappointed after showing up at a club meeting for the express purpose of getting it, only to find Stone absent.[98]

Stone was brought up in Quaker surroundings, but doesn't seem to have been religious. Choate recalled that Stone had "no particular church affiliation."[8] A 1930 note to Stone from a Virginia pastor included, "My Assistant Pastor, the young man whom in your recent letter you spoke of hearing at the church in Cape May, was drowned, and I had the sad duty of accompanying his body to Cape May," which suggests that Stone may have at least occasionally attended church in Cape May.[99] About the only reference by Stone to a deity that I've found in his correspondence or writings is a letter thanking James Peters for help with the AOU check-list that starts off with "God bless you!" – not exactly irrefutable proof of strong religious leanings.[100]

Stone's correspondence has occasional references to politics, and he was a staunch Republican. He particularly detested Woodrow Wilson, once telling a friend who lived in the nation's capital, "I hear you are having a Shakespearean revival in Washington & that the most popular plays are 'The Merry Wives of Wilson' and "McAdoo About Nothing.'"[101] (Wilson was widowed, then remarried, all while in office; McAdoo was Wilson's secretary of the treasury.) Chreswell Hunt's "I suppose you are glad about the Republican landslide, seems most everyone is" in a 1920 missive to Stone could refer to either the presidential election (Warren Harding) or the Philadelphia mayoral one (J. Hampton Moore).[102] And Witmer's quip in a 1936 letter must have been making the rounds then (as it still does): "Christopher Columbus was the first democrat. When he started he had no idea where he was going, when he got there he did not know where he was & when he got back he did not know where he had been & he traveled entirely on other people's money!"[103]

Stone's sociopolitical views could turn up in unexpected places, for example in his *Auk* review of an Althea Sherman article in which she lambasted breeding House Wrens for destroying the eggs and nests of other birds in their vicinity. Stone asserted that the problem was caused by people putting up so many bird boxes that wren numbers had increased artificially, and as a result the wrens' peculiar and unneighborly habit was further magnified. He continued, "In exactly the same way thoughtless and unrestrained charity increases the bad habits of beggars and prevents them from reforming."[104] Spoken like a true Republican, then as now.

Political leanings didn't lessen Witmer's justifiable disgust at Philadelphia Republican mayor W. Freeland Kendrick's handling of the Sesquicentennial in 1926, evidenced in his January statement that Kendrick was intent on rushing through his plans for a hastily-contrived major exposition instead of the originally planned simple historical celebration.[105] Stone was also no boxing fan. The day after the Sesquicentennial's sporting highlight of the Dempsey–Tunney fight, he grumbled to Wetmore, "Did you by any chance ever hear of one Jack Dempsey? We have had ⁹⁄₁₀ of all the nuts, bums & 'plug uglies' of the U.S. here yesterday! A wonderful celebration of the founding of the nation!"[106]

It's difficult to know what other interests Stone may have had outside of his scientific endeavors, but a few odds and ends that have turned up in his correspondence are, despite the trivial nature of some, presented here in order to paint a fuller picture of him. He attended plays by the UP Mask and Wig theater group, which is still active today.[107] He and Lillie bought a phonograph in 1914, and they were delighted with a radio he gave her for Christmas in 1927.[108] He began a rejection of a crossword puzzle submitted to *The Auk* [!] with, "While I take pleasure in working out cross word puzzles and regard them as good mental exercise…"[109]

Witmer also liked to garden. He had a garden in his small Hazel Avenue yard, with fern and wildflower beds, where he grew *Jeffersonia* (Twinleaf), *Trillium sessile* (Toadshade), *Mertensia* (bluebells), *Erythronium albidum* (White Fawnlily/White Trout Lily), *Cubelium* (probably Eastern Greenviolet), *Muscari* (probably grape hyacinths), *Crocus*, and *Galanthus* (snowdrops).[110] He had a garden on Church Lane as well, with the same flowers, and also roses, tulips, daffodils, *Scilla*, and a rock garden planted with *Plox subulata* (Moss Phlox).[111] He and Lillie visited nearby woodlots to bring flowers back for their yard, and similarly transplanted ferns from Cape May.[112] He took the gardening pleasures with the pains, once having to stay home from work for a day nursing a face swollen by poison ivy after he pulled weeds in the garden.[113] By 1932 his health prevented him the pleasure of working in his backyard garden, and he had to hire someone to maintain it for him.[69,114]

☞ ASTONISHING ☜

Stone used the word "astonished" to an amusing extent in *BSOCM* and elsewhere. He seems to have found much to astonish him in life, and was apparently easily and often astonished. He was astonished to find Wood Storks, Louisiana Herons, and Marbled Godwits at Cape May, and was similarly astonished when 20 previously undetected Little Blue Herons suddenly flushed right in front of him from the cover of tall grass.[1] He was astonished by the proliferation of bird check-lists, the volume of bobwhite calls, the ephemeral nature of vulture flocks, and at Edward Forbush's credulousness in publishing questionable bird sightings.[2] Stone wasn't the only one being astonished: Walker Hand was astonished to find Great Crested Flycatchers occupying a nestbox in his yard, campers at Cape May Point were astonished when a young Black-crowned Night Heron strolled through their site, and Stone predicted that *Auk* readers would be astonished by the opinions expressed in a *Science* review of a Joseph Grinnell publication.[3] Even Fish Crows were astonished when they found a normally empty gunner's shack on the Jarvis Sound meadows occupied by Stone and his companions.[4]

16

Travels

U nlike scientists who do fieldwork at exotic locations and attend international conferences in far-flung corners of the globe, Witmer Stone was much more the stay-at-home, museum-bound, administrator and editor type. Outside of attendance at three AOU annual meetings in Canada late in his life, Stone's two early Academy trips to Bermuda and Mexico were the only times he left the country. He did a great deal of local travel and fieldwork, including his summers at Stock Grange and Paradise early in his life, and at Cape May in later life. He took several, if infrequent, trips around the United States and saw a fair portion of the country in his lifetime.

In the late 1890s, Stone began spending time each summer near Lopez, Sullivan County, in northeastern Pennsylvania. He traveled there in the summers of 1898–1901, then at least four times between 1903 and 1918. He was friendly with the Behr brothers, Otto and Herman, who had a lumbering business in the area, and Stone collected birds and plants there.[1] The Behrs were avid naturalists, sending Stone all sorts of natural history specimens, including enormous tree sections from their lumbering operations; Otto participated in the DVOC spring migration study. Stone published "Summer birds of the higher parts of Sullivan and Wyoming Counties, Pa." in *Cassinia* in 1900, in which he recorded – as modern birders sigh wistfully to read – that the Olive-sided Flycatcher was common in some areas, "its penetrating call heard continually."[2] He gave talks to the DVOC and the Philadelphia Botanical Club about his finds in the region.[3]

His visits seem to have decreased in frequency over the years and to have petered out before 1920. In 1935, Stone received a letter from Otto Huch, a relative of the Behrs, asking for a friend if the Academy had any work available. He told Stone, "Though I have not seen you for a number of years, you may remember me as the little chap who used to carry a shot gun around for you, all day, some time back in the wilds of Shady Nook and Sullivan County."[4] In 1936, Stone's lifelong friend Francis Cope Jr., living by then in northeastern Pennsylvania, asked Stone, "Why don't you and Mrs. Stone come to see us some time especially in the beautiful month of May? I know that you cannot tramp the hills as you used to do but we could easily jump in my car and without exertion show you many lovely places including our old North Mountain country."[5] It doesn't appear, however, that Stone took Cope up on his offer to see the area one last time.

Herman Behr was engaged to do some lumbering work at Pine Mountain, Harlan County, in eastern Kentucky in spring 1921, and Stone jumped at Behr's invitation to see a part of the country he had long wanted to visit.[6] They stayed with William R. Creech, son of the founder of the Pine Mountain Settlement School, which is still extant.[7] The trip was a real baptism into the Appalachia lifestyle. Stone told a friend he had "lived in a mountaineer's home with no light but what came from the fire place & little food but salt pork, cornbread, & sorghum syrup & coffee. It is still a place one does not wish to enter without adequate introduction. Your business must be <u>clearly</u> known!...I got a fine series of land Mollusca nearly 50 species, a good series of spring plants & a good bird list."[8] Creech may have been the "Kentucky mountaineer friend" Stone referred to in his talk at the 50th anniversary of the Nuttall Ornithological Club. Stone defended the need for occasional bird collecting, and he quoted the mountaineer as saying, "This is a perfectly law-abiding country: no man ever gets killed here unless he needs killing," to which Stone drily added, "and some birds will always need killing."[9] Stone published an article about his trip in *The Auk*, and gave a talk to the DVOC about his experiences in the "moonshine district" of Kentucky.[10] Behr's lumber work was also Stone's ticket to two short trips to the mountains of western Maryland in 1907 and 1910, where he studied the birds and collected plants, insects, and reptiles.[11] Stone's *Bartonia* memorial by Pennell also mentioned trips to the Catskill Mountains in New York, but that probably refers to trips taken with his family when Witmer was a young man.[12]

Stone first visited Duluth, Minnesota in 1906, and told a friend, "[S]o you see I have at last gotten beyond the boundaries of my native state!!"[13] He and Lillie visited Duluth in late July 1912 and spent most of August along the western end of Lake Superior.[14] They crossed into Wisconsin and had an adventurous canoe trip on the Brule River, where their guide "upset [the] canoe in the rapids, but no serious results – not even a cold!"[15] They probably stayed, at least while in Duluth, with Witmer's UP classmate William Salter, who lived there and attended a UP alumni function with Stone in Duluth that summer.[16,17] Stone spent most of his time on that trip fishing and loafing.[15] The Stones visited Duluth on a return trip from California in 1915, and Duluth and northern Wisconsin for two weeks in 1926.[18]

The 1915 California trip was Witmer's first to the West Coast, and Lillie accompanied him. The AOU annual meeting was held in San Francisco that year – the first time it had ever been held away from the New York–Cambridge–Philadelphia–Washington corridor (away from its "type locality," as Stone facetiously wrote in *The Auk*).[19] The World's Fair, named the Panama Pacific International Exposition for that particular year, was held in San Francisco at the time of the AOU meeting, and a group photograph of the meeting attendees shows the Stones seated front and center, with the Palace of

Horticulture (one of the temporary buildings constructed for the fair) in the background.[20] Stone gave two talks at the meeting, although one was mostly drowned out by a German band playing just outside the auditorium.[21] A group of East Coast AOU members traveled by train to the meeting, with stops at the Grand Canyon, Las Vegas, and Los Angeles. After the meeting the Stones camped in Yosemite for a week; saw the redwoods at the Lagunitas home of C. Hart Merriam; called on friends including transplanted DVOCer Herbert "Curly" Coggins; visited Seattle, Portland, Vancouver, and the Canadian Rockies; and made stops in Minnesota and North Dakota (where Witmer gave a lecture at the state university). Witmer birded to his heart's content, and also made some entomological collections.[21-22] Robert Young, Witmer's University of North Dakota friend who used to sell bird skins to ANSP, wrote to him in July, "I hope that you and Mrs. Stone arrived home safely and without losing any more nights' rests contesting the ground with other occupants. I certainly regret your unpleasant experience."[23] Apparently the train ride wasn't as enjoyable as it might have been.

Lillie had a married sister living in Manning, South Carolina (mother of Witmer Stone Shope), and the Stones took several trips there over the years.[24] They first visited in the spring of 1914, when Witmer did a lot of birding along the Pocotaligo River (tributary of the Black River) and brought back a variety of material for ANSP's collections.[25] They returned to the state in May 1917, and visited Charleston, Columbia, and Rock Hill. Witmer gave lectures to the Charleston Natural History Society, the University of South Carolina, and an audience at a hastily arranged talk in a Manning movie theater. He also published a series of articles on "local birds and their economic value" in the Manning *Times* newspaper.[26-27] He collected for the Academy on that trip as well and, using the reasoning that he was representing the NAAS with his lectures, persuaded NAAS secretary T. Gilbert Pearson into paying $100 for his railroad and incidental expenses.[28] Stone wrote a brief trip report for *Bird-Lore*.[26] Witmer and Lillie visited Charleston and Manning in April 1923 for the annual meeting of the American Association of Museums, being held in conjunction with the 150th anniversary celebration of the Charleston Museum, and Witmer's visits to South Carolina led to his recommending that the AOU hold its annual meeting there in 1928.[29] The Stones attended their last AOU meeting together when it was held again at Charleston in 1937, and they took an excursion to Manning.[30]

There was no Cape May summer in 1919, as the Stones instead took a lengthy, adventurous, but enjoyable trip to Arizona. On their way to Arizona they stopped at New Orleans and made a side trip from there to the Gulf Coast "bird reservations" with a captain recommended by Pearson.[31] According to *PANSP*, "Dr. Stone was granted leave of absence for three months, May 15 to August 15, and visited the Chiricahua Mountains, southern Arizona, the expenses being largely born by the [Academy's] Redfield botanical fund. He obtained a large collection of plants from a region not heretofore represented in the Academy's herbarium."[32] Stone brought back 202 birds, six sets of eggs, 75 reptiles and amphibians, "several" fishes, 4,000 insects, 25 trays of shells, and 1,002 sheets of plants.[33] The Stones were in Arizona May 19 to August 1, and stayed as guests at the Pinery Canyon camp of J. Eugene Law of California, who was business manager of *The Condor*.[34-35] Alexander Wetmore visited the first week of June.[36] Stone summed up some of the birding highlights: "I made the acquaintance of the Red-faced, Grace's, Virginia's and Lucy's Warblers; Painted Redstart, Sulphur-Bellied Flycatcher, Rivoli Hummingbird and hosts of others....A wonderful time altogether!"[37]

The trip wasn't wholly pleasurable, however. Stone told Wetmore about some of the travel hazards: "We had a great time getting over to the S.P. [?] on Aug. 1st. Instead of taking us 3 hrs. it took two days. Our car got stuck in the mud & water time & again & we had to wade in & dig them out. Cowboys & ponies dragged us out once & finally we spent the night out." Stone said he was worried about the ordeal's effects on Law's health, but was thankful his own health had "always been good."[38] Stone sent a letter to an ailing William Brewster, describing the plants, birds and scenery while camped out in the Chiricahuas, but Brewster died before the letter arrived.[9] The area the Stones and their friends explored is part of the Coronado National Forest in southeastern Arizona.

The Stones then did some additional traveling, including a trip to California, where they stopped in San Francisco to visit the California Academy of Sciences museum, and visited Merriam and his wife again.[39] The Northern Division of the Cooper Ornithological Club held a special meeting August 13 to welcome the Stones. Witmer had a brief reunion with Coggins and his wife, which was probably the last time they saw each other.[40] Coggins had moved to California for health reasons in 1907 and became active in the Cooper Club, serving a turn as president.[41] He had married the architect and artist Leola Hall in 1912.[42] He and Witmer had done much fieldwork together in Coggins's East Coast days, and they remained frequent correspondents. Stone's amusing description of Coggins in the *DVOC 1890-1910* souvenir included that he "had the gift of looking at a thing from all sides and he generally took his final stand on the comical side and the worst of it was, things that others looked upon as serious looked comical to him and it was often hard to prove that he was wrong. No amount of rain could dim the sunshine if he was one of a field party."[43]

Witmer developed a carbuncle on his knee on the return trip and ended up in a hospital in Pittsburgh to have it lanced, after which he recovered in bed there for a week.[44] But he and Lillie basked in the afterglow of their Arizona vacation for some time. It was difficult to unwind from it; the sudden transition "from continued out-door life to excessive confinement" was almost too sudden for Witmer to take.[45] He told Wetmore in late October that Lillie was wishing she was back in Pinery Canyon; she had two sotol stalks tied together "which reach to the dining room ceiling," and a stock of pinyon nuts still on hand. He said the plants he collected were being mounted, "after which I hope to tackle <u>portions</u> of it anyway [i.e., identifying them]. [ANSP malacologist Henry] Pilsbry has the mollusks worked up & [ANSP entomologist] Rehn is hard at work on the Orthoptera."[46] Stone gave talks about "one of the finest summers [he] ever had" to the AOU, the DVOC, the Art Club of Philadelphia, the Philadelphia Botanical Club, ANSP, the Audubon Club of Norristown, a UP Class of '87 reunion, and probably anyone else who would agree to listen.[17,35,38,46-47]

An interesting letter from Law in 1921 indicates that Stone had taken Law up on an (open?) invitation to visit again, but Law reneged, saying he wanted to keep his Arizona outings to himself for the time being, "with no distractions."[48] Stone told Wetmore in 1924 that he had just looked at some Arizona pictures and longed to be back there, but sadly he never again visited the area he and Lillie had so enjoyed.[49]

Notes survive that were probably used by Stone for his Arizona talks, and they nicely describe some of the scenery, birds, lizards, and mammals from the trip. In one passage he describes the mammal activity that took place under cover of darkness while the party slept:

> When there are no prairie dog towns mammal life is absent during the day – but what a different condition must prevail at night. We camped out on several occasions on the yucca-covered flats, and as the sun disappeared over the purple mountains to the west in a blaze of red and yellow, and the shadows of the near ranges to the south seemed to gradually creep out over the desert, we set our [mammal] traps about the mesquite bushes, near attractive-looking burrows and about the base of the yucca trunks until it became too dark to see what we were about, although overhead the sky seemed still bright. As we lay in our blankets and the cool night wind blew across the flats we watched the stars coming out, myriads and myriads of them, more it seemed to me than I had ever seen before, and then while still pondering upon the immensity of the universe we slept and then before we realized it, the gray of dawn was spreading over the desert, the stars fading away & the first streaks of light shooting up over the mountain barriers on the east. It seemed but a moment before that we had lain there gazing at the last traces of receding light in the west. But what revels had been going on about us in the interval. Our traps held a stray assortment of night mammals of the desert [– including kangaroo rats, grasshopper mice, and pocket mice].[50]

A pair of binoculars in the Academy archives purportedly belonged to Stone. They were sold to the Academy by Roy Burket of Altoona, Pennsylvania. At the time of her death, Lillie was survived by four sisters, including one in Altoona, and a niece named Thelma Burket, presumably a relative of Roy Burket.[51] In his 1962 letter offering to sell the binoculars to ANSP, Burket wrote that he was told they were given to Witmer "while on a speaking tour in California."[52] Assuming that is correct, his side trip to California after his 1919 collecting trip to Arizona, and the special meeting of the Northern Division of the Cooper Ornithological Club, seems like a possible occasion for the gift, although in a letter written upon his return home, Stone thanked Joseph Grinnell for calling the special Cooper Club meeting but said nothing about a gift of binoculars.[53] I've looked through the binoculars in the ANSP library, and they are still in alignment and produce a sharp image.

In 1935, the Stones spent two weeks at the home of Tabasco tycoon Edward McIlhenny at Avery Island, Louisiana.[54] They took another trip to the deep south in January 1930, traveling by car with DVOCer Richard Erskine and his wife to Florida, Witmer's only visit to that state.[55] The trip was a pleasure/birding jaunt, and Witmer did no collecting. Several DVOC members made visits to Cobb's Island in coastal Virginia, and Stone went on at least one trip there, in 1916.[56] And the Stones traveled to and from the 1932 AOU meeting in Quebec by car (driver unknown), passing through Maine and the White Mountains of New Hampshire on the return trip.[57]

It's difficult to gauge just how strong was Stone's inclination to travel, but for someone with limited funds who never owned an automobile, he managed to visit many regions of the United States. He didn't just make a passing acquaintance with them, as a tourist might, but got to know them intimately through his collecting and exploring.

17

His Heart Was Good to Him

Stone suffered through a variety of ailments and bouts of ill health throughout his life, ranging from abscesses to ear and stomach problems, and he had frequent bouts with "the grippe" (flu).[1] He occasionally dealt with boils, and during a flare-up of one of them W.L. McAtee happened to send him a clipping from a religious magazine that mentioned Stone in one of the articles. Stone replied that he was surprised McAtee read such journals, and "that I should be held up as a shining example by one of them!! I have been suffering the last two weeks from a boil that prevented my sitting down in the way the Creator intended I should. Had the editor of that paper been within hearing of me I doubt I should have been quoted on any subject!!!"[2]

By early 1907, Stone was experiencing problems with his eyes.[3] (Fellow nomenclatural-priority fiend Charles Richmond ribbed him that it was from looking so hard for "old names.")[4] The troubles worsened two years later, and by his 43rd birthday Stone was using reading glasses.[5]

In 1918 he told A.K. Fisher, "I realize that I have lost a whole lot of push & initiative in the last two or three years & none of us are as good for active positions after we pass 50 as we were before."[6] Stone's health problems appear to have increased in the early 1920s. It may be that more correspondence survives starting at that time, making it easier to find more references to his health, but advancing years and the weight of Academy and AOU duties doubtless took a toll. Stone had a very stressful period in November 1921, when in a short span his mother died, Lillie suffered a breakdown in response, there were *Auk* troubles, and a railroad strike loomed over the AOU annual meeting being held in Philadelphia – all after he'd sold his home and was moving around among different locations. Mentions of flu and a severe cold in early 1922 sound commonplace enough, but in a June letter he described something like a nervous breakdown earlier in the year, not just a cold or flu: "As to myself I hope the worst is over. I thought up to last Fall that I could get away with anything I tackled – I have now abandoned that idea. I went completely to pieces this spring after a nerve racking winter & landed in bed & in the doctors' grip."[7] This is one of a couple of references over the next several months to a "breakdown."[8] In September he responded to a query with, "I must fortify my memory, which since my illness last spring, is hazy about what went before."[9] In early 1923 he told a friend, "I am sorry to say I am a good deal worried over my general condition, I hope unnecessarily so, as I have had a pretty bad nervous upset during the past year as you know & am apt to be overexcited."[10] In early 1924 Stone complained he had "been feeling rotten without being able to ascertain any definite cause. The doctors say too much responsibility and worry and trying to do too much which has resulted in a nervous reaction."[11] Another distinct possibility is that continual exposure to arsenic from handling study skins was causing the nervous reactions and breakdowns – a common health problem at the time among Stone's fellow ornithologists.[12]

In 1929, Stone started on a steady, gradual decline in his health. He told Frank Chapman in May, "Since I was in N[ew] Y[ork] I had another attack of oppression about the heart which has troubled me at intervals. At the doctor's suggestion I had my teeth x-rayed & found widespread infection which he thinks is the cause of all my trouble – I hope so! as yesterday I had ten removed 'at one sitting' & am now an Edentate so far as the upper jaw is concerned. I am feeling a bit upset from the ordeal & am home for a few days."[13] Chapman replied, "You certainly are most philosophical and I envy you the temperament which enables you to see anything humorous in your edentatic condition."[14] Stone *was* remarkably blithesome about his ordeal, telling Joseph Grinnell, "I have been ill again from the toxic condition that has been knocking me out from time to time....I have had all my upper teeth removed in an effort to get at the source of infection. I have heard of people being 'on their uppers' [i.e., impoverished] – I am at present on my 'lowers'!"[15]

Stone's physician was clearly enamored with the "focal infection theory," which was hatched in northern Europe before taking hold in American medical circles in the early 1900s. Proponents believed that the microorganisms responsible for a host of bodily ills were harbored in the teeth and tonsils, and there was a craze of tonsillectomies and teeth removals at the time in misguided attempts at cures for a variety of symptoms.[16-17] The unnecessary procedure brought Stone no relief and was doubtless a perfectly ineffectual treatment for what ailed him.

He went to Cape May for the summer, but was largely inactive and felt wiped out. He described his symptoms in early June: "I am condemned to several weeks in bed. The numbness in my chest & arms continues & is now apparent in my legs. The doctors say absolute rest is the only thing & in a month they expect to see improvement due to the teeth extraction & consequent stoppage of the source of infection."[18] He told Chapman in December, "There is something wrong with the nerves or nerve centers in my back which apparently causes the severe pains in my chest muscles & arms whenever I walk even a couple of blocks & I am under observation by a surgeon."[19] But that was a misdiagnosis: the problem wasn't nerve centers in the back, it was full-blown atherosclerosis, and it would only get worse.

Stone's health deteriorated decidedly further in 1931. Early in the year he had the flu, then suffered what he termed a "heart attack" on May 21.[20,21] If stress can contribute to heart problems, Stone had his share leading up to his attack. Just a perusal of his correspondence with T.S. Palmer at the time turns up workplace aggravations such as unpleasant dealings with managing director Charles Cadwalader and an unexpected increase in responsibility for running the Ludwick lecture series; *Auk* finance headaches and endless check-list grind, courtesy of the AOU; preparations for the annual American Society of Mammalogists' meeting, held in Philadelphia that year; writing and production of the annual report of the Philadelphia Zoological Society, for which Stone served on the board of trustees and which had just had all its funding from the city cut, forcing it to fall back on a meager emergency fund; and not least, a string of funerals ("which always depress me") for some old friends and a cousin. In February, with everything rushing in on him at once, he exclaimed, "I don't know when I have been in such a jam as now!"[22]

He didn't take any break from the stress after the "heart attack." Two days later he was writing Palmer about the check-list, saying he feared the doctors might keep him at home "one or two days a week."[21] In June he was flat on his back in bed but, amazingly – and probably unwisely and stubbornly – working on the check-list and getting out the July *Auk*.[23] He began taking digitalis, and rested extensively during his usual sabbatical at Cape May.[24] In July he reported:

> My "knockout" came so suddenly that I really did not think about anything [else] for several weeks....I am perfectly all right sitting here in the house reading or writing with cool breezes from the ocean coming in at the window but I cannot walk much or do anything strenuous without feeling the trouble. It is hardening of the arteries & anything that speeds up heart action causes severe aches in the arms, chest, etc. & general oppression. I have had this for a year or more but failure to heed its warning brought on a severe attack last May. I know now what I am up against and shall be more careful in future.[25]

So in 1931, the doctors realized the true cause of his troubles was arteriosclerosis, and not the focal infection or "problem with his nerve centers" they were pitching in 1929. When Stone returned home from Cape May in September he only went back to the Academy every other day, and stayed on that schedule until January.[26]

The heart condition worsened over the years. By early 1933, Stone had the symptoms of a classic case of angina pectoris: "I cannot maintain steady walking for more than a couple of blocks – no matter how slowly I go....The trouble consists in pains in the arms and chest and a choking sensation in the throat, all of which disappears in a few minutes if I stop and rest."[17,27] A few months later he told a friend, "These hardening arteries are no joke & I suppose the daily struggle to get in town continues to make matters worse. I am all right when I <u>get</u> somewhere but the getting there is the strain. I have no car & could

ASM members attending annual meeting pose with the chimpanzee "Josephine" at the Philadelphia Zoo, May 15, 1931. *Left to right:* Harold Anthony (AMNH), Witmer Stone, T.S. Palmer, Josephine, Marcus W. Lyon Jr., zoo director C. Emerson Brown. The photo was taken six days before Stone's 1931 heart attack. ANSP Archives.

not drive one if I had, or that would solve the problem. As it is I have figured out a street car–subway route which requires only two blocks of walking at each end but <u>one</u> is usually my limit without pain."[28] The increased reliance on public transportation put a strain on his tight budget, but Germantown neighbors with cars helped him out quite a bit – in particular Art Emlen, who dropped Stone off at the trolley in Germantown every morning while taking the Emlen children to school.[27,29,30]

He had boils and pleurisy to add to his woes in 1934, and had some bouts with gallbladder troubles and jaundice starting about that time – an indication that he may have suffered from gallstones.[17,31] In 1935 he predicted, "I am afraid this [heart] disease is getting worse and will eventually get me."[30] In 1936, his doctors prescribed nitroglycerin tablets for relief of the severe pains brought on by the exertion of walking, and Stone commented, "I don't know how much a fellow can take before he blows up! but I do not have an occasion for more than one tablet a day & often not that."[32] Nitroglycerin's symptom-relief benefits for someone with Stone's condition had been known for some time, and it's puzzling that his physicians didn't have him taking it much sooner.[17] Many days he was so tired after coming home from the Academy that he headed directly to bed.[33]

Stone was often sick in late winter, particularly toward the end of his life. An annual pattern developed that saw Stone run down from another winter of bad health; the summer at Cape May would then pick him back up again. In those pre-antibiotics days, winter in particular, with its concomitant illnesses, could be a real minefield to navigate. James Peters once wrote to Stone on the first day of spring, "It has been my experience that if you can survive February you most always live through the rest of the year."[34] Stone noted wryly in early 1936, "This autumn also brings me to the 70th milestone of my life....Next year (1937) our college class holds its 50th reunion...and the following year (1938) I shall have been at the Academy 50 years. So I don't want to be shot until these celebrations are completed."[35]

Once Stone retired as *Auk* editor, he suddenly found himself outside the hub of AOU activity, after decades of being very much at the center of it all. He told McAtee in 1935 that he would attend the upcoming AOU meeting, but that it would be his last except for ones close to home: "I am now in my seventieth year & it is time for me to pull in my horns!"[36] One AOU Fellow remonstrated with him in 1935 after Stone referred to himself as an AOU "has-been."[37] Stone told Fisher in 1937 that it was too bad Fisher, ten years his senior, wouldn't be at the upcoming AOU meeting, because Stone was "getting into the category of the 'oldest one present'!"[38] His correspondence had shrunk almost to nothing after his *Auk* retirement, and he felt he'd lost all his friends along with the job.[39] One reader had already kindly told him, in response to a letter from Stone, "You are far from being out of the thoughts of those who like to claim friendship, although they do not bother you with stuff for the Auk. I appreciate you writing."[40]

Stone was worn out again in the spring of 1938 after another trying winter. His resignation to the effects of the passing years was apparent in such comments to friends as, "Neither Mrs. Stone nor I have been in very good shape this winter. Too much 'anno domini' I guess," and, "I guess we [he & Lillie] both need new 'engines' which are hard to get at our age."[41-42] He summered at Cape May again, but upon returning home in early September his doctor ordered him to bed for a week. A urinary complication had developed over the summer, which at first did not seem serious.[43] But his health quickly deteriorated, and soon he was unable to go to work. His heart condition caused his legs to swell, and he also had a bout with bronchitis.[44] Stone's health was so poor that he wasn't scheduled for any Ludwick lectures for the first time in a donkey's age.

Stone was unable to attend the annual DVOC dinner in January 1939, and members were asked to write to him during his illness.[45] After he missed his UP Class of '87 annual winter reunion, his classmates sent a thoughtful note to their long-serving secretary, saying, "You are the Corner Stone on which the structure of the Class has rested – lo! these many years. Come back to us soon or the whole fabric may collapse."[46] He was confined to the house, but enjoyed a Hermit Thrush and a couple of White-throated Sparrows that had taken cover from the snow under a hedge in his yard.[47] By then, the bladder problem had gotten more serious. In mid-February his doctors told him he had an enlarged prostate, and a few days later he was in Germantown Hospital for surgery to relieve the resultant obstruction of his urinary system.[48-49] Because of his heart condition, his doctors didn't want to remove his prostate, and they used only a local anesthetic for the operation.[50] He returned home, greatly weakened, in mid-March and began to mend.[51]

The situation was stressful for Lillie, and like anyone else going through that kind of pain and discomfort might do, Witmer had bouts of depression, and grew philosophical about suffering.[48,50,52] The DVOC men came by one day for a visit, which must have cheered him quite a bit; he told a friend, "[W]e could almost have held a meeting!"[50] He was eventually diagnosed with prostate cancer, and by early May he was back in the hospital, telling Fisher, "I am still in the hospital but hope to be out soon....I have gone through all stages of prostate operations."[53-54]

At the April 20 DVOC meeting, Art Emlen read a paper about William Bartram as a zoologist, written by Stone, who was of course too ill to attend.[55] It was the last time the club would enjoy a contribution from their old leader. Stone returned home from the hospital May 23, and at 10 a.m. the next morning, his heart gave out.[53] It had taken about all it could stand; the procedures dealing with the prostate problems, including at least one surgery, had pushed it past the breaking point. Stone's physician, Dr. William Hughes, was reported to have said that "his heart was good to him" – that is, spared him further pains, because his condition was bleak.[56]

Wharton Huber – not ANSP president Charles Cadwalader – went to the Stone residence to offer the Academy's condolences to Lillie.[53,57] The funeral service was held in the meeting room of the Germantown Monthly Meeting of Friends on Coulter Street in Philadelphia on Saturday, May 27. DVOC member Ed Weyl later recalled that Emlen and Cornelius Weygandt "successfully sought to have the service take place in the Meeting House rather than in the environment of a funeral home or other site inappropriate for Witmer and his mourners."[58] George M. Sutton wrote to Huber, "News of Doctor Stone's death grieves all of us here [at Cornell] deeply. What a grand old man he was!"[59]

As Stone's surviving spouse, Lillie inherited his estate; interestingly, Witmer's will stipulated that if she had preceded him, half the estate would have gone to ANSP to fund ornithological publications and half to the AOU to finance *The Auk*.[60] George W. Pepper, Witmer's college classmate and friend,

Stone at ANSP, showing the wear of the years, c. 1938. ANSP Archives.

was a successful lawyer and a former U.S. senator. In a compassionate gesture reflecting their friendship, in early 1940 Pepper pitched a plan to Cadwalader that would provide for Lillie's financial needs for the rest of her life. He estimated that Lillie would need $1,000 per year for living expenses over and above her small investment income, and proposed that UP Class of '87 and ANSP each chip in $500 per year. Lillie would arrange her will so that half her estate would go to each as a repayment; in the event the value of her estate was more than the institutions had paid out during her lifetime, they would take only what they had expended and the rest would go to heirs.[61]

An *inter vivos* trust was drawn up, with Emlen acting as trustee, and by mid-June all the parties seemed to be close to a mutual agreement on the matter.[62] Curiously, the Class of '87 was to take the money it received after Lillie's death, equal to what it had paid out while she was alive, and use some or all of the amount (the deed of trust is not explicit) to build a memorial to Witmer in the UP library; the Academy would simply recoup what it paid out with no other obligations.[63] The bottom line appears to have been that the longer Lillie lived, the more ANSP and the UP class would stand to lose, because if she lived long enough that the total they paid out exceeded her assets at death, they would be out of that money. In a sense, they were gambling that she wouldn't live, say, another 20 years.[64]

Lillie attended the wedding of the Wetmores' daughter, Margaret, in mid-June.[65] Alexander sent her a Stone memorial he had written for the American Philosophical Society, and she thanked him for "the excellent tribute paid to my dear Witmer."[66] She had little time left herself, and passed away in Germantown Hospital on August 3, at age 68, only outliving her "dear Witmer" by 14 months.[67] She'd had her share of health woes, and in the last few years of her life she was beset by shingles and high blood pressure.[42,68] According to a newspaper report at the time, she died "from illness aggravated by her grief over her husband's death."[69] That sounds like the work of a melodramatic newspaper writer, although Emlen's daughter Marie once told me that Lillie "died of a broken heart."[70] It was clearly broken in the medical sense: Lillie's death certificate records serious heart problems as the cause of her demise.[71] The trust arrangement to provide for Lillie financially through the rest of her days, the brainchild of a thoughtful and caring George Pepper to take care of the widow of his old college friend, was now a non-issue.

Lillie had been looking to sell Witmer's correspondence, and had some interested potential private buyers.[72] Fortunately, the papers were not sold, and after Lillie's death Cadwalader bought them, anonymously and magnanimously, from the Germantown Trust Company, executors of Lillie's estate, for $125.[73] They are housed in the Academy's archives.

———————— ∽ ————————

Laurel Hill Cemetery is one of the nation's oldest garden cemeteries, and one of its most historic. Hundreds of famous industrialists and financiers, politicians, Revolutionary and Civil War heroes, and other historically important individuals are interred there, many with mausoleums and obelisks designed by some of Philadelphia's most celebrated architects. If you wander over to Section P you'll find the Stone family burial plot, purchased by Frederick Sr. in 1890, where he, Anne, Frederick Jr., and Witmer and Lillie lie under four granite slabs at a pretty little spot overlooking the Schuylkill River.[74] Many of Witmer's relatives – some close, some not-so-close – from the Stone/Steele family tree are buried at Laurel Hill.[75] John Cassin, who preceded Stone at ANSP and put the institution on the ornithological map, and Eliot Underdown, who worked under Stone and died too young after moving on to the Chicago Field Museum, are also buried at Laurel Hill – three generations of Academy ornithologists in one cemetery.

Laurel Hill is a lovely place to visit any time of the year. Pack a picnic some pleasant late-winter or early-spring day, when the bare twigs of the trees between the cemetery and the river are silvery and awash in the sunlight sparkling off the water below. You can sit down at (or on – he won't mind) Witmer's grave. You might say hello, and tell him how may times you've looked up a plant in *PSNJ*, or seen a bird at Cape May and stuck your nose into *BSOCM* to get his say-so on it. You could mention all the times you've almost felt him standing in the spirit at your elbow as you've looked out over the Pond Creek Meadows from the Bayshore dunes by Davis Lake on a fall day with the hawks and falcons shooting past. And maybe as you sit there you'll see the shade of Witmer arise before you, and you'll recognize him instantly: a short, stocky fellow with a bemused smile and twinkling eyes that belie a dry, mischievous sense of humor concealed under the stratas of science; reticent, yet fundamentally merry and whimsical, with a quizzical expression on his interested, searching, but comfortable face, masking his innate kindness; a warm, pacifistic, benign, Quaker-bred gent, and a fading reminder of the good old stock that once made a nation great.

In 1928, Casey Wood, a renowned ophthalmologist and an enthusiastic and active amateur ornithologist, queried Stone about his possible interest in continuing Elliot Coues's old bibliography of North American birds. Stone responded that, in addition to health woes, he was too tied up with ANSP, *Auk*, and AOU check-list work to have any time to spare.[76] Wood advised him to take it easy, telling him – in a sentiment that echoes down through the years, for anyone who's ever been inspired to find a *Polygala*, or been transported back to Old Cape May, or found themselves in the shadow of a kindred spirit who has gone before – "There is only one Witmer Stone!"[77]

It Isn't All Stuck in the Past

P eople may have the impression that the Cape May area was a paradise in Stone's time, but he saw the ruination of much habitat by the time he wrote *BSOCM*. World War I brought a frenzied burst of activity to the town as the navy moved in, building new training facilities in the area of today's Coast Guard base. Walker Hand sensed a permanent change, telling Stone, "I fear that the old quiet days and places are to pass out."[1]

The *Bird-Banding* review of *BSOCM* observed, "A sad note runs through much of the book; the wholesale ditching and draining operations have destroyed the homes of countless birds."[2] Stone *was* a strong critic in *BSOCM* of the draining, ditching, and oiling work of the mosquito commission. During a public lecture in Cape May in 1922, Stone made remarks critical of the mosquito work and draining; only later did he learn that the man who introduced him at the beginning of the talk was the secretary of the mosquito commission![3] By 1937, his beloved Race Track Pond (present again today, but scarcely noticeable through the phragmites, at Bayshore Road and 2nd Avenue) and West Cape May ponds, with their breeding bitterns and rails, were long gone.[4] Price's Pond was drying up as a result of mosquito commission work – "the same fate that has overtaken practically every body of fresh water in the county."[5] The Pond Creek and New England meadows had been salt hay habitat, but by 1937 they were "stretches of dead brush and a waste of weeds."[6] The oil, applied to wetlands to kill mosquito larvae, was more than unsightly: Julian Potter complained to Stone, "They are using so much crude oil along coastal ditches etc. that a fellow can't smell a sea breeze anymore."[7] Oil wasn't the only thing assaulting the nostrils: the Lighthouse Pond was pumped with sewage and had a public dump on its border, complete with a junked Ford.[8] Stone considered the tidewater creeks in the Cape May area to be "little better than open sewers."[9] Conservation and habitat battles have been waged since then, with victories and losses, but thanks to the heroic efforts of individuals and organizations, many of Stone's Cape May birding areas have been preserved and in many cases cleaned up, and would be more or less recognizable to him, if often in altered form. The area has seen less development and more land preservation than most New Jersey shore towns.

So if we could bring Witmer Stone back for a visit to his beloved Cape May, what would he think as we took him around to his once-familiar locales? As he walked from 909 Queen up to the Physick estate, he'd know many of the old houses that were already standing when he started summering there. The lighthouse, Pond Creek Meadows, Higbee's Beach, Hidden Valley Ranch, the Cape Island Creek Meadows – Stone would (eventually, if not sooner) recognize them all. Some places, however, although still intact, have had their immediate surroundings greatly altered. Lake Lily is at about the same size and shape (sans the covering of water lilies, killed by saltwater encroachment during floods), but is completely surrounded now by houses, not the pine woods from Stone's day – it has lost much of its "wildness."[10] The property is maintained as the public park it has essentially become, with the southern half bordered by lawns and benches, and introduced Mute Swans – ecological disasters – are the conspicuous feature of the pond's bird life. Witmer must have laid eyes on the Wesley Hughes house on Sunset Boulevard a few thousand times, but the water treatment plant, cell tower, and other development surrounding it would make it look as if it had been picked up and plopped down in a different location altogether.

He would be heartbroken by many of the changes to the area. The tip of the peninsula was bisected by a canal during World War II, so that the Bayshore Road now ends suddenly just a short stroll from Otway Brown's old property. The lots around Cape May Point sold for $50 each after the war, and they could have been bought up and protected, but that chance came and went. The once sparsely settled southern end of the Point is now blanketed with houses; increasingly, the undeveloped lots and small cottages surrounded by trees and tangles have been replaced with modern monstrosities that take up the whole lot, leaving no room for vegetation and with limited attraction for birds. The town of Cape May, having failed through fires and economic downturns to establish itself as America's premiere oceanside resort, was in the midst of a long slump in Stone's day; it was "an isolated, provincial seaside village" at that time, according to one recent author.[11] Cape May experienced a renaissance beginning in the 1970s; the Victorian homes have been restored, and the town looks lovely, but Stone would sense less of a small-town feel and more that of a trendy, pricey, touristy resort that tries to recreate for vacationers some of the features and ways of life that actually existed in his day. North Cape May and the Villas would be a jolt – his old Price's Pond and southern Bayshore stomping grounds, obliterated. He'd have a tough time recognizing anything in the Wildwoods area.

However, I think he would be equally astonished, but pleased, with other changes. Swarms of birders in the vicinity of the hawkwatch platform and Higbee's Beach on an autumn weekend today might be considered unpleasant even by some birders, but Stone would no doubt recall the gunners lined up along Sunset Boulevard blazing away at everything flying, and sense a change for the better. In fact, he might recognize the realization of a 1936 *Auk* note pitching what we would now call ecotourism: with clairvoyance and business acumen that could have earned him a position with the county's tourism department, Stone wrote, "Similarly, the establishment of [the Stone] sanctuary at Cape May has brought a large number of autumn and winter visitors to the Cape to see the Hawk flights and the abundant winter bird life [at a time when the Cape was a one-season resort]. If this is encouraged it will become a very important factor in increasing the number of visitors to the resort and the return to local hotels and business will far exceed any return from the Hawk shooting there which has caused such wide condemnation."[12] Men hide out in the Higbee's dunes today, waiting for the hawks, as of old – but with digital cameras, not guns.

He would be delighted with the intense coverage the area receives – from the many resident birders, and with the annual migration counts – and with the vast increase in our knowledge of molt, migration, and identification techniques. Hand him a pair of modern binoculars, and like any other birdwatcher from his time, Stone would be impressed with the clarity and crispness of the image; let him look out to the "ripps" through a modern spotting scope and you'd better have the smelling salts on hand. (About the closest thing to a "spotting scope" in Stone's day was to hold two pairs of binoculars in tandem.)[13]

Because many Pine Barrens and Cape May areas familiar to Stone have been preserved, it's possible to get a sense of what he experienced. John E. Pearce wrote in the introduction to his book on the Jersey Pine Barrens, "This is the story of those who have gone before us in this land. I may walk this way but once, but I do not walk it alone."[14] Just as a new spotting scope or pair of binoculars can breathe some new life into your outdoor rambles, as can a new field guide, or a new mentor, or the discovery of a fascinating natural area you hadn't known about before, so too can a newly gained knowledge of the rich ornithological and botanical history (including the ornithologists and botanists) of these beautiful, magical places that have captivated so many naturalists for so long. You don't necessarily have to memorize old DVOC membership lists from 1901 or be able to quote *BSOCM*, chapter and verse, to recognize when you are seeing some of what Stone did at Old Cape May – to find yourself in Witmer's shadow. But the greater your familiarity with the experiences of your naturalist forebears, the more readily you'll be able to recognize that, even today, you can still get little glimpses into their world and experience the things they experienced and wrote about, and that it isn't all stuck in the past, in an old book with grainy photographs.

You can still stand in the "wind-swept vegetation on the Bay-side dunes" at Davis Lake, still "covered with a growth of scrub pine, holly and beach plums with various smaller shrubs and plants," and watch the migrating accipiters zipping by at eye level, so close you could almost reach out and grab them as they "dash through the bayberry bushes and dune thickets…moving silently and at lightning speed and weaving their way through the tangled branches."[15] If the conditions are right, on autumn mornings you can thrill to a stream of warblers, vireos, orioles, flickers, and kingbirds pouring northwards hastily, almost frantically, through the Higbee's treelines, just like "the immense concourse of birds which [Stone] observed on Aug. 26th [1891]."[16] A beach stroll around the Point is sure to turn up some flocks of Sanderlings, those "wild, hardy birds of the sea!"[17] You can still look expectantly out over the ocean with a feeling that "there must always be a chance of sighting something unusual, so great is the waste of waters, with apparently no barriers to hinder visitors from remote seas."[18] And the goldencrest blooms every summer in "truly one of nature's flower gardens" that still "stretches for miles" along the Wading River in the heart of the Pine Barrens.[19] A familiarity with the experiences of those who have gone before in the same places makes for a far more interesting experience today, and fosters an added appreciation for those places, and for the efforts of those who have fought to protect them.

So why should anybody care about what some dead ornithologist saw at Cape May 100 years ago, or what plants he and his fellow botanists used to see in the Pine Barrens? Cape May Point is a birding mecca today, but most of the birders are more interested in today's rarities than yesterday's naturalists. I understand that historians are born, not made, and that some people (I've met a few of them) can go to Cape May for decades and never give a toss about those who came before, the wildlife and plants they found, or what the place looked like then. But for me, knowledge of an area's natural heritage is inseparable from – actually a prerequisite for – any convictions I have about conserving it.

Before Europeans arrived and started devastating the environment, the area later christened the Garden State was truly in a Garden of Eden state. One historian wrote of the conditions c. 1675, "[W]e have nothing to show… that the country from Salem to the sea-shore was other than one primeval and unbroken forest."[20] A string of barrier islands formed the easternmost outposts of land, and immense, *Usnea*-draped forests with impenetrably thick understories rose up behind magnificent dunes. The numbers of nesting birds on the islands during the breeding season cannot be imagined today. In the 1880s, one collector had an extraordinary experience climbing to an Osprey nest on Seven Mile Beach: "'Lookout nest,' the most magnificent eyrie of the entire colony, was built on the top of a mammoth pine exactly ninety feet from the ground, on a piece of higher land than the surrounding meadows and beach, and I was well repaid for a bruising and tiresome climb by a peerless set of four fresh eggs of the brightest red hue, as well as the commanding view of ocean and woodland for miles around."[21] Few other people in history, if any, could claim to have enjoyed such a magnificent and unique view of the pristine New Jersey coastal islands before they were ruined by development.

By Stone's time, the forests were rapidly being replaced by resort towns. In *BSOCM*, he summarized the changes since European settlement, and presented the state of things in the 1920s and 1930s.

Knowledge of a landscape's historical conditions is necessary to serve as a baseline for comparison with what remains, and to recognize which original (or nearly so) landscapes and habitats are imperiled and in need of the greatest conservation efforts and resources. A conservation ethic begins with an innate appreciation for areas and faunas as unsullied by humanity as possible. One has to have the inborn conviction that areas that retain their original, wild, "natural" characteristics are fascinating, to be treasured, and worthy of battles for their protection, and that areas altered by humans are blighted to some extent. And those of us with a conservation bent are so out there with our extreme ideology that we actually think it would be a noble and sensible thing to hang onto what remains of that natural heritage, so that those who come after us can experience it, instead of just reading about it or seeing it in old pictures.

So if some future reader is inspired by Stone's "delightful word pictures" to visit some of his old haunts, hopefully those places won't have been paved and built over (and in New Jersey, the pressure from developers and utilities to do just that never stops). Hopefully they'll be able to stand on the dunes at Cape May Point in late September and watch the peregrines arrowing past at eye level and heading out over the Bay just above the waves, hell-bent for Delaware, or stand in a seaside meadow and listen to the woodcocks' manic twittering in a chilly March twilight. And if some future Mary Brown is charmed and enthused after perusing *PSNJ*, let's trust that she'll be able to go to a unique and interesting place like Bennett's Bog and find her own *Polygala*. How incredible is it that one can – in New Jersey, of all places – walk around Cape May Point or the Pine Barrens today and still get a strong sense of what Stone, Hand, Potter, van Pelt et al. experienced 100 years ago?

Back in the early 1980s, a 20-ish kid thumbed through *Bird Studies at Old Cape May* in a store on the Ocean City boardwalk and decided to fork over $9 for the set, and believe him when he tells you that his subsequent Cape May rambles have been incalculably enriched by what he found between its covers. If this book stirs a similar reaction in its readers, or inspires a closer kinship with those who have gone before, the author's greatest ambitions for the book will have been realized.

APPENDIX 1
Cast of Characters

The following are brief biographical sketches of people whose names appear frequently in the book. Information was gathered mostly from obituaries in *The Auk* and other scientific journals, as well as the *Biographical Dictionary of American and Canadian Naturalists and Environmentalists* (ed. Keir B. Sterling et al. 1997, Westport: Greenwood Press).

Allen, Joel A. ("J.A.") (1838–1921). Worked at MCZ (1871–1875) and AMNH (1885–1921), with a variety of taxa but principally mammals and birds. AOU founder and president (1883–1891); editor of the *Bulletin of the Nuttall Ornithological Club* (1876–1883), then *The Auk* (1883–1911), in addition to all AMNH zoological publications for 32 years. An active conservationist involved with both the original (1886) Audubon Society and the later NAAS. Expert taxonomist; key member of the AOU Classification Committee for over 30 years and edited three AOU check-lists. Among other outstanding contributions, his 1876 book *The American Bisons, Living and Extinct* was an early and important work.

Batchelder, Charles F. (1856–1954). AOU president 1905–1908, and its last remaining founder at his death. Also very active in the Nuttall Ornithological Club, which met at his home for years. Although affiliated in associate capacities with MCZ late in life, he was essentially an amateur naturalist who published little in the way of original research.

Chapman, Frank M. (1864–1945). Worked in AMNH ornithology department 1887–1942. Founder and first editor of *Bird-Lore* magazine, 1899–1934; the magazine promoted conservation issues, including the fight against the use of birds in the millinery trade. AOU president 1911–1914; also active in the Linnaean Society of New York and the NAAS. Author of several books, including an influential field guide (1895). Particular expertise with Central and South American birds.

Dwight, Jonathan (1858–1929). Medical doctor and AOU founder; treasurer 1903–1920; president 1923–1926. His huge private collection of birds was housed at AMNH during his lifetime and passed to the museum at his death. A leading authority on molt.

Fisher, Albert K. ("A.K.") (1856–1948). U.S. Biological Survey employee for 46 years, and headed its predator-control arm for many years. AOU founder and president 1914–1917.

Fleming, James H. (1872–1940). Independently wealthy Canadian amateur ornithologist who amassed a large private collection of birds of the world. AOU president 1932–1935. Corresponded frequently with Stone, particularly during Fleming's AOU presidency; Stone seems to have been one of the older members Fleming relied on for advice.

Fowler, Henry Weed (1878–1965). Began working at ANSP in 1894 and, other than a two-year absence while at Stanford, stayed until his death in 1965. World-renowned ichthyologist who reportedly "ate, drank, and slept fishes." Compiled an amazingly extensive publication record, using his own illustrations in many articles. Was a founder of the American Society of Ichthyologists and Herpetologists and remained active in it, including a term as president.

Grinnell, Joseph (1877–1939). Director of Museum of Vertebrate Zoology 1908–1939; editor of *The Condor* 1906–1939. AOU president 1929–1931; ASM president 1937–1938. Professor at UC Berkeley 1913–1939; many graduate students from his lab went on to become leaders in their natural science fields. Intensively collected and studied western (especially California) vertebrates, with particular interest in their biogeographic distribution.

Huber, Wharton (1877–1942). Began working at ANSP with Stone in the ornithology department in 1920; curator of mammals from 1923 until his death. Active and expert collector and preparator of various taxa. Had a long friendship with Stone and wrote a Stone memorial in the *Journal of Mammalogy*.

McAtee, Waldo Lee ("W.L.") (1883–1962). U.S. Biological Survey/U.S. Fish and Wildlife Service employee for 45 years, and their leading economic ornithologist. Also an entomological curator at the Smithsonian. AOU treasurer 1920–1938.

Murphy, Robert Cushman (1887–1973). Long career in the ornithology department at AMNH (1921–1973). Renowned expert on pelagic birds and early opponent of the use of DDT.

Oberholser, Harry C. (1870–1963). Worked for the U.S. Biological Survey 1895–1941; after retirement, he was curator of ornithology at the Cleveland Museum of Natural History for six years. A talented and enthusiastic avian taxonomist. He was involved in local Audubon societies, the Survey's waterfowl surveys, and academia. Two of his books include *The Bird Life of Louisiana*, and his epic *The Bird Life of Texas*, completed and published posthumously.

Palmer, Theodore S. ("T.S.") (1868–1955). Career U.S. Biological Survey employee (1890–1933). AOU Secretary 1917–1937. An active and highly effective conservationist; vice president of NAAS 1905–1936. Notorious for his obsession with biographies of dead AOU members (which is actually a boon to modern researchers) and for pulling AOU wires to push his own agenda. Although he sometimes complained about Palmer in his personal correspondence, Stone remained good friends with him.

Peters, James L. (1889–1952). Worked in MCZ ornithology department 1921–1952 (as head curator the last 20 years). An outstanding systematist, he published the first seven volumes of his monumental *Check-list of the Birds of the World*; the work was continued by other ornithologists after his death and completed in 1987. Vice president (1938–1941) and president (1942–1945) of the AOU. Also active in the Nuttall Ornithological Club; president the last ten years of his life. Editor of *Bird-Banding* (today's *Journal of Field Ornithology*) 1939–1950.

Rehn, James A.G. (1881–1965). Long tenure at ANSP, beginning in 1900 as a Jessup student and lasting until his death. Academy secretary (1920–1938) and corresponding secretary (1938–1959). World-renowned entomologist, with a particular expertise with Orthoptera. Active in the American Entomological Society; served in a variety of administrative positions over several decades. Had a long friendship with Stone, and wrote two outstanding (and similar) memorials of Stone that appeared in *Cassinia* and *The Auk*.

Richmond, Charles W. (1868–1932). Close friendship with Stone started early in their careers and lasted until Richmond's death. Worked in the USDA's Division of Economic Ornithology and Mammalogy (precursor to the U.S. Biological Survey) 1889–1892, then had a long career at the Smithsonian (1893–1932). An expert in ornithological nomenclature, he created an enormous card catalog of bird names that was published 60 years after his death.

Wetmore, Alexander (1886–1978). Worked for the U.S. Biological Survey 1910–1924, then spent the rest of his life at the Smithsonian. Had particular expertise with fossil birds. AOU president 1926–1929. The Wetmores were close friends of the Stones.

Additionally, some DVOC members who appear throughout the book include William Baily, George Spencer Morris, Julian Potter, Samuel Rhoads, Sam Scoville, Fletcher Street, and Spencer Trotter.

APPENDIX 2

Development of
Bird Studies at Old Cape May

BSOCM's development can be traced to some extent, mostly in *Cassinia* reports of DVOC meetings. The names (or descriptions) and dates of Stone's talks (to the DVOC unless otherwise noted) and Cape May articles, as well as other *BSOCM*-related material, follow:

• Just back from Cape May, where he'd spent July and August 1891, at the 9/1/1891 meeting Stone exhibited some of the bird skins he'd collected there. He read his seminal "The Summer Birds of Cape May, NJ" at the 11/3/1891 meeting.[1]

• "Winter birds of Cape May, New Jersey" in the April 1892 *Auk*. Stone had discussed the trip to Cape May, and probably read this paper, at the 2/2/1892 meeting.[2]

• "Mr. Stone described a trip to Cape May, NJ," May 24–27, 1892 at the 6/7/1892 meeting.[2-3]

• Described a recent trip to Cape May at the 1/3/1893 meeting.[2]

• Read "Birds of the Atlantic City Marshes" at the 2/21/1893 meeting. "Besides delivering in a lively manner the present aspects of bird-life on the New Jersey coasts as observed by members of this Club, the paper was prefaced by an interesting resume of the visits of former naturalists to that region and the great changes in its avifauna since the time of Wilson and Audubon."[4] Remarkably early shades of *BSOCM*.

• *The Birds of Eastern Pennsylvania and New Jersey* published in 1894; *The Birds of New Jersey* published in 1909.[2]

• "Cape May and Its Birds" at the 12/21/1916 meeting.[5] (Note the 23-year gap in time between last Cape May entry and this.)

• Walker Hand to Stone, 2/16/1917: "I will not be able to get up and hear that paper on 'migration at Cape May Point.'"[6] I haven't found where the talk was given, but if Hand's date and topic are correct, it's interesting that Stone was giving talks on the Point migration this soon after he began summering there.

• "Cape May, New Jersey, and its Bird Life" to the AOU annual meeting, 11/13/1917.[7]

• "Additional Observations on Cape May Birds" at the 3/7/1918 meeting.[8]

- "An Intensive Study of Bird Life at Cape May, New Jersey, During the Summer of 1920" at the 10/21/1920 meeting.[9]

- "Field Ornithology as a Study of Animal Behavior – Based on Observations at Cape May, New Jersey in the Summer of 1920" to UP Zoological Laboratory weekly seminar, early 1921.[10]

- "'Additional Notes on Cape May Birds,' reading some biographies [i.e., species accounts] that he had prepared on the Osprey, Spotted Sandpiper, Kingbird, etc., dealing with details of their life histories" at the 2/3/1921 meeting.[11-12] This was presumably similar to a talk of the same title which Stone gave at the AOU annual meeting on 11/9/1920.[13] This is the first reference I've found to the species accounts that would later make up the bulk of *BSOCM*.

- "Cape May Bird Life" on 10/20/1921, in which he "described his experiences with the birds of Cape May, New Jersey, during the past summer; June 30–September 16, 138 species being recorded."[11,14]

- "A Third Season's Study of the Birds of Cape May," at the 10/5/1922 meeting, in which Stone "compar[ed] the species observed between July 3 and October 1 with those of the same period in other years, and describe[d] a trip of several days to Jarvis Sound where the spring migration of shorebirds was studied."[15] Stone's picturesque notes from a May 1921 Jarvis Sound trip were quoted at length in the "Birds of the Salt Meadows" chapter in *BSOCM*.

- "Hawk flights at Cape May Point, N.J." in the October 1922 *Auk*, which included information about the species composition and mechanics of the flights.[16]

- "Wood Ibises and Other Birds at Cape May 1923" at the 11/1/1923 meeting.[17]

- In the 1958 *Cassinia* the DVOC published a "recently-discovered" Stone paper titled "The Mockingbird," which they said dated to "about 1924."[18] Portions of the paper were later used in Stone's mockingbird account in *BSOCM*.

- John Sage to T.S. Palmer, 9/23/1924: Sage wrote that he was glad to hear the Palmers would be vacationing at Cape May, and added, "Stone will be able to prepare an interesting article on the birds of that region. He once told me that he has many records of the rarer species found there."[19]

- "Some Cape May Bird Biographies" at the 1924 AOU annual meeting; Stone "read extracts from his charming biographies of birds observed at Cape May, NJ, including pen pictures of the actions of shorebirds on their feeding grounds and the habits of the Laughing Gull."[20]

• "Past and present bird life of the southern New Jersey coast" in ANSP's 1925 *Year Book*.[21] *BSOCM*'s "The Changing Bird Life of the Cape" chapter had much overlap with the *Year Book* article, and was in fact simply an updated and expanded version of it. Stone had the DeVries date wrong (1637) in the *Year Book* article, but correct (1633) in the *BSOCM* chapter.

• Stone to Alexander Wetmore, 8/11/1925: "I am still amassing notes on Cape May birds & combining them into readable accounts – a combination of field & study work that is very agreeable."[22]

• "More Cape May Notes" at the 10/1/1925 meeting.[23]

• A full page article on Stone's bird migration studies at Cape May appeared in the Philadelphia *Public Ledger* in October 1926. Stone was interviewed, and the article also included a passage from his 1925 ANSP *Year Book* article cited above.[24]

• "The Flicker Flight and Other Migratory Movements at Cape May, NJ" at the AOU annual meeting, 10/24/1926.[25] Doubtless the same material that was read before the DVOC on 11/4/1926.[26]

• Stone read a paper about his Cape May woodcock observations, supplemented by Hand's records, at the 4/21/1927 meeting.[27] From the *Cassinia* description, the paper was clearly an early draft of the eventual *BSOCM* account.

• "Dr. Stone also read a biographical sketch of the Turkey Vulture, which is to be included in his book on Cape May birds" at the 2/2/1928 meeting.[28]

• Stone to Wetmore, 7/15/1928: "I have been resting a good deal & writing up my mss. [i.e., manuscript] on Cape May birds, finished the last one last night but have some revision to make in some of the earlier ones in view of additional data obtained since writing them. They are somewhat like a 'series' never completed! However I am going to draw the line at Dec. 31, 1928 and call it a job!"[29]

• "The Roosting of Herons and Martins at Cape May in 1929" at the 10/31/1929 meeting.[30] Stone had given the same talk at the AOU annual meeting the week before.[31]

• "The Bird-Life of Cape May, Past and Present" at the 12/4/1930 meeting of the Audubon Club of Norristown (Pennsylvania).[32]

• "Bird Life of the New Jersey Sea Coast, Past and Present" to the Ludwick crowd early in 1931.[33]

• Spoke about birdwatching at the 3/17/1932 meeting; "an added attraction was the reading by Dr. Stone of two Cape May Bird biographies on the Green Heron and Sanderling."[34]

• Stone to Wetmore, 7/20/1932: "[I] have been revising my Cape May ms. which is now nearly finished through the Charadriiformes. I hope to get it <u>all</u> done up to & including 1932 before I leave here [i.e., Cape May]. When it will be published (if ever) is another matter."[35]

• Stone to Wetmore, 8/19/1932: "I have nearly finished my Cape May sketches as far as 'water birds' are concerned."[36]

• Clarence Cottam to Stone, 2/7/1933: "May I say that your discussion of Cape May birds at Dr. Wetmore's home at our last Baird [Ornithological] Club meeting [in Washington, D.C.] was most interesting and instructive."[37]

• Stone to James Peters, 4/21/1933: "I hope to finish my <u>ms</u> on Birds of Cape May this summer. Whether it will ever advance beyond the <u>ms</u> stage I do not know!"[38]

• Stone to Palmer, 8/3/1933: "Meanwhile I am typing & revising the 'Birds of Cape May' ms. & collecting some insects."[39]

• Stone to W.L. Stiber of Intelligencer Printing, which printed *BSOCM* (and *The Auk*), 1/26/1936: "It looks now as if the necessary funds would be forthcoming and I am putting what spare time I have on the completion of the manuscript, though it will probably be next fall before I can take up final estimates. You shall hear from me then if not before."[40]

• Stone to Palmer, 2/25/1936: "The DVOC are going to back my Birds of Cape May and I am struggling to get the ms. completed & brought up to date. The latter is a <u>big job</u> as so much seems to have been done in the last 4 years (since most of my sketches were written). However the ms. is <u>nearly</u> done now, up to the song birds, & they, with a few exceptions, can be dismissed quickly. They figure mainly as migrants."[41]

• "[DVOC] President Potter appointed a committee composed of Messrs. Stuart, Street and A.C. Emlen to look into ways and means of publishing Dr. Stone's work on the birds of Cape May County" at the 11/7/1935 meeting.[42] The committee "reported progress" on the book's publication at the 3/5/1936 meeting, and announced its agreement to sponsor the publication at Stone's 70th birthday dinner on 9/22/1936, the same dinner at which Stone announced his retirement as *Auk* editor.[43]

• In a 1/26/1937 letter to Stone, Gustav Swanson mentions that he's "glad to hear that the book on birds of Cape May has already partially reached the printers."[44]

• Stone to Wetmore, 2/20/1937: "I have had more than I bargained for however in getting that 'Birds of Cape May' ready for the press. There seem to have been about a million things to add & check in order to bring it up to Dec 31/[19]36. However the text is practically done & 100 pp in type; all the line cuts drawn & most of them in electrotypes & the photos all in hand & many of them engraved. Mrs. Stone says it is worse than ten Auks!"[45] Stone to Palmer, 2/21/1937: "All the rest of my home time has been taken up with the Cape May book which like everything else of the sort manages to grow as it advances. I had no idea that I had such a job bringing the thing up to date. It is more than Cape May now, as it was thought advisable to take in the entire coastal district of the state as a side issue. The salt marsh is an ecologic unit and it is difficult to draw a line anywhere."[46]

• Stone to Wetmore, 10/27/1937: "The book is practically done except for binding....Mrs. S says it will be as large as 'Gone With the Wind' but it will be in two volumes so it won't look quite so bulky!"[47]

Acknowledgments

The first batch of kudos in any Witmer Stone biography has to go to some Academy of Natural Sciences personnel from long ago whose foresight and passion for Academy history proved to be of incalculable benefit to future researchers. They include Charles M.B. Cadwalader, who personally purchased and donated to the Academy Stone's correspondence (Collection 450 and others); Virginia Campbell, who sorted, filed, and indexed the collection after it came to the Academy; and Venia and Maurice Phillips, who did extraordinary work in the Academy archives in the mid-20th century, and whose guide to the Academy's manuscript collections continues to be an invaluable aid. Modern Academy staff who aided the research for this book include Greg Cowper, Drs. Nathan Rice and Gary Rosenberg, and the library and archives staff, including Joe Annaruma, Cathy Buckwalter, Clare Flemming, Megan Gibes, Eileen Mathias, Danianne Mizzy, Earle Spamer, Dan Thomas, Jennifer Vess, and Catherine Witt. For help with accessing Stone material housed at other archives I'd like to thank Dr. Mark Rabuck at Germantown Academy; James Duffin, Mark Lloyd, and Nancy Miller at the University of Pennsylvania archives; Alex Bartlett and Sam Whyte at the Germantown Historical Society; Drs. Laurie Goodrich and Keith Bildstein at Hawk Mountain Sanctuary; Dr. Paul Sweet at the American Museum of Natural History; Ashley Hamilton at the Reading Public Museum; Stephen Long and Drs. Rauri Bowie and Carla Cicero at the Museum of Vertebrate Zoology at Berkeley; Dana Fisher at the Ernst Mayr Library of the Museum of Comparative Zoology; and the staffs at the Library of Congress, the Smithsonian Institution Archives, and the Cape May Historical and Genealogical Society.

Many others have provided assistance of one type or another along the way: Albert Filemyr, Dr. Art McMorris, Christopher Walters, and the late Sandy Sherman of the DVOC; Jenniffer M. Saucedo and Drs. Michael Carleton and Helen James at the Smithsonian; Ned Barnard; Dr. Lynne Beene; Nick Bolgiano; Dr. Jane E. Boyd; Lou Brownholtz; René Corado at the Western Foundation of Vertebrate Zoology; Meg Diskin; Dr. George W. Drach at the University of Pennsylvania and Drs. Rainer M. Engel and Michael E. Moran of the William P. Didusch Center for Urologic History for insights into Stone's health issues; Tia Farmer; Kathleen and William Finneran; James N. Green at the Library Company of Philadelphia; Cherie Hanscomb; Laura Hedrick; Marie Emlen Hochstrasser; Dr. Art Emlen Jr.; Dr. Stephen T. Emlen; Lynne Flaccus; Joel Fry; Dyana Furmansky; Vicki Henry; Janet Jackson-Gould; Russell Juelg; Kevin Karlson; Sarah and David Larned; Dr. Daniel Lewis; June Lloyd; Turquoise Martin; Richard "Mickey" McPherson; Janet Novak; Julia O'Neil; the late Richard Pough; Dr. Amanda Rodewald; David Rutherford; Helen and

Jack Sayre; Keith Seager; Pat Sutton; Nancy Tanner; Dr. Robert Timm; Scott Weidensaul; Lesley Weissman-Cook for collaboration on the book's design and for expert desktop publishing services; Dr. Kristoffer Whitney; Jean Woodford; and Carol Yaster and the staff at Laurel Hill Cemetery. I'll offer advance apologies to those I've unintentionally neglected to mention.

For their reviews of manuscript chapters, my thanks to Robert M. Peck; Clay Sutton; and Drs. Richard C. Banks, Mark V. Barrow Jr., Frank Gill, Gerry Moore, Steven Peitzman, and Kimberly G. Smith. Dr. William E. Davis Jr. deserves special mention for reviewing five chapters. I was honored to have such a stellar group review a humble scribbler's efforts, and they provided great insights and suggestions. Any errors, inaccuracies, and other examples of scholarly ineptitude that may remain are of course the responsibility of the author.

Cape May Point is rightly renowned as one of the best places in the world to witness and study the phenomenon of fall bird migration. Four great books on the topic have been written: Stone's *Bird Studies at Old Cape May*, Jack Connor's *Season at the Point*, David Sibley's *The Birds of Cape May*, and Clay and Pat Sutton's *Birds and Birding at Cape May*. Meticulously researched and extremely well written, all four of these engaging classics should be on the bookshelves of anyone with an interest in the ornithology of the Cape May area.

What the Rolling Stones' Keith Richards has said of old blues musicians applies equally to birders: "Real gents, the great ones...always." It was my privilege to have a long acquaintance with some great birding gents such as the late Dale Twining, Fred Ulmer and Alan Brady, all of whom knew Stone when they were young men; and the late Charles A. Wonderly, who was my birding mentor when I was growing up in the Roxborough section of Philadelphia. Charlie and his wife, Betty, took me on my first New Jersey Audubon Society Cape May weekend in 1977.

Bibliography

The following books were cited at least twice; all others appear only in the endnotes. Note that due to the number of times cited, in the endnotes I use *PSNJ* for *The Plants of Southern New Jersey*, *TBNJ* for *The Birds of New Jersey*, and *BSOCM* for *Bird Studies at Old Cape May*.

Barrow, Mark V., Jr., *A Passion for Birds: American Ornithology After Audubon*. 1998. Princeton University Press, Princeton.

Broun, Maurice, *Hawks Aloft*. 1948. Kutztown Publishing Company, Kutztown.

Chapman, Frank C., and T.S. Palmer, eds., *Fifty Years' Progress of American Ornithology 1883–1933*. 1933. American Ornithologists' Union, Lancaster, Pa.

Connor, Jack, *Season at the Point*. 1991. The Atlantic Monthly Press, New York.

Dorwart, Jeffery M., *Cape May County, New Jersey: The Making of an American Resort Community*. 1992. Rutgers University Press, New Brunswick, N.J.

Emlen, John T., Jr., *Adventure Is Where You Find It: Recollections of a Twentieth Century American Naturalist*. 1996. Privately published.

Lewis, Daniel, *The Feathery Tribe: Robert Ridgway and the Modern Study of Birds*. 2012. Yale University Press, New Haven.

Newton, Ian, *The Migration Ecology of Birds*. 2008. Academic Press, London.

Peck, Robert M. and Patricia Tyson Stroud, *A Glorious Enterprise: The Academy of Natural Sciences of Philadelphia and the Making of American Science*. 2012. University of Pennsylvania Press, Philadelphia.

Pennypacker, Samuel W., *The Autobiography of a Pennsylvanian*. 1918. The John C. Winston Company, Philadelphia.

Scoville, Samuel, Jr., *Wild Honey*. 1929. Little, Brown, and Co., Boston.

Stevens, Lewis T., *The History of Cape May County, New Jersey*. 1897. Star of the Cape Publishing Company, Cape May.

Stone, Frederick D., Jr. *The Descendants of George Steele*. 1896. Privately published, Philadelphia.

Stone, Witmer, *Bird Studies at Old Cape May*. 1937. Delaware Valley Ornithological Club, Philadelphia.

Stone, Witmer, *The Birds of New Jersey*. 1909. Annual Report of the New Jersey State Museum for 1908. The John L. Murphy Publishing Company, Trenton.

Stone, Witmer, *The Mammals of New Jersey*. 1908. Annual Report of the New Jersey State Museum for 1907. MacCrellish & Quigley, Trenton.

Stone, Witmer, *The Plants of Southern New Jersey*. 1911. Annual Report of the New Jersey State Museum for 1910. MacCrellish & Quigley, Trenton.

Sutton, Clay and Pat Sutton, *Birds and Birding at Cape May*. 2006. Stackpole Books, Mechanicsburg, Pa.

University of Pennsylvania Class of 1887, *Five and Thirty: The Further History of the Class of Eighty-Seven*. 1922. Philadelphia.

Warren, B.H., *Report on the Birds of Pennsylvania*. 2nd ed. 1890. E.K. Meyers, Harrisburg.

Weygandt, Cornelius, *Down Jersey*. 1940. D. Appleton-Century Company, New York.

Weygandt, Cornelius, *On the Edge of Evening*. 1946. G.P. Putnam's Sons, New York.

Weygandt, Cornelius, *Philadelphia Folks*. 1938. D. Appleton-Century Company, New York.

Three helpful websites for finding old books and journal articles are Google Books, the Biodiversity Heritage Library, and the Searchable Ornithological Research Archive. The latter, unfortunately, redesigned its website during my research, and the new one is missing some of the crucial search functions of the older one.

Notes

The DVOC published four proceedings abstracts between 1890 and 1900; the third and fourth volumes included a few articles written by members. In 1901, the club expanded its publication and named it *Cassinia*, but continued with the numbering of the abstracts volumes, so that the first *Cassinia* was numbered Volume V. Some *Cassinia* volumes cover more than one year (the latest one even covered two volumes), and are usually not issued until one to several years after the year(s) denoted on the front cover (e.g., Vol. X for 1906 had an issue date of February 1907; Vol. XXV for 1922–24 had an issue date of February 1926). For simplicity's sake, I have designated the year(s) on the front cover as the publication year(s), instead of using the year of the issue date. I've also cited the early "Abstracts" issues with *Cassinia* titles.

Archives consulted during research:

Academy of Natural Sciences of Philadelphia Archives (ANSP)
American Museum of Natural History, Department of Ornithology Archives (AMNH)
Germantown Historical Society
Harvard University, Ernst Mayr Library of the Museum of Comparative Zoology (MCZ Archives)
Hawk Mountain Sanctuary Archives, Acopian Center for Conservation Learning
Historical Society of Pennsylvania
Library of Congress, Manuscript Division (LOC)
Museum of Vertebrate Zoology, University of California Berkeley (MVZ Archives)
National Audubon Society records. Manuscripts and Archives Division. The New York Public Library. Astor, Lenox, and Tilden Foundations (NYPL)
Smithsonian Institution Archive Collections (SIA)
University of Pennsylvania, Archives and Records Center

Academy of Natural Sciences of Philadelphia Archives Collection 450 is a large collection of Stone's correspondence. It is arranged alphabetically by correspondent, so I do not include box and folder numbers in my citations, and I refer to the collection in the citations as simply "ANSP 450." In a few instances where I cite a non-correspondence document from the collection, or a letter whose correspondents do not include Stone, I have included box number and folder. The Academy's *Proceedings of the Academy of Natural Sciences of Philadelphia* has been abbreviated *PANSP* in the endnotes.

In Witmer's Shadow

1. "Notes and news." *The Auk*, 1929. 46(3):428-30.
2. Weygandt, Cornelius, "A Dearth of Books," in *Down Jersey*. 1940. 151.
3. Peterson, Roger T., "Introduction to the Dover edition," in *Bird Studies at Old Cape May*. 1965, Dover Publications, Inc., New York. vii.
4. Stone, Witmer. "The coastal strip of New Jersey and the rediscovery of Lilaeopsis." *Bartonia*, 1908. 1:20-24.
5. *BSOCM*. 596-97.
6. *BSOCM*. 673.
7. Stone, Witmer. "Notes on winter crow life in the Delaware Valley." *The Auk*, 1903. 20(3):267-71.
8. *BSOCM*. 16.

Chapter 1: An Enthusiasm Centered on Birds

1. Tousey, Thomas G., *Military History of Carlisle and Carlisle Barracks*. 1939. The Dietz Press, Richmond. 236; Coddington, Edwin B., *The Gettysburg Campaign: A Study in Command*. 1968. Charles Scribner's Sons, New York. 202.
2. Hoke, Jacob, *The Great Invasion of 1863*. 1888. W.J. Shuey, Dayton. 254; Boatner, Mark, *The Civil War Dictionary*. 1959. D. McKay Co., New York. 123.
3. Carson, Hampton L. "In memory of Frederick Dawson Stone, Litt.D." *The Pennsylvania Magazine of History and Biography*, 1897. 21(4):v-xxxi.
4. Advertisement in *The West Jersey Pioneer*, March 24, 1855. Bridgeton, N.J.
5. *McElroy's Philadelphia City Directory for 1866*. 1866. A. McElroy, Philadelphia. 708.
6. Stone, Frederick D., Jr., *The Descendants of George Steele*. 1896.
7. Carson, Hampton L. "In memory of Frederick Dawson Stone, Litt.D." *The Pennsylvania Magazine of History and Biography*, 1897. 21(4):v-xxxi. One of the older brothers, Henry Morton Stone, who was the purchasing agent for the company, is buried at Laurel Hill Cemetery with his wife, Louise Besson Stone, adjacent to Frederick's plot.
8. Stone, Witmer. Letter to Theodore S. Palmer, November 17, 1914. LOC, T.S. Palmer papers, Box 10.
9. Stone, Witmer. Letter to Frederic A. Lucas, June 29, 1921. ANSP 450.
10. Stone, Witmer. "Recent Literature: Casey Wood's 'Introduction to the Literature of Vertebrate Zoology.'" *The Auk*, 1932. 49(1):114-16.
11. Pennypacker, Samuel W., *The Autobiography of a Pennsylvanian*. 1918. 157.
12. Stone, Witmer. Letter to Stewardson Brown, June 22, 1884. ANSP Collection 168, Folder 5.
13. Many of Stone's Stock Grange ancestors are interred in the lovely (and easily overlooked) Doe Run Presbyterian Cemetery in Coatesville, Chester County. They include his naturalist aunt Mary and the other "maiden great-aunts," and his great-grandparents John Dutton Steele and Ann Exton Steele, who were married the same year (1805) that John purchased Stock Grange. There is an enormous old White Oak near the family graves that Witmer certainly walked past if he ever visited the cemetery.
14. Stone, Witmer. "I remember: the story of the boyhood adventures of a distinguished naturalist." *Frontiers*, 1936. 1(1):13-15.
15. "Witmer Stone, Sc.D." *Fauna*, 1939. 1(June):36.
16. *BSOCM*. 294-95.
17. Stone, Witmer. "Joseph Crawford." *Bartonia*, 1937. 19:54-55.
18. Stone, Witmer. Letter to John S. Witmer, undated, 1873. ANSP Collection 2009-031, Box 1, Folder 9.
19. Weygandt, Cornelius, "Trenton Oyster Crackers," in *Down Jersey*. 1940. 202.
20. Weygandt, Cornelius, "Twelve Good Men and True," in *Philadelphia Folks*. 1938. 266-69.
21. Stone, Witmer. "George Spencer Morris." *Cassinia*, 1922-24. 25:1-5.
22. Stone, Witmer. "John Cassin." *Cassinia*, 1901. 5:1-7; Stone, Witmer. "Notes and news." *The Auk*, 1922. 39(2):299-304.
23. "Deaths: Frederick D. Stone." *Germantown Telegraph*, Philadelphia, August 18, 1897. "Marriage and Death-related Items from Germantown Newspapers 1891-1907" binder, Germantown Historical Society.
24. Penn Biographies: Witmer Stone (1866-1939). Cited February 7, 2014. Available from http://www.archives.upenn.edu/people/1800s/stone_witmer.html
25. Weygandt, Cornelius, "Street Cries," in *Philadelphia Folks*. 1938. 282-88; Weygandt, Cornelius, *On the Edge of Evening*. 1946. 192.

26. "Germantown and America." A talk given by Cornelius Weygandt to the Art and Science Club of Germantown February 3, 1930. University of Pennsylvania Archives Collection UPT 50, W547.5, Cornelius Weygandt papers, Box 4, Folder 12.

27. Moore, J. Percy. "In memoriam: Witmer Stone (1866-1939)." *PANSP*, 1939. 91:415-418; Stone, Witmer. "Charles J. Pennock. 1857-1935." *Cassinia*, 1933-37. 30:3-6; Trotter, Spencer. "In days before 'the Club.'" *Cassinia*, 1912. 16:26-32.

28. Rehn, James A. G. "In memoriam: Witmer Stone." *The Auk*, 1941. 58(3):299-313.

29. "Many Happy Returns." *Evening Public Ledger*, Philadelphia September 22, 1933.

30. Stone, Witmer. "Changed habits of Blue Jay at Philadelphia." *The Auk*, 1926. 43(2):239.

31. Stone, Witmer. "Stewardson Brown." *Cassinia*, 1920-21. 24:1-7.

32. Stone, Witmer. Undated, but clearly c. March 1934. Untitled notes for talk on *The Gossip* to Germantown Historical Society March 23, 1934. ANSP Collection 2009-031, Box 1, Folder 3.

33. Stone, Witmer. "I remember: the story of the boyhood adventures of a distinguished naturalist." *Frontiers*, 1936. 1(1):13-15. Pine Warblers, particularly the females, have a bland plumage, lacking in strong field marks. Brewster's Warbler is an uncommon hybrid between Golden-winged and Blue-winged Warblers and was little known at the time. Stone sent Pennsylvania state ornithologist B.H. Warren a list of birds, including his Brewster's Warbler (6/19/1889; ANSP 450), and that is presumably the bird referred to obliquely in Warren's 1890 edition of *Birds of Pennsylvania* (p. 277) as an addition to Spencer Trotter's record.

34. Morris, George Spencer. "A day in the salt marshes near Atlantic City." *Cassinia*, 2001. 68:42-46.

35. Stewardson Brown journal. ANSP Collection 486, Folder 7.

36. Stone, Witmer. "Pennsylvania and New Jersey spiders of the Family Lycosidae." *PANSP*, 1890. 42:420-34.

37. Stone, Witmer. Letter to Stewardson Brown, September 21, 1887. ANSP Collection 168, Folder 5.

38. Proceedings of the Wilson Natural Science Association, Vols. 1 & 2. ANSP Collection 2009-031, Box 4, Folders 7 & 6.

39. Brown, Amos P. President's address. Proceedings of the Wilson Natural Science Association, Vol. 1, ANSP Collection 2009-031, Box 4, Folder 7. 133-34.

40. *Oologist* editor Richard M. Barnes gave his two cents about the situation to Stone in a 10/22/1915 letter, writing that "the AOU is a sort of a privately controlled institution run more or less for the benefit of a favored few with the privilege extended to the associate members thereof, of paying the expenses." (ANSP 450).

41. Stone, Witmer. Letter to Stewardson Brown, August 7, 1887. ANSP Collection 168, Folder 5.

42. Stone, Witmer. Letter to Stewardson Brown, August 12, 1886. ANSP Collection 168, Folder 5.

43. *The Gossip*, August, 1882. Extra Number. Germantown Historical Society archives.

44. "Warehouse of A.K. Witmer's Sons - Paradise Pa." Pencil sketch in Witmer Stone's drawing notebook. ANSP Collection 2009-031, Box 3, Folder 2.

45. Stone, Witmer. Letter to Stewardson Brown, July 26, 1886. ANSP Collection 168, Folder 5.

46. Stone, Witmer. Letter to Stewardson Brown, July 15, 1886. ANSP Collection 168, Folder 5.

47. Stone, Witmer. Letter to Stewardson Brown, July 25, 1887. ANSP Collection 168, Folder 5.

48. Stone, Witmer. Letter to Stewardson Brown, July 13, 1887. ANSP Collection 168, Folder 5.

49. Untitled essay. Proceedings of the Wilson Natural Science Association, Vol. 1, p. 100, ANSP Collection 2009-031, Box 4, Folder 7.

50. Huber, Wharton. "Witmer Stone (1866 to 1939)." *Journal of Mammalogy*, 1940. 21(1):1-4.

51. Fowler, Henry W. "Memories of Stock Grange." 1958. ANSP Collection 263, Box 1, Folder 10.

52. Stone, Witmer. "The Turkey Buzzard breeding in Pennsylvania." *The American Naturalist*, 1885. 19(4):407.

53. W.S.M. "Notes from Chester Co., Pa." *Ornithologist and Oologist*, 1884. 9(1):2-3.

54. Stone, Hugh E. Letter to Witmer Stone, September 29, 1910. ANSP 450.

55. Huber, Wharton. Untitled memorial of Witmer Stone. 1939. ANSP Collection 263. A

reminiscence Stone recorded at the end of his 1913 *Bird-Lore* (15:330) catbird article, like the ending to his earlier Orchard Oriole article (*B-L* 12:44-47), recalls Stock Grange and/or Paradise.

56. Jessica Rains on Claude Rains (TCM Original). Cited February 7, 2014. Available from http://www.tcm.com/mediaroom/video/254751/Jessica-Rains-on-Claude-Rains-TCM-Original-.html

57. Larned, David. Email to author, August 8, 2011.

58. Kevinski, J.B. Letter to John S. Witmer, June 11, 1886. ANSP 450.

59. National Register of Historic Places Registration Form for McCalls Ferry Farm. Cited February 7, 2014. Available from https://www.dot7.state.pa.us/ce_imagery/phmc_scans/H112021_01H.pdf

60. Wilson Natural Science Association. York Furnace. 1889. ANSP Collection 2009-031, Box 4, Folder 4.

61. Stone, Witmer. "Amos Peaslee Brown." *Proceedings of the American Philosophical Society*, 1918. 57(7):iii-xv.

62. "Abstract of the proceedings of the DVOC 1892-97." *Cassinia*, 1892-97. 2:1-26; Stone, Witmer. Letter to James L. Peters, August 12, 1935. MCZ Archives.

63. "Additions to the museum." *PANSP*, 1894. 46:485-92; Untitled, undated notes for talk about the ANSP herpetology department given by Stone at the 1917 meeting of The American Society of Ichthyologists and Herpetologists. Private collection of Witmer Stone material.

64. Stone, Witmer. "Lumbriculus limosus (Leidy)." Undated Wilson Natural Science Association paper. Private collection of Witmer Stone material.

65. Perot, Robeson Lea. Letter to Witmer Stone, March 2, 1934. ANSP 450.

66. "To Our Subscribers." *The Gossip*, 1882. 2(10):1. Germantown Historical Society archives.

67. "Philadelphian's Studies of Birds of Cape May." *The Evening Bulletin*, Philadelphia, February 16, 1938; Merriam, C. Hart. Letters to Witmer Stone, December 11, 1888 & December 21, 1889. ANSP Collection 678, Folder 1; Stone, Witmer. "Notes and news." *The Auk*, 1921. 38(2):316-20.

68. Fecht, Sarah. "Relics With Much to Tell About Bird Diets May be Lost to Time." *The New York Times*, May 21, 2012;

Droege, Sam. Email to author, July 17, 2012.

69. Merriam, C. Hart. Letter to Witmer Stone, November 9, 1887. ANSP Collection 678, Folder 1.

70. Stone, Witmer. Letter to Stewardson Brown, July 22, 1884. ANSP Collection 168, Folder 5.

71. Stone, Witmer. Letter to Stewardson Brown, August 1, 1884. ANSP Collection 168, Folder 5.

72. Cope, Francis R., Jr. Letter to Witmer Stone, October 26, 1903.

73. Stone, Witmer. Letter to Stewardson Brown, August 30, 1887. ANSP Collection 168, Folder 5.

74. Merriam, C. Hart. Letter to Witmer Stone, May 9, 1890. ANSP Collection 678, Folder 1.

75. *The DVOC Scrap Book 1890-99*. ANSP Collection 570.

76. Keyser, Naaman H., C. Henry Kain, John Palmer Garber, et al., *History of Old Germantown*. 1907. Horace F. McCann, Philadelphia. 186.

77. Gross, Linda P. and Theresa R. Snyder, *Images of America: Philadelphia's 1876 Centennial Exhibition*. 2005. Arcadia Publishing. 15.

78. "Mr. Cleveland Accepts." *New York Times*, August 24, 1887; Cleveland, S. Grover. Letter to Frederick D. Stone, Sr., August 22, 1887. Historical Society of Pennsylvania, Society Collection; Pennypacker, Samuel W., *The Autobiography of a Pennsylvanian*. 1918. 134.

79. Greenfield, Albert M. Letter to Witmer Stone, August 16, 1937. ANSP Collection 263C, Folder 5.

80. Stone, Witmer. Letter to Stewardson Brown, September 21, 1887. ANSP Collection 168, Folder 5. Witmer was not exaggerating about the level of pageantry – *The Philadelphia Times* ("A Brilliant Ending," 9/18/1887) spent most of the front page detailing the opulence of the celebration at the Academy of Music.

81. Bower, Mark A., *Loudon, Germantown, Philadelphia: Country House of the Armat Family the Years 1801-1835*. Master's thesis, 1984, University of Pennsylvania, Philadelphia.

82. Brown, Herbert. Letter to Witmer Stone, October 14, 1917. ANSP 450; Brown,

Hazen. Letter to Witmer Stone, March 23, 1918. ANSP 450.

83. Stone, Witmer. Letter to Theodore S. Palmer, March 16, 1921. LOC, T.S. Palmer papers, Box 38. A Germantown newspaper at the time (name unknown, 3/19/1921; in Germantown Historical Society archives) listed the ambiguous "apoplexy" as the cause of death.

84. Morris, George Spencer. Letter to Witmer Stone, April 7, 1921. ANSP 450.

85. Saunders, Charles F. Letter to Witmer Stone, February 10, 1925. ANSP 450.

86. Wilde, Mark L. C. Letter to Witmer Stone, February 26, 1896. ANSP 450.

87. *TBNJ*. 230; *BSOCM*. 899.

88. "Members of the Class of '89." *The Academy Monthly*, 1889. 4(9):6-7.

89. Gates, Thomas S. Letter to Witmer Stone, January 11, 1933. ANSP 450.

90. *The Academy Monthly*, January 1889, Vol. 5, No. 4. Germantown Academy archives.

91. Pennsylvania, Philadelphia City Death Certificates, 1803-1915. Film Number (Digital Folder Number) 1011824(004029875), Image 98/631. Cited February 10, 2014. Available from https://familysearch.org/pal:/MM9.3.1/TH-266-13030-113399-45?cc=1320976&wc=MMRX-VT6:93571520

92. "Typhoid fever in Philadelphia." *Journal of the American Medical Association*, 1899. 32(11):620.

93. Dixon, Samuel G. Letter to Witmer Stone, Undated, but clearly c. February 14, 1896. ANSP 450.

94. Purdie, Henry A. Letter to Witmer Stone, February 25, 1896. ANSP 450.

95. Murphy, Robert Cushman. 1955. "Witmer Stone (1866-1939)." Department of Ornithology Archives, AMNH. Written for *Dictionary of American Biography*.

96. Stone, Witmer. Letter to Charles W. Richmond, February 11, 1926. SIA Collection RU-105, Box 27.

97. Will of Lillie May Stone. ANSP Collection 2010-051, Box 7, Folder 13.

98. Stone, Frederick D., Sr. Letter to William Brooke Rawle and Hampton L. Carson, May 25, 1896. Historical Society of Pennsylvania, Society Collection.

99. Rawle, William Brooke. Letter to Gregory B. Keen, May 31, 1900. Historical Society of Pennsylvania, Society Collection.

100. Frederick D. Stone Dead." *New York Times*, August 15, 1897; Pennsylvania, Philadelphia City Death Certificates, 1803-1915. Film Number (Digital Folder Number) 1011826(004008679), Image 425/646. Cited February 10, 2014. Available from https://familysearch.org/pal:/MM9.3.1/TH-267-11842-142440-11?cc=1320976

101. Stone, Witmer. Letter to John W. Jordan, August 13, 1897. Historical Society of Pennsylvania, Society Collection.

102. "Sale of Frederick D. Stone's Library." *New York Times*, October 16, 1897. The sale must have brought in quite a bit of money: another *NY Times* article (10/23/1897) after the sale included a partial list of items sold (out of 1,767 lots). The list may have focused on the items which brought the highest bids, but it totaled nearly $2,000. James N. Green of the Library Company of Philadelphia advises (email to author 7/16/2014) that there were three sales: the first one, discussed here, and two later ones in late October 1897 and February 1898.

103. "Obituary notes." *The Publishers' Weekly*, 1897. 52(1334):259; *See* Carson, "In memory of Frederick Dawson Stone, Litt.D." *The Pennsylvania Magazine of History and Biography*, 21(4):v-xxxi, 1897, for a long discussion of F.D. Stone's historical writings.

104. Batchelder, Charles F. Letter to Witmer Stone, January 15, 1915; Stone, Witmer. Poem for Sam Scoville's 50th birthday. June, 1922; Scoville, Samuel. Letter to Witmer Stone, June 16, 1922. All ANSP 450; Pennell, Francis W. "The botanical work of Witmer Stone." *Bartonia*, 1940. 20:33-37.

105. Stone, Witmer. "Phillips' 'A Sportsman's Scrapbook.'" *The Auk*, 1929. 46(1):133-34.

106. Evans, William Bacon. "Samuel Nicholson Rhoads." *Cassinia*, 1951-52:17-20.

Chapter 2: Class of '87

1. University of Pennsylvania Class of 1887 Scrapbooks. University of Pennsylvania Archives Collection UPT 110.

2. Penn Biographies: Albert Monroe Wilson (1841-1904). Cited February 7, 2014. Available from http://www.archives.upenn.edu/people/1800s/wilson_albert_pomp.html Pomp once showed Penn graduate and professor Cornelius Weygandt a couple of young nighthawks he'd found on the roof of College Hall; Pomp wondered how the

"toads" had managed to clamber up that far. Other than the feathers, his confusion is understandable (Weygandt, unpublished ms. in UP Archives Collection UPT 50, W547.5, Box 1).

3. *University of Pennsylvania: Catalogue and Announcements 1883-84*. 1883, Philadelphia. 18; Duffin, James M. and Mark F. Lloyd. Email to author, November 29, 2012.

4. Price, Eli K. "Rockery at the University of Pennsylvania, built in 1881." *Proceedings of the American Philosophical Society*, 1882. 20(111):118-22.

5. *The Record of the Class of '87*. 1887. Press of Times Printing House, Philadelphia.

6. Academic record for Witmer Stone, University Pennsylvania. 1887. ANSP Collection 2009-031, Box 2, Folder 10.

7. *University of Pennsylvania: Catalogue and Announcements 1883-84*. 1883, Philadelphia.

8. Stone, Witmer. "Joseph Leidy as a botanist." *PANSP*, 1923. 75(The Joseph Leidy Commemorative Meeting supplement):43-48.

9. "Men and Things: Penn's Sons, Crop of '87, in Notable Reunion." *The Evening Bulletin*, Philadelphia, June 4, 1937.

10. Smith, Edgar F. Letter to Witmer Stone, April 16, 1913. ANSP Collection 2009-031, Box 2, Folder 10.

11. "Suggestions for Honorary Degrees, 1912-1913." University of Pennsylvania Archives, Archives General Collection, "1912 - Honorary Degrees" folder; Dixon, Samuel G. Letter to Edgar F. Smith, March 4, 1912. ANSP Collection 241, Box 1, Folder 3.

12. Sage, John H. Letter to Witmer Stone, July 5, 1913. ANSP Collection 541, Folder 3.

13. "Thirty-first annual Congress of the American Ornithologists' Union." *Bird-Lore*, 1913. 15:376-77.

14. Penn archivist James M. Duffin told me (6-28-2012) that was probably still the case, at least with pre-Internet UP classes. Due to the social media phenomenon, the post-graduation activities of recent classes may be more exhaustively covered, at least in cyberspace.

15. Stone, Witmer. Letter to Theodore S. Palmer, June 20, 1932. LOC, T.S. Palmer papers, Box 50.

16. Chambers, George. Letter to Witmer Stone, May 3, 1912. ANSP Collection 263C, Folder 18; Henry, J. Norman. Various letters to Witmer Stone, 1920–1923. ANSP Collection 263C, Folder 20.

17. Report of the subcommittee on policy of the Committee of One Hundred of the alumni of the University of Pennsylvania. 1920. University of Pennsylvania Archives, Alumni Records Collection, "Committee of 100" Folder.

18. Haney, John L. Letters to Witmer Stone July 23 & October 1, 1921, & February 24, 1923. ANSP 450; Several letters between Stone and Edward H. Heffner in late 1921 and early 1922 concern Stone's appointment to the position. ANSP 450.

19. Penn Biographies: Witmer Stone (1866-1939). Cited February 7, 2014. Available from http://www.archives.upenn.edu/people/1800s/stone_witmer.html

20. "Witmer Stone." *Old Penn*, 1913. XI(39).

21. University of Pennsylvania Alumni Award of Merit, 1937. The certificate is in ANSP Collection 2009-031, Box 5, Folder 5. Stone received the award for being "the first [i.e., most prominent] ornithologist of his country." Cornelius Weygandt was chairman of the Committee on Resolutions and Awards of the UP General Alumni Board, and was clearly the impetus behind Stone receiving the award (UP Collection UPT 101 #21).

22. Cope, Francis R., Jr. Letter to Witmer Stone, October 26, 1903. ANSP 450; Kershaw, William. Letters to Witmer Stone, May 26, 1891, October 16, 1893, & March 13, 1895. ANSP 450; Untitled manuscript detailing highlights of Stone's professional career. ANSP Collection 2009-031, Box 1, Folder 4. Undated, but clearly 1937.

23. Montgomery, Thomas. "The bird course at the Marine Biological Laboratory, Woods Holl, Mass., during the summer of 1900." *Bird-Lore*, 1900. 2:153-54; Montgomery, Thomas H. Letters to Witmer Stone, July 19 & September 7, 1900, & July 4, 1901. ANSP 450; Strong, Reuben M. Letters to Witmer Stone, July 11 & 18, 1903. ANSP 450; Ames, Herman V. Letter to Witmer Stone, December 19, 1927. ANSP Collection 2009-031, Box 1, Folder 11.

24. Stiles, C.W. Letter to Witmer Stone, December 2, 1913. ANSP 450.

25. Mumford, Edward W. Letters to Witmer Stone, June 10, 1927 & September 2, 1936. ANSP 450; Cadwalader, Charles M.B. Letter to Witmer Stone, October 2,

1931. ANSP Collection 2009-034, Box 24, Folder 15.

26. Allen, Arthur A., "Ornithological Education in America," in *Fifty Years' Progress of American Ornithology 1883-1933*. 1933. 215-29; Cadwalader, Charles M.B. Letter to Witmer Stone, October 2, 1931. ANSP Collection 2009-034, Box 24, Folder 15.

27. Stone, Witmer. Letter to Theodore S. Palmer, June 24, 1934. SIA Collection 7150, Box 70, Folder 8.

28. University of Pennsylvania: One Hundred and Seventy-Eighth Commencement for the Conferring of Degrees. Cited February 7, 2014. Available from http://www.archives.upenn.edu/primdocs/upg/upg7/1934prog.pdf

29. Dutcher, William. "Report of the AOU Committee on Protection of North American Birds." *The Auk*, 1897. 14(1):21-32.

30. Stone, Witmer. "On looking back fifty years." *Frontiers*, 1938. 2(4):130-32.

31. Lee, Laura. "$5 a Week Feeds Park Birds Here." *The Evening Bulletin*, Philadelphia, April 22, 1935. The occasion may have been the Wissahickon Bird Club spring meeting.

32. Dixon, Samuel G. Letter to Witmer Stone, February 10, 1916. ANSP 450; "Tempting Tenements for Feathered Friends." *Allentown Democrat*, Allentown, June 10, 1916.

33. Ludwick Institute annual board meeting minutes for October 25, 1895. Historical Society of Pennsylvania Collection 1783.

34. The Ludwick Lectures 1938. ANSP Collection 593, Folder 5.

35. Stone, Witmer. Letter to Charles M.B. Cadwalader, April 13, 1934. ANSP Collection 593, Folder 4.

36. *The Ludwick Institute 1799-1947*. 1947. The Ludwick Institute, Philadelphia.

37. The Ludwick Lectures, Spring Season 1925; The Ludwick Lectures, Spring Season, School Course 1922; The Ludwick Lectures 1932; The Ludwick Lectures 1931. All ANSP Collection 593, Folder 5.

38. Stone, Witmer. Letter to Alexander Wetmore, February 21, 1938. SIA Collection 7006, Box 66, Folder 1; Green, Harold T. Letter to Edwin S. Dixon, Jr., August 21, 1939. Historical Society of Pennsylvania Archives Collection 1783.

39. Marie Hochstrasser, interview with author November 17, 2005.

40. The Christopher Ludwick Foundation. Cited February 7, 2014. Available from http://www.ludwickfoundation.org/index.htm

41. Stone, Witmer. "Notes and news." *The Auk*, 1917. 34(1):112-18.

42. DVOC minutes for October 19, 1939. ANSP Collection 74A, Box 2, Folder 2.

43. "Single lectures and courses on Natural History by Witmer Stone, M.A." Pamphlet. ANSP Collection 2009-031 (undated, but pre-1913).

44. Cooke, Wells W. Letter to Witmer Stone, December 6, 1912. ANSP 450.

45. Swisher, Florence. Letter to Witmer Stone, June 24, 1925. ANSP 450.

46. Davison, Alvin. Letter to Witmer Stone, October 2, 1902. ANSP 450.

47. Stone, Witmer. Letter to S. Prentiss Baldwin, March 8, 1923. ANSP 450; Stone, Witmer. Letter to Elizabeth R. Terry, April 20, 1923. ANSP 450.

48. Stone, Witmer. Letter to William A. Whittaker, February 12, 1923. ANSP 450.

49. Volcker, Paul A. Letter to Witmer Stone, February 28, 1927. ANSP 450.

50. Lee, Edith H.M. Letter to Witmer Stone, February 18, 1936. ANSP 450.

Chapter 3: My Establishment Will Not Go On

1. Stone, Witmer. "I remember: the story of the boyhood adventures of a distinguished naturalist." *Frontiers*, 1936. 1(1):13-15.

2. Untitled, undated notes for talk about the ANSP herpetology department given by Stone at the 1917 meeting of The American Society of Ichthyologists and Herpetologists. Private collection of Witmer Stone material.

3. Moore, J. Percy. "In memoriam: Witmer Stone (1866-1939)." *PANSP*, 1939. 91:415-418.

4. Chamberlain, Alexander F. "In memoriam Dr. D. G. Brinton, with a sketch of his archaeological activities." *The American Antiquarian*, 1900. 22(1):37-40; Brinton, D.G. Letter to Frederick D. Stone, Sr., September 30, 1887. ANSP Collection 2009-031, Box 1, Folder 6; Heilprin, Angelo. Letter to Frederick D. Stone, Sr., February 23, 1888. ANSP Collection 2009-031, Box 2, Folder 10.

5. Stone, Frederick D., Sr. Letter to Anonymous, April 11, 1878. ANSP Collection 567, Box 35, Folder 3.

6. Peck, Robert M. and Patricia Tyson Stroud, *A Glorious Enterprise*. 2012. 416.

7. Stone, Witmer. "Joseph Leidy as a botanist." *PANSP*, 1923. 75(The Joseph Leidy Commemorative Meeting supplement):43-48.

8. Stone, Witmer. Letter to Theodore S. Palmer, February 27, 1928. LOC, T.S. Palmer papers, Box 45; Stone, Witmer. "Philadelphia to the coast in early days, and the development of western ornithology prior to 1850." *The Condor*, 1916. 18(1):3-14.

9. Stone, Witmer. "On looking back fifty years." *Frontiers*, 1938. 2(4):130-32.

10. Stone, Witmer. "Mark Catesby and the nomenclature of North American birds." *The Auk*, 1929. 46(4):447-54.

11. Ruschenberger, W.S.W. "Report on the Jessup Fund." *PANSP*, 1892. 44:505-07.

12. Curators' minutes for March 16, 1892. ANSP Collection 86, Folder 1.

13. Fischer, Margaret. Memorandum to Jessup Fund File, February 11, 1992. ANSP Collection 375, Folder 1.

14. Stone, Witmer. "Spencer Trotter: 1860-1931." *Cassinia*, 1929-30. 28:1-8.

15. Stone, Witmer. Letter to Charles M.B. Cadwalader, February 20, 1937. Stone's essay on "The future of zoological research in museums" is attached to the letter. ANSP Collection 2009-034, Box 47, Folder 69.

16. Conant, Roger. "Henry Weed Fowler: 1878-1965." *Copeia*, 1966. 1966(3):628-29; Peck, Robert M. and Patricia Tyson Stroud, *A Glorious Enterprise*. 2012. 392.

17. Stone, Witmer. Letter to Joseph Grinnell, February 16, 1911. MVZ Archives.

18. Work journal of James E. Ives, June 20, 1892–March 30, 1893. ANSP Collection 86, Folder 7. The cover reads "Ives – His book, It's worth a look!"

19. Ruschenberger, W.S.W. Letter to Witmer Stone, October 1, 1892. ANSP Collection 450.

20. Curators' minutes for September 14, 1892. ANSP Collection 86, Folder 1.

21. Jessup and McHenry Awards. Cited February 7, 2014. Available from http://www.ansp.org/research/fellowships-endowments/jessup-mchenry/

22. Heilprin, Angelo. "On some new species of Mollusca from the Bermuda Islands." *PANSP*, 1889. 41:141-42; Heilprin, Angelo. "Contributions to the natural history of the Bermuda Islands." *PANSP*, 1888. 40:302-28.

23. Diary of Witmer Stone from the Yucatan and Mexico expedition sent out by ANSP Feb. 15th–Apr. 21st 1890. ANSP Collection 2009-031, Box 3, Folder 5. (Hereafter "Diary.")

24. Stone, Witmer. "Recent Literature: Barbour's 'Birds of Cuba.'" *The Auk*, 1923. 40(3):548-49.

25. "Geography and Travels." *The American Naturalist*, 1890. 24:761-65.

26. Diary. 171; Baker, Frank C., *A Naturalist in Mexico*. 1895. David Oliphant, Chicago. 80.

27. Diary. 173.

28. Heilprin, Angelo. "Barometric observations among the high volcanoes of Mexico, with a consideration of the culminating point of the North American continent." *PANSP*, 1890. 42:251-65; Newspaper article on ANSP Mexico expedition, title unknown. *The Times of Philadelphia*, Philadelphia, April 24, 1890.

29. Heilprin, Angelo. "Observations on the flora of Northern Yucatan." *Proceedings of the American Philosophical Society*, 1891. 29(136):137-44.

30. Stone, Witmer. "On birds collected in Yucatan and southern Mexico." *PANSP*, 1890. 42:201-18.

31. Diary. 155.

32. Diary. 193-95.

33. Stone, Witmer. "A naturalist in Mexico." *Science*, 1895. 2(44):592-93.

34. Baker, Frank C. Letter to Witmer Stone, November 9, 1895. ANSP 450; Baker, Frank C. "A reply." *Science*, 1895. 2(47):693-94.

35. Baker, Frank C. Letter to Witmer Stone, November 15, 1895. ANSP 450.

36. Baker, Frank C. Letter to Witmer Stone, June 26, 1896. ANSP 450.

37. "International Symposium of Early Man." Pamphlet. 1937. ANSP Collection 263, Box 2, Folder 2.

38. "Abstract of the proceedings of the DVOC 1890-91." *Cassinia*, 1890-91. 1:2-11; "Abstract of the proceedings of the DVOC 1892-97." *Cassinia*, 1892-97. 2:1-26.

39. "Abstract of the proceedings of the DVOC 1929-30." *Cassinia*, 1929-30. 28:48-58.

40. "Dr. Stone 50 Years at Museum Here." *The Evening Bulletin*, Philadelphia, February 28, 1938.

41. Stone, Witmer. "Thomas B. Wilson, M.D." *Cassinia*, 1909. 13:1-6.

42. Stone, Witmer. Letter to Frank M. Chapman, May 25, 1891. Department of Ornithology Archives, AMNH.

43. Undated application for Ornithological Section, Academy of Natural Sciences of Philadelphia. ANSP Collection 297, Folder 5. "Section" is essentially an older term for "department." Spencer Trotter, Benjamin Sharp, William L. Abbott, Samuel N. Rhoads, Isaac Martindale, Edwin Sheppard, Henry A. Pilsbry, George Spencer Morris, Joseph Wilcox, Charles E. Ridenour, and Stewardson Brown were the other signers.

44. Stone, Witmer. "Report of the Ornithological Section." *PANSP*, 1891. 43:502-505.

45. Stone, Witmer. Receipt to Charles P. Perot, February 9, 1893. ANSP Collection 297, Folder 5.

46. Trotter, Spencer. "In days before 'the Club.'" *Cassinia*, 1912. 16:26-32; Stone, Witmer. Letter to Joel Asaph Allen, August 7, 1889. Department of Ornithology Archives, AMNH.

47. Stone, Witmer. "Problems of modernizing an old museum." *Proceedings of the American Association of Museums*, 1909. 3:122-28.

48. Stone, Witmer. Letter to Joel Asaph Allen, March 5, 1894. Department of Ornithology Archives, AMNH.

49. Heilprin, Angelo. "Report of the curators." *PANSP*, 1888. 40:439-42; Heilprin, Angelo. "Report of the curators." *PANSP*, 1889. 41:429-32.

50. Stone, Witmer. Letter to ANSP curators, undated. ANSP Collection 263A, Folder 10.

51. Bendire, Charles. Letters to Witmer Stone, April 24 & 26, September 10, 1890. ANSP 450. Smithsonian ornithologist J.H. Riley eventually had his eye out for it as well (Riley letters to Witmer Stone, 1899–1900, ANSP 450).

52. Bendire, Charles. Letter to Witmer Stone, April 15, 1896. ANSP 450.

53. Stone, Witmer. "An old case of skins and its associations." *The Osprey*, 1899. 3(7):98-99.

54. Stone, Witmer. "Catalogue of the Muscicapidae in the collection of the Philadelphia Academy of Natural Sciences." *PANSP*, 1889. 41:146-54.

55. Allen, Joel Asaph. "Stone's Catalogue of the Muscicapidae in the collection of the Philadelphia Academy of Natural Sciences." *The Auk*, 1889. 6(4):330-31.

56. Rehn, James A. G. "In memoriam: Witmer Stone." *The Auk*, 1941. 58(3):299-313.

57. Stone, Witmer. "The Ornithological Section." *PANSP*, 1904. 56:852-53.

58. Sclater, Philip Lutley. "Notes on the birds in the museum of the Academy of Natural Sciences of Philadelphia, and other collections in the United States of America." *Proceedings of the Zoological Society of London*, 1857. 25:1-9.

59. Sharpe, R. Bowdler. Letter to Witmer Stone, November 12, 1894. ANSP Collection 450.

60. Allen, Joel Asaph. Letter to Witmer Stone, August 12, 1889. ANSP Collection 658, Folder 2.

61. Stone, Witmer. "Report of the Ornithological Section." *PANSP*, 1894. 46:478-79.

62. Stone, Witmer. Letter to Joel Asaph Allen, October 23, 1894. Department of Ornithology Archives, AMNH.

63. Allen, Joel Asaph. Letter to Witmer Stone, October 24, 1894. ANSP Collection 658, Folder 3.

64. Stone, Witmer. "Report of the Ornithological Section." *PANSP*, 1893. 45:567-68.

65. Stone, Witmer. Letter to Leonhard Stejneger, October 30, 1937. ANSP Collection 186, Box 1, Folder 2.

66. Ridgway, Robert. Letter to Witmer Stone, October 27, 1894. ANSP Collection 681, Folder 4.

67. Stone, Witmer. Letter to Charles W. Richmond, December 15, 1897. SIA Collection RU-105, Box 27; Stone, Witmer. "A study of the type specimens of birds in the collection of the ANSP, with a brief history of the collection." *PANSP*, 1899. 51(1):5-62.

68. Stone, Witmer. Letter to Charles W. Richmond, May 17, 1899. SIA Collection RU105, Box 27.

69. DVOC minutes for January 15, 1914. ANSP Collection 74A, Folder 1, Box 5.

70. Stone, Witmer. Letter to Gertrude Shafer, March 3, 1924. ANSP 450; Weygandt, Cornelius, "Tony's Snake Story," in *Philadelphia Folks*. 1938. 62-63.

71. Stone, Witmer. "On some collections of reptiles and Batrachians from the western United States." *PANSP*, 1911. 63:222-32.

72. "Abstract of the proceedings of the DVOC 1906." *Cassinia*, 1906. 10:58-64.

73. Rice, Nathan H. Email to author, January 30, 2013.

74. Stone, Witmer. Letter to Joel Asaph Allen, March 12, 1895. Department of Ornithology Archives, AMNH.

75. Stone, Witmer. Letter to Joel Asaph Allen, March 15, 1895. Department of Ornithology Archives, AMNH.

76. Stone, Witmer. Letter to William B. Scott, May 6, 1924. ANSP 450.

77. Stone, Witmer. Letter to William Brewster, October 30, 1896. MCZ Archives.

78. Stone, Witmer. Letters to R. Bowdler Sharpe, June 9, 1898, & May 15, 1905. Blacker-Wood Collection, Department of Rare Books, McGill University; Stone, Witmer. Letter to Frank M. Chapman, November 1, 1898. Department of Ornithology Archives, AMNH.

79. Stone, Witmer. "Report of the Ornithological Section." *PANSP*, 1901. 53:775-76.

80. Batchelder, Charles F. Letter to Witmer Stone, April 10, 1911. ANSP 450.

81. Stone, Witmer. Letter to "Mr. Andrews" (Roy Chapman?), December 20, 1912. Department of Ornithology Archives, AMNH.

82. Cory, Charles B. Letters to Witmer Stone, March 18 & April 7, 1909. ANSP 450.

83. Grinnell, Joseph. Letter to Witmer Stone, April 2, 1913. ANSP Collection 684, Folder 3.

84. Stone, Witmer. Letter to Joseph Grinnell, April 12, 1913. MVZ Archives.

85. Stone, Witmer. "Ornithological Section." *PANSP*, 1909. 61:584-85.

86. Stone, Witmer. Letter to Frank M. Chapman, January 8, 1918. Department of Ornithology Archives, AMNH.

87. Stone, Witmer. Letter to Albert K. Fisher, April 21, 1918. LOC, A.K. Fisher papers, Box 22.

88. Richmond, Charles W. Letter to Witmer Stone, February 23, 1918. ANSP Collection 675, Folder 7.

89. Stone, Witmer. Letter to Alexander Wetmore, January 8, 1921. SIA Collection 7006, Box 65, Folder 6.

90. Stone, Witmer. Letter to Frank M. Chapman, February 14, 1923. ANSP Collection 679, Folder 11.

91. Stone, Witmer. Letter to S. Prentiss Baldwin, April 6, 1924. ANSP 450.

92. Stone, Witmer. Letter to Robert W. Williams, March 20, 1922. ANSP 450.

93. Grinnell, Joseph. "Editorial notes and news." *The Condor*, 1915. 15(2):95-6.

94. Stone, Witmer. Letter to Theodore S. Palmer, June 7, 1921. LOC, T.S. Palmer papers, Box 38.

95. Stone, Witmer. Letter to John Albert Leach, July 7, 1924. ANSP 450; Rehn, James A. G. Letter to Witmer Stone, November 30, 1928. ANSP Collection 590, Folder 9.

96. "Cadwalader Heads Science Academy." *The Evening Bulletin*, Philadelphia, December 18, 1928.

97. Wetmore, Alexander. "Witmer Stone (1866-1939)." *Year Book of the American Philosophical Society*, 1939:467-69; Rehn, James A. G. "Report of the Secretary." *Year Book of the Academy of Natural Sciences of Philadelphia*, 1928:26-30; Pennell, Francis W. "The botanical work of Witmer Stone." *Bartonia*, 1940. 20:33-37.

98. Bailey, Florence Merriam. Letter to Witmer Stone, August 21, 1928. ANSP 450.

99. Cope, Francis R., Jr. Letter to Witmer Stone, January 2, 1929. ANSP 450.

100. Dixon, Samuel G. Letter to Henry Tucker, December 4, 1911. ANSP Collection 241, Box 2, Folder 2; Pennell, Francis W. Letter to Witmer Stone, July 24, 1925. ANSP Collection 186, Box 3, Folder 1.

101. Stone, Witmer. "On a collection of birds from the Para region, Eastern Brazil." *PANSP*, 1928. 80:149-76.

102. Stone, Witmer. Letter to W.H. Bergtold, April 28, 1935. ANSP 450.

103. Ripley, S. Dillon. "In memoriam: Rodolphe Meyer de Schauensee." *The Auk*, 1986. 103(1):204-06; Parkes, Kenneth C. "In memoriam: James Bond." *The Auk*, 1989. 106(4):718-20.

104. Stone, Witmer. Letter to Charles M.B. Cadwalader, May 15, 1932. ANSP Collection 186, Box 3, Folder 4.

105. Stone, Witmer. Letter to Frank M. Chapman, July 25, 1931. Department of Ornithology Archives, AMNH; Stone, Witmer. Letters to Theodore S. Palmer, July 15 & October 15, 1931. LOC, T.S. Palmer papers, Boxes 48 & 50.

106. Stone, Witmer. Letter to Alexander Wetmore, June 4, 1932. SIA Collection 7006, Box 65, Folder 8; Bowen, W. Wedgwood. "Variation and evolution of Gulf Coast populations of beach mice, Peromyscus polionotus." *Bulletin of the Florida State Museum Biological Sciences*, 1968. 12(1):1-91; Bowen, W. Wedgwood. Letters to Witmer Stone, March 10, April 24, May 7, & June 22, 1934. ANSP 450.

107. Stone, Witmer. Letter to Charles M.B. Cadwalader, September 4, 1933. ANSP Collection 232, Folder 8. Stone actually wrote "instead of a mere collector who does know what he has secured," but it's clear from the context that "doesn't" was intended.

108. Olson, Storrs L. "Correspondence bearing on the history of ornithologist M.A. Carriker Jr. and the use of arsenic in preparation of museum specimens." *Archives of Natural History*, 2007. 34(2):346-51.

109. Stone, Witmer. Letter to George L. Harrison, July 15, 1921. ANSP Collection 186, Box 2, Folder 2; Stone, Witmer. Letter to C.J. Albrecht, November 29, 1927. ANSP Collection 186, Box 1, Folder 1.

110. Elliot, Daniel Giraud. Letter to Witmer Stone, April 23, 1900. ANSP 450.

111. Untitled memo with handwritten "Submitted by Morgan Hebard Jan. 1936" at top of first page. ANSP Collection 590, Folder 10.

112. Miller, Gerrit S. Letter to Witmer Stone, April 13, 1911. ANSP Collection 953, Folder 2.

113. Stone, Witmer. Letter to F.B. Vandergrift Co., June 23, 1926. ANSP Collection 186, Box 1, Folder 7; Stone, Witmer. Letter to W. E. Clyde Todd, December 16, 1921. ANSP Collection 186, Box 3, Folder 4.

114. Carriker, Melbourne A. Letter to Witmer Stone, September 1, 1913. ANSP Collection 186, Box 1, Folder 4.

115. Carriker, Melbourne A. Letters to Witmer Stone, June 19 & 26, 1916. ANSP Collection 186, Box 1, Folder 5.

116. Moffett, Lacey I. Letter to Witmer Stone, July 29, 1925. ANSP Collection 186, Box 2, Folder 6.

117. Stone, Witmer. "Zoological results of the Dolan Expedition of 1931: Part 1. Birds." *PANSP*, 1933. 85:165-222; Stone, Witmer. Letter to T.S. Palmer, November 27, 1932. SIA Collection 7150, Box 70, Folder 6.

118. Montgomery, Thomas H. Letter to Witmer Stone, December 13, 1891. ANSP 450.

119. Stone, Witmer. Letter to Charles M.B. Cadwalader, May 25, 1936. ANSP Collection 2009-034, Box 45, Folder 23.

120. Stone, Witmer. "Report of the Ornithological Section." *PANSP*, 1899. 51:548-49; Rosengarten, J.G. Letter to Witmer Stone, March 15, 1916. ANSP 450; Penrose, Richard A.F. Letter to Witmer Stone, March 18, 1916. ANSP 450; Stone, Witmer, Samuel G. Dixon, Henry A. Pilsbry, et al. "Report of the curators." *PANSP*, 1916. 68:618-25; Stone, Witmer. "Report of the director of the museum." *Year Book of the Academy of Natural Sciences of Philadelphia*, 1928:36-42; Stone, Witmer. Letter to Rufus H. Lefevre, June 14, 1928. ANSP Collection 54, Box 2.

121. Stone, Witmer. Letter to David E. Harrower, May 24, 1923. ANSP Collection 186, Box 2, Folder 2.

122. Henshaw, Samuel. Letter to Witmer Stone, September 15, 1919. ANSP Collection 186, Box 2, Folder 2.

123. Stejneger, Leonhard. Letter to Witmer Stone, September 26, 1919. ANSP 450.

124. Barbour, Thomas. Letter to Witmer Stone, September 5, 1919. ANSP 450.

125. Rehn, James A. G. Letter to Witmer Stone, September 25, 1919. ANSP Collection 682, Folder 1.

126. True, Frederick W. Letter to Witmer Stone, March 17, 1898. ANSP 450. The Smithsonian's True told Stone, "I regret to say that there seem to have been a good many specimens belonging to the Government in Professor Cope's hands at the time of his death" that could no longer be located.

127. Barbour, Thomas. Letter to Witmer Stone, September 15, 1919. ANSP 450.

128. Barbour, Thomas. "Herpetological Notes." *Proceedings of the New England Zoological Club*, 1919. 7:7-13.

129. Stone, Witmer. Letter to Samuel Henshaw, September 17, 1919. MCZ Archives.

130. Barbour, Thomas. Letter to Witmer Stone, September 26, 1919. ANSP 450.

131. Henshaw, Samuel. Letter to Witmer Stone, October 2, 1919. ANSP Collection 186, Box 2, Folder 2; Herpetology R-12457 - *Celestus phoxinus*. Cited February 11, 2014. Available from http://mczbase.mcz.harvard.edu/guid/MCZ:Herp:R-12457

132. Clubb, Joseph A. Letter to Witmer Stone, February 3, 1926. ANSP Collection 54, Box 2, Folder 8.

133. Stone, Witmer. Letter to Joseph A. Clubb, March 18, 1926. ANSP Collection 54, Box 2, Folder 8.

134. "Notes and news." *The Auk*, 1923. 40(2):376-82.

135. Peck, Robert M. and Patricia Tyson Stroud, *A Glorious Enterprise*. 2012. 396.

136. Curators' minutes for February 17, 1890. ANSP Collection 86, Folder 1.

137. Curators' minutes for June 8, 1891. ANSP Collection 86, Folder 1.

138. Fowler, Henry W. Letter to Witmer Stone, August 14, 1902. ANSP 450.

139. Huber, Wharton. Letter to Witmer Stone, July 24, 1923. ANSP 450.

140. Stone, Witmer. Letter to James L. Peters, April 21, 1933. MCZ Archives; Osgood, Wilfred H. Letter to Witmer Stone, August 31, 1921. ANSP 450.

141. De Laguna, Frederica. Letter to Witmer Stone, March 2, 1933. ANSP Collection 186, Box 2 Folder 5.

142. Dixon, Samuel G. Letter to Witmer Stone, May 24, 1913. ANSP 450.

143. Fowler, Henry W. Letter to Witmer Stone, March 23, 1902. ANSP 450.

144. Huber, Wharton. Letter to Witmer Stone, undated. ANSP 450.

145. Cadwalader, Charles M.B. Letter to Witmer Stone, September 15, 1930. ANSP Collection 232, Folder 8.

146. Huber, Wharton. Letter to Greville Haslam, October 5, 1938. ANSP Collection 186, Box 2, Folder 2; Stone, Witmer. Letter to Alexander Wetmore, March 7, 1933. SIA Collection 7006, Box 65, Folder 8.

147. "Memorandum for Members of Council, A.N.S." Undated spreadsheet detailing costs for implementing business office system. Estimated date of 1921–1925, based on mention of Stone's salary of $3.3K, which was his salary during that time frame. ANSP Collection 590, Folder 9. Interestingly, a colleague of Frederick Stone Sr. wrote after his death that in his work at the Historical Society of Pennsylvania, Frederick was burdened with "too much clerical work and detail, which could have been performed just as well by others, and which was unsuited to a man of his ability" (Sydney G. Fisher, "The Late Frederick Stone," *The Philadelphia Times*, 8/18/1897).

148. Undated, handwritten notes by Stone titled "Vertebrate Zool." Staff listed indicates written c. 1930-1934. ANSP Collection 232, Folder 8.

149. Rehn, James A. G. Memorandum to Charles M.B. Cadwalader, March 24, 1936. ANSP Collection 590, Folder 10.

150. Huber, Wharton. Memorandum to Charles M.B. Cadwalader, March 23, 1936. ANSP Collection 232, Folder 8.

151. Dixon, Samuel G. Letter to Witmer Stone, Undated, but clearly c. February 14, 1896. ANSP 450.

152. Penrose, Richard A.F. Letters to Witmer Stone, November 16, 1925 & January 8, 1926. ANSP Collection 186, Box 3, Folder 1.

153. Cadwalader, Charles M.B. Letter to Witmer Stone, June 20, 1929. ANSP Collection 186, Box 1, Folder 4; "Academy of Natural Sciences of Philadelphia Presidents' Office and Administration records, 1874-2003." Finding aid, ANSP Collection 2010-051, prepared by Laurie Rizzo and Eric Rosenzweig; Peck, Robert M. and Patricia Tyson Stroud, *A Glorious Enterprise*. 2012. 208-09, 275-77.

154. Undated, untitled memo, c.1930, about tapping into the vitality of the recent Benjamin Franklin Parkway development to increase the number of ANSP visitors. ANSP Collection 590, Folder 9.

155. Stone, Witmer. Letter to Theodore S. Palmer, January 12, 1931. LOC, T.S. Palmer papers, Box 48.

156. "Academy of Natural Sciences of Philadelphia Presidents' Office and Administration records, 1874-2003." Finding aid, ANSP Collection 2010-051, prepared by Laurie Rizzo and Eric Rosenzweig

157. Peck, Robert M. and Patricia Tyson Stroud, "A Glorious Enterprise," in *A Glorious Enterprise*. 2012. 271.

158. Wardle, H. Newell. "Wreck of the Archaeological Department of the Academy of Natural Sciences of Philadelphia." *Science*, 1929. 70(1805):119-21.

159. Stone, Witmer, Samuel G. Dixon, Henry A. Pilsbry, et al. "Report of the curators." *PANSP*, 1917. 69:346-52; Stone, Witmer and Henry A. Pilsbry. "Report of the curators." *PANSP*, 1918. 70:350-55; Minutes of curators' meeting for June 5, 1923. ANSP Collection 86, Folder 2.

160. Stone, Witmer. Letter to Charles M.B. Cadwalader, April 18, 1934. ANSP Collection 186, Box 3, Folder 4.

161. Cadwalader, Charles M.B. Letter to Witmer Stone, April 18, 1934. ANSP Collection 232, Folder 8.

162. Stone, Witmer. Letter to Charles M.B. Cadwalader, April 27, 1936; Cadwalader, Charles M.B. Letters to Witmer Stone, April 30 & June 8, 1936. All ANSP Collection 2009-034, Box 45, Folder 23.

163. Cadwalader, Charles M.B. Letter to Witmer Stone, April 29, 1937. ANSP 450.

164. Cadwalader, Charles M.B. Letter to Witmer Stone, August 27, 1937. ANSP Collection 2009-034, Box 47, Folder 69; BSOCM. xi.

165. Cadwalader, Charles M.B. Letter to Witmer Stone, December 16, 1937. ANSP Collection 2009-034, Box 47, Folder 69.

166. Huber, Wharton. Letter to Witmer Stone, August 8, 1931. ANSP 450.

167. Huber, Wharton. Letter to Witmer Stone, August 6, 1932. ANSP 450.

168. Cadwalader, Charles M.B. Letter to Witmer Stone, August 27, 1937. ANSP Collection 2009-034, Box 47, Folder 69.

169. Stone, Witmer. Letter to Charles M.B. Cadwalader, November 1, 1937. ANSP Collection 2009-034, Box 47, Folder 69.

170. Curators' minutes for April 24, 1915. ANSP Collection 86, Folder 2.

171. Howell, A. Brazier. Letter to Rosalie Edge, February 10, 1935. Hawk Mountain Sanctuary Archives.

172. Bock, Walter J. "Reviews: Erwin Stresemann (1889-1972)." The Auk, 2001. 118(3):805-06; Stresemann, Erwin. "The Formekreis-theory." The Auk, 1936. 53(2):150-58; Cadwalader, Charles M.B. Letter to Witmer Stone, July 31, 1937. ANSP 450.

173. Cadwalader, Charles M.B. Letter to Witmer Stone, September 16, 1937. ANSP 450.

174. Mayr, Ernst. "Obituary: Erwin Stresemann." Ibis, 1972. 115(2):282-.

175. Curators' minutes for June 26, 1891 & February 24, 1892. ANSP Collection 86, Folder 1.

176. Curators' minutes for October 26, 1896. ANSP Collection 86, Folder 1.

177. Rehn, James A.G. Letter to Witmer Stone, June 8, 1919. ANSP Collection 682, Folder 1; Untitled document showing ANSP salaries 1888-1936. ANSP Collection 186, Folder 2.

178. Cadwalader, Charles M.B. Letters to Witmer Stone, May 27, 1932 & July 7, 1936. ANSP Collection 603, Folder 10 & ANSP Collection 186, Box 1, Folder 4.

179. Stone's handwritten notes for 1925 Ludwick Institute annual board meeting minutes; Dixon, Edwin S., Jr. Letter to Witmer Stone, January 3, 1939. Both Historical Society of Pennsylvania Collection 1783.

180. Stone, Witmer. Letter to Joel Asaph Allen, September 19, 1911. Department of Ornithology Archives, AMNH; Stone, Witmer. Letter to Robert Ridgway, January 18, 1922. Blacker-Wood Collection, Department of Rare Books, McGill University.

181. Stone, Witmer. Letter to Charles M.B. Cadwalader, July 8, 1936. ANSP Collection 2009-034, Box 45, Folder 23; Stone, Witmer. Letter to Frank M. Chapman, December 9, 1935. Department of Ornithology Archives, AMNH.

182. Stone, Witmer. Letter to Frank M. Chapman, September 18, 1932. Department of Ornithology Archives, AMNH; Stone, Witmer. Letter to T.S. Palmer, September 9, 1934. SIA Collection 7150, Box 70, Folder 9; Stone, Witmer. Letter to T.S. Palmer, December ?, 1933. SIA Collection 7150, Box 70, Folder 6.

183. Fleming, James H. Letter to Witmer Stone, December 5, 1933. ANSP 450.

184. Stone, Witmer. Letter to Frank M. Chapman, September 27, 1927. Department of Ornithology Archives, AMNH.

185. Stone, Witmer. Letter to Frank M. Chapman, January 30, 1933. Department of Ornithology Archives, AMNH.

186. Stone, Witmer. Letter to Theodore S. Palmer, November 25, 1933. SIA Collection 7150, Box 70, Folder 6.

187. Roberts, H. Radclyffe. Memo to ANSP curators, December 9, 1954. ANSP Collection 590, Folder 9; Stone, Witmer. Letter to Charles M.B. Cadwalader, February 12, 1938. ANSP Collection 2009-034, Box 50, Folder 34.

188. Stone, Witmer. Letter to John E. Bowers, March 31, 1939. ANSP Collection 2010-051, Box 1, Folder 92.

189. Stone, Witmer. Letter to Waldo Lee McAtee, undated, but clearly mid-1930s. LOC, W.L. McAtee papers, Box 37, Folder 3.

190. McIlhenny, Edward A. Letter to Witmer Stone, October 26, 1937. ANSP 450.

191. Huber, Wharton. Letter to Joseph Grinnell, March 9, 1939. ANSP Collection 186, Box 2, Folder 1; Stone, Witmer. Letter to Charles M.B. Cadwalader, March 15, 1939; Stone, Witmer. Letter to John E. Bowers, March 31, 1939. Latter two ANSP Collection 2010-051, Box 1, Folder 92.

192. Stone, Witmer. Letter to Charles M.B. Cadwalader, January 25, 1939. ANSP Collection 2010-051, Box 1, Folder 92.

Box: Jackrabbit Drives and His Holiness Slides

1. Kirk, Mahlen. Letter to Witmer Stone, June 4, 1904. ANSP 450.

2. Stone, Witmer. "An old case of skins and its associations." *The Osprey*, 1899. 3(7):98-99.

3. Cope, Annie P. Letter to Witmer Stone, March 23, 1901. ANSP 450.

4. "Additions to the museum: fossil vertebrates, fossil invertebrates." *PANSP*, 1901. 53:785-86.

5. Untitled, undated notes for talk about the ANSP herpetology department given by Stone at the 1917 meeting of The American Society of Ichthyologists and Herpetologists. Private collection of Witmer Stone material.

6. Clark, Hubert L. Letter to Witmer Stone, July 12, 1905. ANSP 450.

7. Clark, Hubert L. "The feather tracts of swifts and hummingbirds." *The Auk*, 1906. 23(1):68-91.

8. Calvert, Philip. Letter to Witmer Stone, June 24, 1917. ANSP 450.

9. Stone, Witmer and Henry A. Pilsbry. "Report of the curators." *PANSP*, 1918. 70:350-55.

10. Wood, Horatio C. Letter to Witmer Stone, April 11, 1919. ANSP 450.

11. "Plan to loose rabbit 'corps' in Philadelphia." *Berkeley Daily Gazette*, Berkeley, January 27, 1926.

12. Swarth, Harry S. Letter to Witmer Stone, January 29, 1926. ANSP 450.

13. Stone, Witmer. Letter to Reverend Mother Jane Saul, October 1, 1930. ANSP Collection 2009-034, Box 11, Folder 4.

14. Allen, Glover M. Letter to Witmer Stone, March 9, 1934. ANSP Collection 186, Box 1, Folder 1.

15. "Not a Nature Faker: No! No! No! No!" *Philadelphia Inquirer*, Philadelphia, February 25, 1908. Stone's *Auk* note on the incident (15(4):330) didn't mention the Chuck-will's-widow mistaking the warbler for a butterfly; rather, it said the bird, which was at sea, probably ate the warbler because its usual insect fare wasn't available.

16. "The Double Eagle." *The Ocala Banner*, Ocala, January 3, 1908. I've seen photos of the coin online, and the eagle depiction is not nearly as bad as Stone makes it sound.

17. "Doubt Belgian Met Mr. Brontosaurus." *The Evening Bulletin*, Philadelphia, December 17, 1919.

18. "Squirrels Happy Here, Won't Leave." *Evening Public Ledger*, Philadelphia, December 14, 1933.

Chapter 4: Characters I Have Known

1. History of Ornithology at ANSP. Cited February 7, 2014. Available from http://www.ansp.org/research/biodiv/ornithology/history.php; "The Gift of Caring." Cornelius Weygandt, unpublished manuscript. University of Pennsylvania Archives Collection UPT 50, W547.5, Cornelius Weygandt papers, Box 4, Folder 10.

2. Fingerhood, Edward D. "Origins & founders." *Cassinia*, 1995. 66:28.

3. Rhoads, Samuel N. "Bird clubs in America: The Delaware Valley Club." *Bird-Lore*, 1902. 4:57-61.

4. Street, Phillips B. "A history of the Delaware Valley Ornithological Club." *Cassinia*, 1988-89. 63:2-35.

5. Baily, William L. "The Origin of the Delaware Valley Ornithological Club" in *The DVOC Scrap Book, 1890-1900*. ANSP Collection 570.

6. Delorean Time Machine: Schuylkill Nay Athletic Association. Cited February 22, 2014. Available from http://www.ocfrealty.com/naked-philly/logan-square/delorean-time-machine-schuylkill-navy-athletic-association

7. DVOC minutes for February 3, 1890. ANSP Collection 74A, Box 1, Folder 1.

8. DVOC minutes for March 31, 1890. ANSP Collection 74A, Box 1, Folder 1.

9. DVOC minutes for May 19, 1890. ANSP Collection 74A, Box 1, Folder 1.

10. Weygandt, Cornelius, "Quills and Quillwork," in *A Passing America*. 1932, Henry Holt and Company, New York. 37.

11. *The DVOC Twenty Year Souvenir*. 1910. Privately published.

12. Morris, George Spencer. "The DVOC and its twentieth anniversary." *Cassinia*, 1909. 13:7-10.

13. Trotter, Spencer. "In days before 'the Club.'" *Cassinia*, 1912. 16:26-32. Trotter later said the owl was in the collection at Swarthmore College (DVOC minutes for April 4, 1901; ANSP Collection 74A, Box 1, Folder 4).

14. "Abstract of the proceedings of the DVOC 1909." *Cassinia*, 1909. 13:52-56.

15. Rhoads, Samuel N. "Exit the Dickcissel - a remarkable case of local extinction." *Cassinia*, 1903. 7:17-28.

16. "Abstract of the proceedings of the DVOC 1910." *Cassinia*, 1910. 14:49-53.

17. Trotter, Spencer. "What the DVOC Means to Me." 1909. ANSP Collection 601, Folder 4.

18. Serrill, William J. "William L. Baily." *Cassinia*, 1947-48. 37:17-18.

19. Stone, Witmer. "Spencer Trotter: 1860-1931." *Cassinia*, 1929-30. 28:1-8.

20. "Abstract of the proceedings of the DVOC 1892-97." *Cassinia*, 1892-97. 2:1-26.

21. "Activities of the DVOC." *Cassinia*, 1918. 22:19-21.

22. Ross, C. Chandler. "The DVOC Collection." *Cassinia*, 1972. 53:29-32; Rice, Nathan H. and Robert J. Driver. "History of the DVOC bird collection at the Academy of Natural Sciences." *Cassinia*, 2013. 72-73:58-61.

23. Rhoads, Samuel N. "Bird clubs in America: The Delaware Valley Club." *Bird-Lore*, 1902. 4:57-61. Rhoads reported that all members were 23–30; however, DVOC member Bert Filemyr, who has tenaciously tracked down biographical information and burial sites of the founders, advises that Voelker's gravestone records 1857 as his year of birth, indicating that he was about 32 when the club formed. http://www.dvoc. org/History/Founders/Voelker/Voelker_Charles.htm Cited February 7, 2014.

24. "Abstract of the proceedings of the DVOC 1890-91." *Cassinia*, 1890-91. 1:2-11.

25. DVOC minutes for January 5, 1891. ANSP Collection 74A, Box 1, Folder 1.

26. Baily, William L. Letter to Witmer Stone, January 22, 1891. ANSP Collection 14, Folder 2.

27. DVOC minutes for January 19, 1891. ANSP Collection 74A, Box 1, Folder1.

28. *The DVOC Scrap Book 1890-99.* ANSP Collection 570.

29. DVOC minutes for December 1, 1890. ANSP Collection 74A, Box 1, Folder 1.

30. DVOC minutes for December 20, 1892 & June 6, 1893. ANSP Collection 74A, Box 1, Folders 1 & 2.

31. Stone, Witmer, *The Birds of Eastern Pennsylvania and New Jersey.* 1894. DVOC, Philadelphia.

32. Warren, B.H., *Report on the Birds of Pennsylvania.* 1890; Chapman, Frank M. "Recent Literature: A catalogue of the Birds of New Jersey." *The Auk,* 1891. 8(1):104-05.

33. Chapman, Frank M. "Stone's Birds of Eastern Pennsylvania and New Jersey." *The Auk,* 1895. 12(2):170-71.

34. Batchelder, Charles F. Letter to Witmer Stone, August 20, 1897. ANSP 450.

35. DVOC minutes for March 17, 1898. ANSP Collection 74A, Box 1, Folder 4.

36. Stone, Witmer. Letter to Theodore S. Palmer, June 9, 1926. LOC, T.S. Palmer papers, Box 42; Stone, Witmer. Letter to Frank C. Kirkwood, September 23, 1925. ANSP 450.

37. Moore, Robert T. Letter to Witmer Stone, November 23, 1927. ANSP 450.

38. Moore, Robert T. Letter to Witmer Stone, December 23, 1912. ANSP 450.

39. Moore, Robert T. Letter to Witmer Stone, December 12, 1913. ANSP 450.

40. Rawle, Francis W. Letter to Witmer Stone, March 30, 1908. ANSP 450.

41. Rhoads, Charles J. Letter to Witmer Stone, March 31, 1908. ANSP 450.

42. Wright, Samuel. Letter to James A. G. Rehn, April 7, 1909. ANSP 450.

43. Morris, George Spencer. Letter to Witmer Stone, March 9, 1903. ANSP 450; Moore, Robert T. Letter to Witmer Stone, February 18, 1914. ANSP 450.

44. Stone, Witmer. "George Spencer Morris." *Cassinia*, 1922-24. 25:1-5.

45. Shryock, William. Letter to Witmer Stone, January 30, 1915; Stone, Witmer. Letter to T.S. Roberts, January 24, 1922; Stone, Witmer. Letter to Frederic H. Kennard, September 22, 1922. All ANSP 450.

46. Stone, Witmer. Letter to Theodore S. Palmer, April 21, 1920. LOC, T.S. Palmer papers, Box 37.

47. McMorris, Art. Email to author, October 9, 2012.

48. Wilde, Mark L. C. Letter to Witmer Stone, March 12, 1910. ANSP 450.

49. Trotter, Spencer. "In days before 'the Club.'" *Cassinia*, 1912. 16:26-32.

50. Rhoads, Samuel N. Letter to Witmer Stone, March 8, 1891. ANSP Collection 570.

51. DVOC minutes for March 17, 1891. ANSP Collection 74A, Box 1, Folder 1.

52. DVOC minutes for April 20, 1939. ANSP Collection 74A, Box 2, Folder 2.

53. Brinton, J. Bernard. Letter to Stewardson Brown, November 22, 1892. ANSP Collection 168, Folder 4.

54. Stone, Witmer. "Report of the curators: birds." *PANSP*, 1917. 69:347-48.

55. Apgar, Austin C. Letter to Witmer Stone, March 7, 1894. ANSP 450.

56. Robins, Julia Stockton. "Fifth annual report of the Pennsylvania Audubon Society." *Bird-Lore*, 1902. 4:19-20.

57. The Spencer F. Baird Ornithological Club (Constitution and by-laws). ANSP Collection 104, Folder 2.

58. Sage, John H. Letter to Julia Stockton Robins, December 17, 1900. ANSP Collection 541, Folder 2.

59. "Bird club notes." *Cassinia*, 1901. 5:53-54.

60. "Abstract of the proceedings of the DVOC 1906." *Cassinia*, 1906. 10:58-64.

61. Stone, Witmer. "Notes and news." *The Auk*, 1906. 23(4):485.

62. Thomas, Emily Hinds. Letter to Witmer Stone, August 4, 1906. ANSP 450.

63. Baker, Mary K. Letter to Witmer Stone, February 21, 1910. ANSP Collection 104, Folder 2; Stone, Witmer. "Ornithological Section." *PANSP*, 1910. 62:687-88.

64. Fisher, Elizabeth Wilson. "State reports: Pennsylvania." *Bird-Lore*, 1913. 15:465-66.

65. Deane, Ruthven. Letter to Witmer Stone, January 8, 1910. ANSP Collection 687, Folder 2.

66. Batchelder, Charles F. Letter to Witmer Stone, February 8, 1910. ANSP 450.

67. Stone, Witmer. Letter to Alexander Wetmore, January 13, 1915. SIA Collection 7006, Box 65, Folder 6.

68. Palmer, Samuel C. Letter to Witmer Stone, February 28, 1921. ANSP 450; Stone, Witmer. Letter to Samuel C. Palmer, March 1, 1921. ANSP 450.

69. Stone, Witmer. Letter to Theodore S. Palmer, February 12, 1918. LOC, T.S. Palmer papers, Box 13.

70. The Abbott and Costello Program for Camel Cigarettes (script). Cited February 12, 2014. Available from http://www.otrr. org/FILES/Scripts_pdf/Abbott_And_Costello/Abbott_And_Costello_45-06-07.pdf

71. Potter, Julian K. Letter to Witmer Stone, June 2, 1919. ANSP 450. The ducks proved to be scaups.

72. Haines, Robert L. "Turner E. McMullen." *Cassinia*, 1968-69. 51:45-46.

73. Brady, Alan. Interview with author, August 4, 2011.

74. Brady, Alan. Interview with author, May 3, 2000.

75. Gillespie, John A. Letter to Witmer Stone, July 2, no year. ANSP 450.

76. Reimann, Edward J. "Richard F. Miller." *Cassinia*, 1959. 44:17-18.

77. Weygandt, Cornelius. Letter to Witmer Stone, January 3, 1935. ANSP Collection 76.

78. Stone, Witmer. "Recent Literature: Bennitt's Missouri 'Check-List.'" *The Auk*, 1934. 51(1):112-13.

79. Connor, Jack, *Season at the Point*. 1991. 84.

80. Reimann, Edward J. "Richard F. Miller." *Cassinia*, 1959. 44:17-18. Longtime DVOC member David Cutler (pers. comm. 1/11/2004) once told me that ANSP was offered the collection, but didn't know what to do with it.

81. Carter, John D. Letter to Witmer Stone, April 7, 1925. ANSP 450.

82. Carter, John D. Letter to Witmer Stone, February 24, 1909. ANSP 450. Esther Alsop Carter (d.1989) was born February 24, 1909 (http://www.pennock.ws/surnames/names25.html#CARTER). Cited July 20, 2014.

83. "Abstract of the proceedings of the DVOC 1911." *Cassinia*, 1911. 15:61-66.

84. Kuser, John Dryden. "Egret in northern New Jersey." *The Auk*, 1912. 29(1):100.

85. Johnson, Libbie Harrover, *One Hundred Years and Still Counting*. 1997. Sheridan Press, Hanover. 75; Stone, Witmer. "Recent Literature: Beebe's Monograph of the Pheasants." *The Auk*, 1919. 36(1):119-25.

86. Miller, Judith. "Old Money, New Needs." *New York Times*, November 17, 1991.

87. Gordon, Meryl, "The Family Astor," in *New York Magazine*. August 6, 2006.

88. Falzini, Mark W. Crime of Choice: The Threatened Kidnapping of Senator Dryden Kuser. Cited September 12, 2014. Available from http://njspmuseum.blogspot.com/2007/08/crime-of-choice-threatened-kidnapping_02.html

89. Gordon, Meryl, *Mrs. Astor Regrets*. 2008. Houghton Mifflin, New York. 58.

90. Alan Brady, interview with author August 22, 2013.

91. "Abstract of the proceedings of the DVOC 1929." *Cassinia*, 1929-30. 28:48-52; "Abstract of the proceedings of the DVOC 1927." *Cassinia*, 1927-28. 27:38-41.

92. "Editorial notes and news." *The Condor*, 1910. 12(4):134-35; Pennock, Charles J. Letter to Witmer Stone, August 1, 1903. ANSP Collection 676, Folder 1.

93. Stone, Witmer. Letter to Waldron DeWitt Miller, May 21, 1913. Department of Ornithology Archives, AMNH.

94. Richmond, Charles W. Letter to Witmer Stone, May 20, 1913. ANSP Collection 675, Folder 6; Moore, Robert T. Letter to Witmer Stone, December 12, 1913. ANSP 450.

95. Pennock, Richard W. Letter to Witmer Stone, November 22, 1913. ANSP Collection 676, Folder 2. After Pennock's return, Stone and a few other AOU Fellows chipped in to pay off his dues for the years he was missing, thus keeping his membership continuous (Stone to T.S. Palmer 12/10/1920; LOC T.S. Palmer papers, Box 38; see Stone's attached handwritten note).

96. Palmer, Samuel C. Letter to Witmer Stone, January 27, 1914. ANSP 450.

97. Sharples, Robert P. Letter to Witmer Stone, February 19, 1914. ANSP 450.

98. Williams, John (=Charles J. Pennock). Letter to Witmer Stone, September 23, 1915. ANSP 450.

99. Griscom, Ludlow. Letter to Witmer Stone, November 6, 1919. ANSP 450.

100. Williams, John (=Charles J. Pennock). "Birds about our lighthouse." *The Wilson Bulletin*, 1918. 30(3):87-90.

101. Williams, John (=Charles J. Pennock). Letter to Witmer Stone, October 31, 1919. ANSP 450.

102. Williams, Robert W. Letter to Witmer Stone, November 6, 1919. ANSP 450.

103. Stone, Witmer. "Charles J. Pennock. 1857-1935." *Cassinia*, 1933-37. 30:3-6.

104. Williams, John (=Charles J. Pennock). Letter to Witmer Stone, October 26, 1915. ANSP 450.

105. Stone, Witmer. "Charles J. Pennock. 1857-1935." *Cassinia*, 1933-37. 30:3-6.

106. Williams, John (=Charles J. Pennock). Letter to Witmer Stone, November 8, 1919. ANSP 450.

107. Williams, Robert W. Letter to Witmer Stone, November 28, 1919. ANSP 450.

108. Williams, Robert W. Letter to Witmer Stone, December 3, 1919. ANSP 450.

109. Pennock, Mary S. Letter to Witmer Stone, December 14, 1919. ANSP Collection 676, Folder 2.

110. Pennock, Charles J. Letter to Witmer Stone, December 24, 1919. ANSP 450.

111. Williams, John (=Charles J. Pennock). "Notes on birds of Wakulla County, Florida." *The Wilson Bulletin*, 1920. 32(1):1-12; Pennock, Charles J. "Note on the nesting of Buteo brachyurus at St. Marks, Florida." *The Auk*, 1890. 7(1):56-57.

112. "Bird Expert 'Lost,' is Back." *The Reading Eagle*, January 2, 1920; "Pennock to Come Home: Visits Son." *Evening Public Ledger*, Philadelphia, January 2, 1920.

113. "Story of Birds Brings to Light Missing Man: Lure of the Open Sends Scientist into Seclusion for Six Years." *Harrisburg Telegraph*, Harrisburg, January 2, 1920.

114. Hunt, Chreswell J. Letter to Witmer Stone, January 10, 1920. ANSP 450; "[Title illegible; subtitle 'Recalls Titanic; May Be Oxford Man']." *Chicago Tribune*, January 10, 1920.

115. Pennock, Charles J. Letter to Witmer Stone, March 2, 1920. ANSP Collection 676, Folder 2.

116. Pennock, Mary S. Letter to Witmer Stone, August 24, 1916. ANSP Collection 676, Folder 2.

117. Dawson, W. Leon. Letter to Witmer Stone, October 26, 1917. ANSP 450.

118. Pennock, Charles J. Letter to Witmer Stone, August 9, 1921. ANSP Collection 186, Box 3, Folder 1.

119. Stone, Witmer. Letter to Charles J. Pennock, September 23, 1921. ANSP Collection 186, Box 3, Folder 1.

120. Pennock, Charles J. Letter to Witmer Stone, September 29, 1921. ANSP Collection 186, Box 3, Folder 1.

121. Pennock, Charles J. Letter to Charles M.B. Cadwalader, December 8, 1933. ANSP Collection 186, Box 3, Folder 1.

122. Stone, Witmer. Letter to Charles J. Pennock, December 15, 1933. ANSP Collection 186, Box 3 Folder 1.

123. Pennock, Charles J. Letter to Witmer Stone, December 19, 1933. ANSP Collection 186, Box 3, Folder 1.

124. Pennock, Jean. Letter to Witmer Stone, undated, but 1935. ANSP Collection 676, Folder 2.

125. DVOC minutes for January 2, 1936. ANSP Collection 74A, Box 2, Folder 2.

126. "Abstract of the proceedings of the DVOC 1905." *Cassinia*, 1905. 9:69-76.

127. Biographies of the Birds of Eastern Pennsylvania, New Jersey, and Delaware. ANSP Collection 74A, Box 1, Folder 2.

128. "A prospectus." *Cassinia*, 1910. 14:19-20.

129. Hunt, Chreswell J. Letters to Witmer Stone, September 13 & December 12, 1909. ANSP 450; Hunt, Chreswell J. Letters to Witmer Stone, April 3 & 12, 1919. ANSP Collection 752, Folder 4.

130. "Abstract of the proceedings of the DVOC 1914." *Cassinia*, 1914. 18:62-65; Notes for January 15, 1914 "Present Day Aspects of Ornithology" talk to DVOC in private collection of Witmer Stone material.

131. Stone, Witmer. Letter to Julian K. Potter, November 16, 1918. ANSP 450.

132. DVOC minutes for March 6, 1919. ANSP Collection 74A, Box 2, Folder 1.

133. Undated, untitled check-list of species accounts for DVOC book. ANSP Collection 2009-031, Box 1, Folder 6.

134. DVOC minutes for May 6, 1920. ANSP Collection 74A, Box 2, Folder 1.

135. Scoville, Samuel. Letter to Witmer Stone, June 28, 1926. ANSP 450.

136. Moore, Robert T. Letter to Witmer Stone, May 22, 1926. ANSP 450.

137. Weygandt, Cornelius. Letter to Witmer Stone, October 17, 1910. ANSP Collection 76; Weygandt, Cornelius. Letter to Witmer Stone, September 19, 1913. ANSP Collection 752, Folder 4.

138. Weygandt, Cornelius. Letter to Witmer Stone, December 4, 1929. ANSP Collection 186, Box 3, Folder 7.

139. Stone, Witmer. Letter to Cornelius Weygandt, December 16, 1929. ANSP Collection 186, Box 3, Folder 7.

140. Weygandt, Cornelius. Letter to Witmer Stone, December 10, 1930. ANSP Collection 186, Box 3, Folder 7. A University of Pennsylvania Archives collection (UPT 50) with scores of unpublished Weygandt essays contains several bird biographies, and some of the material was written for inclusion in the DVOC book.

141. Stone, Witmer. Letter to Frank M. Chapman, January 8, 1918. Department of Ornithology Archives, AMNH.

142. "Notes and news." *The Auk*. 36(2):319-24.

143. Stone, Witmer. "Club Notes." *Cassinia*, 1918. 22:42-43.

144. Stone, Witmer. Letter to Albert K. Fisher, June 19, 1917. LOC, A.K. Fisher papers, Box 22.

145. Stone, Witmer. Letter to Harry C. Oberholser, June 28, 1918. LOC, Harry C. Oberholser papers, Box 18; Stone, Witmer. Letters to Theodore S. Palmer, June 28, 1918 & April 20, 1919. LOC, T.S. Palmer papers, Boxes 13 & 36; *Five and Thirty: The Further History of the Class of Eighty-Seven*. 1922. 118.

146. Stone, Witmer. Letter to Harry C. Oberholser, January 23, 1918. LOC, Harry C. Oberholser papers, Box 18.

147. Stone, Witmer. "Recent Literature: Le Gerfaut." *The Auk*, 1920. 37(2):331.

148. Dwight, Jonathan, Jr. Letter to Witmer Stone, June 4, 1918. ANSP Collection 686, Folder 3.

149. Stone, Witmer. Letter to Albert K. Fisher, March 4, 1918. LOC, A.K. Fisher papers, Box 22.

150. Stone, Witmer. Letter to William L. Baily, January 22, 1926. ANSP Collection 398, Folder 7.

151. Stone, Witmer. Letters to Theodore S. Palmer, May 31 & July 6, 1928. LOC, T.S. Palmer papers, Box 45.

152. Stone, Witmer. Letter to Alexander Wetmore, January 22, 1926. SIA Collection 7006, Box 65, Folder 6; Stone, Witmer. Letter to J. Stewart Rodman, October 22, 1926. ANSP 450.

153. "Notes and news." *The Auk*, 1915. 32(3):268-72.

154. Stone, Witmer. Letter to Theodore S. Palmer, November 11, 1935. SIA Collection 7150, Box 70, Folder 10.

155. "Abstract of the proceedings of the DVOC 1935." *Cassinia*, 1933-37. 30:51-55; Eaton, Warren F. Letter to Witmer Stone, November 13, 1935. ANSP 450.

156. Stone, Witmer. Letter to William Vogt, May 29, 1936. ANSP 450.

157. Stone, Witmer. Letter to Julian K. Potter, January 17, 1937. ANSP Collection 2010-113, Box 4.

158. Stone, Witmer. Letter to Theodore S. Palmer, September 27, 1936. SIA Collection 7150, Box 70, Folder 11.

159. "Dr. Stone Honored on 70th Birthday." *Evening Public Ledger*, Philadelphia, September 23, 1936.

160. Untitled list of attendees at DVOC 70th birthday celebration for Stone. ANSP Collection 2009-031, Box 5.

161. DVOC minutes for April 6, 1939. ANSP Collection 74A, Box 2, Folder 2.

162. DVOC minutes for January 19 & March 3, 1891, & January 3, 1893. ANSP Collection 74A, Box 1, Folder 1; Untitled attendance sheets for DVOC meetings, ANSP Collection 74A, Box 2, Folder 1, and ANSP 450, Box 19, Folder 4.

163. Reed, J. Harris. Letter to Witmer Stone, March 17, 1892. ANSP 450. The June 2004 newsletter of the Beverly-Riverside (New Jersey) mason's lodge listed Reed as the "master" of the Beverly Lodge in 1892.

164. DVOC minutes for June 6, 1893. ANSP Collection 74A, Box 1, Folder 2. Fletcher Street later said that Reed's "observations were tinged with an overzealous desire to report the unusual" (*Cassinia* 63:8).

165. Reed, J. Harris. Letter to William E. Hughes, April 16, 1896. ANSP 450; DVOC minutes for April 16, 1896. ANSP Collection 74A, Box 1, Folder 3; Reed, J. Harris. Letter to Charles J. Rhoads, April 21, 1896. ANSP 450.

166. DVOC minutes for February 4, 1897. ANSP Collection 74A, Box 1, Folder 3.

167. Morris, George Spencer. Letter to Witmer Stone, undated, but clearly 1891. Noting Reed's lack of involvement in the new ANSP ornithology section, Morris wrote, "Sorry for Reed and glad for the Section. Hope his little feelings won't be hurt." In another letter, Morris expressed irritation at Reed's reported pique at not being invited to Baily's wedding. ANSP 450.

168. Wilde, Mark L. C. Letter to Witmer Stone, February 21, 1898. ANSP 450.

169. Wilde, Mark L. C. Letter to Witmer Stone, November 20, 1909. ANSP 450.

170. *BSOCM.* xii.

171. List of Active members in DVOC minutes book. ANSP Collection 74A, Box 1, Folder 3; Untitled attendance sheets for DVOC meetings, ANSP 450, Box 19, Folder 4.

172. Voelker, Charles. Letter to Witmer Stone, December 30, 1911. ANSP 450.

173. "Members." *The Cape May Geographic Society Bulletin*, 1948. 2:11-12; Hiers, Mildred D. "Some fragments which have become history." *The Cape May Geographic Society Bulletin*, 1951. 5:8-10.

174. Stone, Witmer. "George Spencer Morris." *Cassinia*, 1922-24. 25:1-5.

175. Trotter, Spencer. Letter to Witmer Stone, March 30, 1892. ANSP Collection 601, Folder 4.

176. Academy of Natural Sciences of Philadelphia board of trustees minutes for March 17, 1925. ANSP Collection 603, Folder 9.

177. Trotter, Spencer. Letter to Witmer Stone, August 30, 1926. ANSP Collection 601, Folder 4; Stone, Witmer. "Spencer Trotter: 1860-1931." *Cassinia*, 1929-30. 28:1-8.

178. Evans, William Bacon. "Samuel Nicholson Rhoads." *Cassinia*, 1953. 39:17-20.

179. Morris, George Spencer. Letter to Witmer Stone, April 1, 1892. ANSP 450.

180. Haverford College Historic Resources Campus Survey. Conducted by George E. Thomas Associates, Inc. Cited February 7, 2014. Available from http://www.haverford.edu/library/special/aids/archives/historic_resources_campus_survey.pdf

181. Serrill, William J. "William L. Baily." *Cassinia*, 1949. 37:17-18.

182. Baily, William L. "William Loyd Baily, Sr." *Cassinia*, 1919. 23:1-13. The senior Baily also wrote a popular book titled *Our Own Birds*, one of the posthumous printings of which was edited by – of all people – Edward Drinker Cope.

183. William L. Baily illustrations of hummingbirds. ANSP Collection 11. Cited February 7, 2014. Available from http://www.ansp.org/research/library/archives/0000-0099/Baily11/

184. DVOC minutes for March 7, 1895. ANSP Collection 74A, Box 1, Folder 3.

185. Jones, Lynds. "Editorial." *The Wilson Bulletin*, 1912. 24(4):194-96.

186. "Notes and news." *The Auk*, 1913. 30(2):318-24.

187. A fascinating tidbit of *Condor* history: In 1914, editor Grinnell actually proposed to change it from a strictly ornithological periodical to one dealing with vertebrates in general. In a straw vote, the membership

responded 2-to-1 in favor of the change, but the dissenters' written objections were so strenuous that the idea was shelved. *The Condor* 16(4):185-86; 16(5):242.

188. "Foreword." *Cassinia*, 1933-37. 30:1-2.

Chapter 5: Conservation Battles

1. "Notes and news." *The Auk*, 1887. 4(2):174-76.
2. Charter of the Pennsylvania Audubon Society. ANSP Collection 398, Folder 8.
3. Stone, Witmer. Letter to Casey A. Wood, December 15, 1921. ANSP 450. Maria Middleton Fisher Coxe was a wealthy Philadelphia socialite engaged in many conservation organizations, and another one that wouldn't be considered particularly progressive today: The Association to Oppose the Further Extension of Suffrage to Women ("Women Object to Equal Suffrage," *New York Times* 3/28/1909).
4. Carter, John D. Letter to Witmer Stone, December 31, 1903. ANSP 450. The Laysan Albatross is 2½ feet long, with a wingspan of 6½ feet.
5. Graham, Frank, Jr., *The Audubon Ark*. 1990. Alfred A. Knopf, New York. 14-15.
6. "Abstract of the proceedings of the DVOC 1892-97." *Cassinia*, 1892-97. 2:1-26.
7. Dutcher, William. "Report of the AOU Committee on Protection of North American Birds." *The Auk*, 1897. 14(1):21-32.
8. PAS minutes for October 21, 1896. ANSP Collection 398, Folder 5.
9. PAS minutes for April 21, 1899. ANSP Collection 398, Folder 5.
10. Robins, Julia Stockton. "Reports from societies: Pennsylvania Society." *Bird-Lore*, 1899. 1:204-05.
11. Stone, Witmer. Letter to William L. Baily, January 11, 1936. ANSP Collection 398, Folder 7.
12. Stone, Witmer. "Report of the Ornithological Section." *PANSP*, 1900. 52:776-78; "Bird club notes." *Cassinia*, 1901. 5:53-54; Robins, Julia Stockton. "Reports of societies: Pennsylvania Society." *Bird-Lore*, 1899. 1:65-66; Robins, Julia Stockton. "Reports of societies: Pennsylvania Society." *Bird-Lore*, 1901. 3:42.
13. Baily, William L. Letter to Witmer Stone, January 15, 1936. ANSP Collection 398, Folder 7.
14. Stone, Witmer. "Report of the AOU Committee on Protection of North American Birds." *The Auk*, 1900. 17(1):51-58; "Notes and news." *The Auk*, 1900. 17(1):91-96.
15. "The aigrette plume and what its use involves." Manuscript written by Stone and dated December 5, 1896. Private collection of Witmer Stone material.
16. Stone, Witmer. "A question of fees." *Bird-Lore*, 1900. 2:95.
17. Fisher, Elizabeth Wilson. Letter to Witmer Stone, March 19, 1901. ANSP Collection 398, Folder 7; Robins, Julia Stockton. "Reports of societies: sixth annual report of the Pennsylvania Audubon Society." *Bird-Lore*, 1903. 5:72-73.
18. "Bird club notes." *Cassinia*, 1902. 6:58-59.
19. PAS minutes for March 29, 1900. ANSP Collection 398, Folder 5.
20. Justice, Hilda. Letter to Julia Stockton Robins, November 7, 1904. ANSP Collection 398, Folder 7.
21. Pearson, T. Gilbert. Letter to Elizabeth Wilson Fisher, May 26, 1916. ANSP Collection 398, Folder 6; "New members and contributors." *Bird-Lore*, 1916. 18:349.
22. Stone, Witmer. "In memoriam." *Bird-Lore*, 1906. 8:142; Stone, Witmer. Letter to Stewardson Brown, July 10, 1906. ANSP Collection 168, Folder 5.
23. Stone, Witmer. "State reports: Pennsylvania." *Bird-Lore*, 1906. 8:270; Janney, Nathaniel E. Letter to Witmer Stone, March 28, 1907. ANSP 450; Fisher, Elizabeth Wilson. "State reports: Pennsylvania." *Bird-Lore*, 1907. 9:353-54.
24. Stone, Witmer. Letter to William L. Baily, January 18, 1936. ANSP Collection 398, Folder 7.
25. "Milliners Driving Birds from Pennsylvania Woods." *The Courier*, Harrisburg, February 23, 1913; Three 1913 *Bird-Lore* articles describe the legislative battle: "Egret protection" (15:147-48), "State legislation" (15:406-07), and "State Audubon reports: Pennsylvania" (15:465-66).
26. "Pennsylvania Audubon Society to be Made an Effective Business Organization With State-wide Activities." Pamphlet. ANSP Collection 398, Folder 8.
27. Fisher, Elizabeth Wilson. Letter to Witmer Stone, October 13, 1914. ANSP Collection 398, Folder 6.
28. Fisher, Elizabeth Wilson. Letters to Witmer Stone, January 26, 1916, & June 2, 1917. ANSP Collection 398, Folder 7; Oldys, Henry. Letters to Witmer Stone, October

26 & November 27, 1916, & W. Stone letter to H. Oldys, December 1, 1916. ANSP Collection 398, Folder 6; Palmer, Theodore S. "Notes and News: Henry Worthington Olds." *The Auk*, 1925. 42(4):616-17.

29. Oldys, Henry. Letter to Witmer Stone, July 29, 1917. ANSP Collection 398, Folder 6.

30. Oldys, Henry. Letters to Witmer Stone, January 29 & September 22, 1924. ANSP Collection 398, Folder 6.

31. Stone, Witmer. Letter to Henry Oldys, February 1, 1924. ANSP Collection 398, Folder 6.

32. Stone, Witmer. Letter to Seth Gordon, March 28, 1921. ANSP 450.

33. Pearson, T. Gilbert. Letter to Witmer Stone, March 31, 1917. ANSP 450.

34. Stone, Witmer. Letter to R. L. Watts, November 3, 1922. ANSP 450.

35. Stone, Witmer. Letter to T. Gilbert Pearson, March 3, 1926. ANSP 450.

36. Stone, Witmer. Letter to A.O. Vorse, May 29, 1925. ANSP 450.

37. Stone, Witmer. Letter to T. Gilbert Pearson, October 4, 1928. New York Public Library Archives Collection 4496, Box A-141, "Pennsylvania" folder.

38. Grinnell, Joseph. Letter to Witmer Stone, May 27, 1930. ANSP Collection 684, Folder 5; Palmer, Theodore S. Letter to Witmer Stone, November 13, 1929. LOC, T.S. Palmer papers, Box 47.

39. Fisher, Elizabeth Wilson. Letter to Witmer Stone, January 22, 1934. ANSP Collection 2009-031, Box 1, Folder 3; Stone, Witmer. Letter to Francis R. Cope, Jr., September 16, 1930. ANSP Collection 2009-034, Box 11, Folder 4; Stone, Witmer. Letter to Elizabeth Wilson Fisher, November 24, 1932, & E.W. Fisher, letter to W. Stone, May 22, 1933. ANSP Collection 398, Folder 6; Stone, Witmer. Letter to Theodore S. Palmer, January 12, 1931. LOC, T.S. Palmer papers, Box 48.

40. Fisher, Elizabeth Wilson. Letter to Witmer Stone, January 15, 1936. ANSP Collection 398, Folder 8.

41. Weyl, Edward S. Letter to Rosalie Edge, December 11, 1935. Hawk Mountain Sanctuary Archives.

42. Robeson, Katherine Morgan. Letters to Witmer Stone, March 6 & 31, 1936. ANSP 450.

43. Stone, Witmer. Letter to William L. Baily, May 29 1936. ANSP Collection 398, Folder 7.

44. "Notes and news." *The Auk*, 1896. 13(1):93-98; Stone, Witmer. Letter to William Brewster, November 26, 1895. MCZ Archives; "Notes and news." *The Auk*, 1898. 15(1):78-80; Dutcher, William. "Results of special protection to gulls and terns obtained through the Thayer Fund." *The Auk*, 1902. 19(1):34-64.

45. "No Hat Feathers Come From the U.S.: Dr. [sic] Witmer Stone Congratulates This Country on its Bird Protection Law." *The Philadelphia Times*, Philadelphia, March 16, 1899.

46. "Bird slaughter in Delaware." *Bird-Lore*, 1900. 2:60.

47. "Notes and news." *The Auk*, 1900. 17(2):193-200.

48. Bush, W.D. Letter to Witmer Stone, March 10, 1900. ANSP 450.

49. Stone, Witmer. "Report of the Committee on the Protection of North American Birds for the year 1900." *The Auk*, 1901. 18(1):68-76.

50. Spaid, A.R. Letter to Witmer Stone, March 9, 1901. ANSP 450.

51. Farmer, Charles W. Letters to Witmer Stone, March 7 & 16, 1900. ANSP 450; "Milliners deny a report." *The New York Press*, March 17, 1900; *The New York Times*, March 25, 1900; "Says birds are bought." *The New York Press*, March 22, 1900.

52. "An agreement." *Bird-Lore*, 1900. 2:98.

53. Stephenson, Louise. Letter to Witmer Stone, undated, but probably May 1900. ANSP 450.

54. Stone, Witmer. Letter to William Dutcher, May 7, 1900. New York Public Library Archives Collection 4496, Box A-6, Folder 1900, Jan-Dec.

55. Stone, Witmer. Letter to Louise Stephenson, May 31, 1900. ANSP 450.

56. Stone, Witmer. Letter to Theodore S. Palmer, June 2, 1900. LOC, T.S. Palmer papers, Box 3.

57. Widmann, Otto. Letter to Witmer Stone, June 9, 1900. ANSP 450.

58. Miller, Olive Thorne. Letter to Witmer Stone, June 8, 1900. ANSP 450.

59. Stone, Witmer. "Report of the Committee on the Protection of North American Birds." *The Auk*, 1902. 19(1):31-34.

60. Rhoads, Samuel N. "'Noxious' or 'beneficial'? False premises in economic zoology." *The American Naturalist*, 1898. 32(380):571-81; Rhoads, Samuel N. "Owls, mice and moles: questions in

economic zoology." *Forest and Stream*, 1898. 51(8):143-44.

61. Stone, Witmer. Letter to Albert K. Fisher, October 15, 1898. LOC, A.K. Fisher papers, Box 13.

62. Dutcher, William. Letter to Witmer Stone, April 15, 1901. ANSP 450.

63. Allen, Joel Asaph. "Rowley's 'Art of Taxidermy.'" *The Auk*, 1898. 15(3):282-83; Dutcher, William. Letter to Witmer Stone, April 13, 1901. ANSP 450.

64. Dutcher, William. Letters to Witmer Stone, May 13 & June 7, 1901. ANSP 450; Pearson, T. Gilbert, "Bird Protection," in *Fifty Years' Progress of American Ornithology, 1883-1933*. 1933. 199-213.

65. Dutcher, William. Letter to Witmer Stone, March 15, 1909. ANSP 450.

66. USDA inspector's permit for Witmer Stone dated August 20, 1900. ANSP 450, Box 25, Folder 1.

67. Stone, Witmer. Letter to Walter Deane, November 21, 1900. MCZ Archives.

68. "To Stop Bird Slaughter." *The New York Times*, November 21, 1902.

69. Rawle, Francis W. Letter to Witmer Stone, April 18, 1907. ANSP 450.

70. Warren, B.H., *Report on the Birds of Pennsylvania*. 1890. 245-46; "Commonwealth of Pennsylvania v. Henry Crumley. Court of Quarter Sessions, Philadelphia County, Appeal from Summary Conviction." ANSP Collection 398, Folder 8.

71. Hornaday, William T. Letter to William Dutcher, December 31, 1897. ANSP 450; Dutcher, William. Note to Witmer Stone, January 3, 1898. ANSP 450, appended to William T. Hornaday letter to William Dutcher 12/31/1897.

72. Hornaday, William T. Letter to Witmer Stone, March 5, 1898. ANSP 450.

73. Cabe, Paul R. 1993. European Starling (*Sturnus vulgaris*), The Birds of North America Online (A. Poole, Ed.). Ithaca: Cornell Lab of Ornithology. Retrieved from: http://bna.birds.cornell.edu.bnaproxy.birds.cornell.edu/bna/species/048. The BNA account states that all starlings in North America are descended from the infamous 1890-91 Central Park introductions, but the Fulton incident suggests there may have been other undetected local introductions that aided the species' spread.

74. Stone, Witmer. Letter to Alexander Wetmore, February 9, 1926. SIA Collection 7006, Box 65, Folder 6.

75. Hornaday, William T. Letter to Witmer Stone, January 26, 1898. ANSP 450.

76. Dutcher, William. Letter to Witmer Stone, January 27, 1900. ANSP 450.

77. Dutcher, William. Letter to Witmer Stone, December 11, 1899. ANSP 450.

78. Stone, Witmer. Letter to William Dutcher, March 16, 1900. New York Public Library Archives Collection 4496, Box A-6, Folder 1900, Jan-Dec.

79. Merriam, C. Hart. Letter to Witmer Stone, October 8, 1900. ANSP Collection 678, Folder 5.

80. Dutcher, William. Letter to Witmer Stone, December 1, 1901. New York Public Library Archives Collection 4496, Box A-6, Folder 1900, Jan-Dec.

81. Stone, Witmer. Letter to William Dutcher, April 2, 1901. New York Public Library Archives Collection 4496, Box A-6, Folder 1901, Jan-July.

82. Dutcher, William. Letter to Witmer Stone, March 17, 1900. ANSP 450.

83. Stone, Witmer. Letters to William Dutcher, November 15 & 17, 1901. New York Public Library Archives Collection 4496, Box A-7, Folder 1902, Jul-Dec.

84. Stone, Witmer. Letters to Theodore S. Palmer, February 11, 1901, & March 29, 1902. LOC, T.S. Palmer papers, Box 4.

85. "Study of Trees, Bird Protection." *The Bucks County Gazette*, Bristol, February 4, 1910.

86. Stone, Witmer. "Recent Literature: Kutchin's 'What Birds Have Done With Me.'" *The Auk*, 1922. 39(3):437-38.

87. Rehn, James A. G. "In memoriam: Witmer Stone." *The Auk*, 1941. 58(3):299-313.

88. Barrow, Mark V., Jr., *A Passion for Birds*. 1998. 134.

89. Stone, Witmer. Letter to J.A. Ferguson, May 12, 1923. ANSP 450, Box 24, Folder 4.

90. Gordon, Seth. Letter to Witmer Stone, October 9, 1922. ANSP 450.

91. Gordon, Seth. Letter to Witmer Stone, March 24, 1921. ANSP 450.

92. Gordon, Seth. Letter to Witmer Stone, March 30, 1921. ANSP 450.

93. Stone, Witmer. Letter to Seth Gordon, March 31, 1921. ANSP 450.

94. Stone, Witmer. Letter to Edward W. Nelson, April 21, 1923. ANSP 450; Henderson,

W.C. Letter to Witmer Stone, April 25, 1923. ANSP 450.

95. Stone, Witmer. Letter to George Wharton Pepper, January 27, 1926; Stone, Witmer. Letter to Robert M. Stanfield, January 27, 1926, & R.M. Stanfield, letter to W. Stone, February 8, 1926. ANSP 450.

96. Stone, Witmer. "Recent Literature: McAtee's 'Woodpeckers in relation to trees and wood products.'" *The Auk*, 1912. 29(1):114.

97. Stone, Witmer. "Recent Literature: Matthews 'The Birds of Australia.'" *The Auk*, 1916. 33(1):91.

98. "Wedge-tailed Eagles in agricultural areas. Fact sheet, September 2012." Published by South Australian Murray-Darling Basin Natural Resources Management Board.

99. Stone, Witmer. "Recent Literature: Annual report of the chief of the Biological Survey." *The Auk*, 1920. 37(1):167.

100. Stone, Witmer. "The hawk question." *The Auk*, 1930. 47(2):208-17.

101. Stone, Witmer. "Recent Literature: Shorter papers. Hadley, Alden H." *The Auk*, 1929. 46(3):413; Stone, Witmer. "Recent Literature: Annual report of the Hawk and Owl Society." *The Auk*, 1933. 50(4):457-58.

102. Pearson, T. Gilbert. Letters to Witmer Stone, January 7 & 14, 1936. ANSP 450.

103. Stone, Witmer. "Recent Literature: Teaching units of the Emergency Conservation Committee." *The Auk*, 1934. 51(3):415-16.

104. Dunlap, Thomas R., *Saving America's Wildlife: Ecology and the American Mind, 1850-1990*. 1988. Princeton University Press, Princeton. 38, 48-50.

105. Stone, Witmer. "Recent Literature: Annual report of the chief of the Biological Survey." *The Auk*, 1921. 38(2):301-02; Stone, Witmer. "Recent Literature: Publications on bird protection. Report of the chief of Bureau of Biological Survey, U.S. Dept. of Agriculture." *The Auk*, 1923. 40(2):370; Stone, Witmer. "Recent Literature: Report of the chief of the Biological Survey." *The Auk*, 1925. 42(2):293-94.

106. Hoffmeister, Donald F. "The influence of university and museum professionals in the formation of the American Society of Mammalogists." *Journal of Mammalogy*, 1994. 75(4):i-ii.

107. Stone, Witmer. "Reader Opinion: The Preservation of Wild Life." *Public Ledger*, Philadelphia, June 15, 1930.

108. Redington, Paul G. Letter to Witmer Stone, April 14, 1931. ANSP 450.

109. Stone, Witmer. Letter to Paul G. Redington, May 2, 1931. ANSP 450.

110. Grinnell, Joseph. "Wholesale poisoning of wild animal life." *The Condor*, 1931. 33(3):131-32; Grinnell, Joseph. Letter to Witmer Stone, May 30, 1931. ANSP Collection 684, Folder 5.

111. "Notes and news." *The Auk*, 1931. 48(3):477-80.

112. Howell, A. Brazier. Letter to Witmer Stone, July 13, 1931. ANSP 450.

113. Fisher, Albert K. Letter to Witmer Stone, August 21, 1931. ANSP Collection 685, Folder 7.

114. Stone, Witmer. Letter to Albert K. Fisher, August 31, 1931. LOC, A.K. Fisher papers, Box 34.

115. Fisher, Albert K. Letter to Witmer Stone, September 15, 1931. ANSP Collection 685, Folder 7.

116. Stone, Witmer. Letters to Albert K. Fisher, October 8, 1938 & May 7, 1939. LOC Archives, A.K. Fisher papers, Box 37.

117. McAtee, Waldo Lee. Letter to Witmer Stone, July 14, 1931. LOC, W.L. McAtee papers, Box 37, Folder 3.

118. Fisher, Albert K., *The Hawks and Owls of the United States in Their Relation to Agriculture*. 1893. USDA Dept. of Ornithology and Mammalogy, Washington, D.C.

119. AOU Council minutes for November 13, 1905. SIA Collection 7150, Box 3.

120. Barrow, Mark V., Jr., "Conserve the Collector," in *A Passion for Birds*. 1998. 141-46; "Abstract of the proceedings of the DVOC 1910." *Cassinia*, 1910. 14:49-53.

121. Stone, Witmer. Letter to Frank M. Chapman, September 13, 1913. Department of Ornithology Archives, AMNH.

122. Stone, Witmer. Letter to Beecher S. Bowdish, December 2, 1920. ANSP 450.

123. Miller, Waldron DeWitt. Letter to Witmer Stone, October 22, 1921. ANSP 450.

124. Stone, Witmer. Letter to Waldron DeWitt Miller, October 24, 1921. ANSP 450.

125. Barrow, Mark V., Jr., "Renewing the Conservation Commitment," in *A Passion for Birds*. 1998. 150-53.

126. "Pennsylvania Conservation Council," in *Forestry Almanac: The American Tree Association*. 1924, J.B. Lippincott Co., Philadelphia. 82; Watts, R. L. Letter to Witmer Stone, October 28, 1922. ANSP 450.

127. Watts, R. L. Letters to Witmer Stone, June 27 & November 20, 1923. ANSP 450.
128. Stone, Witmer. Letter to J.A. Ferguson, May 28, 1924, & J.A. Ferguson, letter to W. Stone, June 2, 1924. ANSP 450.
129. Vorse, A.O. Letter to Witmer Stone, May 21, 1926. ANSP 450.
130. Vorse, A.O. Letter to Witmer Stone, April 20, 1926. ANSP 450.
131. DVOC minutes for December 15, 1891. ANSP Collection 74A, Box 1, Folder 2.
132. "Abstract of the proceedings of the DVOC 1898-99." *Cassinia*, 1898-99. 3:1-13.
133. Carpenter, Benjamin A. Letter to Witmer Stone, November 16, 1898. ANSP 450.
134. Stone, Witmer. "A search for the Reedy Island crow roost." *Bird-Lore*, 1899. 1:177-80.
135. Coggins, Herbert L. "Crow roosts and flight lines in southeastern Pennsylvania and New Jersey." *Cassinia*, 1903. 7:29-42.
136. Stone, Witmer. "Notes on winter crow life in the Delaware Valley." *The Auk*, 1903. 20(3):267-71.
137. "Sport: Vermin" in *TIME*. March 31, 1924.
138. "Notes and news." *The Auk*, 1924. 41(1):201-12.
139. Stone, Witmer. Letters to Edward W. Nelson and T. Gilbert Pearson, April 24, 1924. ANSP 450.
140. "Notes and news." *The Auk*, 1924. 41(4):643-49.
141. "Notes and news." *The Auk*, 1932. 49(1):149-51.
142. "Abstract of the proceedings of the DVOC 1927." *Cassinia*, 1927-28. 27:38-41.
143. "Dr. Stone Denounces Crow Slaughter in New Jersey." *The Evening Bulletin*, Philadelphia, February 23, 1927.
144. *BSOCM*. 725.
145. *BSOCM*. 727.
146. Stone, Witmer. "Report of the Ornithological Section." *PANSP*, 1897. 49:550-51, *PANSP*, 1901. 53:775-76.
147. Stone, Witmer. "Pennsylvania and New Jersey spiders of the Family Lycosidae." *PANSP*, 1890. 42:420-34.
148. Stone, Witmer. "Fishes from Pocotaligo River, South Carolina." *Copeia*, 1914. September 15, 1914. Number 10; "Additions to the museum." *PANSP*, 1914. 66:670-78; "Report of the curators." *PANSP*, 1914. 66:656-64.
149. "Additions to the museum." *PANSP*, 1897. 49:557-64, *PANSP*, 1906. 58(3):595-601,

PANSP, 1902. 54(3):814-23, *PANSP*, 1903. 55:821-29, *PANSP*, 1917. 69(3):358-66, *PANSP*, 1890. 42:492-97.
150. Stone, Witmer. Letter to Charles M.B. Cadwalader, May 17, 1935. ANSP Collection 2009-034, Box 52, Folder 20.
151. Huber, Wharton. Untitled memorial of Witmer Stone. 1939. ANSP Collection 263.
152. Morris, George Spencer. "A day in the salt marshes near Atlantic City." *Cassinia*, 2001. 68:42-46; *The DVOC Twenty Year Souvenir*. 1910. Privately published.
153. *BSOCM*. 908.
154. Shryock, William. Letter to Witmer Stone, February 23, 1898. ANSP 450.
155. Young, Robert T. Letter to Witmer Stone, August 7, 1902. ANSP 450.
156. "Abstract of the proceedings of the DVOC 1892-97." *Cassinia*, 1892-97. 2:1-26; Morris, George Spencer. "A day in the salt marshes near Atlantic City." *Cassinia*, 1999. 68:42-46.
157. DVOC minutes for November 2, 1893. ANSP Collection 74A, Box 1, Folder 2.
158. Morris, George Spencer. "Walks and birds, a May morning at Tinicum." *Cassinia*, 1996-97. 67:9-13. C. Hart Merriam made a similar comment 30 years later, when he objected to some remarks about the decreasing necessity of collecting in a talk given by Stone. Merriam wrote that he didn't "believe that a naturalist was ever made without the actual field experience of collecting specimens. The idea that a man can become a naturalist by studying specimens in the museum and books in the library is to me altogether preposterous. Without the enthusiasm generated by actual field collecting and the exhilaration and thrills incident to the capture of a rare specimen, how can one even hope to become more than the mere vacant shadow of an amateur?" (CHM to Stone 1/15/1924; ANSP Collection 678, Folder 7.)
159. DVOC minutes for May 17, 1894. ANSP Collection 74A, Box 1, Folder 3.
160. Morris, George Spencer. Letters to Witmer Stone, March 27 & April 1, 1892. ANSP 450.
161. Stone, Witmer. "George Spencer Morris." *Cassinia*, 1922-24. 25:1-5; Morris, George Spencer. "Aesthetic and scientific natural history." *Cassinia*, 2000-01. 69:37-39.
162. Reed, J. Harris. Letter to Witmer Stone, May 8, 1891. ANSP 450.

163. DVOC minutes for January 18, 1900. ANSP Collection 74A, Box 1, Folder 4.

164. *BSOCM.* 899; DVOC minutes for January 6, 1910. ANSP Collection 74A, Box 1, Folder 5.

165. Mattern, Edwin Stuart. Letter to Witmer Stone, May 26, 1913. ANSP 450.

166. Mattern, Edwin Stuart. Letter to Witmer Stone, June 23, 1913. ANSP 450.

167. Darlington, Emlen P. Letter to Witmer Stone, February 10, 1917. ANSP Collection 752, Folder 4.

168. Rogers, Charles H. Letter to Witmer Stone, July 9, 1921. ANSP 450.

169. Rogers, Charles H. "Piping Plover breeding in New Jersey." *The Auk*, 1921. 38(4):600-01.

170. Witmer Stone's New Jersey collecting permit for year 1920. ANSP 450, Box 17, Folder 4; Darling, Jay N. Letter to Witmer Stone, July 23, 1936. ANSP 450; Stone, Witmer. Letter to Edward W. Nelson, February 11, 1925. ANSP 450.

171. *BSOCM.* 791; Rice, Nathan H. Email to author, August 16, 2009.

172. *BSOCM.* 823 & 684; Stone, Witmer. Letter to Waldo Lee McAtee, July 12, 1921. LOC, W.L. McAtee papers, Box 10, Folder 4.

173. *BSOCM.* 675-76; Stone, Witmer. Letter to James P. Chapin, June 6, 1923. Department of Ornithology Archives, AMNH.

174. "The trend of the popular ornithological magazine." *The Osprey*, 1901. 5(6):94.

175. Stone, Witmer. "Work of the Delaware Valley Ornithological Club during 1890." *The Auk*, 1891. 8(2):244-45. Stone made the same remark in *TBNJ* in 1909 (p. 275).

176. Stone, Witmer. "Hints to young bird students." *Bird-Lore*, 1899. 1:125-27.

177. Trotter, Spencer. "Some old Philadelphia bird collectors and taxidermists." *Cassinia*, 1914. 18:1-8.

178. Notes for January 15, 1914 "Present Day Aspects of Ornithology" talk to DVOC in private collection of Witmer Stone material. "Abstract of the proceedings of the DVOC 1914." *Cassinia*, 1914. 18:62-65.

179. "Abstract of the proceedings of the DVOC 1922." *Cassinia*, 1922-24. 25:53-57.

180. Stone, Witmer, "The Ornithology of Today and Tomorrow," in *The Fiftieth Anniversary of the Nuttall Ornithological Club*. 1924, Cambridge. 7-25.

181. "Abstract of the proceedings of the DVOC 1933." *Cassinia*, 1933-37. 30:40-44.

182. *BSOCM.* ix.

183. *BSOCM.* viii.

184. Chapman, Frank M. "Book News and Reviews: A Field Guide to the Birds." *Bird-Lore*, 1934. 36:253.

185. Correspondence between Stone and Herbert L. Coggins about collecting Heath Hens, several dates late 1890s; Deane, Walter. Letter to Witmer Stone, June 22, 1899; Wayne, Arthur T. Letters to Witmer Stone, November 2, 1891 & June 26, 1899; Fowler, Henry W. Letter to Witmer Stone, "July" 1900; Peet, Max M. Letter to Witmer Stone, July 23, 1913. All ANSP 450; Stone, Witmer. Letter to William Brewster, June 20, 1899. MCZ Archives.

186. "Passenger Pigeons Again." *Philadelphia Inquirer*, Philadelphia, September 30, 1936.

187. J.M.W. "Among the Buteos." *Ornithologist and Oologist*, 1883. 8(3):17-18.

188. Bent, Arthur Cleveland, *Life Histories of North American Gulls and Terns*. 1921. U.S. Government Printing Office, Washington, D.C. 264; *BSOCM.* 579; Shick, Charles S. "Birds found breeding on Seven Mile Beach, New Jersey." *The Auk*, 1890. 7(3):326-29.

189. Shick, Charles S. Letter to Witmer Stone, December 24, 1890. ANSP 450.

190. Stone, Witmer. "Birds and eggs from the Peary expedition." *Ornithologist and Oologist*, 1892. 17(10):158-59.

191. Stone, Witmer. "Report of the A.O.U. Committee on Protection of North American Birds." *The Auk*, 1899. 16(1):55-74; Zerega, Louis A. "The great American egg-hog." *Ornithologist and Oologist*, 1882. 7(23):183.

192. Brewster, William. Letter to Witmer Stone, April 12, 1899. ANSP 450.

193. Stone, Witmer. "Report of the AOU Committee on Protection of North American Birds." *The Auk*, 1900. 17(1):51-58; PAS minutes for April 21, 1899. ANSP Collection 398, Folder 5.

194. Bond, Frank. Letter to Witmer Stone, April 24, 1900. ANSP 450.

195. Jacobs, J. Warren. Letter to Witmer Stone, October 11, 1899. ANSP 450.

196. "Editorial Notes." *The Condor*, 1899. 1(4):74.

197. "General News Notes." *The Condor*, 1901. 3(5):133.

198. Hornaday, William T. "The destruction of our birds and mammals." *Second Annual*

Report of the New York Zoological Society,
1898:77-126.

199. Norris, J. Parker, Jr. Letter to Witmer Stone,
October 11, 1899. ANSP 450.

200. Norris, J. Parker, Jr. , *Some Facts About
the Consistency of the Chairman of the
AOU Committee on Bird Protection.* 1899.
Privately published.

201. Jackson, Thomas H. Letter to Witmer
Stone, October 23, 1899. ANSP 450.

202. Ladd, Samuel B. "Nesting of the Black and
White Creeper." *Ornithologist and Oologist,*
1887. 12(9):150-51; Ladd, Samuel B. "A
series of eggs of the Worm-eating Warbler."
Ornithologist and Oologist, 1887. 12(9):149-
50.

203. Ladd, Samuel B. "Nesting of the Worm-
eating Warbler." *Ornithologist and Oologist,*
1887. 12(7):110.

204. Norris, J. Parker, Jr. "A reply to the Rev.
W.F. Henninger." *The Osprey,* 1889.
3(9):139.

205. Deane, Ruthven. Letter to Julia Stockton
Robins, October 29, 1899. ANSP Collection 687, Folder 1.

206. Richmond, Charles W. Letter to Witmer
Stone, October 13, 1899. ANSP Collection
675, Folder 3.

207. Barlow, Chester. Letter to Witmer Stone,
November 29, 1899. ANSP 450.

208. DVOC minutes for October 19, 1899.
ANSP Collection 74A, Box 1, Folder 4.

209. Stone, Witmer. Letter to Charles W. Richmond, October 16, 1899. SIA Collection
RU 105, Box 27.

210. Street, Fletcher. "Abstract of the proceedings of the DVOC 1916." *Cassinia,*
1916. 20:42-46; Stone, Witmer. "Notes
and news." *The Auk,* 1916. 33(3):354-56;
Parker, Harry G. Letter to Witmer Stone,
March 17, 1932. ANSP 450; Stone, Witmer. "Nesting of the Connecticut warbler
in Alberta." *The Auk,* 1929. 46(4):552-53;
Stone, Witmer. "Obituaries: Joseph Parker
Norris, Jr." *The Auk,* 1931. 48(2):329-30;
Richard F. Miller, undated, handwritten
notes in the front of the Harry K. Jamison
journals. ANSP Collection 765, Folder 11.

211. *TBNJ.* 18.

212. *TBNJ.* 102.

213. Notes for January 15, 1914 "Present Day
Aspects of Ornithology" talk to DVOC in
private collection of Witmer Stone material.
The article referenced was Wallace Craig's
"Behavior of the young bird in breaking out

of the egg" in the *Journal of Animal Behavior.* See Stone's review in *Auk* 30(2):290-91.
The "blown out of egg shells" comment
refers to the technique of drilling a small
hole at both ends of the egg and blowing
the contents out so that an empty egg shell
is left for preservation; "Abstract of the
proceedings of the DVOC 1914." *Cassinia,*
1914. 18:62-65.

214. Stone, Witmer. "Recent Literature: Burns
on periods of incubation." *The Auk,* 1915.
32(4):516.

215. DVOC minutes for October 15, 1936.
ANSP Collection 74A, Box 2, Folder 2.

216. *BSOCM.* 290 & 307.

217. Brady, Alan. Interview with author, May 3,
2000.

218. Brewster, William and Ralph Hoffman.
"Correspondence: Unsatisfactory records."
The Auk, 1902. 19(4):420.

219. "A question of identity." *Bird-Lore,* 1902.
4:166-67.

220. Saunders, William E. Letter to Witmer
Stone, November 21, 1911. ANSP 450.

221. Taverner, P.A. and Witmer Stone. "Correspondence: Subspecific designations." *The
Auk,* 1917. 34(3):370-76.

222. They're still with us – see today's listserves.

223. "Sight Records." Undated manuscript read
by Stone at 1917 AOU annual meeting.
Concerning the lack of response to his *Auk*
comments, Stone said he was "inclined to
place these correspondence pages in the
same category, except as to position, as the
preface of a book – which a school-boy
once described as the part that comes first
and which nobody reads." Private collection
of Witmer Stone material.

224. Stone, Witmer. "Recent Literature: Griscom
on problems of field identification." *The
Auk,* 1936. 53(2):238-40.

225. Stone, Witmer. "Recent Literature: The
Ornithological Journals. Bird-Lore." *The
Auk,* 1930. 47(2):287.

226. DVOC minutes for April 21, 1904. ANSP
Collection 74A, Box 1, Folder 4.

227. Deane, Ruthven. Letter to Witmer Stone,
October 7, 1908. ANSP Collection 687,
Folder 3.

228. Bowdish, Beecher S. "Justus von Lengerke."
The Auk, 1930. 47(2):306-07.

229. von Lengerke, Justus. Letter to Witmer
Stone, October 28, 1924. ANSP 450;
Broun, Maurice, *Hawks Aloft.* 1948. 6.

230. von Lengerke, Justus. Letter to Witmer Stone, December 13, 1926. ANSP 450.

231. von Lengerke, Justus. Letters to Witmer Stone, March 6, April 11, & November 9, 1927, & W. Stone, letters to J. von Lengerke, March 10, April 13, & December 2, 1927. ANSP Collection 186, Box 3, Folder 6.

232. Wood, Merrill. Letter to Wharton Huber, January 4, 1933. ANSP Collection 186, Box 3, Folder 7.

233. DVOC minutes for December 19, 1935. ANSP Collection 74A, Box 2, Folder 2.

234. DVOC minutes for March 4, 1937. ANSP Collection 74A, Box 2, Folder 2.

235. Broun, Maurice, *Hawks Aloft*. 1948. 143.

236. Sutton, George Miksch. "Notes on a collection of hawks from Schuylkill County, Pennsylvania." *The Wilson Bulletin*, 1928. 40(2):84-95; Sutton, George Miksch. "The status of the Goshawk in Pennsylvania." *The Wilson Bulletin*, 1931. 43(2):108-13; Poole, Earl L. "The hawk migration along the Kittatinny Ridge in Pennsylvania." *The Auk*, 1934. 51(1):17-20.

237. Edge, Rosalie. Letter to Witmer Stone, October 4, 1934. ANSP 450.

238. Edge, Rosalie. "Helping and Hindering Hawk Mountain Sanctuary" in *An Implacable Widow*, unpublished manuscript. Hawk Mountain Sanctuary Archives.

239. Pough, Richard H. "Recollections of a pioneer." *Hawk Mountain News*, 1984. 62(September 1984):15-18.

240. "Abstract of the proceedings of the Delaware Valley Ornithological Club 1934." *Cassinia*, 1933–37. 30:45-50.

241. DVOC minutes for October 4 & November 1, 1934. ANSP Collection 74A, Box 2, Folder 2.

242. Edge, Rosalie. Letter to Witmer Stone, March 19, 1935. ANSP 450.

243. Baker, John H. Letter to Charles M.B. Cadwalader, December 11, 1934. ANSP Collection 2009-034, Box 41, Folder 49.

244. Stone, Witmer. Letter to Rosalie Edge, November 14, 1934. ANSP 450.

245. Baker, John H. Letter to Rosalie Edge, November 13, 1934. Hawk Mountain Sanctuary Archives.

246. Edge, Rosalie. Letter to Witmer Stone, November 17, 1932, & W. Stone, letter to R. Edge, November 21, 1932. ANSP 450.

247. Edge, Rosalie. Letter to Witmer Stone, April 10, 1934. ANSP 450.

248. Stone, Witmer. "Teaching units of the Emergency Conservation Committee." *The Auk*, 1934. 51(3):415-16; "Notes and news." *The Auk*, 1935. 52(3):356-58.

249. Petition dated 1934 to have Mrs. Charles Noel Edge given Associate membership in the AOU. Hawk Mountain Sanctuary Archives.

250. McAtee, Waldo Lee. Letter to Rosalie Edge, October 26, 1938. Hawk Mountain Sanctuary Archives.

251. Fleming, James H. Letter to Witmer Stone, February 26, 1935. ANSP 450.

252. Stone, Witmer. Letter to John H. Baker, November 21, 1934. ANSP 450; "Notes and news." *The Auk*, 1935. 52(1):132-34.

253. Westwood, Richard. Letter to Rosalie Edge, January 7, 1935. Hawk Mountain Sanctuary Archives; Edge, Rosalie. Letter to Witmer Stone, December 19, 1934. ANSP 450.

254. "Deed or Gift." Trust agreement for Hawk Mountain. ANSP 450, Box 7, Folder 6.

255. Lewis, Eleanor L. Letter to Rosalie Edge, May 4, 1935. Hawk Mountain Sanctuary Archives.

256. Stone, Witmer. Letter to Rosalie Edge, January 14, 1935. ANSP 450.

257. Stone, Witmer. Letter to Rosalie Edge, February 6, 1935. Hawk Mountain Sanctuary Archives.

258. Cope, Eliza M. Letter to Rosalie Edge, Undated. Hawk Mountain Sanctuary Archives.

259. Stone, Witmer. Letter to John H. Baker, February 12, 1935. ANSP 450.

260. Foster, Frank B. Letter to Rosalie Edge, February 6, 1935. ANSP 450, Box 7, Folder 6.

261. Edge, Rosalie. Letter to Witmer Stone, February 11, 1935. ANSP 450.

262. Stone, Witmer. Letters to Rosalie Edge, February 24 & March 9, 1935, & R. Edge, letters to W. Stone, February 26 & April 8, 1935. ANSP 450.

263. Edge, Rosalie. Letter to Witmer Stone, August 14, 1936. ANSP 450.

264. Stone, Witmer. "Recent Literature: Framing the Birds of Prey." *The Auk*, 1936. 53(3):356-57.

265. Edge, Rosalie. Letter to Witmer Stone, February 5, 1935. ANSP 450. Edge fatuously accused Baker of a lack of intelligence in a letter to Stone (11/16/1934; ANSP 450). The barb doesn't stick: Baker was a World

War I fighter pilot and a successful invest-
ment banker; he ably steered the NAAS
through a Depression; and he provided very
capable leadership, including recruiting
young men who would go on to be leaders
in conservation. He also expanded Audubon's education, research, and sanctuary
programs, and launched the Audubon Field
Guide series, among other things (Frank
Graham, *The Audubon Ark*, 1990, Alfred
A. Knopf; "Guide to the National Audubon
Society Records, 1883-1990s." Finding aid,
NYPL MssCol 2099, compiled by Valerie
Wingfield).

266. In some 1940s *Altoona Tribune* "This
Morning's Comment" columns (including
11/3/1941 & 1/29/1949), Henry Shoemaker
interestingly used the word "Sparberbarich"
in referring to Hawk Mountain. That was
presumably the old Pennsylvania Dutch
name used for the location by gunners
when Shoemaker first visited there in 1908.

Chapter 6: The Beautiful Science

1. Stone, Witmer. "Spencer Trotter: 1860-
1931." *Cassinia*, 1929-30. 28:1-8.
2. Stone, Witmer, "The Ornithology of Today
and Tomorrow," in *The Fiftieth Anniversary
of the Nuttall Ornithological Club*. 1924,
Cambridge. 7-25. After spending days in
the ANSP library painstakingly trying to
decipher Brewster's horrific handwriting, I
am less enamored of their correspondence.
3. Stone, Witmer. Letter to William Brewster,
January 3, 1917. MCZ Archives.
4. Kennard, Frederic H. Letter to Witmer
Stone, July 14, 1919. ANSP 450.
5. Merriam, C. Hart. Letter to Witmer Stone,
July 21, 1919. ANSP Collection 678, Folder
7.
6. Davis, Jr., William E., *History of the Nuttall
Ornithological Club 1873-1986*. Memoirs
of the Nuttall Ornithological Club, No. 11.
1987. Nuttall Ornithological Club, Cambridge. 18.
7. Stone, Witmer. "Samuel Washington Woodhouse." *Cassinia*, 1904. 8:1-5.
8. Newton, Alfred. Letter to Witmer Stone,
February 17, 1899. ANSP 450.
9. Stone, Witmer. "In memoriam – John Hall
Sage." *The Auk*, 1926. 43(1):1-17.
10. Stone, Witmer. Letters to Albert K. Fisher,
September 14 & December 26, 1915.
LOC, A.K. Fisher papers, Box 21.

11. "Eighth Congress of the American Ornithologists' Union." *The Auk*, 1891. 8(1):80-83.
12. Stone, Witmer. Letter to Anne Stone,
November 19, 1890. ANSP Collection
2009-031, Box 4, Folder 3.
13. Seton, Ernest Thompson. Letter to Witmer
Stone, April 10, 1925, & W. Stone, letter to
E.T. Seton, April 17, 1925. ANSP 450.
14. "Tenth Congress of the American Ornithologists' Union." *The Auk*, 1893. 10(1):63-65.
Stone was elected an "Active" member; the
term for that class was changed to "Fellow"
in 1901.
15. Stone, Witmer. Letter to William Brewster,
October 30, 1896. MCZ Archives.
16. "Notes and news." *The Auk*, 1896.
13(1):93-98; Sage, John H. Letter to
Witmer Stone, November 23, 1895. ANSP
Collection 541, Folder 2; "Notes and news."
The Auk, 1898. 15(1):78-80; Dutcher,
William. "Results of special protection to
gulls and terns obtained through the Thayer
Fund." *The Auk*, 1902. 19(1):34-64.
17. Rehn, James A. G. "In memoriam: Witmer
Stone." *The Auk*, 1941. 58(3):299-313.
18. Stone, Witmer. Letter to Waldo Lee
McAtee, December 18, 1922. LOC, W.L.
McAtee papers, Box 10, Folder 4; Palmer,
T.S. "Thirty-eighth stated meeting of the
American Ornithologists' Union." *The Auk*,
1921. 38(1):89-105; Bent, Arthur Cleveland. Letter to Witmer Stone, December 1,
1936. ANSP Collection 550, Folder 2.
19. "Meetings of the American Ornithologists'
Union." *The Auk*, 1951. 68(3):i-ii.
20. DVOC minutes for April 5, 1894. ANSP
Collection 74A, Box 1, Folder 3; Stone,
Witmer. "Report of the Ornithological Section." *PANSP*, 1898. 50:518-19 & *PANSP*,
1899. 51:548-49.
21. "Meeting of the American Ornithologists
Union." *The Osprey*, 1899. 4(3):44.
22. "Notes and news." *The Auk*, 1916.
33(4):458-62.
23. Merriam, C. Hart. Letter to Witmer Stone,
November 9, 1916. ANSP Collection
678, Folder 7; Palmer, T.S. "Thirty-ninth
stated meeting of the American Ornithologists' Union." *The Auk*, 1922. 39(1):85-94;
Palmer, T.S. "The forty-seventh stated meeting of the American Ornithologists' Union."
The Auk, 1930. 47(2):218-30; DVOC
minutes for November 7, 1929. ANSP Collection 74A, Box 2, Folder 1.

24. Wetmore, Alexander. Letter to Witmer Stone, October 26, 1929. SIA Collection 7006, Box 65, Folder 7.

25. Batchelder, Charles F. Letters to Witmer Stone, November 3 & 27, 1916. ANSP 450.

26. Brewster, William. Letter to Witmer Stone, November 10, 1899. ANSP 450.

27. Grinnell, Joseph. "Editorial notes and news." *The Condor*, 1915. 17(2):103-4.

28. Murphy, Robert Cushman. Letter to Witmer Stone, August 11, 1933. ANSP 450.

29. Kennard, Frederic H. Letter to Witmer Stone, November 24, 1924. ANSP 450.

30. Stone, Witmer. Letter to Frederic H. Kennard, November 28, 1924. ANSP 450.

31. Kennard, Frederic H. Letter to Witmer Stone, November 4, 1916. ANSP 450. "The Appleton Club," pp.12-14 in the 1938 *Auklet*, gives some more insights into the boys' spirituous shenanigans.

32. AOU Council Minutes for October 20, 1930. SIA Collection 7150, Box 3.

33. Stone, Witmer. Letter to Frank M. Chapman, January 30, 1933. Department of Ornithology Archives, AMNH.

34. Stone, Witmer. Letter to Theodore S. Palmer, March 22, 1933. SIA Collection 7150, Box 70, Folder 5; Stone, Witmer. Letter to James L. Peters, April 21, 1933. MCZ Archives.

35. Stone, Witmer. Letter to Alexander Wetmore, June 3, 1933. SIA Collection 7006, Box 66, Folder 18; Stone, Witmer. Letter to T.S. Palmer, August 3, 1933. SIA Collection 7150, Box 70, Folder 6.

36. Chapman, Frank M. Letter to Witmer Stone, October 19, 1933. ANSP Collection 679, Folder 12.

37. Stone, Witmer. Letter to Frank M. Chapman, October 24, 1933. Department of Ornithology Archives, AMNH.

38. Chapman, Frank M. Letter to Witmer Stone, October 4, 1933. Department of Ornithology Archives, AMNH.

39. *Fifty Years' Progress of American Ornithology, 1883-1933*. 1933. Intelligencer Press, Lancaster.

40. Stone, Witmer. Untitled notes for AOU banquet talk. ANSP Collection 2009-031, Box 1. Handwritten notes by Stone. Undated, but certainly 1936.

41. Lee, Laura. Newspaper article, title unknown. *The Evening Bulletin*, Philadelphia, October 5, 1936.

42. Stone, Witmer. "Stewardson Brown." *Cassinia*, 1920-21. 24:1-7; Stone, Witmer. "Notes and news." *The Auk*, 1921. 38(2):316-20; Merriam, C. Hart. Letters to Witmer Stone, December 21, 1889, & January 23, 1891. ANSP Collection 678, Folders 1 & 2.

43. Stone, Witmer. "A migration of hawks at Germantown, Pa." *The Auk*, 1887. 4(2):161.

44. *BSOCM*. 263.

45. Stone, Witmer. "Graphic representation of bird migration." *The Auk*, 1889. 6(2):139-44; Stone, Witmer. "Bird waves and their graphic representation." *The Auk*, 1891. 8(2):194-98.

46. Stone, Witmer. "The Delaware Valley Ornithological Club." *The Auk*, 1890. 7(3):298-99.

47. "Abstract of the proceedings of the DVOC 1890-91." *Cassinia*, 1890-91. 1:2-11.

48. Stone, Witmer. "Report of the spring migration of 1911." *Cassinia*, 1911. 15:42-60.

49. Allinson, Rachel E. Letters to Witmer Stone, February 20, 1901 & (date illegible), 1902; Allinson, Caroline. Letter to Witmer Stone, April 11, 1916. ANSP 450.

50. Stone, Witmer. "Report of the spring migration of 1908." *Cassinia*, 1908. 12:45-64.

51. Fair, William W. Letter to Witmer Stone, November 24, 1907. ANSP 450.

52. Stone, Witmer. "Recent Literature: Forbush's annual report on Massachusetts ornithology." *The Auk*, 1923. 40(1):154-55.

53. Abbott, Charles C. Letter to Witmer Stone, February 22, 1909. ANSP 450.

54. "Notes and news." *The Auk*, 1920. 37(1):182-88.

55. Stone, Witmer. Letter to Raymond Middleton, April 12, 1922. ANSP 450.

56. Stone, Witmer. "Graphic representation of bird migration." *The Auk*, 1889. 6(2):139-44.

57. Peterson, Roger T., *A Field Guide to the Birds*. 1947. Houghton Mifflin Company, Boston. Plates 51-52.

58. Stone, Witmer. "Wetmore's 'The Migration of Birds.'" *The Auk*, 1927. 44(1):123-25.

59. Stone, Witmer. "Report of the spring migration of 1907." *Cassinia*, 1907. 11:54-79.

60. Stone, Witmer. "Report of the spring migration of 1913." *Cassinia*, 1913. 17:37-51.

61. "Report on spring migration for the years 1922–24." *Cassinia*, 1922-24. 25:21-52.

62. Stone, Witmer. "Some light on night migration." *The Auk*, 1906. 23(3):249-52.

63. Marsh, William Barton. *Philadelphia Hardwood, 1798-1948: The Story of the McIlvains of Philadelphia and the Business They Founded*. 1948, William E. Rudge's Sons. 63-65.

64. "Men in Blazing Lanes Fought Fire That Lighted Whole City." *Philadelphia Inquirer*, Philadelphia, March 28, 1906.

65. Brewster, William. Letter to Witmer Stone, July 11, 1906. ANSP 450.

66. Stone, Witmer. "The study of moulting in birds." *Science*, 1893. 21(521):51-52.

67. Stone, Witmer. "The molting of birds with special reference to the plumages of the smaller land birds of eastern North America." *PANSP*, 1896. 48:108-67.

68. Stone, Witmer. "On molt and alleged colour-change in birds." *Ibis*, 1901:177-83.

69. P[almer], W[illiam]. "Recent Literature: Stone on the molting of birds." *The Auk*, 1896. 13(3):240-43.

70. Stone, Witmer. "On the annual molt of the Sanderling." *PANSP*, 1897. 49:368-72.

71. Macwhirter, Bruce, Peter Austin-Smith, Jr. and Donald Kroodsma. 2002. Sanderling (*Calidris alba*), The Birds of North America Online (A. Poole, Ed.). Ithaca: Cornell Lab of Ornithology. Retrieved from: http://bna.birds.cornell.edu.bnaproxy.birds.cornell.edu/bna/species/653; O'Brien, Michael, Richard Crossley, and Kevin Karlson, *The Shorebird Guide*. 2006. Houghton Mifflin, New York. 402.

72. Waterton, Charles, "Notes on the habits of the Mallards," in *Essays on Natural History, Chiefly Ornithology*. 1844, Longman, Brown, Green, and Longmans, London. 202.

73. Stone, Witmer. "The summer molting plumage of certain ducks." *PANSP*, 1899. 51(3):467-72.

74. Allen, Joel Asaph. "Stone on 'The summer molting plumage of certain ducks.'" *The Auk*, 1900. 17(2):183-84.

75. Newton, Alfred, "Moult," in *A Dictionary of Birds*. 1894, Adam and Charles Black, London. 597.

76. Oberholser, Harry C. "The Seventeenth Congress of the AOU." *The Osprey*, 1899. 4:57-58.

77. Dwight, Jonathan, Jr. "The sequence of plumages and moults of the passerine birds of New York." *Annals of the New York Academy of Science*, 1900. 13:73-360; Stone, Witmer. "Recent Literature: Dwight's 'Sequence of plumages and moults of the passerine birds of New York.'" *The Auk*, 1901. 18(1):114-19.

78. Stone, Witmer. "Dwight's 'Gulls of the World.'" *The Auk*, 1926. 43(2):255-57.

79. "Editorial notes and news." *The Condor*, 1916. 18(4):172.

80. Sharpe, R. Bowdler, *A Hand-list of the Genera and Species of Birds*. Vol. 2. 1900. Taylor and Francis, London. vii.

81. "Dr. Witmer Stone, '83, Sc.D." *Germantown Academy Bulletin*. March 15, 1935.

82. "Ornithologist Honored." *Philadelphia Inquirer*, Philadelphia, October 4, 1931.

83. DVOC minutes for March 16, 1933. ANSP Collection 74A, Box 2, Folder 2.

84. Stone, Witmer. Letter to William B. Cadwalader, May 9, 1921. ANSP 450.

85. "Witmer Stone." *Old Penn*, 1913. XI(39); Wetmore, Alexander. "Witmer Stone (1866-1939)." *Year Book of the American Philosophical Society*, 1939:467-69.

86. "The Science and Art Club of Germantown." Pamphlet. ANSP Collection 263C, Folder 17; "Gregory." Letter to Witmer Stone, February 24, 1914. ANSP Collection 209-031, Box 2, Folder 11; Ashhurst, John. Letter to Witmer Stone, December 12, 1912. ANSP 450; Roosevelt, Kermit. Letter to Witmer Stone, October 30, 1936. ANSP Collection 2009-031, Box 1, Folder 11; *Five and Thirty: The Further History of the Class of Eighty-Seven*. 1922. 118. The book said a list of Stone's memberships would "run off the sheet, off the desk, around the block and back again, if the names, we believe, were put end to end. A portentous list, an amazing list: ornithological, philosophical, entomological, ichthological [sic], herpetological and all other 'logicals!'" Meant to be humorous, and a bit hyperbolic – but fairly accurate.

87. Roberts, Isaac. Letter to Witmer Stone, April 24, 1934. ANSP 450; "Notes and news." *The Auk*, 1935. 52(3):356-58.

88. "Pupils Tell How They Saved Birds." *The Evening Bulletin*, Philadelphia, March 20, 1936.

89. "Park Bird Club Formed." November 3, 1922. Clipping from unknown newspaper in ANSP 450, Box 16; Moffett, Caroline T. Letter to Witmer Stone, February 9, 1923. ANSP 450.

90. Stone, Witmer. Letter to Caroline T. Moffett, February 14, 1923. ANSP 450.

91. Lee, Laura. "$5 a Week Feeds Park Birds Here." *The Evening Bulletin*, Philadelphia, April 22, 1935.

92. Friends of the Wissahickon Annual Report 2009. 18 pages.

93. Stone, Witmer. Letter to Charles W. Richmond, May 13, 1898. SIA Collection RU-105, Box 27.

94. Stone, Witmer. Letter to Waldo Lee McAtee, November 23, 1918. LOC, W.L. McAtee papers, Box 10, Folder 4.

95. Stone, Witmer. Letter to Joseph Grinnell, October 23, 1928. MVZ Archives.

96. McAtee, Waldo Lee. "Patrons, fellows, members, and associates of the American Ornithologists' Union, April, 1938." *The Auk*, 1938. 55(2):342-386.

97. Stone, Witmer. Letter to Waldo Lee McAtee, October 21, 1933. LOC, W.L. McAtee papers, Box 37, Folder 3; Stone, Witmer. Letter to Harry C. Oberholser, July 5, 1934. LOC, Harry C. Oberholser papers, Box 18.

98. Richmond, Charles W. Letter to Witmer Stone, March 17, 1929. ANSP Collection 675, Folder 8.

99. DVOC minutes for November 21, 1935. ANSP Collection 74A, Box 2, Folder 2.

100. *The DVOC Twenty Year Souvenir*. 1910. Privately published.

101. T[yler], W[insor] M. "Notes and news: Walter Faxon." *The Auk*, 1921. 38(1):157-58; Faxon, Walter. Letter to Witmer Stone, February 29, 1900. ANSP 450.

102. Stone, Witmer. "Wilson – Father of American Ornithology." *Nature Magazine*, 1926(July):29-30.

103. Stone, Witmer. "Recent Literature: H.O. Bishop. The forest was his studio." *The Auk*, 1931. 48(1):160.

104. Stone, Witmer. "Some early American ornithologists: Alexander Wilson." *Bird-Lore*, 1905. 7:265-68; "Notes and news." *The Auk*, 1913. 30(4):621-24.

105. Sage, John H. "Thirty-first stated meeting of the American Ornithologists' Union." *The Auk*, 1914. 31(1):92-99; Robeson, Katherine Morgan. Letters to Witmer Stone, March 6 & 31, 1936. ANSP 450; Perkins, S. E. III. Letter to Witmer Stone, June 22, 1936. ANSP 450.

106. Stone, Witmer. Stone's Alexander Wilson talk to Gloria Dei Church, April 5, 1936. ANSP Collection 52, Box 1, Folder 2.

107. "Abstract of the proceedings of the DVOC 1892-97." *Cassinia*, 1892-97. 2:1-26.

108. Stone, Witmer. Letter to Joel Asaph Allen, January 18, 1893. Department of Ornithology Archives, AMNH.

109. Allen, Joel Asaph. Letter to Witmer Stone, January 24, 1893. ANSP Collection 658, Folder 2.

110. Coues, Elliott. Letters to Witmer Stone, January 21, 1898 & February 8, 1899. ANSP 450.

111. Stone, Witmer. "Alexander Wilson and the Ipswich Sparrow." *The Osprey*, 1898. 2(9):117.

112. *BSOCM*. 898; Stone, Witmer. "Isaac Norris DeHaven." *Cassinia*, 1925-26. 25:6-9.

113. Calder, Alexander Milne. Letter to ANSP, February 28, 1913.

114. Stone, Witmer. "Wilsoniana." *Cassinia*, 1913. 17:1-5.

115. Brady, Alan. "Alexander Wilson returns to the Academy." *Cassinia*, 1996-97. 67:45-46.

116. Croskey, John Welsh. Letter to Witmer Stone, November 14, 1922. ANSP Collection 186, Box 1, Folder 6. Lawson is buried not far from Stone in Laurel Hill Cemetery.

117. Croskey, John Welsh. Letter to Witmer Stone, December 6, 1922. ANSP Collection 186, Box 1, Folder 6; Curators' minutes for April 3, 1923. ANSP Collection 86, Folder 2.

118. Stone, Witmer. Letter to John Welsh Croskey, May 18, 1923. ANSP Collection 186, Box 1, Folder 6.

119. Stone, Witmer. Letter to John Welsh Croskey, June 9, 1923. ANSP Collection 52, Folder 2.

120. McKenzie, R. Tait. Letter to Witmer Stone, June 13, 1923. ANSP Collection 186, Box 1, Folder 6; Handwritten note by Venia T. Phillips concerning Alexander Wilson tablet, April 2, 1959. ANSP Collection 52, Folder 2.

121. Wood, Casey A. "A plea for the continuation of Elliott Coues' ornithological bibliography." *The Auk*, 1928. 45(2):148-54.

122. "Bird-Lore for 1905." *Bird-Lore*, 1904. 6:210.

123. Stone, Witmer. "Jacob Post Giraud, Jr., and his works." *The Auk*, 1919. 36(4):464-72.

124. Stone, Witmer. "William Gambel, M.D." *Cassinia*, 1910. 14:1-8.

125. Stone, Witmer. Letter to Frank M. Chapman, October 29, 1904. Department of Ornithology Archives, AMNH.

126. Stone, Witmer. Letter to Casey A. Wood, February 25, 1924. Blacker-Wood Collec-

tion, Department of Rare Books, McGill University.

127. Stone, Witmer. Letter to Theodore S. Palmer, September 20, 1934. SIA Collection 7150, Box 70, Folder 9.

128. Stone, Witmer. Letter to Wharton Huber, July 30, 1935. ANSP Collection 186, Box 3, Folder 4.

129. Philips, Venia T. and Maurice E. Phillips, *Guide to the Manuscript Collections in the Academy of Natural Sciences of Philadelphia.* 1963. Academy of Natural Sciences of Philadelphia. 214.

130. Stone, Witmer. Letter to Charles M.B. Cadwalader, January 25, 1939. ANSP Collection 2010-051, Box 1, Folder 92.

131. Stone, Witmer. Unpublished, undated manuscript on history of American ornithology. ANSP Collection 2009-031, Box 2, Folder 11.

132. Payment receipt, Germantown Trust Company for Academy of Natural Sciences of Philadelphia. October 2, 1940; Emlen, Arthur C. Letter to Charles M.B. Cadwalader, October 3, 1940. Both ANSP Collection 2010-051, Box 7, Folder 13. Stone said in 1915 that he still had every letter he'd ever received from an ornithologist (Stone to T.S. Palmer 11/11/1915; LOC, T.S. Palmer papers, Box 11). Unfortunately, a year before he died he was engaged in going through his correspondence and discarding items not of "profound scientific interest" (Stone to W.L. McAtee, 5/21/1938; LOC, W.L. McAtee papers, Box 37, Folder 3).

133. "A Christmas bird-census." *Bird-Lore,* 1900. 2:192.

134. "The Christmas bird census." *Bird-Lore,* 1901. 3:28-33; Stone, Witmer. Letter to Frank M. Chapman, December 29, 1900. ANSP Collection 679, Folder 8.

135. Hiers, Mildred D. "Some fragments which have become history." *The Cape May Geographic Society Bulletin,* 1951. 5:8-10. Hiers states the Browns and Stones spent 14 Christmases together. Her source was presumably Brown, who was a charter member of the CMGS; Brown, Otway. Letters to Witmer Stone, December 6, 1929, December 11, 1930, & December 5, 1932. ANSP 450.

136. Stone, Witmer. Letter to Charles J. Pennock, January 30, 1935. ANSP Collection 676, Folder 1.

137. "Christmas Bird Count, Cape May, N.J." *Bird-Lore,* 1937. 39:40-41.

138. West, Franklin H. "Philip Atlee Livingston, 1901-1986." *Cassinia,* 1989. 63:90-91.

139. Beck, Herbert H. Letter to Witmer Stone, April 18, 1924. ANSP 450.

140. *BSOCM.* 314. Simply saying "the dark appearance of American Kestrels" would have made more sense: young females are no darker than adults, and the sexes are so close in size that the female wouldn't be much closer in size to a Merlin, which is only slightly larger than a kestrel anyway.

141. Bent, Arthur Cleveland, *Life histories of North American birds of prey.* Vol. Two. 1938. U.S. Government Printing Office, Washington, D.C. 81.

142. Connor, Jack, *Season at the Point.* 1991. 28.

143. *BSOCM.* 878-79. Stone also observed in *Auk* 52(3):340 that the cowbirds often walked ahead of the cattle.

144. Stone, Witmer. "Report on the spring migration of 1914." *Cassinia,* 1914. 18:38-61; *BSOCM.* 691.

145. *BSOCM.* 621 & 327.

146. Stone, Witmer, *The Mammals of New Jersey.* 1908. 104-05; Stone, Witmer. Letter to Alexander Wetmore, July 19, 1929. SIA Collection 7006, Box 65, Folder 7.

147. *BSOCM.* 403.

148. *BSOCM.* 643.

149. Stone, Witmer. Letter to J. Percy Moore, August 13, 1926. ANSP 450.

150. Moore, J. Percy. "A crane at Martha's Vineyard, Mass." *The Auk,* 1926. 43(4):538-40; Brooks, S.C. "The Martha's Vineyard crane." *The Auk,* 1927. 44(1):98.

151. *BSOCM.* 258.

152. *BSOCM.* 109.

153. *BSOCM.* 499 & 186.

154. *BSOCM.* 140.

155. *BSOCM.* 839 & 766; Stone, Witmer. "The Catbird." *Bird-Lore,* 1913. 15:327-30.

156. Stone, Witmer. Letter to R. Owen Merriman, November 14, 1922. ANSP 450; Stone, Witmer. "Bird notes." *Cassinia,* 1913. 17:35-36.

157. Anonymous. "City ornithology." *Cassinia,* 1908. 12:65-66.

158. Stone, Witmer. Letter to Mildred H. Miller, May 9, 1921. ANSP 450; Stone, Witmer. Letter to Samuel Scoville, May 28, 1924. ANSP 450.

159. Brady, Alan. "The first roundup." *Cassinia,* 1984. 60:51-52.

160. "Abstract of the proceedings of the DVOC 1929." *Cassinia*, 1929-30. 28:48-52.
161. Stone, Witmer. Letter to William Vogt, May 29, 1936. ANSP 450.
162. Allen, Robert P. Letter to Margaretta Huber, May 28, 1937. ANSP Collection 186, Box 2, Folder 5.
163. Roland, Conrad. Letter to Witmer Stone, June 15, 1935. ANSP 450.
164. DVOC minutes for October 1, 1925. ANSP Collection 74A, Box 2, Folder 1; Stone, Witmer. Letter to Charles M.B. Cadwalader, August 13, 1929. ANSP Collection 2009-034, Box 3, Folder 13.
165. *BSOCM*. x.

Chapter 7: The Custodian of the Bowl

1. Huber, Wharton. "Witmer Stone (1866 to 1939)." *Journal of Mammalogy*, 1940. 21(1):1-4.
2. Will of Lillie May Stone. ANSP Collection 2010-051, Box 7, Folder 13.
3. Stone, Witmer. Letter to Theodore S. Palmer, September 8, 1927. LOC, T.S. Palmer papers, Box 43.
4. "Mrs. Lillie L. Stone." *Evening Public Ledger*, Philadelphia, August 5, 1940.
5. *A History of Blair County, Pennsylvania*, ed. Tarring S. Davis and Lucille Shenk. Vol. 2. 1931. National Historical Association, Inc. 100-01.
6. Morris, George Spencer. Letter to Witmer Stone, July 24, 1904. ANSP 450.
7. "Isaac H. Lafferty: A Well-known Citizen Called Away by Death." *Altoona Tribune*, Altoona, December 4, 1893.
8. Trotter, Spencer. Letter to Witmer Stone, August 7, 1904. ANSP Collection 601, Folder 4.
9. Stone, Hugh E. Letter to Witmer Stone, July 21, 1904. ANSP 450.
10. Fisher, Albert K. Letter to Witmer Stone, August 6, 1904. ANSP Collection 685, Folder 6.
11. Morris, George Spencer. Letter to DVOC, 1904. ANSP Collection 263, Box 1, Folder 10.
12. DVOC minutes for October 6, 1904. ANSP Collection 74A, Box 1, Folder 4.
13. Wemple, Ida M. Letter to Witmer Stone, October 14, 1924. ANSP 450.
14. Stone, Witmer. "Bird notes." *Cassinia*, 1913. 17:35-36.
15. Stone, Witmer. Letter to Theodore S. Palmer, October 18, 1920. LOC, T.S. Palmer papers, Box 37; *BSOCM*. 327 & 505.
16. *BSOCM*. 41.
17. McAtee, Waldo Lee. "Patrons, fellows, members, and associates of the American Ornithologists' Union, April, 1938." *The Auk*, 1938. 55(2):342-386; Bent, Arthur Cleveland. Letter to Witmer Stone, December 1, 1936. ANSP Collection 550, Folder 2.
18. Genoways, Hugh H. and Patricia W. Freeman. "Evolution of a scientific meeting: eighty annual meetings of the American Society of Mammalogists, 1919-2000." *Journal of Mammalogy*, 2001. 82(2):582-603.
19. Stone, Witmer. Letter to Albert K. Fisher, April 16, 1926. LOC, A.K. Fisher papers, Box 29.
20. Stone, Witmer. Letter to Albert K. Fisher, April 26, 1918. LOC, A.K. Fisher papers, Box 22.
21. Stone, Witmer. Letters to Albert K. Fisher, March 4, 1918 & May 13, 1920. LOC, A.K. Fisher papers, Boxes 22 & 23.
22. Stone, Witmer. "A New Hummingbird from Colombia." *PANSP*, 1917. 69:203-04.
23. Lepidopyga lilliae. The IUCN Red List of Threatened Species. Version 2013.2. Cited February 7, 2014. Available from http://www.iucnredlist.org/details/22687417/0
24. Stone, Witmer. Letter to Harry C. Oberholser, November 16, 1920. LOC, Harry C. Oberholser papers, Box 18.
25. Stone, Witmer. Letter to Alexander Wetmore, January 18, 1936. SIA Collection 7006, Box 80, Folder 7.
26. U.S. Census Bureau, Fourteenth Census of the United States, 1920. Washington, D.C. National Archives and Records Administration, 1920. Philadelphia, Pa., Roll T625_1646, Page 4A, Enumeration District 1738, Image 1003.
27. U.S. Census Bureau, Fifteenth Census of the United States, 1930. Washington, D.C. National Archives and Records Administration, 1930. Philadelphia, Pa., Roll 2105, Page 14A, Enumeration District 653, Image 983.0.
28. Cope, Francis R., Jr. Letter to Witmer Stone, September 13, 1897. ANSP 450; Philadelphia Deed Registry Plan 54N15, Plot 163, City Archives of Philadelphia.

29. I heard a singing American Redstart and Blackpoll Warbler on an afternoon visit there in mid-May 2013.

30. U.S. Census Bureau, Twelfth Census of the United States, 1900. Washington, D.C. National Archives and Records Administration, 1900. Philadelphia, Pa., Roll T623_1469, Page 1A, Enumeration District 670.

31. Stone, Witmer. Letter to James P. Chapin, August 10, 1921. Department of Ornithology Archives, AMNH. The UP Class of '87 scrapbooks record Stone at the Regent Street address right up until his wedding, then at 5044 Hazel very shortly thereafter (UP Archives Collection UPT 110); Anonymous. "City ornithology." *Cassinia*, 1908. 12:65-66.

32. Stone, Witmer. Letter to Albert K. Fisher, March 30, 1908. LOC, A.K. Fisher papers, Box 18; Philadelphia Deed Registry Plan 21S22, Plot 38, City Archives of Philadelphia.

33. Stone, Witmer. "The Carolina Wren." *Bird-Lore*, 1911. 13:167-70.

34. U.S. Census Bureau, Thirteenth Census of the United States, 1910. Washington, D.C. National Archives and Records Administration, 1910. Philadelphia, Pa., Roll T624_1413, Page 8A, Enumeration District 1191.

35. Stone, Witmer. Letter to Joel Asaph Allen, September 19, 1911. Department of Ornithology Archives, AMNH.

36. Stone, Witmer. Letter to Theodore S. Palmer, November 14, 1921. LOC, T.S. Palmer papers, Box 38.

37. Stone, Witmer. Letter to Robert Ridgway, January 18, 1922. Blacker-Wood Collection, Department of Rare Books, McGill University.

38. Stone, Witmer. Letter to Frank M. Chapman, October 24, 1921. ANSP Collection 679, Folder 11; Dwight, Jonathan, Jr. Letter to Witmer Stone, October 27, 1921. ANSP Collection 686, Folder 3.

39. Stone, Witmer. Letter to Harry C. Oberholser, June 2, 1922. LOC, Harry C. Oberholser papers, Box 18.

40. Stone, Witmer. Letter to Charles W. Richmond, September 18, 1922. ANSP Collection 675, Folder 7; Bishop, Louis B. Letter to Witmer Stone, June 24, 1923. ANSP 450; Philadelphia Deed Registry Plan 53N22, Plot 226, City Archives of Philadelphia.

41. Brownholtz, Lou. "Memories of Belfield Avenue." *Germantown Crier*, 2006. 56(1):18-23.

42. Stone, Witmer. Letter to Harry C. Oberholser, October 3, 1922. LOC, Harry C. Oberholser papers, Box 18.

43. Stone, Witmer. Letter to Albert K. Fisher, January 10, 1923. LOC, A.K. Fisher papers, Box 26.

44. Stone, Witmer. Letter to Theodore S. Palmer, December 9, 1923. LOC, T.S. Palmer papers, Box 40.

45. Stone, Witmer. Letter to James P. Chapin, February 13, 1932. Department of Ornithology Archives, AMNH.

46. Stone, Witmer. "Changed habits of Blue Jay at Philadelphia." *The Auk*, 1926. 43(2):239.

47. Thomas, George E., Jeffrey A. Cohen, and Michael J. Lewis, *Frank Furness: The Complete Works, Revised Edition*. 1996. Princeton Architectural Press, New York. 225.

48. Stone, Witmer. Letter to Frederic H. Kennard, May 20, 1923. ANSP 450; Stone, Witmer. Letter to Albert K. Fisher, May 30, 1923. LOC, A.K. Fisher papers, Box 26.

49. Oberholser, Harry C. Letter to Witmer Stone, July 15, 1922. ANSP Collection 538, Folder 6. Stone's library was in storage at ANSP while he moved around for a year (Stone to T.S. Palmer 10/2/1921; LOC, T.S. Palmer papers, Box 38).

50. Stone, Witmer. Letter to Albert K. Fisher, December 5, (year not marked, but clearly 1922). LOC, A.K. Fisher papers, Box 27.

51. Grinnell, Joseph. Letter to Witmer Stone, November 3, 1929. ANSP Collection 684, Folder 4.

52. Peterson, C. Bernard. Letter to Charles M.B. Cadwalader and J. Percy Moore, April 11, 1940. ANSP Collection 2010-051, Box 7, Folder 13.

53. "Volumes Valued at $10,000." *Reading Eagle*, Reading, July 25, 1940.

54. The Henry Janssen Foundation, coincidentally, also supplied Rosalie Edge with the last donation needed to finance the purchase of Hawk Mountain. Rosalie Edge to Hanns Gramm, 12/20/1935; Hawk Mountain Sanctuary Archives.

55. "Dr. Stone 50 Years at Museum Here." *The Evening Bulletin*, Philadelphia, February 28, 1938.

56. Stone, Witmer. Christmas card to Alexander Wetmore, 1926. SIA Collection 7006, Box 65, Folder 6.

Chapter 8: Such a Natural Flower Garden

1. Philadelphia Botanical Club minutes for December 1 & 22, 1891. ANSP Collection 88, Box 1, Folder 1; "Introductory." *Bartonia*, 1908. 1:1.
2. Brown, Stewardson. "A brief history of the Philadelphia Botanical Club." *Bartonia*, 1908. 1:2-4.
3. Rehn, James A. G. "Witmer Stone (1866-1939)." *Cassinia*, 1938-41. 31:1-11.
4. Stafleu, Frans A. "Witmer Stone and his 'Plants of Southern New Jersey.'" *Taxon*, 1973. 22(4):467-68.
5. Pennell, Francis W. "The botanical work of Witmer Stone." *Bartonia*, 1940. 20:33-37.
6. Darlington, William, M.D., *Flora Cestrica: An Herborizing Companion for the Young Botanists of Chester County, State of Pennsylvania*. 3rd ed. 1853. Lindsay & Blakiston, Lancaster.
7. Stone, Witmer. "Joseph Leidy as a Botanist." *PANSP*, 1923. 75(The Joseph Leidy Commemorative Meeting supplement):43-48. Darrach was interested in more than botany. He was the Weygandt family physician as well, and in addition to showing author Cornelius some rare plants in the Wissahickon, he "always brought out-of-doors with him into the sickroom.... [H]e was overflowing with anecdotes about purple martins and redpolls, eagles and loons" (Cornelius Weygandt, "How I Came to Care" and "Dawn to Dusk." Unpublished manuscripts. University of Pennsylvania Archives Collection UPT 50, W547.5. Box 1, Folders 34 and 40).
8. Proceedings of the Wilson Natural Science Association, Vols. 1 & 2. ANSP Collection 2009-031, Box 4, Folders 7 & 6.
9. Heilprin, Angelo. "Observations on the flora of Northern Yucatan." *Proceedings of the American Philosophical Society*, 1891. 29(136):137-44.
10. *PSNJ*. 25.
11. *PSNJ*. 520.
12. Bassett, George William. "The trail of the winding water." *Bartonia*, 1912. 5:6-10; *PSNJ*. 528; Stone, Witmer. "Recent Literature: The Ornithological Journals, The Wilson Bulletin." *The Auk*, 1921. 38(1):146.

13. Stone, Witmer. Letter to Alexander McElwee, May 27, 1921. ANSP 450.
14. Stone, Witmer. Letter to Stewardson Brown, November 23, 1893. ANSP Collection 168, Folder 5.
15. Philadelphia Botanical Club/Arthur N. Leeds, treasurer (notebook). ANSP Collection 558, Folder 12.
16. Stone, Witmer. "Summer birds of the Pine Barrens of New Jersey." *The Auk*, 1894. 11(2):133-140.
17. Huber, Wharton. Untitled memorial of Witmer Stone. 1939. ANSP Collection 263.
18. *PSNJ*. 32.
19. *PSNJ*. 29.
20. *PSNJ*. 33.
21. Morris, George Spencer. "Catoxen cabin on the Rancocas." *Cassinia*, 1908. 12:20-24. Morris's hint that one owner was a bird student and "an instructor in one of America's greatest universities" may have referred to Spencer Trotter (Swarthmore) or Cornelius Weygandt (University of Pennsylvania). Why Morris didn't simply name the owners instead of being needlessly coy about it is hard to understand, but other writers at the time (e.g., Sam Scoville, Weygandt) had the same annoying foible; The History of the Washington Biologists' Field Club on Plummers Island. Cited February 7, 2014. Available from http://www.pwrc.usgs.gov/resshow/perry/bios/History.htm; Goodhue, Francis, Jr. Letter to Witmer Stone, May 23, 1910. ANSP 450; Stone, Witmer. Letter to Albert K. Fisher, October 30, 1914. LOC, A.K. Fisher papers, Box 20.
22. Stone, Witmer. Letter to Frank M. Chapman, October 23, 1903. Department of Ornithology Archives, AMNH; Dwight, Jonathan, Jr. Letter to Witmer Stone, October 25, 1903. ANSP Collection 686, Folder 1; Stone, Witmer. Letter to Harry C. Oberholser, October 23, 1903. LOC, Harry C. Oberholser papers; Fisher, Albert K. Letter to Witmer Stone, November 29, 1903. ANSP Collection 685, Folder 6; Sage, John H. Letter to Witmer Stone, October 20, 1903. ANSP Collection 541, Folder 2.
23. DVOC minutes for May 18, 1905. ANSP Collection 74A, Box 1, Folder 4.
24. Stone, Witmer. "George Spencer Morris." *Cassinia*, 1922-24. 25:1-5.
25. Goodhue, Francis, Jr. Letter to Witmer Stone, undated. ANSP 450.

26. Stone, Witmer. Letter to Frank M. Chapman, December 29, 1900. ANSP Collection 679, Folder 8.

27. Stone, Witmer. Letter to Albert K. Fisher, December 15, 1911. LOC, A.K. Fisher papers, Box 19.

28. Coggins, Herbert L. Letter to Witmer Stone, March 10, 1910. ANSP 450. Coggins mistakenly wrote "Pennsauken" instead of Rancocas, but here and in his 1928 letter he was clearly referring to Catoxen cabin.

29. Coggins, Herbert L. Letter to Witmer Stone, January 6, 1928. ANSP 450.

30. Stone, Witmer. Letter to Albert K. Fisher, October 30, 1914. LOC, A.K. Fisher papers, Box 20. Although Morris's 1908 *Cassinia* article clearly indicates five original owners, Stone refers in this letter to "the four original owners." Morris, Brown, Goodhue and Stone were clearly there (G.S. Morris to Stone 10/21/1914; ANSP 450); presumably Morris's "university instructor" (possibly Trotter or Weygandt) had sold out or dropped out by 1914. Previous correspondence about the cabin (F. Goodhue to Stone 7/23/1909 & 5/23/1910; ANSP 450) suggests that the fifth owner dropped out in 1910.

31. Goodhue, Francis, Jr. Letter to Witmer Stone, August 4, 1921. ANSP 450.

32. Anonymous, *Camp Dark Waters: Our 50th Year Celebration.* Undated pamphlet, c. 1977.

33. Stone, Witmer. "Bird-life at Catoxen." *Cassinia,* 1908. 12:25-28.

34. Coggins, Herbert L. "The heart of the New Jersey Pine Barrens." *Cassinia,* 1902. 6:26-31.

35. Stone, Witmer. Letter to ANSP board of curators, June 24, 1901. ANSP Collection 241, Box 1, Folder 3.

36. *The DVOC Twenty Year Souvenir.* 1910. Privately published.

37. Stone, Witmer. "The coastal strip of New Jersey and the rediscovery of Lilaeopsis." *Bartonia,* 1908. 1:20-24.

38. Richards, Annie G. "The ferry boats." *The Cape May Geographic Society Bulletin,* 1955. 9:11-12.

39. *BSOCM.* 690, 317, & 310.

40. Stone, Witmer. "Abama americana (Ker) Morong." *Bartonia,* 1911. 4:1-5.

41. *PSNJ.* 67-68.

42. Stone, Witmer. "Samuel Smyth Van Pelt." *Bartonia,* 1935. 17:1-3.

43. *PSNJ.* 115-17.

44. Stone, Witmer. "Viola renifolia in the Pennsylvanian Alleghanies." *Torreya,* 1902. 2:75.

45. House, Homer D. "Notes on New Jersey violets." *Bulletin of the Torrey Botanical Club,* 1905. 32(5):253-60.

46. Brainerd, Ezra. Letter to Witmer Stone, May 4, 1905. ANSP 450; USDA Plants Database: *Viola × palmata.* Cited February 16, 2014. Available from http://plants.usda.gov/core/profile?symbol=VIPA18

47. Stone, Witmer. "Racial variation in plants and animals, with special reference to the violets of Philadelphia and vicinity." *PANSP,* 1903. 55:656-99.

48. Britton, Nathaniel L. Letter to Witmer Stone, January 18, 1904. ANSP 450.

49. Small, John K. Letter to Witmer Stone, February 27, 1904. ANSP 450.

50. Brainerd, Ezra. Letter to Witmer Stone, March 2, 1904. ANSP 450.

51. Brainerd, Ezra. Letters to Witmer Stone, September 2, 8, & 19, 1905. ANSP 450.

52. Brainerd, Ezra. Letters to Witmer Stone, December 26, 1905, July 26 & September 25, 1906, & May 16, 1907. ANSP 450.

53. Stone, Witmer. "The life-areas of Southern New Jersey." *PANSP,* 1907. 59:452-59.

54. *PSNJ.* 30.

55. Stone, Witmer. Letter to William Brewster, March 25, 1909. MCZ Archives.

56. Deane, Walter. Letter to Witmer Stone, March 2, 1909. ANSP 450.

57. Britton, Nathaniel L. Letter to Witmer Stone, June 8, 1909. ANSP 450.

58. "Abstract of the proceedings of the Philadelphia Botanical Club for 1909." *Bartonia,* 1909. 2:28-31; Pretz, Harold W. "Lehigh County and the Philadelphia Botanical Club" (footnote on p.8-9). *Bartonia,* 1909. 2:3-9.

59. Philadelphia Botanical Club minutes for May 26, 1910. ANSP Collection 88, Box 1, Folder 14.

60. Stone, Witmer. Letter to Albert K. Fisher, August 16, 1910. LOC, A.K. Fisher papers, Box 18.

61. Stone, Witmer. Letter to James A.G. Rehn, September 14, 1910. ANSP 450, Box 22, Folder 2 (under "Witmer Stone").

62. "Abstract of the proceedings of the Philadelphia Botanical Club for 1911." *Bartonia,* 1911. 4:24-27.

63. Philadelphia Botanical Club minutes for April 27, 1911. ANSP Collection 88, Box 1, Folder 14.

64. Stone, Frederick D., Jr., *The Descendants of George Steele*. 1896; Stone, Hugh E. Letter to Witmer Stone, March 16, 1911. ANSP 450.

65. Hugh E. Stone Botanical Illustrations. Cited July 19, 2014. Available from http://www.ansp.org/research/library/archives/0800-0899/stone811b/

66. Stone, Hugh E. Letter to Witmer Stone, June 9, 1910. ANSP 450. At about this time, Hugh also produced a lovely painting of a crow standing amongst emerging skunk cabbages for the title page of *The DVOC Scrap Book 1890-1899* (ANSP Collection 570).

67. Stone, Witmer, *The Plants of Southern New Jersey*. 1911. Annual Report of the New Jersey State Museum for 1910. MacCrellish & Quigley, Trenton.

68. Moore, Gerry. "A review of the nomenclature of Witmer Stone's *The Plants of Southern New Jersey*." *Bartonia*, 2002. 61:27-47.

69. Greenfield, Sydney S. "Book Reviews: The Plants of Southern New Jersey, Witmer Stone." *Plant Science Bulletin*, 1974. 20(4):56.

70. Core, Earl L. "Book Reviews: The Plants of Southern New Jersey." *Castanea*, 1973. 38(4):409-10.

71. *PSNJ*. 34.

72. Bartlett, Harley H. "A flora of the New Jersey Pine Barrens." *Rhodora*, 1912. 14:94-96.

73. Hitchcock, A.S. "Report of the Committee on Generic Types of the Botanical Society of America." *Science*, 1919. 49(1266):333-36; Hitchcock, A.S. "Report of the Committee on Nomenclature of the Botanical Society of America." *Science*, 1921. 53(1370):312-14.

74. Brown, Mary. Letter to Witmer Stone, April 15, 1914. ANSP 450.

75. Philadelphia Botanical Club minutes for September 25, 1913. ANSP Collection 88, Box 1, Folder 14.

76. Bailey, Vernon O. Letter to Witmer Stone, undated, but clearly c. 1913. ANSP 450.

77. Bartsch, Paul. Letter to Witmer Stone, July 5, 1916. ANSP 450.

78. Fisher, Albert K. Letter to Witmer Stone, February 28, 1912. ANSP Collection 685, Folder 6.

79. Morse, Silas R. Letter to Witmer Stone, April 3, 1912. ANSP 450.

80. Morse, Silas R. Letter to Witmer Stone, November 24, 1913. ANSP 450; Gershoy, Alexander. Letter to Witmer Stone, November 8, 1917. ANSP 450.

81. Mousley, Henry. Letter to Witmer Stone, April 29, 1919. ANSP 450; Stone, Witmer. Letter to J.K. Shirk, September 8, 1921. ANSP 450.

82. *PSNJ*. 366.

83. Harshberger, John W., *The Botanists of Philadelphia and Their Work*. 1899. T.C. Davis and Sons, Philadelphia; Harshberger, John W., *The Vegetation of the New Jersey Pine-Barrens*. 1916. Christopher Sower Company, Philadelphia.

84. Brown, Stewardson and Ida A. Keller, *Handbook of the Flora of Philadelphia and Vicinity*. 1905. Philadelphia Botanical Club.

85. *PSNJ*. 608.

86. The taxonomy and nomenclature of many of the plants in *PSNJ* have undergone extensive revision in the intervening century, and it is sometimes difficult to determine with certainty the species being referred to by Stone. Gerry Moore and Russell Juelg have done extensive research to match plants in the modern classification with the ones in *PSNJ*. Russell kindly provided some of the name changes used here (email to author November 27, 2009).

87. *PSNJ*. 356-57.

88. Weygandt, Cornelius. Letter to Witmer Stone, March 24, 1914. ANSP Collection 76.

89. Poyser, William A. Letter to Witmer Stone, March 20, 1912. ANSP 450.

90. Stone, Witmer. Letter to William Brewster, February 5, 1912. MCZ Archives; Stone, Witmer. Letter to Theodore S. Palmer, July 26, 1911. LOC, T.S. Palmer papers, Box 8.

91. "Program of meetings of the Philadelphia Botanical Club from January, 1915, to December, 1923." *Bartonia*, 1924. 8:37-40.

92. Sowden, Lee. Letter to Witmer Stone, September 28, 1917. ANSP 450.

93. Stone, Witmer and Henry A. Pilsbry. "Report of the curators." *PANSP*, 1918. 70:350-55.

94. Bowen, W. Wedgwood. Letter to Witmer Stone, June 28, 1932. ANSP 450.

95. "Report of the curators." *PANSP*, 1919. 71:306-12; John Howard Redfield, Papers 1896. Cited February 7, 2014. Available

from http://www.ansp.org/research/library/archives/0000-0099/coll0062/

96. "Additions to the museum." *PANSP*, 1919. 71(3):317-23.

97. Stone, Witmer. Letter to Alexander Wetmore, October 31, 1919. SIA Collection 7006, Box 65, Folder 6.

98. Standley, Paul. Letter to Witmer Stone, July 26, 1920. ANSP 450.

99. Stone, Witmer. Letter to A. T. Beals, April 8, 1922. ANSP 450.

100. Stone, Witmer. Letter to Merritt L. Fernald, December 16, 1924. ANSP 450; Stone, Witmer. Letter to William C. Ferguson, December 23, 1927. ANSP 450.

101. *BSOCM*. 27 & 320. Stone even gave the date of publication as both 1910 and 1911.

102. Weygandt, Cornelius, "Twelve Good Men and True," in *Philadelphia Folks*. 1938. 266-69.

103. Brown, Herbert. Letter to Witmer Stone, July 23, 1923. ANSP 450; Fisher, Albert K. Letter to Witmer Stone, August 20, 1923. LOC, A.K. Fisher papers, Box 26.

104. Stone, Witmer. Letter to Wharton Huber, August 7, 1929. ANSP Collection 186, Box 3, Folder 4.

105. "Flower Exhibition Cape May Feature." *The Pittsburgh Press*, Pittsburgh, July 20, 1930.

106. Gerry Moore informs me that Scarlet Gilia is also established at the Manumuskin River Preserve in Cumberland County, N.J.; "Dr. Stone Exhibits Flowers at Shore." *The Evening Bulletin*, Philadelphia, July 24, 1930; Stone, Witmer. Letter to Alexander Wetmore, July 24, 1930. SIA Collection 7006, Box 65, Folder 8.

107. Palmer, Theodore S. Letter to Witmer Stone, July 28, 1931. ANSP Collection 680, Folder 1; "Cape May County's Native Flora Still Constitutes a Beauty Show of Rare Attraction." *The Evening Bulletin*, Philadelphia, August 2, 1932; Stone, Witmer. Letter to James L. Peters, August 8, 1932. MCZ Archives.

108. Griscom, Ludlow. Letter to Witmer Stone, August 11, 1933. ANSP 450; Potter, Julian K. Letter to Witmer Stone, July 30, 1933. ANSP 450.

109. "Program of meetings during 1929." *Bartonia*, 1930. 12:60.

110. Stone, Witmer. "John W. Eckfeldt." *Bartonia*, 1933. 15:57-59.

111. Eckfeldt, John W. Letter to Witmer Stone, February 26, 1899. ANSP 450.

112. Gordon, Susan L. "Silas Ruttilus Morse." *The Atlantic County Historical Society: Sixth Yearbook with Historical and Genealogical Journal*, 1953. 2(2):233-41.

113. Morse, Silas R. Letter to Witmer Stone, June 9, 1917. ANSP 450.

Chapter 9: An All-round Naturalist

1. Rehn, James A. G. "Witmer Stone (1866-1939)." *Cassinia*, 1938-41. 31:1-11.

2. Huber, Wharton. "Witmer Stone (1866 to 1939)." *Journal of Mammalogy*, 1940. 21(1):1-4.

3. Pennell, Francis W. "The botanical work of Witmer Stone." *Bartonia*, 1940. 20:33-37.

4. The Academy of Natural Sciences of Philadelphia: Malacology Collection. Cited September 13, 2014. Available from http://clade.ansp.org/malacology/collections/search.php

5. Stone, Witmer. Letter to Stewardson Brown, September 21, 1887. ANSP Collection 168, Folder 5; Stone, Witmer. "Pennsylvania and New Jersey spiders of the Family Lycosidae." *PANSP*, 1890. 42:420-34.

6. Banks, Nathan. Letter to Witmer Stone, February 7, 1891. ANSP 450.

7. Skinner, Henry. "Report of the entomological section." *PANSP*, 1892. 44:497.

8. Stone, Witmer. "A new Evotomys from southern New Jersey." *The American Naturalist*, 1893. 27(313):54-56; Rhoads, Samuel N. "A new Synaptomys from New Jersey." *The American Naturalist*, 1893. 27(313):53-54; Merritt, Joseph F., "Southern Bog Lemming," in *Guide to the Mammals of Pennsylvania*. 1987, University of Pittsburgh Press. 206-08.

9. Stone, Witmer. "Description of a New Species of Neotoma from Pennsylvania." *PANSP*, 1893. 45(1):16-18; *The Allegheny Woodrat: Ecology, Conservation, and Management of a Declining Species*, ed. John D. Peles and Janet Wright. 2008. Springer, New York.

10. Yamada, Fumio and Fernando A. Cervantes, *Pentalagus furnessi*. Mammalian Species, No. 782. 2005. American Society of Mammalogists; Jackson, Stephen M. and Richard W. Thorington, Jr., *Gliding Mammals: Taxonomy of Living and Extinct Species*. Smithsonian Contributions to Zoology, No. 638. 2012. Smithsonian Institution Scholarly Press, Washington, D.C. 48; Stone, Witmer. "Descriptions of a new rabbit from

the Liu Kiu Islands and a new flying squirrel from Borneo." *PANSP*, 1900. 52:460-63.

11. Stokes, John F.G. Lett er to Witmer Stone, July 21, 1915. ANSP 450; Stone, Witmer. "The Hawaiian Rat." *Occasional Papers of the Bernice Pauahi Bishop Museum of Polynesian Ethnology and Natural History*, 1917. 3(4):253-60.

12. Carleton, Michael. Email to author, January 28, 2014.

13. Miller, Gerrit S. Letter to Witmer Stone, January 26, 1899. ANSP Collection 953, Folder 1.

14. Stone, Witmer. Letter to William L. Finley, May 7, 1923. ANSP 450.

15. Lanier, Henry W. Letter to Witmer Stone, September 9, 1901. ANSP 450.

16. Lanier, Henry W. Letter to Witmer Stone, October 15, 1901. ANSP 450.

17. Little Stories of Old New England by William D. and William E. Cram. Cited February 23, 2014. Available from http://www.hampton.lib.nh.us/hampton/history/oral/cram/index.htm

18. Cram, William Everett, *Little Beasts of Field and Wood*, 1899, and *More Little Beasts of Field and Wood*, 1912. Small, Maynard, and Co., Boston.

19. Cram, William Everett. Letter to Witmer Stone, February 11, 1902. ANSP 450.

20. Stone, Witmer and William Everett Cram, *American Animals: A Popular Guide to the Mammals of North America North of Mexico, with Intimate Biographies of the More Familiar Species*. 1902. Doubleday, Page and Co., New York.

21. Stone, Witmer. "Recent Literature: The New Nature Library." *The Auk*, 1914. 31(4):553.

22. Cram, William Everett. Letter to Witmer Stone, December 11, 1913. ANSP 450.

23. Stone, Witmer, *The Mammals of New Jersey*. 1907.

24. Stone, Witmer, *The Mammals of New Jersey*. 1907. 40, 49-50.

25. "Notes and news." *The Auk*, 1919. 36(3):451; Hoffmeister, Donald F. "The influence of university and museum professionals in the formation of the American Society of Mammalogists." *Journal of Mammalogy*, 1994. 75(4):i-ii.

26. Stone, Witmer. Letter to Joseph Grinnell, May 27, 1930. MVZ Archives.

27. Stone, Witmer. "Occurrence of Hyla andersonii at Clementon, N.J." (talk). *PANSP*, 1901. 53:342.

28. Stone, Witmer. "Notes on Reptiles and Batrachians of Pennsylvania, New Jersey, and Delaware." *The American Naturalist*, 1906. 40:159-70.

29. Stone, Witmer. "Terrestrial activity of Spade-Foot Toads." *Copeia*, 1932. 1932(1):35-36.

30. "Report of the curators." *PANSP*, 1919. 71:306-12.

31. Stone, Witmer. Letter to Waldo Lee McAtee, January 17, 1934. LOC, W.L. McAtee papers, Box 37, Folder 3; McAtee, Waldo Lee. Letter to Witmer Stone, October 28, 1919. ANSP Collection 968, Folder 2.

32. Stone, Witmer. Letter to Waldo Lee McAtee, May 28, 1920. LOC, W.L. McAtee papers, Box 10, Folder 4.

33. Rehn, James A. G. "A New Melanoplus from New Jersey." *Entomological News*, 1904. 15:85-87; Brust, Mathew L. et al. "Morphological and genetic analyses in the Melanoplus packardii group (Orthoptera: Acrididae)." 2010. *Faculty Publications: Department of Entomology*, University of Nebraska-Lincoln. Paper 331. Cited February 23, 2014. Available at http://digitalcommons.unl.edu/entomologyfacpub/331.

34. Stone, Witmer. Letter to Albert K. Fisher, April 26, 1918. LOC, A.K. Fisher papers, Box 22.

35. McIlhenny, Edward A. Letter to Witmer Stone, June 20, 1935. ANSP 450.

36. McIlhenny, Edward A. Letter to Witmer Stone, September 24, 1935. ANSP 450.

37. Wetmore, Alexander. "Witmer Stone (1866-1939)." *Year Book of the American Philosophical Society*, 1939:467-69.

38. Rehn, James A. G. Letter to Witmer Stone, July 3, 1933. ANSP Collection 682, Folder 1.

39. McAtee, Waldo Lee. Letter to Witmer Stone, April 25, 1934. LOC, W.L. McAtee papers, Box 37, Folder 3; Morrison, Harold. Letters to Witmer Stone, May 12, 1934 & January 22, 1935. ANSP 450.

40. Huber, Wharton. Untitled memorial of Witmer Stone. 1939. ANSP Collection 263.

41. Bartsch, Paul. Letter to Witmer Stone, 1931. Untitled book of bound letters to Stone in ANSP Collection 2009-031, Box 4, Folder 3.

42. Merriam, C. Hart. Letter to Witmer Stone, March 6, 1915. ANSP Collection 678, Folder 7; Merriam, C. Hart. Letter to Witmer Stone, 1931. Untitled book of bound letters to Stone in ANSP Collection 2009-031, Box 4, Folder 3.

Chapter 10: I Am Asking for More!

1. Stone, Witmer. "The new AOU check-list." *The Auk*, 1931. 48(4):523-31.
2. Sage, John H. "Nineteenth Congress of the American Ornithologists' Union." *The Auk*, 1902. 19(1):64-69.
3. Stone, Witmer. Letter to William Brewster, October 20, 1915. MCZ Archives; "Notes and news." *The Auk*, 1920. 37(1):182-88.
4. Rehn, James A. G. "In memoriam: Witmer Stone." *The Auk*, 1941. 58(3):299-313.
5. Stiles, C.W. Letter to Witmer Stone, July 14, 1927. ANSP 450; Moore, Gerry. "A review of the nomenclature of Witmer Stone's *The Plants of Southern New Jersey.*" *Bartonia*, 2002. 61:27-47.
6. Stone, Witmer (seven articles): "A revision of the species of *Molothrus* allied to *M. bonariensis* (Gm.)." *The Auk*, 1891. 8(4):344-47; "On the genus *Psilorhinus* (Ruppell)." PANSP, 1891. 43:94-96; "A revision of the genus *Anous.*" PANSP, 1894. 46:115-18; "A review of the Old World *Rallinae.*" PANSP, 1894. 46:130-49; "A revision of the North American horned owls with description of a new subspecies." *The Auk*, 1896. 13(2):153-56; "The genus *Sturnella.*" PANSP, 1897. 49:146-52; "A review of the genus *Piaya* (Lesson)." PANSP, 1908. 60(3):492-501.
7. Stone, Witmer. "Recent Literature: The Austral Avian Record." *The Auk*, 1918. 35(4):499-500; Oberholser, Harry C. "The proper generic name of the Ruff." *The Auk*, 1919. 36(2):278.
8. Stone, Witmer. "Proper name for MacGillivray's warbler." *The Auk*, 1899. 16(1):81-82; AOU Checklist of North and Middle American Birds (through 54th supplement). Cited September 13, 2014. Available from http://checklist.aou.org/taxa/
9. Dwight, Jonathan, Jr. Letter to Witmer Stone, November 8, 1905. ANSP Collection 686, Folder 1.
10. Stone, Witmer. "Mark Catesby and the nomenclature of North American birds." *The Auk*, 1929. 46(4):447-54.

11. Taverner, P.A. and Witmer Stone. "Correspondence: Subspecific Designations." *The Auk*, 1917. 34(3):370-76.
12. Stone, Witmer. "An old case of skins and its associations." *The Osprey*, 1899. 3(7):98-99.
13. Stone, Witmer. "Winter plumages:– illustrated by the rose-breasted grosbeak (Zamelodia ludoviciana)." *The Auk*, 1899. 16(4):305-08.
14. Stone, Witmer, "The Ornithology of Today and Tomorrow," in *The Fiftieth Anniversary of the Nuttall Ornithological Club.* 1924, Cambridge. 7-25.
15. BSOCM. 871; Chapman, Frank M. "Further remarks on the relationships of the grackles of the subgenus *Quiscalis.*" *The Auk*, 1935. 52(1):21-29.
16. Peer, Brian D. and Eric K. Bollinger. 1997. Common Grackle (*Quiscalus quiscula*), The Birds of North America Online (A. Poole, Ed.). Ithaca: Cornell Lab of Ornithology. Retrieved from: http://bna.birds.cornell.edu. bnaproxy.birds.cornell.edu/bna/species/271
17. Kennard, Frederic H. Letter to Witmer Stone, August 20, 1920. ANSP 450.
18. Grinnell, Joseph. "Recent additions to the California state list of birds." *The Condor*, 1919. 21(1):41-42.
19. Young, Robert T. Letter to Witmer Stone, [Month illegible] 2, 1905. ANSP 450.
20. Notes for January 15, 1914 "Present Day Aspects of Ornithology" talk to DVOC in private collection of Witmer Stone material; "Abstract of the proceedings of the DVOC 1914." *Cassinia*, 1914. 18:62-65.
21. Stone, Witmer. "Recent Literature: Figgins on subspecies." *The Auk*, 1926. 43(1):118-19.
22. "Notes and news." *The Auk*, 1929. 46(1):151-54.
23. Stone, Witmer. Letter to James P. Chapin, March 23, 1936. Department of Ornithology Archives, AMNH.
24. PSNJ. 36.
25. "Notes and news." *The Auk*, 1915. 32(3):386-90.
26. Ridgway, Robert and Witmer Stone. "Correspondence: 'Generic subdivision'. – 'The genus debased.'" *The Auk*, 1923. 40(2):371-75.
27. Stone, Witmer. "The use and abuse of the genus." *Science*, 1920. 51(1322):427-29.
28. Stone, Witmer. Letter to Harry C. Oberholser, December 26, 1912. LOC, Harry C. Oberholser papers, Box 18; Stone, Witmer.

"Oberholser's one hundred and four new birds from the Barussan Islands and Sumatra." *The Auk*, 1913. 30(1):123.

29. Stone, Witmer. Letter to Frank M. Chapman, February 5, 1917. ANSP Collection 679, Folder 11.

30. Chapman, Frank M. Letter to Witmer Stone, December 8, 1915. ANSP Collection 679, Folder 11.

31. "Notes and news." *The Auk*, 1916. 33(1):111-14.

32. Stone, Witmer. "Recent Literature: The Ornithological Journals. The Austral Avian Record." *The Auk*, 1916. 33(3):345.

33. Stone, Witmer. "Recent Literature: Matthews' 'The Birds of Australia.'" *The Auk*, 1922. 39(3):436.

34. Stone, Witmer. "Recent Literature: The Ornithological Journals. The Condor." *The Auk*, 1932. 49(2):260-61.

35. Stone, Witmer. Letter to Charles M.B. Cadwalader, February 20, 1937. Stone's essay on "The future of zoological research in museums" is attached to the letter. ANSP Collection 2009-034, Box 47, Folder 69.

36. Bridson, G.D.R. "The Zoological Record – a centenary appraisal." *Journal of the Society for the Bibliography of Natural History*, 1968. 5(1):23-34.

37. Stone, Witmer. Letters to P. Chalmers Mitchell, June 28, 1923 & November 19, 1924, & P.C. Mitchell, letters to W. Stone, December 31, 1923 & March 2, 1926. ANSP Collection 186, Box 3, Folder 8.

38. Stone, Witmer. "Recent Literature: 'Aves' for 1924." *The Auk*, 1926. 43(2):261-62.

39. Allen, Joel Asaph. Letter to Witmer Stone, January 18, 1906. ANSP Collection 658, Folder 6.

40. Allen, Joel Asaph. Letter to William Brewster, August 14, 1906 (forwarded to Stone in December). ANSP Collection 658, Folder 10; Allen, Joel Asaph. Letter to Witmer Stone, February 4, 1907. ANSP Collection 658, Folder 11; "Notes and news." *The Auk*, 1907. 24(3):365-68.

41. Stone, Witmer. Letter to William Brewster, April 10, 1907. MCZ Archives.

42. Stone, Witmer. "Brooks' and Swarth's 'Distributional List of the Birds of British Columbia.'" *The Auk*, 1926. 43(1):114-15.

43. Stone, Witmer. Letter to Waldo Lee McAtee, April 20, 1918. LOC, W.L. McAtee papers, Box 10, Folder 4.

44. Stone, Witmer. Letter to R. Bowdler Sharpe, June 12, 1906. Blacker-Wood Collection, Department of Rare Books, McGill University. I have also examined a private collection containing hundreds of pages of Stone's handwritten notes on the subject, which must be the work Stone referred to in this letter.

45. Chapman, Frank M., *Autobiography of a Bird-lover*. 1933. Appleton-Century Co., New York/London. 49.

46. Allen, Joel Asaph. "Note on the generic names *Didelphis* and *Philander*." *Bulletin of the American Museum of Natural History*, 1900. 13:185-90.

47. Stone, Witmer. "The date of publication of Brewster's American Edition of the Edinburgh Encyclopedia." *Science*, 1900. 12(305):685-86.

48. Allen, Joel Asaph. Letter to Witmer Stone, November 3, 1900. ANSP Collection 658, Folder 6.

49. Stone, Witmer. Letter to Joel Asaph Allen, November 5, 1900. Department of Ornithology Archives, AMNH.

50. Allen, Joel Asaph. Letter to Witmer Stone, January 22, 1906. ANSP Collection 658, Folder 6.

51. Allen, Joel Asaph. Letter to Witmer Stone, November 2, 1907. ANSP Collection 658, Folder 11.

52. Coues, Elliott, Joel Asaph Allen, Robert Ridgway, et al., *The Code of Nomenclature Adopted by the American Ornithologists' Union*. 1892. AOU, New York. 44.

53. Dwight, Jonathan, Jr. Letter to Witmer Stone, December 1, 1907. ANSP Collection 686, Folder 1; Osgood, Wilfred H. Letter to Witmer Stone, November 26, 1907. ANSP 450.

54. "Notes and news." *The Auk*, 1914. 31(1):138-48.

55. Batchelder, Charles F. Letter to Witmer Stone, November 4, 1909. ANSP 450.

56. Stone, Witmer. Letter to William Brewster, March 22, 1910. MCZ Archives.

57. Dwight, Jonathan, Jr. Letter to Witmer Stone, April 3, 1910. ANSP Collection 682, Folder 2.

58. Joel Asaph Allen to Robert Ridgway, February 8, 1886. Quoted in Lewis, *The Feathery Tribe*, 167.

59. "Correspondence: The AOU Check-List, Third Edition." *The Auk*, 1913. 30(1):149-54.

60. Wayne, Arthur T. Letter to Witmer Stone, February 5, 1913. ANSP 450.

61. Allen, Joel Asaph. Letter to Charles W. Richmond [JAA mistakenly wrote "Richardson"], January 7, 1914. ANSP Collection 658, Folder 19; Sage, John H. Letter to Witmer Stone, December 15, 1914. ANSP Collection 541, Folder 3.

62. Stone, Witmer. "Notes and news." *The Auk*, 1919. 36(1):152-62; Stone, Witmer. Letter to Albert K. Fisher, March 15, 1915. LOC, A.K. Fisher papers, Box 21; [Committee], "Preface," in *Check-list of North American Birds*. 1931, Lancaster Press, Inc., Lancaster. iii-xv.

63. Dwight, Jonathan, Jr. Letter to Witmer Stone, October 26, 1919. ANSP Collection 686, Folder 3.

64. Stone, Witmer. Letters to Theodore S. Palmer, December 10, 1918 & September 21, 1919. LOC, T.S. Palmer papers, Box 36.

65. Stone, Witmer. Memo to members of AOU Committee on Classification and Nomenclature of North American Birds. Memo is on back of Stone letter to "Mr. Moore." ANSP Collection 186, Box 2, Folder 7. Undated, but c. 1918.

66. Palmer, Theodore S. Letter to Witmer Stone, February 23, 1923. ANSP Collection 680, Folder 2; Stone, Witmer. Letter to Frank M. Chapman, February 14, 1923. ANSP Collection 679, Folder 11.

67. Stone, Witmer. Letter to John Albert Leach, July 7, 1924. ANSP 450.

68. Stone, Witmer. Letter to Jonathan Dwight, Jr., August 6, 1924. ANSP Collection 686, Folder 3.

69. Palmer, Theodore S. Letter to Witmer Stone, September 8, 1924. ANSP Collection 680, Folder 1.

70. Stone, Witmer. Letter to Jonathan Dwight, Jr., October 6, 1924. ANSP Collection 686, Folder 3.

71. Stone, Witmer. Letter to Alexander Wetmore, January 19, 1926. SIA Collection 7006, Box 65, Folder 6.

72. Wetmore, Alexander and Waldron DeWitt Miller. "The revised classification for the fourth edition of the AOU check-list." *The Auk*, 1926. 43(3):337-46; Stone, Witmer. Letter to Alexander Wetmore, February 9, 1926. SIA Collection 7006, Box 65, Folder 6.

73. Stone, Witmer. Letter to Joseph Grinnell, June 2, 1930. MVZ Archives.

74. Wetmore, Alexander. Letters to Witmer Stone, April 6 & 13, 1926. SIA Collection 7006, Box 65, Folder 6.

75. Stone, Witmer. Letters to Alexander Wetmore, September 24, 1926 & June 2, 1929. SIA Collection 7006, Box 65, Folders 6 & 7.

76. Stone, Witmer. "Some aspects of the subspecies question." *The Auk*, 1935. 52(1):31-39.

77. Stone, Witmer. Letter to Alexander Wetmore, January 20, 1928. SIA Collection 7006, Box 65, Folder 7.

78. "Notes and news." *The Auk*, 1930. 47(2):310-12.

79. Stone, Witmer. Letter to Frank M. Chapman, September 27, 1927. Department of Ornithology Archives, AMNH.

80. Dwight, Jonathan, Jr. Letter to Witmer Stone, October 20, 1927. ANSP Collection 686, Folder 3.

81. Dwight, Jonathan, Jr. Letters to Witmer Stone, May 21, 1908 & February 17, 1926. ANSP Collection 686, Folders 2 & 3; Dwight, Jonathan, Jr. "The popular names of birds." *The Condor*, 1909. 11(2):43-45.

82. Dwight, Jonathan, Jr. Letter to Witmer Stone, November 25, 1910. ANSP Collection 686, Folder 2.

83. Dwight, Jonathan, Jr. Letter to Witmer Stone, March 7, 1926. ANSP Collection 686, Folder 3.

84. Allen, Joel Asaph. Letter to Witmer Stone, April 21, 1910. ANSP Collection 658, Folder 14.

85. Stone, Witmer. Letter to Robert Cushman Murphy, January 18, 1930. ANSP 450.

86. Dwight, Jonathan, Jr. Letter to Witmer Stone, December 2, 1915. ANSP Collection 686, Folder 2.

87. "Editorial notes and news." *The Condor*, 1917. 19(5):171-72; Miller, Waldron DeWitt. Letter to Witmer Stone, August 9, 1919, & W. Stone, letter to W.D. Miller, August 28, 1919. ANSP 450.

88. Stone, Witmer. "Recent Literature: Ornithological Articles in Other Journals." *The Auk*, 1921. 38(3):486-89.

89. Grinnell, Joseph. Letter to Witmer Stone, October 20, 1921. ANSP Collection 684, Folder 4.

90. Richmond, Charles W. Letter to Witmer Stone, October 2, 1916. ANSP Collection 675, Folder 6; Chapman, Frank M. Letter to Witmer Stone, October 21, 1927. ANSP Collection 679, Folder 12; Stone, Witmer.

"Recent papers by Oberholser." *The Auk*, 1922. 39(4):585-86.

91. Grinnell, Joseph. Letter to Witmer Stone, February 16, 1929. ANSP Collection 684, Folder 4.

92. Dwight, Jonathan, Jr. Letter to Witmer Stone, October 16, 1919. ANSP Collection 686, Folder 3.

93. Dwight, Jonathan, Jr. Letter to Witmer Stone, April 17, 1925. ANSP Collection 686, Folder 3.

94. Grinnell, Joseph. Letter to Witmer Stone, December 27, 1922, & W. Stone, letter to J. Grinnell, January 6, 1923. ANSP Collection 684, Folder 4; Stone, Witmer. Letter to Harry C. Oberholser, November 29, 1922. ANSP Collection 538, Folder 6.

95. Stone, Witmer, Harry C. Oberholser, Jonathan Dwight, Jr., et al. "Eighteenth supplement to the American Ornithologists' Union check-list of North American birds." *The Auk*, 1923. 40(3):513-25.

96. Wetmore, Alexander. Letter to Witmer Stone, June 4, 1925. SIA Collection 7006, Box 65, Folder 6.

97. Wetmore, Alexander. Letter to Witmer Stone, January 24, 1928. SIA Collection 7006, Box 65, Folder 7.

98. Oberholser, Harry C. Letter to Witmer Stone, May 3, 1927. ANSP Collection 538, Folder 6; *BSOCM*. 417.

99. Oberholser, Harry C. Letter to Witmer Stone, July 5, 1922. ANSP Collection 538, Folder 6.

100. Bishop, Louis B. Letter to Witmer Stone, January 20, 1930. ANSP 450.

101. Peters, James L. Letter to Witmer Stone, May 2, 1930. ANSP 450.

102. Fleming, James H. Letter to Witmer Stone, March 6, 1930. ANSP 450.

103. Stone, Witmer. Letter to Theodore S. Palmer, April 7, 1930. LOC, T.S. Palmer papers, Box 47; Grinnell, Joseph. Letter to Witmer Stone, April 21, 1930. ANSP Collection 684, Folder 5.

104. Swarth, Harry S. Letter to Witmer Stone, August 29, 1930. ANSP 450.

105. Fleming, James H. "In memoriam: Jonathan Dwight." *The Auk*, 1930. 47(1):1-6; Chapin, James P. "In memoriam: Waldron DeWitt Miller." *The Auk*, 1932. 49(1):1-8.

106. Peters, James L. Letter to Witmer Stone, June 23, 1930. ANSP 450.

107. *Check-list of North American Birds, Fourth Edition*, ed. Witmer Stone. 1931. Lancaster Press, Inc., Lancaster. iii-xv.

108. Stone, Witmer. Letter to Alexander Wetmore, November 5, 1926. SIA Collection 7006, Box 65, Folder 6.

109. Stone, Witmer. Letter to Alexander Wetmore, June 27, 1927. SIA Collection 7006, Box 65, Folder 7.

110. Stone, Witmer. Letter to Casey A. Wood, May 21, 1928. Blacker-Wood Collection, Department of Rare Books, McGill University.

111. Stone, Witmer. Letter to James L. Peters, December 30, 1930. MCZ Archives. For what it matters, I've read thousands of letters written by Stone, and this is the only time I've found him using a four-letter word.

112. Chapman, Frank M. Letter to Witmer Stone, April 12, 1930. ANSP Collection 679, Folder 12.

113. Stone, Witmer. Letter to Waldo Lee McAtee, April 29, 1928. LOC, W.L. McAtee papers, Box 10, Folder 4.

114. Grinnell, Joseph. Letter to Witmer Stone, September 7, 1931. ANSP Collection 684, Folder 5.

115. Stone, Witmer. Letter to Samuel F. Rathbun, September 10, 1930. ANSP Collection 2009-034; Stone, Witmer. Letter to Alexander Wetmore, August 18, 1930. SIA Collection 7006, Box 65, Folder 8.

116. Swarth, Harry S. "The subspecies of *Branta canadensis* (Linnaeus)." *The Auk*, 1920. 37(2):268-72.

117. Swarth, Harry S. Letter to Witmer Stone, November 4, 1930. ANSP 450; Mowbray, Thomas B., Craig R. Ely, James S. Sedinger and Robert E. Trost. 2002. Canada Goose (*Branta canadensis*), The Birds of North America Online (A. Poole, Ed.). Ithaca: Cornell Lab of Ornithology. Retrieved from: http://bna.birds.cornell.edu.bnaproxy.birds.cornell.edu/bna/species/682

118. Pickens, Andrew L. Letter to Witmer Stone, February 11, 1929. ANSP 450.

119. Stone, Witmer. Letter to Harry C. Oberholser, April 6, 1931. LOC, Harry C. Oberholser papers, Box 18.

120. Stone, Witmer. Letter to Frank M. Chapman, July 10, 1931. Department of Ornithology Archives, AMNH.

121. Wetmore, Alexander. Letter to Witmer Stone, October 5, 1931, & W. Stone, letter

to A. Wetmore, October 15, 1931. SIA Collection 7006, Box 65, Folder 8.

122. Grinnell, Joseph. Letter to Witmer Stone, October 13, 1931. ANSP Collection 684, Folder 5.

123. Stone, Witmer. Letter to Joseph Grinnell, February 11, 1926. MVZ Archives.

124. Stone, Witmer. Letter to Frank M. Chapman, October 16, 1931. LOC, T.S. Palmer papers, Box 50.

125. Allen, Arthur A. Letter to Witmer Stone, 1931. Untitled book of bound letters to Stone in ANSP Collection 2009-031, Box 4, Folder 3.

126. Rehn, James A. G. "Witmer Stone (1866-1939)." *Cassinia*, 1938-41. 31:1-11.

Chapter 11: The Brave Old Bird Goes On

1. Stone, Witmer. Letter to Casey A. Wood, December 15, 1921. ANSP 450.

2. "Comments: New editors." *The Osprey*, 1899. 4(2):25.

3. Deane, Ruthven. Letter to Witmer Stone, November 2, 1911. ANSP Collection 687, Folder 2.

4. Dwight, Jonathan, Jr. Letters to Witmer Stone, October 8 & November 8, 1911. ANSP Collection 686, Folder 2.

5. Richmond, Charles W. Letter to Witmer Stone, 1931. Untitled book of bound letters to Stone in ANSP Collection 2009-031, Box 4, Folder 3.

6. AOU Council minutes for November 13, 1911. SIA Collection 7150, Box 3.

7. Stone, Witmer. Letter to Arthur Cleveland Bent, May 29, 1936. ANSP Collection 550, Folder 2.

8. Roosevelt, Theodore. "Revealing and concealing coloration in birds and mammals." *Bulletin of the American Museum of Natural History*, 1911. 30:119-231; Thayer, Gerald H., *Concealing Coloration in the Animal Kingdom*. 1909. The MacMillan Co., New York.

9. Allen, Francis H. "Remarks on the case of Roosevelt vs. Thayer, with a few independent suggestions on the concealing coloration question." *The Auk*, 1912. 29(4):489-507.

10. Roosevelt, Theodore. Letter to Witmer Stone, November 22, 1912. ANSP 450; Deane, Ruthven and Witmer Stone. "Correspondence: The concealing coloration question." *The Auk*, 1913. 30(1):146-47.

11. Allen, Francis H. and Witmer Stone. "Correspondence: The concealing coloration question." *The Auk*, 1913. 30(2):311-17.

12. Stone, Witmer. Letter to Frank M. Chapman, December 3, 1912. Department of Ornithology Archives, AMNH.

13. Chapman, Frank M. Letter to Witmer Stone, December 4, 1912. Department of Ornithology Archives, AMNH.

14. Stone, Witmer. Letter to Joel Asaph Allen, February 7, 1913. Department of Ornithology Archives, AMNH.

15. Allen, Joel Asaph. Letter to Witmer Stone, January 7, 1914. ANSP Collection 658, Folder 19.

16. Allen, Joel Asaph. Letter to Witmer Stone, November 20, 1919. ANSP Collection 658, Folder 20. Here's hoping that Allen's poignant comment inspires you to send a note of appreciation to the editor of your favorite journal.

17. Stone, Witmer. Letter to Waldo Lee McAtee, undated, but clearly early autumn 1919. LOC, W.L. McAtee papers, Box 10, Folder 4.

18. Stone, Witmer. Letter to Joseph Grinnell, February 13, 1926. MVZ Archives.

19. Stone, Witmer. "The ornithological journals." *The Auk*, 1912. 29(2):270.

20. Allen, Joel Asaph. Letter to Witmer Stone, March 1, 1912. ANSP Collection 658, Folder 17.

21. Stone, Witmer. Letter to Charles B. Cory, April 14, 1921. ANSP 450.

22. Rehn, James A. G. "In memoriam: Witmer Stone." *The Auk*, 1941. 58(3):299-313.

23. Shufeldt, Robert W. Letter to Witmer Stone, January 4, 1914. ANSP Collection 674, Folder 2; Chapman, Frank M. Letter to Witmer Stone, September 13, 1920. ANSP Collection 679, Folder 11; Grinnell, Joseph, letter to Witmer Stone, July 27, 1931, & Townsend, Charles W., letter to W. Stone, August 27, 1931. Both in untitled book of bound letters to Stone in ANSP Collection 2009-031, Box 4, Folder 3.

24. Wetmore, Alexander. Letter to Arthur Cleveland Bent, May 2, 1936. SIA Collection 7006, Box 80, Folder 7.

25. Stone, Witmer. "Recent Literature: Weygandt's 'The Wissahickon Hills.'" *The Auk*, 1931. 48(1):136-38.

26. Barrow, Mark V., Jr., *A Passion for Birds*. 1998. 201.

27. Stone, Witmer. "Recent Literature: The Ibis. Ornithology of the Maroccan [*sic*] 'Middle Atlas.'" *The Auk*, 1920. 37(2):328.

28. Stone, Witmer. "Recent Literature: Stoner's sketch of the life of Audubon." *The Auk*, 1925. 42(3):457; Stoner, Dayton. Letter to Witmer Stone, August 17, 1925. ANSP 450.

29. Stone, Witmer. "Recent Literature: The Birds of Louisiana." *The Auk*, 1932. 49(3):370-71.

30. Shufeldt, Robert W. Letter to Witmer Stone, April 1, 1913. ANSP Collection 674, Folder 1.

31. Bent, Arthur Cleveland. Letter to Witmer Stone, November 16, 1915. ANSP Collection 550, Folder 2.

32. Grinnell, Joseph. Letter to Witmer Stone, October 17, 1928. ANSP Collection 684, Folder 4.

33. "Notes and news." *The Auk*, 1929. 46(4):584-91.

34. Stone, Witmer. Letter to Frank M. Chapman, June 17, 1920. Department of Ornithology Archives, AMNH.

35. Grinnell, Joseph. Letters to Witmer Stone, December 31, 1911 & January 15, 1912. ANSP Collection 684, Folder 3.

36. A recent *Auk* editor told me he had done the same thing with his *Condor* counterpart.

37. Kennard, Frederic H. Letter to Witmer Stone, January 27, 1919. ANSP 450.

38. Kennard, Frederic H. Letter to Witmer Stone, December 11, 1914. ANSP 450.

39. Bailey, Alfred M. Letter to Witmer Stone, August 20, 1928. ANSP 450.

40. Simmons, George Finlay. Letter to Witmer Stone, April 22, 1914. ANSP 450.

41. Saunders, Aretas. Letter to Witmer Stone, November 11, 1915. ANSP 450.

42. "Notes and news." *The Auk*, 1933. 50(2):262-64.

43. Stone, Witmer. Letter to Thomas E. Penard, April 14, 1921. ANSP 450.

44. Stone, Witmer. Letter to John A. Farley, December 5, 1925. ANSP 450.

45. "Present Day Tendencies and Opportunities in Ornithology." Manuscript of paper read by Stone at AOU annual meeting in 1922 (*Auk* 40(1):114). Private collection of Witmer Stone material.

46. "Notes and news." *The Auk*, 1923. 40(1):182-90.

47. van Tyne, Josselyn. Letter to Witmer Stone, January 30, 1933. ANSP 450.

48. Schorger, A.W. "The contributions of Josselyn van Tyne to the Wilson Ornithological Society." *The Wilson Bulletin*, 1957. 69(4):314-16.

49. Wing, Leonard W. Letter to Witmer Stone, June 16, 1935. ANSP 450.

50. Wing, Leonard W. "The Raven (Corvus corax subspecies) in Dane County, Wisconsin, and a note on its food habits." *The Auk*, 1935. 52(4):455.

51. Wing, Leonard W. Letter to Witmer Stone, November 9, 1935. ANSP 450.

52. Wing, Leonard W. and Witmer Stone. "Correction." *The Auk*, 1936. 53(1):101.

53. Stone, Witmer. Letter to John A. Farley, May 23, 1923. ANSP 450.

54. Farley, John A. Letter to Witmer Stone, May 25, 1923. ANSP 450.

55. Stone, Witmer. Letter to John A. Farley, May 29, 1923. ANSP 450.

56. AOU Council minutes for November 13, 1933. SIA Collection 7150, Box 4, Folder 1; Fleming, James H. Letter to Witmer Stone, February 19, 1934. ANSP 450; Stone, Witmer. Letter to Alexander Wetmore, February 26, 1934. SIA Collection 7006, Box 66, Folder 18.

57. Stone, Witmer. Letter to Frank M. Chapman, July 14, 1936. Department of Ornithology Archives, AMNH.

58. Hicks, Lawrence E. Letter to Witmer Stone, undated. ANSP 450.

59. Clark, Hubert L. Letter to Witmer Stone, December 3, 1917. ANSP 450.

60. Stone, Witmer. Letter to Theodore S. Palmer, November 25, 1933. SIA Collection 7150, Box 70, Folder 6.

61. Stone, Witmer. Letter to Alexander Wetmore, January 9, 1936. SIA Collection 7006, Box 66, Folder 18.

62. Wetmore, Alexander. "The number of contour feathers in Passeriform and related birds." *The Auk*, 1936. 53(2):159-69.

63. Dwight, Jonathan, Jr. Letter to Witmer Stone, December 17, 1912. ANSP Collection 686, Folder 2.

64. Dwight, Jonathan, Jr. Letter to Witmer Stone, January 16, 1921. ANSP Collection 686, Folder 3.

65. Palmer, Theodore S. Letter to Witmer Stone, March 12, 1922. ANSP Collection 680, Folder 3.

66. Richmond, Charles W. Letter to Witmer Stone, August 24, 1923. ANSP Collection 675, Folder 7; Howell, A. Brazier. Letter

to Witmer Stone, January 31, 1934. ANSP 450; Stone, Witmer. Letter to Ludlow Griscom, February 10, 1934. ANSP 450.

67. Strong, Reuben M. Letter to Witmer Stone, August 8, 1923. ANSP 450.

68. Stone, Witmer. Letter to Norman A. Wood, July 26, 1926. ANSP 450.

69. Stone, Witmer. Letter to Alexander Wetmore, August 18, 1935. SIA Collection 7006, Box 66, Folder 18.

70. Wetmore, Alexander. Letter to Witmer Stone, August 26, 1935. SIA Collection 7006, Box 66, Folder 18.

71. Dwight, Jonathan, Jr. Letter to Witmer Stone, March 17, 1920. ANSP Collection 686, Folder 3.

72. Dwight, Jonathan, Jr. Letter to Witmer Stone, October 10, 1920. ANSP Collection 686, Folder 3.

73. Dwight, Jonathan, Jr. Letter to Witmer Stone, November 21, 1920. ANSP Collection 686, Folder 3.

74. McAtee, Waldo Lee. Letter to Witmer Stone, November 20, 1920. ANSP Collection 968, Folder 2.

75. Stone, Witmer. Letter to Waldo Lee McAtee, December 3, 1920. ANSP Collection 968, Folder 2.

76. Dwight, Jonathan, Jr. Letters to Witmer Stone, December 15, 1920 & January 10, 1921. ANSP Collection 686, Folder 3.

77. Stone, Witmer. Letter to C. Hart Merriam, May 9, 1921. ANSP Collection 678, Folder 7.

78. Dwight, Jonathan, Jr. Letter to Witmer Stone, October 23, 1921. ANSP Collection 686, Folder 3.

79. Kalmbach, Edward R. "In memoriam: W.L. McAtee." *The Auk*, 1963. 80(4):474-85.

80. Stone, Witmer. Letter to Jonathan Dwight, Jr., December 13, 1921. ANSP Collection 686, Folder 3.

81. Stone, Witmer. Letter to Theodore S. Palmer, January 28, 1922. LOC, T.S. Palmer papers, Box 38.

82. Stone, Witmer. Letter to Frank M. Chapman, October 13, 1922. ANSP Collection 679, Folder 11; AOU Council Minutes for October 23 & 26, 1922. SIA Collection 7150, Box 3.

83. Stone, Witmer. Letter to Waldo Lee McAtee, September 29, 1922. LOC, W.L. McAtee papers, Box 37, Folder 3. See WLM's handwritten note appended to letter.

84. Forbush, Edward H. Letter to Witmer Stone, February 27, 1922. ANSP 450; Whittle, Charles L. Letter to Witmer Stone, March 15, 1922. ANSP 450.

85. Stone, Witmer. Letter (draft) to Edward H. Forbush, February 28, 1922. ANSP 450.

86. Stone, Witmer. Letter to Edward H. Forbush, March 1, 1922. ANSP 450.

87. Dwight, Jonathan, Jr. Letter to Witmer Stone, July 17, 1922. The letter is incorrectly dated 1921 by Dwight (the letter was written from England, and *Auk* 39:456 puts Dwight in England in summer 1922); Dwight, Jonathan, Jr. Letter to Witmer Stone, August 27, 1922. Both ANSP Collection 686, Folder 3.

88. Fleming, James H. Letter to Witmer Stone, October 30, 1922. ANSP 450.

89. Stone, Witmer. Letter to Jonathan Dwight, Jr., Theodore S. Palmer, and Waldo Lee McAtee, December 14, 1922. ANSP Collection 686, Folder 3.

90. Lincoln, Frederick C. Letter to Witmer Stone, February 19, 1923. ANSP 450.

91. Osgood, Wilfred H. Letter to Witmer Stone, March 13, 1922. ANSP 450.

92. Stone, Witmer. Letter to Henry E. Childs, June 8, 1923. ANSP 450.

93. "Abstract of the proceedings of the DVOC 1922-24." *Cassinia*, 1922-24. 25:53-66; "Notes and news." *The Auk*, 1923. 40(4):716-24.

94. Stone, Witmer, "The Ornithology of Today and Tomorrow," in *The Fiftieth Anniversary of the Nuttall Ornithological Club*. 1924, Cambridge. 7-25.

95. Stone, Witmer. Letter to Charles L. Whittle, March 13, 1922. ANSP 450.

96. Fleming, James H. Letter to Witmer Stone, December 20, 1923. ANSP 450.

97. "Dr. Stone on bird-banding." *Bulletin of the Northeastern Bird-Banding Association*, 1925. 1(1):1-2.

98. Stone, Witmer. Letter to Charles L. Whittle, July 26, 1926. ANSP 450.

99. Dwight, Jonathan, Jr. Form letters to AOU Membership, November 1, 1915 & October 15, 1916. ANSP Collection 498, Box 2, Folder 3; Cole, Leon J. Letter to Witmer Stone, December 10, 1932. ANSP 450; Brooks, Allan. Letter to Witmer Stone, January 10, 1933. ANSP 450.

100. Stone, Witmer. Letter to Henry F. Merriam, May 26, 1917. ANSP 450; Stone, Witmer.

Letter to Edmund Selous, December 9, 1917. ANSP 450.

101. Strong, Reuben M. Letter to Witmer Stone, March 11, 1914. ANSP 450; McAtee, Waldo Lee. Letter to Witmer Stone, September 12, 1916. ANSP Collection 968, Folder 2.

102. Shufeldt, Robert W. Letter to Witmer Stone, December 3, 1914. ANSP Collection 674, Folder 2.

103. Stone, Witmer. Letter to Albert K. Fisher, September 16, 1920. LOC, A.K. Fisher papers, Box 23. The last two pages of this 4-page letter are misplaced in Box 27, with a handwritten "[1924?]" at the top of page 3. The extinct, flightless Great Auk, for which the journal was named, had stubby but visible wings; kiwis have vestigial wings that are not even visible beneath the body plumage.

104. "Notes and news." The Auk, 1920. 37(1):182-88.

105. Stone, Witmer. Letter to Francis H. Herrick, May 4, 1924. ANSP 450.

106. Stone, Witmer. Untitled notes handwritten by Stone for AOU banquet talk. ANSP Collection 2009-031, Box 1. Undated but certainly 1936. Today, thanks to stellar fiscal leadership and financial planning, the AOU has easily the largest endowment of the OSNA organizations.

107. Stone, Witmer. Letter to Waldron DeWitt Miller, March 29, 1926. Department of Ornithology Archives, AMNH.

108. Stone, Witmer. Letter to Ernest G. Holt, December 7, 1925. ANSP 450.

109. Stone, Witmer. Letter to Frank M. Chapman, January 30, 1933. Department of Ornithology Archives, AMNH.

110. Stone, Witmer. "Obituaries: David Galbraith Baird." The Auk, 1935. 52(4):492.

111. Stone, Witmer. "In memoriam: Charles Wallace Richmond." The Auk, 1933. 50(1):1-22.

112. Stone, Witmer. Letter to James L. Peters, June 3, 1933. MCZ Archives.

113. Roberts, Thomas S. Letter to Witmer Stone, June 9, 1933. ANSP 450.

114. Grinnell, Joseph. Letter to Witmer Stone, June 17, 1933. ANSP Collection 684, Folder 5.

115. Murphy, Robert Cushman. Letter to Witmer Stone, May 16, 1933. ANSP 450; Chapman, Frank M. Letter to Witmer Stone, December 5, 1933. ANSP Collec-

tion 679, Folder 12; Foster, Frank B. Letter to Witmer Stone, May 16, 1933. ANSP 450.

116. Stone, Witmer. Letter to Stuart T. Danforth, February 19, 1934. ANSP 450.

117. Nelson, Edward W. Letter to Witmer Stone, October 5, 1912. ANSP 450; Dwight, Jonathan, Jr. Letter to Witmer Stone, August 10, 1912. ANSP Collection 686, Folder 2; ANSP Collection 498, Box 1, Folder 10 contains price estimates to print The Auk from Cosmos, Waverly, and New Era.

118. Stone, Witmer. Letter to Theodore S. Palmer, October 4, 1919. LOC, T.S. Palmer papers, Box 36.

119. Dwight, Jonathan, Jr. Letter to Witmer Stone, January 29, 1919. ANSP Collection 686, Folder 3; Stone, Witmer. Letter to Frank M. Chapman, November 19, 1919. Department of Ornithology Archives, AMNH; Grinnell, George Bird. Letter to Witmer Stone, March 9, 1920. ANSP 450; Stone, Witmer. Letter to Theodore S. Palmer, January 27, 1920. LOC, T.S. Palmer papers, Box 37.

120. "The printers' strike and the publication of 'Science.'" Science. 53(1376):455.

121. Stone, Witmer. Letter to H. Kirke Swann, October 12, 1921. ANSP 450; Stone, Witmer. Letter to Samuel Scoville, December 15, 1921. ANSP 450.

122. Stone, Witmer. Letter to A.E. Urban, April 7, 1922. ANSP Collection 498, Box 2, Folder 6.

123. Stone, Witmer. Letter to A.E. Urban, June 7, 1922. ANSP Collection 498, Box 2, Folder 6.

124. Stone, Witmer. Letter to A.E. Urban, July 19, 1922. ANSP Collection 498, Box 2, Folder 6.

125. Stone, Witmer. Letter to A.E. Urban, November 6, 1922. ANSP Collection 498, Box 2, Folder 6.

126. Stone, Witmer. Letter to Alexander Wetmore, undated but late July (received by Wetmore 8/1), 1927. SIA Collection 7006, Box 65, Folder 7.

127. Strong, J.R. Letter to Witmer Stone, February 17, 1925. ANSP 450; Stone, Witmer. Letter to Theodore S. Palmer, June 5, 1933. SIA Collection 7150, Box 70, Folder 5.

128. "Notes and news." The Auk, 1924. 41(1):201-12. I have read thousands of items of Stone's correspondence, and have often breathed the same sigh of relief he

must have when coming upon letters that are typewritten instead of composed in the awful, semi-legible, fountain pen scrawl so common then.

129. Peters, James L. Letter to Witmer Stone, February 6, 1924. ANSP 450. Recent *Auk* editor Kimberly G. Smith told me there was a similar reaction when the *Auk* submission process went electronic in the early 2000s, with some authors complaining that they didn't use the Internet, etc. So for a time, his staff entered hard copy submissions into the system for authors reluctant to take the digital plunge (KGS pers. comm. to author 1/24/2013).

130. Palmer, Theodore S. Letter to Witmer Stone, February 3, 1921. ANSP Collection 680, Folder 2; Stone, Witmer. Letter to Harry C. Oberholser, January 29, 1921. LOC, Harry C. Oberholser papers, Box 18.

131. "Notes and news." *The Auk*, 1926. 43(2):278-80; Dwight, Jonathan, Jr. Letter to Witmer Stone, February 17, 1926. ANSP Collection 686, Folder 3.

132. Stone, Witmer. Letter to Harry C. Oberholser, March 1, 1926. LOC, Harry C. Oberholser papers, Box 18; AOU Council minutes for October 11, 1926. SIA Collection 7150, Box 3.

133. Stone, Witmer. Letter to Theodore S. Palmer, February 23, 1930. LOC, T.S. Palmer papers, Box 47.

134. Stone, Witmer. Letter to members of AOU Council, January 22, 1932. In James L. Peters correspondence at MCZ Archives.

135. Stone, Witmer. Letter to Alexander Wetmore, January 22, 1932. SIA Collection 7006, Box 65, Folder 8.

136. Peters, James L. Letter to Witmer Stone, January 25, 1932. ANSP 450; Barrow, Mark V., Jr., *A Passion for Birds*. 1998. 202.

137. "Notes and news." *The Auk*, 1932. 49(2):274-78; Stone, Witmer. Letter to James L. Peters, March 17, 1933. MCZ Archives.

138. "Notes and news." *The Auk*, 1935. 52(2):225-26.

139. Stone, Witmer. "Recent Literature: Bird News and Notes." *The Auk*, 1935. 52(3):349.

140. Stone, Witmer. Letter to Waldo Lee McAtee, January 20, 1936. ANSP Collection 498, Box 2, Folder 3.

141. Stone, Witmer. Letter to Barton W. Evermann, March 31, 1921; Stone, Witmer.

Letter to William B. Mershon, June 5, 1920; Stone, Witmer. Letter to Norman A. Wood, February 23, 1921. All ANSP 450.

142. Stone, Witmer. Letter to Alexander Wetmore, January 12, 1920. SIA Collection 7006, Box 65, Folder 6; Wetmore, Alexander. "Observations on the habits of birds at Lake Burford, New Mexico." *The Auk*, 1920. 37(2&3):221-247; 393-412.

143. "Notes and news." *The Auk*, 1921. 38(3):490-500.

144. Stone, Witmer. Letter to Frederick C. Lincoln, February 1, 1921. ANSP 450; Stone, Witmer. Letter to Wilfred H. Osgood, July 12, 1921. ANSP 450.

145. Stone, Witmer. Letter to Laurence Fletcher, March 6, 1922. ANSP 450.

146. Christy, Bayard H. "Topsell's 'Foules of Heauen.'" *The Auk*, 1933. 50(3):275-83; Christy, Bayard H. Letter to Witmer Stone, August 11, 1932. ANSP 450.

147. Stone, Witmer. Letter to Clarence Cottam, September 2, 1932. ANSP 450; Stone, Witmer. Letter to W.H. Bergtold, April 28, 1935. ANSP 450.

148. Stone, Witmer. Letter to Alexander Wetmore, January 10, 1926. SIA Collection 7006, Box 65, Folder 6.

149. Phillips, John C. Letter to Witmer Stone, January 14, 1926. ANSP 450.

150. Allen, Glover M. "In memoriam: John Charles Phillips, M.D." *The Auk*, 1939. 56(3):221-26; Friedmann, Herbert. "In memoriam: Robert Thomas Moore." *The Auk*, 1964. 81(3):326-31; Phillips, John C. Letter to Witmer Stone, November 29, 1933. ANSP 450; Phillips, John C. "John Eliot Thayer. 1862-1933." *The Auk*, 1934. 51(1):46-51; Moore, Robert T. Letter to Witmer Stone, April 21, 1934, & W. Stone, letter to R.T. Moore, April 1, 1935. ANSP 450; Moore, Robert T. "The Mt. Sangay labyrinth and its fauna." *The Auk*, 1934. 51(2):141-56; Moore, Robert T. "A new jay of the genus Cyanocorax from Sinaloa, Mexico." *The Auk*, 1935. 52(3):274-77; Stone, Witmer. Letter to James P. Chapin, February 29, 1932. Department of Ornithology Archives, AMNH; Rockefeller, J. Sterling and Charles B.G. Murphy. "The rediscovery of Pseudocalyptomena." *The Auk*, 1933. 50(1):23-29.

151. Pearson, T. Gilbert. Letter to Witmer Stone, June 23, 1921, & W. Stone, letter to T.G. Pearson, June 24, 1921. ANSP 450.

152. "Notes and news." *The Auk*, 1921. 38(4):621-22.

153. Stone, Witmer. Letter to Theodore S. Palmer, June 24, 1921. LOC, T.S. Palmer papers, Box 38. For Pearson and arms manufacturers, see Frank Graham Jr., *The Audubon Ark*, 1990, pp. 87–89.

154. McIlhenny, Edward A. Letter to Witmer Stone, March 30, 1899. ANSP 450.

155. Stone, Witmer. Letter to William Brewster, April 4, 1901. MCZ Archives.

156. McIlhenny, Edward A. Letter to Witmer Stone, October 22, 1899. ANSP 450.

157. Wiggins, D. A., D. W. Holt and S. M. Leasure. 2006. Short-eared Owl (*Asio flammeus*), The Birds of North America Online (A. Poole, Ed.). Ithaca: Cornell Lab of Ornithology. Retrieved from: http://bna. birds.cornell.edu.bnaproxy.birds.cornell. edu/bna/species/062.

158. McIlhenny, Edward A. Letter to Witmer Stone, August 8, 1912. ANSP 450.

159. McIlhenny, Edward A. Letter to Witmer Stone, August 30, 1912. ANSP 450.

160. McIlhenny, Edward A. Letter to Witmer Stone, September 7, 1912. ANSP 450.

161. McIlhenny, Edward A., *Bird City*. 1934. The Christopher Publishing House, Boston. 112.

162. McIlhenny, Edward A. Letter to Witmer Stone, October 12, 1912. ANSP 450.

163. Stone, Witmer. Letter to Frank M. Chapman, November 18, 1912. Department of Ornithology Archives, AMNH. The relatives referred to doubtless included the Clark family, related to McIlhenny via marriage. Clarence H. Clark Sr. (1833–1906) supplied funds to help ANSP purchase some of McIlhenny's Arctic specimens; he also donated land in West Philadelphia for the creation of Clark Park. Stone lived next to the park for several years. Cited July 10, 2014. Available from http://www.ansp.org/research/systematics-evolution/history/ornithology/clarence-howard-clark/ and http://www.navybook.com/2014/01/12/clarence-clark-park-west-philadelphia/

164. Chapman, Frank M. Letter to Witmer Stone, November 20, 1912. ANSP Collection 679, Folder 9.

165. McIlhenny, Edward A. Letters to Witmer Stone, October 3 & November 27, 1912. ANSP 450.

166. Bent, Arthur Cleveland, *Life Histories of North American Marsh Birds*. 1926. Government Printing Office, Washington, D.C. 180-81.

167. McIlhenny, Edward A. Letters to Witmer Stone, January 29 & May 25, 1932. ANSP 450.

168. McIlhenny, Edward A. Letter to Witmer Stone, February 9, 1932. ANSP 450.

169. McIlhenny, Edward A. Letters to Witmer Stone, May 1, 1934, October 13 & December 17, 1936. ANSP 450.

170. McIlhenny, Edward A. Letters to Witmer Stone, November 17, 1931, August 14, 1934, March 26 & April 5, 1935. ANSP 450.

171. McIlhenny, Edward A. (three articles): "Results of 1936 bird banding operations at Avery Island, Louisiana, with special references to sex ratios and hybrids." *Bird-Banding*, 1937. 3(3):117-21; "Sex ratio in wild birds." *The Auk*, 1940. 57(1):85-93; "A record of birds banded at Avery Island, Louisiana during the years 1937, 1938, and 1939." *Bird-Banding*, 1940. 11(3):105-09; Bellrose, Frank C., *Ducks, Geese, and Swans of North America*. 1976. Stackpole Books, Harrisburg; Brown, David. "Sex ratios, sexual selection and sexual dimorphism in waterfowl." *American Birds*, 1982. 36(3):258-60.

172. Grace, Roger M. "Edward A. McIlhenny: Businessman, Naturalist, Author...Fibber." *Metropolitan News-Enterprise*, Los Angeles, October 21, 2004. Cited September 13, 2014. Available from http://www.metnews.com/articles/2004/reminiscing102104.htm

173. Kennard, Frederic H. Letter to Witmer Stone, June 6, 1935. ANSP 450.

174. McIlhenny, Edward A. "Color of iris in the Boat-tailed Grackle (Cassidix mexicanus major)." *The Auk*, 1934. 51(3):383-84.

175. McIlhenny, Edward A. "A hybrid between Turkey Vulture and Black Vulture." *The Auk*, 1937. 54(3):384; Jackson, Jerome A., "Turkey Vulture," in *Handbook of North American Birds, Vol. 4*, Ralph S. Palmer, Editor. 1988, Yale University Press, New Haven and London. 27.

176. West, Richard L. and Gene K. Hess. 2002. Purple Gallinule (*Porphyrio martinica*), The Birds of North America Online (A. Poole, Ed.). Ithaca: Cornell Lab of Ornithology. Retrieved from: http://bna.birds.cornell.edu.bnaproxy.birds.cornell.edu/bna/species/626; Post, W., J. P. Poston and G. T. Bancroft. 1996. Boat-tailed Grackle (*Quiscalus*

major), The Birds of North America Online (A. Poole, Ed.). Ithaca: Cornell Lab of Ornithology. Retrieved from: http://bna. birds.cornell.edu.bnaproxy.birds.cornell. edu/bna/species/207.

177. McIlhenny, Edward A. "Purple Gallinules are predatory." *The Auk*, 1936. 53(3):327-28.

178. McIlhenny, Edward A., *Bird City*. 1934. The Christopher Publishing House, Boston. 67, 71.

179. McIlhenny, Edward A. "Life history of the Boat-tailed Grackle in Louisiana." *The Auk*, 1937. 54(3):274-95.

180. Barrow, Mark V., Jr., *A Passion for Birds*. 1998. 201. Much of what Barrow wrote here was based on Keir B. Sterling and Marianne G. Ainley's unpublished *A Centennial History of the American Ornithologists' Union*, and a 1995 interview with Ernst Mayr.

181. Evans, Evan. Letter to Witmer Stone, September 30, 1936. ANSP 450.

182. "Notes and news." *The Auk*, 1915. 32(2):268-72.

183. Stone, Witmer. Letter to William R. Maxon, November 26, 1924. ANSP 450.

184. "Notes and news." *The Auk*, 1935. 52(3):356-58. The Fuertes auk might do just that: it had the cover all to itself until 1998, and although it now occupies a much smaller space above a painting or photo unique to each issue, it's still serenely sitting there on its rocky ledge on each cover.

185. Lewis, Daniel, *The Feathery Tribe*. 2012. 79, 81; Johnson, Kristin. "*The Ibis*: transformations in a twentieth century British natural history journal." *Journal of the History of Biology*, 2004. 37:515-55.

186. Barrow, Mark V., Jr., *A Passion for Birds*. 1998. 200.

187. Stone, Witmer. Letter to Reuben M. Strong, January 29, 1923. ANSP 450; Stone, Witmer. Letter to Alfred O. Gross, May 9, 1923. ANSP 450.

188. Allen, Francis H. Letter to Witmer Stone, March 10, 1920. ANSP 450.

189. McAtee, Waldo Lee. Letter to Witmer Stone, March 6, 1920. ANSP Collection 968, Folder 2.

190. Grinnell, Joseph. Letter to Witmer Stone, March 6, 1922. ANSP Collection 684, Folder 4.

191. Stone, Witmer. Letter to Joseph Grinnell, March 13, 1922. ANSP Collection 684, Folder 3.

192. Stone, Witmer. Letter to Joseph Grinnell, June 1, 1930. MVZ Archives.

193. "Notes and news." *The Auk*, 1927. 44(1):156-68.

194. Roads, Myra Katie. "Blue jays gathering twigs for nests." *The Auk*, 1932. 49(2):223; Kalter, Louis B. "A comparatively tame eastern green heron." *The Auk*, 1932. 49(3):342.

195. Stone, Witmer. "Recent Literature: Matthews's 'The Birds of Australia.'" *The Auk*, 1927. 44(3):435-42; Stone, Witmer. "Recent Literature: Beebe's Monograph of the Pheasants." *The Auk*, 1919. 36(1):119-25.

196. Stone, Witmer. Letter to Charles MacNamara, October 9, 1922; Stone, Witmer. Letter to Edwin Ridley, January 3, 1925; Stone, Witmer. Letter to Mrs. Bruce Reid, December 6, 1921. All ANSP 450; Stone, Witmer. Letter to Alexander Wetmore, January 9, 1934. SIA Collection 7006, Box 66, Folder 1.

197. Stone, Witmer. Letter to Theodore S. Palmer, August 26, 1932. LOC, T.S. Palmer papers, Box 50.

198. Stone, Witmer. Letter to Charles M.B. Cadwalader, July 27, 1936. ANSP Collection 2009-034, Box 45, Folder 23; Kelso, Leon and Estelle H. Kelso. "A new screech owl from Colombia." *The Auk*, 1936. 53(4):448.

199. Friedmann, Herbert. Letter to Witmer Stone, March 26, 1935. ANSP 450.

200. Friedmann, Herbert. Letter to Witmer Stone, April 9, 1935. ANSP 450.

201. Bissonnette, Thomas H. and Alphonse J. Zujko. "Normal progressive changes in the ovary of the Starling (Sturnus vulgaris) from December to April." *The Auk*, 1936. 53(1):31-50.

202. Stone, Witmer. Letter to Waldo Lee McAtee, January 14, 1936. LOC, W.L. McAtee papers, Box 37, Folder 3.

203. Griscom, Ludlow. Letter to Witmer Stone, August 12, 1931. ANSP Collection 2009-031, Box 4, Folder 3.

204. Eifrig, C.W. Gustave. "Is photoperiodism a factor in the migration of birds?" *The Auk*, 1924. 41(3):439-44.

205. Strong, Reuben M. "Obituaries: Charles William Gustave Eifrig." *The Auk*, 1951. 68(3):407-08.

206. Palmer, Theodore S. "Fortieth stated meeting of the American Ornithologists' Union." *The Auk*, 1923. 40(1):106-15.

207. Eifrig, C.W. Gustave. Letter to Witmer Stone, August 17, 1922. Eifrig appears to have written the letter before the 1922 AOU meeting, then mailed it to Stone immediately thereafter; Eifrig, C.W. Gustave. Letter to Witmer Stone, February 4, 1924 (Eifrig's "1923" is incorrect); Stone, Witmer. Letter to C.W. Gustave Eifrig, December 13, 1922. All ANSP 450.

208. Stone, Witmer. Letter to C.W. Gustave Eifrig, February 9, 1924, & C.W. Eifrig, letter to W. Stone, February 14, 1924. ANSP 450; English, T.M. Savage. "On the greater length of the day in high latitudes as a reason for spring migration." *Ibis*, 1923. 65(3):418-23; Stone, Witmer. "The ornithological journals." *The Auk*, 1923. 40(4):708-15.

209. Rollo, Marie. "Photoperiodism and migration." *Bird-Banding*, 1941. 12(4):161-64.

210. Schafer, E.A. "On the incidence of daylight as a determining factor in bird-migration." *Nature*, 1907. 77(1990):159-63; Rowan, William. "On photoperiodism, reproductive periodicity, and the annual migrations of birds and certain fishes." *Proceedings of the Boston Society of Natural History*, 1926. 38(6):147-89.

211. Eifrig, C.W. Gustave. Letter to Witmer Stone, February 29, 1924. ANSP 450.

212. Newton, Ian, *The Migration Ecology of Birds*. 2008. 321-23.

213. Murray, James J. Letter to Witmer Stone, January 24, 1933. ANSP 450.

214. Jones, Fred M. Letter to Witmer Stone, October 8, 1932. ANSP 450.

215. Jones, Fred M. Letter to Witmer Stone, November 3, 1932. ANSP 450.

216. Wetmore, Alexander. Letter to Fred M. Jones, November 28, 1932. ANSP 450.

217. Jones, Fred M. Letter to Witmer Stone, December 10, 1932. ANSP 450.

218. Murray, James J. "Breeding of Swainson's Warbler in Robeson County, North Carolina." *The Auk*, 1935. 52(4):459.

219. Jones, Fred M. Letter to Witmer Stone, June 16, 1936. ANSP 450.

220. Wetmore, Alexander. "Notes on the birds of Tennessee." *Proceedings of the United States National Museum*, 1939. 86(3050):175-243.

221. Murray, James J. "Swainson's Warbler in southwest Virginia." *The Raven*, 1939.

10(10&11):9; Anich, Nicholas M., Thomas J. Benson, Jeremy D. Brown, et al. 2010. Swainson's Warbler (*Limnothlypis swainsonii*), The Birds of North America Online (A. Poole, Ed.). Ithaca: Cornell Lab of Ornithology. Retrieved from: http://bna.birds.cornell.edu.bnaproxy.birds.cornell.edu/bna/species/126

222. Jones, Fred M. "Nesting of the Broad-winged Hawk in southwest Virginia." *The Raven*, 1932. 3(7):1-3; Jones, Fred M. "Nesting of the Cooper Hawk." *The Raven*, 1932. 3(6):5-6.

223. Stone, Witmer. Letter to J. Hooper Bowles, May 25, 1917. ANSP 450; Stone, Witmer. Letter to Albert K. Fisher, June 19, 1917. LOC, A.K. Fisher papers, Box 22.

224. Stone, Witmer. Letter to Albert K. Fisher, September 16, 1920. LOC, A.K. Fisher papers, Box 23. The last two pages of this 4-page letter are misplaced in Box 27, with a handwritten "[1924?]" at the top of page 3.

225. Stone, Witmer. Letter to S. Prentiss Baldwin, April 8, 1922. ANSP 450.

226. Stone, Witmer. Letter to Marion A. Boggs, November 5, 1925. ANSP 450.

227. Stone, Witmer. Letter to Alexander Wetmore, January 18, 1936. SIA Collection 7006, Box 80, Folder 7.

228. Dwight, Jonathan, Jr. Letter to Witmer Stone, October 16, 1919. ANSP Collection 686, Folder 3; Clark, Edith Elliott. Letter to A.E. Urban, July 5, 1922. ANSP Collection 498, Box 2, Folder 6. It was a red-letter day when I came across Mrs. Clark's name, since I'd often wondered about the identity of "EEC" in the "WS/EEC" reference initials at the bottom of Stone's professional correspondence in the ANSP archives. Her position seems to have been eliminated when Stone gave up his *Auk* business manager position; Stone, Witmer. Letter to Waldo Lee McAtee, November 18, 1920, and McAtee letter to Stone, December 9, 1920. ANSP Collection 968, Folder 2.

229. Stone, Witmer. Letter to Robert Ridgway, October 13, 1922. Blacker-Wood Collection, Department of Rare Books, McGill University.

230. Fleming, James H. Letters to Witmer Stone, October 3, 1931 & January 18, 1932. ANSP 450.

231. Fleming, James H. Letter to Wharton Huber, April 4, 1934. ANSP Collection 186, Box 1, Folder 8.

232. Kennard, Frederic H. Letter to Witmer Stone, February 16, 1935. ANSP 450.

233. Barrow, Mark V., Jr., *A Passion for Birds*. 1998. 267 (footnote 148).

234. Friedmann, Herbert. Letter to Joseph Grinnell, May 15, 1935. MVZ Archives.

235. Friedmann, Herbert. Letter to Witmer Stone, March 31, 1921, & W. Stone, letter to H. Friedmann, April 2, 1921. ANSP 450.

236. Stone, Witmer. Letter to Frank M. Chapman, December 9, 1935. Department of Ornithology Archives, AMNH.

237. Chapman, Frank M. Letter to Witmer Stone, December 18, 1935. ANSP Collection 679, Folder 12.

238. Stone, Witmer. Letter to Theodore S. Palmer, November 11, 1935. SIA Collection 7150, Box 70, Folder 10.

239. Hicks, Lawrence E. "The fifty-fifth stated meeting of the American Ornithologists' Union." *The Auk*, 1938. 55(2):317-24.

240. Allen, Glover M. Letter to Witmer Stone, October 28, 1936. ANSP Collection 450, Box 1, Folder 3.

241. Butler, Amos W. Letter to Witmer Stone, October 17, 1936. ANSP 450.

242. Witherby, Henry. Letter to Witmer Stone, January 24, 1937. ANSP 450.

243. Stouffer, Philip C. "Editorial: Your new resource for exciting research in applied ornithology." *The Condor: Ornithological Applications*, 2014. 116(1):1-2.

244. Stone, Witmer. Letter to Waldo Lee McAtee, April 9, 1934. LOC, W.L. McAtee papers, Box 37, Folder 3.

245. Smith, Kimberly G. Pers. comm. to author, January 24, 2013.

246. "Dr. Stone Honored on 70th Birthday." *Evening Public Ledger*, Philadelphia, September 23, 1936.

247. Palmer, Theodore S. "The fifty-fourth stated meeting of the American Ornithologists' Union." *The Auk*, 1937. 54(1):117-26.

248. Stone, Witmer. Untitled notes for AOU banquet talk. ANSP Collection 2009-031, Box 1. Handwritten notes by Stone. Undated, but certainly 1936.

249. There has been serious talk recently about dissolving the six major North American ornithological societies (and their journals) and forming a new, single society to take their places. At the Fifth North American Ornithological Conference in August 2012, the various societies voted on the proposed plan, and the upshot was that the AOU and the Cooper Ornithological Society (COS) were interested in moving forward on the plan, the other societies less so. COS and AOU, while not formally merging, soon announced the creation of a single publishing office for their two journals, the names of which were changed (slightly) in 2014 to *The Auk: Ornithological Advances* and *The Condor: Ornithological Applications*.

Box: Lime-lights, Square Roots, and Premeditated Assaults

1. Bergtold, W.H. Letter to Witmer Stone, February 14, 1912. ANSP 450.

2. Bergtold, W.H. Letter to Witmer Stone, August 20, 1912. ANSP 450.

3. Bergtold, W.H. Letter to Witmer Stone, Undated, but clearly in 1913. ANSP 450.

4. Bergtold, W.H. Letters to Witmer Stone, November 14, 1913 & August 27, 1917. ANSP 450.

5. Fisher, Albert K. "In memoriam: William Harry Bergtold." *The Auk*, 1937. 54(1):1-11.

6. Palmer, Theodore S. "The forty-sixth stated meeting of the American Ornithologists' Union." *The Auk*, 1929. 46(1):79-91.

7. Wayne, Arthur T. Letter to Witmer Stone, February 5, 1921. ANSP 450.

8. Jacobs, J. Warren. Letter to Witmer Stone, March 11, 1916. ANSP 450.

9. Mousley, Henry. Letter to Witmer Stone, February 6, 1915. ANSP 450.

10. Storer, Tracy I. Letter to Witmer Stone, July 19, 1919. ANSP 450.

11. Bishop, Louis B. Letter to Witmer Stone, October 20, 1921. ANSP 450.

12. Rehn, James A. G. Letter to Witmer Stone, May 26, 1919. ANSP Collection 682, Folder 1; Stone, Witmer. Letter to S. Prentiss Baldwin, March 24, 1922. ANSP 450.

13. Jacobs, J. Warren. Letter to Witmer Stone, January 31, 1919. ANSP 450.

14. Simmons, George Finlay. Letter to Witmer Stone, October 24, 1917. ANSP 450.

15. Stone, Witmer. Letter to George Finlay Simmons, December 9, 1917. ANSP 450.

16. Stone, Witmer. "Recent Literature: Hicks, Lawrence E." *The Auk*, 1935. 52(3):341.

17. Cory, Charles B. Letter to Witmer Stone, November 25, 1919. ANSP 450.

18. Young, Robert T. Letter to Witmer Stone, April 8, 1908. ANSP 450.

19. Stone, Witmer. "Recent Literature: Burns on periods of incubation." *The Auk*, 1915. 32(4):516.

20. Burns, Frank L. Letter to Witmer Stone, December 1, 1915. ANSP 450.

21. Stone, Witmer. "Recent Literature: Spring migration notes of the Chicago area." *The Auk*, 1920. 37(4):616-17; "Doesn't Know Leopold." *Evening Bulletin*, Philadelphia, August 13, 1924.

22. Leopold, Nathan F., Jr. Letter to Witmer Stone, July 4, 1923. ANSP 450; Palmer, T.S. "The forty-first stated meeting of the American Ornithologists' Union." *The Auk*, 1924. 41(1):122-134.

23. Mark 14:72.

24. Leopold, Nathan F., Sr. Letter to Witmer Stone, undated. ANSP 450.

25. AOU Council minutes for November 10, 1924. SIA Collection 7150, Box 3.

26. Elliott Coues to Joel Asaph Allen January 1, 1884. Quoted in Lewis, *The Feathery Tribe*, 92.

27. Leopold, Nathan F., Jr. 1963. *Checklist of birds of Puerto Rico and the Virgin Islands.* University of Puerto Rico, Agricultural Experiment Station, Rio Pedra. Bulletin 168.

28. Stone, Witmer. Letter to Frederic H. Kennard, March 16, 1925. ANSP 450.

29. Palmer, Theodore S. Letter to Witmer Stone, March 12, 1925. ANSP Collection 680, Folder 1.

30. *The Auk* 42(2):xxiii. Curiously, the AOU's confusion about Brandreth's state of existence continued for some time. He died in 1928, but was on the rolls through 1930. The AOU didn't get around to publishing his death notice, written by Fisher, until 1934 (*Auk* 51(3):432f), and there his year of death was incorrectly reported as 1926. It's given as 1928, however, on his gravestone. Cited July 15, 2014. Available from http://www.findagrave.com/cgi-bin/fg.cgi?page=gr&GRid=92884458

31. Stone, Witmer. Letters to Theodore S. Palmer, August 13, 1930 & September 4, 1931. LOC, T.S. Palmer papers, Boxes 47 & 48; Palmer, Theodore S. Letters to Witmer Stone, September 3 & 8, 1931. ANSP Collection 680, Folder 1.

32. Peters, James L. Letter to Witmer Stone, June 8, 1931. ANSP 450. In Stone's last year as *Auk* editor, Gladys Relyea published "An attempt to measure statistically the difference between eastern and western

subspecies of the same species," which used formulae with square roots to quantify differences (*Auk* 53(1):22-27).

33. Hall, Frank Stevens. Letter to Witmer Stone, July 5, 1934. ANSP 450. Today the organization is called the Society for Northwestern Vertebrate Biology.

34. Stone, Witmer. Letter to Frank M. Chapman, September 21, 1921. ANSP Collection 679, Folder 11.

35. Chapman, Frank M. Letter to Witmer Stone, September 23, 1921. ANSP Collection 679, Folder 11.

36. Evenhuis, Neal L. "Anthony Curtiss (1910–1981): a riddle wrapped in a mystery inside an enigma." *Fly Times*, April, 2010(44):13-16.

37. Curtiss, Roy, *An account of the natural history of New England and of Nova Scotia and lower Canada of the islands of the coasts between the Gulf of St. Lawrence and the Bay of New York; of the mountains wherein the Hudson rises; and all eastward as far as the Bay of Massachusetts; in so far as it applies to beasts, birds, reptiles, whales, fresh and salt water fish and shellfish, worms, insects and pests.* 1924. Privately published; Stone, Witmer. Letter to Roy Curtiss, April 19, 1924. ANSP 450.

Chapter 12: Writing for Fun and Profit

1. Stone, Witmer. Letter to Frank M. Chapman, November 1, 1898. Department of Ornithology Archives, AMNH.

2. Pearson, T. Gilbert. Letter to Witmer Stone, October 3, 1913. ANSP 450.

3. Stone, Witmer. Letter to Frank M. Chapman, December 15, 1911. Department of Ornithology Archives, AMNH.

4. Chapman, Frank M. Letter to Witmer Stone, December 16, 1911. Department of Ornithology Archives, AMNH.

5. Rogers, Charles H. Letters to Witmer Stone, February 2 & 9, 1917. ANSP 450.

6. Keller, Augustus R. Letter to Witmer Stone, December 11, 1902. ANSP 450.

7. Keller, Augustus R. Letter to Witmer Stone, September 18, 1903. ANSP 450.

8. Stone, Witmer and William Draper Lewis, "Roosevelt the Naturalist," in *The Life of Theodore Roosevelt*. 1919. 384-400.

9. "Notes and news." *The Auk*, 1919. 36(1):152-62.

10. Dall, William Healey, *Spencer Fullerton Baird: A Biography.* 1915. J.B. Lippincott & Co, Philadelphia; Anonymous, unaddressed note dated June 28, 1940 regarding Stone's reported involvement in a planned Spencer F. Baird biography. ANSP Collection 2010-051, Box 7, Folder 13.

11. Stone, Witmer. "Recent Literature: Dall's biography of Baird." *The Auk*, 1915. 32(4):505-07.

12. Stone, Witmer. "An anonymous work of John Cassin." *The Auk*, 1921. 38(2):286-87; Baird, Lucy H. Letters to Witmer Stone, October 23, November 3 & 24, 1899. ANSP 450.

13. Sage, John H. "Seventeenth Congress of the American Ornithologists' Union." *The Auk*, 1900. 17(1):58-63; Stone, Witmer. "Cassin on Baird's first paper." *The Osprey*, 1900. 4(11&12):173.

14. Stone, Witmer. Letter to Theodore S. Palmer, July 17, 1915. LOC, T.S. Palmer papers, Box 11.

15. Watson, C.A. Letters to Witmer Stone, August 11 & 14, 1903. ANSP 450. There is also much correspondence about the encyclopedia from George E. Rines in ANSP 450.

16. Carter, A.P. Letters to Witmer Stone, July 15, 23 & 26, 1918. ANSP 450; Untitled document showing ANSP salaries 1888-1936. ANSP Collection 186, Folder 2.

17. Stone, Witmer, "Notes From a Locality Slightly North of Philadelphia, Pa., on the Birds Included in 'Bird-Lore,'" in *Bird-Life: A Guide to the Study of Our Common Birds*, *Teachers' Edition*, Frank M. Chapman, Editor. 1899, D. Appleton & Co., New York. 40-46 (in Appendix); Stone, Witmer. "The migration of birds." *New York Teachers' Monographs*, 1902. 4(1):69-73.

18. Johnson, Allen. Multiple letters to Witmer Stone. ANSP Collection 2009-031, Box 1, Folder 4.

19. Johnson, Allen. Letter to Witmer Stone, March 20, 1929. ANSP Collection 2009-031, Box 1, Folder 4.

20. *Leading American Men of Science*, ed. David Starr Jordan. 1910. Henry Holt and Company, New York.

21. Holt, Henry. Letter to Witmer Stone, April 6, 1909. ANSP 450.

22. Shoffner, Charles P. Letter to Witmer Stone, December 4, 1928. ANSP 450.

23. Shoffner, Charles P. Letter to Witmer Stone, December 1, 1928. ANSP 450.

24. Shriner, Charles A. Letters to Witmer Stone, Various dates, 1896. ANSP 450.

25. Stone, Witmer. Letter to Alexander Wetmore, August 19, 1932. SIA Collection 7006, Box 65, Folder 8.

26. Grosvenor, Gilbert H. Letter to Witmer Stone, January 17, 1933. ANSP 450.

27. Stone, Witmer. "Wilson – Father of American Ornithology." *Nature Magazine*, 1926(July):29-30.

28. *BSOCM*. 637.

29. Stone, Witmer. "I remember: the story of the boyhood adventures of a distinguished naturalist." *Frontiers*, 1936. 1(1):13-15; Stone, Witmer. "On looking back fifty years." *Frontiers*, 1938. 2(4):130-32; Stone, Witmer. Letter to Charles M.B. Cadwalader, August 1, 1937. ANSP Collection 2009-034, Box 47, Folder 69.

30. Untitled, undated notes in Stone's hand on berry picking at Cape May. ANSP Collection 2009-031, Box 1, Folder 3. The "fox grape" Stone refers to is *Vitis labrusca* (*PSNJ*, p. 546-47).

31. Stone, Witmer. Letter to Alexander Wetmore, January 18, 1936. SIA Collection 7006, Box 80, Folder 7.

32. Stone, Witmer. Letter to Alexander Wetmore, December 18, 1937. SIA Collection 7006, Box 66, Folder 1.

Chapter 13: It Is Some Book!

1. Morse, Silas R. Letter to Witmer Stone, February 7, 1910. ANSP 450.

2. Harlow, Richard C. Letter to Witmer Stone, July 11, 1917. ANSP Collection 752, Folder 4.

3. Harlow, Richard C. "Notes on the breeding birds of Pennsylvania and New Jersey." *The Auk*, 1918. 35(1):18-29.

4. Sage, John H. "Twenty-first Congress of the American Ornithologists' Union." *The Auk*, 1904. 21(1):74-78.

5. Stone, Witmer. "Obituaries: Henry Walker Hand." *The Auk*, 1932. 49(4):521.

6. Davenport, Elizabeth B.S. Letter to Witmer Stone, March 20, 1934. ANSP 450. Unfortunately, Mrs. Davenport died a few months after sending Stone the letter, so didn't live to enjoy the book.

7. Stone, Witmer. Letter to Frank M. Chapman, October 16, 1931. LOC, T.S. Palmer papers, Box 50.

8. Weygandt, Cornelius. Letter to Witmer Stone, April 1, 1936. ANSP Collection 76;

Grinnell, Joseph. Letter to Witmer Stone, October 26, 1931. ANSP Collection 684, Folder 5; Stone, Witmer. Letter to James L. Peters, April 21, 1933. MCZ Archives.

9. Stone, Witmer. Letter to Julian K. Potter, July 6, 1930. ANSP Collection 2010-113, Box 4.

10. Stone, Witmer. Letter to T.S. Palmer, August 3, 1933. SIA Collection 7150, Box 70, Folder 6.

11. *A Century After*, ed. Edward Strahan. 1875. Allen, Lane, Scott and J.W. Lauderbach, Philadelphia. 73; *BSOCM*. 3.

12. *BSOCM*. 208 & 534.

13. DVOC minutes for March 17, 1932. ANSP Collection 74A, Box 2, Folder 2.

14. Stone, Witmer. Letter to Edward von Siebold Dingle, September 6, 1922. ANSP 450.

15. Stone, Witmer. "The summer birds of Cape May, N.J." 1891. ANSP Collection 2009-031, Box 1, Folder 2.

16. Stone, Witmer. Letter to Edward J. Nolan, August 23, 1890. ANSP Collection 567, Box 35, Folder 3.

17. Stevens, Lewis T., *The History of Cape May County, New Jersey*. 1897. 393-94.

18. "Abstract of the proceedings of the DVOC 1890-91." *Cassinia*, 1890-91. 1:2-11.

19. Street, Phillips B. "A history of the Delaware Valley Ornithological Club." *Cassinia*, 1988-89. 63:2-35.

20. Brewster, William. "Bird Migration." *Memoirs of the Nuttall Ornithological Club, No. 1*, 1886.

21. DVOC minutes for November 3, 1891. ANSP Collection 74A, Box 1, Folder 2.

22. Stone, Witmer. "Winter birds of Cape May, New Jersey." *The Auk*, 1892. 9(2):203-04.

23. Stone refers, if somewhat obliquely, to his 25-year absence in the Black Skimmer account in *BSOCM* (p. 599).

24. *BSOCM*. 673.

25. Hand, H. Walker, Jr. Letters to Witmer Stone, September 1 & October 12, 1903. ANSP 450.

26. Stone, Witmer. "Report of the spring migration of 1910." *Cassinia*, 1910. 14:37-48.

27. Stone, Witmer. Letter to Albert K. Fisher, September 22, 1917. LOC, A.K. Fisher papers, Box 22. A letter from Walker Hand to Stone on 2/16/1917 (ANSP 450) indicates that Stone may have been giving talks on the Cape May migration at that early date.

28. *BSOCM*. x.

29. Hand, H. Walker, Jr. Letter to Witmer Stone, July 7, 1914. ANSP 450; Sage, John H. Letter to Witmer Stone, July 28, 1913. ANSP Collection 541, Folder 3; Brown, Otway. Letter to Witmer Stone, September 16, 1910. ANSP 450; Stone, Witmer. Letter to Frank M. Chapman, July 24, 1912. Department of Ornithology Archives, AMNH.

30. Hand, H. Walker, Jr. Letter to Witmer Stone, January 17, 1916. ANSP 450.

31. Stone, Witmer. Letter to Albert K. Fisher, September 27, 1916. LOC, A.K. Fisher papers, Box 21.

32. Stone, Witmer. Letter to Julian K. Potter, July 31, 1920. ANSP Collection 2010-113, Box 4. Stone told T.S. Palmer in April 1920, "We have been fortunate in getting our old cottage in Cape May," indicating that they stayed at 211 Perry in at least one of the previous years (Stone to Palmer; LOC, T.S. Palmer papers, Box 37); Urban, A.E. Letter to Witmer Stone, August 27, 1921. ANSP Collection 498, Box 2, Folder 6; Stone, Witmer. Letter to Julian K. Potter, June 27, 1922. ANSP Collection 2010-113, Box 4.

33. Stone, Witmer. Letter to Alexander Wetmore, August 11, 1925. SIA Collection 7006, Box 65, Folder 6.

34. *BSOCM*. xiii. Goff is one of the oldest names in Cape May County (Stevens, *The History of Cape May County, New Jersey*, 1897, p. 39).

35. Sayre, Jack. Interview with author, August 11, 2011; U.S. Census Bureau, Fifteenth Census of the United States, 1930. Washington, D.C. National Archives and Records Administration, 1930. Cape May, N.J., Roll 1325, Page 3B, Enumeration District 3, Image 431.0.

36. *BSOCM*. 769; Stone, Witmer. Letter to Charles M.B. Cadwalader, August 2, 1937. ANSP Collection 2009-034, Box 47, Folder 69.

37. *BSOCM*. 763.

38. *BSOCM*. 866 & 869.

39. Cape May resident Jack Sayre, who caddied at the golf club as a youth, has pointed out the old clubhouse to me; it was moved and stands as a residence at 1033 Lafayette.

40. *BSOCM*. 853.

41. Stone, Witmer. Letters to Charles M.B. Cadwalader, July 1, 1931 & June 20, 1933. ANSP Collection 2009-034, Box 24, Folder 15; *BSOCM*. 909, 338, 307, 689, & 728.

42. *BSOCM.* 679.

43. Stone, Witmer. Letter to Frank M. Chapman, September 18, 1932. Department of Ornithology Archives, AMNH.

44. Stone, Witmer. Letter to Theodore S. Palmer, September 7, 1924. LOC, T.S. Palmer papers, Box 39.

45. Stone, Witmer. Letter to Julian K. Potter, August 11, 1937. ANSP Collection 2010-113, Box 4.

46. Stone, Witmer. Letter to Julian K. Potter, June 13, 1937. ANSP Collection 2010-113, Box 4. The Windsor Hotel burned down in 1979; I don't know what "the Homestead" refers to.

47. U.S. Census Bureau, Fifteenth Census of the United States, 1930. Washington, D.C. National Archives and Records Administration, 1930. Philadelphia, Pa., Roll 2105, Page 14A, Enumeration District 653, Image 983.0.

48. Stone, Witmer. Letter to Julian K. Potter, August 20, 1937. ANSP Collection 2010-113, Box 4; Stone, Witmer. Letter to Theodore S. Palmer, September 11, 1928. LOC, T.S. Palmer papers, Box 45.

49. Roland, Conrad. Letter to Witmer Stone, July 14, 1936. ANSP 450.

50. Stone, Witmer. Letter to Theodore S. Palmer, September 8, 1927. LOC, T.S. Palmer papers, Box 43.

51. Stone, Witmer. Letter to Waldo Lee McAtee, July 5, 1927. LOC, W.L. McAtee papers, Box 10, Folder 4; Stone, Witmer. Letter to Charles W. Richmond, June 28, 1930. SIA Collection RU 105, Box 27; Stone, Witmer. Letter to Albert K. Fisher, October 8, 1925. LOC, A.K. Fisher papers, Box 28. Julia O'Neil, who grew up in Cape May and lived next to 909 Queen since the early 1950s, remembered that Mrs. Goff had the shelves in the basement lined with jars of beach plum jelly (interview with author 4/9/2011).

52. *BSOCM.* 573; "Additions to the museum: birds." *Year Book of the Academy of Natural Sciences of Philadelphia,* 1928:51-53; Ornithology collection search. Cited April 30, 2014. Available from http://clade.ansp.org/ornithology/index.php?page=results&sex=unspecified&ans_number=&genus=Sterna&species=hirundo&country=USA&state_province=&county=

53. Lincoln, Frederick C. Letter to Witmer Stone, August 31, 1928. ANSP 450. Stone also mentioned skinning a field mouse (*Microtus*) brought in by a cat at Cape May during his 1931 vacation – "just to see if I still had the knack" (Stone to T.S. Palmer, 6/22/1931; LOC, T.S. Palmer papers, Box 48).

54. Stone, Witmer. Letter to Alexander Wetmore, July 28, 1930. SIA Collection 7006, Box 65, Folder 8; Stone, Witmer. Letter to Theodore S. Palmer, July 23, 1934. SIA Collection 7150, Box 70, Folder 9.

55. Richmond, Charles W. Letter to Witmer Stone, September 25, 1924. ANSP Collection 675, Folder 7.

56. *The Auklet* is a humorous booklet produced (on an irregular and increasingly infrequent basis) for the AOU annual meeting. It mimics *The Auk* and pokes fun at AOU members. In Stone's day there was talk of discontinuing it, particularly after some of the people who were objects of the lampooning took offense (Stone to W.L. McAtee 2/20/1931 & 1/2/1933; W.L. McAtee papers, LOC).

57. Stone, Witmer. Letter to Theodore S. Palmer, July 9, 1934. SIA Collection 7150, Box 70, Folder 9.

58. Stone, Witmer. Letter to Theodore S. Palmer, September 13, 1926. LOC, T.S. Palmer papers, Box 42.

59. Stone, Witmer. Letter to Alexander Wetmore, August 18, 1930. SIA Collection 7006, Box 65, Folder 8.

60. Shryock, William. Letter to Witmer Stone, July 27, 1933. ANSP 450.

61. Stevens, Lewis T., *The History of Cape May County, New Jersey.* 1897. 349-50.

62. *BSOCM.* 125.

63. Stone, Witmer. "H.W. Hand Dies in Camden." *Cape May Star & Wave,* September 15, 1932.

64. "Shore Man Drops Dead on Way to See Physician." *Cape May County Gazette,* September 16, 1932.

65. Stone, Witmer. "Henry Walker Hand: 1870-1932." *Cassinia,* 1931-32. 29:18.

66. "Hand-Hughes Wedding." *Cape May Wave,* April 21, 1906.

67. Howe, Paul S., *Mayflower Pilgrim Descendants in Cape May County, New Jersey.* 1921. Albert R. Hand, Cape May. 251. Laura Hedrick, granddaughter of Walker and Laura Hand, told me (5/10/2013) that Caroline Hughes may have died from complications of an early-term miscarriage;

"Town of Mohawk Native Succumbs." *Evening Recorder*, Amsterdam, N.Y., May 18, 1960.

68. "Abstract of the proceedings of the DVOC 1900." *Cassinia*, 1900. 4:1-6.

69. Scoville, Samuel, Jr., *Wild Honey*. 1929. 59-75.

70. The same or a similar incident was recorded in Charles Tomlin's book of Cape May history (*Cape May Spray*, 1913; Bradley Brothers, Philadelphia, p. 76). Lifelong Cape May resident Jack Sayre told me he has heard the story but doesn't know the location of the "cow pen" (interview with author 8/11/2011).

71. Stone, Witmer. Letter to Alexander Wetmore, July 22, 1927. SIA Collection 7006 Box 65 Folder 7.

72. Hand, H. Walker, Jr. Letter to Witmer Stone, September 25, 1925. ANSP 450.

73. Hand, H. Walker, Jr. Letters to Witmer Stone, February 3, 1908 & September 22, 1913. ANSP 450.

74. Hand, H. Walker, Jr. Letter to Witmer Stone, April 20, 1902. ANSP 450.

75. Hand, H. Walker, Jr. Letter to Witmer Stone, January 6, 1914. ANSP 450.

76. Fowler, Henry W., "The King Crab Fisheries in Delaware Bay, and Further Notes on New Jersey Fishes, Amphibians and Reptiles," in *Annual Report of the New Jersey State Museum for 1907*. 1908, MacCrellish & Quigley, Trenton. 111-202.

77. *PSNJ*. 151; Hand, H. Walker, Jr. Letter to Witmer Stone, January 6, 1908. ANSP 450.

78. *BSOCM*. 894; "Abstract of the proceedings of the DVOC 1909." *Cassinia*, 1909. 13:52-56.

79. Stone, Witmer. "Report of the spring migration of 1907." *Cassinia*, 1907. 11:54-79.

80. *BSOCM*. 212.

81. Hagar, Joseph A., "American Black Duck," in *Handbook of North American Birds: Waterfowl, Part 1*, Ralph S. Palmer, editor. 1976, Yale University Press, New Haven. 344.

82. Hand, H. Walker, Jr. Letter to Witmer Stone, June 29, 1907. ANSP 450.

83. T.R.B. "Cape May City Comment." *The Cape May Gazette*, Cape May, September 18, 1903; "Cape May Storm Swept." *The Star of the Cape*, Cape May, September 19, 1903.

84. *BSOCM*. 694. New Jersey isn't the only place where weather-stressed swallows have gotten a helping hand from sympathetic humans: in Europe they've packed swallows downed by cold snaps into airplanes to move them to warmer climes (Newton, *The Migration Ecology of Birds*, p. 815).

85. *BSOCM*. 516.

86. Stone, Witmer. Letter to Waldo Lee McAtee, May 30, 1918. LOC, W.L. McAtee papers, Box 10, Folder 4.

87. Hand, H. Walker, Jr. Letters to Witmer Stone, May 12 & 20, 1920. ANSP 450; Stone, Witmer. Letter to Albert K. Fisher, May 18, 1920. LOC, A.K. Fisher papers, Box 23.

88. *BSOCM*. 491; Hand, H. Walker, Jr. Letter (tide table) to Witmer Stone, undated, 1922. ANSP 450; Stone, Witmer. Letter to Harry C. Oberholser, June 2, 1922. LOC, Harry C. Oberholser papers, Box 18; *BSOCM*. 337, 18, & 476-77.

89. *BSOCM*. xiv.

90. Stone, Witmer. Letter to Theodore S. Palmer, June 8, 1924. LOC, T.S. Palmer papers, Box 40.

91. Hand, H. Walker, Jr. Letter to Witmer Stone, May 5, 1924. ANSP 450.

92. Allen, Robert P. and Roger T. Peterson. "The hawk migrations at Cape May Point, New Jersey." *The Auk*, 1936. 53:393-404.

93. *BSOCM*. 42-43.

94. Sutton, Clay and Pat Sutton, *Birds and Birding at Cape May*. 2006. 32, 90-91; Author Deborah Cramer called my attention (pers. comm. 5/21/2013) to a tantalizing passage in *BSOCM* (p. 400) that indicates Hand and others may have been aware of the annual springtime shorebird/horseshoe ("king") crab phenomenon on the Delaware Bayshore, even if they didn't recognize that the birds were feeding on the crab eggs.

95. Nichols, John T. Letter to Witmer Stone, October 2, 1926. ANSP 450.

96. Hand, H. Walker, Jr. Letter to Witmer Stone, January 7, 1930. ANSP 450. Hand was a diabetic, and at that time living to the age of 62 was an accomplishment for someone with the disease. Heart disease is a common complication of diabetes. According to Laura Hedrick (interview with author 5/10/2013), Hand's wife Laura was the first certified home economics teacher in New Jersey, and she had Hand on a special diet to control his diabetes. It seems to have worked.

97. *BSOCM*. 847.

98. Brown, Otway. Letter to Witmer Stone, September 4, 1919. ANSP 450. Laura Hedrick told me (5/10/2013) that the official cause of death was whooping cough.

99. Stone, Witmer. Letter to Theodore S. Palmer, September 18, 1932. LOC, T.S. Palmer papers, Box 50.

100. *BSOCM*. xi.

101. *BSOCM*. xiii.

102. Brown, Otway. Letter to Witmer Stone, May 24, 1907. ANSP 450.

103. "Officers and members of the Philadelphia Botanical Club." *Bartonia*, 1908. 1:27-29.

104. Hiers, Mildred D. "Some fragments which have become history." *The Cape May Geographic Society Bulletin*, 1951. 5:8-10.

105. "Married." *The Cape May Gazette*, Cape May, June 20, 1903.

106. Brown, Otway. Letters to Witmer Stone, April 9, 1930 & December 1, 1937. ANSP 450.

107. Richard "Mickey" McPherson, interview with author September 1, 2013. Brown's house occupied the lot at 678 New England Road in Lower Township, Cape May County. The land had belonged to Brown's parents since 1888, and Otway and Edith appear to have moved onto it in 1916 (Deeds of property, private collection). Brown was living at 906 Lafayette Street in Cape May in 1907 (O. Brown to W. Stone 5/24/1907, ANSP 450). Mr. McPherson said his father, Edgar, bought the house from Edith after Otway's death and used it as lodgings for migrant workers employed on his farm. It fell into disrepair, and Edgar donated it to the local fire company, which sacrificed it as part of a firefighting exercise. Thanks to William and Kathleen Finneran and Cherie Hanscomb for help and information; Alexander, Robert C., *Noteworthy Trees of Cape May County*. 1949. Cape May County Geographic Society, Cape May. 17.

108. Stone, Witmer. Letter to Charles J. Pennock, January 30, 1935. ANSP Collection 676, Folder 1; Brown, Otway. Letters to Witmer Stone, December 6, 1929 & October 5, 1930. ANSP 450; Stone, Witmer. Letter to Alexander Wetmore, December 24, 1929. SIA Collection 7006, Box 65, Folder 7.

109. *BSOCM*. 44.

110. Brown, Otway and Edgar T. Wherry. "Check-list of the vascular flora of Cape May County, New Jersey." *Bartonia*, 1970. 40:1-18.

111. "The Otway H. Brown Memorial Driveway." *The Cape May Geographic Society Bulletin*, 1948. 2:9-10; "Otway Brown memorial trees." *The Cape May Geographic Society Bulletin*, 1952. 6:1.

112. Alan Brady, interview with author May 3, 2000; Dale Twining, interview with author December 14 & 18, 1999.

113. Page, Charles C. Letter to Witmer Stone, April 12, no year. ANSP 450.

114. *BSOCM*. 47.

115. Shryock, William. Letter to Witmer Stone, July 30, 1929. ANSP 450.

116. "Abstract of the proceedings of the DVOC 1921." *Cassinia*, 1920-21. 24:55-59.

117. Urgo, Jacqueline L. "Island is a living laboratory." *Philadelphia Inquirer*, November 16, 2005.

118. Potter, Julian K. "A season's study of some of our water birds." *Cassinia*, 1922-24. 25:10-20.

119. "The Gift of Caring." Cornelius Weygandt, unpublished manuscript. University of Pennsylvania Archives Collection UPT 50, W547.5, Cornelius Weygandt papers, Box 4, Folder 10. Typically, Weygandt is coy about the identity of the hiker, but based on his description - and even the story - it must have been Miller.

120. "Abstract of the proceedings of the DVOC 1901." *Cassinia*, 1901. 5:45-52.

121. Stone, Witmer. Letter to Charles W. Richmond, June 29, 1929. SIA Collection RU 105, Box 27. The Cape May County library system owns several original sets of *BSOCM* today, and is one of the few libraries that has an online subscription to *Birds of North America* accessible to cardholders, so it has shown much improvement since then.

122. Tanner, James Taylor. Cape May Reports. James Taylor Tanner papers. 1931-36. Division of Rare and Manuscript Collections, Cornell University Library.

123. *BSOCM*. 637; Page, Charles C. Letter to Witmer Stone, January 6, 1936. ANSP 450; *BSOCM*. 849 & 873; Fowler, Henry W. Letter to Witmer Stone, June 30, 1920. ANSP 450; Palmer, T.S. Letter to Witmer Stone, August 7, 1922. ANSP Collection 680, Folder 2; Stone, Witmer. Letter to T.S. Palmer, September 9, 1934. SIA Collection 7150, Box 70, Folder 9; Stone, Witmer. Letter to Harry C. Oberholser, July 8,

1937. LOC, Harry C. Oberholser papers, Box 18; Schroeder, Ida. Letter to Witmer Stone, August 4, 1934. ANSP 450; Palmer, T.S. Letter to Witmer Stone, September 22, 1922. ANSP Collection 680, Folder 3; Stone, Witmer. "Audubon's Shearwater at Cape May, N.J." *The Auk*, 1926. 43(4):536; Brooks, Allan. Letter to Witmer Stone, July 22, 1928. ANSP 450; Stone, Witmer. Letter to Albert K. Fisher, April 6, 1924. LOC, A.K. Fisher papers, Box 27; Stone, Witmer. Letter to Art Emlen Jr., July 30, 1935. Art Emlen, Jr. personal collection; Rehn, James A. G. Letter to Witmer Stone, July 3, 1933. ANSP Collection 682, Folder 1.

124. Wetmore, Alexander. "Witmer Stone (1866-1939)." *Year Book of the American Philosophical Society*, 1939:467-69.

125. "Abstract of the proceedings of the DVOC 1937." *Cassinia*, 1933-37. 30:62-68; Stone, Witmer. "The Mississippi Kite (*Ictinia mississippiensis*) at Cape May, NJ." *The Auk*, 1924. 41(3):477-78.

126. *BSOCM*. vii.

127. Stone, Witmer. Letter to Harry C. Oberholser, July 9, 1922. LOC, Harry C. Oberholser papers, Box 18.

128. Stone, Witmer. Letter to Albert K. Fisher, September 19, 1924. LOC, A.K. Fisher papers, Box 27.

129. Stone, Witmer. Letter to Alexander Wetmore, July 15, 1928. SIA Collection 7006, Box 65, Folder 7.

130. Stone, Witmer. Letter to Alexander Wetmore, July 20, 1932. SIA Collection 7006, Box 65, Folder 8; Stone, Witmer. Letter to James L. Peters, April 21, 1933. MCZ Archives.

131. Weygandt, Cornelius. "The writing of Witmer Stone." *Frontiers*, 1939. 4(1):29.

132. "The Blessing of Birds." Cornelius Weygandt, unpublished manuscript. University of Pennsylvania Archives Collection UPT 50, W547.5. Box 1, Folder 33.

133. Rehn, James A. G. "In memoriam: Witmer Stone." *The Auk*, 1941. 58(3):299-313.

134. Roland, Conrad. Letter to Julian K. Potter, August 23, 1934. ANSP Collection 2010-113, Box 4.

135. Stone, Witmer. Letter to William L. Baily, January 11, 1936. ANSP Collection 398, Folder 7.

136. Stone, Witmer. Letter to William L. Baily, January 18, 1936. ANSP Collection 398, Folder 7.

137. "Abstract of the proceedings of the DVOC 1935." *Cassinia*, 1933-37. 30:51-55; Stone, Witmer. Letter to Charles M.B. Cadwalader, August 1, 1937. ANSP Collection 2009-034, Box 47, Folder 69.

138. Stone, Witmer. Letter to Theodore S. Palmer, February 25, 1936. SIA Collection 7150, Box 70, Folder 11.

139. Stone, Witmer. Letter to Theodore S. Palmer, February 21, 1937. SIA Collection 7150, Box 70, Folder 12.

140. Stone, Witmer. Letter to Alexander Wetmore, February 20, 1937. SIA Collection 7006, Box 66, Folder 1.

141. Sherman, Sandra L. "Tracking Stone's tome: the dispersal of 1,400 copies of 'Bird Studies at Old Cape May.'" *Cassinia*, 1999. 68:51-60.

142. Stone, Witmer. Letter to Alexander Wetmore, October 27, 1937. SIA Collection 7006, Box 66, Folder 1.

143. Stone, Witmer. Letter to Albert K. Fisher, April 27, 1937. LOC, A.K. Fisher papers, Box 36.

144. Brown, Herbert. Letter to Witmer Stone, August 3, 1937. ANSP 450.

145. Stone, Witmer. Letter to Albert K. Fisher, November 13, 1937. LOC, A.K. Fisher papers, Box 36; Vogt, William. Letter to Witmer Stone, December 1, 1937. ANSP 450.

146. "Abstract of the proceedings of the DVOC 1937." *Cassinia*, 1933-37. 30:62-68.

147. *BSOCM*. 880.

148. Sherman, Sandra L. "Tracking Stone's tome: the dispersal of 1,400 copies of 'Bird Studies at Old Cape May.'" *Cassinia*, 1998-99. 68:51-60.

149. Alan Brady told me a story about a DVOC outing in New Jersey to look for some rare bird (a godwit, I think) that had been seen recently. During a search thorough a marsh they sat down to take a lunch break. Fletcher Street didn't bring food on these outings, and was, as usual, mooching from everyone else. Potter was the only one who kept looking for the bird, and after wandering off a distance, started gesticulating wildly to them – he had found the godwit. Alan said he realized that day that persistence was the hallmark of a great birder.

150. Stone, Witmer. Letter to Julian K. Potter, August 4, 1936. ANSP Collection 2010-113, Box 4.

151. Stone, Witmer. Letter to William Vogt, June 23, 1936. ANSP 450.

152. Stone, Witmer. Letter to Alexander Wetmore, August 16, 1936. SIA Collection 7006, Box 66, Folder 18.

153. *BSOCM*. ix.

154. *The DVOC Scrap Book 1890-99*. ANSP Collection 570; Stone, Witmer. Letter to Alexander Wetmore, March 20, 1920. SIA Collection 7006, Box 65, Folder 6; Merriam, C. Hart. Letter to Witmer Stone, September 28, 1915. ANSP Collection 678, Folder 7; Sage, John H. Letter to Witmer Stone, November 25, 1919. ANSP Collection 541, Folder 3.

155. Hickey, Joseph J. "Book News and Reviews." *Bird-Lore*, 1938. 40:130-31.

156. Murphy, Robert Cushman. "Ornithology at its Best." *New York Herald*, New York, October 2, 1938.

157. Nice, Margaret M. and Thomas T. McCabe. "Bird Studies at Old Cape May. An Ornithology of Coastal New Jersey by Witmer Stone." *Bird-Banding*, 1938. 9(2):113-14.

158. Moore, J. Percy. "In memoriam: Witmer Stone (1866-1939)." *PANSP*, 1939. 91:415-418.

159. Stephens, T.C. "Bird Studies at Old Cape May, an Ornithology of Coastal New Jersey." *The Wilson Bulletin*, 1938. 50(2):147.

160. Stone, Witmer. Letter to Robert Cushman Murphy, December 18, 1937. Department of Ornithology Archives, AMNH.

161. Weygandt, Cornelius, *On the Edge of Evening*. 1946. 182-83.

162. Stone, Witmer, "The Ornithology of Today and Tomorrow," in *The Fiftieth Anniversary of the Nuttall Ornithological Club*. 1924, Cambridge. 7-25.

163. *BSOCM*. 575.

164. *BSOCM*. 775-76.

165. *BSOCM*. 370.

166. *BSOCM*. 538.

167. Potter, Julian K. Letter to Witmer Stone, April 11, 1937. ANSP 450.

168. *BSOCM*. 242-43.

169. *BSOCM*. 16. Incidentally, the full moon mentioned in the passage is not artistic license: May 21 was in fact the date of a full moon.

170. *BSOCM*. 339, 471, 489, 756-57, 691, & 818-20.

171. *BSOCM*. 660-61.

172. *BSOCM*. 338.

173. Stone, Witmer. "McAtee on local names of migratory game birds." *The Auk*, 1924. 41(1):186-87.

174. Taylor, John. Letter to Witmer Stone, November 2, 1893. ANSP 450.

175. Laurent, Philip. Letter to Witmer Stone, September 8, 1893. ANSP 450.

176. Dorwart, Jeffery M., *Cape May County, New Jersey: The Making of an American Resort Community*. 1992. 197; U.S. Census Bureau, Sixteenth Census of the United States, 1940. Washington, D.C. National Archives and Records Administration, 1940. Philadelphia, Pa., Roll T627_2324, Enumeration District 5-5. Jack Sayre (interview with author 8/11/2011) thought Otter may have also been a house painter.

177. Stone, Witmer. Letter to Harry C. Oberholser, October 11, 1932. LOC, Harry C. Oberholser papers, Box 18.

178. *BSOCM*. 344; Rusling, William, "Bird Flights Characteristic of Cape May Point," in *Cape May Hawk Flights and Witmer Stone Wildlife Sanctuary*. NAAS manuscript in private collection.

179. *BSOCM*. 347.

180. *BSOCM*. 660, 703, 692, & 770.

181. Urner, Charles A. and Robert W. Storer. "The distribution and abundance of shorebirds on the north and central New Jersey coast, 1928-1938." *The Auk*, 1949. 66(2):177-94.

182. Tyler, Winsor M. "The call-notes of some nocturnal migrating birds." *The Auk*, 1916. 33(2):132-41.

183. *BSOCM*. 778-79.

184. *BSOCM*. 76; Roland, Conrad. Letter to Witmer Stone, February 6, 1935. ANSP 450; Roland, Conrad. Letter to Julian K. Potter, September 12, 1934. ANSP Collection 2010-113, Box 4.

185. Hand, H. Walker, Jr. Letter to Witmer Stone, September 13, (no year). ANSP 450.

186. *The Birds of New Jersey*. 26.

187. Stone told a newspaper reporter, "There are not so many summer land birds at Cape May, although there are many water birds," which indicates that he thought the water birds were the characteristic species of the area (*Times Recorder*, Zanseville, Ohio; 10/10/1926).

188. Palmer, Theodore S. Letter to Witmer Stone, September 8, 1924. ANSP Collection 680, Folder 1; Stone, Witmer. Letter to Julian K. Potter, August 30, 1935. ANSP

189. archives; Stone, Witmer. Letter to Theodore S. Palmer, September 7, 1923. LOC, T.S. Palmer papers, Box 39.
189. *BSOCM.* 803.
190. *BSOCM.* 690 & 640.
191. Potter, Julian K. "The Season, Philadelphia Region." *Bird-Lore*, 1922. 24:349. Monarch numbers have declined alarmingly, due to a potpourri of threats, and it is hoped that the spectacle of their migration will be enjoyed by future generations.
192. *BSOCM.* 822.
193. *Birds of New Jersey*, ed. Joan Walsh et al. 1999. New Jersey Audubon Society. 524.
194. Squires, Walter A. "The Cerulean Warbler at Cape May, N.J." *Bird-Lore*, 1926. 28:398-99.
195. "Bibliography of publications relating to the birds of Pennsylvania, New Jersey, and Delaware, 1925-28." *Cassinia*, 1927-28. 27:50-57.
196. *Birds of New Jersey*, ed. Joan Walsh et al. 1999. New Jersey Audubon Society. 525.
197. Ashley, Linda Ramsey, *In the Pilgrim Way; The First Congregational Church, Marshfield, Massachusetts, 1640-2000*. 2001. Powderhorn Press.
198. Squires, Walter A. "Birds which are coming back to New Jersey shores." *Bird-Lore*, 1925. 27:395-96.
199. Squires, Walter A. "Black Duck nesting at Cape May Point, N.J." *Bird-Lore*, 1931. 33:257.
200. Squires, Walter A. Letter to Witmer Stone, April 22, 1931. ANSP 450.
201. Sibley, David, *The Birds of Cape May, 2nd edition*. 1997. New Jersey Audubon Society. 31.
202. Fisher, Muriel B. Letter to Witmer Stone, Undated, probably late May/early June, 1928; Fisher, Muriel B. Letter to Witmer Stone, Undated, probably late March/early April, 1929; Fisher, Muriel B. Letter to Witmer Stone, February 4, 1935. All ANSP 450.
203. *BSOCM.* 348.
204. The Suttons have covered the changes in species composition in the Cape May area so well in their book *Birds and Birding at Cape May* that I have left the topic in their far more capable hands.
205. Stone, Witmer. "Report on the spring migration of 1902." *Cassinia*, 1902. 6:32-48.
206. *BSOCM.* 324.
207. *TBNJ.* 149; *BSOCM.* 326.
208. *BSOCM.* 535.
209. *BSOCM.* 552.
210. *BSOCM.* 547.
211. Bowers, John E. Letter to Charles M.B. Cadwalader, September 13, 1940. ANSP Collection 2010-051, Box 7, Folder 13.
212. Bowers, John E. Letter to Charles M.B. Cadwalader, October 4, 1940; Bowers, John E. Letter to Margaretta Huber, September 27, 1940. Both ANSP Collection 2010-051, Box 7, Folder 13.
213. Stone, Witmer. Letter to Alexander Wetmore, December 18, 1937. SIA Collection 7006, Box 66, Folder 1; Stone, Witmer. Letter to John K. Terres, April 14, 1938. Private collection of Witmer Stone material.
214. Bowers, John E. Letters to A.B. Walker, June 20, 1939 and to Arthur C. Emlen, June 16, 1939. ANSP Collection 2010-051, Box 1, Folder 93; Smyth, C.S. Letter to Charles M.B. Cadwalader, September 27, 1940. ANSP Collection 2010-051, Box 7, Folder 13.
215. Huston, McCready. Letter to Charles M.B. Cadwalader, September 14, 1940. ANSP Collection 2010-051, Box 7, Folder 13.
216. Cadwalader, Charles M.B. Letter to Arthur C. Emlen, November 4, 1940. ANSP Collection 2010-051, Box 7, Folder 13.
217. Bowers, John E. Memo to ANSP staff, March 14, 1947. ANSP Collection 2010-051, Box 33, Folder 24.
218. Sherman, Sandra L. "Tracking Stone's tome: the dispersal of 1,400 copies of 'Bird Studies at Old Cape May.'" *Cassinia*, 1998-99. 68:51-60. See the DVOC website for further information about them: http://www.dvoc.org/Publications/Publications.htm. At least one set, #578, has not been relocated and probably never will be: it was returned to the Academy after being purchased by a book dealer because it had several blank pages, and was presumably discarded (Fred Pierce, letter to ANSP, 3/7/1947. ANSP Collection 2010-051, Box 33, Folder 24).
219. "Relatives Share $16,000 Estate." *The Evening Bulletin*, Philadelphia, August 20, 1940; Will of Lillie May Stone. ANSP Collection 2010-051, Box 7, Folder 13; DVOC minutes for October 3, 1940. ANSP Collection 74A, Box 2, Folder 2.
220. Stone, Witmer. Letter to Alexander Wetmore, September 22, 1938. SIA Collection 7006, Box 66, Folder 1.

221. Stone, Witmer. Letter to Theodore S. Palmer, October 8, 1938. LOC, T.S. Palmer papers, Box 27.

222. Stone, Witmer. Letter to Charles M.B. Cadwalader, July 29, 1938. ANSP Collection 2009-034, Box 50, Folder 34.

223. Lanier, Henry W. Letter to Witmer Stone, October 15, 1901. ANSP 450.

224. Stone, Witmer. Letter to William Brewster, August 2, 1906. MCZ Archives.

225. "The William Brewster Memorial." *The Auk*, 1920. 37(1):29-32; Hicks, Lawrence E. "The fifty-seventh stated meeting of the AOU." *The Auk*, 1940. 57(1):141-49. Some of the AOU's future references to the work left a bit to be desired. In the *Auk* announcement of the award in 1940, it misreported the title as *The Birds of Old Cape May*, and in 2006 I emailed a testy note of correction to the AOU when I found "Whitmer [sic] Stone" listed on its website as the recipient of the 1939 Brewster Medal. It's also curious that the AOU took two years to publish a Stone memorial in *The Auk*.

226. Weygandt, Cornelius, "A Dearth of Books," in *Down Jersey*. 1940. 151.

227. "The Out-of-door Books of Pennsylvania." Cornelius Weygandt, unpublished manuscript. University of Pennsylvania Archives Collection UPT 50, W547.5. Box 2, Folder 19.

228. Bent, Arthur Cleveland, *Life Histories of North American Birds of Prey*. Vol. One. 1937. United States Government Printing Office, Washington, D.C. 78.

Chapter 14: A Sanctuary in Which to House It

1. Dunne, Peter and Karen Williams. "Hawk shooting at Cape May, New Jersey." *Cape May County Magazine of History and Genealogy*, 1982. 7(2):107-16.

2. Stone, Witmer. Letter to Beecher S. Bowdish, December 2, 1920. ANSP 450.

3. Potter, Julian K. "The Season, Philadelphia Region." *Bird-Lore*, 1921. 23:306-07.

4. DVOC minutes for October 20, 1921. ANSP Collection 74A, Box 2, Folder 1.

5. Stone, Witmer. "Hawk flights at Cape May Point, N.J." *The Auk*, 1922. 39(4):567-68. Stone included some hawk numbers from September 1920, but they are similar to those in his DVOC talk from the year before and it seems likely that 1921 was the year intended.

6. Potter, Julian K. "The Season, Philadelphia Region." *Bird-Lore*, 1923. 25:399-400.

7. "Report on spring migration for the years 1922-24." *Cassinia*, 1922-24. 25:21-52.

8. Potter, Julian K. "The Season, Philadelphia Region." *Bird-Lore*, 1925. 27:404-06.

9. Carey, Henry R. "Correspondence: Hawk extermination." *The Auk*, 1926. 43(2):275-76.

10. Potter, Julian K. "The Season, Philadelphia Region." *Bird-Lore*, 1927. 29:424-25.

11. Potter, Julian K. "The Season, Philadelphia Region." *Bird-Lore*, 1928. 30:399-400.

12. Potter, Julian K. "The Season, Philadelphia Region." *Bird-Lore*, 1929. 31:409-10.

13. Craighead, Frank C., "Notes on the Hawk Migration at Cape May, September 22 and 23, 1933," in *Cape May Hawk Flights and Witmer Stone Wildlife Sanctuary*. NAAS manuscript in private collection.

14. Stone, Witmer. "The hawk question." *The Auk*, 1930. 47(2):208-17.

15. *BSOCM*. 265-66.

16. "Report on the Cape May hawk situation." *Bird-Lore*, 1932. 34:171-73.

17. *BSOCM*. 662.

18. "Hawk-killing at Cape May, New Jersey." *Bird-Lore*, 1931. 33:97-98.

19. Potter, Julian K. "The Season, Philadelphia Region." *Bird-Lore*, 1930. 32:430-31. In an *Auk* note in 1932, Stone added Barn Owls, nighthawks, and Whip-poor-wills to the list of birds besides hawks being shot (*Auk* 49(3):384).

20. McDonald, Norman J. Letter to Witmer Stone, November 15, 1930. ANSP 450.

21. Stone, Witmer. "Recent Literature: The Ornithological Journals. Bird-Lore." *The Auk*, 1931. 48(2):308.

22. DVOC minutes for April 16, 1931. ANSP Collection 74A, Box 2, Folder 2.

23. Reeves, Henry M. "In memoriam: George B. Saunders." *The Auk*, 2001. 118(4):1030-31; Allen, Arthur A. Letter to Witmer Stone, December 10, 1929 and W. Stone, letter to A.A. Allen, January 7, 1930. ANSP Collection 186, Box 1, Folder 1.

24. Stone, Witmer. Letter to Albert K. Fisher, December 19, 1927. ANSP Collection 685, Folder 7.

25. Hand, H. Walker, Jr. Letter to Witmer Stone, December 12, 1928. ANSP 450.

26. Redington, Paul G. Letter to Witmer Stone, December 4, 1929. ANSP 450.

27. "Notes and news." *The Auk*, 1931. 48(2):331-34.

28. Chapman, Ellwood B. Letter to Wharton Huber, April 17, 1931. ANSP Collection 186, Box 1, Folder 5.

29. Huber, Wharton. Letter to Ellwood B. Chapman, April 23, 1931. ANSP Collection 186, Box 1, Folder 5.

30. Stone, Witmer. "Recent Literature: The Ornithological Journals. Bird-Lore XXXIV No. 2." *The Auk*, 1932. 49(3):384.

31. Stone, Witmer, "The Autumn Hawk Flights," in *BSOCM*. 262-68.

32. Allen, Robert P. and Roger T. Peterson. "The hawk migrations at Cape May Point, New Jersey." *The Auk*, 1936. 53:393-404.

33. Saunders, George B., "Report of George B. Saunders, Field Representative, National Association of Audubon Societies. Cape May, New Jersey. October 20, 1931," in *Cape May Hawk Flights and Witmer Stone Wildlife Sanctuary*. NAAS manuscript in private collection.

34. Tanner, James Taylor. Cape May Reports. James Taylor Tanner papers. 1931-36. Division of Rare and Manuscript Collections, Cornell University Library. Sharp-shinneds with food present in the gut averaged 1.3 birds/stomach, Cooper's Hawks 1.7, and Peregrine Falcons 2.8. Merlin stomachs averaged <1 bird each, and numerous dragonflies (4.4/stomach of the 26 which contained dragonflies).

35. "Law-enforcement at Cape May." *Bird-Lore*, 1932. 34:445.

36. Stone, Witmer, "The Autumn Hawk Flights," in *BSOCM*. 262-68. Note that in *BSOCM*, Stone erroneously reported that Allen counted 5,765 hawks for the season; that was actually only the Sharpie count.

37. Allen, Robert P., "Hawk Flights and Law Enforcement at Cape May, September 15–October 29, 1932," in *Cape May Hawk Flights and Witmer Stone Wildlife Sanctuary*. NAAS manuscript in private collection. 19-20, footnote.

38. *The Birds of New Jersey*. 164.

39. Allen, Robert P., "Hawk Flights and Law Enforcement at Cape May, September 15–October 29, 1932," in *Cape May Hawk Flights and Witmer Stone Wildlife Sanctuary*. NAAS manuscript in private collection. 8.

40. DVOC minutes for October 6, 1932. ANSP Collection 74A, Box 2, Folder 2.

41. Sprunt, Alexander, IV. "In memoriam: Robert Porter Allen." *The Auk*, 1969. 86(1):26-34.

42. Page, Charles C. Letter to Witmer Stone, September 21, 1933. ANSP 450.

43. Tanner, James Taylor. Cape May Reports. James Taylor Tanner papers. 1931-36. Division of Rare and Manuscript Collections, Cornell University Library.

44. Potter, Julian K. "The Season, Philadelphia Region." *Bird-Lore*, 1933. 35:327-28.

45. Potter, Julian K. "The Season, Philadelphia Region." *Bird-Lore*, 1934. 36:370-71.

46. Roland, Conrad. Letter to Julian K. Potter, September 12, 1934. ANSP Collection 2010-113, Box 4.

47. Roland, Conrad. Letter to Witmer Stone, February 6, 1935. ANSP 450.

48. "The Audubon Societies: New Jersey." *Bird-Lore*, 1934. 36:209.

49. Tanner, James Taylor, "Witmer Stone Wildlife Sanctuary, 1936," in *Cape May Hawk Flights 1936-1937*. NAAS manuscript in private collection.

50. Lincoln, Alexander, Jr. Untitled report, in *Cape May Hawk Flights and Witmer Stone Wildlife Sanctuary*. NAAS manuscript in private collection.

51. Eaton, Warren F. Letter to Witmer Stone, November 15, 1934. ANSP 450.

52. Eaton, Warren F. Letter to Witmer Stone, June 12, 1935. ANSP 450.

53. Eaton, Warren F. Letter to Witmer Stone, June 18, 1935. ANSP 450.

54. Eaton, Warren F. Letter to Witmer Stone, June 24, 1935. ANSP 450.

55. Eaton, Warren F. Letter to Witmer Stone, July 1, 1935. ANSP 450.

56. Baker, John H. Letter to Witmer Stone, July 25, 1935. ANSP Collection 2009-031, Box 1.

57. Baker, John H. Letter to Witmer Stone, August 6, 1935. ANSP 450.

58. Stone, Witmer. Letter to Alexander Wetmore, August 18, 1935. SIA Collection 7006, Box 66, Folder 18.

59. Wetmore, Alexander. Letter to Witmer Stone, August 26, 1935. SIA Collection 7006, Box 66, Folder 18.

60. Stone, Witmer. Letter to Frank M. Chapman, August 20, 1935. Department of Ornithology Archives, AMNH.

61. Fleming, James H. Letter to Witmer Stone, September 9, 1935. ANSP 450.

62. Lincoln, Alexander, Jr. Untitled report, in *Cape May Hawk Flights and Witmer Stone Wildlife Sanctuary.* NAAS manuscript in private collection. Stone's notes about Warden Steel's disinterest in a conservation matter brought to his attention by Stone is appended to Lincoln's report.

63. *Harvard University Catalogue of Names, 1922-23.* 1922. Harvard University, Cambridge. 346; Urner, Charles A. "Obituaries: Warren Francis Eaton." *The Auk,* 1936. 53(2):255-56.

64. Allen, Robert P. "Sanctuary established at Cape May." *Bird-Lore,* 1935. 37:348-49.

65. Rusling, William J. Letter to Witmer Stone, December 19, 1935. ANSP 450. It was 1958 before a Sandhill Crane was convincingly reported from Cape May (*Cassinia* 43:24-30), and the closest we've come to the warbler may have been the time in about 1990 when a loud and unfamiliar vocalization brought a few of us tumbling off the hawkwatch platform at a run to where some nitwit was broadcasting a Kirtland's song with a tape recorder, saying he thought he'd just seen one.

66. Bryant, Harold C. "Report of the Committee on Bird Protection American Ornithologists' Union." *The Auk,* 1936. 53(1):70-73.

67. Pough, Richard H. Letter to Witmer Stone, August 3, 1936. ANSP 450.

68. Jordan, Joe J., *Cape May Point: Three Walking Tours of Historic Cottages.* 2004. Schiffer Publishing, Atglen, Pa. 79.

69. Tanner, James Taylor. Cape May Reports. James Taylor Tanner papers. 1931-36. Division of Rare and Manuscript Collections, Cornell University Library. Stone didn't refer to Tanner's data in *BSOCM,* presumably because it wasn't yet available to him when he was wrapping up the book.

70. Allen, Robert P. Letter to I. Grant Scott, August 16, 1935. ANSP 450.

71. Pough, Richard H. Letter to Witmer Stone, July 1, 1936. ANSP 450.

72. *BSOCM.* 280.

73. Allen, Robert P., "Hawk Flights and Law Enforcement at Cape May, September 15–October 29, 1932," in *Cape May Hawk Flights and Witmer Stone Wildlife Sanctuary.* NAAS manuscript in private collection. 6.

74. Kuerzi, Richard, "Witmer Stone Wildlife Sanctuary Report for 1937," in *Flights, Cape May Point 1936-1937.* NAAS manuscript in private collection. 15.

75. Allen, Robert P., "Sanctuary or slaughter pen?" in *Nature Magazine.* March, 1936.

76. Allen, Robert P. Letter to Witmer Stone, August 29, 1935. ANSP 450.

77. "Audubon Association Establishes Wildlife Sanctuary in New Jersey." NAAS press release, 1935. ANSP Collection 263; Allen, Robert P. Letter to Witmer Stone, August 16, 1935. ANSP 450.

78. Allen, Robert P. Letter to D.L. Reeves, August 21, 1935. ANSP 450.

79. Baker, John H. Letter to Witmer Stone, September 4, 1935. ANSP 450.

80. Stone, Witmer. Letter to Julian K. Potter, August 30, 1935. ANSP archives.

81. David Rutherford, interview with author August 30, 2011.

82. Allen, Robert P. Letter to I. Grant Scott, August 21, 1935. ANSP 450.

83. Riley, George. "Heading South: Birds from Far and Near Get Second Wind at Cape May on Long Trek." *The Evening Bulletin,* Philadelphia, October 13, 1939.

84. Pough, Richard H. "The Witmer Stone Wildlife Sanctuary." *Audubon Magazine,* 1942. 44(4):201-05.

85. Abbott, Gertrude. Letter to Witmer Stone, April 6, 1937; Baker, John H. Letters to Witmer Stone, March 29 & April 13, 1937. All ANSP 450.

86. Rusling, William, "Witmer Stone Wildlife Sanctuary," in *Cape May Hawk Flights and Witmer Stone Wildlife Sanctuary.* NAAS manuscript in private collection.

87. Fry, Gladys Gordon. "Note from the Witmer Stone Sanctuary." *Bird-Lore,* 1935. 37:473.

88. Brown, Otway. Letters to Witmer Stone, September 6, 1936 & February 3, 1937. ANSP 450.

89. "Nature notes: wildlife sanctuaries." *The Cape May Geographic Society Bulletin,* 1950. 4:2; Clark, George A. "The character of Cape May." *The Cape May Geographic Society Bulletin,* 1975. 29:1-4.

90. Jordan, Joe J., *Cape May Point: The Illustrated History, 1875 to the Present.* 2003. Schiffer Publishing, Atglen, Pa. 139. The magnesite plant was torn down in 1989, and the area is now part of the Higbee Beach Wildlife Management Area (Sutton and Sutton, *Birds and Birding at Cape May.* 243).

91. "Program for summer 1947: The Audubon Society." *The Cape May Geographic Society Bulletin,* 1947. 1:5-6; Sutton, Clay and

Pat Sutton, *Birds and Birding at Cape May.* 2006. 469.

92. Sutton, Clay and Pat Sutton, *Birds and Birding at Cape May.* 2006. 134-38.
93. Mendenhall, Matt. "Watching hawks: 25 best places to watch hawks." *Birder's World,* 2010(October):35-38.
94. *BSOCM.* 268.

Box: Contemplating Counts

1. Allen, Robert P. and Roger T. Peterson. "The hawk migrations at Cape May Point, New Jersey." *The Auk,* 1936. 53:393-404.
2. Tanner, James Taylor. Cape May Reports. James Taylor Tanner papers. 1931-36. Division of Rare and Manuscript Collections, Cornell University Library.
3. Baker, John H. Letter to Witmer Stone, September 1, 1936. ANSP 450.
4. Rusling, William J. "Flight - Cape Charles - 1936. The study of the habits of diurnal migrants, as related to weather and land masses during the fall migration on the Atlantic Coast, with particular reference to the hawk flights of the Cape Charles (Virginia) region." Presumably Rusling's report for the NAAS.

Chapter 15: A Genius for Friendship

1. Murphy, Robert Cushman. 1955. "Witmer Stone (1866–1939)." Department of Ornithology Archives, AMNH. Written for *Dictionary of American Biography.*
2. Morris, George Spencer. Letter to Witmer Stone, July 2, 1894. ANSP 450; Morris, George Spencer. "Catoxen cabin on the Rancocas." *Cassinia,* 1908. 12:20-24.
3. University of Pennsylvania Class of 1887 Scrapbooks. University of Pennsylvania Archives Collection UPT 110.
4. *BSOCM.* 618 & 88; Stone, Witmer. "Audubon's Shearwater at Cape May, N.J." *The Auk,* 1926. 43(4):536.
5. Photograph labelled (on back) "August 29, 1926." ANSP Collection 2009-031, Box 2, Folder 10.
6. *BSOCM.* xi.
7. *BSOCM.* x. I think the late Tom Parsons (1930–2011), a retired university professor who lived at Cape May Point and who, like Stone, didn't drive, was the only person in recent times who did anything close to the kind of walking they did in Stone's day.

8. Woodford, Elizabeth M., "Foreword," in *Plants of Southern New Jersey.* 1973, Quarterman Publications, Inc., Boston.
9. Page, Charles C. Letter to Witmer Stone, December 5, 1934. ANSP 450; Stone, Witmer. Letter to Charles J. Pennock, January 30, 1935. ANSP Collection 676, Folder 1; Stone, Witmer. Letter to Alexander Wetmore, July 8, 1931. SIA Collection 7006, Box 65, Folder 8; Stone, Witmer. Letters to Theodore S. Palmer, July 8, 1931 & August 26, 1932. LOC, T.S. Palmer papers, Boxes 48 & 50.
10. Hochstrasser, Marie. Interview with author, November 17, 2005; Stone, Witmer. Letter to Alexander Wetmore, January 14, 1935. SIA Collection 7006, Box 66, Folder 18.
11. Rehn, James A. G. "Witmer Stone (1866-1939)." *Cassinia,* 1938-41. 31:1-11.
12. Scoville, Samuel. Letter to Witmer Stone, November 15, 1916. ANSP 450.
13. Weygandt, Cornelius, "Twelve Good Men and True," in *Philadelphia Folks.* 1938. 266-69.
14. Wetmore, Alexander. Letter to Witmer Stone, June 13, 1933, & W. Stone, letter to A. Wetmore, June 16, 1933. SIA Collection 7006, Box 66, Folder 1.
15. Scoville, Samuel, Jr., *Wild Honey.* 1929. 68-69.
16. Stone, Witmer. Letter to Charles M.B. Cadwalader, July 29, 1938. ANSP Collection 2009-034, Box 50, Folder 34.
17. *The DVOC Twenty Year Souvenir.* 1910. Privately published.
18. Huber, Wharton. "Witmer Stone (1866 to 1939)." *Journal of Mammalogy,* 1940. 21(1):1-4.
19. Street, Phillips B. "A history of the Delaware Valley Ornithological Club." *Cassinia,* 1988-89. 63:2-35.
20. Kennard, Frederic H. Letter to Witmer Stone, October 29, 1920. ANSP 450.
21. DVOC minutes for March 20, 1919. ANSP Collection 74A, Box 2, Folder 1.
22. *Dictionary of American Regional English,* ed. Joan Houston Hall. Vol. 4. 2002. Belknap Press.
23. Sage, John H. Letter to Witmer Stone, June 23, 1920. ANSP Collection 541, Folder 3.
24. DVOC minutes for January 8, 1931. ANSP Collection 74A, Box 2, Folder 2.
25. *BSOCM.* 292-93.
26. DVOC minutes for October 19, 1939. ANSP Collection 74A, Box 2, Folder 2.

27. Howell, A. Brazier. Letter to Witmer Stone, January 18, 1928. ANSP 450.

28. Stone, Witmer. Letter to A. Brazier Howell, January 20, 1928. ANSP 450.

29. Snyder, Lester L. Letter to Witmer Stone, September 20, 1935. ANSP 450.

30. Batchelder, Charles F. Letter to Witmer Stone, November 22, 1907. ANSP 450.

31. Bowdish, Beecher S. Letter to Witmer Stone, January 12, 1925. ANSP 450. Stone's notes are on the back of the letter. "Whiskey Jack" is a colloquial name for the Gray Jay. Thrushes have a continuous, non-scaly bony covering over their "legs" (tarsi), giving them a "booted" appearance. The "booted tarsi" is presumably a pun on "bootleg." Another possibility suggests itself: in the 1935 Three Stooges episode "Pardon My Scotch," they use a rubber boot to mix an alcoholic concoction; there may have been a standing joke at the time that illicit booze manufacturers used a boot as a shaker.

32. Pennell, Francis W. "The botanical work of Witmer Stone." *Bartonia*, 1940. 20:33-37.

33. Burr, Charles W. Letter to Witmer Stone, July 21, 1932. ANSP 450.

34. Mumford, Edward W. Letter to Witmer Stone, July 21, 1932. ANSP 450.

35. "The Out-of-door Books of Pennsylvania." Cornelius Weygandt, unpublished manuscript. University of Pennsylvania Archives Collection UPT 50, W547.5. Box 2, Folder 19.

36. Weygandt, Cornelius. "The writing of Witmer Stone." *Frontiers*, 1939. 4(1):29; "The Blessing of Birds." Cornelius Weygandt, unpublished manuscript. University of Pennsylvania Archives Collection UPT 50, W547.5. Box 1, Folder 33.

37. Stone, Witmer. Letter to Joseph Grinnell, December 22, 1911. MVZ Archives.

38. Huber, Wharton. Letter to Witmer Stone, August 28, (no year). ANSP 450.

39. Moore, J. Percy. "In memoriam: Witmer Stone (1866-1939)." *PANSP*, 1939. 91:415-418.

40. Weygandt, Cornelius, *On the Edge of Evening*. 1946. 182.

41. Stone, Witmer. Letter to Waldo Lee McAtee, February 26, 1937. LOC, W.L. McAtee papers, Box 10, Folder 4.

42. Chapman, Frank M. Letter to Witmer Stone, November 21, 1925. ANSP Collection 679, Folder 12.

43. Stone, Witmer. Letter to Frank M. Chapman, September 27, 1936. Department of Ornithology Archives, AMNH.

44. Chapman, Frank M. Letter to Witmer Stone, March 1, 1938. ANSP Collection 2009-031, Box 1, Folder 11.

45. Chapman, Frank M. Letter to Witmer Stone, November 30, 1929. ANSP Collection 679, Folder 12; Stone, Witmer. Letter to Frank M. Chapman, December 7, 1929. Department of Ornithology Archives, AMNH. The Barro Colorado Island research station is now part of the Smithsonian Tropical Research Institute (*85th Anniversary, BCI: History and Research*; 2008, STRI).

46. Wetmore, Alexander. Letter to Witmer Stone, January 24, 1939. SIA Collection 7006.

47. Stone, Witmer. Letter to Albert K. Fisher, February 23, 1939. LOC, A.K. Fisher papers, Box 37.

48. Wetmore, Alexander. Telegram to Charles M.B. Cadwalader, May 26, 1939. SIA Collection 7006.

49. Wetmore, Alexander. "Witmer Stone (1866-1939)." *Year Book of the American Philosophical Society*, 1939:467-69.

50. Wetmore, Alexander. Letter to Lillie M. Stone, June 21, 1940. SIA Collection 7006.

51. Grinnell, Hilda Wood. "Joseph Grinnell: 1877-1939." *The Condor*, 1940. 42(1):3-34.

52. Miller, Alden H. "Dedication." *The Condor*, 1940. 42(1):91. Alice Fitch Echelle, whose father, herpetologist Henry S. Fitch, earned a master's degree and a Ph.D. at UC Berkeley with Grinnell as his advisor, told me (email 6/9/10) that during his grad school days her father received a letter from Grinnell that didn't seem to require a reply. Grinnell must have expected one, for when Fitch saw him a few weeks later, Grinnell refused to shake his hand and told Fitch to learn to "heed the proprieties." The two got along fine, but the story is illustrative of how formal the advisor-student relationship could be at that time.

53. Grinnell, Joseph. Letter to Witmer Stone, September 26, 1900. ANSP Collection 684, Folder 3.

54. Grinnell, Joseph. Letter to Witmer Stone, May 6, 1903. ANSP Collection 684, Folder 3.

55. "Notes and news." *The Auk*, 1915. 32(3):386-90; Allen, Amelia S. "Minutes of Cooper Club meetings." *The Condor*, 1919. 22(1):46; Grinnell, Joseph. Letter to

Witmer Stone, November 3, 1929. ANSP Collection 684, Folder 4.

56. Grinnell, Joseph. Letter to Witmer Stone, October 13, 1931. ANSP Collection 684, Folder 5.

57. Grinnell, Joseph. Letter to Witmer Stone, July 27, 1931. Untitled book of bound letters to Stone in ANSP Collection 2009-031, Box 4, Folder 3.

58. Stone, Witmer. Letter to Theodore S. Palmer, June 4, 1931. LOC, T.S. Palmer papers, Box 48.

59. Grinnell, Hilda Wood. Letter to Theodore S. Palmer, June 25, 1939. LOC, T.S. Palmer papers, Box 27; Linsdale, Jean M. "In memoriam: Joseph Grinnell." *The Auk*, 1942. 59(2):269-85.

60. Stone, Witmer. "Isaac Norris DeHaven." *Cassinia*, 1922-24. 25:6-9.

61. Stone, Witmer. "Charles Sumner Williamson." *Bartonia*, 1914. 7:1-5.

62. *BSOCM*. xiii-xiv. In a 1934 letter, Stone referred to the Cape May Court House restaurant where the roundup was held as "Stone's Restaurant," adding that he wasn't related to the owner (Stone to Muriel B. Fisher, 1/31/1934; ANSP 450).

63. Gardner, Bessie. Letter to Witmer Stone, October 24, 1920. ANSP 450.

64. Gardner, Aston. Letter to Witmer Stone, October 28, 1920. ANSP 450.

65. Rehn, James A. G. "In memoriam: Witmer Stone." *The Auk*, 1941. 58(3):299-313.

66. Pearson, T. Gilbert. Letter to Witmer Stone, April 25, 1917. ANSP 450.

67. Huber, Wharton. Letter to Witmer Stone, July 24, 1927. ANSP Collection 186, Box 2, Folder 2; Dwight, Jonathan, Jr. Letter to Witmer Stone, September 5, 1927. ANSP Collection 686, Folder 3; Richmond, Charles W. Letter to Witmer Stone, October 30, 1927. ANSP Collection 675, Folder 7; Murphy, Grace. Letter to Witmer Stone, November 5, 1927. ANSP 450.

68. Stone, Witmer. Letter to Theodore S. Palmer, May 5, 1930. LOC, T.S. Palmer papers, Box 47; Howell, A. Brazier. Letter to Witmer Stone, May 14, 1930. ANSP 450.

69. Stone, Witmer. Letter to Frank M. Chapman, November 24, 1932. Department of Ornithology Archives, AMNH.

70. Tanner, James Taylor. Cape May Reports. James Taylor Tanner papers. 1931-36. Division of Rare and Manuscript Collections, Cornell University Library.

71. "Who's who at the AOU." *Bird-Lore*, 1935. 37:446-47.

72. Alan Brady, interview with author May 3, 2000.

73. Dale Twining, interview with author December 14 & 18, 1999.

74. Mayer, Charles R. Letter to DVOC, January 23, 1922. ANSP 450.

75. Stone, Witmer. Letter to Charles R. Mayer, January 24, 1922. ANSP 450.

76. DVOC minutes for February 1, 1923. ANSP Collection 74A, Box 2, Folder 1.

77. Stone, Witmer. Letter to Theodore S. Palmer, November 25, 1933. SIA Collection 7150, Box 70, Folder 6.

78. Stone, Witmer. Letter to Art Emlen Jr., July 30, 1935. Art Emlen Jr. personal collection.

79. Peterson, Roger T., "Introduction to the Dover edition," in *Bird Studies at Old Cape May*. 1965, Dover Publications, Inc., New York. vii.

80. Moore, Robert T. Letter to Witmer Stone, July 31, 1931. Untitled book of bound letters to Stone in ANSP Collection 2009-031, Box 4, Folder 3.

81. Peters, James L. Letter to Witmer Stone, 1931. Untitled book of bound letters to Stone in ANSP Collection 2009-031, Box 4, Folder 3.

82. Griscom, Ludlow. Letter to Witmer Stone, February 26, 1913; Harlow, Richard C. Letter to Witmer Stone, January 16, 1933; Friedmann, Herbert. Letter to Witmer Stone, March 31, 1921; Grange, Wallace B. Letter to Witmer Stone, November 2, 1922; Stone, Witmer. Letter to Wallace B. Grange, November 7, 1922; Stone, Witmer. Letter to Bryant Teachers Bureau, September 24, 1926; Roland, Conrad. Letters to Witmer Stone, June 14&22, 1928, and October 17, (no year); Surface, H.A. Letters to Witmer Stone June 18 and October 17, 1900, and December 18, 1902; Stone, Witmer. Letter to Ernest G. Holt, November 23, 1935; Holt, Ernest G. Letter to Witmer Stone, November 27, 1935. All ANSP 450; Worth, George S. Letter to Witmer Stone, October 4, 1930. ANSP Collection 186, Box 3, Folder 7; Emlen, John T., Jr., *Adventure is Where You Find It*. 1996. 40 & 68; Lanyon, Wesley E., Stephen T. Emlen, and Gordon H. Orians. "In memoriam: John Thompson Emlen, Jr., 1908-1997." *The Auk*, 2000. 117(1):222-27.

83. Yarnall, Stanley R. Letter to Witmer Stone, September 22, 1921. ANSP 450.

84. "Abstract of the proceedings of the DVOC 1922." *Cassinia*, 1922-24. 25:53-57.

85. Stone, Witmer. "C. Eliot Underdown." *The Auk*, 1932. 49(2):272-3.

86. Underdown, C. Eliot. Letter to Witmer Stone, August 20, 1929. ANSP Collection 186, Box 3, Folder 6; Bond, James. Letter to Witmer Stone, July 30, 1931. ANSP 450; Stone, Witmer. Letter to Wharton Huber, undated. ANSP Collection 186, Box 3, Folder 4.

87. Cadwalader, Charles M.B. Letter to Witmer Stone, July 13, 1931, & W. Stone, letter to C.M.B. Cadwalader, July 1, 1931. ANSP Collection 2009-034, Box 24, Folder 15.

88. Underdown, C. Eliot. Letter to Witmer Stone, September 24, 1931. ANSP 450.

89. Underdown wasn't the first young ornithologist to die of pneumonia shortly after moving to Chicago: in 1901, Audubon Ridgway, only son of ornithologist Robert Ridgway, met the same unfortunate fate just a few months after his start at the same museum (*Auk* 18(2):221-22).

90. Fulweiler, John H. Letters to Witmer Stone, July 12 & 15, 1937. ANSP 450.

91. Hamill, Stuart. "Scientist Takes a Busman's Holiday - With Variations." *The Evening Bulletin*, Philadelphia, August 10, 1937.

92. Stone, Witmer. Letter to Charles M.B. Cadwalader, August 23, 1937. ANSP Collection 2009-034, Box 47, Folder 69; Rusling, William, "Witmer Stone Wildlife Sanctuary," in *Cape May Hawk Flights and Witmer Stone Wildlife Sanctuary*. NAAS manuscript in private collection.

93. Schroeder, Ida. Letter to Witmer Stone, August 4, 1934. ANSP 450.

94. "Mastodon Molars Netted by Fishermen Off Jersey." *New York Herald Tribune*, New York, July 2, 1931.

95. Volcker, Paul A. Letter to Witmer Stone, February 28, 1927. ANSP 450.

96. Shields, Catherine. Letter to Lillie M. Stone, October 2, 1935. ANSP 450.

97. Stone, Witmer. Letter to Alexander Wetmore, January 18, 1936. SIA Collection 7006, Box 80, Folder 7; Stone, Witmer. Letter to Theodore S. Palmer, February 25, 1936. SIA Collection 7150, Box 70, Folder 11.

98. Moffett, Caroline. Letter to Witmer Stone, October 30, 1933. ANSP 450.

99. Murray, James J. Letter to Witmer Stone, May 29, 1930. ANSP 450.

100. Stone, Witmer. Letter to James L. Peters, December 12, 1930. MCZ Archives.

101. Stone, Witmer. Letter to Waldo Lee McAtee, July 19, 1920. LOC, W.L. McAtee papers, Box 10, Folder 4; Stone, Witmer. Letter to Harry C. Oberholser, February 25, 1918. LOC, Harry C. Oberholser papers, Box 18.

102. Hunt, Chreswell J. Letter to Witmer Stone, November 4, 1920. ANSP 450.

103. Stone, Witmer. Letter to Alexander Wetmore, May 11, 1936. SIA Collection 7006, Box 66, Folder 18.

104. Stone, Witmer. "Recent Literature: Miss Sherman on the House Wren problem." *The Auk*, 1925. 42(3):460-61.

105. Stone, Witmer. Letter to Alexander Wetmore, January 22, 1926. SIA Collection 7006, Box 65, Folder 6.

106. Stone, Witmer. Letter to Alexander Wetmore, September 24, 1926. SIA Collection 7006, Box 65, Folder 6.

107. Wright, Samuel. Letter to Witmer Stone, April 9, 1893. ANSP 450; Brown, Otway. Letter to Witmer Stone, March 30, 1931. ANSP 450.

108. Richmond, Charles W. Letters to Witmer Stone, May 7, 1914 & January 22, 1927. ANSP Collection 675, Folders 6 & 7; Stone, Witmer. Letter to Theodore S. Palmer, January 4, 1927. LOC, T.S. Palmer papers, Box 43.

109. Stone, Witmer. Letter to E.D. Slawson, January 4, 1925. ANSP 450. Although the submission seems peculiar today, crossword puzzles were a recent creation and the country was in the midst of a craze over them.

110. Stone, Witmer. Letters to Albert K. Fisher, March 30 & April 7, 1908. LOC, A.K. Fisher papers, Box 18; Stone, Witmer. Letter to Waldo Lee McAtee, May 17, 1912. LOC, W.L. McAtee papers, Box 10, Folder 4; Stone, Witmer. Letter to William Brewster, March 22, 1910. MCZ Archives.

111. Stone, Witmer. Letters to Albert K. Fisher, April 16, 1926 & April 27, 1937. LOC, A.K. Fisher papers, Boxes 29 & 36; Stone, Witmer. Letter to Waldo Lee McAtee, April 9, 1934. LOC, W.L. McAtee papers, Box 37, Folder 3.

112. Stone, Witmer. Letter to Albert K. Fisher, April 15, 1925. LOC, A.K. Fisher papers, Box 28; Stone, Witmer. Letter to Theodore

S. Palmer, June 9, 1926. LOC, T.S. Palmer papers, Box 42.

113. Stone, Witmer. Letter to Alexander Wetmore, September 17, 1928. SIA Collection 7006, Box 65, Folder 7.

114. Stone, Witmer. Letter to T.S. Palmer, November 27, 1932. SIA Collection 7150, Box 70, Folder 6.

Box: Astonishing

1. *BSOCM.* 163, 127, 499, & 137.
2. Stone, Witmer. "Recent Literature: Check List of the Birds of Essex County, Mass." *The Auk*, 1922. 39(3):438; *BSOCM.* 324 & 254; Stone, Witmer. "Recent Literature: Forbush's annual report on Massachusetts ornithology." *The Auk*, 1923. 40(1):154-55.
3. *BSOCM.* 679 & 154; Stone, Witmer. "Notes and news." *The Auk*, 1915. 32(2):268-72.
4. *BSOCM.* 728.

Chapter 16: Travels

1. Conant, Roger "Skip." "A birding history of Dutch Mountain, Pennsylvania." *Cassinia*, 1990. 63:57-60.
2. Stone, Witmer. "Summer birds of the higher parts of Sullivan and Wyoming Counties, Pa." *Cassinia*, 1898-99. 3:20-23.
3. "Abstract of the proceedings of the DVOC 1898-99." *Cassinia*, 1898-99. 3:1-13; "Abstract of the proceedings of the DVOC 1901." *Cassinia*, 1901. 5:45-52; Philadelphia Botanical Club minutes for January 23, 1914. ANSP Collection 88, Box 1, Folder 14.
4. Huch, Otto Frederick. Letter to Witmer Stone, December 2, 1935. ANSP 450. Huch was an electrical engineer who lived in the Philadelphia area, and the son of Carl Frederick Huch, treasurer for a time of MacKellar, Smiths, and Jordan, the oldest type foundry in America.
5. Cope, Francis R., Jr. Letter to Witmer Stone, March 28, 1936. ANSP 450. Much of the property around Cope's Dimock Township, Susquehanna County home has been put into the care of land conservation organizations, including The Nature Conservancy ("Woodbourne Orchards and Family of Francis R. Cope, Jr." Finding aid, Haverford College Quaker & Special Collections, HC.Coll.1230).
6. Behr, Herman. Letter to Witmer Stone, April 20, 1921. ANSP 450; Stone, Witmer. Letter to Frank M. Chapman, April 26,

1921. ANSP Collection 679, Folder 11; Stone, Witmer. Letter to C. Hart Merriam, April 26, 1921. ANSP Collection 678, Folder 7.

7. Creech, William R. Letter to Witmer Stone, May 31, 1921. ANSP 450; Pine Mountain Settlement School. Cited February 7, 2014. Available from http://www.pinemountainsettlementschool.com/

8. Stone, Witmer. Letter to Harry C. Oberholser, May 28, 1921. LOC, Harry C. Oberholser papers, Box 18.

9. Stone, Witmer. "The Ornithology of Today and Tomorrow," in *The Fiftieth Anniversary of the Nuttall Ornithological Club*. 1924, Cambridge. 7-25.

10. Stone, Witmer. "Some birds observed at Pine Mountain Kentucky." *The Auk*, 1921. 38(3):464-65; "Abstract of the proceedings of the DVOC 1922." *Cassinia*, 1922-24. 25:53-57.

11. Stone, Witmer. Letter to S.S. Dickey, October 7, 1929. ANSP 450; "Additions to the museum." *PANSP*, 1907. 59:579-85; "Abstract of the proceedings of the DVOC 1907." *Cassinia*, 1907. 11:81-86; "Abstract of the proceedings of the Philadelphia Botanical Club for 1912." *Bartonia*, 1912. 5:16-21; Stone, Witmer. Letter to Frank C. Kirkwood, September 23, 1925. ANSP 450.

12. Pennell, Francis W. "The botanical work of Witmer Stone." *Bartonia*, 1940. 20:33-37; Proceedings of the Wilson Natural Science Association, Vol. 1. ANSP Collection 2009-031, Box 4, Folder 7; Stone, Witmer. Letter to Stewardson Brown, August 15, 1883. ANSP Collection 168, Folder 5; Stone, Witmer. Letter to John W. Jordan, August 13, 1897. Historical Society of Pennsylvania, Society Collection.

13. Stone, Witmer. Letter to Theodore S. Palmer, August 27, 1906. LOC, T.S. Palmer papers, Box 6.

14. Stone, Witmer. Letter to Frank M. Chapman, July 24, 1912. Department of Ornithology Archives, AMNH; Stone, Witmer. Letter to Theodore S. Palmer, August 24, 1912. LOC, T.S. Palmer papers, Box 9.

15. Stone, Witmer. Letter to Frank M. Chapman, August 30, 1912. Department of Ornithology Archives, AMNH.

16. Stone, Witmer. Letter to Joel Asaph Allen, July 26, 1912. Department of Ornithology Archives, AMNH; *Five and Thirty: The*

Further History of the Class of Eighty-Seven. 1922. 105.

17. University of Pennsylvania Class of 1887 Scrapbooks. University of Pennsylvania Archives Collection UPT 110.

18. Stone, Witmer. Letter to Frank M. Chapman, July 14, 1926. ANSP Collection 679, Folder 12.

19. "Notes and news." *The Auk*, 1915. 32(3):386-90. The 1903 meeting in San Francisco was a "special," not annual, one (*Auk* 20(3):299-302).

20. The Exposition featured three sculptures by Philadelphia-born sculptor Alexander Sterling Calder, who would subsequently create the figures in the Swann Fountain adjacent to the Academy of Natural Sciences.

21. DVOC minutes for October 21, 1915. ANSP Collection 74A, Box 1, Folder 5.

22. Stone, Witmer. Letter to Edward J. Nolan, June 15, 1915. ANSP Collection 567, Box 35, Folder 3; Street, Fletcher. "Abstract of the proceedings of the DVOC 1915." *Cassinia*, 1915. 19:56-60.

23. Young, Robert T. Letter to Witmer Stone, July 2, 1915. ANSP 450.

24. Stone, Witmer. Letter to Edward von Siebold Dingle, January 16, 1922. ANSP 450; Wayne, Arthur T. Letter to Witmer Stone, May 31, 1920. ANSP 450.

25. DVOC minutes for November 5, 1914. ANSP Collection 74A, Box 1, Folder 5; "Report of the curators." *PANSP*, 1914. 66:656-64.

26. Stone, Witmer. "Report of Dr. Witmer Stone, special field agent for South Carolina." *Bird-Lore*, 1917. 19:432.

27. Untitled announcement of "a series of articles on bird life" by Stone, commencing with the 7/4 issue. Stone wrote about meadowlarks on 7/4, and woodpeckers on 7/11. *The Manning Times*, Manning, July 4 & 11, 1917.

28. "Curators' Report." *PANSP*, 1917. 69:347; Pearson, T. Gilbert. Letters to Witmer Stone, December 4, 1916 & June 25, 1917. ANSP 450.

29. DVOC minutes for May 3, 1923. ANSP Collection 74A, Box 2, Folder 1; Stone, Witmer. Letter to Harry C. Oberholser, March 15, 1923. LOC, Harry C. Oberholser papers, Box 18; Bragg, Laura M. Letter to Witmer Stone, November 3, 1927. ANSP 450.

30. Stone, Witmer. Letter to Albert K. Fisher, November 13, 1937. LOC, A.K. Fisher papers, Box 36; Hicks, Lawrence E. "The fifty-fifth stated meeting of the American Ornithologists' Union." *The Auk*, 1938. 55(2):317-24. Witmer attended his last AOU meeting, sans Lillie, in Washington, D.C. in 1938 (*Auk* 56(1):120).

31. Arthur, Stanley Clisby. Letter to Witmer Stone, September 9, 1919. ANSP 450; Stone, Witmer. Letter to T. Gilbert Pearson, August 28, 1919. ANSP 450; "Abstract of the proceedings of the DVOC 1920." *Cassinia*, 1920-21. 24:50-54.

32. "Curators' Report." *PANSP*, 1919. 71:307.

33. "Additions to the museum." *PANSP*, 1919. 71(3):317-23.

34. "Notes and news." *The Auk*, 1919. 36(4):628-36.

35. DVOC minutes for December 19, 1919. ANSP Collection 74A, Box 2, Folder 1.

36. "Editorial notes and news." *The Condor*, 1919. 21(4):174-76.

37. Stone, Witmer. Letter to Robert Ridgway, March 4, 1920. Blacker-Wood Collection, Department of Rare Books, McGill University

38. Stone, Witmer. Letter to Alexander Wetmore, September 23, 1919. SIA Collection 7006, Box 65, Folder 6.

39. Stone, Witmer. Letter to Joseph Mailliard, August 30, 1919. ANSP 450; Merriam, C. Hart. Letter to Witmer Stone, August 2, 1919. ANSP Collection 678, Folder 7.

40. Allen, Amelia S. "Minutes of Cooper Club meetings." *The Condor*, 1919. 22(1):46.

41. "Abstract of the proceedings of the DVOC 1907." *Cassinia*, 1907. 11:81-86.

42. Leola Hall Coggins (1881-1930). Cited September 15, 2014. Available from http://www.medicinemangallery.com/bio/bio.lasso?url=Leola-Hall-Coggins

43. *The DVOC Twenty Year Souvenir.* 1910. Privately published.

44. Stone, Witmer. Letter to C. Hart Merriam, August 30, 1919. ANSP Collection 678, Folder 7.

45. Stone, Witmer. Letter to Theodore S. Palmer, September 21, 1919. LOC, T.S. Palmer papers, Box 36.

46. Stone, Witmer. Letter to Alexander Wetmore, October 31, 1919. SIA Collection 7006, Box 65, Folder 6.

47. Palmer, Theodore S. "The thirty-seventh stated meeting of the American Ornitholo-

gists' Union." *The Auk*, 1920. 37(1):110-25; Cooper, Samuel W. Letter to Art Club of Philadelphia membership, April 5, 1920. ANSP 450; "Program of meetings of the Philadelphia Botanical Club from January, 1915, to December, 1923." *Bartonia*, 1924. 8:37-40; Walker, Isabella. "Reports of the affiliate organizations: Audubon Club of Norristown (Pa.)." *Bird-Lore*, 1920. 22:408; *Five and Thirty: The Further History of the Class of Eighty-Seven*. 1922. 16.

48. Law, J. Eugene. Letter to Witmer Stone, February 16, 1921. ANSP 450.

49. Stone, Witmer. Letter to Alexander Wetmore, September 22, 1924. SIA Collection 7006, Box 65, Folder 6.

50. Untitled notes for talk on Stone's Arizona trip. Private collection of Witmer Stone material.

51. Will of Lillie May Stone. ANSP Collection 2010-051, Box 7, Folder 13.

52. Burket, A. Roy. Letter to ANSP, June 21, 1962. ANSP Collection 263, Box 1, Folder 10.

53. Stone, Witmer. Letter to Joseph Grinnell, August 29, 1919. MVZ Archives.

54. "Abstract of the proceedings of the DVOC 1936." *Cassinia*, 1933-37. 30:56-61; Stone, Witmer. Letter to W.H. Bergtold, April 28, 1935. ANSP 450.

55. Stone, Witmer. "To Florida by the Buick route." Unpublished diary. ANSP Collection 2009-031, Box 1, Folders 1,4, and 6.

56. Fingerhood, Edward D. "The George Spencer Morris collection." *Cassinia*, 1994. 65:12-14; Pearson, T. Gilbert. Letter to Witmer Stone, June 20, 1916. ANSP 450; Rathbun, Samuel F. Letter to Witmer Stone, July 26, 1916. ANSP 450.

57. Stone, Witmer. Letter to T.S. Palmer, November 27, 1932. SIA Collection 7150, Box 70, Folder 6.

Chapter 17: His Heart Was Good to Him

1. The earliest reference I found to Stone ill with the grippe is in an 1890 letter (Frank C. Baker to Stone, 1/8/1890; ANSP 450).

2. Stone, Witmer. Letter to Waldo Lee McAtee, October 6, 1925. LOC, W.L. McAtee papers, Box 10, Folder 4.

3. Allen, Joel Asaph. Letter to Witmer Stone, January 14, 1907. ANSP Collection 658, Folder 11.

4. Richmond, Charles W. Letter to Witmer Stone, January 16, 1907. ANSP Collection 675, Folder 5.

5. Pennock, Charles J. Letter to Witmer Stone, August 11, 1909. ANSP Collection 676, Folder 2; Handwritten note from Stone to Samuel Rhoads in the front pages of Rhoads's copy of *The Birds of New Jersey*, dated September 22, 1909. Copy of book found online; DeHaven, Isaac Norris. Letter to Witmer Stone, September 24, 1909. ANSP Collection 559, Folder 17.

6. Stone, Witmer. Letter to Albert K. Fisher, December 7, 1918. LOC, A.K. Fisher papers, Box 22.

7. Stone, Witmer. Letter to Waldo Lee McAtee, February 20, 1922. ANSP Collection 498, Box 2, Folder 3; Stone, Witmer. Letter to Laurence Fletcher, March 6, 1922. ANSP 450; "Secretary." Letter to Isaac Roberts, May 9, 1922. ANSP 450; Stone, Witmer. Letter to Harry C. Oberholser, June 2, 1922. LOC, Harry C. Oberholser papers, Box 18.

8. Bent, Arthur Cleveland. Letter to Witmer Stone, September 13, 1922. ANSP Collection 550, Folder 2; Moore, Robert T. Letter to Witmer Stone, March 3, 1923. ANSP 450.

9. Stone, Witmer. Letter to Harry C. Oberholser, September 29, 1922. ANSP Collection 538, Folder 6.

10. Stone, Witmer. Letter to Harry C. Oberholser, February 11, 1923. LOC, Harry C. Oberholser papers, Box 18.

11. Stone, Witmer. Letter to S. Prentiss Baldwin, April 6, 1924. ANSP 450.

12. Lewis, Daniel, *The Feathery Tribe*. 2012. 95-97.

13. Stone, Witmer. Letter to Frank M. Chapman, May 14, 1929. Department of Ornithology Archives, AMNH.

14. Chapman, Frank M. Letter to Witmer Stone, May 15, 1929. Department of Ornithology Archives, AMNH.

15. Stone, Witmer. Letter to Joseph Grinnell, June 3, 1929. MVZ Archives.

16. Pallasch, Thomas J. and Michael J. Wahl. "The focal infection theory: appraisal and reappraisal." *Journal of the California Dental Association*, 2000. 28(3):194-200.

17. Peitzman, Steven J. Email to author, August 23, 2012.

18. Stone, Witmer. Letter to Alexander Wetmore, June 7, 1929. SIA Collection 7006, Box 65, Folder 7.

19. Stone, Witmer. Letter to Frank M. Chapman, December 7, 1929. Department of Ornithology Archives, AMNH. Stone to T.S. Palmer 8/19/1929 referred to "a nerve affection" (LOC, T.S. Palmer papers, Box 46).

20. Stone, Witmer. Letter to Glover M. Allen, January 21, 1931. MCZ Archives; Stone, Witmer. Letter to Waldo Lee McAtee, May 25, 1931. LOC, W.L. McAtee papers, Box 37, Folder 3.

21. Stone, Witmer. Letter to Theodore S. Palmer, May 23, 1931. LOC, T.S. Palmer papers, Box 48.

22. Stone, Witmer. Letters to Theodore S. Palmer, January 12, February 20, March 4, & April 29, 1931. LOC, T.S. Palmer papers, Box 48.

23. Stone, Witmer. Letter to James L. Peters, June 4, 1931. MCZ Archives; Stone, Witmer. Letter to Alexander Wetmore, June 10, 1931. SIA Collection 7006, Box 65, Folder 8.

24. Stone, Witmer. Letter to Charles M.B. Cadwalader, 1931. ANSP Collection 2009-034, Box 24, Folder 15; Stone, Witmer. Letter to Glover M. Allen, June 22, 1931. MCZ Archives.

25. Stone, Witmer. Letter to Frank M. Chapman, July 10, 1931. Department of Ornithology Archives, AMNH.

26. Stone, Witmer. Letter to Frank M. Chapman, September 24, 1931. Department of Ornithology Archives, AMNH; Stone, Witmer. Letter to Robert T. Moore, January 19, 1932. ANSP Collection 2009-034, Box 27, Folder "Stone."

27. Stone, Witmer. Letter to Alexander Wetmore, January 9, 1933. SIA Collection 7006, Box 65, Folder 8.

28. Stone, Witmer. Letter to James L. Peters, April 21, 1933. MCZ Archives.

29. Stone, Witmer. Letter to Theodore S. Palmer, February 25, 1936. SIA Collection 7150, Box 70, Folder 11; Stone, Witmer. Letter to Alexander Wetmore, January 14, 1935. SIA Collection 7006, Box 66, Folder 18.

30. Stone, Witmer. Letter to John K. Terres, November 24, 1935. ANSP 450.

31. Stone, Witmer. Letter to Wharton Huber, February 2, 1934. ANSP Collection 186, Box 3, Folder 4; Stone, Witmer. Letters to Alexander Wetmore, September 20, 1934 & February 20, 1937. SIA Collection 7006, Box 66, Folders 18 & 1.

32. Stone, Witmer. Letter to Alexander Wetmore, May 11, 1936. SIA Collection 7006, Box 66, Folder 18.

33. Stone, Witmer. Letter to W. E. Clyde Todd, May 29, 1936. ANSP 450.

34. Peters, James L. Letter to Witmer Stone, "First Day of Spring," no year. ANSP Collection 186, Box 3, Folder 1. Peters lived to be 62, dying in April 1952 despite having survived another February.

35. Stone, Witmer. Letter to Albert K. Fisher, February 10, 1936. LOC, A.K. Fisher papers, Box 36.

36. Stone, Witmer. Letter to Waldo Lee McAtee, October 12, 1935. LOC, W.L. McAtee papers, Box 37, Folder 3.

37. Swarth, Harry S. Letter to Witmer Stone, June 1, 1935. ANSP 450.

38. Stone, Witmer. Letter to Albert K. Fisher, November 13, 1937. LOC, A.K. Fisher papers, Box 36.

39. Stone, Witmer. Letter to Waldo Lee McAtee, May 21, 1938. LOC, W.L. McAtee papers, Box 37, Folder 3.

40. Wood, Harold B. Letter to Witmer Stone, July 25, 1937. ANSP 450.

41. Stone, Witmer. Letter to Alexander Wetmore, February 21, 1938. SIA Collection 7006, Box 66, Folder 1.

42. Stone, Witmer. Letter to Harry C. Oberholser, April 3, 1938. LOC, Harry C. Oberholser papers, Box 18.

43. Stone, Witmer. Letter to Alexander Wetmore, September 22, 1938. SIA Collection 7006, Box 66, Folder 1.

44. Stone, Witmer. Letter to John E. Bowers, December 16, 1938. ANSP Collection 2009-034, Box 50, Folder 34; Stone, Witmer. Letter to Charles M.B. Cadwalader, December 24, 1938. ANSP Collection 2010-051, Box 1, Folder 92.

45. DVOC minutes for January 5, 1939. ANSP Collection 74A, Box 2, Folder 2.

46. University of Pennsylvania Class of 1887 Scrapbooks. University of Pennsylvania Archives Collection UPT 110.

47. Stone, Witmer. Letter to Alexander Wetmore, January 25, 1939. SIA Collection 7006, Box 66, Folder 1.

48. Stone, Witmer. Letter to Charles M.B. Cadwalader, February 19, 1939. ANSP Collection 2010-051, Box 1, Folder 92.

49. Stone, Witmer. Letter to Albert K. Fisher, February 23, 1939. LOC, A.K. Fisher papers, Box 37.

50. Stone, Witmer. Letter to Robert Cushman Murphy, March 12, 1939. Department of Ornithology Archives, AMNH.

51. Stone, Witmer. Letter to John E. Bowers, March 21, 1939. ANSP Collection 2010-051, Box 1, Folder 92.

52. Stone, Witmer. Letter to Albert K. Fisher, February 21, 1939. LOC, A.K. Fisher papers, Box 37; Stone, Witmer. Letter to Charles M.B. Cadwalader, January 25, 1939. ANSP Collection 2010-051, Box 1, Folder 92.

53. Huber, Wharton. Letter to Theodore S. Palmer, May 24, 1939. LOC, T.S. Palmer papers, Box 27.

54. Stone, Witmer. Letter to Albert K. Fisher, May 7, 1939. LOC, A.K. Fisher papers, Box 37.

55. "Abstract of the proceedings of the DVOC 1938-41." *Cassinia*, 1938-41. 31:52-61.

56. Rehn, James A.G. Letter to Constance J. Sherman, December 21, 1955. ANSP Collection 263. Rehn also stated that Stone died of a heart attack while in the hospital for "cancer of the bladder." However, Huber (note 53, above) said Stone died at home, and he visited there shortly after Stone's death. Additionally, Stone's death certificate lists prostate cancer and heart disease as the cause of death, and modern urologists who reviewed Stone's symptoms didn't see evidence of bladder cancer (Commonwealth of Pennsylvania, Department of Health, Bureau of Vital Statistics. Certificate of death for Witmer Stone. Obtained from Pennsylvania Department of Health, Division of Vital Records; Drs. George W. Drach [email to author 8/27/2013], Rainer M. Engel [email to author 6/28/2013], and Michael E. Moran [email to author 7/1/2013] provided written comments after reviewing a chronology of Stone's health issues in his final months that I compiled from his correspondence).

57. Cadwalader, Charles M.B. Letter to William J. Fox, May 24, 1939. ANSP Collection 263.

58. "Dr. Witmer Stone to be Buried Saturday." *Cape May Star & Wave*, May 25, 1939; Weyl, Edward S. Letter to Alan Brady, November 22, 1993. Alan Brady private collection.

59. Sutton, George Miksch. Letter to Wharton Huber, May 30, 1939. ANSP Collection 186, Box 3, Folder 4.

60. Bowers, John E. Letter to Charles M.B. Cadwalader, August 16, 1940. ANSP Collection 2010-051, Box 7, Folder 13.

61. Pepper, George Wharton. Letter to Charles M.B. Cadwalader, February 26, 1940; Bodine, William C. Letter to Arthur C. Emlen, May 7, 1940. Both ANSP Collection 2010-051, Box 7, Folder 13.

62. Drinker, Biddle and Reath. Letter to Charles M.B. Cadwalader, June 14, 1940. ANSP Collection 2010-051, Box 7, Folder 13.

63. Deed of trust between Lillie May Stone, Settlor, and Arthur E. (*sic*) Emlen, Trustee. ANSP Collection 2010-051, Box 7, Folder 13.

64. This was not the only time the Class of '87 took care of a woman left behind by one of their own. When L.V. Newlin died in 1927, the class provided for his daughters until they married (UP Class of 1887 Scrapbooks. UP Archives Collection UPT 110).

65. Wetmore, Alexander. Letter to Lillie M. Stone, June 21, 1940. SIA Collection 7006, Box 66, Folder 1; "Margaret Wetmore Harlan." *Daily Press*, Hampton Roads, August 27, 2000.

66. Stone, Lillie M. Letter to Alexander Wetmore, June 23, 1940. SIA Collection 7006, Box 66, Folder 1.

67. "Mrs. Lillie May Stone." *The Evening Bulletin*, Philadelphia, August 5, 1940.

68. Stone, Witmer. Letter to Albert K. Fisher, April 27, 1937. LOC, A.K. Fisher papers, Box 36.

69. "Mrs. Lillie L. Stone." *Evening Public Ledger*, Philadelphia, August 5, 1940.

70. Hochstrasser, Marie. Interview with author, November 17, 2005.

71. Commonwealth of Pennsylvania, Department of Health, Bureau of Vital Statistics. Certificate of death for Mrs. Lillie M. Stone. Obtained from Pennsylvania Department of Health, Division of Vital Records.

72. Wetmore, Alexander. Letter to Lillie M. Stone, November 22, 1939. SIA Collection 7006, Box 66, Folder 1; Wetmore, Alexander. Letter to Lillie M. Stone, November 24, 1939. SIA Collection 7006, Box 66, Folder 1.

73. Cadwalader, Charles M.B. Letter to Arthur C. Emlen, September 25, 1940, & A.C. Emlen, letter to C.M.B. Cadwalader, October 3, 1940. Both ANSP Collection 2010-051, Box 7, Folder 13. Stone said

in 1915 that he still had every letter he'd ever received from an ornithologist (Stone to T.S. Palmer 11/11/1915; LOC, T.S. Palmer papers, Box 11). Unfortunately, a year before he died he was engaged in going through his correspondence and discarding items not of "profound scientific interest" (Stone to W.L. McAtee, 5/21/1938; LOC, W.L. McAtee papers, Box 37, Folder 3).

74. "Copy of Sales Book." Laurel Hill Cemetery receipt for Frederick D. Stone for purchase of Section P, Lot number 50, south half. February 12, 1890. Laurel Hill Cemetery records.

75. Stone, Frederick D., Jr., *The Descendants of George Steele*. 1896.

76. Stone, Witmer. Letter to Casey A. Wood, May 21, 1928. Blacker-Wood Collection, Department of Rare Books, McGill University.

77. Wood, Casey A. Letter to Witmer Stone, May 29, 1928. ANSP 450.

It Isn't All Stuck in the Past

1. Hand, H. Walker, Jr. Letter to Witmer Stone, June 17, 1917. ANSP 450.

2. Nice, Margaret M. and Thomas T. McCabe. "Bird Studies at Old Cape May. An Ornithology of Coastal New Jersey by Witmer Stone." *Bird-Banding*, 1938. 9(2):113-14.

3. Stone, Witmer. Letter to Theodore S. Palmer, September 25, 1922. LOC, T.S. Palmer papers, Box 38. This was probably Stone's 8/10 talk to the "[Women's?] Community Club" at "the [First] Presbyterian Church" (Stone to T.S. Palmer 8/20/1922; LOC, T.S. Palmer papers, Box 38).

4. *BSOCM*. 36.

5. *BSOCM*. 25.

6. *BSOCM*. 37.

7. Potter, Julian K. Letter to Witmer Stone, August 11, 1929. ANSP 450.

8. *BSOCM*. 24; Rusling, William, "Bird Flights Characteristic of Cape May Point," in *Cape May Hawk Flights and Witmer Stone Wildlife Sanctuary*. NAAS manuscript in private collection.

9. *BSOCM*. 834.

10. Page, Charles C. Letter to Witmer Stone, January 6, 1936. ANSP 450.

11. Salvini, Emil R., *Historic Cape May, New Jersey: The Summer City by the Sea*. 2012. The History Press, Charleston. 123.

12. Tanner, James Taylor, "Witmer Stone Wildlife Sanctuary, 1936," in *Cape May Hawk Flights 1936-1937*. NAAS manuscript in private collection; "Notes and news." *The Auk*, 1936. 53(2):259-60.

13. Wood, Harold B. "Increasing the power of field glasses." *The Auk*, 1930. 47(3):429-30.

14. Pearce, John E., *Heart of the Pines*. 2000. Batsto Citizens Committee. xvi.

15. *BSOCM*. 49 (facing) & 270.

16. Stone, Witmer. "The summer birds of Cape May, N.J." 1891. ANSP Collection 2009-031, Box 1, Folder 2.

17. *BSOCM*. 507.

18. *BSOCM*. 8.

19. *PSNJ*. 357.

20. Beesley, Maurice, "Sketch of the Early History of Cape May County," in *Geology of the County of Cape May, State of New Jersey*. 1857, Trenton. 160.

21. H.A.R. "A trip to Seven-Mile Beach, New Jersey." *Ornithologist and Oologist*, 1889. 14(1):1-4.

Appendix 2: Development of *BSOCM*

1. "Abstract of the proceedings of the DVOC 1890-91." *Cassinia*, 1890-91. 1:2-11; Stone, Witmer. "The summer birds of Cape May, N.J." 1891. ANSP Collection 2009-031, Box 1, Folder 2.

2. "Abstract of the proceedings of the DVOC 1892-97." *Cassinia*, 1892-97. 2:1-26.

3. *BSOCM*. 705.

4. DVOC minutes for February 21, 1893. ANSP Collection 74A, Box 1, Folder 2.

5. Street, Fletcher. "Abstract of the proceedings of the DVOC 1916." *Cassinia*, 1916. 20:42-46.

6. Hand, H. Walker, Jr. Letter to Witmer Stone, February 16, 1917. ANSP 450.

7. Palmer, T.S. "Thirty-fifth stated meeting of the American Ornithologists' Union." *The Auk*, 1918. 35(1):65-73.

8. "Abstract of the proceedings of the DVOC 1918." *Cassinia*, 1918. 22:38-41.

9. "Abstract of the proceedings of the DVOC 1920." *Cassinia*, 1920-21. 24:50-54.

10. Stone, Witmer. Letter to Clarence E. McClung, January 21, 1921. ANSP 450.

11. "Abstract of the proceedings of the DVOC 1921." *Cassinia*, 1920-21. 24:55-59.

12. DVOC minutes for February 3, 1921. ANSP Collection 74A, Box 2, Folder 1.

13. Palmer, T.S. "Thirty-eighth stated meeting of the American Ornithologists' Union." *The Auk*, 1921. 38(1):89-105.

14. DVOC minutes for October 20, 1921. ANSP Collection 74A, Box 2, Folder 1.

15. "Abstract of the proceedings of the DVOC 1922." *Cassinia*, 1922-24. 25:53-57.

16. Stone, Witmer. "Hawk flights at Cape May Point, N.J." *The Auk*, 1922. 39(4):567-68.

17. "Abstract of the proceedings of the DVOC 1922-24." *Cassinia*, 1922-24. 25:53-66; DVOC minutes for November 1, 1923. ANSP Collection 74A, Box 2, Folder 1.

18. Stone, Witmer. "The Mockingbird." *Cassinia*, 1958. 43:13-19.

19. Sage, John H. Letter to Theodore S. Palmer, September 23, 1924. LOC, T.S. Palmer papers, Box 40.

20. Palmer, T.S. "The forty-second stated meeting of the American Ornithologists' Union." *The Auk*, 1925. 42(1):105-15.

21. Stone, Witmer. "Past and present bird life of the southern New Jersey coast." *Year Book of the Academy of Natural Sciences of Philadelphia*, 1925:19-29.

22. Stone, Witmer. Letter to Alexander Wetmore, August 11, 1925. SIA Collection 7006, Box 65, Folder 6.

23. DVOC minutes for October 1, 1925. ANSP Collection 74A, Box 2, Folder 1; "Abstract of the proceedings of the DVOC 1925." *Cassinia*, 1925-26. 26:30-33.

24. "New Facts About Migratory Birds." *Times Recorder*, Zanesville (Ohio), October 10, 1926. The article notes "Copyright by Public Ledger" in the bottom corner, so had presumably been published there recently.

25. Palmer, T.S. "The forty-fourth stated meeting of the American Ornithologists' Union." *The Auk*, 1927. 44(1):73-84.

26. "Abstract of the proceedings of the DVOC 1926." *Cassinia*, 1925-26. 26:34-38; DVOC minutes for November 4, 1926. ANSP Collection 74A, Box 2, Folder 1.

27. "Abstract of the proceedings of the DVOC 1927." *Cassinia*, 1927-28. 27:38-41.

28. DVOC minutes for February 2, 1928. ANSP Collection 74A, Box 2, Folder 1.

29. Stone, Witmer. Letter to Alexander Wetmore, July 15, 1928. SIA Collection 7006, Box 65, Folder 7.

30. "Abstract of the proceedings of the DVOC 1929." *Cassinia*, 1929-30. 28:48-52.

31. "Forty-sixth [sic] annual meeting of the American Ornithologists' Union." *Bird-Lore*, 1929. 31:418-19; Palmer, T.S. "The forty-seventh stated meeting of the American Ornithologists' Union." *The Auk*, 1930. 47(2):218-30.

32. Walker, Isabella. "Audubon Club of Norristown, PA." *Bird-Lore*, 1931. 33:497-98; Middleton, Raymond. Letters to Witmer Stone, October 30 & November 1, 1930. ANSP 450.

33. "Lectures of the Philadelphia Academy of Natural Sciences." *Science*, 1931. 73(1887):228.

34. "Abstract of the proceedings of the DVOC 1932." *Cassinia*, 1931-32. 29:60-64.

35. Stone, Witmer. Letter to Alexander Wetmore, July 20, 1932. SIA Collection 7006, Box 65, Folder 8.

36. Stone, Witmer. Letter to Alexander Wetmore, August 19, 1932. SIA Collection 7006, Box 65, Folder 8.

37. Cottam, Clarence. Letter to Witmer Stone, February 7, 1933. ANSP 450. The Baird Ornithological Club referred to was formed in Washington, D.C. in 1922, and has been defunct for decades.

38. Stone, Witmer. Letter to James L. Peters, April 21, 1933. MCZ Archives.

39. Stone, Witmer. Letter to T.S. Palmer, August 3, 1933. SIA Collection 7150, Box 70, Folder 6.

40. Stone, Witmer. Letter to W. L. Stiber, January 26, 1936. ANSP Collection 498, Box 2, Folder 5.

41. Stone, Witmer. Letter to Theodore S. Palmer, February 25, 1936. SIA Collection 7150, Box 70, Folder 11.

42. "Abstract of the proceedings of the DVOC 1935." *Cassinia*, 1933-37. 30:51-55.

43. "Abstract of the proceedings of the DVOC 1936." *Cassinia*, 1933-37. 30:56-61; *BSOCM*. xi; "Dr. Stone Honored on 70th Birthday." *Evening Public Ledger*, Philadelphia, September 23, 1936.

44. Swanson, Gustav A. Letter to Witmer Stone, January 26, 1937. ANSP 450.

45. Stone, Witmer. Letter to Alexander Wetmore, February 20, 1937. SIA Collection 7006, Box 66, Folder 1.

46. Stone, Witmer. Letter to Theodore S. Palmer, February 21, 1937. SIA Collection 7150, Box 70, Folder 12; *BSOCM*. vii.

47. Stone, Witmer. Letter to Alexander Wetmore, October 27, 1937. SIA Collection 7006, Box 66, Folder 1.

Index

Italicized page numbers reference photographs. Species names are not included in the index, and only place names of locations that figure prominently in the book are included. Witmer Stone is abbreviated WS.

www.ingramcontent.com/pod-product-compliance
Lightning Source LLC
Chambersburg PA
CBHW072042020426
42334CB00017B/1361